JIM CROW

Jim Crow

VOICES FROM A CENTURY OF STRUGGLE

Part Two: 1919–1976
Tulsa to the Boston Busing Crisis

Tyina L. Steptoe, *editor*

THE LIBRARY OF AMERICA

JIM CROW: VOICES FROM A CENTURY OF STRUGGLE
PART TWO: 1919–1976

Published in the United States by Library of America.
14 East 60th Street, New York, NY 10022, U.S.A.
Visit our website at www.loa.org.

This paper exceeds the requirements of
ANSI/NISO Z39.48–1992 (Permanence of Paper).

Distributed to the trade in the United States
by Penguin Random House Inc.
and in Canada by Penguin Random House Canada Ltd.

Library of Congress Control Number: 2024952066
ISBN 978–1–59853–801–4

The authorized representative in the EU for product safety
and compliance is eucomply OÜ,
Pärnu mnt 139b-14, 11317 Tallinn, Estonia.
hello@eucompliancepartner.com

First Printing
The Library of America—387

Manufactured in the United States of America

Contents

1946–1963

1964–1976

Introduction

BY TYINA L. STEPTOE

ON THE NIGHT of Thanksgiving in 1915, a flaming cross blazed from Georgia's Stone Mountain. The fiery symbol announced a rebirth. William Joseph Simmons, a Methodist preacher with a love for fraternal organizations, brought over a dozen of his friends to the landmark, located fifteen miles east of Atlanta. That night the southern white men launched a new version of the Ku Klux Klan. The secretive Reconstruction-era terrorist organization had lain dormant for decades, but the premiere of the film *The Birth of a Nation* earlier that year inspired Simmons to bring the KKK into the twentieth century. He conceptualized the organization as a fraternal order for white, native-born Anglo-Saxon Protestant men who wanted to protect their families and communities from the destabilizing forces of immigration and urbanization. One of the Klan's new slogans was "100% Americanism," a sign of the intense anti-immigrant sentiment that targeted Jewish and Catholic Americans. The ongoing Great Migration further stoked white supremacist anxieties as the urban Black population spiked across the nation.

Although reborn in the Deep South, the new Klan became national in its scope and scale in the 1920s. Approximately five million people joined klaverns in different parts of the United States from 1915 to 1930. This time, they didn't hide their membership. Women of the Ku Klux Klan formed in 1923, and like the men, they exerted political influence in places like Indiana. Klan newspapers appeared in different cities. Texas sent a Klansman to the Senate, and Rice Institute in Houston had a student chapter of the KKK. The Klan's national popularity and the "Red Summer" of 1919 showed that violent white supremacy was not unique to the South in the age of Jim Crow.

Yet a palpable spirit of hope and optimism characterized Black America, even as stories of lynchings, massacres, and the destruction of Black communities filled newspapers of the early 1920s. From the emerging cultural center of Harlem, Alain Locke proclaimed the arrival of the New Negro: "With this renewed self-respect and self-dependence, the life of the Negro community is bound to enter a new dynamic phase . . ." As his peers noted, white violence often targeted Black success, like the destruction of the Black business district of Tulsa, Oklahoma, in 1921 and the violence directed at the Sweet family in 1925 after they moved into a white neighborhood in Detroit. When Dr. Ossian Sweet and his family and friends stood trial for shooting a white man in the mob attacking his house, communities across the nation rallied in support of the Black physician. The *Amsterdam News* referred to the trial as "[p]ossibly the most important court case the Negro has ever figured in in all the history of the United States," noting how the Sweets "dared to protect themselves and their property against mob violence."

New Negro activism had local, national, and international reach in the decade following World War I. Activists and allies launched a renewed effort to influence federal policy by pushing for anti-lynching legislation. In 1928 Black Chicagoans, some of whom voted for the first time after migrating from the South, elected Oscar De Priest to Congress, making him the first Black representative to serve since 1901. Meanwhile Marcus Garvey's Universal Negro Improvement Association flourished, becoming a transnational mass movement with Harlem as its headquarters. But the New Negro was not strictly a northern phenomenon. When Texan C. F. Richardson justified why he would remain in the South and fight Jim Crow in his home state, he captured the mood of countless Black southerners.

The Great Depression saw the growth of the Black Left, with Socialists and Communists linking race and economics. An increasing number of intellectuals and unemployed workers found Marxism appealing, as the Depression led them to question the durability of an economy built on competition. The Communist Party had launched the American Negro Labor Congress in 1925 (renamed the League of Struggle for Negro Rights five years later), hoping to make inroads with Black workers. In the 1930s, Communists agitated against segregation and lynching, and became vocal allies of the

"Scottsboro Boys," nine Black teenagers accused of raping two white women on a train in Alabama in 1931. The Communist Party also appealed directly to rural Black southerners, resulting in the creation of the Sharecroppers Union by 1931. Men like Ned Cobb, who detailed his struggles as a sharecropper in his autobiography *All God's Dangers*, joined the Alabama Sharecroppers Union to advocate for other poor farmers in the Black Belt.

Labor organizing drew intense backlash from white landowners and law enforcement officials. Nineteen-year-old Angelo Herndon, who became a labor organizer after reading the *Communist Manifesto*, was arrested in Atlanta, Georgia, in 1932 after leading a demonstration of over 1,000 unemployed workers in that city. Herndon eventually served two years in prison before the Supreme Court overruled his conviction. The CPUSA made what was perhaps its boldest display of support for racial equality in 1932 by nominating James W. Ford as its candidate for vice president of the United States, running alongside presidential nominee William Z. Foster. The nomination made Ford the first Black vice-presidential candidate in U.S. history.

The federal government, especially the Democratic Party, paid increasing attention to the growing number of Black voters in migration cities. In 1936, when Franklin D. Roosevelt ran for a second term, he won 76 percent of the Black vote, making him the first Democratic presidential candidate to secure the Black vote. Roosevelt won Black support, in part, by appointing Black Americans to important positions. He appointed Mary McLeod Bethune as director of the Negro Affairs Division of the National Youth Administration, and he appointed the first Black federal judge, William H. Hastie. The crew of Black advisors operated as an informal network with Bethune as the group's unofficial leader and one of its most influential members. Historian Nancy Weiss describes FDR's so-called Black Cabinet as "the most important racial symbol of the New Deal."

As the United States prepared for World War II, the Socialist labor union organizer A. Philip Randolph began pressuring Roosevelt to desegregate the defense industry. Randolph was the president of the Brotherhood of Sleeping Car Porters, a union of railway workers that numbered in the thousands. Early in 1941 Randolph called for 10,000 Black activists to march on Washington, D.C., and helped organize the March on Washington Committee, which demanded a presidential order forbidding companies with government contracts from discriminating by race, and the elimination of racial exclusion from all branches of the armed services. In response to mounting threats of a massive demonstration, in June 1941 President Roosevelt established the Fair Employment Practices Committee (FEPC) to investigate discrimination, and issued Executive Order 8802, which banned racial and ethnic discrimination in the employment of workers in the defense industry or government. The expansion of the war industry during World War II helped motivate a second Great Migration. This time, the migrants also relocated to the West Coast, eventually sending a new wave of Black congressional representation to Washington, D.C., from places like Los Angeles. For Black Americans during the war, the "Double V" campaign—named by the *Pittsburgh Courier*—called for a victory abroad in the war effort and a victory against Jim Crow at home in the United States.

During the war, membership in the NAACP increased by 900 percent. In order to raise money to fight for civil rights in the courts, the organization in 1940 established the Legal Defense and Educational Fund, a tax-exempt agency that pursued justice through the courts. The national office appointed Thurgood Marshall, a Baltimore-bred attorney, as director of the LDF, and he worked with local NAACP branches in filing civil rights lawsuits. Marshall had one of his first major successes in 1944, when he partnered with the Houston branch of the NAACP to overturn the white primary in the Supreme Court case *Smith v. Allwright*. Buoyed by civil rights successes, civil rights activists entered the postwar years with a sense of optimism.

Black soldiers, sailors, and airmen returned from World War II with a renewed spirit of activism, but they faced a segregated country, as the lyrics to Big Bill Broonzy's "When Will I Get to Be Called a Man" attest. New organizations formed in the aftermath of the war. Black veterans realized that fighting fascism abroad did not translate to equality in the United

States, and their experiences helped launch a new era in the fight against Jim Crow.

Rosa Parks began working as a secretary at Maxwell Air Force Base in Montgomery in 1941, and her wartime experience shaped her postwar activism. The Alabama native was struck by the contrast between the desegregated trolley cars on the base and the Jim Crow buses she took in Montgomery. She experienced the possibilities of a desegregated society when she went to work each day. As a member of the NAACP, Parks investigated the rape of a Black Alabama woman named Recy Taylor by a gang of white men. She cofounded the Committee for Equal Justice for Mrs. Recy Taylor and sponsored a letter-writing campaign to Alabama governor Chauncey Sparks. These war-era experiences strengthened Parks's commitment to civil rights activism long before her historic stand against segregation on a Montgomery bus in December 1955.

The cause of Black civil rights got a boost during the presidency of Harry S. Truman. Truman formed the interracial Committee on Civil Rights, which recommended passage of anti-lynching legislation, ending voter discrimination, and desegregating the military. Truman's boldest move toward civil rights came on July 26, 1948, when he ordered the desegregation of the military. Earlier that summer, at the Democratic National Convention, Hubert Humphrey praised his party's "great fight for civil rights in America," prompting the "Dixiecrat revolt" by some white southerners within the Democratic Party. Led by then-governor of South Carolina Strom Thurmond, the fledgling States' Rights Democratic Party opposed Democrats' growing support for desegregation. Thurmond ran for president as a Dixiecrat, securing just over 2 percent of the national vote, but winning the states Louisiana, Mississippi, Alabama, and South Carolina. Truman won the election, and Thurmond and other Dixiecrats returned to the Democratic Party, but for the next twenty years, the rift in the party over civil rights would only deepen, especially as civil rights organizations claimed more victories against Jim Crow.

The 1954 Supreme Court ruling in *Brown v. Board of Education of Topeka* declared racial segregation in public schools unconstitutional and sparked the emergence of a "Second Reconstruction." Like the first Reconstruction that followed the

Civil War, the civil rights era of the 1950s provoked organized white resistance. The Ku Klux Klan reemerged after losing its power during the Great Depression, and Confederate flags became symbols of national white rebellion against the federal government and desegregation. The White Citizens Council, typically affluent members of the business community, used economic intimidation in addition to violent reprisals to terrorize Black activists. The idea of integrated schools intensified segregationists' fears of "miscegenation." The 1955 killing of fourteen-year-old Chicago native Emmett Till during his visit with family in Money, Mississippi, by several white men for allegedly behaving or speaking to a white woman in ways that defied Jim Crow mores, showed how race, gender, and sex fueled hysteria over school desegregation.

Yet the civil rights movement continued to claim victories. Building on the energy of the Montgomery bus boycott and the international attention garnered during the desegregation of Little Rock's Central High School in 1957, college students began using the tactic of nonviolent direct action in 1960. Ella Baker corralled the energy of the sit-in movement into a new organization called the Student Nonviolent Coordinating Committee, or SNCC. She also helped organize the coalition of ministers that became the Southern Christian Leadership Conference, with clergymen like Ralph Abernathy, Martin Luther King, Jr., and Fred Shuttlesworth as members.

As historian Barbara Ransby argues, Baker was guided by the idea that the process of overhauling an oppressive system had to involve ordinary people. SNCC and SCLC partnered with local activists to mount campaigns in small towns and big cities. They used modern telecommunications technology and the international politics of the Cold War to sway public opinion and prompt federal response. People across the nation learned about Fannie Lou Hamer, the former plantation worker, SNCC field secretary, and cofounder of the Mississippi Freedom Democratic Party who captured media attention during the Democratic National Convention of 1964. They watched footage of marches in the town of Selma, Alabama, in March of 1965. Grassroots campaigns fueled passage of the Civil Rights Act of 1964 and Voting Rights Act of 1965.

Stone Mountain continued to serve as a symbol of resistance for those opposed to Black equality. In 1965, a public park opened at the site where Simmons and his friends relaunched the Ku Klux Klan fifty years earlier. The opening date, April 14, 1965, marked the one-hundredth anniversary of the assassination of President Abraham Lincoln. Visitors could revel at the Confederate memorial carving of Jefferson Davis, Robert E. Lee, and Thomas J. "Stonewall" Jackson. But the memorial was not just a commemoration of a Confederate past. The date signified a continued defiance of federal intervention in racial matters of the South. The Klan terrorized and murdered activists and "outside agitators" who mounted civil rights campaigns. "Much of the Klan's terrorism is handled by goon squads with such picturesque names as 'The Holy Terrors' and 'The Secret Six,'" noted *Time* magazine in April 1965. "Such groups were held responsible for the mutilation and murder of three civil rights workers who were found in an earthen dam in Mississippi last June, for the killing of Washington, D.C., Educator Lemuel Penn in Georgia last July, and for the death of Mrs. Viola Liuzzo in Selma last month."[1] FBI investigators found the murderers in some of the cases, but federal intervention did not quell the killings.

As white supremacist violence persisted, veterans of southern civil rights campaigns began to question the efficacy of nonviolent direct action. Segregationists shot and wounded James Meredith during his 1966 "March Against Fear" campaign to register Black voters. SNCC continued Meredith's march, chanting "Black Power" during rallies. The Trinidad-born Bronx native Stokely Carmichael became the chairman of SNCC that year, and he was just one member of the group whose ideological and tactical stance shifted. Later known as Kwame Ture, he and others refocused their attention away from desegregation campaigns in favor of self-government, economic self-sufficiency, armed self-defense, and Black pride.

Advocates of Black Power drew inspiration from activists like Malcolm X and local NAACP leader Robert F. Williams

[1]"Nation: The Various Shady Lives of the Ku Klux Klan," *TIME*, April 9, 1965. Andrew Goodman, Michael Schwerner, and James Chaney were murdered on June 21, 1964; their bodies were found on August 4.

of Monroe, North Carolina. Williams had caused a rift in the organization by staging public protests and championing "armed self-reliance." Lowndes County in Alabama became testing grounds for the tenets of Black Power. Local activists and SNCC volunteers created the Lowndes County Freedom Organization, and like the Mississippi Freedom Democratic Party, the LCFO sought to overturn white Democratic control. Carmichael and more than a dozen field secretaries spent January through April 1966 canvassing Lowndes and hosting biweekly meetings in an effort to build support for the LCFO. They chose for their symbol a black panther, an image that helped inspire the creation of the Black Panther Party for Self-Defense in Oakland, California. The imagery and rhetoric of Black Power shook white supremacists, white moderates, and some Black activists who championed nonviolence. Shirley Chisholm, who in 1968 became the first Black woman elected to Congress, said one year later during a speech at Howard University, "everybody is so hysterical and panic stricken because of the adjective that precedes the word power—'black.' You know it would have been hoped in this country that we would never have to use the word 'black' before the word 'power,' because America has been built on a series of immigrants coming into this land, rising up and moving out in terms of achieving power to control their lives."

By the late 1960s, coverage of civil rights activity increasingly focused on places outside of the South. In Milwaukee, the Italian American Catholic priest Father Groppi marched and organized with Black activists like lawyer Vel Phillips to protest housing discrimination. Their activism prompted violent white backlash, earning the city the nickname "Selma of the North." Just a few years later, Boston became known as the "Little Rock of the North" due to violent resistance to a federal judge's school busing plan. Angry white mothers screamed abuse as teenagers threw rocks at school buses full of Black children. Places like Milwaukee and Boston showed the persistence of Jim Crow even after the passage of legislation like the Civil Rights Act.

When Barbara Jordan delivered the keynote address at the Democratic National Convention in 1976, she acknowledged the problems facing the United States while expressing confidence in the country's ability "to fulfill our national purpose, to create and sustain a society in which all of us are equal." Jordan spoke at the Democratic convention one hundred years after Frederick Douglass addressed the Republican National Convention, and she saw her presence as proof that the nation could change. In 1966, at the age of thirty, Jordan had become the first Black American elected to the Texas Senate since 1883 and the first Black woman ever elected to the Texas state legislature. The Houstonian became the first Black woman from the South to serve in the U.S. Congress in 1973. For Jordan, these political triumphs did not mean the long civil rights struggle had reached a victorious conclusion. The United States had not overcome, but she encouraged her party to believe that it could. "We have a positive vision of the future," she reminded the rapturous crowd at Madison Square Garden, "founded on the belief that the gap between the promise and reality of America can one day be finally closed."

1919–1945

A MASSACRE IN PHILLIPS COUNTY

WALTER WHITE

The Race Conflict in Arkansas

The Survey, December 13, 1919

THE RACE CONFLICT IN ARKANSAS

ASSOCIATED PRESS dispatches of early October informed the country in detail of a plot, by a fortuitous circumstance checked, of Negro assassins conspiring to stage a massacre and to murder, without reason or warrant, twenty-one white citizens of Phillips county, Arkansas. Following closely upon the widespread publicity given this account, an investigation was made by the National Association for the Advancement of Colored People who sent me as their representative into the county. The facts thus secured are totally at variance with the published accounts sent out from the community.

The trouble began on October 1, when W. D. Adkins, special agent for the Missouri Pacific Railway, Charles Pratt, deputy sheriff, and a Negro trusty were driving past a Negro church at Hoopspur in Phillips county, Arkansas, where a meeting of a branch of the Progressive Farmers and Household Union of America was being held. According to Pratt's story, Negroes without cause fired at the party from the church, killing Adkins and wounding Pratt. Negroes in the church at the time, however, declare that Pratt and Adkins fired into the church apparently to frighten the Negroes gathered there, and that the Negroes returned the fire. This started the conflict which spread to all parts of Phillips county.

About the same time that the meeting was being held at Hoopspur, sixty-eight Negro farmers at Ratio, another small town in the county, had met for conference with the son of a white lawyer of Little Rock, to pay retainers' fees for the prosecution, in court, of their landlord who they alleged had seized their cotton and was about to ship it away. During 1918 these same share-croppers charged that their cotton had been taken from them and a settlement had not been made until

July, 1919. Fearing that this action would be repeated with this year's crop, the Negroes were taking legal means to prevent it. The lawyer's son and all of the Negroes in the conference were arrested. The white man was kept in jail thirty-one days without a hearing, charged with "barratry"—fomenting legal action. He was finally released on his own recognizance.

When the news of the killing of Adkins spread—vague rumors of the farmers' organization having meanwhile come to the ears of the whites—the entire community was at once thrown into a state of antagonism. White men poured into Helena, the county seat of Phillips county, from all parts of Arkansas, Mississippi, and Tennessee; Negroes were disarmed and arrested; their arms were given to the whites who rapidly thronged the little town of Helena. Those Negroes who escaped arrest took refuge in the canebrakes near the town where they were hunted down like animals. According to the final death list, five whites and twenty-five Negroes were killed. Several white men in Helena told me that more than one hundred Negroes were killed, and that in his opinion the total death list would never be known. The Negroes arrested were herded together in a stockade and were refused communication with relatives, friends, or attorneys. Though a Negro might have been able to prove his innocence, he was released only when a white man vouched for him; a thing which was not done until the Negro agreed to work for the white man for a period of time and for wages determined upon by the employer.

Five times as many Negroes as white persons were killed, according to statements given out in the community, and many more times as many according to unofficial statements. According to the census of 1910, there were 7,176 white people and 26,354 Negroes in the county.

When the alleged conspirators were brought up for trial they were assigned counsel by the court; witnesses for the defense were not allowed to testify; no change of venue was asked, although the trials were held in Phillips county one month after the alleged massacre took place while the feeling was still intense. The first six defendants were jointly indicted, tried and found guilty in exactly seven minutes by a jury from which Negroes were excluded. The six were sentenced to electrocution on December 27, for murder in the first degree. In all, twelve Negroes have been sentenced to death and eighty have been sentenced to terms ranging from one to twenty years—all of these convictions taking place within five days.

These Arkansas Negroes like others in certain parts of the South, have been living under a state of subjection for more than fifty years. The system, known as "share-cropping" or "tenant farming," had become so abusive that these farmers felt its continuance meant nothing except peonage.

The basis of the system in theory is this: Land together with implements, seed, and supplies, is furnished by a landlord; labor is furnished by the share-croppers; and at the end of the year the crop is divided share and share alike. The system, however, rarely works out in actual practice according to this theory. When the season is ended the cotton is taken by the owners, ginned at the plantation gin, and sold. The Negro share-cropper is not allowed to know the weight of the cotton which he raised nor the price at which it is sold. Instead of an itemized statement of the goods received during the year from the plantation commissary (where in most cases he is compelled to purchase his supplies), the Negro is given a lump statement generally marked "to balance due." By always having the charge for goods received larger than the value of the Negro's share of the crop the owner can keep him perpetually in debt. There is an unwritten law which is rigidly observed in this Arkansas district that no Negro can leave a plantation while he is in debt. Thus the owner not only takes the Negro's crop out but is assured of his workers for the following year.

Attempts had been made by individuals to protest against their failure to secure from landlords itemized statements of their accounts and equitable settlements; these resulted not only in failure but in many cases in further persecution of the worker. The organization of the Progressive Farmers and Household Union of America was the Negro's answer—a legitimate alliance of colored farmers in Phillips county to end a vicious system of economic exploitation.

A few of the actual cases taken from court records and from personal interviews with share-croppers, owners, and their agents, will show how the system has worked there and the condition which the farmers' union attempted to remedy.

A Negro raised during the season of 1918, 40 bales of cotton. An average bale of cotton weighs 500 pounds, and at the time that this crop was sold cotton was selling at $.28 a pound.

To every bale of cotton there is approximately one-half ton of seed which sells at $70 a ton. The total value of the Negro's crop was, therefore, $7,000, and when this Negro asked for a settlement he was told that he had not only "taken up" goods worth over $7,000 but that his "balance due" amounted to over $1,000.

During the same year in Keo, Lonoke county, Arkansas, a Negro by the name of George Conway, raised 20 bales of cotton, the value of which was $3,500. His landlord refused to furnish him shoes or clothing, so that he was forced to work his crop bare-footed and often hungry. The worker's family consisted of himself, a wife, and two children. Although the value of goods he "took up" did not amount to more than $300, when he asked for an itemized statement at the end of the year he was told that his purchases amounted to $40 more than the value of his crop. When he demanded a settlement and an itemized statement his landlord beat him severely and threatened to kill him if he persisted in his demand. For the $40, balance due, the landlord seized the Negro's household goods and drove him off the plantation, penniless.

A Negro who lived at Watson, Arkansas, produced, during the year 1919, a crop of which his share was 14 bales. The price of cotton when his crop was sold was $.43 a pound, so that the value of the 14 bales with the seed was $3,500. The man "took up" during the year goods valued at $23.50, yet in the statement he received the value of the goods received exactly equaled the value of his crop. This man, though paralyzed in his right leg, walked 122 miles to Little Rock, hoping to secure a lawyer to bring suit against the landlord. But being without funds he was unable to secure one.

Phillips county, in October, is relatively unimportant as an isolated case. As an example of the underlying corruption and injustice that will lead to further and more disastrous conflicts, it is of grave import. Unless there is immediate interference on the part of federal or state officials—and there is little hope of the latter—twelve Negroes will be legally lynched and eighty will continue to serve prison sentences in Arkansas, victims of America's negligence and denial of common justice to men.

RAISING FUNDS FOR THE DEFENSE

IDA B. WELLS-BARNETT

Condemned Arkansas Rioters Look to Chicago for Help

The Chicago Defender, December 13, 1919

CONDEMNED ARKANSAS RIOTERS LOOK TO CHICAGO FOR HELP

GOV. BROUGH'S PROMISE TO LET SUPREME COURT REVIEW CASES GIVES HOPE TO ALLEGED RIOTERS

The following press dispatch under date of Nov. 28, is interesting to all of our people:

"Of the twelve Negroes sentenced to death for participating in the uprising in Phillips county, six are scheduled to be executed Dec. 26 and six Jan. 2. Governor Brough, however, has announced that he would postpone the executions. The governor declared that he desired to have the Arkansas Supreme court pass on the cases of the Negroes in order that there might be no doubt that they received justice."

This is especially gratifying to those of us here in Chicago who are preparing to put the resolution we passed a few weeks ago into effect. All the resolutions and protests sent from other parts of the country simply protested against the outrage of condemning eleven men to the electric chair in eight minutes, and appealed to the governor of Arkansas and to the President and congress to do something to save these men, whose crime (?) had been that they had organized their forces to protect the labor of their hands.

PASS RESOLUTIONS

The resolutions passed by the Equal Rights League, the People's Movement and the Negro Fellowship League said that if those men were electrocuted because they had defended themselves when fired upon, the people of those organizations would immediately take steps to see that thousands more of our people who had enriched the South by their labor would leave Arkansas, never to return. That was the resolution which caused Governor Brough to call a meeting of whites and blacks and try to get them to say that it was all right to electrocute eleven of our Race for the killing of two whites who were firing on them.

UNITY SHOWN

This show of unity among Chicago Negroes has already brought forth splendid fruit. Especially so when the Chicago Defender goes everywhere to tell Negroes what we are doing in their behalf. No wonder Governor Brough took occasion to denounce the Defender before the State Baptist Association. But the Defender goes on defending the rights of the Race, just the same.

WILL APPEAL CASE

But while we are thanking God for this reprieve for those eleven men who were fighting for the right to organize for their own protection, let us not sit down in idleness, believing all is well. The Arkansas Supreme court may affirm the decision of the lower court. If it does, the Negro race of this country ought to be prepared to appeal the case to the United States Supreme court. To do this will take the biggest lawyers in the country. We should begin raising a fund for that purpose right now! I have already spoken to some, and as chairman of the publicity committee of the National Equal Rights League and president of the Negro Fellowship League, will be glad to receive and acknowledge receipt of said funds, and solemnly pledge myself to see that every dollar raised will be applied to the purpose for which it was given.

WEALTHY SOCIETIES AND CHURCHES

Every organization in the country, which has thousands of dollars of the people's money in their treasuries, should send in from $100 to $500 and quickly get a fund of $10,000 for the purpose of defending these men. The principle at stake involves every one of us—the right to organize for our own protection! The man or woman who does not see that does not deserve the liberty he or she enjoys. If they are not willing to aid in this fight they will not long enjoy that liberty, for already word comes that all Negro organizations which whites do not approve must be stamped out. That's why they killed the Johnson family. Already in Georgia, Alabama, as well as Arkansas, churches and lodges have been burned down.

DRIVEN FROM HOMES

Already in Mississippi N. S. Taylor has had to leave his home and the accumulations of thirty years—without time to realize a dollar—because he accepted the presidency of the National Equal Rights League. The Defender reported last week that a prominent educator of South Carolina, who had been a teacher and respected citizen of the community for thirty years, who had built a school which was an honor and credit to the Race and state, was driven from his home because he, too, had become president of an organization, and the whites demanded his resignation! Is the Race going to sit still and permit these outrages to continue without doing something in its own behalf? I do not believe it will.

WHAT CAN YOU DO?

You ask what can you do? And my reply is, send me the money and I will show you what we can do. You furnish me with the sinews of war and I will fight your battles just as I have done for twenty-five years—only this time you will be helping. Will you do it?

If the Arkansas Supreme court reverses the decision of the lower court the cases of these eleven condemned men and the three score who are in prison for long terms will be tried again in the lower courts. These men must have the best lawyers in the country to take their cases again. This will take money. If the Arkansas Supreme court affirms the finding of the lower court we should be in position to appeal to the United States Supreme court. It can and will be done if we have money enough that is available. Will you do it? If so, let me hear from individuals, churches, secret societies, business men's leagues and women's clubs at once, wherever the Defender is read. Quick action is needed. Your confidence will be respected. No one but yourselves will know of your contribution, and you will know as soon as I receive it.

MRS. IDA B. WELLS-BARNETT.

3006 S. State St., Chicago.

“MARCHING THROUGH . . . AN ENEMY’S LAND”

ARCHIBALD H. GRIMKÉ

The Shame of America: Or the Negro’s Case against the Republic

December 29, 1919

THE AUTHOR of the Declaration of Independence said once that he trembled for his country when he remembered that God was just. And he did well to do so. But while he was about it he might have quaked a little for himself. For he was certainly guilty of the same crime against humanity, which had aroused in his philosophic and patriotic mind such lively sensations of anxiety and alarm in respect to the Nation. Said Jefferson on paper: “We hold these truths to be self-evident, that all men are created equal; that they are endowed by their Creator with certain unalienable rights; that among these are life, liberty and the pursuit of happiness,” while on his plantation he was holding some men as slaves, and continued to hold them as such for fifty years thereafter, and died at the end of a long and brilliant life, a Virginia slaveholder. And yet Thomas Jefferson was sincere, or fancied that he was, when he uttered those sublime sentiments about the rights of man, and when he declared that he trembled for his country when he remembered that God was just. This inconsistency between the man’s magnificence in profession and his smallness in practice, between the grandeur of what he promised and the meanness of what he performed, taken in conjunction with his cool unconsciousness of the discrepancy, is essentially and emphatically an American trait, a national idiosyncrasy. For it has appeared during the last one hundred and forty-four years with singular boldness and continuity in the social, political, and religious life of the American people and their leaders. I do not recall in all history such another example of a nation appearing so well in its written words regarding human rights, and so badly when it comes to translating those fine words into corresponding action, as this Republic has uniformly exhibited from its foundation, wherever the Negro has been concerned.

Look at its conduct in the War of the Revolution, which it began with the high sounding sentiments of the Declaration of Independence. The American colonists rose in arms because they were taxed by England without their consent, a species of tyranny which bore no sort of comparison to the slavery which they themselves were imposing on the Negro. But with such inconsistency of conduct the men of the Revolution bothered not their heads for a simple, and to them, a sufficient reason. They were white and the Negro was black and was their property. Since they were fighting for a political principle in order the better to protect their pockets, they were not disposed to give up their property rights in anything, not even in human beings. They were contending for the sacred right of loosening their own purse strings, not for the sacred privilege of loosening the bonds of their slaves. Not at all. Millions they were willing to spend in defense of the former, but not a cent to effect the latter, their loud talk in the Declaration of Independence to the contrary, notwithstanding.

Their subsequent conduct in respect to the Negro was of a piece with this characteristic beginning. First they accepted the services of the blacks, both bond and free, as soldiers, and then they debated the expediency and justice of their action, not from the point of view of the slaves but from that of the masters, and later decided upon a policy of exclusion of the slaves from the Continental army. With the adoption of such a policy the chattel rights of masters in those poor men would be better conserved. Hence the policy of exclusion. But when the British evinced a disposition to enlist the slaves as soldiers, a change passed quickly over the leaders of the Revolution, with Washington at their head. The danger to the master of a policy of inclusion was overridden readily enough in the greater danger to the cause of one of exclusion. Without a thought for the slave, he was put on the military chessboard, withdrawn, then put back in response to purely selfish considerations and needs.

Thus it happened that black men fought in that war shoulder to shoulder with white men for American Independence. In every colony from Massachusetts to Georgia, they were found faithful among the faithless, and brave as the bravest during those long and bitter years, fighting and dying with incomparable devotion and valor, by the side of Warren at Bunker Hill, and of Pulaski at Savannah.

The voluntary surrender of life for country has been justly held by all ages to be an act of supreme virtue. It is in the power of any man to give less; it is in the power of none, however exalted in station, to give more. For to lay down one's life at the call of Duty is to lay down one's all. And this all of the General weighs no more than the all of a common soldier. Weighed in the scales of truth this supreme gift of the beggar on foot balances exactly that of the Prince on horseback. When Prince or beggar, master or slave, has given his life to a cause, he has given his utmost. Beyond that absolute measure of devotion neither can add one jot or tittle to the value of his gift. Thank God there is no color line in acts of heroism and self-sacrifice, save the royal one of their blood-tinted humanity. Such was the priceless contribution which the poor, oppressed Negro made to American Independence.

What was his guerdon? In the hour of their triumph did the patriot fathers call to mind such supreme service to reward it? In the freedom which they had won by the aid of their enslaved countrymen, did they bethink them of lightening the yoke of those miserable men? History answers, no! Truth answers, no! The descendants of those black heroes answer, no! What then? What did such bright, such blazing beacons of liberty, the Washingtons, Hamiltons, Madisons and Franklins, the Rufus Kings, Roger Shermans, and Robert Morrises? They founded the Republic on slavery, rested one end of its stately arch on the prostrate neck of the Negro. They constructed a national Constitution which safeguarded the property of man in man, introducing into it for that purpose its three-fifths slave representation provision, its fugitive slave clause, and an agreement by which the African slave trade was legalized for nineteen years after the adoption of that instrument. That was the reward which the founders of the Republic meted out with one accord to a race which had shed freely its blood to make that Republic a reality among the nations of the earth. Instead of loosening and lifting his heavy yoke of oppression, they strengthened and tightened it afresh on the loyal and long suffering neck of the Negro. Notwithstanding this shameful fact, the founders of the Republic were either so cooly unconscious of its moral enormity or else so indifferent to the amazing contradiction between what they said and what they did, as to write over the gateway of the new Constitution this sonorous preamble: "We the people of the United States, in order to form a more perfect union, establish justice, insure domestic tranquillity, provide for the common defense, promote the general welfare, and secure the Blessings of liberty to ourselves and our posterity, do ordain and establish this Constitution for the United States of America."

"We the people!" From the standpoint of the Negro, what grim irony; "establish justice!" What exquisitely cruel mockery; "to insure domestic tranquillity!" What height and breadth and depth of political duplicity; "to provide for the common defense!" What cunning paltering with words in a double sense; "to promote the general welfare!" What studied ignoring of an ugly fact; "and secure the blessings of liberty to ourselves and posterity!" What masterly abuse of noble words to mask an equivocal meaning, to throw over a great national transgression an air of virtue, so subtle and illusive as to deceive the framers themselves into believing in their own sincerity. You may ransack the libraries of the world, and turn over all the documents of recorded time to match that Preamble of the Constitution as a piece of consummate political dissimulation and mental reservation, as an example of how men juggle deliberately and successfully with their moral sense, how they raise above themselves huge fabrics of falsehood, and go willingly to live and die in a make-believe world of lies. The muse of history, dipping her iron pen in the generous blood of the Negro, has written large across the page of that Preamble, and the face of the Declaration of Independence, the words, "sham, hypocrisy."

It is the rage now to sing the praises of the fathers of the Republic as a generation of singularly liberty-loving men. They were so, indeed, if judged by their fine words alone. But they were, in reality, by no means superior to their sons in this respect, if we judge them by their acts, which somehow speak louder, more convincingly to us than their words, albeit those words proceed out of the Declaration of Independence and the Preamble of the Constitution. If the children's teeth today are set on edge on the Negro question, it is because the fathers ate the sour grapes of race-wrong, ate those miserable grapes during their whole life, and, dying, transmitted their taste for oppression, as a bitter inheritance to their children, and children's children, for God knows how many black years to come.

Take the case of Washington as an example. He was rated an abolitionist by his contemporaries. And so he was if mere words could have made him one. On paper he was one person, but on his plantation quite another. And as far as I know his history, he never made any effectual attempt to bring this second self of his into actual accord with the first. In theory he favored emancipation, while in practice he was one of the biggest, if not the biggest slaveholder in the country, who enriched himself and his family out of the unpaid toil of more than two hundred slaves. The father of his country did not manumit them during his lifetime, or of that of his wife. Not until his death, not until the death of his widow, did he, as a matter of fact, release his hold upon the labor of those people, did they escape from his dead hands. As first President, moreover, he signed the first fugitive slave law, and was not ashamed to avail himself of its hateful provisions for the reclamation of one of his runaway slave-women. And yet Washington, and Jefferson also, are the two bright, particular stars of our American democracy. They had very fine words for liberty, no two men ever had finer, but when it came to translating them into action, into churning them into butter for the poor Negro's parsnips, no atom of butter did they yield, or will ever yield, churn them ever so long. *Ex pede Herculem.*

Naturally enough under the circumstances of its origin and antecedents, American democracy has never cared a fig in practice for the fine sentiments of its Declaration of Independence, or for the high sounding ones of the Preamble to its Constitution, wherever and whenever the Negro has been concerned. It used him to fight the battles for its independent political existence, and rewarded his blood and bravery with fresh stripes and heavier chains.

History repeats itself. In America, on the Negro question, it has been a series of shameful repetitions of itself. The Negro's history in the first war with England was repeated exactly in the second. In this conflict no more loyal and daring hearts bled and broke for the country than were those of its colored soldiers and sailors. On land and water in that war the Negro died as he fought, among the most faithful and heroic defenders of the American cause. But to praise him is to condemn the country, which in this instance I will leave to no less an American than General Jackson. Out of his mouth shall this condemnation be spoken. Said Jackson three weeks before the battle of New Orleans to the black soldiers who had rallied at his summons to repel a formidable invasion of our national domain by a powerful foreign enemy:

"From the shores of Mobile I called you to arms. I invited you to share in the perils and divide the glory of your white countrymen. I expected much from you, for I was not uninformed of those qualities which must render you so formidable to an invading foe. I knew you could endure hunger and thirst, and all the hardships of war. I knew that you loved the land of your nativity, and that, like ourselves, you had to defend all that is most dear to men. But you surpass my hopes. I have found in you united to those qualities, that noble enthusiasm that impels to great deeds.

"Soldiers: The President of the United States shall be informed of your conduct on the present occasion, and the voice of the representatives of the American nation shall applaud your valor, as your General now praises your ardor. The enemy is near. His sails cover the lakes, but the brave are united, and if he finds us contending among ourselves, it will be for the prize of valor, and fame its noblest reward."

Jackson's black troops proved themselves in the actions of Mobile Bay and New Orleans entitled to every mouthful of the ringing applause which Old Hickory gave them without stint. They got fair enough words as long as the enemy was in sight and his navy covered the waters of the country. But as soon as the peril had passed those fair words were succeeded by the foulest ingratitude. On every hand Colorphobia reared its cursed head, and struck its cruel fangs into those brave beasts which had just received the swords and the bullets of a foreign foe. They were legislated against everywhere, proscribed by atrocious laws everywhere. They had given the nation in its dire need, blood and life, and measureless love, and had received as reward black codes, an unrelenting race prejudice, and bondage bitterer than death.

Strange irony of fate which reserved to Andrew Jackson, whose mouth overflowed with praise in 1814 for his black soldiers and with fair promises of what he intended to do for them—strange irony of fate, I say, which reserved to that man, as President in 1836, the elevation of Roger B. Taney to the Chief-Justiceship of the United States, of Taney, the infamous slave Judge who wrote the Dred Scott Decision, which argued that black men had no rights in America which white men were bound to respect. The downright brutality of that opinion was extremely shocking to some sensitive Americans, but it was no more so than was the downright brutality of the facts, which it reflected with brutal accuracy. The fell apparition of American inhumanity, which those words conjured up from the depths of an abominable past and from that of a no less abominable present, was indeed black, but it was no blacker than the truth. The dark soul of the nation was embodied in them, all of its savage selfishness, greed and iniquity. There they glared, large and life-like, a devil's face among the nations, seamed and intersected with the sinister lines of a century of cruelty and race hatred and oppression. Of course the fair idealism of the Declaration of Independence was wanting in the photographic naturalism of the picture, and so was the fictive beauty of the Preamble of the Constitution, because they were wanting in the terrible original, in the malignant, merciless, and murderous spirit of a democracy which the dark words of the dark judge had limned to the life.

God has made iniquitous power ultimately self-destructive. Into every combination of evil He puts the seed of division and strife. Without this effective check wickedness would conquer and permanently possess the earth. The law of the brute would rule it forever. Where today are the empires of might and wrong, which men reared in their pride and strength, on the Nile, the Tigris, and the Euphrates, on the Tiber, the Bosporus, and the Mediterranean? They flourished for a season and seasons, and spread themselves like green bay trees. But behold they are gone, perished, burnt up by the fires of evil passions, by the evil power which consumed them to ashes. Centuries have flown over their graves, and the places once cursed by their violence, and crushed by their oppressions, shall know them and their vulture laws and trampling armies no more forever.

So it happened in the case of the American people when in order "to form a more perfect union," they ordained and established their Constitution. Within the "more perfect union" was enfolded a fruitful germ of division and discord. No bigger at first than the smallest of seeds, the germ grew apace with the growth of the new nation, drawing abundant nourishment from the dark underworld of the slave. Slender sapling in 1815, it was a fast growing tree in 1820, bearing even then its bitter apples of Gomorrah. Where its bitter fruit fell, there fell also on the spirit of the people mutual distrust, and incipient sectional hate. And no wonder, for when the North clasped hands with her Southern sister in "a more perfect union," she did so the better to conserve a set of interests and institutions peculiar to herself and inherently hostile to those of the South, and vice versa with respect to the action of the latter in the premises. The "more perfect union" had, thank God, effected a conjunction, under a single political system, of two sets of mutually invasive and destructive social ideas and industrial forces. Differences presently sprang up between the partisans of each set, and discontent, and wide-spreading fear and contention. National legislation which oxidized and enriched the blood of the North, not only impoverished but actually poisoned that of the South. And so it came to pass that the compromise Constitution which was designed "to form a more perfect union," failed of its purpose, because with human slavery at the core of it, it brought two warring social systems face to face, whose unappeasable strife it had not the secret or the strength to subdue.

As in Egypt more than three thousand years ago, the Eternal spoke to the master-race at divers times and with divers signs, saying, "let my people go," so he spoke to the master-race in this land through divers omens and events, saying likewise, "let my people go." Those with ears to hear might have heard that divine voice in the Hartford Convention and the causes which led to its call; in the successive sectional conflicts over Missouri, the Tariff, and Texas; in the storm winds of the Mexican war, as in the wild uproar which followed the annexation of new national territory at its close; in the political rage and explosions of 1850 and 1854, and in the fierce patter of blood-drops over Kansas. They might have surely heard that commanding voice from the anointed lips of holy men and prophets, from the mouths of Garrison and Sumner, and Phillips, and Douglass, from the sacred gallows where John Brown heard and repeated it while his soul went marching on from city to city, and State to State, over mountain and river, across a continent, and from the Lakes to the Gulf with rising accent saying, "let my people go." Alas! the nation hearkened not to the voice of justice, but continued to harden its heart, until thunder-like that voice broke in the deep boom of Civil War.

When masters fall out a way oftentimes opens for the escape of their slaves. In the death grapple of the sections for political supremacy, the dead weight of two centuries of oppression lifted from the neck of the Negro. The people and their leaders of both sections despised him to such a degree that neither would in the beginning enlist his aid against the other. "We the people" of the glorious union of 1789 had quarrelled like two bloody scoundrels over their ill-gotten gains, and had come to murderous blows. Yet in spite of their deadly hatred of each other, they said in their mad race-pride and prejudice, the North to the South, and the South to the North, "go to, shall we not settle our differences without the aid of him who is our slave? Shall not we white men fight our duel to a finish; shall either of us appeal for help to that miserable being who by our laws, written and unwritten, has never possessed any rights among us which we have ever respected?" They chose to forget how in two wars this faithful man had for their sakes, received into his sad but brave breast the swords and the bullets of a foreign enemy, and all unmindful of self had helped them to achieve and maintain their liberty and independence. And thus choosing to forget his past services and to remember only their bitter race-prejudice against him, they fought on with deadly malice and violence, the one side against the other, rending their dear Union with fraternal strife, and drenching it with fraternal blood.

Perceiving the unlimited capacity of mankind for all sorts of folly, no wonder Puck exclaimed "What fools these mortals be!" Yes, what fools, but of all the fools who have crawled to dusty death the most stupendous and bedeviled lot are those who strut their fool's feet and toss their fool's heads across their little stage of life, thanking their fool's selves that God made them different from other men—superior to other men—to rule over other men. Puffed up with their stupid race-pride and prejudice, inflated to the bursting point with their high and mighty notions, and *noli me tangere* airs, the North and the South went on for nearly two years goring and tearing each other like two infuriated bulls of nearly equal strength, before either would call on the Negro for assistance. Not until bleeding at every pore, sickened at the loss of its sordid dollar, and in despair at the threatened destruction of that to which it ascribed, as to the Almighty, all of its sectional progress, prosperity and power, viz: the dear Union, did the North turn for help to the Negro, whom, it had despised and wronged, and whom it even then, in its heart of hearts, despised and intended, upon occasion, to wrong anew.

Think of the incredible folly and selfishness of a people fighting for existence and yet begrudging freedom to an enslaved race, whom it had called upon to help defend that existence; doling out to its faithful black allies, with miserly meanness, its blood-money and its boasted democratic equality and fair play; denying to its colored soldiers equal pay and promotion with its white ones, albeit many of those white ones were mercenary aliens from Europe. Nevertheless, of such bottomless depths of folly and meanness was the National Government certainly guilty. The Fifty-fourth and the Fifty-fifth Massachusetts regiments enlisted to fight the battles of the country, with the understanding that there would be no discrimination against them on account of their color. Yet the government violated its understood pledge, and proceeded to pay, or tried to pay those men ten dollars a month where it was paying other men, because they were white, thirteen dollars a month for the same service. All honor to Massachusetts for objecting to this shameful act, and, for offering to make up to her colored regiments the three dollars out of which the National government was endeavoring to cheat them. Three times three cheers for the brave and true men who had the sagacity, and the courage, and the self-respect to resist the injustice of the government, and to refuse firmly to compromise by a cent their right to equality of pay in the army.

Take another instance of the meanness of the government's conduct toward its colored defenders. In January of 1864, Henry Wilson embodied, in a bill to promote enlistments, a clause which provided that when "any man or boy of African descent, in service or labor in any State under its laws, should be mustered into the military or naval service of the United States, he and his mother, wife and children, shall be forever free." Now will you believe that this just and moderate measure took thirteen long months before its friends could get Congress to enact it into law? "Future generations," exclaimed Charles Sumner in closing his remarks on the subject, "Future generations will read with amazement, that a great people when national life was assailed, hesitated to exercise a power so simple and beneficient; and this amazement will know no bounds, as they learn that Congress higgled for months on a question, whether the wives and children of our colored soldiers should be admitted to freedom."

Need I repeat in this presence the old, grand story, how in numbers nearly two hundred thousand strong our colored boys in blue, left their blood and their bones in every State from Virginia to Louisiana? How, like heroes, they fought and died for the Union at Port Hudson, and Fort Wagner, and Petersburg, and Honey Hill, and Olustee, and Milliken's Bend? How in winter and summer, in cold and heat, in valley and on hilltop, on horse and on foot, over rivers and swamps, through woods and brakes, they rushed to meet the foe? How leaving behind them fields strown thick with their dead and wounded, they mounted the blazing sides of grim fortresses, climbing on great deeds and self-sacrifices through storms of shot and shell, to death and a place among the stars?

No, no, it is not required of me on this occasion to read afresh that glorious record. Sufficient then this: The Northern arm, reinforced by the strength which it drew from that of the Negro, broke in time the back of the Rebellion, and saved the Union, so that in 1865 the flag of the nation floated again over an undivided country, and the Republic, strong and great beneath that flag, launched anew to meet the years, and to reach her fair ideals of liberty and equality which were flashing like beacon lights upon her way.

Amid widespread rejoicing on the return of peace and the restoration of the Union, the Negro rejoiced among the gladdest, for his slave fetters were broken, he was no longer a chattel. He imagined in his simple heart, in his ignorance and poverty, that he had not only won freedom, but the lasting affection and gratitude of the powerful people for whom he had entered hell to quench for them its raging fires with his blood. Yes, although black and despised, he, the slave, the hated one, had risen above his centuries of wrongs, above their bitter memories and bitterer sufferings to the love of enemies, to the forgiveness of those who had despitefully used him, ay, to those moral heights where heroes are throned and martyrs crowned. Surely, surely, he, who had been so unmindful of self in the service of country, would not be left by that country at the mercy of those who hated him then with the most terrible hatred for that very cause. He who had been mighty to save others would surely, now in his need, be saved by those whom he had saved. "Oh! Justice thou hast fled to brutish beasts, and men have lost their gratitude."

I would gladly seal forever the dark chapter of our history, which followed the close of the war. Gladly would I forget that record of national shame and selfishness. But as it is better to turn on light than to shut it off, I will, with your forebearance, turn it on for our illumination and guidance, in the lowering present.

The chapter opened with an introduction of characteristic indifference on the part of the country in respect to the fate of the Negro. With his shackles lying close beside him, he was left in the hands of his old master, who seizing the opportunity proceeded straightway to refit them on the disenthralled limbs of the former slave. State after State did so with such promptitude and to such effect that within a few months a formidable system of Negro-serfdom had actually been constructed, and cunningly substituted in place of the system of Negro slavery, which the war had destroyed. An African serf-power, Phoenix-like, was rising out of the ashes of the old slave power into national politics. At sight of this truly appalling apparition, the apparition of a returning slave power in thin disguise, all the old sectional fear and hatred which had existed against it in the free States before the Rebellion, awoke suddenly and hotly in the breast of the North. Thinking mainly, if not wholly of its own safety in the emergency which confronted it, and how best to avert the fresh perils which impended in consequence over its ascendency, the North prepared to make, and did in fact make, for the time being, short shrift of this boldly retroactive scheme of the South to recover within the Union all that it had lost, by its defeated attempt to land itself outside of the Union.

Having tested to its entire satisfaction the Negro's value as a soldier in its war for the preservation of the Union, the North determined at this juncture to enlist his aid as a citizen in its further conflicts with the South, for the preservation of its sectional domination in the newly restored Union. To this end the Fourteenth and the Fifteenth Amendments to the Constitution were in the progress of events, incorporated into that instrument. By these two great acts, the North had secured itself against the danger of an immediate return of the South to anything like political equality with it in the Republic. Between its supremacy and the attacks of its old rival, it had erected a solid wall of Negro votes. But immensely important as was the ballot to its black contingent, it was not enough to meet all of his tremendous needs. Nevertheless, as the North was considering mainly its own and not the Negro's necessities at this crisis, and as the elective franchise in his hands was deemed by it adequate to satisfy its own pressing needs, it gave the peculiar wants of the Negro beyond that of the ballot but scant attention.

Homeless, landless, illiterate, just emerging from the blackness of two centuries of slavery, this simple and faithful folk had surely other sacred claims on the North and the National Government than this right to the ballot. They had in truth a strong claim to unselfish friendship and statesmanship, to unfaltering care and guardianship, during the whole of their transition from slavery to citizenship. They needed the organized hands, the wise heads, the warm hearts, the piled up wealth, the sleepless eyes, the faith, hope, and charity of a Christian people and a Christian government to teach them to walk and to save them from industrial exploitation by their old masters, as well as to vote. Did they receive from the Republic what the

Republic owed them by every consideration of justice, gratitude and humanity, as of enlightened self-interest? Alas! not a tithe of this immense debt has the Republic ever undertaken to pay to those who should have been, under all circumstances, its sacredly preferred creditors. On the contrary they were left to themselves by the government in the outer darkness of that social state which had been their sad lot for more than two centuries. They were left in that darkest night of moral and civil anarchy to fight not alone their own terrible battle with poverty, ignorance, and untutored appetites and passions, but also the unequal, the cruel battle for the preservation of Northern political domination in the Union. For ten awful years they fought that battle for the North, for the Republican party, in the face of persecutions and oppressions, terrors and atrocities, at the glare of which the country and the civilized world shrunk aghast.

Aghast shrank the North, but not for the poor Negro, faithful unto death to it. For itself rather it shrank from the threatening shadows which such a carnival of horrors was casting athwart its vast and spreading network of trade and production. The clamor of all its million-wheeled industry and prosperity was for peace. "Let us have peace," said Grant, and "let us have peace" blew forthwith and in deafening unison, all the big and little whistles of all the big and little factories and locomotives, and steamships from Maine to California. Every pen of merchant and editor scratched paper to the same mad tune. The pulpit and the platform of the land cooed their Cuckoo-song in honor of those piping times of peace. The loud noise of chinking coin pouring into vaults like coal into bins, drowned the agonized cry of the forgotten and long-suffering Negro. Deserting him in 1876, the North, stretching across the bloody chasm its two greedy, commercial hands, grasped the ensanguined ones of the South, and repeated, "let us have peace." Little did the Northern people and the government reck then or now that at the bottom of that bloody chasm lay their faithful black friends. Little did they care that the blood on those Southern hands had been wrung drop by drop from the loyal heart of the Negro. But enough.

Years of struggle and oppression follow and we come to another chapter of American history; namely, the Spanish-

American War. In the Spanish-American War the Negro attracted the attention of the world by his dashing valor. He attracted the attention of his country also. His fighting quality was of the highest, unsurpassed, and perhaps unequalled in brilliancy by the rest of the American army that invaded Cuba. He elicited applause and grudging justice from his countrymen, dashed with envy and race prejudice. Still it seemed for a brief time that his conspicuous service had given his case against the Republic a little better standing in Court—a little better chance for a fair hearing at the Bar of Public Opinion. But our characteristic national emotionalism was too shallow and insincere to last. In fact it died aborning. The national habit of a century and a half reasserted itself. There was no attempt made to square national profession and national practice, national promise and national performance. The Negro again had given his all to his country and had got in return at the hands of that country wrong and injustice. Southern propaganda presently renewed all of its vicious and relentless activity against the Negro. He was different, he was alien, he was unassimilable, he was inferior, and he must be kept so, and in the scheme of things he must be made forever subordinate to the white race. In this scheme of things white domination could best be preserved by the establishment of a caste system based on race and color. And so following the Spanish-American War the North and the South put their heads together to complete their caste system. Everywhere throughout the Republic race prejudice, color proscription grew apace. One by one rights and privileges which the Negroes had enjoyed for a brief space were withdrawn and the wall of caste rose higher and higher. He was slowly and surely being shut out from all the things which white men enjoyed by virtue of their citizenship, and shut within narrowing limits of freedom. Everywhere within his prison house he read in large and sinister letters, "Thus far and no farther." He was trapped, and about to be caged. In spite of the Emancipation Proclamation and the Three War Amendments he found that white men were becoming bolder in ignoring or violating his freedom and citizenship under them. The walls of the new bondage were closing about his right to life, liberty and the pursuit of happiness in this boasted Land of The Free and Christian Home of Democratic Hypocrisy and Cruelty.

Then Mr. Taft appeared upon the scene and became famous or infamous as a builder on the walls of the Temple of the New American Jerusalem, where profession is High Priest to the God of Broken Promises. He proved himself a master workman in following the lines of caste, in putting into place a new stone in the edifice when he announced as his policy at the beginning of his administration that he would not appoint any colored man to office in the South where the whites objected. Caste had won and the Negro's status was fixed, as far as this bourgeois apostle of American Democracy was able to fix it. His adds but another illustrious name to the long list of those architects of national dishonor who sought to build the Temple of American Liberty upon a basis of caste.

Then in the fullness of time came Woodrow Wilson, the ripe, consummate fruit of all this national contradiction between profession and practice, promise and performance. He can give Messrs. Washington, Jefferson, Jackson and Company odds and beat them in the subtle art of saying sonorously, grandiosely, what in action he does not hesitate to flout and spurn. When seeking the Negro's vote in 1912 he was the most profuse and generous in eloquent profession, in irridescent promises, but when he was elected he forgot straightway those fair professions and promises and began within a week after he entered the White House to put into office men filled with colorphobia, the better to finish the work of undoing, in the government the citizenship of the Negro, to whom he had promised not grudging justice but the highly sympathetic article, heaping up and running over. Mr. Taft had established the principle that no Negro was to be appointed to office in the South where the whites objected—Mr. Wilson carried the principle logically one step farther, namely, no Negro was to be put to work in any department of the Government with white men and women if these white men and women objected to his presence. Segregation along the color line in Federal employment became forthwith the fixed policy of the Wilson administration.

There sprang up under the malign influence of this false prophet of the New Freedom all sorts of movements in the District of Columbia and in the Federal Government hostile to the Negro—movements to exclude him from all positions under the Civil Service above that of laborer and messenger and charwoman, to jim-crow him on the street cars, to prohibit him from intermarrying with the whites, to establish for him a residential pale in the District; in short, to fix forever his status as a permanently inferior caste in the land for which he had toiled in peace and bled and died in war. The evil influence of this false apostle of freedom spread far and wide and spurred the enemies of the Negro to unwonted activity. The movement of residential segregation and for rural segregation grew in volume and momentum in widely separated parts of the country until it was finally checked by the decision of the Supreme Court in 1917.

The condition of the Negro was at its worst and his outlook in America at its darkest when the Government declared war against Germany. Then was revived the Republic's program of false promises and hypocritical professions in order to bring this black man with his brawn and brains, with his horny hands and lion heart, with his unquenchable loyalty and enthusiasm to its aid. No class of its citizens surpassed him in the swiftness and self-forgetfullness of his response to the call of country. What he had to give he brought to the altar and laid it there —labor and wealth, wounds and death, with unsurpassed devotion and patriotism. But what he received in return was the same old treatment, evil for his good, ingratitude and treachery for his loyalty and service. He was discriminated against everywhere—was used and abused, shut out from equal recognition and promotion with white men and women. Then when he went overseas he found American colorphobia more deadly than the gun and poison gas of the Germans. In the American army there was operated a ceaseless propaganda of meanness and malice, of jealousy and detraction against him. If our Expeditionary Force had given itself with a tithe of the zeal and industry to fighting the Germans, which a large section of it devoted to fighting the black soldier it would have come out of the war with more honor and credit, and left behind in France a keener sense of gratitude and regard than exists for them in that country today. But alas, thousands of them were more interested in watching the Negro and his reception by the French, in concocting villainous plots to degrade him in the eyes of that people, in segregating him from all social contact with them, and in keeping him in his place, within the hard and fast lines of caste which they had laid for him in America.

But the Negro went and saw—saw the incredible meanness and malice of his own country by the side of the immense genius for Liberty and Brotherhood of France. There he found himself a man and brother regardless of his race and color. But if he has seen these things in France he has also conquered certain other things in himself, and has come back not as he went but a New Negro. He has come back to challenge injustice in his own land and to fight wrong with a courage that will not fail him in the bitter and perhaps bloody years to come. For he knows now as he has never known before that he is an American citizen with the title deeds of his citizenship written in a century and a half of labor and suffering and blood. From his brave black lips I hear the ringing challenge, "This is my right and by the Eternal I have come back to claim all that belongs to me of industrial and political equality and liberty." And let us answer his high resolve with a courage and will to match his own, and so help to redeem our country from its shame of a century and a half of broken promises and dishonored ideals.

But be not deceived, friends. Let us like brave men and women face the stern reality of our situation. We are where we are. We are in the midst of a bitter and hitherto an invincible race-prejudice, which beats down into the dust all of our rights, all of our attainments, all of our aspirations after freedom and excellence. The North and the South are in substantial accord in respect to us and in respect to the position which we are to occupy in this land. We are to be forever exploited, forever treated as an alien race, allowed to live here in strict subordination and subjection to the white race. We are to hew for it wood, draw for it water, till for it the earth, drive for it coaches, wait for it at tables, black for it boots, run for it errands, receive from it crumbs and kicks, to be for it, in short, social mudsills on which shall rest the foundations of the vast fabric of its industrial democracy and civilization.

No one can save us from such a fate but God, but ourselves. You think, I know, that the North is more friendly to you than the South, that the Republican party does more for the solution of this problem than the Democratic. Friends, you are mistaken. A white man is a white man on this question, whether he lives in the North or in the South. Of course, there are splendid exceptions. Scratch the skin of Republican or Democrat, of Northern white men or Southern white men, and you will find close to the surface race prejudice, American colorphobia. The difference, did you but know it, is not even epidermal, is not skin-deep. The hair is Democratic Esau's, and the voice is Republican Jacob's. That is all. Make no mistake here, for a true understanding of our actual position at this point is vital.

On Boston Commons stands a masterpiece in bronze, erected to commemorate the heroism and patriotism of Col. Robert Gould Shaw and his black regiment. There day and night, through summer and winter, storm and shine are to march forever those brave men by the side of their valiant young leader. Into the unknown they are hurrying to front and to fight their enemies and the enemies of their country. They are not afraid. A high courage looks from their faces, lives in the martial motion of their bodies, flashes from the barrels of their guns. On and yet ever on they are marching, grim bolts of war, across the Commons, through State Street, past the old State House, over ground consecrated by the martyr's blood of Crispus Attucks, and the martyr's feet of William Lloyd Garrison. Farther and farther they are pressing forward into the unknown, into the South, to Wagner and immortal deeds, to death and an immortal crown.

Friends, we too are marching through a living and lowering present into the unknown, through an enemy's land, at the summons of duty. We are to face great labors, great dangers, to fight like men our passions and American caste-prejudice and oppression, and God helping us, to conquer them.

MILITARY INTELLIGENCE DIVISION

Memorandum on Marcus Garvey

May 5, 1921

Panama, May 5th 1921

SUBJECT MARCUS GARVEY IN PANAMA. (POLITICAL FACTOR NO. 75) MONOGRAPH REPORT.

MARCUS GARVEY arrived in Panama about a week ago. Since then he has spoken in Bocas del Toro, Guabito, Colón and Panama. He is boosting the Black Star Line and urging "Africa for the Negroes." The only thing objectionable in his speeches is his repeated statement that "the whites must be driven from Africa, even if armed force is required."

It is clearly evident that the primary object of Garvey's presence here is to get some easy money. He charges a dollar admission to each lecture and all are more than crowded. He sells stock in the Black Star Line on every occasion, and in fact "grabs" money in the most brazen way. The working negroes here are all enthusiastic about him, but the more influential seem to see through his game and are publishing criticisms and warnings against him. From his actions here I should class him as a pure grafter, agitating only for the money in it, and with no real convictions at all on what he preaches.

To date Garvey has taken in the following sums:

	Admissions.	*Stock sold.*
Bocas del Toro.	$ 300.00	None.
Guabito.	700.00	$ 5000.00
Colón.	4000.00	10000.00
Panama.	5000.00	10000.00
TOTAL	$10,000.00	$25,000.00

Source of information: Newspapers and personal observation.

THE DESTRUCTION OF A BLACK COMMUNITY

MARY E. JONES PARRISH
from *Events of the Tulsa Disaster*

1921

MY EXPERIENCE IN TULSA.

AFTER VISITING Tulsa in 1918, I returned to Rochester, and remained there only five months before being called to McAlester, to the bedside of my dear mother who departed this life after six months of patience and care by the children who loved her so dearly. I then decided to locate in Tulsa. I had heard of this town since girlhood and of the many opportunities here to make money. But I came not to Tulsa as many came, lured by the dream of making money and bettering myself in the financial world, but because of the wonderful co-operation I observed among our people, and especially the harmony of spirit and action that existed between the business men and women.

On leaving the Frisco station, going north to Archer Street one could see nothing but Negro business places. Going east on Archer Street for two or more blocks there you would behold Greenwood Avenue, the Negro's Wall Street, and an eyesore to some evil minded real estate men who saw the advantage of making this street into a commercial district. This section of Tulsa was a city within a city, and some malicious newspapers take pride in referring to it as "Little Africa." On Greenwood one could find a variety of business places which would be a credit to any section of the town. In the residential section there were homes of beauty and splendor which would please the most critical eye. The schools and many churches were well attended.

Space will not permit me to give a full description of the Tulsa folk here. "Tulsa, Then and Now," by Prof. G. A. Gregg, A.B., which follows will give a mental view of our group in Tulsa.

After spending years of struggling and sacrifice, the people had begun to look upon Tulsa as the Negro Metropolis of the Southwest. Then the devastating Tulsa Disaster burst upon us, blowing to atoms ideas and ideals no less than mere material evidence of our civilization.

A Colored boy accidentally stepped on a white elevator girl's foot. An evening paper hurled the news broadcast, with the usual "Lynching is feared if the victim is caught." Then the flames of hatred which had been brewing for years broke loose.

Since the lynching of a White boy in Tulsa, the confidence in the ability of the city official to protect its prisoner had decreased; therefore, some of our group banded together to add to the protection of the life that was threatened to be taken without a chance to prove his innocence. I say innocence because he was brought to trial and given his liberty; the girl over whom the trouble was caused failed to appear against him.

On the evening of May 31st, I was busy with a class in Typewriting until about 9 P.M. After my pupils were gone I immediately began reading a book which I was very anxious to finish (must admit, however, that I was never able to complete it), so did not notice the excitement until a late hour. The evening being a pleasant one, my little girl had not retired, but was watching the people from the window. Occasionally she would call to me, "Mother, look at the cars full of people." I would reply, "Baby, do not disturb me, I want to read." Finally she said, "Mother, I see men with guns." Then I ran to the window and looked out. There I saw many people gathered in little squads talking excitedly. Going down stairs to the street I was told of the threatened lynching and that some of our group were going to give added protection to the boy.

I am told that this little bunch of brave and loyal Black men who were willing to give their lives, if necessary, for the sake of a fellow man, marched up to the jail where there were already over 500 white men gathered, and that this number was soon swelled to over a thousand. Someone fired a stray shot and, to use the expression of General Grant, "All hell broke loose." From that moment quiet and peaceful Tulsa was turned into a hot-bed of destruction.

My little girl and I watched the excited groups from our window until a late hour, when I had her lie down and try to rest while I waited and watched. Waited and watched, for what

—I do not know. One could hear firing in quick succession and it was hours before the horror of it all dawned upon me. I had read of the Chicago Riot and of the Washington trouble, but it did not seem possible that prosperous Tulsa, the city which was so peaceful and quiet that morning, could be in the thrall of a great disaster. When it dawned upon me what was really happening I took my little girl in my arms, read one or two chapters of Psalms of David and prayed that God would give me courage to stand through it all.

The Frisco tracks and station form a dividing line between the business section of White Tulsa and Black Tulsa. It was here that the first battle was staged. Like mad bulls after a red flag or blood thirsty wolves after a carcass, so did these human wolves called men rave to destroy their fellow citizens. But these brave boys of ours fought gamely and held back the enemy for hours. Owing to the shortage of ammunition they were forced to retreat from Cincinnati, and immediately the advancing force began to pillage and burn that section.

About 1:30 o'clock the firing had somewhat subsided and it was hoped that the crisis had passed over. Some one on the street cried out, "Look, they are burning Cincinnati!" On looking we beheld columns of smoke and fire and by this we knew that the enemy was surging quickly upon Greenwood. Like Stonewall Jackson of old our boys stood "Like a stone wall," offsetting each and every attempt to burn Greenwood and the immediate vicinity. I had no desire to flee but my heart went out in sympathy for those who were fighting so bravely against such tremendous odds. I forgot about personal safety and was seized with an uncontrollable desire to see the outcome of the fray. The firing and burning continued at long intervals. In the early morning, about 3 or 4 o'clock, the Midway Hotel was seen to be burning. A friend in the building with me called up the Fire Department. The answer was, "They will be out right away," but they failed to show up. About 5 o'clock a lady friend called up the Police Department and asked how soon the Militia would reach Tulsa, and the reply was, "About 7 o'clock." Looking south out of the window of what then was the Woods Building, we saw car loads of men with rifles unloading up near the granary, which is located on the railroad tracks near First Street. Then the truth dawned upon us that our men were fighting in vain to hold their dear Greenwood. A fit of restlessness seized us and Mrs. Jones and I walked the halls, looking first out of the windows and then out of the doors. In our excitement we would sometimes forget ourselves and lean out of the window, when we would receive a timely warning to get back or be shot. At an early hour the lights were all out, so we prayed for daylight in hope that the worst would be over, but not so, for daylight had a distressing surprise in store for us.

After watching the men unload on First Street where we could see them from our windows, we heard such a buzzing noise that on running to the door to get a better view of what was going on, the sights our eyes beheld made our poor hearts stand still for a moment. There was a great shadow in the sky and upon a second look we discerned that this cloud was caused by fast approaching aeroplanes. It then dawned upon us that the enemy had organized in the night and was invading our district the same as the Germans invaded France and Belgium. The firing of guns was renewed in quick succession. People were seen to flee from their burning homes, some with babes in their arms and leading crying and excited children by the hand; others, old and feeble, all fleeing to safety. Yet, seemingly, I could not leave. I walked as one in a horrible dream. By this time my little girl was up and dressed, but I made her lie down on the dufold in order that the bullets must penetrate it before reaching her. By this time a machine gun had been installed in the granary and was raining bullets down on our section. Looking out of the back door I saw people still fleeing and the enemy fast approaching. I heard a man groan; looking up just in time to see him fall, and was pulled into the house. Still I could not flee. Finally my friend called her husband, who was trying to take a little rest and they decided to try to make for a place of safety, so called to me that they were leaving. By this time the enemy was close upon us, so they ran out of the south door, which led out on Archer Street, and went east toward Lansing. I took my little girl by the hand and fled out of the west door on Greenwood. I did not take time to get a hat for myself or baby, but started out north on Greenwood, running amidst showers of bullets from the machine gun located in the granary and from men who were quickly surrounding our district. Seeing that they were fighting at a disadvantage our men had taken shelter on the buildings and in other places out of sight of the enemy. When Florence Mary and I ran into the street it was vacant for a block or more. Someone called to me to "Get out of the street with that child or you both will be killed." I felt that it was suicide to remain in the building, for it would surely be destroyed and death in the street was preferred, for we expected to be shot down at any moment, so we placed our trust in God, our Heavenly Father, who seeth and knoweth all things, and ran on out Greenwood in the hope of reaching a friend's home who lived over the Standpipe Hill in the Greenwood Addition. As I neared the hill I could see homes on Eastern and Detroit burning, and also discovered that the enemy had located on the hill and that our district was entirely surrounded. We thought that we were leaving the firing behind, but found that our danger was increasing for a machine gun was located on the hillside. As we neared the addition we caught up with other people fleeing in the same direction. We finally reached my friend's home, but to our disappointment found that she and her family had fled after watching for me all through the night. I then decided to follow the crowd in the hope of reaching safety. On and on we went toward the section line, the crowd growing larger and larger. The question on every lip when a newcomer from town would arrive was, "How far had they burned when you left town?"

At the section line I met Mrs. Thompson, her husband and family. They were on a truck and had started east. She called to me and I ran to them and got on the truck. Soon we had started again on our quest for safety. On and on we went, past many farm houses, mostly White. They looked at us as if we were animals escaping a forest fire. We passed many of our group. The most pathetic sight was an old couple struggling along on foot. How I longed to get off and give them my seat, but I dared not leave my little girl alone to perish. When we passed, the old lady asked us to take her coat; it was too heavy. We did but have never been able to find her again. After we had gone several miles we began to see automobile loads of men with guns going east ahead of us. We wondered where they were going but we were not destined to wonder long, for as we neared the aviation fields we saw their destination. The planes were out of the sheds, all in readiness for flying, and these men with highpowered rifles were getting into them. As we went further we saw several men leaving the fields, going to the house, returning with guns and heading towards Tulsa.

After we had traveled many miles into the country and was turning to find our way to Claremore, we looked up the road and saw a race lady coming toward us. My lady friend and I went to meet her. She advised us to not try to pass through a little adjoining town, for they were treating our people awfully mean as they passed through, taking their guns from them and threatening to place them in prison. She made us welcome to come to her home and remain until it was safe to return to Tulsa. We gratefully accepted her hospitality and returned with her to her home. There we rested and were as comfortable as could be expected under the circumstances. Having been out in the hot sun all day without hats—only make-shifts made from leaves—we found the shelter of a roof very refreshing.

A bread wagon met the fleeing people on the roadside and sold the bread. On the way we bought bread so when we stopped to rest we had bread and water, whenever and wherever we could get it. Ofttimes the men would stop and dip water from a branch, using their hats for cups. In France? No, in Oklahoma. After reaching this home the crowd thronged there was too large to supply them out of a pail so a washtub was drafted into service and pride cast to the wind. We were so famished and our lips parched, the children crying for a drink, that this was the best tasting water we could remember of having tasted. I can never forget a family who started out and had the misfortune to lose one wheel off of their wagon and, therefore, had to get out and walk. In that number was a mother and father with a six-months-old infant—such a fine and healthy baby. The father would run along and carry it awhile when the mother would take it until she was tired out. When they both were just about exhausted the father cried out, "Will some one help us?" Being a mother, naturally my heart was in deep sympathy for them, so I called to them to bring the baby to me and I would care for it awhile and let them rest. They finally succeeded in getting another wheel, after going miles on the hub of the broken wheel.

The aeroplanes continued to watch over the fleeing people like great birds of prey watching for a victim, but I have not heard of them doing any harm to the people out in the direction where we were. I have been reliably informed, however, that they fired on the people who were gathered in groups in the colored park close to town.

Everything went well until late in the afternoon. An elderly man with some daughters and grand-children came to where we were stopping. He was sent to a nearby farm store to procure food for the family. There he was told that the Red Cross workers were coming out in trucks to bring food to the suffering people and to take back to town all who desired to go. Instead of buying food, as he was instructed to do by his daughters, he informed the store people that there were "lots of people" up where he came from desiring food. They told him that they would send the trucks right up on their return from town, which they did, but when the trucks came they found no one to take back. After spending such a dreadful night and day and witnessing so much destruction, how could we trust a race that would bring it about? At that hour we mistrusted every person having a white face and blue eyes. Since, we have learned that the Red Cross workers came like angels of mercy to heal and help suffering humanity. When the man told us what he had done the crowd started out to look for another haven of rest. We walked about two miles across the prairie, most of the way having to carry the children to keep the weeds from stinging their tired little limbs. We were well paid for the walk for these kindly people prepared hot lunch for the bunch and provided us with a place to sleep, so we remained here for the night. Altho we were over thirteen miles from Tulsa we could, at about 10 P.M., see the smoke rising from the ruins.

NAME WITHHELD BY REQUEST

Tulsa, Okla., June 24, 1921.

ON TUESDAY evening we heard the shooting and several friends came to my home for shelter until about 2 o'clock. Then in the early morning the Whites were stationed on the hill with machine guns and high powered rifles, firing upon our people as they tried to run for safety.

About seven o'clock the Whites or Home Guards came for the men. Then they took the women and children, promising them safety. After they had the homes vacated one bunch of whites would come in and loot. Even women with shopping bags would come in, open drawers, take every kind of finery from clothing to silverware and jewelry. Men were carrying out the furniture, cursing as they did so, saying "These d— Negroes have better things than lots of white people." I stayed until my home was caught on fire, then I ran to the hill side where there were throngs of White people; women, men and children, even babies, watching and taking snap shots of the proceedings of the mob. Some remarked that "The city ought to be sued for selling D— niggers property so close to the city." One woman noticed the First Baptist Church, which is a beautiful structure located near a White residence district. She said, "Yonder is a nigger church, why ain't they burning it?" The reply was, "It's in a White district."

I saw an old Colored man, Mr. Oliver, who stayed with Dr. Jackson. I hailed him and asked him to help me with my handbag. He told me that Dr. Jackson was killed with his hands up. He said the ruffians ordered him out of his beautiful home. He came out with his hands up and said, "Here I am boys, don't shoot," but they shot him just the same. About this time some Home Guards appeared and ordered Mr. Oliver to come to them. While doing so a bunch of rifles were raised to shoot. The guards fell down and Mr. Oliver took shelter behind a post just in time to save his life. Then Mr. Oliver went to the Guards and they searched him, with hands up, and took over $50.00 from him, which they failed to return, and then took him to Convention Hall.

Then the horde of ruffians went down on Detroit, looting those beautiful homes of everything valuable and then burned them, even breaking the phones from the walls. The machine guns just shattered the walls of the homes. The fire department came out and protected the White homes on the west side of Detroit Street while on the east side of the street men with torches and women with shopping bags continued their looting and burning of Negro homes, while aeroplanes flew over head, some very low.

I watched this awful destruction from where I sat on the hill side. As I sat watching my modern 10-room and basement home burn to ashes an old White man came by. Addressing me as "Auntie," he said, "It's awful, ain't it?" and offered me a dollar to buy my dinner with.

NAME WITHHELD BY REQUEST.

“FIENDISHNESS AND BARBARITY”

B. C. FRANKLIN

The Tulsa Race Riot and Three of Its Victims

1921

IT WAS IN the month of October, 1917 and the leaves were browning on the trees and the grass had taken on a golden tint. A mighty crowd had gathered from all over McIntosh and adjoining counties and had congregated in the little town park, near the depot, at Eufaula, Oklahoma.

The man in charge of the meeting—a white gentleman—arose on the speaker’s stand and said:

“Fellow-citizens: I feel happy to have the privilege of introducing to you the speaker of the hour. Many, if not all, of you know him. He practiced his profession here in our little city for several years and had the esteem and respect of both the bench and the bar. He has become so very greatly interested in the prosecution of the war against the German Government until he has actually, for the time being, foresaken his own personal business and, at his own expense, is traveling all over this state and speaking in our campaign for the sale of the present liberty bonds. He is also urging the young men of his race to enlist in the service of our common country. I take great pleasure, therefore, in presenting attorney B. C. Franklin.” (Great applause.)

I spoke in part as follows: “Master of Ceremonies, and fellow citizens:

“We are met together here for a three-fold purpose, namely, to impress upon you the importance of buying as many of these Fourth Liberty Bonds as possible, to urge upon you—young men—the imperative necessity of immediate enlistment and to bid farewell to those splendid young men here who are soon to entrain.

“We who are too old to enlist, or who are exempted from enlisting for any other cause, should remember that it is both our moral and financial duty to see to it that these young men and others like them shall not want for anything while 'over there' fighting our battles.

"Young men, you are here in answer to your country's call to duty. Yours is an honorable heritage; yours is a remarkable reputation to uphold and defend. You have come from the loins of a race that has never produced a traitor, nor a coward when summoned in the defense of this nation and its flag. It is gratifying to note the spirit of comradeship already in evidence here and to see the smiles with which your faces are wreathed. A few days ago, I attended a similar meeting, the difference being that the other gathering was composed of all white people, except myself. At that other gathering, the war cry was, 'On to France.' But here, there is no such cry. As I look into your faces, I divine your thoughts. Your cry is, 'On to Berlin.'" (Thunderous applause rent the air.)

When I had finished my little speech, a young colored couple made their way through that vast throng to the speaker's stand. The young man was dressed in the uniform of his country. He spoke to me: "My name is John Ross and this is Mrs. Ross, my wife. I understand you are from Tulsa. My home is there, although I have not spent very much time there for the past three years or more."

"I am very glad to meet both of you," I said. Continuing, "May I ask you, Mr. Ross, where you have been? I know your mother quite well."

"I left home in the early spring of 1914 and by mid-summer of that year, I was in Europe. I had the wanderlust, I was adventurous and wanted action. I succeeded in joining the British army. I got plenty of action and adventure—then, I quit the army in August 1916 and returned to this country. I again enlisted for service in New York last January and have been stationed there ever since. I secured a leave of absence a few days ago to visit mother. Within thirty days, we are to sail for Europe. I mean my company. Mrs. Ross will live with mother until the war is over."

And so young Ross returned to Europe and fought for his country until the armistice was signed. Over there he, like hundreds of his buddies, was simply a cog in the great machinery of war. He did his bit in comparative obscurity—he was known only to a few. Providence was kind to him and he, like a few others—just a few others—returned home sound in mind and in body.

Life—sordid at times—is made up of many changes and vicissitudes, and so the scene shifts back to Tulsa.

It is now May 31st, 1921. The day is just beginning. Sweet-throated birds warble their songs of joy in the tree-tops, fanned by the refreshing zephyr, and the dew sparkles upon the grass like countless little diamonds, as old Sol rises above the eastern horizon and, shining in all his resplendent glory, thrusts his myriad rays upon the busy world below. An unbroken stream of pedestrians—male and female—passes down Greenwood Avenue. It is made up of laborers, some empty-handed and others with dinner pails, on their way to work. They hurry along as if they are late. A few of the more pretentious ones pass in their own cars, or in jitneys, or upon busses. Then comes a lull—a lull before the storm.

It is now 11:30 A.M. of the same day and the first edition of the Tulsa Daily Tribune is out. The newsies are hawking their wares. Listen: "Tulsa Daily Tribune, Mister? Tribune, Mister? All about a Negro assaulting a white girl—read about it—Tribune, Mister?"

And so thousands of people buy the Tribune and scan its pages for the article about the alleged assault. They find it tucked away in a small space on one of the inside pages of the paper. In the twinkling of an eye, a part of Tulsa is changed from the happy, joyous, care-free to looks of grim determination.

It is also the commencement season and the streets of the city are filled all day long with happy, innocent, care-free graduates, colored and white, walking proudly in their caps and gowns. The colored graduates are dreaming, building air-castles and, in their waking dreams, they see themselves rising, mounting higher and higher up the ladder of recognition and renown. But, alas, their dreams are like Ponzi's financial bubbles.

The day wears on, and the shadows of evening lengthen and soon darkness comes on apace. Now it is night and all law-abiding citizens, except those attending some commencement program or detained on business in shop or office, are at home. Possibly a few are out with their families for a drive in the cool of the night. The night grows a little older and a few shots are heard—in the distance. One first thinks it's fire signals. The night grows older and the shooting increases and becomes less intermittent. One becomes, by the peculiar working of one's mind, slightly disturbed and distressed. One's mind goes back to that news article about that purported assault, and then still farther back—about a month—to the lynching of that white man in West Tulsa. (This white man was taken from the Tulsa County Jail by a mob and hung, I believe, to a telephone pole.) My mind becomes thoroughly aroused.

I had had an unusually hard day of it at court and in my office. By noon, I had finished the trial of a land case that was begun two days before. I had spent the entire afternoon briefing a law suit docketed for trial the following week. And so, I retired rather early. But the shooting continued. I arose, dressed and went to the 'phone to call the sheriff's office to find out the trouble. I could not make connection. The next thought was my office and to it I hastened. Upon reaching Greenwood Avenue, the same street upon which my office was then, and is now, located, I found the street congested with humanity and vehicles of all kinds and descriptions. Everybody, except the business men, was running about excitedly. The business men remained in their places of business, looking distressed and deeply concerned. Pushing and elbowing my way through the crowd, I finally reached my office. Again I tried to call the sheriff's office and again I failed to get connection. I was puzzled. I of course knew that there was trouble—that a race riot —or race war, as it afterward proved to be—was in the making and that we would soon be in the midst of a great catastrophe if something was not done at once to avert it. I went down upon the streets and tried to get the heads and tails of things. I found no one in any mood to talk with me about the trouble, except a few of the business men and they could tell me nothing and knew nothing that they could do or assist me in doing. We were not organized for such an emergency. No one could reach the sheriff's office and no one knew where he was. I started to town; but did not get very far before I concluded that such a move was both foolish and suicidal. I could do neither myself, nor anybody else any good by attempting such a course. So, after remaining on the streets for an hour or more, I returned to my room. I slipped out of my top shirt and lay down and tried to think—sleeping was out of the question. I soliloquized, "Here I am, a peaceable and law-abiding citizen, I have harmed no one—just like thousands of others of my race here—and yet I cannot now walk the street, upon a peaceful mission, in safety." This seemed hard to me. You see, I had never been in a mob before. Up to then, I knew absolutely nothing about mob-psychology. Since becoming a man, I have always been kept busy and never had had an occasion to study the mob-spirit. I had thought, foolishly, I suppose, that a peaceable, law abiding citizen could go wherever he had business—upon the streets. I was rudely disillusioned.

About mid-night, I arose and went to the north porch on the second floor of my hotel and, looking in a north-westerly direction, I saw the top of stand-pipe hill literally lighted up by the blazes that came from the throats of machine guns, and I could hear bullets whizzing and cutting the air. There was shooting now in every direction, and the sounds that came from the thousands and thousands of guns were deafening.

When the eastern sky reddened, announcing the approach of day, I was still standing on that upper porch thinking—thinking—thinking. And how different was the coming of this day from that of the day before. Now, one could see no stream of laborers passing down Greenwood Avenue, happy and care-free as on the morn before; no birds warbled their sweet songs, or, if they did, their voices were hushed in the din of battle. The grass was wet again with the morning dew and the sun rose again to travel the path known to his feet since time began, but neither had any charm on that morning for the sons of Ham in Tulsa.

I went from the front porch into the bathroom and washed my face, and thereafter went into my room and dressed. I left the building for my office. As I reached the side-walk a shrill whistle sounded from the direction of stand-pipe hill. And then, immediately thereafter, five thousand feet, it seemed, were heard descending that hill in my direction. On they rushed, whooping to the top of their voices like so many cowboys, and firing their guns every step they took. I quickened my pace and, cutting across vacant lots and dodging behind buildings, I finally reached Frankfort Place, about the middle of the three hundred block. Just as I emerged upon the street,

I came face to face with a fine-looking young man, with soldierly bearing, leading an elderly woman and with a young lady following close behind. I knew mother Ross, but at the time did not recognize the other two.

"Why, hello Lawyer Franklin," the young man spoke between clenched teeth. His face was grim and bore a determined look and his eyes sparkled and flashed defiance. He continued, hurriedly, "I have not seen you since you delivered that memorable address at Eufaula in October, 1917. How different is this occasion of our meeting from that. Then we were all filled with patriotism—love of country—and—standing erect—were recognized as the equal of our other fellow men. Now, now," he continued choking with rage, "we, after going through hell once for our country—now, I say, we are chased, driven and hunted as wild, hateful, dangerous things."

"What in the world, Ross—where have you been and where are you going," I hurried to ask him. For I now recognized both the soldier and his wife, the young lady with him and his mother.

"Just some more of my wanderlust, I suppose," he answered hurriedly, "I have been out of the State until this morning. Yesterday I became restless. Something within me told me that all was not well at home. I followed my mind. I reached Tulsa not more than one hour ago. How I got through the mountain of white men on the other side of the city, will always be a miracle to me. Judge, we are literally surrounded. I reached Greenwood and, luckily for me, I found my mother and my wife wandering about the street, panic stricken. In terror, they had fled from home. I'm going back home to defend it or die in the attempt." And, without another word, he grabbed his aged mother in his arms and fled on toward his home.

When young Ross and his family left me, I pushed on toward my office. On the way, I thought of those stirring words of our war president, "We must fight to make the world safe for democracy." I repeated those words aloud and they sounded like hollow-mockery. They seemed to have rattled like those dry bones in the valley, spoken of in the scriptures. I thought too of that other saying found in the scriptures, "He saved others; but himself he cannot save." That saying seemed so applicable to my race. We had saved others any number of times. We had saved, or helped mightily to—save, this nation from the enemy upon countless battle fields. And now, young Ross and I and the whole race were unable to save ourselves. The thought was bitter—it chided me and made me feel ashamed. Then my face burned with anger. But what could I do? I was unarmed—did not have even a pocket knife. I was not looking for such as was happening all around me and was therefore unprepared. My thought reverted to Ross again and my bosom swelled with pride and hope for the Race. Here was one young man who regarded it as a solemn duty to die, if needs be, in the defense of his home—for the protection of his fire-side. There must be others like him who think to lose their lives in such undertaking they shall find them again in greater abundance. Surely any man who fights to protect his home and fire-side from pollution and desecration of barbarians and infidels is doing the will of the Master.

I reached my office in safety; but I knew that that safety would be short-lived. I now knew the mob-spirit. I knew too that government and law and order had broken down. I knew that mob law had been substituted in all its fiendishness and barbarity. I knew that the mobbist cared nothing about the written law and the constitution and I also now knew that he had neither the patience nor the intelligence to distinguish between the good and the bad, the law abiding and the lawless in my race. From my office window, I could see planes circling in mid-air. They grew in number and hummed, darted and dipped low. I could hear something like hail falling upon the top of my office building. Down East Archer, I saw the old Mid-Way hotel on fire, burning from its top, and then another and another and another building began to burn from the top. "What, an attack from the air too?" I asked myself. Lurid flames roared and belched and licked their forked tongues in the air. Smoke ascended the sky in thick, black volumes and amid it all, the planes—now a dozen or more in number—still hummed and darted here and there with the agility of natural birds of the air. Then a filling station farther down East Archer caught on fire from the top. I feared now an explosion and decided to try and move to safer quarters. I came out of my office, locked the door and descended to the foot of the steps. The side-walks were literally covered with burning turpentine balls. I knew all too well where they came from and I knew all too well why every burning building first caught from the top. I paused and waited for an opportune time to escape. "Where, oh where is our splendid fire department with its half dozen stations?" I asked myself. "Is the city in conspiracy with the mob?" I again asked myself. As I stood there in contemplation of these and other gruesome facts, I saw two sights that will live in my memory to my dying day. One was a woman on the opposite side of the street. She was traveling south, hair disentangled and disheveled—in the very path of whizzing bullets. She was calling wildly to a little tot that, a few moments before, had dashed in panic before her and turned off Greenwood on Archer at the corner. I hollered to her, "Turn back woman, for God's sake turn back. You will be mown down." Never turning her head, she answered, as she hurried on, "I must follow my child." And so she did follow her child and not a bullet touched her although they literally rained down the street. This brave self-denying mother lives today here in Tulsa and with her that tot—now a splendid young lady—whom she risked her life to save. The other sight was occasioned by the Piro building catching on fire from the top. (This was a frame building then.) The fire dislodged those in the building—a woman, two children and three men. They emerged in wild confusion and came on in my direction. The little children—they were both girls—outran the others and passed the place where I was standing with the speed of the wind. The woman ran across the street and into the foot of the steps of my office building—right where I was standing—and fell upon her knees and commenced to pray, totally oblivious of my presence. I don't think she ever saw me. And such a prayer!—She asked God to save her and her children from whom she had just been separated. This prayer was uttered over and over. I am unable to say whether that prayer was answered or not. I have lived in Tulsa continuously ever since that memorable morning, but I have never seen that woman since. I know I would know her if I were to meet her, even today. The three men—one of whom lugged a heavy trunk on his shoulder—were all killed as they were crossing the street—killed before my very eyes. The man who carried the trunk was very old. Likely, he had in that trunk many things of great value (Negroes in Tulsa then were as a rule, very wealthy) and thought as much of the contents thereof as he did of his own life. When the old man was hit —no doubt by a dozen bullets—he dropped his burden and shrieked and fell sprawling upon the hard paved street. Blood gushed from every wound and ran down the street. I turned my head from the scene.

From every direction, except the North, we were surrounded, and the mob was closing in upon me. Across the street, directly in front of me, stood the Gurley Building, property of a very wealthy and—up to that time—a very influential colored man. I heard shots fired from behind that building and heard angry and profane voices, saying "Come out of there, Gurley—you black s—o—a—b." I saw an opening to move on and so I sped North, out Greenwood Avenue. About one hundred yards on the way out, I was joined by I. H. Spears, another colored attorney and we proceeded on together. I thought that may be I could make it back to my hotel and find a gun of some sort there—in some of those rooms. At the intersection of North Greenwood and East Easton—the point at which I intended to turn west—I looked across to my left and there, in stone's cast, stood the Ross residence—burning from the top. On the front porch stood Mother Ross, with outstretched and trembling hands, begging a mob that was approaching from the northwest to spare her home and family. (Evidently she had not then discovered her house on fire.) From within I could hear the report of some high-powered rifles. I remembered the words of young Ross that morning and knew that he was making good his threat. Every time there was a report of a gun from within, one of the members of the mob would fall, never to rise again. I somehow, felt happy. I cannot explain that feeling. I never felt that way—before nor since. I looked North and directly in front of us stood a thousand boys, it seemed, with guns pointed at our heads. They commanded us to "right about face." Then one half-starved ruffian came forward to search us. Finding no weapon, he started to take my money. At this I balked. This was the last straw. I had endured about all I could and decided then and there to die, if necessary before I would be robbed by that bunch of hungry out-laws. I have always thanked my God that none of the other members of my family were in the city. My wife and three children were down on the farm—one hundred miles away—and my oldest child—a daughter—was in college in Tennessee. The next day, I got a chance to route her away from Tulsa on her trip from school.

The ruffians marched us back down Greenwood to First Street, thence on First Street to Main Street, thence on Main Street to Brady Street and thence on Brady Street to convention hall. You see, this was one of the many places of detention, refuge or whatever you wish to call it, to which my Race was taken when dislodged from its home. Here, those who cared to accept the fare, the people were fed and watered like so many cattle by the benefactors (?) who had allowed the mob to take their government away from them and trample their laws and constitution under their unhallowed and barbarous feet. Here, I saw the colored lady of refinement, culture and good breeding placed on an absolute equality with the prostitute and street walker of the Race. Here, I saw some of the fine matrons of the Race wrapped only in their night gowns, having been ejected from their homes so hurriedly until they did not even have time to dress. Here, I saw a mother, in a dark corner of that mammoth building, giving birth—premature birth—to a babe and I heard its husky cries, for the first time, amid this strange, unseemly and wicked surrounding. And from sun rise to sun set, I passed through scenes and experiences that beggar description. They were like unto—if not worse than—The Last Days of Pompeii, as described by Bulwer Lytton. During that bloody day, I lived a thousand years, in the spirit, at least. I lived the whole experiences of the Race; the experiences of royal ancestry beyond the sea; experiences of the slave ships on their first voyage to America with their human cargo; experiences of American slavery and its concomitant evils; experiences of loyalty and devotion of the Race to this nation and its flag in war and in peace; and I thought of Ross back yonder, out yonder, in his last stand, no doubt, for the protection of home and fire side and of old Mother Ross left homeless in the even-tide of her life. I thought of the place the preachers call hell and wondered seriously if there was such a mystical place —it appeared, in this surrounding—that the only hell was the hell on this earth, such as the Race was then passing through.

For fully forty-eight hours, the fires raged and burned everything in its path and it left nothing but ashes and burned safes and trunks and the like where once stood beautiful homes and business houses. And so proud, rich, black Tulsa was destroyed by fire—that is its buildings and property; but its spirit was neither killed nor daunted. It is however not within the purpose of this true story to dwell on this; nor is it our purpose to discuss here the cause or causes of this great shame, except to say that the chief cause was economic. The Negroes were wealthy and there were too many poor whites who envied them. Within two hours after the alleged assault had been reported, there were not a dozen white men here who did not know that this alleged assault consisted of a poor laboring, Negro boy accidentally stepping on the foot of a very poor but worthy white girl while the two were on a very crowded elevator in one of the down town business buildings; nor yet is it our purpose here to discuss the wonderful, almost miraculous come-back of the Race here in the accumulation of property and in the acquiring of a larger, richer and fuller spiritual life.

How the years have flown and how changed and changing is the whole face of this nation. It is now August 22nd, 1931 as this is being written. A little more than ten years have passed under the bridge of time since the great holocaust here. Young Ross, the veteran of the world war, survived the great catastrophe, but lost both his mind and eye sight in the fires that destroyed his home. With a burned and scarred face and a mindless mind, he sits today in the asylum of this State and stares blankly into space. At the corner of North Greenwood and East Easton, sits Mother Ross with her tin cup in hand, begging alms of the passers-by. They are nearly all new comers and have no knowledge of her tragic past, hence they pay her little attention. Young Mrs. Ross is working and doing the best she can to carry on in these times of depression. She divides her visits between her mother-in-law and her husband at the asylum. Of course, he has not the slightest recollection of her or of his mother. All yesteryears are only blank pieces of paper to him. He cannot remember one thing in the living, breathing, throbbing present.

"WHITES WERE JEALOUS OF US"

OTIS CLARK

Oral History Interview on the Tulsa Race Massacre

1921

John Erling: Would you state your name and your date of birth?

Otis Clark: Otis Granville Clark, February 13th, 1903.

JE: So how old are you right now?

OC: About 106 years old.

JE: Where were you born?

OC: Meridian, Oklahoma.

JE: What was your father's name?

OC: Henry Clark.

JE: And where was he raised?

OC: He was from Tulsa, Oklahoma, to my knowledge.

JE: Do you know how old he was when he died?

OC: He was supposed to have been about 97 years old when he died. He died in California.

JE: Your mother's name?

OC: Effie Clark.

JE: Was she from Tulsa as well?

OC: To the best of my knowledge, she was from Meridian, Oklahoma.

JE: And how old was she when she died?

OC: I think she was around 94 years old, somewhere in there. She died in Guthrie, Oklahoma, where she was buried.

JE: Did you have brothers and sisters?

OC: Yes, I had a brother, Bernard Clark. And I had two sisters. Gladys was one, and Almida was one. Both of them died in Tulsa.

JE: Where did you grow up?

OC: I grew up in the north end of Los Angeles, California.

JE: How did you make your way to Tulsa?

OC: We were born in the Meridian, Oklahoma, and my folks took me to Tulsa when I was a baby. And I grew up in

Tulsa until we had, what you might say are the race riots, they called it.

JE: Yes.

OC: That was in 1921.

JE: Right, we'll get to that in a moment. Where did you go to school in Tulsa for elementary school?

OC: It was a little country school they called Hartford School.

JE: And then you went on to junior high school, is that so?

OC: I went to Booker T. Washington.

JE: Oh, you went to Booker T.?

OC: Yes, they transferred us from Hartford over to the Booker T. school and at the same time, just before we got settled in at the Booker T. school, they had the race riots.

JE: Yes.

OC: And the school was torn up in the riots, and burned, or something. And anyway, I went to California with some of my friends.

JE: Yes. In 1914, World War I broke out and you were 13 years old. Do you remember hearing anything about World War I?

OC: No, I didn't hear too much about World War I.

JE: Okay. As you grew into your teen years, tell us what it was like to be growing up in Tulsa.

OC: Oh, to tell the truth about it, just before the riots we boys just played ball and skated after school-time, at a little school that was called Hartford School, just a block or so off of Archer. Greenwood was our main little business street, and it ran up to Archer. We lived on Archer Street.

JE: Do you remember your address?

OC: To the best of my knowledge, it was around 802 or somewhere in there.

JE: Can you name any of your friends?

OC: To tell the truth about it, the riots broke up everything and I had to run off to California. One of them was named Clifton, and he stayed right there pretty close to Archer Street.

JE: Did you go to movies? Did you go to the theater?

OC: Yes. At that time, they didn't have anything but writing. They didn't have talkies, they were silent pictures as they called them. But I think it was Charlie Chaplin and Stepin Fetchit. They were the ones that were in the movies back then.

JE: And you remember going to the movies?

OC: Yes. That's all I did back then. That was our pastime, going to the movies. That was on Greenwood Avenue.

JE: On Memorial Day 1921, do you remember the days leading up to that day? Did you go downtown in Tulsa?

OC: I went downtown. I was about 12 or 13. I wrote a bicycle and delivered medicine for the drugstore and 12th in Main Street.

JE: Sure.

OC: Shackles Drug Store. Dr. Shackles, I worked for him. And we had, what you might say is a disease hit Tulsa and a lot of the rich folks died. I delivered medicine. We had what you might say was kind of an epidemic or something. A lot of rich folks died around 21st Street in Tulsa. That was on the south side of the city.

JE: Were they dying from a certain kind of flu?

OC: Yes. I didn't ever know what it was, but some kind of disease hit Tulsa and a lot of folks died. A lot of rich, white people died.

JE: That would have been about 1918, I think.

OC: Somewhere, in there.

JE: Do you recall as a black person in Tulsa that you could only go to certain lunch counters and restrooms?

OC: Yes.

JE: The theater that you went to was only for blacks, is that true?

OC: You're right. It was only for blacks. Whites couldn't come, or didn't come on that side. And the colored people weren't allowed on the white side. That's the way that was.

JE: Do you remember the names of any of the other stores that were in downtown Tulsa?

OC: We colored folks weren't allowed in the downtown stores. We had to stay over on the Greenwood side of the city, on the north side of downtown.

JE: But they let you come downtown to work, right?

OC: Oh yes.

MEMORIAL DAY—1921

John Erling: On May 30, 1921, Memorial Day, you are 18 years old. Do you remember that day? Say in the morning—what the day was like? What the weather was like?

Otis Clark: Oh, that was the earliest part of the summer. It was just getting warm at that time. Because I didn't have on anything but trousers when the riots started. Then I had to run off, a lot of the colored folks had to run off from their businesses to keep from being killed. The whites were taking over the colored city altogether.

JE: Well let me just recap here what I know about this and then we'll talk about it. Because sometime that afternoon, Dick Rowland who worked on the ground of the Drexel building, at 319 S. Main, Dick Rowland, shining shoes, and he went on to the elevator and Sarah Page was the elevator operator. Dick Rowland was 19 and she was 17. And he had been to the top floor to use the restroom. When he came down, as he stepped out, we believe he put his hand on her arm, and Sarah screamed. He was black and she was white. That's what the history books say about this.

OC: That's about right too.

JE: He was 19, so he was your age. Did you know Dick Rowland at all?

OC: No, I was in grade school, and I think he was probably in high school at that time. He was a little older than me. They arrested him for saying something to this little white girl. They said he said something to the girl and the white men didn't like it and they jumped on him. And they took him and arrested him and put them in jail. And while he was in jail, some of the colored boys, to the best of our knowledge, went down to the courthouse to try to keep the folks from killing him. At that particular time, we made up our mind to try to leave Tulsa to go where my father was. My father was a pullman on the Frisco Train. He had left and gone to the other side of Chicago —to Milwaukee, Wisconsin. He'd gone to Milwaukee, Wisconsin working for some of the leading white people on the train. He had sent letters to my grandmother, and I was staying with my grandmother, his mother. We went up there to try to catch him. We learned that he had left Wisconsin, and we came back to Tulsa. We were riding the freight train. We didn't have any money. But we got back to Tulsa, and found out that he had written to my grandmother that he was in California. So, my little-old Grandmother and me made up our minds we would try go to California too. So I went to California.

JE: Otis, on that day of this elevator scene, do you remember the first time you heard something was wrong? Something was going on in town? Do you remember that moment?

OC: To tell the truth about it, we didn't get that news. We'd run off and left Tulsa going up to Milwaukee, Wisconsin.

JE: But how did you know that day that something had happened?

OC: Because, they had gone and started what you might say is a little war so to speak. And the whites were running the colored folks out of town. We lived with a man that ran the little theater at that time on Greenwood. But, they didn't spare him either. They didn't spare any of the rich colored folks. If they were colored, they had to run off and leave their stuff.

JE: The Tulsa Tribune, the afternoon newspaper, carried the headline: Nabbed Negro for Attacking Girl in Elevator. And it said that Dick Rowland tore her clothes and scratched her face. And it said that Dick Rowland had been arrested and they alluded to attempted rape.

OC: I heard that.

JE: Did you ever see that newspaper? Or know about that newspaper?

OC: No. I'd run off and left everything. I'd run off and tried to catch up with my father.

JE: Whom did you live with?

OC: My grandmother. My father had built a home for my grandmother up on Archer Street, that wasn't too far up from Greenwood.

JE: Did your mother live there too?

OC: No, she lived in different places. But, she worked downtown—down on 1st Street. I didn't get a chance to even see my mother very much. She hardly ever came out there to check on us.

JE: Your grandmother had a garden?

OC: Oh yes. When I was a little boy she made me carry some of the stuff to sell to the sportin' folks, right back behind us on Archer. No, it was on 1st Street. The sportin' folk, what you might say sportin' women and stuff like that lived over on 1st Street. I remember carrying groceries and stuff over to the whites, they were sportin' women.

JE: What do you mean by sportin' women?

OC: Back then what we knew was that they would sell their bodies to men, white men. They had a regular little settlement that they lived in, right across from the Frisco tracks, right behind us. Just the Frisco train tracks separated 1st Street from Archer Street. And I had to carry groceries that my grandmother would send over to these sportin' women.

JE: And so you'd charge them for their vegetables?

OC: Yes.

JE: And they would pay you then?

OC: Yes.

JE: You'd bring that back to your grandmother?

OC: Yes. We were living well until the riot broke out. They tell me whites were jealous of us, of what you might say is—you some of the Colored people over on that side. Some of the main folk were working for the rich, white folks that were down on the south side of the city. And they were living well. And there was a jealousy they tell me. They were living too well, and they wanted to run them out of town, and take that part of town and give it back to the white folks.

BULLETS FIRED AT OTIS

John Erling: On that day, Memorial Day of 1921, do you recall hearing bullets and shooting?

Otis Clark: Oh yes. I got shot at. Come to think about it, I had a friend there at the Jackson funeral home. He was what you might say was the father of my sister's two little boys. I was down there at the funeral home when the riot broke out.

JE: When you went to the garage of that funeral home, tell me what happened as your friend was opening the garage door?

OC: While he was trying to open it, Jackson had come to the knowledge that we better get the colored folks out of that part of town. You see, we were the closest to the white section of town. Archer was the first street on what you might say is the north side of town.

JE: When you were there at the garage, Otis is it true that somebody shot and a bullet struck your friend's hand?

OC: That's right. Just across the Frisco tracks, on 1st Street, there was a mill. And the white men worked in that mill. It was some kind of grain mill, three or four stories high. And they (white men) could get up at the top of that mill and look across the tracks and see what we colored folks were doing. And sure enough we got shot at from the men over across the tracks. And it hit the boy in the hand, and I'm standing right behind him. He dropped his keys and we left the old car in the garage, and ran off and left it.

JE: You tried to run home?

OC: No, because the whites had then covered our home, which was about, three or four blocks up from the funeral home.

JE: Did you stay with your friend? His hand had a bullet in it?

OC: No, I ran off and left him.

JE: When you tried to go home, the whites were blocking your way home, is that true?

OC: Oh Lord. Yes. And they even burned it up.

JE: They burned your house?

OC: Oh yes, they burned up where we lived.

JE: But do you recall that night, you couldn't go to your house, it was burning. Didn't you go to your cousin's house? They were planning to go to Claremore?

OC: That was in the riot. The riot was just starting. The whites were taking over that section of the city, which was closest to them, just across the Frisco tracks. My cousin, they lived way out on Greenwood and had a little café way up out on Greenwood there. So we made up our minds to try to get out to where they lived. But when we got out there, they were fixing to go to Claremore to kind of get out of the troubled area. So we went to Claremore. But on our way to Claremore, after we crossed the little old

Verdigris River, and then came out with their guns and stopped the car.

JE: When the white men stopped your car, were they asking for anything? Or did you think that was going to be the end of you there?

OC: We didn't know about all this race trouble that they had started. They knew about it, and so after they found out we didn't have anything, no guns and stuff, they let us go on to Claremore. But then in Claremore, at a little hotel where we stayed, they found out that the soldiers had come in there and stopped some of the riots, so we could come on back home. And the next morning we came back to Tulsa. But when we got back there, they had burned up everything. And so the little Salvation Army had come over and built some little-old building for the colored folks that were left there to live in. My mother and some of them had a little building and that's where I had to stay too, because all of the big buildings were burned up.

JE: When you came back then, you found your home was destroyed. I think even your dog was gone, right?

OC: Oh yes, yes. We didn't see him anymore.

TREATMENT OF BLACKS

John Erling: So that night, May 31, in 1921, you left town?

Otis Clark: Yes.

JE: And that's when you hopped a freight train?

OC: Yes. A little-old freight train all the way to Chicago because we found out that we could get the train out of Chicago over to Milwaukee, Wisconsin. That's where we wanted to go to find my father. But he had already left and gone to California.

JE: Do you have any other memories of what you saw when you came back on the 31st? Did you see smoke or buildings on fire? Did you see dead bodies in the street?

OC: Oh, I don't know how many days that it was before we got back to Tulsa on the freight train. But when we got back to Tulsa the soldiers had come there and stopped all the shooting and stuff and everything was kind of calm then. But they killed a lot of the poor colored folks. That's the worst thing in all of the United States. They got away with killing 300 folks they claim, but it was even more than that. My stepfather, he was dead and gone. There was nobody that knew where he was. They didn't have any funeral for anybody. Ku Klux Klan they came in and had taken over and they didn't let the folks have any law or anything like that, they just killed the folks, all that they wanted to kill. And they let some of the folks live. But it was the Ku Klux Klan taken over the city of Tulsa. And they had taken over power there for three or four years and the colored folks couldn't do anything. We didn't have anything. And all the rich colored folks that owned the theaters and barbershops and all that stuff, they were what you might say out of jobs. All of them had become poor folks from then on.

JE: Did you see the courthouse and the mob that was beginning to build around the courthouse? Did you know that the mob was there and they wanted to lynch Dick Rowland?

OC: We were living down in the colored section, and didn't know anything about this at all. We just heard that they had arrested a boy. Though we didn't get the chance to see anything about it at all.

JE: Was your grandmother—what happened to her? Where did she go?

OC: My grandmother was—they had protected all the old folks and taken them downtown and put them in a ballpark in different big places to protect them from being destroyed.

JE: Well, they put some in jail, and they put some at the fairgrounds—was your mother taken to the fairgrounds?

OC: She worked downtown. We didn't get the chance to see her much at all. She was a young woman, so we didn't know what she was doing.

JE: Did anybody try to capture you?

OC: No. We stayed over on the colored side. They called it the nigger side back then. All the niggers had to stay back on the north side of the city where they were burning them up. They didn't tell the whole truth about it in the papers. But more colored folks were killed in that riot than anyplace in America. It was the worst thing in all of America—the Tulsa Race Riots.

JE: So then you decided to leave Tulsa?

OC: Oh yes. I decided to catch up with my father, and he had gone to California. My grandmother got a letter from him, which (by the way) they didn't ever leave Tulsa, they stayed right there in Tulsa, my grandmother and my mother and some of them stayed there in Tulsa. The Salvation Army built some little-old shack and so they stayed in a little shack. But I went to California.

BUTLER FOR JOAN CRAWFORD

John Erling: Okay, you took a freight train to California, is that true?

Otis Clark: Yes. We were on a freight train, riding in a boxcar. That's where I saw some of the best grape orchards where they grow grapes. And for miles and miles those folks had nothing but grape farms where they grew different kinds of grapes. We were happy to see all of that. We hadn't seen anything like that before we went to California. But anyway, we had a nice time. And we got out there in California, and then I went to work for my father. My father was working for the rich sportin' folks, so I got a job working for the movie star folks. And I worked for Clark Gable and Charlie Chaplin and Stepin Fetchit. I worked as a butler for Joan Crawford, the movie star. I got what you might say on big-time. To tell the truth, I forgot all about our troubles that we had in Tulsa, Oklahoma.

JE: Didn't you marry—you married a woman out there in California?

OC: Yes, I married a woman out there, but she died. I married more than one. My last wife was named Bessie.

JE: But this woman you married in California, she was a cook?

OC: I married her in Tulsa, Oklahoma. And then we moved to California. She was a good cook in Tulsa. So when we got to California, she got a good job cooking for—what was that movie star?

JE: Joan Crawford?

OC: Yes! She got a job cooking for Joan Crawford. That's right. And so I got along nicely then.

JE: And then you had a job, what did you do? You were a butler?

OC: Yes. I worked as a butler and I worked as a driver for some rich doctors.

JE: You mentioned Clark Gable, can you tell us what he was like?

OC: I only took care of him when he came to the house. I worked as a butler for Joan Crawford, and they would come to her house and have dinner. My job was to help serve them.

JE: Charlie Chaplin came to the house too?

OC: Oh yeah. Oh yes. But they had moved over to England. I didn't know just whereabouts in England, but they were over there in England. London or somewhere over there. They went over there because they didn't want to pay taxes, but they didn't talk about it, so I didn't know too much about it. But all of these new movie stars went over to England.

JE: California was taxing them too much.

OC: That's right.

JE: All of this time that you were living in California, were you hearing anything about Tulsa and the aftermath of the race riots? Did you stay in touch with anybody?

OC: No. My mother and my grandmother, they got along so nice after they calmed down everything. They didn't want to leave Tulsa. So they stayed around in Tulsa and those little shacks that they built them, because their real homes had been burned down.

JE: You lived in California until about 1998, and you came back to Tulsa?

OC: I had come back to Tulsa every now and then to see about my mother and my grandmother and others and visit with them a while. But I made my own home, really, in California.

JE: When you would come back to visit, what did you think about Tulsa? And what did your grandmother and mother say about that? Because here this riot had gone on, what were they talking about?

OC: The Ku Klux Klan had taken over the power of the city, and they didn't allow the colored folks to have anything to do with what was going on downtown, and what those folks were up to. They had to be, what you might say, kind of like prisoners. They had to be quiet, and they couldn't say anything. They tell me that lasted around three or four years that the Ku Klux Klan wouldn't let them have anything to say. And, they wouldn't let any other towns come in and help us. The Ku Klux Klan kept us bound down for three or four years.

OTIS AND JAILHOUSE CONVERSION

John Erling: When you were in California, I think for some reason, you landed in jail for about 20 days?

Otis Clark: You got that right. I had forgotten about that. I got acquainted with some of my old boyfriends that used to live in Oklahoma, in Tulsa, and they were selling whiskey, bootlegging we called it. And I got to selling whiskey. And somehow or another, I sold whiskey to the wrong guys. The little guy was a stool pigeon they called him. And he would tell the law about you. And I guess he made his living telling on folks selling whiskey. He told on me about having whiskey in my room. And sure enough, they put me in jail. My father was moving pretty well. He was in the Baptist Church. It was quite a nice big church, one of the leading churches of the city. It was the second Baptist Church they called it.

JE: Did the Salvation Army send preachers to the jail?

OC: Yes! They did that. The Salvation Army on Saturday and Sunday, they would let little young preachers and workers come to the jail and preach to us in jail. And I happened to be one of those that got converted in jail. They told me I had to get to the Lord and repent. So I repented and had one of the most beautiful dreams that I ever had in my life in the Los Angeles jail. I got to be a member then of the Baptist Church.

JE: What was the dream you had?

OC: I dreamed that I was over in heaven, over in the heavenly pastures. I don't know whether I had wings or what. But I could see all of the beautiful trees. Trees all beautiful with flowers all over them. More beautiful than anything I'd ever seen in my life. And so I made up my mind that

I was going to be a good Christian. And so I got to be, what you might say after that, is something of a preacher myself. And I would tell the folks to repent and get on God's side. And if you're on God's side, you were on the winning side. And if you weren't on God's side, you were a loser, and the devil had the power over you. So I had a good time then. I got to be a little evangelist traveling all around all over the country. I even went to Chicago and New York and traveled around the main big cities as an evangelist of the Church of God in Christ. And Bishop Mason was the head of the Church of God in Christ at that time. I served Bishop Mason and a lot of the big elders of the Church of God in Christ.

JE: You were a minister and in the church for many years then weren't you?

OC: That's right.

JE: Today you are a Bishop, Bishop Clark?

OC: They gave me that title. My little youth group gave me that title. I just call myself an evangelist. And an evangelist is one that travels to different places and goes to different church buildings and stuff like that.

JE: Did you ever come back to Oklahoma to preach?

OC: Oh Lord. Yes. I tried to tell the folks in Oklahoma how to get on God's side.

JE: Did you preach in Tulsa?

OC: Oh yes.

JE: What effect did the race riots have on your life and the way you view things?

OC: The race riots didn't have too much of a real effect on me after getting to California and getting with these leading sportin' folks. I forgot all about some of the troubles that we had there in Tulsa, Oklahoma. That's the way that turned out. Then, when I got to preaching—it was then that I was able to tell the folks about what a difference it would make, to be safe from the powers of the devil to the glory of God.

LIFE AND ADVICE AT 106 YEARS OLD

John Erling: You came back to Tulsa in 1998, and you lived here then for some time?

Otis Clark: Yes, I spent a little time because my sister had bought a home place for us in Tulsa. I didn't stay there. I just stayed in California. But I would come back and check with them and spend time with them and then go on back to California. But, I fooled around then and made up my mind to live there in Tulsa and then I married there. Then after we were married, I made up my mind to take my wife and go back to California.

JE: We should point out that we are talking to you now from your home in Seattle, Washington.

OC: That's right. Auburn.

JE: Auburn, Washington. Otis, but we think back on the race riot, and the fact that the city was really silent about the riot for about 75 years, and that many Tulsans grew up, attended school, studied Oklahoma history and said that many years ago they did not know about the riot, that the city was quiet about it. What are your feelings about that?

OC: That's about right. The Ku Klux Klan was in power, and they stayed in power for years. The Negroes had to stay on one side of town and the whites on the other.

JE: Actually, the race riot sent you to California and you started living a better life out there than if you had stayed right here in Oklahoma. Now you are 106 years old today. To what do you owe this long life of 106? Why do you think you've lived to be 106?

OC: I don't know myself other than trying to warn the folks that if you were on God's side, you were on the right side.

JE: How strong are you here at 106 years old? Do you walk with a cane or walker?

OC: No, I don't use either one.

JE: You are absolutely amazing. What do your doctors say about your condition?

OC: I'm not on medication or anything.

JE: You're not on any medication?

OC: No.

JE: You're absolutely amazing.

OC: I just have to thank God. I try to tell the younger folks to get on his side, and that is best side to be on.

JE: Otis, how would you like to be remembered?

OC: As being blessed to be saved from the powers of Satan

unto God. I wasn't on God's side all the time. I was on Satan's side. I was doing everything I thought the world was doing—doing bad things. But through the goodness of God, he let me get saved, and get on his side. And I'm telling the young folks that if you're on God's side, you're on the winning side. And if you're not on God's side, you're a loser. The devil can't save you. The devil is going to lose. The devil is going to get put in hell. (Laughter.) So if you follow him, you'll have to go to hell, so you don't want to go to hell. You want to get on God's side and go to heaven and live with God. You can't beat that can you?

JE: No, you can't beat that. When they were talking about reparations or paying money to those who were survivors, which you were, did you believe that you should be paid money by the state or the federal government?

OC: I heard that but it never did materialize into anything, or in other words, to reality in my life.

JE: You know, you could possibly have, as other blacks may have, resentment toward whites in what they did to Tulsa. Do you feel any of that resentment?

OC: Well, you're taught that, but if you get converted, God forgives you, and you don't bother about it at all. Real Christians don't bother about the riots and stuff anymore. Somehow or another, God has just taken it out of their minds. We don't have the mind of what we used to suffer. We have the mind of Christ. And the Book tells us, to let your mind be used for Christ—a mind to love and to do right.

JE: Well, you have done a great job here, and it's just hard to believe that I'm talking to a 106-year-old man. You're the oldest man I've ever talked to. And, by your pictures, you sure do not look 106.

OC: That's God's doing.

JE: Well God bless you. Thank you for telling us this story and for taking the time with us today. We really appreciate it very, very much.

OC: Thank you John. May God bless you, too.

“THE GLORIOUS CAUSE OF AFRICAN FREEDOM”

MARCUS GARVEY

Membership Appeal to the Negro Citizens of New York

July 1921

FELLOW MEN AND WOMEN:

I greet you in the name of the Universal Negro Improvement Association, and African Communities League of the World.

You may ask what Organization is that? It is for me to inform you that the Universal Negro Improvement Association, is an Organization that seeks to unite into one solid body, the 400 million Negroes of the world, to link up the 15 million Negroes of the United States of America, with the 20 million Negroes of the West Indies, the 40 million Negroes of South and Central America, with the 280 million Negroes of Africa for the purpose of bettering our industrial, commercial, educational, social and political condition.

As you are aware, the world in which we live to-day, is divided into separate race groups, and distinct nationalities. Each race, and each nationality endeavoring to work out its own destiny, to the exclusion of other races, and other nationalities. We hear the cry of England for the English, of France for the French, of Germany for the Germans, of Ireland for the Irish, of Palestine for the Jew, of Japan for the Japanese, of China for the Chinese. We of the Universal Negro Improvement Association are raising the cry of Africa for the Africans, those at home and those abroad.

There are 400 million Africans in the world who have Negro blood coursing through their veins, and we believe that the time has come to unite these 400 million people for the one common purpose of bettering their condition.

The greatest problem of the Negro for the last five hundred years, has been that of disunity.

No individual or no Organization ever succeeded in uniting the Negro race, but within the last four years, the Universal

Negro Improvement Association has worked wonders in bringing together in one fold, four million organized Negroes, who are scattered in all parts of the world, being in the 48 States of the American Union, all the West Indian Islands, and the countries of South and Central America, and in Africa. These four million people are working to convert the rest of the 400 millions scattered all over the world, and it is for this purpose that we are asking you to join our ranks, and do the best you can to help us to bring about an emancipated race in the strictest sense of the word.

You will realise that this is an age of Organization. The individual cannot live by himself, he can accomplish very little by himself. If anything praiseworthy is to be done, it must be done by united effort; and it is for that reason that the Universal Negro Improvement Association calls upon every Negro in the State of New York to rally to its standard. We want to unite the Negro race in this State. We want every Negro to work for one common object, that of building a nation of his own on the great continent of Africa. That all Negroes all over the world are working for the establishment of a Government in Africa, means that it will be realised in another few years.

We want the moral and financial support of every Negro to make the dream a possibility. Already this Organization has established itself in Liberia, West Africa, and is endeavouring to do all that is possible to develop that Negro country into a great industrial and commercial commonwealth.

Pioneers have been sent by this Organization to Liberia and they are now laying the foundations upon which the 400 million Negroes of the world will build. If you believe that the Negro has a soul, if you believe that the Negro is a man, if you believe the Negro was endowed with the senses commonly given to other men by the Creator, then you must acknowledge that what other men have done, Negroes can do. We want to build up Cities, Nations, Governments, Industries of our own in Africa, so that we will be able to have a chance to rise from the lowest to the highest positions in the African commonwealth.

The Universal Negro Improvement Association does not seek to set race against race, but seeks to elevate the Negro. We have no time to preach race hatred, because all of our time is given to the spreading of the doctrine of unity among Negroes everywhere. In our desire to build a nation for Negroes, we are doing so without prejudice to any other nation, Government, or race in the world. If the Englishman has the right to rule himself, if the German has the right to rule himself, if the Frenchman has the right to rule himself, if the Chinese has the right to rule himself, if the Japanese has the right to rule himself, on the same principle, we believe that the Negro has the right to rule himself. When God created the world He gave [ ] common rights and intended that all of us should be the lords of creation. Under our common [ ] therefore as a race, we demand a place in the political sun of the world. We demand our portion, which is Africa. The Almighty Architect, when He created the world, designed that black men should inherit the land of Africa. Our country is being robbed and despoiled by the avaricious races and nations of the world, but by their injustice, and by their unrighteous methods, they will fall, and by their fall will come the rise of the African Empire upon which the sun will never set. Let us work toward the end of the glorious cause of African freedom caring not how long we have been out of Africa. Although we have been slaves in these parts for nearly three hundred years, it goes without argument that we are still citizens of Africa. From Africa our parents were robbed three hundred years ago. Nevertheless, when they were robbed from Africa, they never gave over their rights of ownership in the land to any other race or any individual. By right of heritage therefore, each and every Negro in the Western world has a moral and a legal claim to Africa. As Africans abroad, we should lend out assistance morally and financially for the redemption of our Motherland.

This is what the Universal Negro Improvement Association seeks to do by inculcating race pride, and race consciousness in the mind and heart of every Negro. There are some Negroes who think themselves too educated, too successful to lend an ear to the common plea, and the common cry of Mother Africa. How unfortunate that this should be. These people are indeed narrow minded, and have no vision, because every careful student of political science can foresee a future world of tears for those who are not prepared to defend themselves by strong political organization. When we say political organization we do not mean as confined to one's domestic district, where you live, as a subject or as a citizen of the Government that is controlled by an alien race. We mean political organization that is indeed independent to race, that political organization that will make you an independent political unit among the nations and races of the world. We mean the political organization called independent Government. No Negro with all his success, is secure in any community where the Government is vested in an opposite race, when that opposite race is prejudiced to the Negro. There is no guarantee of the safety of any such Negro, because by mob violence and by lynch law, the outcome of race prejudice, one's success can be overthrown overnight, and one transformed from a prosperous subject or citizen, to a refugee. That has been demonstrated in many communities and it should act as a warning to the educated and prosperous Negro, and let him realise that the best thing for every one to do, is to unite, and so fortify ourselves by building up a strong Government in Africa, that as citizens of that Government we can claim protection in any part of the world we happen to find ourselves. Why should not Africa have a Navy? Why should not Africa have a standing Army? Why should not Africa have a Government second to none in the world, controlled and dominated by Negroes? Do you mean to say that 400 million Negroes cannot govern themselves? Do you mean to say that 400 million Negroes cannot work to build up themselves, and to protect Civilization? Men and women of the race in New York, the Universal Negro Improvement Association appeals to you at this hour, for unity. "United we stand, divided we fall."

This, we believe, is your last chance to come together as a race, because if, in the reorganization of the world, you do not demonstrate your fitness to exist, you shall be completely wiped out in the question of the survival of the fittest. We of the Universal Negro Improvement Association are longing for the day, when the other races of the world will respect Negroes for what Negroes have done on their own initiative to demonstrate their ability as a race. We are longing for the day when Presidents and Princes shall come out of Africa. We are longing for the day when the children of Africa will have respect and homage paid to them, even as are paid to the other races of the world to-day. We can do it, but we cannot do it living separately and individually. We can only do it when we work collectively and unitedly, so let all the Negroes of the State of New York come together and join the Universal Negro Improvement Association and African Communities League, and support the program morally and financially. It is only by the pooling of our own resources your dollar with mine, and our dollars with the other fellow's, that we can accumulate sufficient money to put over big programs, industrially, commercially and politically, in the name of our race.

The Universal Negro Improvement Association is the strongest Negro Organization in the world. It has no selfishness about it. It is not for one class of Negroes as against another class, it is for all Negroes. If you are poor, you can come into the Universal Negro Improvement Association, if you are rich you can come into the Universal Negro Improvement Association, if you are educated, you can come into the Universal Negro Improvement Association. It is for everybody, so long as you have one drop of Negro blood in your veins. We want to build factories. We want to build and run steamships, and that is why we have the Corporation known as the Black Star Line with its shares selling at $5.00 each. Already those who have joined our Organization have bought their shares, some one, some two, some ten, 20, 50, 200, and by what they have done by purchasing shares in this Corporation, we have been able to place ships on the ocean, thus demonstrating to the world, that Negroes are able to enter into maritime commerce, but we want more money now, to build and buy more ships. We want more money now to build factories. We want more money now to finance our industries in Africa. Why not make up your mind to come over and help the Universal Negro Improvement Association carry through this program, so that you and your children can be insured forever.

We are asking you to communicate at once with, or call at the office of the Universal Negro Improvement Association, 56 W. 135th street, New York City, N.Y., U.S.A., for all information about the Universal Negro Improvement Association, and for membership. You can send $1.00, which will, if you are a Negro, make you a member of the Organization, with all the necessary supplies furnished for membership. If you desire shares in the Black Star Line, so as to enable us to float a bigger merchant marine, you can write to the Black Star Line

Steamship Corporation, 56 W. 135th street, New York City. You can send from $5.00 to $1,000.00 for shares, in that the shares are sold at $5.00 each, and you can buy as many as you want. In buying shares in the Black Star Line, you will be investing to make profit which will be declared by way of dividends, once a year, according to the success of the Corporation for that year. Outside of the profits they will give to you as individuals, there is the satisfaction that you have helped to build up a great merchant marine, to be owned and controlled by the Negro race.

Men and women of New York, let us be up and doing, turn not a deaf ear to this place, but right away let us make up our minds to be whatsoever we can for the glorification of this race of ours.

Write, or call, Department of Information, Universal Negro Improvement Association, 56 West 135th street, New York City, or Department of Information, Black Star Line, 56 W. 135th street, New York City. If you want to help this movement, you may also send us a donation for the continuance of our work.

This Organization meets in Liberty Hall, 120–148 W. 138th street, New York City, every night at 8:30. Yours for racial uplift,

UNIVERSAL NEGRO IMPROVEMENT ASSOCIATION
MARCUS GARVEY, President General

APPLICATION BLANK FOR MEMBERSHIP IN UNIVERSAL NEGRO IMPROVEMENT ASSOCIATION

Secretary, Universal Negro Improvement Association.

56 W. 135th street, New York.

Dear Sir:—Enclosed and attached hereto please find one dollar. For this amount register me as an active member of the U.N.I.A. and send me all supplied by an officer of the organization.

NAME . . . .
ADDRESS . . . .

SCIPIO AFRICANUS JONES

Petition for Writ of Habeas Corpus in Moore v. Dempsey

September 21, 1921

YOUR PETITIONERS, Frank Moore, Ed. Hicks, J. E. Knox, Ed. Coleman and Paul Hall, state that they are citizens and residents of the State of Arkansas, and are now residing in Little Rock, confined in the Arkansas State Penitentiary, in the Western Division of the Eastern District of Arkansas, within the jurisdiction of this court; that the defendant is the keeper of the said Arkansas State Penitentiary, and as such is unlawfully restraining your petitioners of their liberty, and will, unless prevented from so doing by the issuance of the writ herein prayed for, deprive them of their life on the 23rd day of Sept., 1921, in violation of the Constitution and laws of the United States, and the Constitution and laws of the State of Arkansas.

Petitioners further say that they are Negroes, of African descent, black in color, and that prior to the times hereinafter mentioned were citizens and residents of Phillips County, Arkansas, at Elaine; that on the —— day of October, 1919, they were arrested, placed in the Phillips County jail and thereafter until their trial were kept in close confinement upon an alleged charge of murder in the first degree for the killing of one Clinton Lee, a white man, said to have occurred on the 1st day of October, 1919; that said Clinton Lee was killed, as they are informed, while a member of a posse of white men who were said to be attempting to quell a race riot, growing out of the killing of W. A. Adkins on the night of September 30, 1919, at Hoop Spur in said County and State; that said Adkins was killed, as they are advised, under these circumstances and conditions: Petitioners and a large number of the members of their race were peaceably and lawfully assembled in their church house at or near Hoop Spur, with no unlawful purpose in view, and with no desire or purpose to injure or do any wrong to any one; that while they were thus assembled, white persons began firing guns or pistols from the outside into and through said church house, through the windows and shooting the lights out therein, causing a great disturbance and stampede of those assembled therein; that the white persons so firing on said church came there in automobiles, of which there were several, and came for the purpose of breaking up said meeting; that said Adkins was killed either by members of his own party or by some other persons unknown to your petitioners; that the white men sent out the word to Helena, the county seat, that said Adkins had been killed by the Negroes, shot down in cold blood while on a peaceable mission, by an armed force of Negroes, assembled at the church, which caused great excitement all over the City of Helena and Phillips County; that the report of said killing spread like wild-fire into other counties, all over the State of Arkansas, and into other States, notably the State of Mississippi; that early the next day a large number of white men of said County armed themselves and rushed to the scene of the trouble and to adjacent regions, the vicinity of Elaine being one of them, and began the indiscriminate hunting down, shooting and killing of Negroes; that in a short time white men from adjoining counties and from the State of Mississippi likewise armed themselves, rushed to the scene of the trouble and began the indiscriminate shooting down of Negroes, both men and women, particularly the posse from the State of Mississippi, who shot down in cold blood innocent Negro men and women, many of whom were at the time in the fields picking cotton; that highly inflammable articles were published in the press of Arkansas and especially of Helena and throughout the United States, in which the trouble was variously called a "race riot," "an uprising of the Negroes," and a "deliberately planned insurrection among the Negroes against the whites" of that part of Phillips County; that the officers of Phillips County, especially the Sheriff, called upon the Governor of the State, and the Governor in turn called upon the Commanding Officer at Camp Pike for a large number of the United States soldiers to assist the citizens in quelling the so-called "race riot", "uprising", or "insurrection"; that a company of soldiers was dispatched to the scene of the trouble who took charge of the situation and finally succeeded in stopping the slaughter.

Your petitioners further say that they, together with a large number of their race, both men and women, were taken to the Phillips County jail, at Helena, incarcerated therein and charged with murder; that a committee of seven, composed of leading Helena business men and officials, to wit: Sebastian Straub, Chairman; H. D. Moore, County Judge; F. F. Kitchens, Sheriff; J. G. Knight, Mayor; E. M. Allen, E. C. Hornor and T. W. Keesee, was selected for the purpose of probing into the situation and picking out those to be condemned to death and those to be condemned and sentenced to the penitentiary; that said Committee assumed charge of the matter and proceeded to have brought before them a large number of those incarcerated in jail and examined them regarding their own connection and the connection of others charged with participation in said trouble; that if evidence unsatisfactory to said Committee was not given they would be sent out and certain of their keepers would take them to a room in the jail which was immediately adjoining, and a part of the Court House building where said Committee was sitting, and torture them by beating and whipping them with leather straps with metal in them, cutting the blood at every lick until the victims would agree to testify to anything their torturers demanded of them; that there was also provided in said jail, to frighten and torture them, an electric chair, in which they would be put naked and the current turned on to shock and frighten them into giving damaging statements against themselves and others, also strangling drugs were put up their noses for the same purpose and by these methods and means false evidence was extorted from Negroes to be used and was used against your petitioners.

Petitioners further say that on every day from October 1, until after their trial on November 3, 1919, the press of Helena and the State of Arkansas carried inflammatory articles giving accounts of the trouble, which were calculated to arouse and did arouse bitter feeling against your petitioners and the other members of their race;

. . . that shortly after being placed in jail, a mob was formed in the City of Helena, composed of hundreds of men, who marched to the county jail for the purpose and with the intent of lynching your petitioners and others, and would have done so but for the interference of United States soldiers and the promise of some of said Committee and other leading officials that if the mob would stay its hand they would execute those found guilty in the form of law.

Petitioners further state that prior to October 1, 1919, they were farmers and share croppers; that nearly all the land in Phillips County is owned by white men; that some is rented out to share croppers to be tilled on shares, one-half to the tenant and the other half to the owner; that some years past there has grown up a system among the land owners of furnishing the Negro tenants supplies on which to make crops and which is calculated to deprive and does deprive the Negro tenants of all their interest in the crops produced by them; that in pursuance of this system, they refused to give the share croppers any itemized statement of account of their indebtedness for supplies so furnished, refused to let them move or sell any part of their crops, but themselves sell and dispose of the same at such prices as they please, and then give to the Negroes no account thereof, pay them only such amount as they wish, and in this way keep them down, poverty stricken and effectually under their control; that for the purpose of protecting themselves, if possible, against the oppressive and ruinous effects of this system, the Negro farmers organized societies, with the view of uniting their financial resources in moral and legal measures to overcome the same, which fact became quickly known to the plantation owners; that such owners were bitterly opposed to such societies, sought to prevent their organization, ordered the members to discontinue their meeting and sought by every means they could employ to disrupt them; that on the 30th day of September, 1919, petitioners and other members of the Ratio Lodge, near Elaine, learned that some of the Negro farmers of a nearby plantation had employed U. S. Bratton, an attorney of Little Rock, Arkansas, to represent them in effecting a settlement for them with their landlords, or, if he could not, to institute legal proceedings to protect their interests, and that either he, or his representative, would be there on the following day to meet with all parties concerned, perfect the arrangements, and learn all the facts as far as possible, and decided to hold a meeting with the view of seeing him while there, and engaging him as an attorney to protect their interest; that accordingly they met that night in the Hoop Spur church, which resulted, as hereinbefore set out, in the killing of said Adkins and the breaking up of said meeting; that on the morning of October 1, Mr. O. S. Bratton, son and agent of Attorney U. S. Bratton, arrived in Elaine for consultation with those who might desire to employ his father, was arrested, hardly escaped being mobbed, notwithstanding it was well known that he was there only for the purpose of advising with those Negroes as to their rights, and getting from them such facts as would enable his father intelligently to prepare for their legal rights; that he was carried thence to the County jail, thrown into it and kept closely confined on a charge of murder until the 31st day of the same month, when he was indicted on a charge of barratry, without any evidence to sustain the charge; that on that day he was told by officials that he would be discharged, but not to go on the public streets anywhere, to keep the matter a secret, to leave secretly in a closed automobile and to go to West Helena, four miles away, and there take the train, so as to avoid being mobbed; that he was told he would be mobbed, or would be in great danger of being mobbed if his release became known publicly before he was out of reach; that the Judge of the Circuit Court, the Judge of the same court before whom petitioners were tried, facilitated the secret departure and himself went to West Helena and there remained until he had seen said Bratton safely on the train and the train departed.

Petitioners further say that the Circuit Court of Phillips County convened on October 27, 1919; that a grand jury was organized composed wholly of white men, one of whom, T. W. Keesee, was a member of the said Committee of Seven, and many of whom were in the posse organized to fight the Negroes; that during its sessions, petitioners and many others of the prisoners were frequently carried before it in an effort to extract from them false incriminating admissions and to testify against each other, and that both before and after, they were frequently whipped, beaten and tortured; that those in charge of them had some way of learning when the evidence was unsatisfactory to the grand jury, and this was always followed by beating and whipping; that by these methods, some of the Negro prisoners were forced to testify against others, two against your petitioners, though no one could truthfully testify against them; that on October 29, 1919, a joint indictment was returned against petitioners accusing them of the murder of said Clinton Lee, a man petitioners did not know and had never, to their knowledge, even seen; that thereafter on the 3rd day of November, 1919, petitioners were taken into the court room before the judge told of the charge, and were informed that a certain lawyer was appointed to defend them; that they were given no opportunity to employ an attorney of their own choice; that the appointed attorney did not consult with them, took no steps to prepare for their defense, asked nothing about their witnesses, though there were many who knew that petitioners had nothing to do with the killing of said Lee; that they were immediately placed on joint trial before an exclusively white jury and the trial closed so far as the evidence was concerned with the State's witnesses alone; that after the court's instructions, the jury retired just long enough to write a verdict of guilty of murder in the first degree, as charged, and returned with it into court—not being out exceeding two or three minutes, and they were promptly sentenced to death by electrocution on December 27, 1919.

Petitioners further say that during the course of said trial, which lasted less than an hour, that only two witnesses testified to anything to connect them in any way with the killing of said Clinton Lee; that said witnesses were Walter Ward and John Jefferson, both of whom are Negroes and were under indictment at the same time for the killing of said Lee; that they were compelled to testify against them by the same methods and means hereinbefore described; that their testimony was wholly false and that they gave such testimony through fear of torture and were further told that if they refused to testify they would be killed, but that if they did so testify, and would plead guilty their punishment would be light; that they thereafter pleaded guilty to murder in the second degree and were sentenced to terms of imprisonment; that they attach hereto the affidavits of each of said witnesses showing the falsity of their testimony and the means of its acquisition.

Petitioners further say that large crowds of white people bent on petitioners' condemnation and death thronged the courthouse and grounds and streets of Helena all during the trial of petitioners and the other Negro defendants; that on account of the great publicity given theirs and the other cases, on account of their being charged with connection with an insurrection against the white people, and that four or five white men were killed, on account of the fact that they are Negroes, and those who run the court, the Judge upon the bench, the Sheriff, the Clerk and all the jurors are white men, on account of the fact that it was stated and widely published that the purpose of the Negroes was to kill the whites and take their property, and on account of all the race prejudice which normally exists and which was enhanced a thousandfold at the time, by bitterness beyond expression, it was impossible for them to get a fair and impartial trial in said court before a jury of white men; that the attorney appointed to defend them knew that the prejudice against them was such that they could not get a fair and impartial trial before a white jury of said county, yet he filed no petition for a change of venue, did not ask the court for time to prepare for a defense, and did nothing to protect their interests; that the court did not ask them whether they had counsel, or desired to employ counsel, or were able to do so, but simply said a lawyer, whom he named, would defend them; that they have, therefore, not had a trial, have had no opportunity to make a defense but that their case was closed against them as virtually and effectually as if on a plea of guilty; that if they had been given the opportunity they would have employed counsel of their own choice and have made a defense, their ability to do so having been demonstrated since their conviction; that the feeling against petitioners was such that it overawed the Judge on the bench, the jury, the attorney appointed to defend them and every one connected with said court; that all, Judge, jury and counsel, were dominated by the mob spirit that was universally present in court and out, so that if any juror had had the courage to investigate said charge with any spirit of fairness, and vote for an acquittal, he, himself, would have been the victim of the mob; that such was the intensity of feeling against petitioners and the other defendants, that had counsel for them objected to the testimony of the three witnesses against them said Ward, Green and Jefferson, on the ground that it was extorted by beating and torture, as they are advised he should have done, he himself would have been the victim of the mob; that it is possible counsel did not know how the evidence against them was obtained, and they do not desire to appear to criticize him, yet he knew that if the evidence against them was acquired as before stated, it was incompetent and should have been excluded, a fact which petitioners did not know, that petitioners were ignorant of their rights, had never been in court before, and had counsel asked them about this testimony they would have told him how it was obtained, that through fear of the mob spirit no witness was called in their behalf and they themselves were advised not to take the stand on their own behalf; that as a result of the mob domination of court, counsel and jury, the court, although a court of original jurisdiction in felony cases, lost its jurisdiction by virtue of such mob domination and the result was but an empty ceremony, carried through in the apparent form of law, and that the verdict of the jury was really a mob verdict, dictated by the spirit of the mob and pronounced and returned because no other verdict would have been tolerated, and that the judgment against them is, therefore, a nullity.

Petitioners further say that the entire trial, verdict and judgment against them was but an empty ceremony; that their real trial and condemnation had already taken place before said Committee of Seven; that said Committee, in advance of the citing of the court, had sat in judgment upon them and all the other cases and had assumed and exercised the jurisdiction of the court by determining their guilt or innocence of those in jail had acquired the evidence in the manner herein set out, and decided which of the defendants should be electrocuted and which sent to prison and the terms to be given them, and which to discharge; that when court convened, the program laid out by said Committee was carried through and the verdict against petitioners was pronounced and returned, not as the independent verdict of an unbiased jury, but as a part of the prearranged scheme and judgment of said Committee; that in doing this the court did not exercise the jurisdiction given it by law and wholly lost its jurisdiction by substituting for its judgment the judgment of condemnation of said Committee.

Petitioners further say that, ever since the law of Arkansas for the selection of jury commissioners was enacted, all of the judges of the courts have been and are now white men, and that ever since then said judges have appointed, without exception, white commissioners to select the jurors, both grand

and petit, and that such commissioners have uniformly selected only white men on such juries; that all of this has been done in discrimination against the Negro race, on account of their color; that such has been the unbroken practice in Phillips County for more than thirty years, notwithstanding the Negro population in said county exceeds the white population by more than five to one, and that a large proportion of them are electors and possess the legal, moral and intellectual qualifications required or necessary for such jurors; that the exclusion of said Negroes from the juries was, at all times, intentional and because of their color, of their being Negroes; that such was the case on the grand jury by which petitioners were indicted, and of the petit jury that pronounced them guilty; that under the law of Arkansas, as construed by the Supreme Court of the State, an objection to an indictment on the ground that it was found by a grand jury composed only of white men to the exclusion of Negroes on account of their color, must be made at the impanelling of the grand jury and objection to the petit jury must be made before a plea is entered to the indictment; that at the time said indictment was found petitioners were confined in jail and did not know the grand jury had been organized, did not know it was in session, did not know they were to be indicted for the killing of said Lee or any other person and did not know they were charged therewith; that it was impossible for them to make any objection to the organization of said grand jury for the very simple reason that they were closely confined, had no attorney, and no opportunity to employ an attorney; that at their trial, counsel appointed to defend them made no objection to the petit jury or to any previous proceeding; that their failure to do so was through fear of the mob for petitioners and himself, as they believe.

Petitioners further say that after their conviction and sentence to death, their friends employed other counsel to represent them; that through such counsel they filed a motion for a new trial, which was promptly overruled and an appeal was taken to the Supreme Court of Arkansas, the highest court in said State, where, on the 29th day of March, 1920, the judgment of the Phillips Circuit Court was affirmed; that thereafter they applied to the Supreme Court of the United States for a writ of certiorari to the Supreme Court of Arkansas, praying that said court be required to send up the record and proceeding in said cause for review by the Supreme Court of the United States, but that on the 11th day of October, 1920, the application for said writ was denied; that the Governor of the State of Arkansas did on the —— day of August, 1921, issue a proclamation carrying into effect the judgment and sentence of the Phillips Circuit Court against petitioners and in which he fixed Sept. 23, 1921, as the date of their execution.

Petitioners further say that on the 19th day of October, 1920, the Richard L. Kitchens Post of the American Legion of Helena, Arkansas, an organization composed of approximately three hundred white ex-service men living in every part of Phillips County, passed a resolution calling on the Governor of the State of Arkansas, for the execution by death of petitioners and the seven other Negroes condemned to death by said Circuit Court at the same time and under the same circumstances as petitioners, and protesting against the commutation of the death sentence of any of said Negroes, which said Resolution was presented to the then Governor of Arkansas; that at a meeting of the Rotary Club of Helena, Arkansas, attended by seventy-five members, representing as many leading industrial and commercial enterprises of said city, and of the Lion's Club of said city, attended by sixty-five members, representing as many of the same kind of enterprises of said city each adopted a resolution approving the action of the Richard L. Kitchens Post of the American Legion in the premises, which said resolutions were presented to the then Governor of the State of Arkansas; that said resolutions further and conclusively show the existence of the mob spirit prevalent among all the white people of Phillips County at the time petitioners and the other defendants were put through the form of trials and show that the only reason the mob stayed its hand, the only reason they were not lynched was that the leading citizens of the community made a solemn promise to the mob that they should be executed in the form of law. Petitioners further say that to further show the overwhelming existence of the mob spirit and mob domination of their and other trials of Negro defendants at the October term, 1919, of the Phillips Circuit Court, there were six defendants convicted of murder in the first degree, to wit: John Martin, Alf Banks, Will Wordlow, Albert Giles,

Joe Fox and Ed. Ware, whose cases were also appealed to the Supreme Court of Arkansas which were reversed on account of bad verdicts, due to the extreme haste in securing convictions and executions (Banks vs. State, 143 Ark. 154), and remanded for a new trial; that upon a retrial of said cases, defendants were again reversed (Ware vs. State, Vol. 4 Sup. Court Rep. No. 11, Page 674), and remanded for a new trial on December 6, 1920; that said cases were coming on for trial at the May term of the Phillips Circuit Court, which convened May 2nd, 1921, and it was represented to the Governor of the State of Arkansas by the white citizens and officials of Phillips County that unless a date of execution was set for petitioners there was grave danger of mob violence to the other six defendants whose cases would be called for trial at the May term of said Court and that in all probability they would be lynched; that in order to appease the mob spirit still prevalent in Phillips County and in a measure to secure the safety of the six Negroes whose cases were to be called for trial and were called on May 9th, 1921, the Governor issued a proclamation fixing a date of execution of Petitioners for June 10, 1921, which was stayed by Court Proceedings; that these facts conclusively show that mob spirit and mob domination are still universally present in Phillips County.

Petitioners further say that on the 8th day of June, 1921, they filed a petition in the Pulaski Chancery Court for a Writ of Habeas Corpus setting out the matters and things herein stated, and that on said date the Pulaski Chancery Court issued its Writ of Habeas Corpus, directed to the defendant, E. H. Dempsey, keeper of the Arkansas State Penitentiary, commanding him to have the bodies of the Petitioners in Court at 2 o'clock P.M. on the 10th day of June, 1921, and then and there state in writing the term and cause of their imprisonment; that on the 9th day of June, 1921, the Attorney General for the State of Arkansas filed with the Supreme Court of Arkansas a Petition for Writ of Prohibition against J. E. Martineau, Chancellor of the Pulaski Chancery Court, and your petitioners, and that on the 20th day of June, 1921, the Supreme Court of the State of Arkansas issued its Writ of Prohibition against the Judge of the Pulaski Chancery Court, prohibiting him from hearing the Petitions for Habeas Corpus pending in his court and quashed the Writ of Habeas

Corpus theretofore issued; that thereafter, to wit, on the 4th day of August, 1921, your petitioners made application to the Hon. Oliver Wendell Holmes, Associate Justice of the Supreme Court of the United States, for a Writ of Error to the Supreme Court of the State of Arkansas in the matter of said Writ of Prohibition, but same was denied.

Petitioners, therefore, say that by the proceedings aforesaid, they were deprived of their rights and are about to be deprived of their lives in violation of Section II, of the 14th Amendment of the Constitution of the United States and the laws of the United States enacted in pursuance thereto, in that they have been denied the equal protection of the law, and have been convicted, condemned and are about to be deprived of their lives without due process of law; that they are now in custody of the defendant, E. H. Dempsey, Keeper of the Arkansas State Penitentiary, to be electrocuted on the 23rd day of September, 1921; that they are now detained and held in custody by said Keeper and will be electrocuted on said date unless prevented from so doing by the issuance of a Writ of Habeas Corpus.

Petitioners therefore pray that a Writ of Habeas Corpus be issued to the end that they may be discharged from said unlawful imprisonment and unlawful judgment and sentence to death.

—

The writ of Habeas Corpus asked for above was granted. Later a demurrer was sustained and the writ discharged. Thereupon the attorneys appealed to the Supreme Court of the United States and their appeal was allowed in the United States District Court. Thus, the greatest case against peonage and mob-law ever fought in the land and involving 12 human lives, comes before the highest court.

Reader, we have already spent $11,299 *to save these poor victims; we need* $5,000 *more. Can you help?*

A PLEA FOR POLITICAL AND ECONOMIC EQUALITY

WARREN G. HARDING

Address in Birmingham, Alabama

October 26, 1921

MR. MAYOR, CITIZENS OF BIRMINGHAM, AND PEOPLE OF THE SOUTH:

I have been wondering, as we have seen the Birmingham district and the marvels of this region's industrial development, whether any of us have yet quite realized the significance of the fact that Birmingham has been called "The Magic City." The basic, characteristic industry on which modern civilization rests is iron and steel; and Birmingham is the world's last word in development of the iron and steel industries.

We have come here to pay tribute to the marvelous achievement of a brief half century to which this city and its industries stand as a monument. They testify to us how far the South has progressed in a single generation: the generation since slavery was abolished and the rule of free labor and unfettered industrial opportunity became the rule of all of our great Republic.

Somewhere my attention has been called to the legend, possibly a historical fact, that when Fernando De Soto was leading his expedition of exploration and conquest from Florida to the Mississippi, some of his metal workers not only discovered the wonderful deposits of coal, limestone, and iron ore in this area and told De Soto that here was an even greater treasure house than that which he was seeking; not an El Dorado of precious metals, but the opportunity for making the world's dominating iron industry. I have been told, I do not know whether it is literally true, that the first reduction of iron in this district was actually accomplished by members of the De Soto party who supplied certain of the expedition's needs by smelting some of these wonderful ores. But De Soto was led on by the mirage which filled his vision, and instead of the pot of gold he sought, he found the mighty Mississippi, and in it his grave.

So far as concerns more modern development, it appears that General Andrew Jackson also utilized your mineral and metal riches. When he was on his march to New Orleans for the great battle in which the yeomanry of the South won the single notable land victory of the War of 1812, his metallurgists discovered that from these easily smelted ores they could supply their requirements of iron, of which they stood in great need. Accordingly, they erected rude furnaces and reduced considerable quantities of iron. From that time on there appears to have been more or less sporadic and intermittent utilization of these deposits, and during the Civil War they provided a considerable part of the needs of the South.

In this connection I have many times wished that there might be a wider appreciation of the energy, resourcefulness, and genius for industrial development which the people of the South demonstrated during that war. Essentially an aristocratic agricultural region, the South suddenly confronted the need to turn out iron and steel, and a vast complexity of their products which were absolutely essential to the conduct of the war. Not only did they arise to the occasion, but they gave what I have regarded as one of the greatest demonstrations in all history of the possibilities of adaptation, organization, and industrial development under stress of great necessity. We will do well to recognize that the industrial achievement of the South during the Civil War was one of the marvels resulting from that unhappy conflict. It marked the beginning of that diversification of industry which has made the South of to-day an industrial as well as an agricultural empire. I have often wished that some inspired son of the South might one day devote the time and effort necessary to record the history of that Aladdin-like industrial wonder which was a large part of the story of the South in the civil contest. It is one of the phases of American history that has had too little understanding attention. When we have studied the Civil War we have been so engrossed with military and political aspects that we have slighted the industrial and economic phases. I am going to venture, therefore, the suggestion that a comprehensive study of that aspect of the war period would be of inestimable value to the South and to the great story of our national progress. Not only would it constitute an eloquent testimony to the genius and devotion of our southern people, but it would present a picture of opening opportunity and widening horizon whose contemplation would challenge every remaining vestige of prejudice and sectional antagonism.

It has been a truism that the War between the States started the Nation as a whole in its way of colossal industrial growth. But I have wished that the particular story of that war-time experience in the South might be better known. I have been told of the almost overnight development of munition factories out of smithies: of the expansion of railroad repair shops into locomotive works: how shipyards, ordnance plants, powder factories were conjured up and put at work almost in the twinkling of an eye: of improvised industrial processes and mechanical contrivances, not a few of which have been of permanent value, some of them fairly revolutionary. We will, I am sure, be forgiven if, as Americans, we remind ourselves that wooden navies had fought each other for thousands of years until Americans fell to fighting among themselves. Then came iron fighting craft—came so quickly and unanimously that both sides had their first armored warships ready at the same moment, so well matched that they fought to a draw. It was a revolution; yet it was only one incident in this matching of American genius and resourcefulness in titanic struggle.

The railway and the telegraph were first bidden to the service of war on a great scale during our civil contest. The huge ordnance which both North and South created and used was as sensational in that day as the most startling constructions of the World War were more than a generation later. In both South and North our people learned and demonstrated what it means to mobilize all the human, industrial, financial, scientific resources of a great community for the purposes of war. That, indeed, was the most characteristic and most revolutionary development of the struggle. When we had done with our war we had well-nigh made over the whole art of war. The old things were gone forever. By land or by sea both its material and its methods were sweepingly changed. Glory and glamour had been taken out of it and in their place had been put the grim, hard reality of whole peoples measuring against each other their last ounce of power and resources.

In that contest of industry and resources the South started with a fearful handicap; a handicap so great that its accomplishments constituted one of the industrial wonders of all time. It is to this wonder that I have wanted to call attention to-day, for I have felt that it has never been appraised as it ought to be. From that contest the South emerged, not only with the foundation of industrial greatness securely laid but freed from the incubus of a labor system that had from colonial times chained it to the status of an almost purely agricultural community.

The industrial and commercial development of States and peoples has always been strikingly influenced by their wars; perhaps even more than their social and political development. That older war founded industry in the South under stress of sternest necessity; and so we may recognize in your Birmingham district and its industrial splendor one of the fine products of the industrial revolution which was forced upon the whole South.

We are gathered to-day to celebrate the semicentenary of the founding of Birmingham. That this wonder could be wrought in so brief a time tells us how fast our modern world moves; so fast that we are wont to forget our yesterdays before our to-days are fairly begun; so absorbing in its concerns of the present that too often we have neither time nor interest for the morrow. Yet there never was a time when we needed so much to study our past and, in the light of its lessons, give earnest thought to the to-morrows. So I have thought that here in your Magic City, whose story seems a very compress of yesterday, to-day, and to-morrow, it may be proper to suggest a few thoughts regarding the critical times which are faced by our country and all countries and some of the issues which command our consideration.

Exhausted and affrighted by the horrors of the World War, the nations are seeking means to prevent repetition of such an experience. They see the need for effective reform in international relationships and, along with this, for many alterations and adaptations of domestic institutions which will better fit them for the new time. Our own country, though its necessities are less onerous, its difficulties not so grievous as those of many others, has yet occasion to consider wherein it may better its methods, adjust itself to the new relationships, and equip itself for the new sort of struggle that lies ahead. Concerning one phase of this national problem, I want to say a few words.

If the Civil War marked the beginnings of industrialism in a South which had previously been almost entirely agricultural, the World War brought us to full recognition that the race problem is national rather than merely sectional. There are no authentic statistics, but it is common knowledge that the World War was marked by a great migration of colored people to the North and West. They were attracted by the demand for labor and the higher wages offered. The slow movement had been in progress for decades before, but it was vastly accelerated because of the war, and has continued at only a slackened pace since. It has brought the question of race closer to North and West, and I believe it has served to modify somewhat the views of those sections on this question. It has made the South realize its industrial dependence on the labor of the black man and made the North realize the difficulties of the community in which two greatly differing races are brought to live side by side. I should say that it has been responsible for a larger charity on both sides, a beginning of better understanding; and in the light of that better understanding perhaps we shall be able to consider this problem together as a problem of all sections and of both races, in whose solution the best intelligence of both must be enlisted.

Indeed, we will be wise to recognize it as wider yet. Whoever will take the time to read and ponder Mr. Lothrop Stoddard's book on The Rising Tide of Color, or, say, the thoughtful review of some recent literature of this question which Mr. F. D. Lugard presented in a recent Edinburg Review, must realize that our race problem here in the United States is only a phase of a race issue that the whole world confronts. Surely we shall gain nothing by blinking the facts, by refusing to give thought to them. That is not the American way of approaching such issues.

In another way the World War modified the elements of this problem. Thousands of black men, serving their country just as patriotically as did the white men, were transported overseas and experienced the life of countries where their color aroused less of antagonism than it does here. Many of them aspire to go to Europe to live.

A high-grade colored soldier told me that the war brought his race the first real conception of citizenship—the first full realization that the flag was their flag, to fight for, to be protected by them, and also to protect them. He was sure that the opportunity to learn what patriotism meant was a real opportunity to his race.

These things lead one to hope that we shall find an adjustment of relations between the two races, in which both can enjoy full citizenship, the full measure of usefulness to the country and of opportunity for themselves, and in which recognition and reward shall at last be distributed in proportion to individual deserts, regardless of race or color. Mr. Lugard, in his recent essay, after surveying the world's problem of races, concludes thus:

"Here then is the true conception of the interrelation of color—complete uniformity in ideals, absolute equality in the paths of knowledge and culture, equal opportunity for those who strive, equal admiration for those who achieve; in matters social and racial a separate path, each pursuing his own inherited traditions, preserving his own race purity and race pride; equality in things spiritual; agreed divergence in the physical and material."

Here, it has seemed to me, is suggestion of the true way out. Politically and economically there need be no occasion for great and permanent differentiation, for limitations of the individual's opportunity, provided that on both sides there shall be recognition of the absolute divergence in things social and racial. When I suggest the possibility of economic equality between the races, I mean it in precisely the same way and to the same extent that I would mean it if I spoke of equality of economic opportunity as between members of the same race. In each case I would mean equality proportioned to the honest capacities and deserts of the individual.

Men of both races may well stand uncompromisingly against every suggestion of social equality. Indeed, it would be helpful to have that word "equality" eliminated from this consideration; to have it accepted on both sides that this is not a question of social equality, but a question of recognizing a fundamental, eternal, and inescapable difference. We shall have made real progress when we develop an attitude in the public and community thought of both races which recognizes this difference.

Colonizing countries everywhere have in recent times been more and more dealing with the problem from this point of view. The British commonwealth of nations and races confronts it, and has been seeking its solution along the lines here suggested. There is possibility of our learning something applicable to our own country from the British. It is true that there is a great difference between bringing into our own land the colonists of another race and going out to another land and subjecting it and its people to the rule of an alien race. Yet the two cases have so many elements of similarity that it seems to me the experience of each must furnish some light upon the other.

Take first the political aspect. I would say let the black man vote when he is fit to vote: prohibit the white man voting when he is unfit to vote. Especially would I appeal to the self-respect of the colored race. I would inculcate in it the wish to improve itself as a distinct race, with a heredity, a set of traditions, an array of aspirations all its own. Out of such racial ambitions and pride will come natural segregations, without narrowing any rights, such as are proceeding in both rural and urban communities now in Southern States, satisfying natural inclinations and adding notably to happiness and contentment.

On the other hand I would insist upon equal educational opportunity for both. This does not mean that both would become equally educated within a generation or two generations or ten generations. Even men of the same race do not accomplish such an equality as that. They never will. The Providence that endowed men with widely unequal capacities and capabilities and energies did not intend any such thing.

But there must be such education among the colored people as will enable them to develop their own leaders, capable of understanding and sympathizing with such a differentiation between the races as I have suggested—leaders who will inspire the race with proper ideals of race pride, of national pride, of an honorable destiny, an important participation in the universal effort for advancement of humanity as a whole. Racial amalgamation there can not be. Partnership of the races in developing the highest aims of all humanity there must be if humanity, not only here but everywhere, is to achieve the ends which we have set for it.

I can say to you people of the South, both white and black, that the time has passed when you are entitled to assume that this problem of races is peculiarly and particularly your problem. More and more it is becoming a problem of the North: more and more it is the problem of Africa, of South America, of the Pacific, of the South Seas, of the world. It is the problem of democracy everywhere, if we mean the things we say about democracy as the ideal political state.

Coming as Americans do from many origins of race, tradition, language, color, institutions, heredity; engaged as we are in the huge effort to work an honorable national destiny from so many different elements; the one thing we must sedulously avoid is the development of group and class organizations in this country. There has been time when we heard too much about the labor vote, the business vote, the Irish vote, the Scandinavian vote, the Italian vote, and so on. But the demagogues who would array class against class and group against group have fortunately found little to reward their efforts. That is because, despite the demagogues, the idea of our oneness as Americans has risen superior to every appeal to mere class and group. And so I would wish it might be in this matter of our national problem of races. I would accept that a black man can not be a white man, and that he does not need and should not aspire to be as much like a white man as possible in order to accomplish the best that is possible for him. He should seek to be, and he should be encouraged to be, the best possible black man, and not the best possible imitation of a white man.

It is a matter of the keenest national concern that the South shall not be encouraged to make its colored population a vast reservoir of ignorance, to be drained away by the processes of migration into all other sections. That is what has been going on in recent years at a rate so accentuated that it has caused this question of races to be, as I have already said, no longer one of a particular section. Just as I do not wish the South to be politically entirely of one party; just as I believe that is bad for the South, and for the rest of the country as well, so I do not want the colored people to be entirely of one party. I wish that both the tradition of a solidly Democratic South and the tradition of a solidly Republican black race might be broken up. Neither political sectionalism nor any system of rigid groupings of the people will in the long run prosper our country. I want to see the time come when black men will regard themselves as full participants in the benefits and duties of American citizenship; when they will vote for Democratic candidates, if they prefer the Democratic policy on tariff or taxation, or foreign relations, or what-not; and when they will vote the Republican ticket only for like reasons. We can not go on, as we have gone for more than a half century, with one great section of our population, numbering as many people as the entire population of some significant countries of Europe, set off from real contribution to solving our national issues, because of a division on race lines.

With such convictions one must urge the people of the South to take advantage of their superior understanding of this problem and to assume an attitude toward it that will deserve the confidence of the colored people. Likewise, I plead with my own political party to lay aside every program that looks to lining up the black man as a mere political adjunct. Let there be an end of prejudice and of demagogy in this line. Let the South understand the menace which lies in forcing upon the black race an attitude of political solidarity. The greater hope, the dissipation of hatred, the discouragement of dangerous passions lie in persuading the black people to forget old prejudices and to have them believe that, under the rule of whatever political party, they would be treated just as other people are treated, guaranteed all the rights that people of other colors enjoy, and made, in short, to regard themselves as citizens of a country and not of a particular race.

Every consideration, it seems to me, brings us back at last to the question of education. When I speak of education as a part of this race question, I do not want the States or the Nation to attempt to educate people, whether white or black, into something they are not fitted to be. I have no sympathy with the half-baked altruism that would overstock us with doctors and lawyers, of whatever color, and leave us in need of people fit and willing to do the manual work of a workaday world. But I would like to see an education that would fit every man not only to do his particular work as well as possible but to rise to a higher plane if he would deserve it. For that sort of education I have no fears, whether it be given to a black man or a white man. From that sort of education, I believe, black men, white men, the whole Nation, would draw immeasurable benefit.

It is probable that as a nation we have come to the end of the period of very rapid increase in our population. Recent legislation to restrict immigration will be in part responsible for a slacking ratio of increase. The new immigrants have multiplied in numbers much the more rapidly, but as the immigrants become Americanized, amalgamated into the citizenry, the tendency has been toward less rapid multiplication. So restricted immigration will reduce the rate of increase, and force us back upon our older population to find people to do the simpler, physically harder, manual tasks. This will require some difficult readjustments. It has been easy, indeed, but it has not been good for the people of our older stock, that a constant inflow in immigration made it possible to crowd off these less attractive and profitable tasks upon the newcomers. I don't think it has been good for what the old Latins called the national *virtue*. That is a word I have always liked, employed in the Roman sense. I wish we might have adopted it into our vocabulary, in this sense. It strikes me as a good deal better than *morale*. Anyhow, we are under necessity to raise honest, hard, manual work to a new dignity if we are to get it done. We will have to make its compensations more generous, materially, and, if I may say it, spiritually; to make usefulness of service, rather than spotlessness of hands, the test of whatever social recognition depends on the individual's occupation. I confess a large disgust with all such classifications, and I earnestly bespeak an attitude toward good, honorable, hard work that will end them. I do not want to coddle and patronize labor; I want us all to get out, put on blue denims, roll up our sleeves, let our hands be honorably soiled, and do the work. That's what we've got to do, if we are to get on. We must do it, and be glad we can; for there is small chance that we will ever again have such armies of laborers landing on these shores, as have come in the past.

In anticipation of such a condition the South may well recognize that North and West are likely to continue their drafts upon its colored population, and that if the South wishes to keep its fields producing and its industry still expanding it will have to compete for the services of the colored man. If it will realize its need for him and deal quite fairly with him, the South will be able to keep him in such numbers as your activities make desirable. At any rate, here is a problem and it is pressing for settlement.

Is it not possible, then, that in the long era of readjustment upon which we are entering for the Nation to lay aside old prejudices and old antagonisms and in the broad, clear light of nationalism enter upon a constructive policy in dealing with these intricate issues? Just as we shall prove ourselves capable of doing this we shall insure the industrial progress, the agricultural security, the social and political safety of our whole country regardless of race or sections and along the line of ideals superior to every consideration of groups or class, of race or color or section or prejudice.

Here are the reflexes of magical industrial development, here are the fruits in the making of a nation and its commitment to free productivity and trade. There is a materialism which sometimes seems sordid, but on the material foundation we have expanded in soul, and we have seen this Republic the example to freedom aspiring throughout the world. We wish to cling to all that is good. We want to preserve the inheritance over which we fought because our conflict made it more precious. But we wish to go on as well as preserve.

The march of a great people is not a blind one. We can not be unmindful of human advancement. We wish to be more than apace with progress—we wish our America leading and choosing safe paths. Fifty years is a narrow span. Yet the marvel of Birmingham is less than the marvel of our astounding America. And we mean to go on. If we are just and honest in administering justice, if we are alive to perils and meet them in conscience and courage, the achievement of your first half century will be magnified tenfold in the second half, and the glory of your city and your country will be reflected in the happiness of a great people, greater than we dream, and grander for understanding and the courage to be right.

RAYMOND CLAPPER

Timely Talk on Race Issue

Riverside Daily Press (California), October 26, 1921

TIMELY TALK ON RACE ISSUE

President Protests Against Lining Up Negroes as Political Asset

SPEECH AT BIRMINGHAM

Negro Should Be Best Possible Black
Man and Not Imitation of White Man

BIRMINGHAM, Ala., Oct. 26.—The negro must be given a chance to make good, President Harding declared in a frank discussion of the race problems in the heart of the south today.

The black man, he said, must be given political and economic equality as a matter of justice and national welfare.

"Surely we shall gain nothing by blinking at the facts," President Harding said in bringing up the subject in his main speech at the Birmingham semi-centennial celebration.

"Political and economic equality," he explained, "does not mean social equality. On the other hand, he urged that both sides recognize the "absolute divergence on things social and racial."

Harding, in a rather startling fashion, protested against his own party's use of the black man as a mere political tool and urged the negroes to vote either the Democratic or Republican ticket on the merits of the two parties.

"I plead with my own political party to lay aside every program that looks to lining up the black men as a mere political adjunct," he said. The south should cease narrowing the negro's political rights, Harding added. The real menace, he warned, lies in forcing political solidarity on the negro. The negro, the president continued, should seek the best possible black man and not the possible imitation of a white man.

"Racial amalgamation cannot be," he declared.

"Men of both races may well stand uncompromisingly against every suggestion of social equality . . .

"I would say let the black man vote when he is fit to vote; prohibit the white man voting when he is unfit to vote. Especially would I appeal to the self-respect of the colored race. I would inculcate in it the wish to improve itself as a distinct race, with a heredity, a set of traditions, an array of aspirations all its own. Out of such racial ambitions and pride will come natural segregations, without narrowing any rights."

The negro should have equal educational advantages so he can develop his own leaders, President Harding said.

President Harding's plea for economic and political equality for the negro brought only dead silence from thousands of white listeners whose thundered cheers only a few minutes before rang in his ears.

The president's ire was frankly stirred up by this apparent coldness.

During one tense pause, he squared his jaw and pointed straight at the white section of the crowd.

"Whether you like it or not, unless our democracy is a lie, you must stand for that equality," he declared, referring to political equality.

The negro section cheered loudly, but there was only silence from the white portion.

President Harding reached the part of his prepared speech that touched on the race question, he turned to the negro section.

"I want to look at you directly as I say this," he told them, "because I am never going to say anything that I can't say to every section and to all the people:

"I am thinking of the north and the south, the white and the black in terms precisely alike."

JAMES WELDON JOHNSON

The Passage of the Dyer Bill

New York Age, February 4, 1922

THE DYER Anti-Lynching Bill passed the House of Representatives on Thursday, January 26, by a vote of 230 to 119, almost two to one. And so, more than half the battle to have a law on the Federal statute books making lynching a crime has been won.

The two last days of this fight in Congress were not without their spectacular features. As late as eleven o'clock on Tuesday morning, the 24th, the Republican leaders in the House were not wholly decided that they would make a final attempt to put the Bill over. A conference was held in the Speaker's office between that hour and the convening of the session at noon. It was then decided to begin the final push on Wednesday and to keep it up until the Bill was put through.

The colored people of Washington had heard that the Bill was to be taken up on Tuesday and there was quite a number of them in the galleries. They went away disappointed, but on the next day when the House convened at noon every available niche in the galleries was packed with colored spectators. The presence of so many colored people created a tenseness in the situation which otherwise would have been lacking. It produced a strong psychological effect even upon the members on the floor. When Mr. Mondell, Republican floor leader, rose to make the first speech of the day in support of the Bill, his voice was trembling with suppressed emotion. The pent-up feelings, both of the men on the floor and the people in the galleries, broke loose when a colloquy took place between Mr. Sissoms of Mississippi and Mr. Cooper of Wisconsin.

Mr. Sissoms in closing his speech declared that lynching would never stop until "the black rascals keep their hands off the throats of white women." Representative Cooper retorted that it was the first time he had heard lynch law justified on the floor of the House. The rest of Mr. Cooper's remarks were lost in the confusion, but Mr. Sissoms shouted, "I dare you to say that again in any other place." At Mr. Cooper's statement five hundred or more colored people in the galleries rose as one man and cheered. Southern Democrats sprang to their feet and shouted at the colored people in the galleries. Some voice from the floor yelled out, "Sit down, niggers!" and some voice from the galleries cried out, "We are not niggers; you are a liar." For several minutes the entire chamber was in an uproar despite the efforts of Chairman Campbell of Kansas to restore order. Notwithstanding this, the presence of the colored people in the galleries had a decidedly good effect upon all of the deliberations.

When the Bill was taken up on Thursday there were not quite so many colored people present; yet, there was a large number, three hundred or more. The Republican leaders pressed the passage of the Bill as fast and as hard as it was possible to do so. By parliamentary strategy, they cut off the delaying tactics of the Democrats. The Bill, therefore, reached a vote much earlier than anyone had expected. The roll call on the final vote began at 3:02 in the afternoon and at 3:30 the Speaker declared the Bill passed.

During the last hours of the debate Southern members exceeded in violence and truculency all that they had said and done during the previous sessions. For example, Blanton of Texas virtually said, "You can pass this law if you want to, but whenever we think it necessary we will lynch Negroes just the same."

The Anti-Lynching Bill passed the House with fewer amendments than even its most sanguine supporters expected. Those amendments which were added do not in any way weaken the effectiveness of the Bill. The thing that was most feared by friends of the Bill was that emasculating amendments would be hitched on to it. At only one time during the debate under the five-minute rule was the real strength of the Bill in danger. A Republican member offered an amendment striking out the $10,000 penalty on those counties where a mob originated and where a lynching took place. The amendment would have been carried had it not been for the tactics adopted by the Democrats. The Democrats, in order to retain as many as possible of the features which they considered obnoxious in the

Bill, voted to defeat the amendment. Therefore, the clauses providing the penalty of $10,000 were retained in the Bill. It was in this way that the real teeth were kept in the Bill.

It is true that a great deal will be gained by having men indicted for lynching tried in the Federal courts rather than in the state courts. When an attempt is made to try lynchers in the state courts, it is always made in the county in which the lynching is perpetrated, and everybody connected with the trial, from the judge down, is a neighbor, or a friend, or a relative of the accused. For these reasons it has been a matter of impossibility to secure convictions.

Under the jurisdiction of Federal courts such trials will be removed from the immediate vicinity, and men charged with the commission of lynching in one part of the state will be tried before strangers in another part of the state.

But after all, the main strength of the Bill is in the clauses providing for a penalty of $10,000 upon the county in which a mob seizes its victim and upon the county in which the victim is lynched. Trial or no trial, jury or no jury, communities will soon find a way to stop lynchings when they become expensive.

Under present conditions lynching in most Southern communities is an entertainment; it is a circus, the only difference being that no admission fee is charged. But when a lynching means an increase in taxes on the whole community, the whole community is going to make it its business to see that lynching is stopped.

The Dyer Anti-Lynching Bill now goes to the Senate. The fight to make it a law is a little more than half won; but it is going to take hard work to put it through the upper house. Colored people and law loving citizens everywhere should unite in an effort to see that it is done.

COLONEL MAYFIELD'S WEEKLY
Negro Porter Whipped by Masked Citizens of Abilene

February 18, 1922

NEGRO PORTER WHIPPED BY MASKED CITIZENS OF ABILENE

Day of Date-Making Porters Has Passed in Texas; White Citizens Are Determined to Break Up Practice.

As predicted in this paper last week, negro hotel porters making dates for white women, would be roughly dealt with. A dispatch from Abilene states that Littleton Oaks, negro porter at a local hotel, was seized by a group of masked men, carried into the country and whipped almost to death. The negro had been making dates for a white woman who was a guest at the hotel, similar to the actions of negro porters in Houston, Fort Worth and Dallas, and many other places.

The Klan is everywhere; it sees everything; hears everything, and negro porters engaged in the pursuit above mentioned are going to have a hard year.

Last week I mentioned that the practice was going on in Houston. The hotels are known and the negroes are known.

Let me say right here, the Rice Hotel has no such practice going on there. The Rice Hotel is managed by Barney Morton. It imploys no negro porters, and is watched like a hawk by a staff of plain clothes men. Barney won't stand a minute for the least semblance of shady work going on in that hotel. It is a great big family hotel, conducted on clean, high-toned and correct principles. It is a great credit to the South, both in its size, its magnificence and manner of operation.

W. P. EVANS

To the Editor of the Observer

The Charlotte Observer, May 20 and June 3, 1923

THE NEGRO MOVEMENT.

THE WHITE MAN'S RELATION TO IT DISCUSSED BY A NEGRO LEADER.

To the Editor of the Observer:

I want to say first that this condition is deplored by the thrifty industrious leading colored men of the south just as intensely and seriously as by the most patriotic southern white citizen, and to supply a remedy is as much the concern of the bonafide colored citizen as it is the white citizens. To find the remedy we must hunt with in the premises of cause and effect. Naturally the negro deep down in his undesigning heart, loves sincerely this sunny south. The recollection of its low grounds indented with hospitable cabins, bearing the latch strings on the outside of their doors and the old camp meeting grounds are still dear to his soul. Primarily, his devotion to the south and the good "White Folk" was as heart felt and as true as "Ruth to Naomi." If his devotion, and loyalty is now divorced, it must have come about by his Naomi's chilly attitude towards him in denying him a man's chance, in the upward and onward movement of higher civilization and financial progress. I understand in communities away down south where migration is the greatest and thousands of fertile acres and as many negro shanties are abandoned that in those communities my people are now held like slaves and peonage a predominant spirit of some of the white land lords; and might, alone is right. If this be true then we must commend those negroes for their long endurance and patience and ask God for his forgiveness of the sins of their land lords.

Is this all of their grievance? Upon investigation we find down there on plantation after plantation, the negro tenant farmer, works himself, his wife and all the family from January to Christmas upon the promise that he is to receive for his services a third of the crop made, but when the crop is made and the thousands of bales of cotton gathered and sold; around Christmas eve the poor laborer stands outside the commissary awaiting for his portion of the crop made, with which to buy his wife a new dress and his children shoes and clothes; his boss man says to him: "Well Sandy you did little better this year, you're paid all of your back debt and don't owe but $119. on this year's debt." The negro is not shown by an itemized statement what this year's debt is for; he knows all he was allowed to take up was some coarse rations to the amount of $10 or $12 per month. He did get one humspun work dress for his wife and a pair of work shoes and overalls for himself. He also knows that on his two horse farm he made and gathered 40 bales of cotton, 1,200 bushels of cotton seed and 150 bushels of corn. He doesn't know, but he heard cotton was selling for $75 a bale and cotton seed 60 cents a bushel, out of which he was to get one third. However, the poor negro tenant returns to his shanty, crest-fallen and discouraged to greet the anxious hearts of his naked and barefoot children around Christmas time, with disappointment and nothing to warm the winter of his family's discontent, except smooky lightwood knots on the hearth stone of a dillapidated home. Ask yourself the question: could you still follow Naomi? It's learned that these conditions surround largely the lives of negroes who were born before the war and possibly immediately after the war; hence this unparalled patience and endurance. The new negro, born in the new south, and under new conditions possibly, is the cause of the revolt. Schooled in the white man's language, mathematics reasoning and equations; he is not content in his settlements by saving, this leaves you owing $119 on this year's debt. They must show him by itemized statement what makes this year's debt: in too many, many cases the land lord being unused to this new demand, deems it impudence on the part of the new negro; resistance sets up and the negro, conscious of his weak standing falls back on the power of "Least Resistance" and the next year that farm is vacant and the negro is in the iron works of Pennsylvania. New conditions require the wisdom to accept the fundamental fact, that all employes are partners to an appreciable extent in the business as operated and that the success of the same must come through frank open hearted co-operation and that the humblest members of the business must be made to feel that it's "Our" business so much so that in speaking of the business there will be such cordiality in it that the term "We" instead of "I" will be the slogan.

It is said that Henry Ford, the greatest manager of men and the financial wonder of the world, recognizes with all his soul that his humblest employee (the floor sweeper) is his partner, to an appreciable extent, and that he too must share and does share in the wonderful dividends of the great business to which he is an accessory. I believe that if our southern white people will encouch this spirit in all their business relationship, with the negroes in all industrial activities, the exodus would at once cease and all prohibition laws and restricted immigration would automatically be done away with.

I know my people; I meet them in our churches, lodge rooms and homes; therefore I can say no man has a greater love for this south land than does the negro. But it must be remembered that the father of the home can by his indifference and misrule, many times drive members of his loving family away into distant and frigid communities and they are forced to fly to ills they know not of.

Some sections speak of importing, Porto Ricians and West Indians, but let me say they will never contentedly accept the stars and stripes for the English jack. But better than that, let me advise negro and white man, in the language of the late Booker T. Washington, "Cast down your buckets where you are."

Let the negro cultivate thoughtfulness, respectfulness, town pride, economy and commercialize his activities. Let the white man cast down his bucket and draw it up brim full of the golden rule, "do unto the negro as you would have him do unto you." The negro is blind yet to the many ways of preparation necessary to rounded citizenship, but he is credulous and believe as a race that what a white man says or does is right. Therefore take him as it were by the hand and show him how. The majority of domestic help has an abiding faith in the white ladies of the homes; therefore let me ask the white ladies to do more missionary work among their help, teaching economy and how many times to take an old dress and make a new one out of it. We are all craving for the know how, maybe it would help the cause by using more money for home missions than for foreign missions. Let the relationship to negro women, be such as not to cause such confusion in distinguishing some negro people from other nationalities. It's tacitly admitted that the negro is an asset of the south. We are inclined to believe this is true, circumstances warrants the belief. The white man's brain and negro's brain have tunnelled every mountain in North Carolina, razed the hill tops and drove the spikes into every rail that the foundation for the great rail-roads to carry civilization into the remotest parts of our great state. Did his toil end with this? No, every new ground has been grubbed by his aid and vegetation watered by the sweat of his brow. Truly then he is an asset.

If the white man's bank account is an asset and when he gets his monthly statement, finds an error to his loss, he immediately inquires into it, that he may duly come into his own. The negro is the white south's asset and now that 350,000 of its assets are short, why not look over the statement, find the error or trouble, get expert accountants together and if it will accept, I warrant you that the leading negroes of the south will voluntarily join the board of accountants and bring about a correction of the errors that are causing our south this vital loss.

W. P. EVANS

Laurinburg, May 18.

THE NEGRO SITUATION.

LAURINBURG LEADER OF THE RACE THINKS NORTH CAROLINA, ALREADY NEGRO'S MOST LIBERAL FRIEND, MUST LEAD IN KEEPING HIM HERE.

To the Editor of The Observer:

I had the privilege to contribute an article several Sundays ago to your great paper setting forth some of the reasons for the exodus of so many of my people from away down south. The truths have reverberated throughout North Carolina and negro leaders stand ready to co-operate in "locking the stables before all the horses go to other pastures." It is utterly useless for the south to sit down and bewail the hard fate that is threatening to strip its fields of laborers. Wailing will do no one any good. Work alone is capable of changing the conditions that have brought about the movement; and it must be head work; team work, conciliatory efforts that have been too rare among the white south. In the race for negro labor the south has the advantage of the north. The negro is at home here; his first love for country was conceived here; his social and religious charms surround him; his older friends are here; he is amidst the origination of folk lore music and nowhere can those soul stirring spirituals be sung with more fervor and embellishment than in the open air camp meetings and August revival meetings of his sunny hospitable southland. Aye, more than this, is to the advantage of the south in the race for negro labor, all the leading negro college professors and teachers throughout the south are agitating that the white south make new contracts and conditions to encourage the negro to stay home. I submit that every commencement address in every negro school in the south was froth with advice to stay in the south and that in no other section of the country are the opportunities for commercial and financial success greater than in this part of our common country. And most of all some day the negro will come into possession of more of the lands that he has helped to clear up and make tenable. He is already in control and ownership of one million acres.

The south has still another great advantage in the contest, she has the influence of thousands of bona fide negro leaders in church, state, profession and business and real estate who are determined to stay in the south, and because of their interest here, have sacrificed their citizenship right to vote that they may remain peacefully and harmoniously in the land of their nativity and the birthplace of their fathers. What other educated leaders anywhere in the world would accept such capitulations? The foregoing enumerates the olive branches that the negro leaders have sent and are sending out during this flood of migration. The ark of our life insurance companies, our real estate, churches and professions will be more or less affected; therefore we see the wisdom of armistice; giving the white south chance to create new living conditions in every phase of human life for the black man. Some of the south's editors and citizens are treating the migration lightly and with apparent unconcern, stating that the negro will come back; but let me tell you, don't fool yourselves, for possibly this class of advisers is like the majority of the migrants. It is the landless negro who is going away and the man who is not tied to the land by a deed. The real south is not treating the situation lightly, but is like a certain white landlord in South Carolina who has a 13-horse plantation plowed and planted and in January had plenty of labor, is now with 13 head of mules and only two plow hands on his plantation; he is not treating the condition lightly. The old saying, that the negro will come back has been exploded, because thousands and thousands who left during the war have never come back, but instead are writing letters back to the friends they left behind, urging them to come on. God gave the lion strength for his defense; the rabbit flight for his defense; what can the poor negro do but run; telling the negro that he will die from cold in the north and that the north does not understand him; if all this be true, as long as the south does not improve conditions for the negro, telling the negro of the danger before him in the north will not keep him in the south. No: when the rabbit is in flight for his life, no use telling him what is before, when the rabbit gets to running, he is more afraid of what is behind him than he is of what is before him. To save the rabbit here in the south you must hasten to remove the scare crows. This migration is like a snowball, the farther it rolls the bigger it gets. The world's eyes are upon it. In 1920 the total amount of cotton made was 19,500,000 bales. 13,250,000 bales were made by negroes. The revenue derived from the negro's portion of the crop was very great. The increasing migration of the negro and his abandonment of so many plantations portends a serious money loss to the south and not only to the south but the textile industry of America and Great Britain. It is said Great Britain has long wanted to end her dependence on America for cotton. She has recently found that Australia can grow as fine cotton as Georgia, but it's too hot for the white people over there to work in cotton fields; who would dare say that England won't some day induce the southern negro to make cotton for her over there; guaranteeing better living conditions to the black man, she might induce him.

France imported the southern negro to save the world's war. Why wouldn't England import him to save Europe's textile industries? It's thought by some that if ever foreign immigration starts up again then the negro will be turned back south; not so, but instead, he will become the northern man's problem. Investigation, however, reveals that the northern employer is agreeably surprised with negro labor and is taking steps to hold him permanently. He feels that he is more or less immune to strikes, anarchistic and bolshevik tendencies to which the south, because of the character of its labor has hitherto been immune. No one successfully charges the Yankee with overlooking a good business proposition.

Geographically North Carolina is the most northern of all the cotton growing states: her attitude towards the negro has been more liberal, so much so that negroes from away down south, when they reach here seem to feel an air of security. Her own colored citizens have an abiding faith in the ultimate betterment of their conditions. I believe therefore, right now is the psychological moment for the white people to act so as to prevent any restlessness that might be growing on the part of any of its colored citizens. And since she is the first state of the south to lead in good roads and superior educational advantages for the negro, she might right now lead in showing the south how to keep its labor here. Start a campaign of, every member canvass. (I suggest this because I understand that in some parts of the south the cooks and tenants leave without the slightest indication of their intention so to do.) Inquire if your help has any grievance, discuss the matters freely, assuring that you are willing to adjust them profitably and satisfactorily. If the tenant's family has outgrown his two room shanty, add more room; if he is planning to slip off, because he isn't getting his one-third of the cotton seeds; give him his third, or its equivalent; make a new contract with him, because this will be far cheaper than an abandoned plantation. Market the cotton so that he can see his boy whom he has been schooling figure out what his part comes to. If he has been tempted to steal a chicken or watermelon, because of hunger, see that the courts don't give him a longer road sentence than it does the cashier, who robbed the bank and made widows and orphan children penniless. If poolrooms and immoral women are menacing his thrift and morality drive them out of the com- him and his family better coach accommodation or reduce his cost of transportation and by all means make sanitary their waitingrooms. See that the railroad policemen keep negro loafers, who hold no transportation from imposing themselves on our wives and daughters in all railroad waitingrooms.

Let all town and cities extend sewerage, water, and lights in all negro communities. Sell him land on terms so he can pay for it. Place financial responsibilities upon him. No citizen can come up without bearing burdens of responsibilities; he must have some load upon him so that he will walk steady and straight, otherwise he will be light and chaffy and any wind will beat him about. Seed we sow in our gardens must have the weight of the soil upon it before it can or will come up.

The chamber of commerce of Jackson, Mississippi, has called a conference of its white and colored citizens with the hope of mutual benefit. Last, but not least the negroes know that our southland hasn't the wealth of the north and therefore cannot measure arms in the high prices offered for labor; along that line he is in perfect sympathy with the south and is satisfied with far less per diem, provided the south will show a spirit of fairness along all other human lines. The masses are not clamoring for the ballot, and they are not going north to vote, because some democratic leaders said "If they ever wanted to vote they would have to go there." But deep down in the hearts of the educated negro land owner, he is praying that the legislature of North Carolina will enact a property and educational qualification, so that he can exercise his franchise as a citizen, not under the leadership any more of the carpetbagger, but under the leadership of the best white citizens of North Carolina and the south as well and he no longer will be the ridicule of northern and West Indies negroes, in saying "you can't vote."

W. P. EVANS

Laurinburg, May 20.

GEORGE BROOKS

Far Away Blues

Recorded 1923

We left our southern home and wandered north to roam
Like birds, went seekin' a brand new field of corn
We don't know why we are here
But we're up here just the same
And we are just the lonesomest girls that's ever born

Some of these days we are going far away
Some of these days we are going far away
Where we have got a lots of friends and don't have no
roof rent to pay

Oh, there'll come a day when from us you'll hear no news
Oh, there'll come a day when from us you'll hear no news
Then you will know that we have died from those
lonesome far away blues.

WALTER WHITE

Report on the Lynching of Sammie Smith

December 1924

FROM Sammie's relatives and many others I got the story. A bit of information here. A bit there. Put together here it is. Until last May, Sammie worked for a white man named Preston Lee at Smyrna Tenn., eight or ten miles from Nashville. One day in that month Lee beat Sammie Smith. Sammie quit and went to Nashville where he got a job with the Atlantic Ice Company. All summer he worked there turning over his wages to his mother to help provide for the mother and nine children. Cold weather came and the need of ice dropped off so Sammie was discharged. He then went to live alternately with his uncle, Eugene Smith, and grandmother at Arrington.

On Friday, December 12th, Sammie and his uncle went to Nashville in the latter's Ford. Late that night they started back to Arrington. As they hurried along near Nolansville about one o'clock in the morning the car went into a ditch, turning over. The man and boy righted it but found one of the parts broken. Leaving Sammie in the car, Eugene went to a garage nearby to get a new part for his car. When Eugene did not return Sammie went to search for him. He met Eugene coming towards the car and behind him walked a white man holding a gun on Eugene. The garage belonged to the owner of the gun and he had caught Eugene in the act of stealing what he needed.

"This boy with you?" the white man asked Eugene.

"Yes sir," was the answer.

"Then come along with me—I'm going to put you in jail, too!" the white man declared to Sammie.

Sammie whipped out a gun and fired. The white man returned the fire, shooting Sammie through the stomach. Sammie dropped his gun and fled while the white man held his gun on Eugene until others roused by the shots came and took him to jail. All the rest of the night they sought Sammie. Early the next morning they found him in a field nearby, lying unconscious from the loss of blood and the raw, stinging cold. Sheriff Bob Briley carried him to the county jail but soon removed him to the Nashville General Hospital on Nance Street. There it was seen at once that Sammie's wound was a fatal one —but they took no chances with this desperate fifteen-year-old, 110 pound criminal—they chained him to the iron bed.

Through Saturday, Sunday and Monday he lingered on while life slowly slipped away from him. On Sunday afternoon around two o'clock two white boys from Smyrna called at the hospital to see if Sammie was yet alive. Monday afternoon two others from the same neighborhood called and told the dying lad, according to one of the last statements he made, "It won't do you no good to get well for if you do, we're going to put you in the electric chair." They more than hinted he wouldn't live twenty-four hours longer. Of them more will be said later.

Just after midnight Monday Larry Hardeman, custodian of the hospital was sitting in his office, according to his story. Hearing a noise he turned and looked into the barrels of several shotguns. Leaving him covered by two of the masked men, ten or twelve others cut the telephone wires and hurried towards the Negro ward on the west end of the first floor. One of the masked figures clad in khaki was left to guard the hallway with orders to let no one pass. In the Negro ward there was a lone nurse, Miss Amy Weagle, all the other attendants being, according to later statements issued, "at the time eating their supper." The mob demanded of Miss Weagle that she point out the bed in which Sammie Smith lay. She refused. The mob began a systematic search of the ward examining each bed to see in which the occupant was chained. Miss Weagle stood in front of Sammie's bed trying to hide the tell-tale chain. Helpless, his eyes wide in terror, his life so far gone already he could not possibly live until morning Sammie Smith, fifteen-year-old desperado watched the half-score of his executioners approach. A shout of exultation greeted the discovery of the chain. Miss Weagle was thrust aside. The chain was rapidly sawed apart. "Get up!" demanded the leader. "I can't—I can't!" tremblingly, piteously pleaded the terrified, half-dead boy. . . . . . .

Forty-five minutes later the telephone rang in the office of the Nashville *Tennessean*. "It's all over, partner," the newspaper office was informed. The unknown voice went on to tell where Sammie Smith's body was to be found. "The members of the mob have disappeared to the four winds of the earth," he ended after describing the lynching in detail.

Out near Nolansville at the spot where he had been found unconscious on Saturday morning hung the naked body of Sammie Smith. Around his ankle the manacle was yet clamped. From it dangled the severed chain. A plow rope was about his neck, the other end tied firmly to the branch of an oak tree. Through his abdomen forty, perhaps fifty, loads of buckshot had plowed their way. My young undertaker friend must have been right—Sammie's abdomen must have looked "like a sifter. . . ."

Nashville awoke the next morning horrified. Apparently everything that can be done *after* a lynching was done. The Chamber of Commerce held an indignation meeting, denounced the mob, and offered a reward of $5000 for the arrest and conviction of the lynchers. One member, W. D. Trabue, moved that the amount be made $15,000. After some argument the amount was reduced to $10,000. Still later it dropped to $5000 . . . Governor Austin Peay offered on behalf of the state an additional $1500 and denounced the lynching as "a horrible thing" and added, "Nothing has happened since I have been governor so regrettable. . . ." Hilary E. Howse, mayor of Nashville declared the lynching was like a "horrible dream," and asserted that "the fair name of this city has been besmirched. . . ." Sheriff Bob Briley daily stated through the press that arrests were momentarily expected but on Friday following the lynching when I was in Nashville no arrests had been made—Resolutions condemning the mob were passed by the men's club of the First Lutheran Church, the Lions Club, the faculty of Treveca College, the Rotary and Exchange Clubs, the heads of all the educational institutions (white and colored) in Nashville, and others—The Negroes of Nashville were not to be outdone—even they met and passed a resolution expressing gratification that "the law-abiding and better class of our white citizens had taken such a bold and strong stand—both by resolutions and the subscribing of a reward . . ." I don't think their act was intended as irony . . .

But with all the reservations in their disapproval of the mob, the city- and state-wide excoriation of the lynching does indicate a very distinct advance on the part of the South. Twenty—fifteen—even ten years ago it will hardly be claimed by even the most ardent champion of the South that a lynching like that of Sammie Smith would have brought forth so unified and articulate an expression of condemnation from those who represent the very best elements of a city like Nashville. With all due credit for what was done in this particular case, the problem of Nashville, of Tennessee, of the South, and of the United States lies much deeper than in this isolated case. The remedy must go much further than the offering of rewards and the writing of forceful editorials. The lynching of Sammie Smith is not a phenomenon but instead fits very snugly into the frame of absolute disregard of the right to protection of life, person and property of Negroes in Nashville and Tennessee and the South and the United States. As long as Negroes can be murdered with impunity, as long as they can be denied even elemental decency other Sammie Smiths can and will be lynched in Nashville, even in New York City.

Do my statements savor of bombast? Do they have an echo of Fourth of July or Emancipation Day Speeches? Then let me give just a few of the things that have taken place almost without comment in Nashville during the past few years. One can then more easily understand why Sammie Smith was murdered.

On Thanksgiving Day of this year a respectable colored woman, working as a domestic in the home of a prominent citizen of Nashville, boarded a street car and sat on the end of the long seat at the rear of the car—a seat to which she had every right under the "Jim-Crow" law of the state. A well-dressed white man sat on the other end. He jumped up when she sat down, seized her by the throat and neck, pulled her out of the seat and shouted at her, "You sit down there again and what I did won't be a patching to what I will do to you!" There were no colored men on the car—only women. The conductor and motorman said and did nothing—nor did any of the white passengers. The white man rode on to his destination while the colored woman stood up.

During the same month a young colored girl, a student at the State Agricultural and Industrial School for Colored Youth, started to board a Jefferson Street car. Waiting for the same car was a notorious gambler who operates unmolested a gambling place in the heart of Nashville. With him was a white woman. The colored girl, being nearest the door when the car stopped, started to board it. The white man jerked her off the step, struck her in the face breaking her nose, and got aboard the car with his companion. He was not arrested nor molested in any way until the mother of the girl at the insistence of colored citizens of Nashville swore out a warrant for his arrest. He immediately swore out one for the girl. The mother, knowing the man's reputation as a professional "bad man" became frightened and dropped the case.

Early this year the Rev. W. C. Matthews, a Negro minister was returning to Nashville in his Ford one night after holding a service in his church just outside of Nashville. He was hailed by an officer who noticed that one of his lights had gone out, unknown to the minister. When Rev. Mr. Matthews did not stop as quickly as the officer thought he should have, the latter jumped on the running board and began cursing the minister. He protested that he had stopped as quickly as he could. The officer drew his revolver and killed the minister. Nothing has ever been done to the officer.

Two colored men by the name of Patton owned in Nashville a prosperous pressing and cleaning business. They owned their own trucks and were reputed to be good, law-abiding citizens. A certain notorious divekeeper, a white man, king of the bootleggers of Nashville, suspected one of the Patton brothers of interfering with a colored woman with whom the white man was living. The latter sought out one day Tom Patton in a business place on Cedar Street telling two police officers before entering the place he was "going to shoot a nigger." He walked in the store and shot Patton killing him instantly. He walked out, went with the two policemen to a nearby police station and in five minutes returned to the place of his crime. He has never been indicted. Six months ago he shot and killed another man, this time a white one, who was blind, shooting him on the blind side. The grand jury then in session refused to indict him even for the latter crime and he went unmolested until the local newspapers began to agitate the matter. He was then indicted but when placed on trial the jury was hung. It is generally felt that he will not have to stand trial again.

Just one more case. Last summer Lem Motlow, owner of the Jack Daniel Distillery in Kentucky and who lives at Lynchburg, Tenn., got into an altercation with a Pullman porter on a train as it left St. Louis for Nashville. The Negro porter was too wise to argue with Motlow and reported the trouble to Pullis, the Pullman conductor on the train. Motlow drew his revolver and killed Pullis. When placed on trial Governor Austin Peay, ex-Governor M. R. Patterson, W. R. Cole, President of the Nashville, Chattanooga and St. Louis Railroad and other prominent Tennesseans went to St. Louis and testified as character witnesses for Motlow. Motlow was acquitted. It is interesting to note that the town in which are Motlow's distillery and warehouses is on the N.C. and St. L. Railroad, which covers most of Tennessee. Even the Pullman Company which put all its weight behind the prosecution of Motlow was powerless.

And the other side when Negroes are suspected of crime? Last September a policeman by the name of True was killed at midnight at the corner of Fourth and Peabody Streets. By daybreak thirteen Negros had been lodged in the city jail. Some were released in a few days—others some weeks later. Three weeks after the murder the guilty Negro was captured at Columbia, Tenn. Three weeks after his arrest the newspapers reported he "had hung himself with a shoestring in his cell."

Though I was in Nashville but a short time, I gathered data regarding a great many more cases like those given above, every one authenticated. Even Negroes themselves have gotten so hardened to them that many of them do not see the direct connection between them and the lynching of Sammie Smith. It is quite easy to understand the psychology of the mob that murdered him, when one views his lynching against this background. Other Negroes had been killed and no one punished for their murder—why should there be any fear that they would be punished for killing Sammie Smith? Instead, their action would doubtless be approved by many people in Nashville!

But the causes go even further. I asked many reputable citizens of Nashville if they felt the Klan had had any part in the lynching. No one knew positively—in fact, the Klan had hastily come out in the local press to disclaim any connection with the crime and declared instead that "this organization is grieved always at instances of mob violence." But always I found myself listening to the ominous and meaningful statement: "The Klan's mighty strong out around Nolansville." It's strong in Nashville, too. The Klan has purchased a home at Sixteenth and Laurel Streets, just five blocks from the exclusive Ward-Belmont School for Girls, only ten blocks from Vanderbilt University and the same distance from the Peabody Teachers Training School. There they hold their meetings without fear of molestation and the site is, as may be judged from its contiguity to the institution's named, in an exclusive neighborhood. As one man said to me: "The Nashville Klan mightn't have had anything to do with this lynching; but I'm pretty sure the rural Klans did." And his feeling was not an isolated one . . .

And when I asked several other colored men why Sammie Smith had a revolver if he was such a good boy, never had been in trouble before, and gave his wages to his widowed mother, in every instance I received the same two words as answer. Those words were "The Klan."

But to go back to the four young white men who called at the hospital to see Sammie Smith before he died. I have furnished their names and addresses to Gov. Peay, Mayor Howse, Sheriff Briley, Chief of Police Smith and to the Chamber of Commerce. Those four may not have had anything to do with the lynching—but at least an investigation can be started there —since according to the local authorities no clues have been found as yet.

I talked with one of the most prominent colored men of Nashville. "It's mighty fine for them to offer a reward, don't you think?" I asked him. "They might as easily have offered a million," he returned cynically, "They know they'll never have to pay any of it!"

"But the editorials and resolutions were fine, anyhow, weren't they?" I inquired. "Oh, they're for Northern consumption," was his reply.

DISCRIMINATION IN THE DENVER SCHOOLS

THE ROCKY MOUNTAIN NEWS
Decision Rendered in Students' Row

January 8, 1925

DECISION RENDERED IN STUDENTS' ROW

Negroes Can Attend Parties
Unless Similar Gathering
Is Provided, Says Board.

NEGRO STUDENTS at local high schools are not entitled to attend dances or other entertainments given for white students, so long as provision has been made for separate dances for the negro students, according to a decision of the state board of education yesterday. The board dismissed an appeal from a recent decision by Jesse H. Newlon, city superintendent of schools, in which he declared that negro students were not being discriminated against in local high schools.

The order by Newlon was an outgrowth of a fight several months ago at the East Denver High school, when several negro students who attended a social hour with negro partners were ordered from the dance floor. The negro students resented being ordered off and the fight ensued.

The matter was appealed thru George Ross, the negroes' attorney, to Newlon and later to the state board of education. Ross claimed that rights under the state constitution were impaired by Newlon's order. He also claimed that discrimination was being shown against negro students at the Morey Junior High school swimming pool. The board held that there was no evidence of such discrimination at the Morey pool.

Yesterday's decision, adopted after consultation with the state attorney general's office, provided also that negroes might attend entertainments given for white students so long as similar entertainments were not provided for them.

Mrs. Mary C. C. Bradford, state superintendent of public instruction, Attorney General Wayne C. Williams and Secretary of State Carl S. Milliken are members of the state board.

"A SPIRITUAL COMING OF AGE"

ALAIN LOCKE

Enter the New Negro

Survey Graphic, March 1925

IN THE LAST decade something beyond the watch and guard of statistics has happened in the life of the American Negro and the three norns who have traditionally presided over the Negro problem have a changeling in their laps. The Sociologist, The Philanthropist, the Race-leader are not unaware of the New Negro, but they are at a loss to account for him. He simply cannot be swathed in their formulae. For the younger generation is vibrant with a new psychology; the new spirit is awake in the masses, and under the very eyes of the professional observers is transforming what has been a perennial problem into the progressive phases of contemporary Negro life.

Could such a metamorphosis have taken place as suddenly as it has appeared to? The answer is no; not because the New Negro is not here, but because the Old Negro had long become more of a myth than a man. The Old Negro, we must remember, was a creature of moral debate and historical controversy. His has been a stock figure perpetuated as an historical fiction partly in innocent sentimentalism, partly in deliberate reactionism. The Negro himself has contributed his share to this through a sort of protective social mimicry forced upon him by the adverse circumstances of dependence. So for generations in the mind of America, the Negro has been more of a formula than a human being—a something to be argued about, condemned or defended, to be "kept down," or "in his place," or "helped up," to be worried with or worried over, harassed or patronized, a social bogey or a social burden. The thinking Negro even has been induced to share this same general attitude, to focus his attention on controversial issues, to see himself in the distorted perspective of a social problem. His shadow, so to speak, has been more real to him than his personality. Through having had to appeal from the unjust stereotypes of his oppressors and traducers to those of his liberators, friends and benefactors he has subscribed to the traditional positions from which his case has been viewed. Little true social or self-understanding has or could come from such a situation.

But while the minds of most of us, black and white, have thus burrowed in the trenches of the Civil War and Reconstruction, the actual march of development has simply flanked these positions, necessitating a sudden reorientation of view. We have not been watching in the right direction; set North and South on a sectional axis, we have not noticed the East till the sun has us blinking.

Recall how suddenly the Negro spirituals revealed themselves; suppressed for generations under the stereotypes of Wesleyan hymn harmony, secretive, half-ashamed, until the courage of being natural brought them out—and behold, there was folk-music. Similarly the mind of the Negro seems suddenly to have slipped from under the tyranny of social intimidation and to be shaking off the psychology of imitation and implied inferiority. By shedding the old chrysalis of the Negro problem we are achieving something like a spiritual emancipation. Until recently, lacking self-understanding, we have been almost as much of a problem to ourselves as we still are to others. But the decade that found us with a problem has left us with only a task. The multitude perhaps feels as yet only a strange relief and a new vague urge, but the thinking few know that in the reaction the vital inner grip of prejudice has been broken.

With this renewed self-respect and self-dependence, the life of the Negro community is bound to enter a new dynamic phase, the buoyancy from within compensating for whatever pressure there may be of conditions from without. The migrant masses, shifting from countryside to city, hurdle several generations of experience at a leap, but more important, the same thing happens spiritually in the life-attitudes and self-expression of the Young Negro, in his poetry, his art, his education and his new outlook, with the additional advantage, of course, of the poise and greater certainty of knowing what it is all about. From this comes the promise and warrant of a new leadership. As one of them has discerningly put it:

We have tomorrow
Bright before us
Like a flame.

Yesterday, a night-gone thing
A sun-down name.

And dawn today
Broad arch above the road we came.
We march!

This is what, even more than any "most creditable record of fifty years of freedom," requires that the Negro of today be seen through other than the dusty spectacles of past controversy. The day of "aunties," "uncles" and "mammies" is equally gone. Uncle Tom and Sambo have passed on, and even the "Colonel" and "George" play barnstorm roles from which they escape with relief when the public spotlight is off. The popular melodrama has about played itself out, and it is time to scrap the fictions, garret the bogeys and settle down to a realistic facing of facts.

First we must observe some of the changes which since the traditional lines of opinion were drawn have rendered these quite obsolete. A main change has been, of course, that shifting of the Negro population which has made the Negro problem no longer exclusively or even predominantly Southern. Why should our minds remain sectionalized, when the problem itself no longer is? Then the trend of migration has not only been toward the North and the Central Midwest, but city-ward and to the great centers of industry—the problems of adjustment are new, practical, local and not peculiarly racial. Rather they are an integral part of the large industrial and social problems of our present-day democracy. And finally, with the Negro rapidly in process of class differentiation, if it ever was warrantable to regard and treat the Negro en masse it is becoming with every day less possible, more unjust and more ridiculous.

The Negro too, for his part, has idols of the tribe to smash. If on the one hand the white man has erred in making the Negro appear to be that which would excuse or extenuate his treatment of him, the Negro, in turn, has too often unnecessarily excused himself because of the way he has been treated. The intelligent Negro of today is resolved not to make discrimination an extenuation for his shortcomings in performance, individual or collective; he is trying to hold himself at par, neither inflated by sentimental allowances nor depreciated by current social discounts. For this he must know himself and be known for precisely what he is, and for that reason he welcomes the new scientific rather than the old sentimental interest. Sentimental interest in the Negro has ebbed. We used to lament this as the falling off of our friends; now we rejoice and pray to be delivered both from self-pity and condescension. The mind of each racial group has had a bitter weaning, apathy or hatred on one side matching disillusionment or resentment on the other; but they face each other today with the possibility at least of entirely new mutual attitudes.

It does not follow that if the Negro were better known, he would be better liked or better treated. But mutual understanding is basic for any subsequent cooperation and adjustment. The effort toward this will at least have the effect of remedying in large part what has been the most unsatisfactory feature of our present stage of race relationships in America, namely the fact that the more intelligent and representative elements of the two race groups have at so many points got quite out of vital touch with one another.

The fiction is that the life of the races is separate, and increasingly so. The fact is that they have touched too closely at the unfavorable and too lightly at the favorable levels.

While inter-racial councils have sprung up in the South, drawing on forward elements of both races, in the Northern cities manual laborers may brush elbows in their everyday work, but the community and business leaders have experienced no such interplay or far too little of it. These segments must achieve contact or the race situation in America becomes desperate. Fortunately this is happening. There is a growing realization that in social effort the cooperative basis must supplant long-distance philanthropy, and that the only safeguard for mass relations in the future must be provided in the carefully maintained contacts of the enlightened minorities of both race groups. In the intellectual realm a renewed and keen curiosity is replacing the recent apathy; the Negro is being carefully studied, not just talked about and discussed. In art and letters, instead of being wholly caricatured, he is being seriously portrayed and painted.

To all of this the New Negro is keenly responsive as an augury of a new democracy in American culture. He is contributing his share to the new social understanding. But the desire to be understood would never in itself have been sufficient to have opened so completely the protectively closed portals of the thinking Negro's mind. There is still too much possibility of being snubbed or patronized for that. It was rather the necessity for fuller, truer, self-expression, the realization of the unwisdom of allowing social discrimination to segregate him mentally, and a counter-attitude to cramp and fetter his own living—and so the "spite-wall" that the intellectuals built over the "color-line" has happily been taken down. Much of this reopening of intellectual contacts has centered in New York and has been richly fruitful not merely in the enlarging of personal experience, but in the definite enrichment of American art and letters and in the clarifying of our common vision of the social tasks ahead.

The particular significance in the reestablishment of contact between the more advanced and representative classes is that it promises to offset some of the unfavorable reactions of the past, or at least to re-surface race contacts somewhat for the future. Subtly the conditions that are moulding a New Negro are moulding a new American attitude.

However, this new phase of things is delicate; it will call for less charity but more justice; less help, but infinitely closer understanding. This is indeed a critical stage of race relationships because of the likelihood, if the new temper is not understood, of engendering sharp group antagonism and a second crop of more calculated prejudice. In some quarters, it has already done so. Having weaned the Negro, public opinion cannot continue to paternalize. The Negro today is inevitably moving forward under the control largely of his own objectives. What are these objectives? Those of his outer life are happily already well and finally formulated, for they are none other than the ideals of American institutions and democracy. Those of his inner life are yet in process of formation, for the new psychology at present is more of a consensus of feeling than of opinion, of attitude rather than of program. Still some points seem to have crystallized.

Up to the present one may adequately describe the Negro's "inner objectives" as an attempt to repair a damaged group psychology and reshape a warped social perspective. Their realization has required a new mentality for the American Negro. And as it matures we begin to see its effects; at first, negative, iconoclastic, and then positive and constructive. In this new group psychology we note the lapse of sentimental appeal, then the development of a more positive self-respect and self-reliance; the repudiation of social dependence, and then the gradual recovery from hyper-sensitiveness and "touchy" nerves, the repudiation of the double standard of judgment with its special philanthropic allowances and then the sturdier desire for objective and scientific appraisal; and finally the rise from social disillusionment to race pride, from the sense of social debt to the responsibilities of social contribution, and off-setting the necessary working and commonsense acceptance of restricted conditions, the belief in ultimate esteem and recognition. Therefore the Negro today wishes to be known for what he is, even in his faults and shortcomings, and scorns a craven and precarious survival at the price of seeming to be what he is not. He resents being spoken for as a social ward or minor, even by his own, and to being regarded a chronic patient for the sociological clinic, the sick man of American Democracy. For the same reasons, he himself is through with those social nostrums and panaceas, the so-called "solutions" of his "problem," with which he and the country have been so liberally dosed in the past. Religion, freedom, education, money—in turn, he has ardently hoped for and peculiarly trusted these things; he still believes in them, but not in blind trust that they alone will solve his life-problem.

Each generation, however, will have its creed and that of the present is the belief in the efficacy of collective effort, in race cooperation. This deep feeling of race is at present the mainspring of Negro life. It seems to be the outcome of the reaction to proscription and prejudice; an attempt, fairly successful on the whole, to convert a defensive into an offensive position, a handicap into an incentive. It is radical in tone, but not in purpose and only the most stupid forms of opposition, misunderstanding or persecution could make it otherwise. Of course, the thinking Negro has shifted a little toward the left with the world-trend, and there is an increasing group who affiliate with radical and liberal movements. But fundamentally for the present the Negro is radical on race matters, conservative on others, in other words, a "forced radical," a social protestant rather than a genuine radical. Yet under further pressure and injustice iconoclastic thought and motives will inevitably increase. Harlem's quixotic radicalisms call for their ounce of democracy today lest tomorrow they be beyond cure.

The Negro mind reaches out as yet to nothing but American wants, American ideas. But this forced attempt to build his Americanism on race values is a unique social experiment, and its ultimate success is impossible except through the fullest sharing of American culture and institutions. There should be no delusion about this. American nerves in sections unstrung with race hysteria are often fed the opiate that the trend of Negro advance is wholly separatist, and that the effect of its operation will be to encyst the Negro as a benign foreign body in the body politic. This cannot be—even if it were desirable. The racialism of the Negro is no limitation or reservation with respect to American life; it is only a constructive effort to build the obstructions in the stream of his progress into an efficient dam of social energy and power. Democracy itself is obstructed and stagnated to the extent that any of its channels are closed. Indeed they cannot be selectively closed. So the choice is not between one way for the Negro and another way for the rest, but between American institutions frustrated on the one hand and American ideals progressively fulfilled and realized on the other.

There is, of course, a warrantably comfortable feeling in being on the right side of the country's professed ideals. We realize that we cannot be undone without America's undoing. It is within the gamut of this attitude that the thinking Negro faces America, but the variations of mood in connection with it are if anything more significant than the attitude itself. Sometimes we have it taken with the defiant ironic challenge of McKay:

Mine is the future grinding down today
Like a great landslip moving to the sea,
Bearing its freight of debris far away
Where the green hungry waters restlessly
Heave mammoth pyramids and break and roar
Their eerie challenge to the crumbling shore.

Sometimes, perhaps more frequently as yet, in the fervent and almost filial appeal and counsel of Weldon Johnson's:

O Southland, dear Southland!
Then why do you still cling
To an idle age and a musty page,
To a dead and useless thing.

But between defiance and appeal, midway almost between cynicism and hope, the prevailing mind stands in the mood of the same author's To America, an attitude of sober query and stoical challenge:

How would you have us, as we are?
Or sinking 'neath the load we bear,
Our eyes fixed forward on a star,
Or gazing empty at despair?

Rising or falling? Men or things?
With dragging pace or footsteps fleet?
Strong, willing sinews in your wings,
Or tightening chains about your feet?

More and more, however, an intelligent realization of the great discrepancy between the American social creed and the American social practice forces upon the Negro the taking of the moral advantage that is his. Only the steadying and sobering effect of a truly characteristic gentleness of spirit prevents the rapid rise of a definite cynicism and counter-hate and a defiant superiority feeling. Human as this reaction would be, the majority still deprecate its advent, and would gladly see it forestalled by the speedy amelioration of its causes. We wish our race pride to be a healthier, more positive achievement than a feeling based upon a realization of the shortcomings of others. But all paths toward the attainment of a sound social attitude have been difficult; only a relatively few enlightened minds have been able as the phrase puts it "to rise above" prejudice. The ordinary man has had until recently only a hard choice between the alternatives of supine and humiliating submission and stimulating but hurtful counter-prejudice. Fortunately from some inner, desperate resourcefulness has recently sprung up the simple expedient of fighting prejudice by mental passive resistance, in other words by trying to ignore it. For the few, this manna may perhaps be effective, but the masses cannot thrive on it.

Fortunately there are constructive channels opening out into which the balked social feelings of the American Negro can flow freely.

Without them there would be much more pressure and danger than there is. These compensating interests are racial but in a new and enlarged way. One is the consciousness of acting as the advance-guard of the African peoples in their contact with Twentieth Century civilization; the other, the sense of a mission of rehabilitating the race in world esteem from that loss of prestige for which the fate and conditions of slavery have so largely been responsible. Harlem, as we shall see, is the center of both these movements; she is the home of the Negro's "Zionism." The pulse of the Negro world has begun to beat in Harlem. A Negro newspaper carrying news material in English, French and Spanish, gathered from all quarters of America, the West Indies and Africa has maintained itself in Harlem for over five years. Two important magazines, both edited from New York, maintain their news and circulation consistently on a cosmopolitan scale. Under American auspices and backing, three pan-African congresses have been held abroad for the discussion of common interests, colonial questions and the future cooperative development of Africa. In terms of the race question as a world problem, the Negro mind has leapt, so to speak, upon the parapets of prejudice and extended its cramped horizons. In so doing it has linked up with the growing group consciousness of the dark-peoples and is gradually learning their common interests. As one of our writers has recently put it: "It is imperative that we understand the white world in its relations to the nonwhite world." As with the Jew, persecution is making the Negro international.

As a world phenomenon this wider race consciousness is a different thing from the much asserted rising tide of color. Its inevitable causes are not of our making. The consequences are not necessarily damaging to the best interests of civilization. Whether it actually brings into being new Armadas of conflict or argosies of cultural exchange and enlightenment can only be decided by the attitude of the dominant races in an era of critical change. With the American Negro his new internationalism is primarily an effort to recapture contact with the scattered peoples of African derivation. Garveyism may be a transient, if spectacular, phenomenon, but the possible role of the American Negro in the future development of Africa is one of the most constructive and universally helpful missions that any modern people can lay claim to.

Constructive participation in such causes cannot help giving the Negro valuable group incentives, as well as increased prestige at home and abroad. Our greatest rehabilitation may possibly come through such channels, but for the present, more immediate hope rests in the revaluation by white and black alike of the Negro in terms of his artistic endowments and cultural contributions, past and prospective. It must be increasingly recognized that the Negro has already made very substantial contributions, not only in his folk-art, music especially, which has always found appreciation, but in larger, though humbler and less acknowledged ways. For generations the Negro has been the peasant matrix of that section of America which has most undervalued him, and here he has contributed not only materially in labor and in social patience, but spiritually as well. The South has unconsciously absorbed the gift of his folk-temperament. In less than half a generation it will be easier to recognize this, but the fact remains that a leaven of humor, sentiment, imagination and tropic nonchalance has gone into the making of the South from a humble, unacknowledged source. A second crop of the Negro's gifts promises still more largely. He now becomes a conscious contributor and lays aside the status of a beneficiary and ward for that of a collaborator and participant in American civilization. The great social gain in this is the releasing of our talented group from the arid fields of controversy and debate to the productive fields of creative expression. The especially cultural recognition they win should in turn prove the key to that revaluation of the Negro which must precede or accompany any considerable further betterment of race relationships. But whatever the general effect, the present generation will have added the motives of self-expression and spiritual development to the old and still unfinished task of making material headway and progress. No one who understandingly faces the situation with its substantial accomplishment or views the new scene with its still more abundant promise can be entirely without hope. And certainly, if in our lifetime the Negro should not be able to celebrate his full initiation into American democracy, he can at least, on the warrant of these things, celebrate the attainment of a significant and satisfying new phase of group development, and with it a spiritual Coming of Age.

HOUSING SEGREGATION IN THE NORTH

W.E.B. DU BOIS

The Challenge of Detroit

The Crisis, November 1925

THE CHALLENGE OF DETROIT

IN DETROIT, MICHIGAN, a black man has shot into a mob which was threatening him, his family, his friends and his home in order to make him move out of the neighborhood. He killed one man and wounded another.

—

Immediately a red and awful challenge confronts the nation. Must black folk shoot and shoot to kill in order to maintain their rights or is this unnecessary and wanton bloodshed for fancied ill? The answer depends on the facts. The Mayor of Detroit has publicly warned both mob and Negroes. He has repudiated mob law but he adds, turning to his darker audience, that they ought not to invite aggression by going where they are not wanted. There are thus two interpretations:

1. A prosperous Negro physician of Detroit, seeking to get away from his people, moves into a white residential section where his presence for social reasons is distasteful to his neighbors.

2. A prosperous Negro physician of Detroit, seeking a better home with more light, air, space and quiet, finds it naturally in the parts of the city where white folk with similar wants have gone rather than in the slums where most of the colored are crowded.

Which version is true? See the figures:

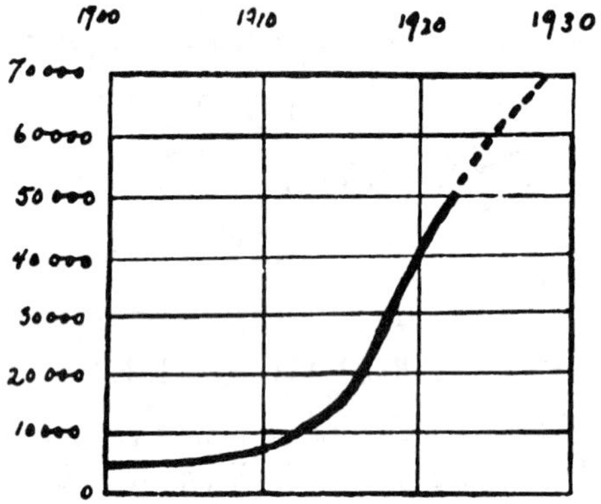

Negro Population of Detroit

1900 4,111
1910 5,741
1920 40,838
1925 . . . . . 60,000 (estimated)

Two thirds of this population in 1920 were crowded into three wards—the Third, Fifth and Seventh. Meantime the total population of Detroit has more than doubled in ten years and the people have reached out on all sides to new dwelling places. Have the Negroes no right to rush too? Is it not their duty to seek better homes and, if they do, are they not bound to "move into white neighborhoods" which is simply another way of saying "move out of congested slums"?

Why do they not make their own new settlements then? Because no individual can make a modern real estate development; no group of ordinary individuals can compete with organized real estate interests and get a decent deal. When Negroes have tried it they have usually had miserable results; in Birmingham, Alabama, twenty years since, they bought a nice street and lined it with pretty homes; the city took all its prostitutes and stuck them into a segregated vice district right behind the pretty homes! In Macon, Savannah, New Orleans and Atlanta crime and prostitution have been kept and protected in Negro residence districts. In New York City, for years, no Negro could rent or buy a home in Manhattan outside the

"Tenderloin"; and white Religion and Respectability far from stretching a helping hand turned and cursed the blacks when by bribery, politics and brute force they broke into the light and air of Harlem. Some great leaders in Negro philanthropy like Clarence Kelsey formed a financial bloc to push the Negroes out of Harlem, to refuse mortgages to landlords renting to them; but only one practical project of furnishing them decent quarters came to fruition.

—

Dear God! Must we not live? And if we live may we not live somewhere? And when a whole city full of white folk led and helped by banks, Chambers of Commerce, mortgage companies and "realtors" are combing the earth for every decent bit of residential property for whites, where in the name of God can we live and live decently if not by these same whites? If some of the horror-struck and law-worshipping white leaders of Detroit instead of winking at the Ku Klux Klan and admonishing the Negroes to allow themselves to be kicked and killed with impunity—if these would finance and administer a decent scheme of housing relief for Negroes it would not be necessary for us to kill white mob leaders in order to live in peace and decency. These whited sepulchres pulled that trigger and not the man that held the gun.

—

But, wail the idiots, Negroes depress real estate values! This is a lie—an ancient and bearded lie. Race prejudice decreases values both real estate and human; crime, ignorance and filth decrease values. But a decent, quiet, educated family buying property in a decent neighborhood will not affect values a bit unless the people in that neighborhood hate a colored skin more than they regard the value of their own property. This has been proven in a thousand instances. Sudden fall in values comes through propaganda and hysteria manipulated by real estate agents or by Southern slave drivers who want their labor to return South; or by ignorant gossip mongers. Usually Negroes do not move into new developments but into districts which well-to-do whites are deserting. The fall in values is not due to race but to a series of economic readjustments and often, as in Baltimore, real estate values were actually saved and raised, not lowered, when black folk bought Druid Hill Avenue and adjacent streets. Certainly a flood of noisy dirty black folk will ruin any neighborhood but they ruin black property as well as white, and the reason is not their color but their condition. And whom, High Heaven, shall we blame for that?

—

But these facts make no difference to organized American Negro haters. They are using every effort to maintain and increase race friction. In the South time and time again communities have almost forgotten race lines until the bitter, hate-preaching liar stirred it up again. The whole present "Anglo-Saxon" and "race purity" agitation in Virginia has arisen because one white family openly acknowledged its colored grandmother! The whole crusade in Detroit has come to a head because, in 1920, 663,000 Southern whites had migrated and were living in Wisconsin, Michigan, Illinois, Indiana and Ohio. Their numbers are swelling. They are largely clerks, artisans and laborers, not illiterate but ignorant of the modern world and forming by habit the lawless material of mobs. They are ruining the finer democracy of the Middle West and using the Negro as an excuse.

What shall we do? I know a black man. He is a professional man and a graduate of a great eastern school. He has studied abroad. His wife was educated in a good western school and is a quiet housewife. His son is a college graduate and a high school teacher. They have never been arrested. They conduct themselves as cultured folk. This man is living in an apartment in Harlem. He would like more air and sunlight and less noise. He would like a new, small, modern house in the further Bronx or in the hills of Westchester or New Jersey or in the higher part of Queens. He sees daily in the papers new homes advertised suitable to his means—$500, $1,000 even $2000 down, the rest as rent. Can he buy one of these? Not without plotting, deception, insult or murder.

For instance: A man bought a modest home in Staten Island. He was a mail carrier with a fine record; his wife was a school teacher, educated and well-bred. They had four sturdy children in school. As a result he has been mobbed and insulted, his property injured, his glass and shrubbery broken, his insurance cancelled, his life threatened, his existence made miserable. His neighbors do everything to insult him and his, even to crossing the street to avoid passing him. He sticks to his home even though offered a profit to sell, "on principle." He is "colored."

Another man in Detroit bought a fine home in a former exclusive district which is now changing. He was a physician with a large practice, the founder of a hospital, public-spirited and well-liked. He had married the daughter of perhaps the greatest of the interpreters of Negro folk songs with world-wide reputation. He moved in. A mob of thousands appeared, yelling and cursing. They broke his windows, threw out his furniture and he and his family escaped under police protection. He gave up his home, made no resistance, moved back whence he came, filed no protest, made no public complaint. He was "colored."

A little later another physician in Detroit bought another beautiful home and moved in. A mob—almost the same mob—came, cursed, threw stones and ordered him to move. He gathered his family and friends within and locked the door. Five or six thousand people lined the streets. The police set traffic officers to divert the traffic that could not get through. The mob invaded his yard and approached his doors. He shot and shot to kill. His wife and his friends are now in jail charged with *Murder in the first degree*! He was "colored."

Gentle Reader, which of these three examples shall my friend of Harlem follow? Which would you follow if you were "free," black and 21?

“DR. SWEET’S BATTLE . . . IS OUR BATTLE”

THE NEW YORK AMSTERDAM NEWS

We Must Fight If We Would Survive

November 18, 1925

AN EDITORIAL

POSSIBLY the most important court case the Negro has ever figured in in all the history of the United States is being heard out in Detroit, Michigan, where Dr. Ossian Sweet, his wife and nine other defendants are on trial for their lives, because they dared to protect themselves and their property against mob violence.

To get a true picture of what is going on, turn the matter around and imagine that a mob of Negroes has resented a white family’s moving into a colored neighborhood; and, in defending themselves, the besieged white family had shot and killed a colored man. What grand jury in the United States would indict the white family for murder in the first degree? What police officer would take the stand and testify that they were not acting within their rights in protecting themselves? Why, then, should Negroes be charged with murder who dare to defend themselves and their property?

The outcome of the Sweet case means everything that is dear to the Negro in America. If a colored man is not secure in his own home, in a northern community, where there is a semblance of civilization, where under heaven in the United States is he secure? Dr. Sweet’s battle in Detroit is our battle; just as much so as if we had been in the besieged dwelling. He and the other brave defendants could easily have avoided the many discomforts they must bear as prisoners charged with murder by not moving into the house after he purchased it. He could have sold it, possibly at a higher figure than he paid for it.

But, thank god, Dr. Sweet moved in! Thank God that his noble wife moved in with him! And, thank God, nine of their relatives and friends came in with them! Wisdom dictated that they should not go in empty handed. They determined to fight fire with fire, and, according to reports, had ten separate fire-arms in the house. Not one of them knew whether he would come out of that house alive, once he went in, but fear of death did not deter them.

This is the spirit of unity the Negro must more and more evidence if he is to survive. He must face death if he would live! He must be willing to die fighting when he is right! When police authorities fail to protect him and his family; when courts of law desert him; when his own government fails to take a stand in his behalf, he faces death anyway, and might just as well die fighting!

Join in the fight by subscribing to the fund necessary for the defense of Dr. Sweet, his noble wife and the other defendants in this case. Send your contribution to the National Association for the Advancement of Colored People, 69 Fifth avenue, or to the Editor of The Amsterdam News, who will see that the Association gets it. ACT AT ONCE.

"MY BACK WAS UP AGAINST THE WALL"

NETTIE GEORGE SPEEDY

"Not Guilty," Dr. Sweet Tells Jury

The Chicago Defender, November 28, 1925

DR. SWEET GOES ON STAND

DETROIT, MICH., Nov. 27.—The merciless, pitiless and gruelling cross-examination to which Dr. Ossian H. Sweet was subjected for two days by Prosecutor Robert Toms failed to shake his story which he had told on direct examination conducted by Arthur Garfield Hayes.

Dr. Sweet, his wife, Mrs. Gladys Sweet, his two brothers, Otis and Henry, and seven friends are on trial for the killing of Leon Briener which occurred Sept. 9 last while a howling mob was in front of Dr. Sweet's home because he had moved into a neighborhood inhabited entirely by white people.

Dr. Sweet and the 10 other defendants were charged with murder and conspiracy to commit murder. They have been in jail since the night of the shooting, with the exception of Mrs. Sweet, who was granted bail by Judge Frank Murphy, the trial judge. She was allowed her liberty after 30 days' confinement in the county jail.

"When I opened the door and saw the mob I realized in a way that I was facing the same mob that has hounded my people throughout its entire history. I was confident of what I was up against. I realized that my back was up against the wall. I was filled with a peculiar fear—a fear which can only be felt by those who have experienced that to which my people have been subjected. I know what mobs have done to my people before," declared Dr. Sweet when asked to express his feelings on that night.

He described the events leading up to the shooting. How a crowd had surrounded the house the night before, and of the much larger crowd the night of the trouble. He declared that there had been some shooting from his home, but he did not know who had done the firing.

The house was being continuously pelted with rocks, the windows had been broken, and when he realized that the police on the outside were doing nothing to protect him or his property, he decided that the time for action had come.

He armed himself and waited for the onslaught. But when he had gone downstairs to admit his brother and a friend, who had come to his rescue, the mob stoned the house with renewed vigor, and he heard firing a few seconds later.

TELLS OF ARRESTS

He admitted seeing his brother Henry with a rifle and he admitted having a gun himself, but this testimony could not connect either of them with the death of Briener, as the state's witnesses had testified that the deceased had died from the effects of a pistol shot, and the gun Sweet had was never fired, and Henry was armed with a rifle.

His description was graphic as he told of the arrival of the police. His home had been in darkness, but when the officers came, they lighted all the lights, pulled up every window shade, handcuffed them to each other and exposed them to the mob.

The moment was tense when he described the mob as "a human sea," he crouched in his chair, unconsciously he placed his hand over his eyes, as if to shut out the sight which had gripped his soul in terror.

The scene was being lived again. A slight shudder shook his diminutive form. He faltered in his speech. Then suddenly he was alert, he looked quickly to the space where his wife was seated, and a wan smile played about his features when he awoke to the realization that he had been in the painful throes of a past nightmare. Ossian Sweet asserted himself again.

He related how the timely arrival of Lieut. John Hayes had possibly saved them from a much worse fate. He told of being taken to police headquarters, and after being denied counsel, he was forced to make a statement. He asserted that he had made some false answers in his statement because he was afraid that the police would misconstrue them. He also stated that he was afraid that the police would beat him up.

"Since I have been in jail I have learned many things regarding the beatings of prisoners. It is commonly known that the officers beat up Negro prisoners. Mr. Kennedy, your assistant prosecutor, even framed a mock trial for us. After the day of the trial had been set, he even then tried to intimidate us.

"He, Lieutenant Johnson and his partner came to the jail, handcuffed us, brought us out under the tunnel, declaring that we were going to our trial. He carried us to some strange room where there was a piano, and asked us if we wanted to verify whatever we had said the night of our arrest.

"I soon realized that we were being hoaxed and I refused to answer any questions, and advised the others not to answer any. When the three realized that we were not to be made fools, they carried us back to jail. I advised my attorney of their actions as soon as I could communicate with him."

Dr. Sweet stated that he does not believe and has never believed that a shot from his home killed Briener. In a statement introduced by the state coming from Henry Sweet he admitted firing twice from the house, but claimed that the first time he fired up in the air to scare the people, but the second time he fired over their heads. He declared that he was armed with a rifle.

The defense gained a strong point at the expense of the state when Fred Hyde (white) was ushered to the witness chair. It was noticeable that Prosecutor Toms rubbed his hands with a satisfied air. Hyde was a surprise witness called to refute the testimony of the defense witnesses that there was a mob in front of the Sweet home that evening.

WITNESS CONFUSED

Hyde said that he was working at a filling station on Sept. 9, one block from the Sweet home. He declared that he saw no crowd there, heard no shouting and saw no one throwing stones. He stated that the occupants of a machine had not been set upon by a mob in front of his place.

He broke under the cross-examination of Mr. Darrow and declared that shortly after he went to work he heard people talking about the "excitement down at the corner." He understood them to mean there was excitement because Colored people had moved into the neighborhood. He added that there were a large number of people congregated at the corner where he was working, and he was so busy that if a car had been attacked he possibly would not have seen it.

Attorney Charles H. Mahoney testified that he, Attorney Julian Perry and Cecil Rowlette had gone to police headquarters the evening of Sept. 9 and asked to see the prisoners, which permission was denied. It was not until after they had filed a petition for a writ of habeas corpus that they were allowed to see the prisoners.

At this juncture a whisper was traveling through the courtroom. It had just been learned that some one had set fire to the garage of Dr. Sweet, although it was supposed to be under police surveillance. Mr. Darrow demanded that officers who were supposed to be guarding the house be brought before the court.

Stephan Tickey, a commercial photographer, was called by the defense to identify two photographs which he had taken. The defense intends to use the pictures to show that the bullet which killed Briener might have been fired by Officer Frank Gill and not from the guns fired from the Sweet home.

The officer had testified during the early stages of the trial that he had fired a shot at two of the defendants when he saw them appear on an upper porch during the firing that evening.

The photographer testified that when he took the first picture he placed himself in the same spot where Gill was supposed to have been standing when the shots were fired. The other picture was taken at the opposite end of the supposed course of the bullet.

Lieut. William Johnson, in charge of the case, and whom Dr. Sweet had testified had asked him "Why in the h—— did you move in a neighborhood where you were not wanted?" was compelled to change collars after his grilling cross-examination by Mr. Darrow.

COP GIVES "ADVICE"

Johnson denied using the language stated, but admitted that he had advised Dr. Sweet to move into some other neighborhood. He added that he had later learned that Sweet was decidedly not wanted where he had moved.

"Did you ever stop to learn whether you were wanted in the neighborhood where you lived?" thundered Mr. Darrow. "Possibly if you investigated that end of the matter you may learn that you are not the most desirable citizen where you live."

Mr. Darrow drew from the witness the admission that he would not have allowed Dr. Sweet the opportunity of consulting an attorney had he seen Mr. Mahoney that evening.

Harry L. Diehl (white), law partner of Walter Nelson, associate counsel for the defense, testified that he walked over the roof of the Sweet home and found many stones there and in the gutters of the roof.

Prosecutor Toms tried in vain to introduce additional testimony, but Mr. Darrow gave him a lesson in law regarding rebuttal. Mr. Darrow's objection was sustained by the court. Toms sought to have a newspaper reporter testify as to the condition of the streets regarding the gathering of people the night in question.

The color line was ruthlessly torn asunder by Attorney Darrow when the defense got under full sway. He had succeeded in locating two white witnesses who were truthful enough to come to court and admit what they saw that evening.

Phillip Adler, 9412 Richter St., a newspaper reporter, was an eye-witness to the mob which had formed outside the home of Dr. Sweet. He described the formation of two very large number of persons and declared that he had asked a woman what was the matter, and she had told him that "a 'nigger' family had moved into the neighborhood and they were going to put them out."

He stated that he heard continuous clouting of stones against the Sweet home, so fast that it sounded as if it was hail. The missiles were being thrown from directly across the street. He declared that he knew none of the defendants and had never seen any of them until he faced them in court.

The other white witness, testifying as to the mob outside the Sweet home, was Lloyd Lorenze, 2978 Merrill Ave., who testified that he was in an accessory store near the vicinity of the Sweet home that evening and saw the large number of people, which amounted to several hundred. He stated that he was working in the store and could not leave it to ascertain what had caused the gathering.

James Smith, 932 Elliot St., described by Mr. Darrow as one

of the best witnesses he had ever heard in his 40 years of practice of criminal law, declared that on the evening of the trouble he was driving in the neighborhood of the Sweet home, when he and the occupants of the car were assaulted by the mob.

He declared that he noticed a large number of persons on the corner, and curiosity caused him to drive in the direction of the crowd. As he came to the intersection of the streets, he was diverted from his course by a traffic policeman, who told him to "step on it."

"By this time the people had seen us and came running toward us. They were yelling, 'There goes some "niggers" now. They are going to the Sweet home. Lynch them, kill them!' They were throwing stones and bricks at the car. One of the stones broke the window of the car.

MOB CHASES CAR

"One of the fellows, a little more daring than the rest, jumped on the running board of the car. There were two cars directly in front of us and the mob screamed, 'Stop them!' The man riding with me and my uncle put one foot on the running board and pretending that he had a gun yelled, 'Don't stop or I will shoot.'

"The man who had jumped on our running board was trying to reach in the window and strike me. At the corner the car in front of us turned off and I gave my car gas and the sudden jerk caused the man to fall off of the car."

His testimony was corroborated by his uncle, Alonzo Smith, and Henry Smith, their guest of the evening.

Charles Schoffner, a chef living at 1731 Seminole Ave., exhibited a large scar upon his forehead, declaring that it was the result of being stoned and hit by the mob that night. He stated that he and his wife were riding near the Sweet home and when the mob spied them they began to throw stones at them. They broke his car to pieces and threatened to kill them, but the pleadings of his wife possibly saved them from mortal injury.

Bruce Spaulding, a letter carrier, and his wife, Mrs. Mary L. Spaulding, a social service worker with the Detroit Urban league, 4708 St. Antoine St., told of driving through the neighborhood of the Sweet home that evening and seeing a large mob of people.

Miss Edna Butler, 31 Robinwood Ave., employed in the needlecraft division of the Woman's Exchange, testified that she went to the Sweet home the night before the trouble to discuss the interior decorations of the home and that such a large crowd gathered in front of the place that she was afraid to leave and had to spend the night there.

She telephoned Mrs. Sweet of a conversation she heard between the motorman of the car and a white woman passenger who boarded the car at the same time with her the next morning. She related that the motorman asked the woman what caused the crowd in the street the night before and the woman replied: "Some 'niggers' have moved there, and we are going to get rid of them. They stayed there last night, but they will be put out tonight."

Miss Ferrena Rochelle, 6373 Beagle St., an interior decorator for a white firm, who accompanied Miss Butler to the Sweet home, stated that while they were in the house that evening the people who had gathered outside had rocked the home and caused her to be afraid to leave the house.

John W. Fletcher, 4585 Roosevelt St., related how he had purchased a home in a white neighborhood, lived there one day and was forced to leave it. He had bought a place in Stoble St. Mr. Hays asked him where did he go and he replied, "To jail."

Wellington Bristol, 7804 American Ave., stated that he had built his home at the present address, how it had remained vacant for a long time, because the white people would allow no one to rent it. He decided to move into the place himself, and they tried to drive him away, but he was living there today under police protection.

Dr. D. A. Stewart, 3855 Montclair Ave., succeeded Bristol on the stand. He related that he was sitting in his car in front of the Sweet home on the 9th of September, talking to Dr. Sweet's brother, Henry, when an officer approached them.

The policeman had told them that "the white people had held an indignation meeting last night and the whole crowd have decided to come back tonight double force, so you had better be on the alert."

DOCTORS TESTIFY

Judge Murphy ruled that the recital of other racial troubles be admitted as evidence as they tended to prove the state of Dr. Sweet's mind on the night of the shooting. Counsel for the defense had contended that these disturbances had a direct bearing on the case, inasmuch as Dr. Sweet had heard of them and was influenced by them with reference to his conduct that night.

With this object in view, the defense called Dr. Edward Carter, 620 Chandler St., to the stand. Dr. Carter is an unusually brilliant man, with several degrees attached to his name. He has been the intimate friend of Dr. Sweet for many years.

He stated that Dr. Sweet had talked with him about the purchase of a home. Had asked his advice about moving into a neighborhood which was practically destitute of Race home-owners. They had discussed about what happened to Dr. A. L. Turner when he bought property on Spokane Ave. in a white neighborhood.

"Dr. Sweet and I were both present at a doctors' meeting when Dr. Turner told of buying his home. The day he moved in, he said, a large crowd began to assemble early in the morning, increasing in size during the day. Two men called at the house in the afternoon, representing that they had come from the mayor's office. When they were admitted, a crowd rushed in. Dr. Turner was forced to sign some kind of a document, and his furniture was moved out into the street. Broke his automobile and struck him, and he was driven from the house."

Dr. Carter added that he and the other doctors talked of the other racial differences which had developed from the purchasing of homes in exclusive white neighborhoods by Race men. He also testified to the good character of each of the prisoners.

At the conclusion of Dr. Carter's testimony, Prosecutor Robert Toms sought to show that Dr. Sweet had been greatly influenced by reading from Race periodicals which were in sympathy with the Race men. Numerous Race papers were mentioned by the prosecutor as spreading propaganda.

In order to disprove the statement of Mr. Toms that the report prepared by the National Association for the Advancement of Colored People covering 30 years of lynchings from

1889 to 1918, which Dr. Sweet had read and had learned that 3,500 lynchings had occurred during that period, was a Race pamphlet, the defense called Walter F. White to the stand.

Mr. White stated that he was assistant executive secretary of the association, which is financing the trial of Dr. Sweet, and declared that the association is composed of white and Race people. He mentioned that Judge Ira W. Jayne, Edsel Ford, the late J. J. Crowley and other representative white citizens of Detroit were affiliated with the association.

A TEXAS EDITOR'S "BURNING ZEAL"

CLIFTON F. RICHARDSON

Why I Stay in Texas and Fight

Pittsburgh Courier, September 24, 1927

WHY I STAY IN TEXAS AND FIGHT

Houston Editor Criticizes Leaders Who Live in Safety Zone and Direct Affairs At Long Range.

HOUSTON, TEXAS, Sept. 22.—The query is often propounded to the author of this article by Negro residents of other sections of the country, particularly those of the North and East, as to why this writer prefers to remain in Texas (and the South) and endanger his life in the defense of justice, right and a square and fair deal for his race in particular and humanity in general, when he could remove to other sections of the republic and be assured of more protection and a larger degree of liberty in his editorial utterances and observations.

In response to this interrogation and manifest interest on the part of so many of my friends and well-wishers in other parts of the country I wish to assert that I have a "burning zeal" for my race. Their trials are my trials; their sufferings my sufferings; their heartaches my heartaches; their successes and triumphs my successes and triumphs, and whatever affects them, for weal or for woe, affects me similarly. The attitude of Moses, who elected to endure the hardships and sufferings with his own race during Egyptian bondage rather than enjoy the luxury, security, ease and comfort of Pharaoh's palace, has played no small part in inspiring and actuating me in my determination to remain in Dixie and fight wrong and unrighteousness wherever it exists, and to that end it is my aim to "fight it out along these lines if it takes all summer."

I was born, reared and educated in Texas, and thus I am an integral part (small though it may be) of the Lone Star State commonwealth. I consider myself a member of the Texas household, and, as a member of such family, I deem it my sacred, inherent, God-given and constitutional right to preach an uncompromising gospel for the ultimate triumph of democracy and Christianity, and to contend with might and main for the final reign of the doctrine of the "fatherhood of God and brotherhood of man;" for the advent of the day when man's humanity to man will make countless thousands rejoice and be exceedingly glad.

This writer (readers will pardon the personal reference, yet the article is largely personal in its aspect) was born at Marshall, a small city in East Texas, and educated at Bishop College, an institution for the higher education of Negro youths, founded and supported by the American Baptist Home Mission Society of New York City, located in the "Athens of Texas" (Marshall, also home of Wiley College).

It was while a student in the department of printing and journalism at Bishop College that the writer became imbued with a desire to devote his life to the cause of racial and social uplift through the instrumentality of the written and printed word, and to some day edit a newspaper through whose columns he could attack and expose the evils and ills, the injustices and inequalities heaped with impunity upon his race in Texas and the South.

The South is yet, and will remain for many years to come, the chief place of abode for the majority of our people, and, since this is an undeniable fact, most assuredly these people, denied and refused so many of their inalienable and constitutional rights because of their color and previous condition of servitude, ought receive some substantial and constructive assistance from those who are able to render certain types of help and succor.

If I were to answer this question point blank, I would reply by simply stating that I remain in Texas (and the South) and fight because my people need me, and because I believe that I can perform some kind of service (whether they appreciate my efforts or properly evaluate the contributions I am striving to make in their behalf or not) which should play an important part in changing Nordic sentiment, à la Dixie, concerning the Negro race, and thereby promote and advance our racial cause.

Furthermore, never in the history of martial conflicts has any notable military victory been achieved by the army which flees from the line of danger; by soldiers who try to snipe the enemy many miles removed from the field of battle and carnage. No baseball pitcher ever won a diamond classic by failing to get on the hillock and hurl the spheroid at opposing batsmen. To win the battle soldiers must stay in there and fight, and to win a ball game the pitcher must stay in there and pitch!

The soldier who is unwilling to face shot and shell and even death itself in the cause he represents is unworthy to wear the uniform of his country, and is classified as a slacker, coward or even traitor. Likewise, no pitcher ever won a ball game by refusing to mount the box and hurl his shoots, benders, curves and twisters in an effort to fool the batters and bring victory to his team. A "yellow" fellow is of very little service to any cause, whether in military, athletic, political, commercial or civic life.

Very few cases of illness are cured by "long-distance" doctors—where the ailing patients live in one section of the country, and the doctor, living in another section and unable to take the patient's pulse and scientifically and properly diagnose the case, endeavors to prescribe medicine for said patient. When a person becomes seriously ill, the doctor must be seen in person, either by the patient being carried to the physician, or the physician coming to see the patient.

The Negro race in the South is sick—not unto death, however; and those who would essay to affect a cure and place the patient (racially speaking) on the road to complete recovery, must be in a position to understand, appreciate and examine the condition of the patient and then remain on the scene and write the prescription for the necessary medicine to bring about a marked improvement in the patient's condition. Doctors from "afar," who endeavor to prescribe medicine for this ailing patient, are not to be victims of base ingratitude on the part of the Southern patient of color; but it is our opinion (knowing the South and Southerners as I do) that the "resident" physician is better situated (if he will do his holden duty without fear or favor) to render the type of service best calculated to restore the health of this racial patient.

In other words, the status of the Negro in Texas and the South must be improved principally by and through the efforts—sanely and properly directed—of Negroes with courage, vision and intelligence; Negroes who accept no place as "their place," unless that place is where they can best serve their race and the social family; Negroes who are not afraid or too cowardly to "stay in there and pitch the old horsehide," and to thus "carry on" right in the heart of Dixieland, rather than from some securely sheltered and safely protected sector far removed from the scene of daily—yes, hourly—conflict and strife.

In this brief article the writer has not attempted to throw any bouquets at himself, nor indulge in self-laudation; but merely to give, as best he possibly can, his reasons for remaining in Texas and fighting the wrongs and evils of our day and generation:

"For right is right, since God is God,
And right the day must win;
To doubt would be disloyalty;
To falter would be sin."

AN ALABAMA SHARECROPPER REMEMBERS

NED COBB

from *All God's Dangers: The Life of Nate Shaw*

1904–08, c. 1930

MAYNARD CURTIS was old man Jim Curtis's son. And durin of my correspondin Waldo Ramsey's daughter I had to go right by Mr. Maynard Curtis's house any time I went to her house. Waldo Ramsey and Mr. Curtis owned land joinin—houses didn't set over two hundred yards apart. Mr. Curtis had known of me through I used to work for his daddy—choppin cotton, pullin fodder, strictly day labor. I was well known by Maynard Curtis. So he knowed who it was correspondin this girl that lived up the road from him.

Of course, quite naturally, Mr. Curtis owned both sides of the road there, right and left; that road come along and divided his plantation. Public road; and right up above his house a piece I'd turn to my right and go out to Hannah's house.

And so he caught on to me goin over there regular and he figured I was liable to marry over there and I believe he might have heard something about it. So, me and Mr. Curtis agreed—he got at me bout buildin me a house, before we married, and I traded with him and he went on and built it. But at the time we married, in the Christmas, he didn't have the house completed. My wife's daddy told me, "Nate, go ahead and make yourself at home until Mr. Curtis gets your house finished. Stay right here in the house with us; it won't cost you a thing."

We stayed there a month and a half, until some time in February. Old man Waldo Ramsey forbid me of buyin any groceries at all. He said, "We got plenty. Just make yourself at home, you and your wife, until your house gets done."

They had two underage children, a boy and a girl, called em little Waldo and Mattie, only boy they had and the baby girl—they was in the house with us, they wasn't grown. But the rest of em—her parents didn't have but five children—the two older girls was grown and married and out of the house at that time. Old man Waldo and old lady Molly Ramsey treated me as they did their own dear children. I called the old man "Pa" and I called his wife "Ma"; Ma and Pa and not for no hearsay, but to recognize em.

Mr. Curtis soon got the house done. Just a old plantation style house, built for colored folks, no special care took of how it was built. But it'd keep you out the rain, it'd keep you out the cold; just a old common-built house, board cabin. In them days they weren't buildin no houses for white men. It was a actual fact: the white folks mixin up and one livin on the other one's place, it was quickly becomin a thing of the past in this country. They wanted all colored people on their places and they built the house accordin to the man and because it was a nigger they just put up somethin to take care of him. And the white man would cut his britches off if the nigger fooled around in that house too much. Whenever a white man built a house for a colored man he just run it up right quick like a box. No seal in that house; just box it up with lumber, didn't never box it up with a tin roof. They'd put doors to the house and sometimes they'd stick a glass window in it, but mostly a wood window. Didn't put you behind no painted wood and glass, just built a house for you to move in then go to work.

So, Mr. Curtis built me a cheap house with wood windows and put a chimney to it. We moved in the house—and when we moved in I was ready to go to work with Mr. Curtis on halves, 1907. He put me on the sorriest land he had and he took all the best. Couldn't complain, no complainin come. I was the underdog and as a colored man I taken what he prepared for me and stuck out there with him; went on to the field and went to work. And when I went to work I worked the sorriest land he had—that was the whole proposition. Land so doggone thin—and what was said about the grade of land Mr. Curtis put me on to make a crop? People would laugh and talk: never knowed about or seed a crop growed on that grade of land. They'd say, "God, that land's so poor it won't sprout unknown peas."

He worked all the land out on front of his plantation. And at the time I moved there, there wasn't a full one-horse farm cleared up on the side he gived me to work. Some of it was timbered land; some of it was swamp land, disused land.

And he had a brother-in-law, Mr. Calvin Culpepper—Mr. Curtis married a Culpepper woman, Miss Beatrice Culpepper, Mr. Calvin Culpepper's sister, Mr. John Culpepper's children. Single man, Mr. Calvin moved out from up in them hills across Sitimachas when he become of age, down over there this side of Sitimachas with his sister and brother-in-law. Mr. Curtis rented him a small one-horse farm. And he had his own animal to plow—he had a gray mare and a buggy, was all I seed Mr. Calvin Culpepper had. And Miss Beatrice, his sister, washed and ironed and cooked for him, and he lived there that year, and also 1908, in the house. Just before I left there he married Mr. Avery Brown's daughter, Miss Ruth Brown. And I moved from there in the fall of 1908, to Mr. Gus Ames' place, and Mr. Calvin Culpepper remained right on there someways and he worked all the open land that I had worked, same sorry land, workin it with his brother-in-law.

Before I moved away from there I bought Mr. Calvin's buggy. I'd scuffled to save enough off my basketmaking to buy that buggy. And before I moved away from there I had that buggy some—I'd hitch Mr. Curtis's mule to it, the mule I plowed. He called the little old mule Nate. He had two mules, a mare mule and a horse mule, both of em was good mules. Mr. Curtis plowed the mare mule; her name was Clyde. Nate was a horse mule. And Mr. Curtis would tell me, if there was some place I wanted to go, "Nate, you drive the mule you plow."

So I'd hitch Nate up on Sundays and go visitin, hitch him up and go to church. Practically whenever I went to church, I'd take Nate and hitch him to Mr. Curtis's two-horse wagon, beside of my daddy-in-law's mule, and all of us would get on that wagon and go to church, come back, stop Mr. Curtis's wagon, me and my daddy-in-law would separate the mules and he'd carry his mule home and I'd leave Mr. Curtis's mule and wagon there. But if just me and my wife was goin somewhere, I'd drive Nate alone to the buggy I bought from Mr. Calvin Culpepper.

Moved away from there and I used the buggy right on with the mule I plowed of Mr. Ames, and her name was Sally; she was a young mule, youngest of a pair of mules Mr. Ames had when I moved on his place.

I moved away from Mr. Curtis because I seed I couldn't make nothin on that sorry land he gived me to work. That was one reason. But Mr. Curtis also done this—and that was a great disconsolation to me. I bought me a cow—I had a little old poor yearlin, bull yearlin, I paid for workin for Mr. Jack Knowland in 1904. I worked hard for the man—of course, Mr. Knowland didn't give me no hard time but it just meant *work* as I was hired to him. I tried my best to please him and nothin ever come between me and Mr. Knowland. So, my daddy come over there one day—and Mr. Knowland was a cow man. He was pickin up good cows, sorry cows, and all kinds nearly. And he had a heifer yearlin there, a Jersey heifer yearlin. My daddy wanted to buy a cow and Mr. Knowland sold him that heifer *and* her calf—Jersey heifer, crumple horn. He charged my daddy sixteen dollars and a half for the both of em. I worked there and paid for em; my daddy took the cow and her calf and carried em home. My daddy kept that cow and made a good cow out of her—she was a good-blooded heifer, Jersey milk type.

So, 1904, Mr. Knowland sold the heifer and her yearlin to my daddy; my daddy had me hired to Mr. Knowland by the month. 1905, Mr. Knowland wanted to hire me right on, my daddy wouldn't let me work for him, took me back home under his administration. I worked there, had tribulations and trials with my daddy that year but I stuck there. 1906, he hired me to Mr. Jim Barbour in Apafalya and just before he done that, he gived that cow to Mr. Barbour on a debt—at forty-five dollars on the debt. And kept that calf until the time I went off to Stillwell and got me a job at the sawmill and begin to come home with money in my pocket and he standin there with his hands open, ready for it, all he could get of it. And he told me one Saturday night when I come in off my job, "Son, I owe Mr. Roy Bacon in Apafalya—" givin him money and he wanted me to trace around and pay off his debts for him—"I owe Mr. Roy Bacon in Apafalya—" that's where he traded, at Mr. Roy Bacon's a whole lot and at Mr. Richard Tucker's, them was his two main places to trade. So, I was comin backwards and forwards every other week, givin him money; told me one

Saturday night, "Son, I owe Mr. Roy Bacon in Apafalya five dollars and sixty cents and if you'll pay the debt for me, I'll give you Dolly's calf."

1906, and he'd paid Mr. Knowland for the cow and her calf both with my labor in 1904. I thought, when he done it—I didn't have no better sense than to think it—as close as I was to grown, I'd get a good part of that, maybe I might stand a chance to get the cow. Shit! Get nothin. Gived the cow to Mr. Jim Barbour on his debt. He still had that bull yearlin there but he hadn't growed worth a damn hardly. It was the heifer's first calf and as a rule, unless they're mighty well treated, a heifer's first calf don't grow good—knotty and small. If you just leave off a little of that care for your animal, he aint goin to prosper. That's what my daddy done. Didn't pay no attention to that calf, but he made a nice cow out of that cow. But he gived that cow away on his debt—that put the cow gone, out the way. He kept the little old bull yearlin there but he never did grow good; he never would amount to nothin.

That Monday mornin when I went to Apafalya to catch the train for Stillwell, first thing I done—I thought that was a dickens of a deal but I went right on just like I was due to do—paid my daddy's debt for five dollars and sixty cents. And in the end of the deal he gived me the yearlin. But I looked at it this way: done paid Mr. Knowland, worked hard and paid him for the cow and calf both and my daddy done sold the cow and I had to pay for the calf again. Calf weren't worth a bit more than what I paid neither.

Well, I took the calf when I married and carried her on to Mr. Curtis's place. I kept the calf a few months in Mr. Curtis's pasture—he let me pasture the calf. One day, in the fall of the year, I traded the yearlin—he done picked up but still he weren't nothin but a little knot—traded him to Mr. Carl Fagan for a nice heifer and she was with calf, 1907. Mr. Fagan lived at that time just about a mile west of Pottstown; he was a farmin man. I put a rope on that yearlin, not valuin the yearlin at all, and drove him over there. Mr. Fagan looked at him and told me he'd trade with me. I give him twelve dollars and a half, to boot, between that bull calf and that heifer. I'd call that reasonable. Taken that heifer home and in a few months she come in.

I made somethin out of that heifer, I improved her by takin care of her. She made me a milk cow that everybody that seed her wanted her if they had any use for a cow at all. Now I aint goin to lie: she was a mischievous heifer, she'd get out and ramble. She got out one day in Mr. Curtis's cotton—had his cotton growin right there close to his house and barn. She got out in his cotton and he was fractious as the devil. He runned out there and commenced chunkin rocks at the cow and he hit her on the bone of one of her front legs and he broke her down practically. The cow limped and hopped several weeks after that.

He told me, "Nate, I hated to do it, but through a mistake I throwed and hit her with a rock."

Well, the rock cut her hide and left a print. She hopped, she limped—I doctored her and eventually she got over it. 1908, I moved to Mr. Gus Ames', I carried that cow—that calf she had, I sold it; it was a bull calf, had no use for a bull calf at that present time.

I didn't make two good bales of cotton the first year I stayed with Mr. Curtis. Sorry land, scarce fertilize, Mr. Curtis not puttin out, riskin much on me and I a workin little old fool, too. I knowed how to plow—catch the mule out the lot, white man's mule, bridle him, go out there and set my plow the way I wanted—I knowed how to do it. Bout a bale and a half was what I made.

The second year he went out there and rented some piney wood land from Mr. Lemuel Tucker, sixteen acres bout a half mile from his plantation and he put me on it. Well, it was kind of thin but it was a king over Mr. Curtis's land. I worked it all in cotton; what little corn I had I planted on Mr. Curtis's place. Well, I made six pretty good bales of cotton out there for Mr. Curtis and myself. When I got done gatherin, wound up, by havin to buy a little stuff from Mr. Curtis at the start, in 1907—it sort of pulled the blinds over my eyes. It took all them six bales of cotton to pay Mr. Curtis. In the place of prosperin I was on a standstill. Second year I was married it took all I made on Mr. Tucker's place, by Mr. Curtis havin rented it from Mr. Tucker for me, to pay up 1908's debts and also 1907's debts—as I say, by me buyin a right smart to start me off to housekeepin, cleaned me. I had not a dollar left out of the cotton.

And also, Mr. Curtis come in just before I moved off his place —I was determined to pay him and leave him straight; in fact, I reckon I just had to do it because he'd a requested it of me, movin from his place, clean up and leave myself clear of him.

Mr. Curtis had Mr. Buck Thompson to furnish me groceries. Mr. Curtis knowed all of what Mr. Thompson was lettin me have; kept a book on me. See, he was standin for everything Mr. Thompson gived me; he paid Mr. Thompson and I paid him—the deal worked that way—out of my crop. So he made somethin off my grocery bill besides gettin half my crop when the time come.

Took part of my corn to pay him. He come to my crib, him and Mr. Calvin Culpepper come together to my crib and got my corn, so much of it. And what I had he got the best of it, to finish payin him on top of them six bales of cotton.

Then I moved to Mr. Gus Ames', 1908. Mr. Ames' land was a little better than Mr. Curtis's, but it was poor. Worked his pet land hisself and whatever he made off me, why, that was a bounty for him. I didn't make enough there to help me.

Hannah was dissatisfied at it, too. We talked it over and our talk was this: we knew that we weren't accumulatin nothin, but the farmin affairs was my business, I had to stand up to em as a man. And she didn't worry me bout how we was doin —she knowed it weren't my fault. We was just both dissatisfied. So, we taken it under consideration and went on and she was stickin right with me. She didn't work my heart out in the deal. I wanted to work in a way to please her and satisfy her. She had a book learnin, she was checkin with me at every stand. She was valuable to me and I knowed it. And I was eager to get in a position where I could take care of her and our children better than my daddy taken care of his wives and children.

Mr. Curtis and Mr. Ames both, they'd show me my land I had to work and furnish me—far as fertilize to work that crop, they'd furnish me what *they* wanted to; didn't leave it up to me. That's what hurt—they'd furnish me the amount of fertilize they wanted regardless to what I wanted. I quickly seed, startin off with Mr. Curtis in 1907, it weren't goin to be enough. First year I worked for him and the last year too he didn't allow me to use over twenty-two hundred pounds of guano—it come in two-hundred-pound sacks then—that's all he'd back me up for all the land I worked, cotton and corn. It was enough to start with but not enough to do any more. Really, I oughta been usin twice that amount. Told him, too, but he said, "Well, at the present time and system, Nate, you can't risk too much."

I knowed I oughta used more fertilize to make a better crop—if you puts nothin in you gets nothin, all the way through. It's nonsense what they gived me—Mr. Curtis and Mr. Ames, too—but I was a poor colored man, young man too, and I had to go by their orders. It wasn't that I was ignorant of what I had to do, just, "Can't take too much risk, can't take too much risk." Now if you got anything that's profitable to you and you want to keep it and prosper with that thing, whatever it is, however you look for your profit—say it's a animal; you're due to look for your profit by treatin him right, givin him plenty to eat so he'll grow and look like somethin. Or if you fertilize your crop right, if you go out there and work a row of cotton—that's evidence of proof—I have, in my farmin, missed fertilizin a row and it stayed under, too. Them other rows growed up over it and produced more. If you don't put down the fertilize that crop aint goin to prosper. But you had to do what the white man said, livin here in this country. And if you made enough to pay him, that was all he cared for; just make enough to pay him what you owed him and anything he made over that, why, he was collectin on his risk. In my condition, and the way I see it for everybody, if you don't make enough to have some left you aint done nothin, except givin the other fellow your labor. That crop out there goin to prosper enough for him to get his and get what I owe him; he's makin his profit but he aint goin to let me rise. If he'd treat me right and treat my crop right, I'd make more and he'd get more—and a heap of times he'd get it all! That white man gettin all he lookin for, all he put out in the spring, gettin it all back in the fall. But what am I gettin for my labor? I aint gettin nothin. I learnt that right quick: it's easy to understand if a man will look at it.

I worked four years on halves, two with Mr. Curtis. I was just able when I moved from his place to leave him paid. What did I have left? Nothin. Of course, if I'm left with nothin, no cash in my pocket, I can look back and say what I paid for I got. But what little I did get I had to work like the devil to get it. It didn't profit me nothin. What little stuff I bought to go in my house—it set in my house! What is that worth to me in my business out yonder? It aint prosperin me noway in my work. I'm losin out yonder to get a little in my house. Well, that's nothin; that aint to be considered. You want some cash above your debts; if you don't get it you lost, because you gived that man your labor and you can't get it back.

Now it's right for me to pay you for usin what's yours—your land, stock, plow tools, fertilize. But how much should I pay? The answer ought to be closely seeked. How much is a man due to pay out? Half his crop? A third part of his crop? And how much is he due to keep for hisself? You got a right to your part—rent; and I got a right to mine. But who's the man ought to decide how much? The one that owns the property or the one that works it?

—

If you want to sell your cotton at once, you take it to the market, carry it to the Apafalya cotton market and they'll sample it. Cotton buyin man cuts a slug in the side of your bale, reaches in there and pulls the first of it out the way and get him a handful, just clawin in there. He'll look over that sample, grade that cotton—that's his job. What kind of grade do it make? You don't know until he tells you. If it's short staple, the devil, your price is cut on that cotton. Color matters too, and the way it was ginned—some gins cuts up the cotton, ruins the staple.

They had names for the cotton grades—grade this, or grade that or grade the other. Didn't do no good to argue with the man if you didn't agree with the grade. Thing for you to do if he graded your cotton, examined it and gived you a low bid, take it to the next man.

Much of it is a humbug just like everything else, this gradin business. Some of em don't pay you what that cotton's worth a pound. They want long staple, clean cotton: the cleaner and the prettier it is and the nearer it comes to the specification of the staple they lookin for, the more they'll offer you. Generally, it's a top limit to that price and that's what they call the price cotton is bringin that year. If it's forty-cent cotton or six-cent cotton, it don't depend much on *your* cotton. It's a market price and it's set before you ever try to sell your cotton, and it's set probably before you gin your cotton and before you gather it or grow it or even plant your seed.

You take that cotton and carry it around to the cotton buyers. You might walk in that market buildin to a certain cotton buyer and he'll take your sample and look it over, look it over, give it a pull or two and he just might if he's very anxious for cotton, offer you a good price for it. But if he's in no hurry to buy your cotton and he gives you a price you don't like you can go to another buyer.

Heap of em buyin that cotton to speculate; he got plenty of money, wants to make more money, he buyin that cotton for himself and he don't care what company buys it from him. Maybe he might be buyin for a speculatin company, a company what does business in speculation. Or he might be buyin for a company that uses that cotton. Or if he can handle the matter, he buys for two companies.

Niggers' cotton didn't class like a white man's cotton with a heap of em. Used to be, when I was dealin with them folks in Apafalya, some of em you could have called em crooks if you wanted to; they acted in a way to bear that name, definitely. Give a white man more for his cotton than they do you.

I've had white men to meet me on the streets with a cotton sample in my hand, say, "Hello, Nate, you sellin cotton today?" White men, farmers like myself, private men; some of em was poor white men.

I'd tell em, "Yes sir, I'm tryin. I can't look like get what my cotton's worth."

"What you been offered?"

"Well, Mr. So-and-so—"

"O, I see here such-and-such a one offered you so-and-so-and-so—"

Heap of times the scaper that I offered to sell him my cotton had a knack of puttin his bid on the paper that the cotton was wrapped up in. I didn't want him to do that. The next man would see how much this one bid me and he wouldn't go above it.

And so, I'd have my cotton weighed and I'd go up and down the street with my sample. Meet a white man, farmin man like myself, on the street; he'd see what I been offered for my sample—the buyer's marks would be on the wrapper—or I'd tell him. And he'd take that sample, unwrap it, look at it;

he'd say, "Nate, I can beat you with your own cotton, I can get more for it than that."

Aint that enough to put your boots on! The same sample. He'd say, "Let me take your sample and go around in your place. I can beat what they offered you."

Take that cotton and go right to the man that had his bid on it and he'd raise it; right behind where I was, had been, and get a better bid on it. I've gived a white man my sample right there on the streets of Apafalya; he'd go off and come back. Sometime he'd say, "Well, Nate, I helped you a little on it but I couldn't help you much."

And sometime he'd get a good raise on it with another fellow out yonder. He'd bring my sample back to me with a bid on it. "Well, Nate, I knowed I could help you on that cotton."

That was happenin all through my farmin years: from the time I stayed on the Curtis place, and when I moved to the Ames place, and when I lived with Mr. Reeve, and when I moved down on Sitimachas Creek with Mr. Tucker, and when I lived up there at Two Forks on the Stark place, and when I moved down on the Pollard place and stayed there nine years. Colored man's cotton weren't worth as much as a white man's cotton less'n it come to the buyer in the white man's hands. But the colored man's labor—that was worth more to the white man than the labor of his own color because it cost him less and he got just as much for his money.

ELIZABETH LAWSON

They Shall Not Die! Stop the Legal Lynching: The Story of Scottsboro in Pictures

1932

INTRODUCTION

Scottsboro is a small town with a population of 2,000, located in the Eastern part of the state of Alabama. The eyes of the world are today focused on this typical Southern village, with its backward hill people. Overnight, all over the world, the name of Scottsboro was written big upon the front pages of newspapers large and small, and uttered by the lips of black and white, native and foreign people.

The Scottsboro case has been a thunderbolt that has moved the Negro masses and advanced white workers into stubborn struggle to resist the sharpening terror. It has hurled these peoples into powerful mass action. It has ripped the cover off the monstrous system of national oppression of the Negro peoples, exposing it in all its vicious nakedness. It has brought quaking fear to the murderous landowners and capitalists and their hangers-on.

Why such mighty mass action? Why such furious mass anger? Why have the white ruling class officials of the state of Alabama trembled in their boots upon receiving thousands of protest telegrams and resolutions from the angered masses all over the world? Why have government officials in foreign countries, and especially in the United States, hidden in deadly fear before the mass protest demonstrations of Negro and white toilers against this hideous frame-up? Why have mayors and other city officials been forced by the mass pressure of the working class to send their protests to the Alabama authorities? Why have scores of prominent men and women—famous writers, scientists and artists such as Albert Einstein, Theodore Dreiser, Langston Hughes, Edna Vincent Millay, Lincoln Steffens, John Dos Passos, Franz Boas, Malcolm Cowley, Maxim

Gorky, Leo Tolstoi, Eugene Gordon, Henri Barbusse, Sherwood Anderson, Waldo Frank, Mary Heaton Vorse, Michael Gold, Charles R. Walker, Floyd Dell, and many others—joined with the hosts of angered and aroused masses in protest and demanded the immediate release of the innocent boys? Why have the workers, black and white, faced the nightsticks and tear-gas bombs of the bosses' savage and blood-thirsty police, the gunfire of uniformed thugs, to protest the Scottsboro verdict? Why have the boss-controlled reformist organizations, the National Association for the Advancement of Colored People, the International Ministers Alliance, etc., betrayed at every turn the nine Scottsboro boys? What is the role of the working class organizations of Negro and white, the League of Struggle for Negro Rights and the International Labor Defense, in the case, together with many other organizations?

These questions of vital importance, which concern the lives and liberty of the nine boys, are answered graphically in the following pages, in the pictures and the running story that accompanies them.

The Scottsboro case is a symbol of the bloody reign of American white ruling class persecution of the Negroes. It reveals the robbery and slavery of the Negro masses. It lays bare the fact that the barbarous oppression of the Negroes is a link in the chain of American capitalist exploitation and plunder of the entire working class. It has thrown the light on the close relationship between the Negro misleaders and organizations, e. g. the N. A. A. C. P., and the white ruling class, in their betrayal of the struggles of the Negro masses.

Revolutionary organizations are building up a mighty mass defense campaign against this special terror. They have appealed to the world's toilers to join the united front movement of the Negro masses and black and white workers. The response to this appeal has shown the willingness and readiness of broad sections of the working people to struggle, to take the streets and demonstrate, before American consuls and embassies and ruling class officials, demanding the immediate release of the nine boys.

The toiling masses throughout the world will not allow the capitalists and their courts in Alabama to carry through unnoticed their intended legal lynching of these nine victims of

American "democracy." Thousands upon thousands of workers have joined the mass defense movement and have pledged themselves to fight to save these boys as part of the struggle of the working class for better conditions.

The compilation of the facts in this pamphlet has been the result of the energetic labor of worker-artists and worker-writers. This pamphlet can help to build up the defense movement and spread broadcast the revolutionary working-class ideas of solidarity of black and white, and build a fighting alliance of black and white workers as the only method that will force the bosses to open the prison doors that hold these youthful victims.

The sketches in this pamphlet were drawn by a worker-artist, A. Refregier, a member of the John Reed Club, and were first printed in the LIBERATOR, the fighting organ of the League of Struggle for Negro Rights. The running story that accompanies them was written by Elizabeth Lawson, Managing Editor of the LIBERATOR.

The toiling masses throughout the world are asked to read this pamphlet, arm themselves with the facts in the Scottsboro lynch frame-up, pass them on to their employed and unemployed worker-brothers, and assist the Negro masses and white workers to build up this mighty mass protest movement for the unconditional release of the nine Negro boys.

B. D. AMIS.

THE STORY OF SCOTTSBORO IN PICTURES

In 1931, in the Southern part of the United States, where Negroes are still held in virtual slavery and subjected to the most brutal terror, there lived nine young Negro boys of working-class families.

In Chattanooga, Tennessee, lived Haywood Patterson, 17 years old; Eugene Williams, 13; and the brothers Roy and Andy Wright, 17 and 14 years old. In Atlanta, Georgia, lived Clarence Norris, 19; Charlie Weems, 20; and Ozie Powell, 14.

Olen Montgomery, 17 years old, lived in Monroe, Georgia, and Willie Roberson, 17, lived in Columbus, Georgia.

Like millions of other young and adult workers, these boys were out of work. Dying capitalism can no longer provide jobs for its workers. Tens of thousands of working-class families are starving today. The families of these boys were starving. Negro workers are always hardest hit in times of unemployment and mass misery. These nine boys tried desperately to help their starving families. But there was no work to be found. Conditions went from bad to worse. No food. Rent due. Mothers and little sisters and brothers hungry, facing death by starvation.

The nine boys determined to leave home to try to find work. Their families gave reluctant permission.

On March 25, 1931, a freight train running through Jackson County, Alabama, carried many "passengers," most of them being jobless Negro workers bound for Memphis and other places in search of jobs on the river boats.

Among these "passengers" were the nine young Negro boys. They had jumped on the train at various places. Most of them had never seen each other before. They travelled in different parts of the train.

There were also on the freight train seven white men and two girls dressed in men's clothing—mill girls who had been forced into prostitution by low wages and lack of work.

A white boy moving about the train pushed against a Negro worker, who protested. All of the workers on the freight, white and Negro, would be branded by the bosses as bums. But so rigid is the system of Jim Crowism in the South, that even on freight trains "niggers" must "keep in their place." In the fight that followed between some of the white boys and some of the Negroes, the Negroes got the better of the scrap and the whites jumped off the train.

Their minds inflamed by the race hatred poison of the bosses and the licking they had been given, the white boys on leaving the train went to a station and told the story of the fight—in their own way, of course. This story was telegraphed to Paint Rock, Alabama, where the train was due to stop.

Now, in the South, it is a "crime" for a Negro to defend himself when attacked by a white man. The bosses determined to make an example of the Negroes. A deputy sheriff and many deputized mountaineers and business men surrounded the train when it stopped at Paint Rock.

The Negroes who had been involved in the fight had jumped off the train before it reached Paint Rock. The only Negroes left on the train were the nine young Negro boys. A few white men and the two white girl hoboes dressed in men's clothing were still on the train. Armed deputies arrested the nine Negro boys. The charge at first was that of fighting with white boys.

In searching the train, the deputies saw three white hoboes getting out of the gondola car. But two turned out to be women in men's clothing.

Here were all of the elements for a fine Southern frame-up! The charge against the Negro boys of beating up the white boys was quickly dropped. Eagerly the bosses raised the old lying charge of "rape."

The Negro masses were showing signs of revolt against their terrible conditions. Negroes were even daring to demand payment of their wages! And most horrible in the eyes of the bosses —white and Negro workers were uniting in struggle under revolutionary leadership in some sections even of the South. The carefully built-up wall of race prejudice with which the bosses seek to separate white and Negro toilers was crumbling!

Here was the chance to throw nine dead young bodies into the face of the Negro masses! Here was a fine chance to terrorize the Negro workers and poor farmers. Here was a chance to stir up race hatred among the white masses by painting the Negro workers as "born rapists," by pretending that white women were always in danger from Negro "rapists."

And trade was dull. A lynching or a lynch trial would bring out great crowds and help the business men.

And—thought the lynchers—nobody would bother about the fate of nine "niggers"—and working-class "niggers" at that!

The two white prostitutes, when first questioned, said plainly that the Negro boys had nothing to do with them. But the state solicitor urged them on. "Go ahead and say they did it," he told the two women. "That boy attacked you, didn't he? Go ahead and say that he did it!" And finally the girls, both of whom were well known in Chattanooga and elsewhere as prostitutes, were prevailed upon to "identify" the boys and to tell an unbelievable story of "rape."

The two white women now ceased to be arrested vagrants and became "pure" and holy examples of "outraged white womanhood."

The boys were thrown into the Gladsden jail, where they were brutally beaten with clubs and blackjacks until they presented a picture of bruised heads, swollen and discolored eyes, cut lips and blood streaming from many wounds.

Finally they were arraigned at the County seat, Scottsboro. Monday, April 6, was selected as the day of the trial, because it was "Fair Day," or "Horse Swapping Day," when thousands of mountaineers would come into town.

On April 6, the little town of Scottsboro, inhabited by two thousand people, held ten thousand mountaineers, many of them armed. The usually deserted streets were crowded with automobiles.

The boss-incited lynch-mob of the most backward people packed the court-house and surrounded it. A brass band was provided by the bosses to serenade the jury as soon as guilty verdicts could be brought in.

The whole Scottsboro trial was just a legal substitute for a lynching. The judge, and a hand-picked jury of white business men and backward mountaineers, were to act as lynchers; the court-room would take the place of the woods, where lynchings are usually committed; and instead of a rope, there would be waiting—the state's electric chair.

The nine victims, caught in the trap of boss-justice, were denied the right to inform their parents of their plight, denied the right to choose a lawyer. The only lawyers the boys had were two who actually helped in the lynch frame-up. Stephen Roddy, the drunkard Klansman sent by the boot-licking Ministers Alliance of Chattanooga, stated openly that he was there merely as an "observer."

Inside the court a ghastly farce was played. Within a few hours, without the calling of a single witness for the defense outside of the framed-up boys themselves, and on the unsupported evidence of the two white prostitutes, the first two Negro lads, Charlie Weems and Clarence Norris, were sentenced to die. In quick succession, Haywood Patterson and then five more in a group, quickly followed by the last little boy, Roy Wright, were put on "trial." All but Roy were swiftly sentenced to death. In Roy's case, the bosses made a "mere" life imprisonment in southern dungeons for this child. A small minority of the jurors held out for a life imprisonment for Roy. This caused a mistrial to be declared. The brass band furnished by the mill-bosses hailed the first death verdict. The boss-incited, backward crowd cheered. The jurors listened, and speeded through the other death verdicts.

Little Roy was thrown into Birmingham County Jail to await a new "trial." The eight boys railroaded to the electric chair were hurried off to Montgomery, there to begin the torture of waiting in the death cells at Kilby prison.

But now a furious storm of protest broke over the heads of the astonished boss-lynchers. The Communist Party and its press had exposed the lynch frame-up. The League of Struggle for Negro Rights, the International Labor Defense and the Communist Party roused the masses, black and white, to angry protests. A mass defense movement was built up and a mass fight begun against the legal lynchings and for the unconditional release of the nine innocent boys.

On May 1, 1931, more than 300,000 Negro and white workers, East and West, North and South, demonstrated in 110 cities in the United States, demanding the release of the Scottsboro victims. Conferences of working-class organizations met in many cities to build a mass defense for the boys. One of the most remarkable of these conferences was the All-Southern Scottsboro United Front Defense Conference held in Chattanooga, May 31, 1931. It was attended by over 200 Negro and white *Southern* delegates. Everywhere, the white workers were coming to a recognition of the fact that the Scottsboro lynch verdicts were an attack on the entire working-class, white and black. Everywhere, they rallied to the building of a fighting alliance of white and Negro workers against the white ruling class.

Tens of thousands of telegrams were sent to Gov. B. M. Miller of Montgomery, Alabama, demanding the release of the Scottsboro lynch-verdict victims. In faraway countries

—the Soviet Union, Germany, France, Cuba, Mexico, etc., millions of workers added thunderous voices to the roar of protest.

Competent lawyers were engaged by the International Labor Defense, an organization of Negro and white workers, to defend the boys.

Frightened by the sight of Negro and white workers joining hands to fight against the lynch verdicts, the bosses, North and South, tried desperately to stop the protest meetings and telegrams, to prevent the building of a mass defense movement.

In this attempt, the bosses were ably aided by the leadership of the National Association for the Advancement of Colored People. This group, far too respectable to enter into the case of nine poor working-class boys charged with "rape," had not stirred a finger until the fury of the masses forced them to act. They then tried to head the movement in order to behead it. They refused to have anything to do with the organizations defending the boys, the International Labor Defense and other groups. Shamelessly they lied about the facts of the case, tried to cover up the hideous crime of the bosses against the toiling masses.

The N. A. A. C. P. screamed with fury—but not at the lynchers! It screamed at the workers, Negro and white, because they were throwing a glaring spotlight upon the lynchers and exposing the whole rotten capitalist system. More—the workers were exposing the alliance of the N. A. A. C. P. with the boss-lynchers and their system.

Taking the fight for a new trial for the boys to the Alabama Supreme Court, the International Labor Defense exposed the Scottsboro case as a murderous frame-up.

The bosses had thought that no one would care about the fate of nine jobless "niggers." And now were heard the voices of millions, roaring protest.

The bosses had hoped to throw in the faces of the downtrodden Negroes, nine charged young bodies, as another warning to these oppressed masses. And now these same nine boys have become symbols of a relentless fight of the Negro masses for their rights.

Always the bosses had tried to divide the white workers from the Negroes—and here were white workers, taking their places in the very forefront of the struggle for the freedom of nine black boys!

Scottsboro stands today as a symbol of the national oppression of the Negroes, of the bosses' oppression of the whole working-class. The cause of the nine Scottsboro boys is the cause of all the workers, Negro and white.

The working-class must renew and intensify its protests. A fighting alliance of Negro and white workers, giant militant demonstrations, a flood of protest telegrams that will throw fear into the white rulers, the building of a powerful mass defense movement of the Negro masses and black and white workers—these alone will break open the doors of Kilby Prison and free the nine framed Scottsboro boys.

THE ADVOCATE
Calls Negro Masses to Unite

June 19, 1932

CALLS NEGRO MASSES TO UNITE

FORD, FIRST NEGRO VICE-PRESIDT'L NOMINEE SAYS COMMUNISM RACE'S ONLY SALVATION

FORD CALLS UPON MASSES TO UNITE FORCES

ERIE, PA., JUNE 16—James W. Ford, Vice-Presidential candidate of the Communist Party, issued here today the following statement:

"To the Negro Masses:

Starvation and misery confront the workers, farmers and oppressed masses, Negro and white. The ruling class refuses to grant any relief and when the pennies are doled out the Negro worker is greatly discriminated against. The Negro masses are again being appealed to by the capitalist politicians and their own misleaders for votes. And in return these politicians will give us what they have given us in the past: starvation, lynching, war, jim-crow, and death. We, on the other hand, the oppressed people of America, must turn this election campaign into a struggle against hunger, for bread and jobs; for unemployment and Social insurance without discrimination as to color; for equal political, economic and social equality for the Negro and self determination for the millions of Negroes in the Black Belt. We, the Negro people, must join in firm solidarity under the banners of the Communist Party for this struggle, and ultimately victory will be ours."

ABOLISHING CONFEDERATE MONUMENTS

THE CHICAGO DEFENDER

What Do You Say About It?

September 10, 1932

WHAT DO YOU SAY ABOUT IT?

A question of general interest will be asked in this column each week. The Chicago Defender invites answers from its many readers. Letters should be brief—not over 100 words. A postcard will serve for your reply. Sign name, address and city.

—

THIS WEEK'S QUESTION:

Would you favor a federal law to abolish all patriotic monuments erected in the South to the memory of Confederate soldiers?

I am highly in favor of such a law. It is with much regret that the federal government tolerates the unpatriotic spirit of the South to the Stars and Stripes. The rebels are extolled as gentlemen of the first rank in every so-called Christian institution below the Mason-Dixon line. Every white Y. M. C. A. is a Confederate museum. There you see the sword of Stonewall Jackson, or the badge of Robert E. Lee, also the flag carried against the Union forces. Rebels should not be honored, and any section of the country producing traitors should be ashamed of them.

SPENCER HILT.
Columbus, Ga.

—

Yes, I am in favor of a federal law to abolish all patriotic monuments erected in the South to the memory of Confederate soldiers. Every time children of the men look at the monuments it gives them a greater desire to put forth stronger efforts to carry out the wishes of their forefathers. If those monuments weren't standing the white South wouldn't be so encouraged to practice hate and discrimination against our people. They stand as emblems of hate and envy. In the first place the South shouldn't have been permitted to erect them.

JOHN F. UPCHER.
Omaha, Neb.

The dirtiest blot on the pages of American history was written by rebel statesmen of the South. Why honor them? If monuments to Confederate veterans, despoilers of the American flag, are in order anywhere in this country then congress should vote funds to erect a monument to the memory of Benedict Arnold, the arch traitor. The South has always held this nation back. America can never expect to advance as a highly civilized people as long as it erects statues to its most dishonorable citizens. Only fools would want to glorify men who fought in defense of human slavery.

SCOTT W. BOYDSTON.
Birmingham, Ala.

The South has never admitted defeat because the North dealt too kindly with the rebel leaders after the Appomattox surrender. Jeff Davis should have been shot at sunrise and his whole staff imprisoned for life. To honor these skunks with monuments for the future generation to gaze upon is the rawest insult to the memory of noble men like Lincoln and Grant. Some idiot even had the nerve to propose that we place Robert E. Lee's picture on our paper money. What a travesty on freedom and justice. I fail to see the good to result from glorifying traitors to this country. I favor a federal law to abolish these monuments.

M. K. QUIGLEY.
Marietta, Ga.

America should move forward by showing disgust for that element of citizens who tried to drag the Stars and Stripes in the dust. It is a blot on civilization to think that at this time and day we are faced with granites that depict men who attempted to perpetuate human slavery. Pride, if nothing more, should force the South to discontinue lauding traitors to the cause of the Union.

MARSHFIELD GREGG.
Waynesboro, Ga.

"A BLOODY CARNIVAL" IN MARYLAND

BALTIMORE AFRO-AMERICAN

The Lynching of George Armwood

October 28, 1933

ROMAN HOLIDAY AS ARMWOOD IS HANGED, BURNED

PRINCESS ANNE, Md.—This town took on a festive atmosphere when a mob, estimated at 2,000, participated in the lynching of George Armwood, Wednesday night.

Four teachers of the public school who were bold enough to venture out in an automobile witnessed the mob howling and stamping and creating a general disorder while state police looked on.

Lieutenant Ruxton K. Ridgeley, white, who had charge of the state troops, told the AFRO that although he had orders to shoot to kill, he could not permit his men to use anything other than their fists.

The crowd assailed the enforcers of the law with bricks and whatever other weapons happened to come into their hands.

After they had succeeded in taking the prisoner from the jail, many of them went home for small children and brought them to view the scene.

WATCHED THE "BARBECUE"

A little girl who protested against watching was scored by her mother and told to come and "watch the N—— being barbecued."

Another man, when asked by his small son what was a lynching, was about to reply when he discovered the house near which he was passing had colored residents and were listening so he refrained.

All in all, it had the general atmosphere of a bloody carnival. Boys just out of their teens were seen to help in wielding the battering ram which demolished the door of the jail.

A student who lives nearby declared that he heard an

anguished cry of "My God, it ain't me!" when attackers went in search of the victim and got into the wrong cell.

There seems to be a general atmosphere of tension on the streets of Princess Anne, and reporters from the AFRO were frequently warned by state police to avoid being conspicuous. Nevertheless, representatives persisted in gaining admittance to the inquest, which was held on Thursday morning.

One of the passing young white women designated an AFRO reporter with the audible phrase, "That's one of them," when he passed through the door of the Washington Hotel where the activities of the previous night were being freely discussed by an assembled group of whites.

Colored people who ventured on the courthouse side of the main street heard groups of disheveled whites sneer and wisecrack about the death of Armwood.

MOB MEMBERS KNEW PREY WAS FEEBLE-MINDED

BY CLARENCE MITCHELL

PRINCESS ANNE, Md.—George Armwood, 22, who was murdered by Eastern Shore whites on Wednesday night, was an old offender, according to some of the town's prominent residents.

Some years ago, Armwood is said to have raped a woman of our race, but escaped penalty of the law when white people for whom he was working declared that he was a "good boy" and they would be responsible for him.

He was generally recognized as a feeble-minded person.

UNDERTAKER REFUSED TO SERVE

After the crime, a civil officer called John M. Dennis, prominent Princess Anne undertaker, and asked him to take care of the mutilated body of Armwood. The request was met by a refusal on the grounds that it was the city's duty to remove the murdered man.

The final way of meeting the issue was to toss the body into a lumber yard owned by Mrs. D. M. Doughtery, white, who registered violent protest against this in the morning.

Silent groups of our people on their way to work, or with nothing in particular in view, solemnly gazed at the horribly-mangled corpse which had been stripped of all clothing and was covered with two sacks.

The skin of George Armwood was scorched and blackened while his face had suffered many blows from sharp and heavy instruments. A cursory glance revealed that one ear was missing and his tongue, between his clenched teeth, gave evidence of his great agony before death. There is no adequate description of the mute evidence of gloating on the part of whites who gathered to watch the effect upon our people.

Some of the school children who were bold enough to venture out carried a reporter to the high school and explained on the way that most of the people were afraid to come out during the night but a few of them had been seen darting through alleys and dark streets when the activity of the mob was at its height.

MOTHER'S HEART IS BROKEN FROM LYNCH TRAGEDY

Told on Day of Crime Son Would Be Safe in Jail.

POSSE BROKE IN WITH SHOTGUNS

Saw Men Dragging Youth Across Field.

BY LEVI JOLLEY

[*Staff Correspondent*]

MANOKOO, Md.—A broken-hearted mother sank into a chair in abject resignation when rumors that had drifted to her ears concerning the fate of her son were confirmed when AFRO reporters informed Mrs. Etta Armwood, 40, that her son, George Armwood, 22, had been lynched Wednesday night.

A sixteen-mile dash into the almost barren area of the Eastern Shore, over dirt, cement, and mud roads to a dilapidated two-story building, sadly in need of repairs, brought Mrs.

Armwood the horrible tidings of the death of her son, the night before, at the hands of a mob.

Mrs. Armwood, who admitted that she seldom went to Princess Anne, declared that she had been in the town just the day before, several hours before her son was lynched, and was assured that he would be safe. Although she visited officials, the mother stated that she did not see her son.

After becoming reconciled to the tragedy, Mrs. Armwood told of her son's life.

Starting off very composedly the mother stated that George was born at Westover, Maryland, February 28, 1911.

GAVE SON TO WHITES

"During his childhood," she said, "George was always quiet. When very young, he was inclined toward athletics. He attended the public schools at Manokoo, Md., and remained there until he was 15 years of age. After that, Mr. John H. Richardson, white, and his wife requested that George be given to them."

"Mr. Richardson, as you know," she said, "is the man who was accused of sheltering and assisting my son to escape. George is the oldest of my three children, the next two being Clifford, who is 20, and Irema, 17. During his entire life, he has given me little trouble. I have prayed to the Lord that He would protect my son as I knew that his mental condition was not the best."

Apparently grief-stricken at this point of her story, Mrs. Armwood went on to describe her first knowledge of the affair.

BROKE INTO HOME

"It was Monday afternoon and I was standing in the kitchen of my home here when 13 men, with guns, revolvers and rifles, broke into the home and, without a word to me, went to the second floor and conducted a search.

"When I questioned them about it, they told me they were looking for George, who had attacked some woman a few miles from here. The last I had seen of my son George was Sunday when he made his usual visit home.

"It was sometime later that they brought George across the field from Mr. Richardson's home. Their conduct toward him forced me to go to the second floor as I feared that they would kill him there. It was only by persuasion from a sheriff that they did not.

"The death of my son is horrible, but God knows I did everything possible for him and his safety. Had he been sick and died here, I would not feel so badly."

At this point of her story, the mother began weeping violently and, midst tears and sobs, continued:

"He didn't have a chance, not even to repent if he did attack this woman. My heart is broken, and I shall never recover from the shock. I was unaware of his death until you reporters came, but the sight of you made me fear that something had happened to him. I can only live now for my other two children. This thing shall worry me the rest of my life.

"I have not been notified by any of the officials of the city as to what has happened. I do not know where his body is now or what to do."

It was then that AFRO reporters volunteered to make necessary arrangements for his funeral.

HOME WAS NEAT

The information had been given the heart-broken mother, in a room which served as both kitchen and living room. In this large, barren inclosure there was an old organ, a cot, a large, flat-top stove, a kitchen table covered with oil cloth, and four chairs, including a rocker.

Mrs. Armwood was neatly dressed in a pink flowered gingham dress while her daughter, Miss Irema Armwood, wore a similar outfit. The dilapidated home, despite its aged condition and the poor surroundings and furniture, was neat and clean.

On the stove, apparently what was to consist of their breakfast, were seven slices of sweet potatoes. On the rear of the stove was a pot containing either tea or coffee. When reporters entered the house with Joshua Benson, the woman's brother, the daughter was slicing bread. When informed that the two men were reporters, the young woman stopped and did not resume her breakfast.

The family readily consented to be photographed, the mother fixing her hair and changing shoes, apparently put on her best.

ARMWOOD QUIT SCHOOL IN 5TH GRADE, SAYS PAL

BY LEVI JOLLEY

MANOKOO, Md.—In an exclusive interview given an AFRO reporter, John Waters, 21, Kelton Road, a fellow worker of George Armwood, told Thursday morning of the lynched youth's life.

Waters, who had acted as guide in assisting to locate Mrs. Etta Armwood, the youth's mother, and Joshua Henson, his uncle, during the conversation said:

"George and I have been friends ever since we were very small. Living in a community like this, naturally our parents were friends. When we were about seven or eight years of age, we started to school. We went to the public school of Manokoo which goes as high as the eighth grade. George only went to the fifth grade and then quit school.

"I continued in school, however, and naturally I did not see him very often, but I knew he was working and living at the home of Miss Gertie Blades. She is now the wife of John Richardson, the man who helped George to get away from that mob which was hunting him."

WAS GOOD WORKER.

"After I came out of school there was nothing to do but farm. On numerous occasions I met him when we were either employed at the same place or by neighboring farmers. I can assure anyone that George was a good worker. He labored hard, never complained and was liked by everyone who saw him. I do think that guy was a little off at times. Whether this caused him to grab the old lady or not, I could not say."

SEIZED WOMAN.

"Last year during the summer they accused George of grabbing Mrs. Zelpa Wilson, wife of James Wilson, who runs a little place up at Jamestown. His white people Mr. Richardson, were able to get him off.

"After that occurrence last year, George and I, during harvest time, were working on the same farm for a short time. I liked to work with him because he was easy to get along with, never fussing and squabbling. Whenever you needed help to finish your work, if George was finished his work, he would help you out. He wasn't like the rest of the fellows around here who always wanted you to help them but in time of need never wanted to help you.

WAS QUIET FELLOW.

"George was a very quiet fellow. He never engaged in any quarrels with people he worked with. In fact, I can't recall anyone who didn't like him. He was considered a good, reliable worker. He knew what he was supposed to do and did it without anyone watching him.

"He was faithful and conscientious while at work. He worked relentlessly. He was the type of person who always went alone. He never went around with a group.

"I was around when the mob was hunting him, Monday afternoon. They caught him some place over on the other side," he indicated, pointing south of Manokoo, "and brought him through the fields here. After they had caught him, the officers started to beat him. Some of them struck him with their fists and others punched him in the sides with revolvers."

GET AT THE ROOTS

The belief and contention of the International Labor Defense that exploitation and race prejudice go hand in hand, and upon these mob violence and lynching flourish, was given additional credibility this week in the case of George Armwood, alleged Eastern Shore attempted rapist.

Armwood was rushed to the Baltimore city jail this week to escape from a lynching party of white hoodlums which threatened to storm the jail at Princess Anne.

Armwood, the AFRO learned, was reared by a white family and was recognized by many to be feeble-minded and a fit subject for a psychopathic ward. He was not put in one because, in spite of his mental infirmity or because of it, he was a good workman and an inexpensive one. The influence of his white employers saved him from a jail term when he committed a similar crime against a colored woman last year.

Now friends and neighbors of that same employer rise up and demand Armwood's blood because he is alleged to have attacked a 71-year-old white woman. The physical aspects of the attack themselves prove his insanity.

If Armwood had been properly incarcerated the crime of this week would have been avoided, racial feeling would not have been aroused, the State of Maryland would have been saved the disgraceful recurrence of the 1931 mob orgy and the man himself would have been saved from facing the horrible death which he suffered.

The case of Matthew Williams, who was lynched at Salisbury two years ago, was similar. He was conceded by both colored and white to be demented, but allowed to work at starvation wages until he allegedly slew his own employer and exploiter.

George Davis, who now is serving a 15-year term in the Maryland penitentiary for an alleged rape attempt on his white mistress near the same scene, was a feeble-minded, underpaid laborer and he barely escaped being lynched.

Euel Lee, now in the Maryland penitentiary awaiting the noose for having slain a whole family over a one-dollar debt, is unequivocally incompetent.

The time is now ripe for the State of Maryland to clean house, if repetitions of Wednesday's disgrace are to be avoided in future.

Negroes held in peonage, ignorance and serfdom on the Eastern Shore of Maryland should be rounded up and placed in an institution for the sub-normal at the expense of the State.

White farmers should be prevented by law from "rearing" these unbalanced Negroes which is merely a polite term for slavery.

If this is done, Maryland will have taken steps to get at the roots of the evil which is fast hurling us into the chasm of barbarity and savagery which has made Alabama, Georgia, South Carolina, Florida and Mississippi infamous in the eyes of the civilized world.

RAISING FUNDS FOR AN APPEAL

CALIFORNIA EAGLE

Scottsboro Youths in Greatest Danger; Organizations Asked to Send Delegates to Congress

July 20, 1934

SCOTTSBORO YOUTHS IN GREATEST DANGER, ORGANIZATIONS ASKED TO SEND DELEGATES TO CONGRESS

POINTING OUT that the Scottsboro Boys are in greatest danger now than at any time since their original trial in Alabama's lynch courts, the Scottsboro Action Committee and the International Labor Defense today broadcast an appeal for every possible organization to send delegates to a united front conference scheduled to be held at 3015 South San Pedro street, Friday, 8 P.M., July 20 and Friday, July 27.

The calling of the local conference is a part of a nation wide campaign launched by the defense organization to secure $30,000 with which to perfect an appeal to the supreme court and to make vocal the tremendous wave of underground sentiment that is welling up against the Alabama supreme court's cynical assertion that there was "no error to reverse" in the trial before Judge W. W. Callahan last fall.

Trade unions, clubs, civic, community and religious organizations and every group of every nationality that is opposed to legal lynching is being appealed to send delegates to the July 20 conference.

Combined with the appeal for the Scottsboro Boys is the question of Angelo Herndon, 20 year old Negro, who is facing 20 years.

BEN DAVIS, JR.

Scottsboro Attorneys in High Court

The Daily Worker, February 16, 1935

SCOTTSBORO ATTORNEYS IN HIGH COURT

Defense Proves Negroes Were Excluded from Jury Service

WASHINGTON, Feb. 15.—We are in the court chambers of the United States Supreme Court. The justices of the Supreme Court are preparing to hear the appeals of Clarence Norris and Haywood Patterson, two of the nine innocent Scottsboro Negro boys.

Perched near the bench is a table containing the forged jury rolls used by the Alabama lynch court officials.

NEGROES SYSTEMATICALLY EXCLUDED

The case is called at 3:10 P.M. Attorney Leibowitz begins the argument for Haywood Patterson and Clarence Norris. He states the facts of the lower court procedure. He states that Negroes were systematically excluded from the entire jury system in Jackson and Morgan counties. He states that the Alabama law did not specifically exclude Negroes but that the administration of the law was unconstitutional.

"Not so much whether Negroes sat but whether they were called for jury service." This was the interruption of Justice Van Devanter. Leibowitz answered that no Negroes "in the memory of man" had ever been seen on either the grand or petit jury.

The entire Court was plainly attentive. The Justices asked questions frequently. Mr. Leibowitz answered them all as he narrated the whole system of exclusion of Negroes. A dramatic moment occurred when he exhibited the book containing the alleged forged jury rolls. The entire bench and audience became quiet. He turned the book towards the judges and showed them how the names of Negroes were forged.

The Justices asked many detailed questions about the forgery. Justice Van Devanter presses Mr. Leibowitz on the motive for writing in the names. Justice Van Devanter impresses the audience as a Prosecutor rather than an "impartial" Judge.

Chief Justice Hughes has the book brought up to him. Everyone is amazed at the unusual proceeding.

The fictions of judicial impartiality disappeared completely —and significantly.

Justice Stone, former U. S. Attorney General, examines the book spectacularly with large magnifying glass.

Mr. Pollak begins argument. He cleared up masterfully a point raised by Justice Butler. He makes it clear that Negroes not only never sat on grand or petit juries but even never were called for jury service. Mr. Pollak shows that in Morgan County Negroes frequently qualified—many had had high school qualifications. Some had even been students of Phillips Andover, wealthy, exclusive academy in Massachusetts, some were lawyers, etc.

At 4:30 the Chief Justice adjourned the court. The case will be resumed Monday at 12 noon. Mr. Pollak was speaking beautifully and brilliantly when the session ended.

Pollak will complete his argument Monday, following which Mr. Frankel and Lieutenant Governor Tom Knight will present testimony. Knight, although no longer Attorney General of Alabama, has been named Special Prosecutor in charge of prosecution of the Scottsboro boys.

MARGUERITE YOUNG
Knight Has No Answer to the Scottsboro Defense

The Daily Worker, February 19, 1935

KNIGHT HAS NO ANSWER TO SCOTTSBORO DEFENSE

I. L. D. Attorney's Proof of Exclusion of Negroes from Jury Unassailed in Arguments Before U. S. Court—Recess for 2 Weeks

WASHINGTON, D. C., Feb. 18.—Attorney General Thomas E. Knight of Alabama today failed to give the United States Supreme Court a single reply to repeated sharp questions on the Scottsboro boys' plea that proof of the denial of their constitutional rights lies in the uncontested evidence that none of their race "in the memory of man" has served on a jury in the counties where they were convicted by all-white juries.

"The sum total of the State's case," Knight frankly admitted, "is that if there were no Negroes on the jury roll, it was not because of color."

Walter H. Pollak, retained by the International Labor Defense to argue the appeals before the obviously tense tribunal, unleashed a drumfire of uncontested evidence and legal precedents to prove the defense's case.

TWO WEEKS' RECESS

"The case in its cardinal issue (the denial to Negroes of their right to serve on juries) is way beyond the need of further evidence," Pollak argued. "Half a century ago the fact of the qualification of Negroes for jury service was undubitably proved. . . ." And yet in the Scottsboro case, "It was proved without contradiction . . . not only that no Negro had ever served on a jury within a generation, but also that no Negro ever was called to serve on a jury."

The Supreme Court recessed for two weeks on the conclusion of argument by Attorney General Knight. As he neared his finish, one of the justices by inference indicated that the Court might sit again tomorrow—but Knight hastily urged, "Oh, no."

ADMITS MARKS ON ROLLS

Attorney General Knight boldly admitted to the Supreme Court that the names of Negroes are customarily marked "Col." to show that they are Negro voters, on the rolls of voters in the State of Alabama. He did this in an effort to maintain that it was rolls of voters—and not lists of jurymen, as the defense showed, on which the special designation was given to Negroes' names. Pointing to the red books containing the jury rolls, on which the defense contends that the names of six Negroes were forged, Knight said:

"I cannot tell you today that those names were or were not forged . . . I simply take the position that I don't know how, when or whether, and I consider it immaterial whether they were or were not placed there."

KNIGHT CAN'T ANSWER

Justice Willis Van Devanter of Wyoming, seemingly irked at Knight's striking failure to even approach the defense's main issue, called the attention of the shouting prosecutor to the fact that out of the "box" containing the names of qualified voters "no colored man's name ever came," and "that no colored man ever was called." Then the justice asked Knight, "What is your answer to that?"

"I understand that the Jury Commission has the discretion——" Knight began.

"It has not the right to exclude colored men," the Justice shot in.

"I don't contend that it has," said Knight.

"But the colored men didn't get on," Van Devanter complained.

Instead of answering, Knight retorted that it was for the Supreme Court to decide whether the evidence warrants "the presumption that the Jury Commission did what they said they did."

HUNDREDS WAIT TO HEAR

The Court, according to its custom, set no definite time for rendering its decision on the appeals.

Osmond K. Fraenkel, the other lawyer retained by the I. L. D., sat beside Pollak, ready to offer rebuttal argument. Attorney Samuel S. Leibowitz, who presented the facts for the defense last Friday, was not present today.

The session opened with hundreds of Negro and white persons waiting outside to hear the case. Many of them waited in vain.

FOUR MAIN POINTS

The four main points, hammered by Pollak with the calm of his judicial listeners perched high on the bench above him, were:

1. That the indictment of a member of the Negro race and his conviction by juries from which Negroes are systematically excluded is a denial of the equal protection of the law.

2. That the court (in Alabama) denied the boys' constitutional rights in refusing to quash the indictments by the grand juries in Jackson County where Negroes had for years been excluded from jury service.

3. That the court denied the boys' constitutional rights in refusing to quash the venire of the petit jury in Morgan County where Negroes had for years been excluded.

4. That the court denied their constitutional rights in refusing to permit them full opportunity to prove that Negroes were systematically excluded.

Pollak cited the uncontested testimony by a jury commissioner, Stewart, that the names of Negroes on the lists from which jurymen were drawn were followed by the designation, "Col."

Attorney-General Knight, wearing a deep flush with his black cutaway coat, told the court that jury commissioner Stewart was “confused” when he testified to that fact, and “was thinking of the voting list.”

“Is that the custom there?” Justice Butler asked Knight, referring to the custom of designating Negroes as to color on voting lists.

“It’s been done ever since I can remember,” Knight replied. “But that’s on voting rolls, not on jury rolls.”

“Why didn’t Mr. Steward say so?” asked Chief Justice Charles Evans Hughes.

“He said the roll did not systematically exclude Negroes,” was Knight’s only answer.

His only answer to the exclusion of qualified Negroes was, “I can’t conceive of this court constituting itself a jury commission.”

The defense’s plea is that the jury commission and all other agencies of the State of Alabama concerned with the case violated the constitution—the protection of which is the duty of the Supreme Court of the United States.

BALTIMORE AFRO-AMERICAN
Watching the Scottsboro Case in Supreme Court

February 23, 1935

WATCHING THE SCOTTSBORO CASE IN SUPREME COURT

(AFRO Bureau)

WASHINGTON—The United States Supreme Court was packed on Friday, with the interested and merely curious, when the case of the Scottsboro boys was called, shortly after 2:30.

It was as impressive as a scene from the Roman Senate, all centering around the august judges in their high-backed chairs, appearing fully as aloof and impartial as the law and legend require them to be.

In the center, Chief Justice Hughes, impressive, with the ascetic Justice Van Devanter, and the lion-headed Brandeis on his right.

At the counsel's desk stood Samuel Leibowitz, white, capable and cool, pleasantly presenting his damaging evidence against the state of Alabama—no oratory or display of emotion—just facts, facts, facts.

Near him, smiling incessantly and nervously, sat Attorney-General Knight, white, of Alabama, watching the evidence pile up; watching the cumbersome jury list, which he had fought to exclude from the evidence, carried up and placed before Justice Hughes; watching the sudden eager stir among the justices, as they leaned forward, examining the alleged forgeries minutely.

Crowding the spectators' benches were students from Howard University, reporters from the weekly papers, and a few observers from out-of-town.

Dean Charles Houston, recently appointed legal advisor for the N.A.A.C.P., sat on the benches reserved for members of the bar.

At each new evidence of the sheer effrontery of Southern procedure, audible gasps of amazement rose from the spectators' benches, and questions of incredulity from the justices.

Court adjourned promptly at 4:30, with the assurance that every opportunity to fully present the case would be given when it sits again on Monday.

EXCLUDING BLACK MEN FROM JURIES

LOUIS R. LAUTIER

Highest Court Hears Scottsboro Case

Baltimore Afro-American, February 23, 1935

HIGHEST COURT HEARS SCOTTSBORO CASE

Supreme Court Is Interested in the Scottsboro Jury

Justices Pert as Leibowitz Accuses Alabama Court of Gross Fraud.

STATE LACKS CHOICE SAYS VAN DEVANTER

Can't Exclude Men from Jury on Account of Color.

WASHINGTON, D.C.—During the argument of the so-called Scottsboro cases in the United States Supreme Court last Monday, Justice Willis Van Devanter critically questioned Thomas E. Knight, former attorney-general of Alabama, now lieutenant-governor, to elicit from him the truth respecting the exclusion of colored persons from jury duty in Alabama.

Mr. Knight started badly. He began by telling the court he did not know how two big books containing the names of men eligible for jury duty in Jackson County, Alabama, had got before the Supreme Court.

KNIGHT CHIDED

"Come, come, now!" Justice Van Devanter chided him.

Samuel S. Leibowitz, of New York, who twice tried the cases at Decatur, Alabama, had shown one of the books to the court last Friday when argument was commenced.

Mr. Leibowitz startled the court by charging that the names of six colored men appearing in the book had been forged after the question of the exclusion of colored persons from jury duty had been raised.

FRAUD ALLEGED

He declared that the names of the colored men had been entered after the jury commission which made up the jury rolls, from which the grand jury which returned the indictments, had gone out of power "for the purpose of depriving the defendants of their constitutional rights and in all probability preventing a review by this court."

He explained that red lines had been drawn on each page by the new jury commission to show where the work of the old commission had ended and the work of the new commission had begun. He stated that an expert witness had testified that the names of the colored men, arranged alphabetically and according to precincts, had been superimposed upon the red lines indicating that they were inserted after the red lines had been put there.

JUDGES QUESTION

Chief Justice Charles E. Hughes and Justices Van Devanter, Owen J. Roberts, Pierce Butler and Harlan F. Stone questioned him, one after another, to ascertain how the clerk of the old jury commission had got possession of the book after he went out of office and what explanation he had made with respect to the alleged spurious names.

Mr. Leibowitz replied that he himself would like to find out how the old clerk had got access to the book and that no explanation had been given when the old clerk testified regarding the jury rolls and the alleged forged names were brought to his attention.

RIGHTS VIOLATED

Mr. Leibowitz contended that the rights of the petitioners had been violated by the systematic exclusion of colored persons from jury service solely because of race and color.

He made no complaint with respect to the Alabama statute prescribing the qualifications of jurors, but contended that "the administration of the statute is the gravamen of the complaint we lay before you."

ALWAYS LILY-WHITE JURIES

He said, "we were able to show that no colored person has ever served within the memory of man on grand or petit juries in Jackson County."

"Do you mean by that," asked Justice Van Devanter, "that they were never called, or, although called, they were excused?"

CUSTOM FOR 60 YEARS

Mr. Leibowitz replied that it is a matter of custom in Jackson County that no colored person can sit on juries. That custom, he said, has prevailed for at least 60 years.

He asserted it was proved there are colored persons in Jackson County qualified to serve. He said it was testified there were those in the county who had served on Federal juries.

"We showed not only the absence of service on juries by colored persons," he declared, "but we actually produced living specimens in the court who we contended were legally qualified and whose qualifications were not challenged by the state."

POLLAK COLORS CASE

Taking up the argument where Mr. Leibowitz had left off, Walter H. Pollak, of New York, who presented the first appeal in the Supreme Court which resulted in a reversal of the conviction of seven youths for alleged attacks on two white women, described the situation in Morgan County, Alabama, where the second and third trials were held after a change of venue had been granted.

"As to Morgan County," said Mr. Pollak, "no claim is made by the state that the names of colored persons appeared on the jury rolls, although the proportion of colored people to whites is even considerably larger than in Jackson County."

NEAL CASE

Mr. Pollak pointed out that the Scottsboro case had arisen fifty years after the case of Neal against Delaware in which the court found that there was a presumption of qualified persons.

"Colored people obviously have progressed immeasurably in the interval," declared Mr. Pollak, "and we have a case where there is no problem of relying upon the presumption of qualified colored people because we have proof of the existence of them."

ARGUMENT RESUMED MONDAY

When argument was resumed after the court had handed down its decision in the gold clause cases on Monday, Mr. Pollak took up the question of the striking of the motion for a new trial and the bill of exceptions in the case of Haywood Patterson.

But Mr. Pollak contended that the striking of the bill of exceptions did not affect the constitutional question because the issue of exclusion of colored persons from jury duty was raised by separate motions in writing.

KNIGHT'S REPLY

Mr. Knight declared that the issue was solely whether or not colored persons were systematically excluded from jury service. He said he was not concerned with whether the names of the six colored men had been placed on the jury list illegally or not. He added that the state of Alabama was not concerned with whether or not the name of a single colored person appeared on the book which Mr. Leibowitz had produced in court.

"I am not telling the court those names were forged in there," he declared. "I am not telling you they were not."

Mr. Knight was then subjected to a series of questions respecting the meaning of testimony that race or color was not discussed by the jury commissioners in making up the jury rolls.

DISCRETION?

"No colored man was ever called or served on the jury," commented Justice Van Devanter. "What answer do you make to that?"

Mr. Knight said he was inclined to think that the commissioners had acted within their discretionary powers.

JUDGE'S REBUKE

"I do not understand they had any discretion to exclude colored people because they were colored," replied Justice Van Devanter.

Justice James C. McReynolds, who dissented when the Supreme Court reversed the convictions, did not sit during the argument of the case.

By stipulation Mr. Leibowitz argued the appeal of Haywood Patterson and Mr. Pollak the appeal of Clarence Norris, both of whom are under death sentence in Kilby Prison, Montgomery, Ala.

Patterson and Norris were found guilty in December, 1933, of attacking Victoria Price, a white mill worker. Appeals from their convictions were taken to the Supreme Court of Alabama. That court affirmed their convictions. From the decision of the Alabama Supreme Court the cases are now before the United States Supreme Court for review for the second time.

“THE COMMON SENSE OF HUMANITY”

GRACE MOTT JOHNSON

Draft Letter to the Editor on the Scottsboro Case

April 6, 1936

April 6, 1936

To the Editor:

The “Scottsboro Case” is now at the bar of the common sense of humanity, which is outraged at the previous trials and verdicts, and at the years in jail which the young men are spending.

For this no redress is possible either to them or their families and friends.

The ill fame of the white citizens of Alabama and the United States will not be lessened even if any or all are adjudged not guilty of violence, given light sentences, or acquitted.

We have to prove to the world that any *white* boy or man accused by any *colored* girl or woman will be subject to the same trial, punishment, and publicity as colored accused by white.

The social insult to the manhood and womanhood of millions of our colored birthright citizens, which is universal in this country, their economic and educational pauperization by prejudicial discrimination, and advertised lynchings by “unknown” whites, constitute a vital menace to the peaceful evolution of American democracy.

The rest of the world follows the Scottsboro cases, aware of this fact, more intelligently than we do.

I am a non-partisan, white Anglo-Saxon American acquainted with north, south, and west.

Grace Mott Johnson
Pleasantville, N. Y.

A "SCOTTSBORO BOY" WRITES FROM JAIL

Haywood Patterson to Anna Damon

October 12, 1937

Haywood Patterson
Jeff. County Jail
Birmingham Ala
October 12, 1937

MY DEAR ANNA, I am writing you once again, although I have written you but an yet I haven't Heard anything at all from you and I begins to wonder why? In that letter I suggested a favor and my reason for asking you for an extra $5.00 is because I want only to get me a few articles of cheap clothing. An most of my clothing was destroyed and that is because I wasn't allowed to carry them into Prism with me. Now in your letter you asked me if there was anything I would like or need let you know, so I did. And I fail to understand why you Havent written me in & regarding my letter well maybe you will when you get this one. I do Honestly hope so anyway, Dear Anna an I understand from some friends that the boys hav deserted the I.L.D. and Insure them selves with some sort of Show. I am quite sorry for that if they have done such a thing. Of course I didn't so much an expect that those Boys would be of any aid or assistance to me or the remaining Boys, but I did so thought that they should go out with a determined mind to do all there was in their power to strengthen the I.L.D. the ones whom fought for them and saved their lives and saved them from Prison because you all knew that they was all innocent Boys.

I have nothing against either one of the boys nothing more than that they are most disagreeable at all times, but still I hope that the I.L.D. and Mr. Leibowitz do not hold anything in their hearts against these boys for they are rather young and stands in state ignorance of a great many things and can easy be deceived but after all they knew right from wrong. After we are all freed I think they would want to come back to you all, most likely they will. Why I myself can never forget the wonderful deeds and splendid cooperating that the I.L.D. Have shown me through all these years of misery and hardship and therefore my gratitude goes out to you all for the wonderful service you are daily rendering.

You know I haven't heard from the Committee for a good longtime now and I certainly miss the aid and assistance of the Committee and I wonder why such kindness should be taken a way from me especially when I am so appreciative. Now I am Honestly hoping for an answer from you please let it be soon

Yours Sincerely Haywood

A WARNING AND AN AGENDA

MARY MCLEOD BETHUNE

Draft Letter to Franklin D. Roosevelt

November 27, 1939

MY DEAR MR. PRESIDENT:

For several weeks I have made it my business to talk with thoughtful and informed Negroes in various parts of the country. Those conferences and reports which have come to me cause me to place before you these observations on what appears to be a situation serious enough to merit careful study by yourself and others concerned with the continuation of the ideals of your administration.

I have found deep affection for you and Mrs. Roosevelt among colored Americans in all walks of life. They share the feeling of many other Americans that at least so far as the heart is concerned you are genuinely concerned with the well being of and improvement of opportunities for all Americans, and particularly those who are disadvantaged. But over and above this personal regard for yourselves is a widespread and growing feeling of despair, distrust, and even bitterness because of the apparently increasing control of party policy, so far as Negroes are concerned, by southern congressmen, senators and others who are bitterly anti-Negro. I refer to such figures as Senators Connally, Byrnes, Glass, Smith, George, Harrison and Bilbo whose Negro-phobia reached its climax in the vicious attacks on the Negro during the filibuster against the Anti-Lynching Bill. There is puzzlement and bitterness among Negroes because even northern Democratic senators did not raise their voices against the ofttimes ridiculous attacks on the Negro. However, they are not unaware of the fact that Republican senators were equally mute.

It is my conviction that it would be a serious mistake to believe that the Negro vote is irrevocably fixed in the Democratic ranks. It would be equally a mistake to believe that not only the leaders of Negro opinion but the rank and file are satisfied with the deal the Negro has received even under your administration.

I have also found that very extensive plans are being made by the Republicans who are determined to win back the Negro vote in the 1940 election. Intelligent Republicans know that the seventeen states where the Negro vote potentially holds the balance of power may and probably will determine the outcome of the next election, particularly in such pivotal states as Illinois, Indiana, Ohio, Pennsylvania, New Jersey, New York, Maryland, Kentucky and Missouri.

I have encountered evidence of liberal spending by Republicans already. The Party will doubtless spend much more not only in attempting to purchase purchasable Negro (and white) votes but in legitimate propaganda. For example, the Republican National Committee about a year ago employed Prof. Ralph J. Bunche of Howard University to make a study of the reasons why Negroes left the Republican Party. This report has been kept secret but we shall see during the next twelve months how many of its recommendations will be followed. Senator Taft has employed Perry W. Howard, Republican National Committeeman from Mississippi, to line up southern delegates, white and Negro, in his behalf. Thomas E. Dewey has appointed three high type Negro assistants in his office—which is in marked contrast to the fact that there are no Negroes in the United States Attorney's office in New York City. And he sent a very strong letter of greeting to the recent Richmond convention of the National Association for the Advancement of Colored People, a copy of which is enclosed.

In addition, more Republican members of the House of Representatives signed the Discharge Petition on the Gavagan Anti-Lynching Bill than Democrats and this fact has been widely publicized in the Negro press. Emmett J. Scott, former secretary to Booker T. Washington, and also former Secretary-Treasurer of Howard University, has been employed by the Republican National Committee to handle publicity among Negroes.

The results are already being seen in recent elections in Pennsylvania, Ohio, New York and other states. In the *New*

York Times of November 26 Arthur Krock features the efforts of the Republicans to win the support of farmers, white collar workers, possible labor, and particularly Negroes in order to win in 1940. These are but straws in the wind which I think it is imperative we pay attention to.

As I have already said, Negroes generally are grateful to you and Mrs. Roosevelt for the attitude which you have shown, but the status of the Negro is so desperate that they are naturally disturbed about the many things which could have been done but which have not been done by the present administration. For example, your silence during the filibuster against the Anti-Lynching Bill has been widely commented upon among Negroes. The appointment of a Negro as District Judge in the Virgin Islands has been heralded, but Negroes know that it is not a District judgeship of a constitutional court, with the indefinite tenure of office of Federal judges.

Discrimination against Negroes by such agencies as the Federal Housing Administration, the Tennessee Valley Authority in the office personnel, and on other federal-financed projects, have added to this unrest.

Permit me to summarize some of the shortcomings which I have found Negroes to feel exist and which should be remedied if we are to continue to have the support of Negro voters:

1. Some tangible means of securing enactment of federal legislation against lynching and particularly limiting filibuster with its vicious attacks upon Negroes by southern senators.
2. Support of federal legislation against discrimination in federal-financed projects similar to that provided in contracts of the WPA under Mr. Ickes and of the United States Housing Authority under Mr. Straus.
3. Active administration support for safeguards in proposed legislation for federal aid to education and health which would insure equitable distribution of federal moneys for these purposes in states where there are separate schools, hospitals, clinics, etc., for Negroes.
4. The issuance of an executive order abolishing the use of photographs with civil service applications and the

substitution therefore of fingerprints or some other suitable method; and (b) ordering appointment from competitive registers strictly according to rank instead of giving the appointing officer, as at present, the right to select any one of the three certified by the Civil Service Commission. There are undoubted advantages to honest appointing officers in this latitude but it has been used in both the North and the South to pass over Negroes and select white persons who made lower marks.

5. At least one qualified Negro lawyer of ability and character should be appointed to one of the present vacancies on the federal bench in continental United States, either in the District Court or the Circuit Court of Appeals. It is interesting to note that the press generally and Negro newspapers in particular are featuring the recent suggestion that Charles H. Houston of Washington be appointed to the United States Supreme Court bench.
6. There should be three or four outstanding appointments in Washington of qualified Negroes to posts where they can render services directly affecting pressing needs of Negro citizens. By this I do not mean Negro advisory jobs but posts of real authority where their mere presence will help to establish the fact that the Negro is an integral and important part of the American government. I have in mind such posts as a member of the Civil Service Commission, an assistant secretaryship of labor and important posts of that sort.
7. Appointment of a Negro assistant in the division of personnel supervision and management in every department and independent establishment, one of whose main duties shall be that of assisting the director of the division in integrating qualified Negroes more widely into the department or establishment.
8. Next to the matter of jobs, the Negro is more concerned than ever before over the right to vote. He is not naive enough to believe that this is a panacea but he does recognize fully the value of the ballot. He knows that if he had the same access to the ballot box as other citizens he could help elect officials ranging from the occupant of the White

House down to local school boards who would thereby be sensitive to protests against racial discrimination from which the Negro suffers. Any movement, therefore, by the administration which will accelerate the removal or the easement of the restrictions now affecting the exercise of the ballot will earn the gratitude of the Negro and will deprive the Republicans of one of their chief arguments.

In addition to the preceding specific items there may be mentioned the following:

More than six and a half million of the twelve million American Negroes are engaged in agriculture either as farm owners, tenants, or sharecroppers. Anything which can be done towards relief of the distress of Negro agricultural workers would be welcomed.

The administration's record so far as housing is concerned is, on the whole, excellent. Mr. Straus, as administrator of the United States Housing Authority, appears to have done all he could to keep down discrimination both in employment in construction of housing projects and also in occupancy. But more can be done to back up Mr. Straus' efforts and particularly in extending the benefits of housing as far as Congress will appropriate funds for such furtherance of decent housing.

One of the sorest points among Negroes which I have encountered is the flagrant discrimination against Negroes in all the armed forces of the United States. Forthright action on your part to lessen discrimination and segregation and particularly in affording opportunities for the training of Negro pilots for the air corps would gain tremendous good will, perhaps even out of proportion to the significance of such action.

In conclusion, we are dealing with an increasingly independent and thinking group. The Negro has done a good deal of housecleaning during recent years in getting rid of venal politicians of his own race. At the same time he is looking with an increasingly skeptical eye upon the lip service of white politicians of all parties. I have found him increasingly aware of how he and other members of his race have been used and are being used. Deeds rather than empty promises are increasingly important to perpetuate the support of this important group. I trust, therefore, that serious consideration may be given to the urgent necessity of specific action on the above issues and any others which may occur to you. Unless this is done I seriously doubt that we shall have the support of any considerable percentage of this group in 1940.

"THE RIGHT TO FIGHT"

WALTER WHITE

It's Our Country, Too

Saturday Evening Post, December 14, 1940

IT'S OUR COUNTRY, TOO

The Negro Demands the Right to be Allowed to Fight for It

FROM the man-power angle, the largest defense headache ahead of the United States Government is likely to be the status of that 10 per cent of our population which is Negro. The Negro insists upon doing his part, and the Army and Navy want none of him.

Charging wholesale discriminations in both the military and industrial defense services, the 250 papers which make up the nation's Negro press have been clamoring more loudly and with greater unanimity than at any time since the Scottsboro case. National Negro organizations, like the National Association for the Advancement of Colored People, have accumulated files full of case records and put the problem in the No. 1 position on their fighting agenda. For several months the War and Navy departments and the Advisory National Defense Commission have been on the receiving end of a considerable outpouring of Negro complaints, suggestions and indignant resolutions. Mr. Roosevelt has given ear to the problem in conference with Negro leaders at the White House. In the late August debates on the Burke-Wadsworth Conscription Bill the matter was brought to the floor of the United States Senate and given a gingerly airing.

The issue got to the Senate through the efforts of senators Wagner and Barbour sure-fire friends of Negro causes. Senator Wagner offered an amendment to that portion of the bill which had to do with voluntary enlistments. His amendment proposed that the opportunity to volunteer in the land or naval forces should be offered "regardless of race or color." After seven Congressional Record pages of debate, the phrase was accepted, 53 to 21.

Although through the National Association for the Advancement of Colored People I had something to do with this amendment, its adoption appears to have left Negro opinion and the military and defense status of the Negroes about where they were. The good intentions expressed by its mollifying phrase are pretty well nullified in the next sentence of the bill. That sentence provides "that no man shall be inducted for training and service under this act unless and until he is acceptable to the land or naval forces. . . ."

After considerable research, it seems clear to me that the land and naval forces have not managed to find a way by which Negroes can be "acceptably" inducted. The bars likewise appear to be up in many of the industrial establishments engaged on defense orders.

As far as the Army is concerned, it is possible that this situation will be helped by Mr. Roosevelt's recent proposal to utilize Negro troops "on a fair and equitable basis" in the various branches of the Army service. The results of that declaration remain to be seen. Meanwhile, the Negroes' fight for the right to fight has only started. It will continue till, all along the line, Negroes receive their fair share in the task of national defense.

Of the wartime loyalty of Negroes and the value of Negro troops, I do not believe that there is any longer much question. There is no known case of Negro treason or sabotage against the United States. No minority group in the country has been freer from Fifth Columnist suspicions. In the numerous photographs of those companies of young men who lately flocked to the marriage-license bureaus hoping to escape the draft, I have yet to find a Negro.

Negroes have fought in every war in our history and have been lauded for their bravery by commanding generals from Andrew Jackson to John J. Pershing. Two Negro regiments —the 9th and 10th Cavalry—saved the day for Theodore Roosevelt's Rough Riders at San Juan Hill. In the World War, another Negro Regiment—Harlem's 369th—lost 1100 men, killed and wounded, won 172 individual French and American decorations and never surrendered a foot of ground to the enemy. When, early in 1919, the 369th marched up Fifth Avenue, its regimental standard bore the ribbons of the Croix de Guerre.

Despite this record, the United States—in the preparation for and the fighting of the next war—hesitates to make use of its reservoir of Negro man power or has used it as little or as insignificantly as possible.

Negro youths, like other young Americans, have recently become acutely air-minded. There is every reason to believe that many of them would make good aviators. "The first requisite of a military flier," says the Chicago Tribune, "is quick nervous responses. He should have a superior sense of balance, excellent muscular co-ordination, a good sensory apparatus, a sound body. In short, the qualities which make a good athlete are required of a flier. Of course he should have physical and moral courage as well. In all of these qualifications Negroes have given ample demonstration of their fitness. A race which has produced, in the span of a few years, Joe Louis, Henry Armstrong, Jesse Owens, Kenny Washington of U. C. L. A., Jefferson of Northwestern—All-American halfback—Ozzie Simmons of Iowa—All-American halfback—a substantial number of Golden Gloves champions and other absolutely top-notch athletes, provides a rich resource which ought not to be lost to the country through prejudice. In the face of this roster of world champions, the physical fitness and courage of their race cannot be questioned by any reasonable man. The record suggests that the country would lose less by refusing to train Harvard, Yale and Princeton men for the flying corps than by refusing to train Negroes."

Up to the present, however, this source of aviation man power has not been touched for either the Army or the Navy. Testifying recently before a committee of the House of Representatives, Gen. George C. Marshall, Army Chief of Staff, declared, "As to pilots, there is no such thing as colored aviation at the present time." He added, however, that "a start has been made and I think the CAA—Civil Aeronautics Authority—is the proper place for that start or beginning to be made."

What General Marshall apparently had in mind when he referred to a start having been made, was the 1939 Army expansion act, which authorized the Secretary of War to lend military equipment to at least one accredited civilian aviation school to train Negro fliers. That concession was won only after a vigorous struggle. Eventually, in line with the law, the War

Department designated the Chicago School of Aeronautics, at Glenview, Illinois, to train Negro pilots, and lent equipment to the school for that purpose. What the general's testimony did not bring out was the fact that the Army Air Corps, to date, has not enlisted or sent any Negroes to the Glenview school for training. There being no Negro units in the Air Corps, the Army, presumably, wouldn't know what to do with a Negro pilot if it trained one.

Even in those few instances where Negroes have been permitted to take training courses from the Civil Aeronautics Authority in American universities, they are left—so far as American military aviation is concerned—with no place to go to use their training. Recently, Walter L. Robinson, a Negro, was given flight training under the CAA at the University of Minnesota. He finished with a standing of thirteenth in a class of 300. When, along with some of his fellow graduates, he applied for enlistment in the Army Air Corps, he was told by the lieutenant in charge that it was useless for him to apply. "There is no place for a Negro," said the lieutenant, "in the Air Corps."

Robinson, knowing that the British—with their backs to the wall—had opened the Royal Air Force both to Negroes and to Indians, went to Canada and applied for service. He was almost instantly accepted.

The Robinson case has become a *cause célèbre* among Negroes and in the Negro press. Thoughtful Negroes, says a Negro educator, "are wondering whether it will take the national humiliation of military defeat such as France now knows," to establish, for American Negroes, the right to fight for America.

But the no-place-for-Negroes policy of the Air Corps does not differ greatly from that of other branches of the Army. According to its own official statements, the Army is badly in need of pharmacists. Recently a Negro pharmacist took the prescribed examinations, passed with a high average and applied for service. He was told, "We're not going to have any black pharmacists in the Army."

During the Army's high-pressure drive for enlistments, it has been virtually impossible for Negroes to volunteer in any branch of the service. Negro volunteers are taken only for service in Negro regiments. On September first, in those regiments there were only 304 vacancies. At that time, in the 2nd Corps Area, embracing New York, New Jersey and Delaware, voluntary enlistment of whites had fallen far below the number hoped for. But Negroes seeking to enlist in that area were turned down. Late in August, a Negro high-school teacher—holding, incidentally, a master's degree from Columbia University—took four of his pupils to the Army recruiting station at Charlotte, North Carolina, to help them enlist. They were told that the recruiting station was for "whites only." When the teacher asked for further particulars, he was assaulted by men in Army uniform and thrown out with a fractured jaw.

No Negro has ever served, either as an officer or an enlisted man, in the Marine Corps. During the last thirty years, one Negro has been graduated from West Point. At present there are five Negro officers in the Regular Army. Three of them are chaplains. Two are combat officers. Of these latter, one is Brig. Gen. Benjamin O. Davis, commander of the famous 369th. He came up from the ranks, served for a time as military attaché in Liberia, and since then has taught military science at Negro colleges. The other is his son, Lt. Benjamin O. Davis, Jr., the West Point graduate. He finished in 1936, ranking thirty-fifth in a class of 276. He now commands the R. O. T. C. at the Negro Tuskegee Institute.

There are, however, 500 Negro officers in the Army reserve. Most of these are men commissioned during the World War. Up to mid-September, not one of these reserve officers had been called for service or training. According to Mr. Roosevelt's recent statement, these men apparently will not be entirely ignored. More of them will probably be needed, since some 1,000,000 Negroes are due to be called under the draft.

Judged by the practices which have prevailed, the plans of the War Department called for drawing as meagerly as possible upon the military resources or the patriotism of the nation's Negroes. Recently a War Department order was issued requiring two Negro National Guard regiments—Harlem's 369th and the 8th Illinois—to add to their names the word "Colored."

There was an immediate uproar, on the ground that, since predominantly Jewish or German or Irish units of the National Guard were not designated as such, there should be no singling out of Negro regiments. The order was rescinded.

But the Negroes believe that, designated or not, their fighting services will be used only if present policies can be widely changed. It is true that the 369th has been recently converted into an antiaircraft regiment. That, however, was due to the vigorous intercession of Gov. Herbert H. Lehman and Gen. William N. Haskell, of the New York National Guard. The department's plan, as reported to the governor, had been to convert the 369th into a labor regiment.

A mounting storm of protests from white as well as Negro Americans against discrimination in the armed forces, which coincided with the presidential campaign, resulted in the promotion of Col. Benjamin O. Davis, of the 369th New York Antiaircraft Regiment, to brigadier general, the first instance of a Negro becoming a general in the United States Army. On the same date, Dean William H. Hastie, of the Howard University Law School, was appointed civilian aide to the Secretary of War; Major Campbell Johnson, a third Negro, was made executive assistant to Dr. Clarence Dykstra, director of the draft. On October twenty-fifth the President wrote a letter announcing a relaxation of the previously announced plans to continue existing conditions which had aroused nationwide protest. Some Negroes promptly labeled these appointments as "appeasement jobs," while others, more realistic, attributed them to the successful protests and recognized that one gets something in this world only when he has something—in this case, the vote—which the other fellow wants and needs.

SERVANTS IN KHAKI

Negro apprehensions have been further increased by the present fate of the Negro regiments of the regular Army—the 9th and 10th Cavalry and the 24th and 25th Infantry regiments. "Today and for some years past," says the Chicago Tribune, "the bulk of the regiment—the 10th Cavalry—has been split between West Point and Fort Leavenworth. Its members are employed chiefly as grooms and horse holders for officers and cadets."

Troop F of the 10th Cavalry is doing the same menial work at Fort Myer, Virginia. A recent investigation at Fort Riley, Kansas, revealed that, as late as mid-August, "not a single member of the 9th Cavalry was being trained in any capacity to fight, but, to the contrary, they are merely hostlers. . . . Many of them are well educated . . . but they are simply not being trained as combat troops."

Inquiry at Fort Benning, Georgia, regarding the 24th Infantry brought the reply that this "is not a combat unit." They serve in the capacity of a service unit. Most of the men are given some form of training as truck drivers, cooks, caretakers of horses and in other menial tasks. A few are also serving in the band and as clerks and as caretakers of the equipment.

Henry L. Stimson, the Secretary of War, stated in August that "in the augmentation of the Army now under way, additional colored units have been authorized. These include one field artillery regiment, two coast artillery antiaircraft battalions, one engineer regiment for general service, twelve quartermaster companies and one chemical decontamination company."

That, on the face of it, looked like a good beginning. But it did not take the Negro press very long to break down those "authorizations" into more specific and less satisfactory terms. Quartermaster companies, said the Negroes, are service and not combat units. The engineer regiment, according to my information, is also due to be a service unit, which is another word for a labor battalion. The chemical decontamination company evidently will be trained in the arts of delousing, garbage removal and the care of latrines.

The Negro field artillery regiment referred to by Mr. Stimson was to be established at Fort Sill, Oklahoma. Several weeks after the announcement of the organization of such a regiment was made, inquiries at Fort Sill revealed that the Negro soldiers there were chiefly employed in washing dishes, shining boots, cleaning the houses and mowing the lawns of the officers at the post. When the Oklahoma National Guard came to Fort Sill for training, the Negro troops performed the same services for the Guard officers.

Negroes and Negro soldiers know perfectly well that some white soldiers are required to perform menial tasks in the Army.

Negroes do not object to some Negro soldiers doing the same kind of work. But they do vigorously object against all Negro soldiers, regardless of training and qualifications, being relegated to the role of hewers of wood and drawers of water.

"We will be American soldiers," says William H. Hastie. "We will be American ditchdiggers. We will be American aviators. We will be American laborers. We will be anything that any other American should be in this whole program of national defense. But we won't be black auxiliaries."

When a Negro desiring a combat post turns from the Army to the Navy he runs into even more insurmountable difficulties. Life aboard ship presents problems which are likely to be more acute than in any Army post. Moreover, although the Army has had all-Negro regiments, there has never been an all-Negro naval vessel. Thus, no Negro has ever graduated from Annapolis, and only two Negroes, during the past seventy years, have been permitted to enter it.

Until the World War it was possible for Negroes in the Navy to attain the rank of petty officer. Nowadays they are permitted to enlist only as menials. They can rise only to the position of officers' cook or steward. If a Negro youth enlists, he is rated as a mess attendant, third class, at twenty-one dollars a month. He is obliged to remain in that classification for a year. A white boy enlisting at the same time is eligible for promotion in rating every three months and, at the end of the year, may have become a petty officer with a fifty-four-dollars-a-month salary.

"After many years of experience," says the chief of the Bureau of Navigation, writing on behalf of the Secretary of the Navy, "the policy of not enlisting men of the colored race for any branch of the naval service except messman branch was adopted to meet the best interests of general ship efficiency. . . . This policy not only serves the best interests of the Navy and the country but serves the best interests of the men themselves."

THE INDUSTRIAL PICTURE

A somewhat similar policy appears to be in operation in some of the navy yards. At the Charleston, South Carolina, yard Negro employees in the powerhouse are used to teach white employees. The whites thus are advanced to the engine room, classified as engineers and given higher pay. The Negro teacher remains in the fireman's classification.

Due, perhaps, to the fact that the mechanics union bars Negroes from membership, Negroes in the machine shop at Charleston are not permitted to rise above the position of mechanic's helper. Formerly the renovating division was entirely manned by Negroes. Pay in that division was recently raised from $3.84 to $5.20 a day. Immediately all the Negroes were displaced by whites. One Negro, admitted to the renovating division as a "trainee," was assigned to the janitor service at $3.84 a day. A white applicant who entered at the same time and also did janitor work was rated as an explosives operator and paid $5.20 a day. When an educated Negro took the civil-service examination as explosives operator and passed, he was notified by the board of civil-service examiners that his rating was "canceled—unsuitable for position of explosives operator."

As far as the industrial side of the defense program is concerned, the Negroes constitute a great reservoir of trained and skilled workers. Since the Civil War, public and private moneys have been spent in increasing volume for this type of Negro education. Within the last ten years more than 30,000 Negroes have graduated from colleges, universities, graduate and professional schools. During the same period more than 200,000 have finished high school. A considerably larger number have graduated from trade, industrial and mechanical-arts schools or finished courses given by the WPA, the NYA or other state and Federal agencies.

Despite the fact that thousands of them are trained workers and, therefore, assets in the nation's defense-construction program, the evidence seems to indicate that here, too, the policy seems to be to get along without Negroes. In some instances, at least, this policy is adhered to regardless of the consequences to defense.

One large airplane-manufacturing company with a huge Government contract happens to be located in a New England state near the large estate of a wealthy and patriotic woman. One of her gardeners was of German birth. When she found that he was a leading figure in the local Nazi Bund and aggressively pro-Hitler and anti-American in his opinions, she promptly fired him. Twenty-four hours later he landed a job —apparently with no questions asked—in the airplane plant. American Negroes, however, are refused employment in that plant, regardless of their training. One young Negro recently applied. He was a graduate of an excellent trade school. His average of grades for his course had been 98.4 per cent. But good as his record was and badly as skilled men were needed, he was turned down. Subsequently this concern notified the state and Federal employment office that henceforth Negro applicants should not be sent and that if they were sent they would not be hired. Having discovered that the defense program—which made a place for anti-American aliens—had no place for his loyalty and skill, the Negro with the 98.4 per cent average took a job in a garage washing automobiles.

I have made an extensive survey of the policy toward the employment of Negroes of a large number of the several hundred plants which are working on defense orders for the United States Government. Some of these concerns did not reply. A number of them replied that they were prevented, by their contract with the Government, from disclosing the information desired. From out of the voluminous replies which were received, however, it is fairly clear that the Army policy toward Negroes has been established, in varying degrees, in many of these industrial establishments.

One of the plants where that policy is not in operation is a Southern concern—the Newport News Shipbuilding and Dry Dock Company, of Newport News, Virginia. According to J. B. Woodward, Jr., vice-president and general manager of that company, 3000 of the 12,000 men employed at the plant on August twenty-second were Negroes. "Many of them," he said, "are helpers in skilled trades. There are also many Negroes in service jobs as chauffeurs, porters and messengers. All laborers and nearly all our riveters, chippers and drillers are Negroes. There is no ban, written or unwritten, on the employment of Negroes, and the company has always found them, as a class, loyal and efficient employees. The total pay roll of this company is now averaging more than $400,000 per week and the amount received by any employee is determined by the kind of job he holds, and not by his color."

THE NEGRO AND THE UNIONS

In the shipbuilding industry new workers are qualified for skilled classification largely through the apprenticeship system. From the standpoint of the younger Negro worker, therefore, even the Newport News company offers little for the future, since the apprenticeship schools which it maintains are open only to white workers.

The Government itself maintains apprenticeship schools at the Pensacola naval air base. There the Government offers a four-year course and pays the trainee $2.88 a day while taking it. Negroes are barred from these courses. Among the several thousand skilled workers at the Pensacola base there are about ten Negroes.

The Tampa Shipbuilding and Dry Dock Company has contracts from the Maritime Commission amounting to about $17,000,000. The management wrote to me that it was not only willing but, skilled labor being hard to get, eager to employ qualified Negroes. The snag at Tampa is certain AFL unions, such as the International Boilermakers Union, which, by constitutional clauses, bar from membership all who are not "members of the white race."

At this plant, in 1936, the employees, led by twelve Negroes, organized and won a strike for higher wages. The plant then was unorganized. The success of the strike brought in, posthaste, the organizers. When a closed shop was asked for, the question was raised about the status of the Negroes who constituted 50 per cent of the employees. The organizers promised that the Negroes would be taken care of with a special charter. Immediately after the closed-shop agreement was signed, however, the organizers double-crossed both the Negroes and the management, and demanded that all workers not bona-fide union members be discharged. There was no out. The Negroes —many of them highly skilled workers—were fired. They appealed to William Green, president of the AFL, and to other union officials. Neither Mr. Green nor any of his subordinates took any corrective action. Last June a regional official of the AFL promised an investigation. The promise is still unkept.

For three months two colored aviation mechanics sought employment at the Boeing Aircraft plant at Seattle, which, to date, has received Government contracts totaling nearly

$32,000,000. Late in July, the Boeing Company apparently withdrew its refusal to employ Negroes and announced that it would take on qualified Negro mechanics, provided they were members of Aeronautical Mechanics Union No. 751, with which the company had a contract. Application forms were issued to the two Negroes. Whereupon it was discovered that the Aeronautical Union likewise has a clause in its constitution which bars Negroes from membership.

UNSEEN BARRIERS

My survey indicates that many of the industrial concerns which are reluctant to hire Negroes or which bar them altogether do so because of the objections of their own employees or because of labor-union regulations. For these reasons, also, a good many concerns which have no actual ban on the employment of Negroes, even in skilled occupations, nonetheless seem to make it a point to hire as few as possible. The few hired are generally for unskilled jobs of a sort least likely to throw them into competition with white employees or—even more important—with the all-white labor unions. At Wichita, Stearman Aircraft, a division of Boeing, has received orders from the Government for $5,713,389 worth of planes; another Boeing plant in Wichita has a contract for $2,041,947.97 for planes, making a total of $7,755,336.97. Stearman officials write that the number of persons employed and the total pay roll are confidential. The company does disclose, however, that only three Negroes are employed, at a total pay-roll cost of $239 a month. Two of them are porters, one an assistant cook.

The Rev. S. L. McDowell, a Negro Baptist minister of Nashville, recently wrote to Stinson Aircraft regarding possible work for Negroes in the Nashville plant, which is expected to employ 7000 to 8000 men. Rudolph Funk replied: "I am not certain at the present time how many colored people will be employed in our plant. As far as I know, there will be very few. There possibly will be some porters and truckmen."

To fulfill contracts for planes for the Federal Government this company will do most of its employing through tax-supported employment agencies jointly run by the Federal Government and the state of Tennessee. This public agency maintains separate offices for the registration of white and Negro workers.

The Negro division is listed as a bureau for "domestic and personal service." Skilled Negro workers are required to register as common laborers and, if they insist, are given a second classification in the skills which they possess. Even then, requests for skilled workers are never sent to the Negro office until all available whites listed at the "white" office have been given employment. Repeated protests to Washington have been unavailing.

Westinghouse has Government contracts to manufacture radio apparatus and communications equipment totaling $8,024,892. In its Baltimore plant, at present, 800 persons are employed, of which normally three are Negroes. They are laborers and porters. No skilled Negro workers are hired, but there is no ban, according to the company, on the employment of Negroes. The Virginia Engineering Company, at Norfolk, to which have been awarded contracts totaling $13,125,000, reports that it is now employing 1500 persons, of which probably 500 are Negroes. All of them are unskilled laborers.

According to the Baltimore Urban League, the Glenn L. Martin Company, already employing more than 10,000 workers, most of them on Government orders, has never employed a single Negro. The Colt Arms Company, of Hartford, refused to give any information. But a number of young Negroes have recently been turned away with the assertion that "we are not hiring any Negroes today." W. G. Skelly, of the Spartan Aircraft Company, of Tulsa, doubts "very much that even later, when we get to manufacturing the planes, we will require any colored help, with the exception of possibly using a few laborers." In Cleveland, neither General Motors nor the White Motor Company—both of which are working on large Government orders—employs Negroes. This again is largely a result of the policy of the International Association of Machinists in barring Negroes from membership.

The Federal Government, in the interest of speeding up defense, has begun slowly to move in on the problem of Negro employment in defense industries.

Recently, Sidney Hillman, of the National Defense Advisory Commission, appointed Dr. Robert C. Weaver as administrative assistant in the commission's labor-supply division. Doctor Weaver is a Negro. His duties will include the integration of qualified Negroes in the vocational and apprenticeship courses which are to be established to train workers and to supply such skilled workers to the plants working on defense contracts. The Defense Commission itself has issued a statement of labor policy which includes the admonitory statement that "workers should not be discriminated against because of age, sex, race or color."

In the administration of the draft law, the President has appointed a Negro member of the six-man Advisory Committee on Selective Service. He is Channing H. Tobias, national Negro secretary of the Y. M. C. A. Particularly in the larger cities, Negroes are being appointed to many of the city and local draft boards.

When, during the summer, the NAACP appealed to Secretary Stimson for a greater combat opportunity for Negroes, the Secretary's reply was a veiled warning that to criticize the department's policies was to obstruct defense. "The success of the national-defense program," wrote Mr. Stimson, "can best be established by united support of the War Department plans, which have been worked out after years of study by those who have devoted their lives to these questions. Unity can be destroyed by attempting to establish a program which is contrary to the War Department's plans by those who are not familiar either with the principles involved or the requirements of such plans."

On a small minority of Negroes, these repeated rebuffs have had a disillusioning effect. That, in the opinion of many Negro leaders, explains why both Fascists and Communists, of late, have increased their proselytizing work in the country's Negro communities.

It is the Negroes' hope that Mr. Roosevelt's recent declaration will have a remedial effect in this situation. The overwhelming majority of American Negroes regard the United States as a country which they helped to build, and which, rebuffed or not, they propose to help defend. Unsatisfactory as conditions are, the average Negro, up to now, doesn't believe that either Hitler or Stalin has anything better to offer. He is, therefore, hanging on to his faith in democracy and going grimly ahead, determined to carry on his shoulders a fair share of the burden of its defense.

FIGHTING FOR A DOUBLE VICTORY

JAMES G. THOMPSON

Should I Sacrifice To Live "Half-American?"

Pittsburgh Courier, January 31, 1942

SHOULD I SACRIFICE TO LIVE "HALF-AMERICAN?"

Suggest Double VV for Double Victory Against Axis Forces and Ugly Prejudices on the Home Front.

(EDITOR'S NOTE: A young man, confused and befuddled by all of this double talk about democracy and the defense of our way of life, is asking, like other young Negroes, some very pertinent questions. We reprint this letter in full because it is symbolic.)

DEAR EDITOR:

Like all true Americans, my greatest desire at this time, this crucial point of our history; is a desire for a complete victory over the forces of evil, which threaten our existence today. Behind that desire is also a desire to serve, this, my country, in the most advantageous way.

Most of our leaders are suggesting that we sacrifice every other ambition to the paramount one, victory. With this I agree; but I also wonder if another victory could not be achieved at the same time. After all the things that beset the world now are basically the same things which upset the equilibrium of nations internally, states, counties, cities, homes and even the individual.

Being an American of dark complexion and some 26 years, these questions flash through my mind: "Should I sacrifice my life to live half American?" "Will things be better for the next generation in the peace to follow?" "Would it be demanding too much to demand full citizenship rights in exchange for the sacrificing of my life? Is the kind of America I know worth defending? Will America be a true and pure democracy after this war? Will Colored Americans suffer still the indignities that have been heaped upon them in the past? These and other questions need answering; I want to know, and I believe every colored American, who is thinking, wants to know.

This may be the wrong time to broach such subjects, but haven't all good things obtained by men been secured through sacrifice during just such times of strife.

I suggest that while we keep defense and victory in the forefront that we don't lose sight of our fight for true democracy at home.

The V for victory sign is being displayed prominently in all so-called democratic countries which are fighting for victory over aggression, slavery and tyranny. If this V sign means that to those now engaged in this great conflict then let we colored Americans adopt the double VV for a double victory. The first V for victory over our enemies from without, the second V for victory over our enemies from within. For surely those who perpetrate these ugly prejudices here are seeking to destroy our democratic form of government just as surely as the Axis forces.

This should not and would not lessen our efforts to bring this conflict to a successful conclusion; but should and would make us stronger to resist these evil forces which threaten us. America could become united as never before and become truly the home of democracy.

In way of an answer to the foregoing questions in a preceding paragraph I might say that there is no doubt that this country is worth defending; things will be different for the next generation; colored Americans will come into their own, and America will eventually become the true democracy it was designed to be. These things will become a reality in time; but not through any relaxation of the efforts to secure them.

In conclusion let me say that though these questions often permeate my mind, I love America and am willing to die for the America I know will someday become a reality.

JAMES G. THOMPSON

"WINNING DEMOCRACY"

MARCH ON WASHINGTON MOVEMENT

Why Should We March?

Summer 1942

WHY SHOULD WE MARCH?

15,000 Negroes Assembled at St. Louis, Missouri
20,000 Negroes Assembled at Chicago, Illinois
23,500 Negroes Assembled at New York City
Millions of Negro Americans all Over This Great Land Claim the Right to be Free!

FREE FROM WANT!
FREE FROM FEAR!
FREE FROM JIM CROW!

"Winning Democracy for the Negro is Winning the War for Democracy!" — A. Philip Randolph

WHAT IS THE MARCH ON WASHINGTON MOVEMENT?

It is an all Negro Mass Organization to win the full benefits of democracy for the Negro people. It is pro-Negro but not anti-white nor anti-American.

WHAT HAS THE MOVEMENT DONE?

1. Won Executive Order No. 8802 from the President of the United States of America barring discrimination in war industries, government agencies and defense training because of race, creed, or national origin, the only such order issued since the Emancipation Proclamation.
2. Won the appointment of the Fair Employment Practices Committee to enforce this order.
3. Won thousands of jobs for Negroes in defense industries.
4. Brought together millions of Negroes in key cities all over the United States of America to protest against injustice and to demand redress of their grievances.

WHAT IS ITS PURPOSE?

1. To develop a disciplined and unified program of action for the masses of Negro people directed toward abolishing all social, economic and political discrimination.
2. To develop a strategy for non-violent struggle against jim crow and for the full integration of Negroes into every phase of American life.
3. To develop leadership from the mass of Negro people to struggle in their own behalf.

WHO CAN BELONG?

Every Negro who believes in our purpose and who wants freedom so much that he is willing to struggle for his own liberation.

WHERE CAN YOU JOIN?

There is a Branch of our Movement in your city. If there is not, you and your friends may start one by writing to the national office.

HOW MUCH DOES IT COST?

The yearly membership fee is ten cents per person, five cents of which is to remain in your local treasury and five cents to be sent to the National office.

WHO ARE ITS OFFICERS?

A. Philip Randolph, National Director

B. F. McLaurin, National Secretary

E. Pauline Myers, National Executive Secretary

WHAT ARE OUR IMMEDIATE GOALS?

1. To mobilize five million Negroes into one militant mass for pressure.
2. To assemble in Chicago the last week in May, 1943, for the celebration of

"WE ARE AMERICANS—TOO" WEEK

And to ponder the question of Non-Violent
Civil Disobedience and Non-Cooperation,
and a Mass March On Washington.

— —

I enclose my membership fee in the Cause For Freedom—ten cents (10c).

Name ______________________________

Address ______________________________

City ______________ State ______________

Mail to: E. Pauline Myers, March On Washington Movement, Hotel Theresa Building, 2084 Seventh Avenue, New York, N. Y.

THE POLICE ROLE IN A DEADLY RIOT

THURGOOD MARSHALL
The Gestapo in Detroit

The Crisis, August 1943

THE GESTAPO IN DETROIT

RIOTS are usually the result of many underlying causes, yet no single factor is more important than the attitude and efficiency of the police. When disorder starts, it is either stopped quickly or permitted to spread into serious proportions, depending upon the actions of the local police.

Much of the blood spilled in the Detroit riot is on the hands of the Detroit police department. In the past the Detroit police have been guilty of both inefficiency and an attitude of prejudice against Negroes. Of course, there are several individual exceptions.

The citizens of Detroit, white and Negro, are familiar with the attitude of the police as demonstrated during the trouble in 1942 surrounding the Sojourner Truth housing project. At that time a mob of white persons armed with rocks, sticks and other weapons attacked Negro tenants who were attempting to move into the project. Police were called to the scene. Instead of dispersing the mob which was unlawfully on property belonging to the federal government and leased to Negroes, they directed their efforts toward dispersing the Negroes who were attempting to get into their own homes. All Negroes approaching the project were searched and their automobiles likewise searched. White people were neither searched nor disarmed by the police. This incident is typical of the one-sided law enforcement practiced by Detroit police. White hoodlums were justified in their belief that the police would act the same way in any further disturbances.

In the June riot of this year, the police ran true to form. The trouble reached riot proportions because the police once again enforced the law with an unequal hand. They used "persuasion" rather than firm action with white rioters, while against

Negroes they used the ultimate in force: night sticks, revolvers, riot guns, sub-machine guns, and deer guns. As a result, 25 of the 34 persons killed were Negroes. Of the latter, 17 were killed by police.

The excuse of the police department for the disproportionate number of Negroes killed is that the majority of them were shot while committing felonies: namely, the looting of stores on Hasting street. On the other hand, the crimes of arson and felonious assaults are also felonies. It is true that some Negroes were looting stores and were shot while committing these crimes. It is equally true that white persons were turning over and burning automobiles on Woodward avenue. This is arson. Others were beating Negroes with iron pipes, clubs, and rocks. This is felonious assault. Several Negroes were stabbed. This is assault with intent to murder.

All these crimes are matters of record: Many were committed in the presence of police officers, several on the pavement around the City Hall. Yet the record remains: Negroes killed by police—17; white persons killed by police—none. The entire record, both of the riot killings and of previous disturbances, reads like the story of the Nazi Gestapo.

Evidence of tension in Detroit has been apparent for months. The *Detroit Free Press* sent a reporter to the police department. When Commissioner Witherspoon was asked how he was handling the situation he told the reporter: "We have given orders to handle it with kid gloves. The policemen have taken insults to keep trouble from breaking out. I doubt if you or I could have put up with it." This weak-kneed policy of the police commissioner coupled with the anti-Negro attitude of many members of the force helped to make a riot inevitable.

SUNDAY NIGHT ON BELLE ISLE

Belle Isle is a municipal recreation park where thousands of white and Negro war workers and their families go on Sundays for their outings. There had been isolated instances of racial friction in the past. On Sunday night, June 20, there was trouble between a group of white and Negro people. The disturbance was under control by midnight. During the time of the disturbance and after it was under control, the police searched the automobiles of all Negroes and searched the Negroes as well. They did not search the white people. One Negro who was to be inducted into the army the following week was arrested because another person in the car had a small pen knife. This youth was later sentenced to 90 days in jail before his family could locate him. Many Negroes were arrested during this period and rushed to local police stations. At the very beginning the police demonstrated that they would continue to handle racial disorders by searching, beating and arresting Negroes while using mere persuasion on white people.

THE RIOT SPREADS

A short time after midnight disorder broke out in a white neighborhood near the Roxy theatre on Woodward avenue. The Roxy is an all night theatre attended by white and Negro patrons. Several Negroes were beaten and others were forced to remain in the theatre for lack of police protection. The rumor spread among the white people that a Negro had raped a white woman on Belle Island and that the Negroes were rioting.

At about the same time a rumor spread around Hastings and Adams streets in the Negro area that white sailors had thrown a Negro woman and her baby into the lake at Belle Isle and that the police were beating Negroes. This rumor was also repeated by an unidentified Negro at one of the night spots. Some Negroes began to attack white persons in the area. The police immediately began to use their sticks and revolvers against them. The Negroes began to break out the windows of stores of white merchants on Hastings street.

The interesting thing is that when the windows in the stores on Hastings street were first broken, there was no looting. An officer of the Merchants' Association walked the length of Hastings street, starting 7 o'clock Monday morning and noticed that none of the stores with broken windows had been looted. It is thus clear that the original breaking of windows was not for the purpose of looting.

Throughout Monday the police, instead of placing men in front of the stores to protect them from looting, contented themselves with driving up and down Hastings street from time to time, stopping in front of the stores. The usual procedure was to jump out of the squad cars with drawn revolvers and riot guns to shoot whoever might be in the store. The policemen would then tell the Negro bystanders to "run and not look back." On several occasions, persons running were shot in the back. In other instances, bystanders were clubbed by police. To the police, all Negroes on Hastings street were "looters." This included war workers returning from work. There is no question that many Negroes were guilty of looting, just as there is always looting during earthquakes or as there was when English towns were bombed by the Germans.

CARS DETOURED INTO MOBS

Woodward avenue is one of the main thoroughfares of the city of Detroit. Small groups of white people began to rove up and down Woodward beating Negroes, stoning cars containing Negroes, stopping street cars and yanking Negroes from them, and stabbing and shooting Negroes. In no case did the police do more than try to "reason" with these mobs, many of which were, at this stage, quite small. The police did not draw their revolvers or riot guns, and never used any force to disperse these mobs. As a result of this, the mobs got larger and bolder and even attacked Negroes on the pavement of the City Hall in demonstration not only of their contempt for Negroes, but of their contempt for law and order as represented by the municipal government.

During this time, Mayor Jeffries was in his office in the City Hall with the door locked and the window shade drawn. The use of night sticks or the drawing of revolvers would have dispersed these white groups and saved the lives of many Negroes. It would not have been necessary to shoot, but it would have been sufficient to threaten to shoot into the white mobs. The use of a fire hose would have dispersed many of the groups. None of these things was done and the disorder took on the proportions of a major riot. The responsibility rests with the Detroit police.

At the height of the disorder on Woodward avenue, Negroes driving north on Brush street (a Negro street) were stopped at Vernor Highway by a policeman who forced them to detour to Woodward avenue. Many of these cars are automobiles which appeared in the pictures released by several newspapers showing them overturned and burned on Woodward avenue.

While investigating the riot, we obtained many affidavits from Negroes concerning police brutality during the riot. It is impossible to include the facts of all of these affidavits. However, typical instances may be cited. A Negro soldier in uniform who had recently been released from the army with a medical discharge, was on his way down Brush street Monday morning, toward a theatre on Woodward avenue. This soldier was not aware of the fact that the riot was still going on. While in the Negro neighborhood on Brush street, he reached a corner where a squad car drove up and discharged several policemen with drawn revolvers who announced to a small group on the corner to run and not look back. Several of the Negroes who did not move quite fast enough for the police were struck with night sticks and revolvers. The soldier was yanked from behind by one policeman and struck in the head with a blunt instrument and knocked to the ground, where he remained in a stupor. The police then returned to their squad car and drove off. A Negro woman in the block noticed the entire incident from her window, and she rushed out with a cold, damp towel to bind the soldier's head. She then hailed two Negro postal employees who carried the soldier to a hospital where his life was saved.

There are many additional affidavits of similar occurrences involving obviously innocent civilians throughout many Negro sections in Detroit where there had been no rioting at all. It was characteristic of these cases that the policemen would drive up to a corner, jump out with drawn revolvers, striking at Negroes indiscriminately, ofttimes shooting at them, and in all cases forcing them to run. At the same time on Woodward avenue, white civilians were seizing Negroes and telling them to "run, nigger, run." At least two Negroes, "shot while looting," were innocent persons who happened to be in the area at that time.

One Negro who had been an employee of a bank in Detroit for the past eighteen years was on his way to work on a Woodward avenue street car when he was seized by one of the white mobs. In the presence of at least four policemen, he was beaten and stabbed in the side. He also heard several shots fired from the back of the mob. He managed to run to two of the policemen who proceeded to "protect" him from the mob. The two policemen, followed by two mounted policemen, proceeded down Woodward avenue. While he was being escorted by these policemen, the man was struck in the face by at least eight of the mob, and at no time was any effort made to prevent him from being struck. After a short distance this man noticed a squad car parked on the other side of the street. In sheer desperation, he broke away from the two policemen who claimed to be protecting him and ran to the squad car, begging for protection. The officer in the squad car put him in the back seat and drove off, thereby saving his life.

During all this time, the fact that the man was either shot or stabbed was evident because of the fact that blood was spurting from his side. Despite this obvious felony, committed in the presence of at least four policemen, no effort was made at that time either to protect the victim or to arrest the persons guilty of the felony.

In addition to the many cases of one-sided enforcement of the law by the police, there are two glaring examples of criminal aggression against innocent Negro citizens and workers by members of the Michigan state police and Detroit police.

SHOOTING IN YMCA

On the night of June 22 at about 10 o'clock, some of the residents of the St. Antoine Branch of the Y.M.C.A. were returning to the dormitory. Several were on their way home from the Y.W.C.A. across the street. State police were searching some other Negroes on the pavement of the Y.M.C.A. when two of the Y.M.C.A. residents were stopped and searched for weapons. After none was found they were allowed to proceed to the building. Just as the last of the Y.M.C.A. men was about to enter the building, he heard someone behind him yell what sounded to him like, "Hi, Ridley." (Ridley is also a resident of the Y.) Another resident said he heard someone yell what sounded to him like "Heil, Hitler."

A state policeman, Ted Anders, jumped from his car with his revolver drawn, ran to the steps of the Y.M.C.A., put one foot on the bottom step and fired through the outside door. Immediately after firing the shot he entered the building. Other officers followed. Julian Witherspoon, who had just entered the building, was lying on the floor, shot in the side by the bullet that was fired through the outside door. There had been no show of violence or weapons of any kind by anyone in or around the Y.M.C.A.

The officers with drawn revolvers ordered all those residents of the Y.M.C.A. who were in the lobby of their building, to raise their hands in the air and line up against the wall like criminals. During all this time these men were called "black b—— and monkeys," and other vile names by the officers. At least one man was struck, another was forced to throw his lunch on the floor. All the men in the lobby were searched.

The desk clerk was also forced to line up. The officers then went behind the desk and into the private offices and searched everything. The officers also made the clerk open all locked drawers, threatening to shoot him if he did not do so.

Witherspoon was later removed to the hospital and has subsequently been released.

VERNOR APARTMENT SIEGE

On the night of June 21 at about eight o'clock, a Detroit policeman was shot in the two hundred block of Vernor Highway, and his assailant, who was in a vacant lot, was, in turn, killed by another policeman. State and city policemen then began to attack the apartment building at 290 E. Vernor Highway, which was fully occupied by tenants. Searchlights were thrown on the building and machine guns, revolvers, rifles, and deer guns were fired indiscriminately into all of the occupied apartments facing the outside. Tenants of the building were forced to fall to the floor and remain there in order to save their lives. Later slugs from machine guns, revolvers, rifles, and deer guns were dug from the inside walls of many of the apartments. Tear gas was shot into the building and all the tenants were forced out into the streets with their hands up in the air at the point of drawn guns.

State and city policemen went into the building and forced out all the tenants who were not driven out by tear gas. The tenants were all lined up against the walls, men and women alike, and forced to remain in this position for some time. The men were searched for weapons. During this time these people were called every type of vile name and men and women were cursed and threatened. Many men were struck by policemen.

While the tenants were lined up in the street, the apartments were forcibly entered. Locks and doors were broken. All the apartments were ransacked. Clothing and other articles were thrown around on the floor. All of these acts were committed by policemen. Most of the tenants reported that money, jewelry, whiskey, and other items of personal property were missing when they were permitted to return to their apartments after midnight. State and city police had been in possession of the building in the meantime.

Many of these apartments were visited shortly after these events. They resembled part of a battlefield. Affidavits from most of the tenants and lists of property destroyed and missing are available.

Although a white man was seen on the roof of an apartment house up the street from the Vernor apartments with a rifle in his hand, no effort was made to either search that building or its occupants. After the raid on the Vernor apartments, the police used as their excuse the statement that policeman Lawrence A. Adams had been shot by a sniper from the Vernor apartments, and that for that reason, they attacked the building and its occupants. However, in a story released by the police department on July 2 after the death of Patrolman Lawrence A. Adams, it was reported that "The shot that felled Adams was fired by Homer Edison, 28 years old, of 502 Montcalm, from the shadows of a parking lot. Edison, armed with a shot gun, was shot to death by Adams' partner." This is merely another example of the clumsy and obvious subterfuges used by the police department in an effort to cover up their total disregard for the rights of Negroes.

Justification for our belief that the Detroit police could have prevented the trouble from reaching riot proportions is evidenced in at least two recent instances. During the last month in the town of Atlanta, Georgia, several white youths organized a gang to beat up Negroes. They first encountered a young Negro boy on a bicycle and threw him to the ground. However, before they could beat this lone Negro, a squad car drove up. The police promptly arrested several of the white boys, and dispersed the group immediately, thus effectively forestalling and preventing what might have resulted in a riot. On the Sunday preceding the Detroit riots, Sheriff Baird, of

Wayne County, Michigan, with jurisdiction over the area just outside Detroit, suppressed a potential riot in a nearby town. A large group of Negroes and a large group of white people were opposing each other and mob violence was threatened. The sheriff and his deputies got between the two groups and told them that in case of any violence, the guilty parties would be handled and that the law enforcement officers would do everything possible to prevent the riot. Because of this firm stand, the members of both groups dispersed.

If similar affirmative action had been taken by the Detroit police when the small groups were running up and down Woodward avenue beating, cutting and shooting Negroes, the trouble never would have reached the bloody and destructive magnitude which has shocked the nation.

This record by the Detroit police demonstrates once more what all Negroes know only too well: that nearly all police departments limit their conception of checking racial disorders to surrounding, arresting, maltreating, and shooting Negroes. Little attempt is made to check the activities of whites.

The certainty of Negroes that they will not be protected by police, but instead attacked by them is a contributing factor to racial tensions leading to overt acts. The first item on the agenda of any group seeking to prevent rioting would seem to be a critical study of the police department of the community, its record in handling Negroes, something of the background of its personnel, and the plans of its chief officers for meeting possible racial disorders.

DETON J. BROOKS, JR.

Morale Sags at Camp Forrest as Jim Crow Rules

The Chicago Defender, November 6, 1943

TULLAHOMA, Tenn.—This little town tacked on the map just a stone's throw from Camp Forrest is where General Sherman started his march to the sea during the Civil War.

And the whites both in town and in camp never seem to forget it. They seem determined to convince Negro troops here that war is just what General Sherman said it was.

Jim Crow rules the roost with an iron hand at Camp Forrest. Colored soldiers at this Tennessee army post bitterly complain at the treatment they get here.

War is what General Sherman called it—at least to the Negro soldiers.

In talking to hundreds of soldiers and officers during a recent tour of this maneuver area, they cited any number of humiliating incidents which they have suffered and which tend to eat away morale so necessary in developing an effective fighting force.

Here's a description one northern-born soldier gave me of Camp Forrest: "My unit as well as all colored units, with the exception of the WACs, are isolated in one section of the camp, as if by contact we'd give our white brothers-in-arms the 'black plague.'

"When we are fortunate enough to get into the camp theatre, we're segregated. Any time there's a good picture, they won't let us in. They tell us it's crowded.

"They bar us from the camp library. Why they even refused to let a captain of the 931st Field Artillery Battalion stay in there. Yet there's no library for us. Since they put the captain out, they're building a dinky addition to our recreation hall. But as yet that's not finished.

"The facilities that we do have, like our recreation hall, and Post Exchange, are small and inadequate. While the white boys have large buildings with separate game room and reading rooms, ours are one-room affairs.

"The post command seems to spare no efforts to let us know that we are different, something apart from the other soldiers."

I visited in Tullahoma and found conditions equally as bad as the soldiers described within it. The colored USO center is located near the end of town in what is known as the Negro district. There is one medium-sized lounge room, a kitchen and a room which could pass for an office. This in contrast to four large, spacious buildings for white troops which are strategically located in various sections of the village.

The very location is depressing. All around the center are hovels and shacks, as bad as the worst to be found elsewhere in the South. The director of the USO club is a Chicagoan and former football player of Fenger high school by the name of Emmet Spurlock. Together with his wife and curly-headed little 10-year-old son, he is forced to live in a trailer because the whites won't rent him a decent house. He is striving manfully to carry on a real recreation program under the most impossible handicaps.

The railroad station is another rotten spot. Colored soldiers complain that they often miss their train when leaving on short precious furloughs because the clerks in the station won't sell them tickets until after all the whites have been waited on. Then it is too late to catch the train.

The soldiers say further that no matter how many men are travelling, they are allowed only one Jim-Crow car. If this is overcrowded they either have to ride in the baggage car or forfeit their travel privilege.

With the exception of the colored USO club, there is no decent place for a Negro soldier to go in town. Tullahoma is the typical southern village which is still fighting the Civil War. It will be remembered that it was from this town that a white soldier attached to the Illinois 33rd division had to be escorted back to camp by military police as a protective measure for asking to see where General Sherman started his march to the sea.

Investigation shows that all attempts to improve conditions for Negro troops in this camp have been blocked by post commanders. It was during the administration of Col. Millard F. Waltz that the theatre incident involving officers of the 931st

Field Artillery Battalion occurred. It was Col. Waltz who, backed by MP's carrying tommy guns, ordered these officers to leave the theatre for sitting in the non-segregated section. Col. Waltz, a southerner by birth, made no provision for Negro troops.

He has since been relieved by Col. Frank T. Addington, another southerner who boasts Virginia as his home. It is reported that he is an ardent believer in segregation although he is trying to make some provision for the recreation of colored troops. It is he who is building the "dinky" library addition. And he has given Negroes a couple of nights a month in the post dance hall.

The net effect of these conditions is extremely low morale among the troops. The northern boys and the more intelligent southern ones are bitterly and deeply resentful. They only go into Tullahoma when they have to. They spend most of their time in the camp areas.

The lower calibre southern boys, most of whom are in the engineering units, are not as resentful, but their appearance belies the state of their morale.

They are dirty, some of them look as if they haven't had a bath for a month. Their uniforms are untidy. They don't have the snap and zip which is a natural part of a fighting man.

Apparently, their white officers are doing nothing to inject into them the feeling that they are part of a proud fighting American army, which is destined to make a world safe for the democratic ideology.

PRAISE FOR A WAR DEPARTMENT FILM

JAMES AGEE

The Negro Soldier

Time, March 27, 1944

THE NEGRO SOLDIER (U.S. Army Signal Corps). This short moving picture has been two years in the making. The War Department authorized the film, but Lieut. Paul Vogel, the chief cameraman, had to do his job with old cameras which he pilfered (for the occasion) from Universal. During the shooting of one snowy sequence these tired machines froze up and he had to use an Eyemo 16 mm.

As anyone can see who knows or cares anything about the seriousness of the subject, the makers of the film have not included any of the dynamite implicit in a truly forthright treatment of the subject. There is no mention of segregation, of friction between Negro soldiers and white soldiers and civilians. But Carlton Moss, a Negro who wrote the film's script, was overall adviser for the production and acted in it, assured white friends who were discouraged by its mildness that the picture would mean more to Negroes than most white men could imagine.

Sneak-previews for Negro soldiers proved that Mr. Moss was right. At first the men, who have learned to expect veiled contempt in most Hollywood handling of Negroes, froze into hostile silence. But after 20 minutes they were applauding. For just about the first time in screen history their race was presented with honest respect. Many wanted to know: "Are you going to show this to white people?" Asked why, they replied: "Because it will change their attitude."

The Negro Soldier opens in a Negro church with the sermon of a Negro preacher (Carlton Moss). From its first moment, it is arresting. For the preacher is no Uncle Tom. He does not talk minstrel-show dialect or advise his flock that, for those who bear their afflictions meekly, there will be watermelon by & by, or the Hall Johnson Choir in the sky. He talks sober, unrhetorical English, and before long he is reading aloud (from

Mein Kampf) some of Hitler's opinions about those "born half-apes." While he reads, the camera moves among his listeners, quietly contradicting Hitler by the most powerful shots in the film—the intent faces of proud, enduring, mature human beings.

They continue to listen gravely while their minister tells them of the Negro's part in the making of America. The screen fills with historical paintings and with statuary, with bits from U.S. films which record the Negro's work in U.S. industry and warfare. They nod and smile when a mother interrupts to read a letter from her boy at camp. Then the screen fills with his Army story, from the day of his induction, and with images of Negroes at work in all branches of the service.

With deep feeling, the Negro congregation sings *Onward, Christian Soldiers.* In 46 minutes there has taken place on the screen (despite the bitter facts left out) a brave, important and hopeful event in the history of U.S. race relations.

FLETCHER P. MARTIN

Negro Marines Win Admiration Of Vets in Southwest Pacific

The Apache Sentinel, April 7, 1944

NEGRO MARINES WIN ADMIRATION OF VETS IN SOUTHWEST PACIFIC

ADVANCE BASE, South Pacific.—(By Courier)—Negro Marines, upholding a tradition which has blazed from the Halls of Montezuma to the Shores of Tripoli, have the situation well in hand in the Pacific perimeter. Young and tough, cocky yet serious, these United States Marines have landed, dug in, and won the admiration from battle-scarred veterans who expressed surprise at seeing Negroes wearing the coveted green of the corps.

The newest unit shoved into a Pacific post during the rainy season and has shown such boyish enthusiasm in living and working in ankle-deep mud, the commandant found it necessary to warn against over-confidence.

Trained especially for combat, and with the commendations of Navy Secretary Knox and Admiral Bill Halsey behind them, they wait the order to plunge into battle and defend the title of "the finest bunch of fighting men in the world."

The schoolish-looking Marines are aware they're the Negroes first to wear the red, white and blue of the 169-year-old branch of the service. Fully trained in the use of automatic weapons, small arms, invasion tactics and assault, they want to justify months of strenuous training and hard living during the "boot" days at Camp Lejeune, N. C.

Led by the highest ranking Negro Marine in the South Pacific, First Sgt. Nolan A. Marshall of New Orleans, over half of the unit volunteered for the service and expect 30 months overseas duty.

Capt. James R. Adams, Plainsfield, N. J., pulls no punches in praising his troops, especially Sgt. Marshall. The long and slightly built Negro has just turned 20 and gained his rank in 13 months to become one of the first in Marine history. The unit has 26 non-coms, and is the only one with a Negro holding first sergeant rank.

At headquarters, Admiral Halsey, theater commander, especially emphasized that his Negro Marines are the "best disciplined group" in the command. They were the only group emphasized during the interview with this correspondent.

Negro Marines are spread from Pearl Harbor to the Russell Islands, or roughly 3,000 miles. Unofficially, the number exceeds 10,000 now serving in the corps. Defense battalions as well as service units have been formed and are thought functioning.

COMMITTEE FOR EQUAL JUSTICE FOR MRS. RECY TAYLOR

The Woman Next Door: A Story of Unequal Justice

1945

A STORY OF UNEQUAL JUSTICE

The woman next door . . .

A Woman You Don't Know . . .

Mrs. Recy Taylor doesn't actually live next door to you. She might have. She is like your neighbor and hundreds of other Americans. Twenty-four now, she grew up in the country, and then moved to town (not a big town, Abbeville is about 2,000). After a while she got married and had a baby. When little Joyce was old enough to be left with friends Mrs. Taylor worked in the daytime (for things must be better for the baby).

Nights she'd sew, perhaps, or sit on the porch talking with Will, her husband.

Her life was like that—until something happened.

Last September 3rd, Mrs. Taylor left her child with Will, and went to church with Mrs. Daniels, a friend, and Mrs. Daniels' son. After the services they started walking home through the moonlit night.

The Car Passed . . .

The walkers didn't pay much attention until it passed again, then they noticed the seven young men inside. When the car stopped beside them, they drew together.

Mrs. Taylor was forced into the car at the point of a gun.

The Daniels, unable to find the Sheriff, found the Deputy, who started the hunt for the kidnappers. While he was at the home of Mrs. Taylor's father, Mrs. Taylor staggered in. She had been taken out into the country and criminally assaulted by six of the hoodlums. She gave the Deputy a description of the rapists and the car.

Confession

The car—and its driver—was found. The young man confessed, and is reported to have named the others.

Yet none of the rapists were detained in jail.

Mrs. Recy Taylor is a Negro

When Henry County's Grand Jury met on October 9th they refused to indict the rapists, in spite of the confession and the testimony of the Daniels and Mrs. Taylor.

But a new South has come into being. Forward-looking Southerners are fighting to wipe out the blot of unequal citizenship. It used to be said that in the South "A Negro has no rights a white man is bound to respect." There are sections where this is still true, such as the section of Alabama where Abbeville lies. Alabamans are refusing to allow this situation to continue. They asked for help in focusing national attention on the case. A Committee was formed, to make the facts and issues known. Alabama's governor was informed of the case. He assigned investigators to collect evidence. Again the confession.

Pressure's Result: A Special Grand Jury Meeting

The Governor asked the Grand Jury to meet again. Once more feudal attitudes prevailed. The twelve to six vote necessary for indictment was not obtained. But Alabamans are demanding justice. *The Birmingham News*, foremost Alabama daily, insists that Henry County bring the rapists to trial.

Equal Justice Can Be Won

1. Send letters, telegrams, resolutions to Gov. Chauncey M. Sparks, State Capitol, Montgomery, Alabama, commending his forthright stand. Urge him to use his powers as Chief Executive of the state to see that justice is done.

2. Send financial contributions to the Committee for Equal Justice for Mrs. Recy Taylor, Room 204, 112 East 19th St., New York 3, N. Y.

COMMITTEE FOR EQUAL JUSTICE FOR MRS. RECY TAYLOR

MISS HENRIETTA BUCKMASTER
REV. DR. BENJAMIN C. ROBESON
Co-Chairmen
REVELS CAYTON
CAREY MCWILLIAMS
Los Angeles, Calif.
REV. STEPHEN FRITCHMAN
Boston, Mass.
HON. MICHAEL J. QUILL
LYMAN BEECHER STOWE
New York, N. Y.
HON. C. PAT QUINN
FRANK X. MARTEL
Detroit, Mich.
DR. IRA DE A. REID
Atlanta, Ga.
HOBSON R. REYNOLDS
Philadelphia, Pa.
JOHN H. SENGSTACKE
Chicago, Ill.
SIDNEY WILLIAMS
Cleveland, Ohio
Vice-Chairmen
MISS GLENDA SULLIVAN
Executive Secretary
HON. HULAN E. JACK
Treasurer

COMMITTEE OF SPONSORS

(partial list)

Alabama
MISS CAROLINE COLLIER BALLIN
LOUIS E. BURNHAM
MRS. PAULINE DOBBS
CLYDE GANAWAY
CHARLES G. GOMILLION
J. P. MOONEY

Arizona
RT. REV. WALTER MITCHELL

Arkansas
DR. M. LA FAYETTE HARRIS

California
PHILIP M. CONNELLY
THEODORE DREISER
FRED FINKELHOPPE
MISS ELLA LOGAN
EMIL LUDWIG
LEWIS MILESTONE
HON. ELLIS B. PATTERSON
REV. CLAYTON D. RUSSELL
FRANZ WERFEL
MONTY WOOLLEY

Colorado
REV. J. A. THOMAS HAZELL
REV. W. T. LIGGINS
REID ROBINSON

Connecticut
MRS. RUTH DEMBO
CROCKETT JOHNSON
MRS. FLORENCE SMEDLEY

Delaware
REV. DELOS O'BRIEN

Washington, D. C.
DEAN WILLIAM C. HASTIE
REV. DR. WILLIAM H. JERNAGIN
LEE PRESSMAN
MRS. MARY CHURCH TERRELL

Florida
PROF. ROYAL WILBUR FRANCE
DANIEL R. FRANCIS
REV. EDWARD MAXTED
REV. M. D. POTTER

Georgia
BISHOP W. Y. BELL
DEAN BRAILSFORD R. BRAZEAL
DR. J. W. HAYWOOD
DR. BENJAMIN E. MAYS
MISS LILLIAN SMITH

Illinois
FRANK MARSHALL DAVIS
HON. WILLIAM L. DAWSON
GRANT W. OAKES

Indiana
WALTER FRISBIE
REV. FRANK A. HAMILTON

Iowa
REV. G. S. NICHOLS

Kansas
REV. JOHN WARREN DAY
BISHOP NOAH W. WILLIAMS

Kentucky
PROF. JOHN KUIPER
DR. WALTER W. SIKES

Louisiana
HERMAN C. GRAY
C. C. DEJOIE

Maine
REV. ROBERT MAYHEW

Maryland
DR. J. E. T. CAMPER

WALTER MACMANAMON
FRANK RHOAD
LEON SACHS
MISS ESTHER STAMATS

Massachusetts

CONRAD AIKEN
DEAN HARRIET M. ALLYN
WALDO FRANK
REV. F. HASTINGS SMYTH

Michigan

JUDGE LILA M. NEUENFELDT
JUDGE PATRICK H. O'BRIEN
C. LEBRON SIMMONS
SHELTON TAPPES

Missouri

REV. DAVID D. BAKER
MRS. RUTH H. PAGE
REV. CLAUDE WILLIAMS

Minnesota

JUDGE WILLIAM A. ANDERSON
MISS ANNE GERLOVICH

Mississippi

THOMAS SANCTON
REV. PAUL M. SHURTLEFF
H. RAYMOND VOSS

Montana

REV. WALTER B. SPAULDING

Nebraska

REV. CARL A. STORM
REV. W. B. WALTMIRE

New Hampshire

MRS. DILYS BENNETT LAING
REV. A. BROWNLOW THOMPSON

New Jersey

JAMES G. HUTCHINSON
JOHN A. MACKAY
DR. HARRY F. WARD

New Mexico

WITTER BYNNER
JOHN SLOAN

New York

JAMES EGERT ALLEN
MISS ELIZABETH BERGNER
LEONARD BERNSTEIN
REV. SHELTON HALE BISHOP
HON. PETER V. CACCHIONE
DONALD B. CLOWARD
COUNTEE CULLEN
HON. BENJAMIN J. DAVIS, JR.
MISS AGNES DE MILLE
HON. SAMUEL DICKSTEIN
OLIN DOWNES
DR. W. E. B. DU BOIS
MISS KATHERINE DUNHAM
RABBI MAX FELSHIN
ABRAM FLAXER
JAMES W. FORD
OSCAR HAMMERSTEIN, 2ND
LANGSTON HUGHES
CANADA LEE
HON. VITO MARCANTONIO
REV. WILLIAM HOWARD MELISH
MISS SONO OSATO
ARTHUR UPHAM POPE
HON. ADAM CLAYTON POWELL, JR.
C. B. POWELL
MISS HAZEL SCOTT
HERMAN SHUMLIN
MISS THELMA STEVENS
REV. CARL HERMAN VOSS
RT. REV. MSGR. H. WILKIE
MRS. STEPHEN S. WISE

North Carolina

DR. CHARLOTTE HAWKINS BROWN
PROF. CHARLES A. ELLWOOD
DR. C. H. HAMLIN
PROF. ELBERT RUSSELL
EUGENE SMITH

Ohio

HON. GEORGE H. BENDER
WILLIAM O. WALKER
BISHOP R. R. WRIGHT, JR.

Oklahoma

ROSCOE DUNJEE
REV. JOHN B. THOMPSON

Oregon

PROF. WILLIAM C. SMITH

Pennsylvania

RAYMOND PACE ALEXANDER
RT. REV. C. C. ALLEYNE
RABBI W. H. FINESHIBER
DONALD HENDERSON

Puerto Rico

HON. JESUS T. PINERO

South Carolina

REV. W. R. HAYNSWORTH
OSCEOLA MCKAINE
REV. CARL NIELSEN

Tennessee

JAMES DOMBROWSKI
DR. ALVA W. TAYLOR
REV. H. M. RATLIFF, JR.

Texas

MRS. ETHEL BLOOMFIELD BOGDANOW
RABBI HENRY COHEN
REV. JOHN C. GRANBERY
A. MACEO SMITH

Utah

JUDGE CLARENCE E. BAKER
REV. J. RAYMOND COPE
HON. SOL. J. SELVIN

Vermont

MISS GENEVIEVE TAGGARD
REV. A. RITCHIE LOW

Virginia

ROSCOE E. LEWIS
REV. J. OSCAR LEE
DR. HARRY W. ROBERTS
REV. C. W. SYDNOR, JR.

Washington
HON. JOHN M. COFFEE
HON. CHARLES R. SAVAGE

West Virginia
PROF. J. SAPOSNEKOW

Wisconsin
HAROLD CHRISTOFFEL
REV. MALCOLM DE PUI MAYNARD

Wyoming
KATHERINE NEWLIN BURT
REV. J. CLYDE KEEGAN

"AN ATTACK ON ALL WOMEN"

EARL CONRAD, EUGENE GORDON, AND HENRIETTA BUCKMASTER

Equal Justice Under Law

1945

EQUAL JUSTICE UNDER LAW

—

FOREWORD

American women have waged a long fight for social, economic and political freedom. Great American women have fought with their hearts and minds and bodies for these ideals. We know the names of some—Lucretia Mott, Susan B. Anthony, Lucy Stone, Harriet Tubman. Of hundreds of thousands whose names we do not know we do know that in kitchens and marketplaces, at desks and in schools they have fought to bring dignity, equal opportunity, and full citizenship to the life-bearers of our country.

When indignities occur, when humiliation is thrust upon any woman, in Alabama, in New York, in California, it is an indignity which must strike the nervecenter of everyone who deserves the name of human being. The sacred white-woman-cult of the South is a blood-sucking disease which affronts me as it affronts you. It robs the white woman of hope and self-respect, and it strips the Negro woman of dignity and confidence.

Let us acknowledge then what Recy Taylor represents to us. She represents more than a woman who chances to be a Negro in Alabama. She represents all the past and the future—our hope of a free new world, our passionate conviction that the day has almost come when women everywhere may raise their children without fear, and love their husbands with assurance, and be the individuals to which their highest hopes and capacities entitle them. This is what we are fighting for. When we say "Equal Justice for Recy Taylor!" we are also saying, "Equal Hope, Equal Joy, Equal Dignity for every woman, child and man the wide world over!"

Is that too much to ask? Why, that is the very meaning of life itself!

HENRIETTA BUCKMASTER

—

THE PEOPLE'S CASE . . .

By EARL CONRAD

On the night of September 3rd, 1944, a Methodist revival meeting was on in the small town of Abbeville, Alabama. That place, with about 2,000 people, black and white, lies in Henry County, in the heart of a great peanut plantation country only a few miles north of Florida, only a few miles west of Georgia. It was a warm night; a rich, full moon was rising, and the atmosphere inside the church was languid. The town, too, lay quiet. At about nine o'clock the church meeting broke up. A young man of seventeen took up a collection, turned it in to the pastor, then went out to meet his gang.

Mrs. Recy Taylor

The group of seven, aged 14 to 19, piled into a green, rattlebang automobile owned by a farmer lad, and they set out, as a white townsman later put it, "to see what they could find." They looked over the white girls who strolled along Abbeville's short main street, and then they rode out into the country.

They passed the Rock Hill Holiness Church where the Negroes were meeting and they noticed a crowd inside. They slowed down, peered inside the one-story wooden house of worship, and then turned back toward town. They halted idly for awhile, started up again, went back toward the Negro church.

It was eleven o'clock by now, perhaps eleven thirty, and the Negro church had let out. The people were going home in twos and threes. They strolled along, light of heart, in the moonlight, passing the orchards of pecan trees, passing the green-covered peanut plantations. The boys in the sputtering green car moved along the road, and in the full night light they could see the church people going homeward.

In one long stretch of the road a party of three moved leisurely ahead. The auto slowed down, and the boys looked over

Mrs. Fanny Daniels, 61, her son, West Daniels, 17, and the shapely young woman in the center, Mrs. Recy Taylor, 24, the mother of a two-year-old daughter.

The car snorted as it passed the walkers, went beyond a hundred yards or so, returned hesitantly and glided past the group again. The young men were debating an approach. And Mrs. Taylor was remarking nervously that the occupants seemed intent on them.

Suddenly the green auto swept up close to them, stopped abruptly, and the young men leaped out.

"Halt!" cried one.

"What for?" answered Mrs. Daniels.

The youths closed in on the churchgoers, one packing a rifle, others flashing knives, and the leader approached Mrs. Taylor, saying, "We want you . . . you in the middle . . . for a cutting in Clopton."

Mrs. Daniels protested that they couldn't want Mrs. Taylor: she had been at the Daniels home all day.

Now the young white men surrounded the party, the rifle pointed at the young matron.

"The sheriff wants to see you," they lied. "If you aren't the one, we'll bring you home."

Mrs. Daniels kept protesting; Mrs. Taylor thought of fleeing, and the gang spokesman now threatened to shoot. Then the boys clutched her, pulled her into the auto, fled off down the road.

The car headed for Abbeville, and, so Mrs. Taylor thought, toward the sheriff's. But the party turned off on a road that led away from the sheriff's office. Mrs. Taylor tried to leap out, but someone grabbed her wrist, held her tightly, as the car raced down the Old Columbia Highway.

Now, she thought, they're going to lynch me for something I didn't do.

"Don't kill me," she pleaded. "I got a little baby. Don't kill me!"

They told her to shut up; someone threatened to kill her then and there; another, shamming solicitousness, remonstrated, "Don't kill the girl."

The car sped for a mile until she heard someone direct, "Turn at the first fork in the road."

The car turned, then it moved over a cowpath a few yards and came to a halt.

The boys jumped out, and one threw a raincoat on the ground.

At gunpoint they forced Mrs. Taylor to get out, and pushed her over across the patch of ground . . . and now she knew what it was they wanted.

Her pleas for her child and for herself brought only curses and threats of death.

When the young men were finished with her, they told her to get her dress on, thrust her into the car, took her back toward Abbeville, dropped her blindfolded at the outskirts of the town and said to her, "If you tell, we'll lynch you sure."

Meantime the Danielses had hurried on home and aroused Mrs. Taylor's father, Mr. Benny Corbett. Then they awakened a nearby white neighbor, and at once they started to hunt for the sheriff. They succeeded in finding Deputy Sheriff Louis Corbett, and now the whole party went on a hunt for the kidnappers.

They drove around nearby roads; they sought but they did not find the young gang.

One other thing happened: the parents of the young men, wondering what kept them out so late, went into the center of the town to find them. There in the town main street, in the bright moonlight, the two searching parties met.

In the middle of the night Recy Taylor staggered into her home. The deputy sheriff was there at the time.

Deputy Sheriff Corbett vowed he would find the attackers—and he did, the next morning. He wasn't long in hauling in the driver of the car, and that young man named his accomplices. But the driver remained in jail only one day. The others never saw the inside of the place.

A significant thing happened on the day after the attack. Mrs. Taylor guided the authorities, including High Sheriff George Gamble, to the scene of the crime, and officials reportedly admitted seeing evidence of the attack.

Knowledge of the attack swept through the small community. Black and white received a shock. A pall hung over the Methodist revival which continued through the week. Mrs.

Taylor was known as a woman of excellent character. She worked at various white homes. Even the parents of the attackers, we are told on unimpeachable authority, knew her as a devoted mother, as a working woman who minded her own affairs, who went straight home from work. Mrs. Taylor, who spent the first fifteen years of her life on a plantation, has three brothers and sisters. Her husband worked in Abbeville at a sawmill and as a peanut thresher.

On October 9th a Grand Jury met in Henry County. Mrs. Taylor and the Danielses were questioned. The Danielses described the kidnapping. Mrs. Taylor told of the attack. But the jury split, returned a "no bill," meaning the youths were not indicted.

The failure to indict the Abbeville gang for the crime against Mrs. Taylor was serious enough without the need of any relief background to limn its horror. But there was, in the South, at the very time of the attack on her, a parallel situation whose handling by the authorities brought into contrasting focus the injustice of the "no bill" against the attackers. In Quincy, Florida, three young Negro men, accused of raping a white woman, were arrested, indicted, tried, convicted, and *electrocuted* in two short months!

The consequences in that case, and the callous indifference in the Recy Taylor case, sent a quiver of horror through right-minded whites in Alabama. They met quietly and talked it over. They drew Negroes into their conversations. The idea of making a fight for equal justice for Mrs. Taylor spread across the Alabama border, into other southern states, then northward. Now it is a national movement.

A few months ago, Mrs. Taylor wrote a letter to Eugene Gordon, a Negro newspaperman, who, like hundreds of others, had become interested in this case. She said:

"Afterward nobody in the town came to see me and nobody offered to provide a doctor . . . I hope and trust God something will be done about it . . . I can do nothing."

And now I want to turn you over to Mr. Gordon, who will describe how the people have been answering Mrs. Taylor's appeal. He'll discuss the pattern that made possible this crime and tell you of its political significance in this crucial war year.

. . . FOR EQUAL JUSTICE

By EUGENE GORDON

Of course, the raping of Mrs. Recy Taylor was a vicious crime. It was a fascist-like, brutal violation of her personal rights as a woman and as a citizen of a democracy.

The State of Alabama, with a highly efficient legal apparatus for punishing rapists, acts slowly, with deep reluctance. Its machinery, as smooth as oil in prosecuting the innocent Scottsboro boys, creaks and hesitates. Indeed, certain persons in Alabama are suspected of being ready to resort to almost any tricks to absolve the criminals.

But there is more to this than the raping of a Negro wife and mother in a feudal-minded Alabama town.

Negro women have been raped in the South for more than three hundred years. And the rapists got away with it. When I was there on the Taylor case last December I heard of a number of cases.

There is the case of a little girl in Montgomery. Unspeakably bestial, it was just ordinary for some parts of the South. Little Amanda Baker had been picked up in a car, carried outside the town, raped and killed. The murderer poured hydrochloric acid down her throat. He was white. He has never been arrested. Apparently neither Montgomery nor state police have interested themselves in trying to find him. She was just a little Negro girl.

I learned, when I was in Birmingham, about the Simpson case: white man took possession of a black man's wife when she moved into a little Alabama town ahead of her husband to prepare their new home; husband was waylaid and nearly killed by white men to scare him away from his own wife; she, helpless: the law, indifferent.

In Decatur, Georgia, three white youths admitted to police officers that they had severely beaten 20-year-old Walter Berry, Jr., a Negro, stolen Berry's car and forced his 17-year-old girl companion, also Negro, into a deserted cabin six miles away, where they criminally assaulted her in bestial fashion. The criminals were given their freedom under a total of $6,000 in bail. Both rape and sodomy are capital offenses in Georgia and the customary procedure is not to allow bail.

Horror stories whispered to me in Abbeville showed that town's treatment of Mrs. Taylor to be part of a pattern:

Fred Ward, Negro, 16, had recently been chased out of town for defending two young girl acquaintances from a group of white bullies.

Lee Ward, Negro, 17, was beaten by a mob. He had been accused of stealing five dollars.

Peter Johnson, Negro soldier, home in Abbeville after two years overseas, was beaten by a mob.

Robert Fagor, Negro youth, was threatened with lynching because, according to gossip, he had "insulted" a white woman. The "insulted" woman, it was later learned, had been friendly with the youth.

Wesley Johnson, Negro, jailed for "insulting" a white woman, was taken out and lynched. Bibb Graves, Governor of Alabama at that time, sought to impeach the High Sheriff —J. L. Corbitt. The first Grand Jury in session when this impeachment case was reported to them stayed deadlocked—11 to 7 in favor of indictment.

Yes, there is more to Mrs. Taylor's case than her having been raped. Mrs. Taylor is not the first Negro woman to be outraged, but it is our intention to make her the last. "White-supremacy" imitators of Hitler's storm troopers shrink under the glare of the nation's spotlight. They know that so long as that spotlight exposes them to the gaze of Americans they can neither escape responsibility for old crimes nor commit new ones.

Focusing national attention on the case, in support of Alabamans who are determined to wipe the blot of unequal justice from the South, the Committee for Equal Justice for Mrs. Recy Taylor brought powerful national support to Governor Chauncey M. Sparks of Alabama, who promised to investigate the case. As a result of the investigation, the case was presented once more to a Grand Jury, specially called to consider it, on February 14, 1945. But again—"no bill"—the boys went free again. Temporarily.

You, who read these words: think what this case means to you.

We are united in a war against fascism. We must not allow fascist-like acts to breach that unity. The boys lined up against

Hitlerism must know that their wives, their sweethearts, their sisters, their mothers can not be mistreated with impunity as was Mrs. Taylor. They must know that those they love are secure and safe in a democratic America, where laws apply equally to all citizens.

Sixty million jobs—such a post-war program demands our strength and our unity to a greater degree than ever before. We can strengthen our unity. We can do it, together, by proving to all of the peoples of the United States that our democracy is growing.

The attack on Mrs. Taylor was an attack on all women. Mrs. Taylor is Negro. But the only reason a black woman was singled out was that owing to economic, social and political inequality established during and held over from slavery, she was unprotected, and, therefore, easy prey. A part of her helplessness came from the fact that the criminals believed they wouldn't be punished. The black woman, and not the white, is generally the object of debasement, but only because the black woman is less well protected economically and socially. The white woman is safe only to a degree above the safety of the black woman. No woman is safe or free until all women are free. A fight to free all women is a fight for widespread and complete democracy in the United States.

All sorts of benefits have come to the Negro people—and, consequently, to the whole country—as a result of our fighting fascist tendencies at home while fighting armed fascism on the battlefield. There are Negroes in every branch of the armed services; Negroes in every branch of industry; Negroes integrated in the trade union movement, North and South; preparations under way to preserve the Negro's war gains for peacetime; Negroes elected to office by black and white voters; increasing numbers of white citizens in the South joining the fight for Negro rights in the South on a basis of equality rather than on a basis of paternalism.

But there are still the Fred Wards, the Lee Wards, the Peter Johnsons, the Robert Fagors, the Simpsons, the little Amanda Bakers, and all the countless fine and decent people who have had to suffer indignities, brutalities and death because they were black.

The fight for justice for Mrs. Taylor is a fight for them, too.

It is the duty—as well as the right and privilege—of every American to see that this fight is successful.

I am sure that you are doing your part to win the war. I know that the demands on your energies are greater than ever before—so much so that it may seem difficult to take this added responsibility for yourself and your organization. But, while this was being written, a letter came to our office. It came from thirty-three very busy people, enclosing a letter they had sent to the Governor of Alabama. The date line on the letter is "Somewhere in Belgium"—and the signers are soldiers.

Committees for Equal Justice for Mrs. Recy Taylor have been formed in a dozen states. More are in formation. Organizations of the people in almost every state have sent letters, telegrams, resolutions to Governor Sparks and his Attorney-General. Hundreds of meetings have been, and are being, held. Still—it is not enough. Her attackers still swagger on the streets of Abbeville.

This fight for equal justice can be won. The criminals can be indicted and tried under Alabama law for the crime of rape—if the voices of millions of Americans who believe that unity must be strengthened, that every fascist-like act against any minority group is an attack on democracy, are heard in Alabama.

The Governor and Attorney-General of Alabama must be aided in their pledge to do something about this case. They have at various times expressed determination to protect their womanhood: let us pledge our unqualified support. Let us insist that the letter and the spirit of Alabama's law against rape be enforced.

Mrs. Recy Taylor has become the symbol of free womanhood. The fight for justice for her has become the fight for equal justice and democracy.

COMMITTEE FOR EQUAL JUSTICE
FOR MRS. RECY TAYLOR

CO-CHAIRMEN

MISS HENRIETTA BUCKMASTER REV. DR. BENJAMIN C. ROBESON

VICE-CHAIRMEN

REVELS CAYTON
CAREY MCWILLIAMS
Los Angeles, Cal.

REV. STEPHEN FRITCHMAN
Boston, Mass.

HON. MICHAEL J. QUILL
LYMAN BEECHER STOWE
New York, N. Y.

HON. C. PAT QUINN
FRANK X. MARTEL
Detroit, Mich.

DR. IRA DE A. REID
Atlanta, Ga.

JOHN H. SENGSTACKE
Chicago, Ill.

SYDNEY WILLIAMS
Cleveland, Ohio

MISS GLENDA SULLIVAN
Executive Secretary

HON. HULAN E. JACK
Treasurer

YOUR SHARE IN THE FIGHT FOR EQUAL JUSTICE

1. Send letters, telegrams, resolutions to Governor Chauncey M. Sparks, State Capitol, Montgomery, Alabama, commending his action in bringing the case before the Grand Jury. Urge him to use his powers as Chief Executive of the State to see that these criminals are brought to justice. Send copies to the Committee, to your union publication, and local newspapers.
2. Initiate community or organizational membership meetings around the case. Copies of this pamphlet, a leaflet and petition collection-sheets are available for distribution.
3. Write the Committee, so that you may be kept informed of new developments. Whenever possible, groups in each community should work together on the case. We can help you by putting you in touch with other local groups.
4. Funds are urgently needed to carry out this program of national action. Send your personal contribution today, and see that your organization sends a generous contribution. Send checks to Hulan Jack, Treasurer, Room 204, 112 East 19th Street, New York 3, N. Y.

"A GRIEVOUS INJURY"

RAYMOND AND ROSA PARKS TO CHAUNCEY SPARKS

March 16, 1945

ALABAMA COMMITTEE
FOR EQUAL JUSTICE
POST OFFICE BOX 1589
BIRMINGHAM, ALA.

March 16, 1945

Hon. Chauncey Sparks
Governor of Alabama
State Capitol
Montgomery, Alabama

Dear Governor Sparks:

I should like to commend you for the action you have so far taken on the Recy Taylor Case of Abbeville, Alabama.

As a citizen of the state of Alabama, I urge you to use your high office to reconvene the Henry County Grand Jury on the Taylor case at the earliest possible date. As you know, four of the accused youth have confessed. Therefore, I am certain that you will see that all obstacles which are preventing justice in this case, be removed, in order that at the next meeting of the Grand Jury indictments will be returned.

Such crimes as this one are far reaching in their devastating effect upon our state and nation. There has been a grievous injury done to an individual. Because six months have elapsed and there has been no equal justice in the case, a shadow has been cast over our state. Such a crime also has a definite reflection upon the war effort. Alabama's Negro citizens have accepted their full share of responsibility in this war. Negro men and women have maintained an excellent record in the armed services, in our war plants and on the farms. Such injustice can only serve to disunite our people at a time when the united effort of all is essential to speed victory.

Therefore, I am sure that you will not fail to let all Alabamians know that their state and Governor stand for equal justice for all of our citizens, regardless of race, creed or color.

Respectfully yours,
Mr. & Mrs. R. A. Parks
22 Mill St. City 5

"THE GOOD THINGS OF LIFE
. . . MUST BE FOUGHT FOR"

THEODORE STANFORD
Reporting from Europe

Pittsburgh Courier

784TH WINS BATTLE HONORS IN CAPTURING GERMAN TOWNS

IN THE FIELD WITH THE U. S. NINTH ARMY—(By Cable)—The 784th Tank Battalion, crack Negro unit, which recently received its first real baptism of fire during savage offensive action against Nazi bastions in Holland and Germany, has won for itself the general reputation of being "the fightingest tank outfit in the European Theatre of Operations."

Accounts of the kind of fight these men put up at such bitterly contested towns as Sevelen, Straseelin, Kamperbruck and Rheinburg have become favorite topics of conversation among hard-bitten soldiers whose day-to-day lives are filled with the whiplash of snipers' bullets and the sudden terror of artillery fire and the strangely sickening odor of newly spilled blood.

MOST MEN FROM DIXIE

Most of these tankmen are of very ordinary education, coming chiefly from towns deep in Mississippi, Alabama, the Carolinas and Texas. They handle their cumbersome and complicated vehicles with the ease and sureness of a middle-aged matron trundling a baby carriage. Intensely conscious of the special role which the Negro soldier must play in this war, they have left a trail of goodwill behind them on their passage through five countries.

I have seen sober-faced Europeans of all ranks and ages remove their hats and stand respectfully at attention as the armored battlewagons manned by these tankmen thundered by.

I was the first Negro war correspondent to drop in and eat chow with the tankmen of the 784th, and to most of them, I was the first war reporter of their race they had seen. They received me with the calm reserve of men who have seen their best friends killed at their sides amid all the din and horror of modern military combat.

OFFERED GIFTS

When I left them a few days later they tried to force on me gifts of chocolate, cigarettes and souvenirs hoarded from their wanderings and battles. Most of these gifts I refused with a friendly handclasp. I was profoundly impressed because I knew that the actual cost of those gifts could be estimated only in the coin of agony and blood.

The story of the hotly fought battle for Sevelen already had been reported in the American newspapers. It was a good story, although war reporters realize how limited words can be when they are used in an attempt to describe such scenes. Sevelen, however, was not an isolated encounter. It was merely typical of the brutal opposition which these Negro tankmen have faced with gallantry and honor. The shell fire of other conquered towns still haunts their thoughts.

ATLANTAN IS HERO

Corp. James Rice of Atlanta, Ga. told me of his experience during the battle for Rheinburg, Germany. Said he: "We were moving up into the town when something suddenly hit our tank and our tank commander fell down, striking me in my back. I looked around and saw that he had been shot. I tried to keep him from falling down into the edge of the turret and held his head in my arms.

"Since we were under terrific small and heavy arms fire at the time, I rested the commander against my leg as carefully as I could. This allowed me to look through the turret so that I could tell the cannoneer what kind of ammunition to use. Continuing to fire, we backed our tank up to the edge of the woods. We had no sooner reached there when our gun jammed and we were forced to stop firing. We pulled back into cover of the woods and I think that is the only thing that saved us.

"The medics came and removed our tank commander who died shortly afterwards.

"He had been shot in the head and his brains and blood had splashed on my back when he fell."

CORPORAL TAKES COMMAND

The shot which hit the tank commander had immediately rendered him speechless and Corporal Rice, the tank gunner, took command of the vehicle throughout the rest of the action.

Sgt. Barney Ross of Dunbar, S. C., one of the battalion tank commanders, also participated in the conquest of Rheinburg. "We were the second tank in the leading column," he said, "and when we were about 500 yards from the town we drew fire from eighty-eights, mortars and small arms. For about twenty minutes we were pinned down behind a couple of small buildings. Then we pulled out, advanced about 250 yards and opened up with all we had. Bazooka shooters and automatic riflemen among the Germans continued to make it pretty hot for us, but we were able to advance about seventy-five yards under fire before we were pinned down again. It was about this time that one of our light tanks was knocked out by an eighty-eight shell.

PINNED DOWN NINE HOURS

"The Nazis kept us pinned down in that spot from ten o'clock in the morning until seven o'clock that night. However, during that time we killed quite a few of the enemy with our 37-mm. and small calibre guns. The Germans came out by the hundreds and surrendered to us. We waved them back to our infantrymen in our rear.

"We had entered the town with infantrymen on our tanks but the heavy fire had forced the doughboys to take cover in cellars of houses along the way. Finally the artillery fire got so hot that we were forced to withdraw. After we withdrew I set up a radio control station and called for more support. When I failed to get support I called back for further orders and was told to use my best judgment.

"I withdrew to the rear and that ended the part which my tank played in the action."

CHICAGOAN PRAISED

Sgt. James Mines of Chicago was one of the several men whom the commanding officers of the battalion pointed to with particular pride. In the assault of a small German town, Sergeant Mines led the attack column in the first tank. As his tank entered the town it was knocked out by the first round of fire from a concealed enemy anti-tank gun. Sergeant Mines remained in the turret of his tank and continued to fire on the anti-tank gun until his platoon leader ordered him to dismount and to set up a machine-gun outpost.

DIRECTED FIRE

After dismounting and consulting with his platoon leader, Sergeant Mines went to his platoon leader's tank and directed fire on the enemy anti-tank gun until it was silenced. This accomplished, he accompanied his platoon leader on a foot reconnaissance of the town. They were under constant sniper fire. Returning from the reconnaissance, they boarded the platoon leader's tank and moved into the town. The tank they were in was knocked out by another anti-tank gun. The platoon leader ordered the crew to dismount, covered them with machinegun fire and instructed them to seek shelter inside a building while he returned to the rest of his tanks for help. Disregarding his own safety, Sergeant Mines again set out with his platoon leader until ordered to take rest and cover.

OUTSTANDING COURAGE

His courage, alertness and attention to his mission greatly contributed to the ultimately successful effort of the task force.

T./4 Robert Smith of Detroit is another tankman of whom the battalion is especially proud. During the action in Straelen, Germany, a tank in his company was set on fire by enemy mortar shells. Sergeant Smith, who was riding with the maintenance crew of his company, was ordered to set up a defense. This having been accomplished, he assisted his maintenance sergeant in fighting the fire and in evacuating a wounded tankman who had been left behind for dead by the tank crew.

FIRES FROM HIP

While assisting in aiding the wounded crew member, Sergeant Smith was fired on by an enemy sniper from a nearby house. Grasping a 30-calibre machinegun, he fired it from his hip, spraying the house with bullets and killing one sniper. Directing the removal of the wounded man to a safer place, Sergeant Smith covered the movement of the rescue crew with continuous machinegun fire until the snipers were silenced. His hand was severely burned from holding the barrel of the overheated gun.

During an hour of holding the crossroads, Sergeant Smith alternately helped by firing various small arms and by assisting in the direction of 37-mm. fire against approaching enemy bazooka teams. His tank was withdrawn to a roadblock outside of Straelen where the rest of the task force was pinned down. There he helped to cover the repair of the roadblock by alternately firing and directing the 37-mm. machinegun fire from his tank.

March 31, 1945

DEMOCRACY GOAL OF TAN YANKS ABROAD

PARIS (By Cable)—Our Negro soldiers are tired of Europe and its battles, its mud, its story book cities and its prostitutes . . . Many Tan Yanks were little more than mere unshaven boys when they first touched these shores a year or so ago. Most of them will return to the United States seriously aware of the responsibilities that await them as "free male citizens of the world's greatest democracy."

The great majority are convinced that the security of human freedom and the dignity of human equality are as desirable for the black man in Mississippi as they are for the paler peoples of the European continent. The war has accomplished infinitely more than the simple uprooting of several hundreds of thousands of colored fighting men from their native soil.

EAGER TO RETURN

There is every good reason to believe that a more matured and democratically determined Negro will return to the States after the victory over foreign fascism has been achieved . . . The European beast is dead now and the Negro soldiers in the European Theatre of Operations are eager to return home.

But they are by no means weary of well doing. Most of them are determined to turn their newly found strengths to the task of helping American democracy realize its finest dreams.

I sat in the half shadows of a Dutch tile factory on a cold damp night two months ago talking to First Sgt. Morris Harris of New York City. The miscellaneous gear of an Army in bivouac cluttered about us . . . stacked carbines, duffle bags, messkits and empty jerricans.

AN "OLD" SOLDIER TALKS

At my right hand a "liberated" German kerosene lamp threw a feeble cone of light against one wall, and at my feet a home-made stove created a temporary illusion of warmth. All about us battle-weary tankmen snored in their sleeping bags on the unyielding brick floor.

Sergeant Harris was an "old" soldier as "old" soldiers go in this war. As he put it, he had been "sweating it out" with the 764th Tank Battalion for three of his three years and ten months in the Army. There was no question that he knew how to wear the six stripes and diamond on his left sleeve. He was proud of his wife and mother back home in New York City and therefore had the right to be considered a family man.

ASKS IMPORTANT QUESTION

There was a question on my mind as we sat there in the alien lamplight, chain smoking, chuckling at the assorted snores of the sleeping men, and remembering all the silly, useless things that a soldier likes to think of when the stars are bright at mid-night in a lonely night. It was a question that had followed me through four countries. I had tried to find the answer. I had formed some conclusions, but I wanted to be sure.

So I waited until the sergeant finished telling me one of his choice yarns and then said: "Sergeant, how has Army life affected the ordinary colored soldier? Has there been any fundamental change in his attitude towards life and times? What do you think will be on the average colored soldier's program when he gets back home?"

What Sergeant Harris told me that night corresponds in overall detail with statements that I have gathered from all over the ETO. These things represent, I believe, what goes on in the mind of the common every-day black fighting man when he sits down to think of the wife, the mother, the children and the country he left behind.

WANTS TO DO SOMETHING CONSTRUCTIVE

"First of all," Sergeant Harris said, "your colored GI wants to get back to the good old USA. Secondly, he wants to do something constructive. The Army has done a great deal for these men. It has given them time and cause to think. Many men want to go into business, the trades or the professions. They want more education because they see that education is required to fight the opposition which Negroes must face everywhere. They see that the world is moving and they must move forward with it.

"Fifty per cent of the colored soldiers that I know feel that they are playing a definite role in aiding the advancement of the race. Most of the men regret the fact that they are unable to keep up with the day-to-day news development. They are almost pathetically eager to learn of the things that are happening to colored people in America. The average Negro soldier is losing the habit of taking other people's words. He is asking more and more questions. He is tired of promises and wants definite security. Three-fourths of the men who lived in the South are determined not to return to their original home.

FEEL THEY DESERVE THE BEST

"They have traveled at home and abroad with the Army and have enjoyed greater opportunities in communities where there is less racial friction. They have fought and they have seen their friends lose their lives. They feel that they deserve the best that America can offer its citizens. The Negro soldier isn't living any sleepless nights worrying about how he can marry outside of his own race when he returns home. He is convinced that his own women are as fine as any in the world. His conception of democracy is simply equality of opportunity in all things."

In conclusion, Sergeant Harris said: "We soldiers learned that the good things of life are not dropped into a man's hand. They must be fought for."

I scribbled down the last words and slipped the notebook into my jacket pocket. We sat there for a while, saying nothing . . . the sergeant, with his helmet cupped in his hands, the dark lean contours of his face lost in the shadows.

Those were good things he has said and they were true. I knew that they were not simply personal because I had heard them from the lips of too many other colored fighting men. And as I sat there I couldn't help but think how proud all America should be of such builders from democracy as those . . . And also proud of one, Sergeant Harris, whom some of the tankmen called "The Ramrod," but whom his friends all affectionately referred to as "Doctor Boo."

May 19, 1945

GERMAN WOMEN SEE TAN YANKS AS MEN ONLY

Miss "Superwoman" Has Own Ideas About Males

PARIS—(Via Bomber Pouch)—I have yet to see a German woman who gave the slightest indication that she preferred the white American soldier to the Negro fighting man. The Nazi "superwomen" seem to look upon all of us, black and white, simply as what we are—Americans.

And if any illegitimate children crop up among this people during the coming year it's a pretty safe guess that the skins of many of these infants will register some familiar shades of brown.

In those early April days as we fought our way eastward to the rim of the Ruhr Valley there was something more than the mere instinct of "self-preservation" in the minds of many of the young German women and wartime widows. There was a look in their eyes, a swing in their hips, and a certain lingering hesitation in their steps as they passed us in the streets.

It was the same that we had seen in the companionable women of Belgium, of Holland and of France. And its meaning was the same.

To a great many of the German women, the arrival of our soldiers freshened the hopes of passions long deferred. A most natural reaction. The male Nazi youth had been a long time at the wars. And, to the burdens of those whom they left behind the weight of loneliness had been added. It was not strange, then, that many of these women should feel their blood warm at the sight of an Allied soldier.

MEN ARE MEN

They are women of the Nazi state. Yes. But, first of all, they were women. And, under the circumstances, they found it difficult to close the doors of their starved lives to this sudden possibility of affection. Would male companionship be anything less than male companionship, simply because it chanced to arrive wearing the combat boots and steel helmets of the American Army? They didn't think so—not if they had their way.

Such always has been.

Thus long before the broken Nazi armies had capitulated it was obvious that the Army was going to face some stiff trials in its attempt to enforce a rigid "non-fraternization" policy. And, weeks before the shooting had stopped, white and Negro GI's in Germany were being grilled on charges of "fraternization" and "rape."

Frankly, I had gone into Germany intensely interested in observing the reaction of its people to the Negro fighting man. Hitler had directed the main bulk of his race-hate philosophy against the Jew, chiefly because that unhappy people offered the most convenient target. But it was known that, on the Nazi calendar of human evolution the Negro was rated as little better than a beast.

The flaxen-haired young woman, who chatted pleasantly with me at the edge of the captured town, confided that she thought I had a beautiful coat of tan. Under the Linden tree, in the blue spring morning she held her thin, pale forearm up to mine to emphasize the thought.

HATED NAZIS

Because I understood the language poorly I was under the impression that she was a Dutch slave-girl. She insisted that she hated the Nazis. They had forced her to toil for long hours in a nearby munitions plant, she explained. "The Germans are good," she remarked repeatedly, "but the Nazis are no good." I was surprised when one of the battalion's white officers later told me that the girl was of ordinary German peasant stock.

Once, in the center of a town we had just taken a young housewife walked up carrying in her arms one of the healthiest looking infants I have ever seen. The attack on the town had been made by a combination of white infantrymen and Negro tankmen. There were at least half a hundred of these white soldiers within a few feet of the spot where I stood leaning against a jeep. Because our battle dress was the same I looked no different from any of the white infantrymen—except for the darker color of my skin.

AGAINST REGULATION

Completely ignoring the white American soldiers the young mother walked confidently up to me and begged me for a bit of chocolate for her baby. I declined. The woman fastened her large, pleading eyes on my face for a long moment, then turned and walked away. Some of the infantrymen were catching the little scene with open interest. But the woman ignored them and moved on without another word. Her narrow shoulders drooped and she appeared badly let down at my seeming lack of kindness.

As I watched her pass slowly down the street I was reminded of an old American Negro proverb: "A down-and-out white man will ask a Negro for help before he will go to the people of his own color." I felt a faint twinge of regret. It was against regulations to be friendly with these people—and my pockets were empty of chocolate. Sadly, I wondered if the poor woman thought I was prejudiced.

QUESTIONS FAMILY

On another occasion I followed a couple of heavily armed tankmen into the pitch black cellar of a large urban apartment house. By the dim glow of their flashlights the soldiers attempted to question several assorted members of a German family who were clustered together in the blackness of a low-ceilinged room. Nothing doing. No one spoke English. There was a helpless waving of Nazi hands.

Feeling a bit uneasy I fished my own torch out of a back pocket and began to play its beams, inch by inch, along the walls of the room. I had heard stories about what happened to American GI's who pushed their way into German cellars without first tossing in a hand grenade.

As I slowly inched the rays of the flashlight along the walls its beams suddenly fell dull on the face of a young woman who had been sitting motionless and without sound on a pile of straw mattresses. The effect was startling. She was one of those lush, honey-haired, blue-eyed, nineteen-year-old looking things. The kind that easily would have driven a Hollywood movie scout into raves. As I stood there staring at her I heard myself blurt out: "Say, fellows! Take a look at this beautiful blonde!"

And, that did it. Vanity had its way. The young lady of the mattresses blushed and dropped her eyes. She giggled and clasped both hands. She waggled her feet and wriggled delightedly where she sat. In general she gave every indication of the delicious embarrassment which a self-conscious and vain young woman feels when she has just been complimented on her good looks.

YIELDS TO FLATTERY

"So we do have someone here who understands English, after all, don't we?" I shifted the light partly from her face. She looked up, giggled foolishly again and answered "Yes."

By a stroke of vanity we discovered that someone in that cellar spoke something other than the German language. The girl had studied English for eight years at a local school. It was pleasant to hear her talk. When it became obvious that we were not there for the purpose of harming civilians one of the older men stepped forward and confessed that he spoke a little English. By way of explanation he said that he was a miner. I couldn't get the connection between a Nazi coal mine and the English language, but decided to let it go at that.

The miner thoughtfully apologized for the fact that he had no "Schnapps" on hand to give us. "You are not the first soldiers here," he said—or words to that effect. Whereupon we hastened to inform him that as model representatives of the American armed forces we never touch strong liquids anyway.

As we pulled up out of the cellar into the clean sunlight I was impressed by the fact that I had seen at least one of Herr Adolph's "superwomen" who didn't consider it beneath her blonde and Aryan dignity to relish the compliment of an ordinary black man.

To tell the truth, as I stepped across the body of a Nazi sniper whom some of the boys had neutralized that morning, I was rapidly becoming persuaded that Hitler had wasted a good portion of his racial theories on the German female population.

June 9, 1945

“I INTEND TO DESTROY SEGREGATION”

PAULI MURRAY

An American Credo

Common Ground, Winter 1945

AN AMERICAN CREDO

I AM an American. I lay no claim to an ancestry which arrived here by the *Mayflower* or by the slave-ship of 1619. I do regard myself, however, as a representative of blended humanity, carrying in my bloodstream the three great races of man—Caucasian, Negroid, and Mongolian. Some of my ancestors came from Ireland, Scotland, Wales, and England. Others came over in chattel-ships from Africa. Others were indigenous to American soil and met the colonists when they arrived. They all fought it out here and fused their bloods. I am the product. Therefore I will resist every attempt to categorize me, to place me in some caste, or to assign me to some segregated pigeonhole.

Nobody gave me my freedom. I owe it to no political party or the goodwill of any group. I inherited it. Some of my forefathers fought for it at Appomattox, Petersburg, and Richmond. Others toiled for it in Carolina tobacco fields, paying their masters dollar for dollar, and bought it. Others paid for it with their health, sanity, and their lives, jumping overboard from slave vessels or lying in swamps and crawling through the night into the shelter of the Underground Railroad. Others pulled a “mass strike” when the Union Armies invaded the Confederacy and helped disintegrate the labor force of the rebellious South. The Proclamation of Emancipation which Lincoln signed in 1863 was but the historical and documentary recognition of an accomplished fact.

As an American I inherit the magnificent tradition of an endless march toward freedom and toward the dignity of all mankind. And though my country has not always loved me, yet in the words of the poet, Claude McKay, “I must confess I love this cultured hell which tests my strength.” Loving it as I do, I am determined that my country shall take her place among nations as a moral leader of mankind. No law which imprisons my body or custom which wounds my spirit can stop me.

That my country may accomplish this great task of history, I must make myself worthy to be called an American. I would bring shame and disgrace upon the United States' flag if I tolerated for one moment any practice of discrimination, segregation, or prejudice against any human being because of an accident of birth which has determined race, color, sex, or nationality and helped to shape his or her creed.

For history moves in strange and unpremeditated ways. But for an error in navigation or a perverse trade wind the pioneers who reached Massachusetts would have landed in Virginia. As it was, the Virginia cousins became great slaveholders and slave breeders. The Massachusetts cousins became great slave traders and great Abolitionists. The North Carolina cousins became small cells of Unionism within a slaveholding state. The Pennsylvania cousins became Quakers and operators of the dramatic Underground Railroad.

Many of these ancestors of the 19th century had the vision of men who saw that a country cannot exist half-slave and half-free. They saw the abolition of slavery as the logical extension of the 18th century Declaration of Independence and the Constitution of the United States. The record of that vision is scattered on historical markers by gullies and streams in Maryland, Virginia, Pennsylvania, and Tennessee, and up and down the southeastern coast. They knew of no other way to destroy the slave mart save through sword and fire and blood.

But they have left for me and my contemporaries of the 20th century the task of destroying the incidents of slavery—segregation, discrimination, and prejudice. The Civil War was an inadequate answer to the slavery issue. Families were hopelessly divided among themselves; brothers and cousins fought on opposite sides of the lines. Spiritual and psychic wounds still fester in the Southland. The virus of an understandable hatred, the hatred of a conquered and expropriated people, has spread to every corner of our country. Its tentacles will engulf us unless we reach the heart of the monster.

And so, with my feet rooted firmly in the moral precepts of the Declaration of Independence and the Constitution of the

United States and all the preachments of humanitarian tradition throughout the history of man, I take my stand against the institution of segregation and all of its incidents. For segregation is a monster, dividing peoples, thwarting personalities, breeding civil wars. It must be rooted out of our national life. It must be replaced by individual codes of conduct and by federal and state laws which recognize and protect the individual. It must go during our life time.

But even while taking this stand, we must learn from the mistakes of our ancestors. Force is not the way. Bloodshed is not the answer. We deserve to go down in history as the most bankrupt generation ever produced, if with the total cultural and spiritual resources of the globe at our disposal, we cannot fashion superior instruments to those of civil war, of riots, of personal retaliation, and of mass resentment. We must span the chasms of internecine strife. We must heal the wounds even while removing the cancerous growth. It can be done. It must be done.

For me the process means an individual revolution in my thinking. I must see each man or woman as the product of his biological and environmental background. The forces of history of which he may be totally unaware have helped to shape his attitudes. His immediate environmental experiences have moulded his conduct. A lyncher in Texas may become a liberal leader in California. Had he been born in Africa, Mr. Bilbo might have become a great protagonist for the freedom of colonial peoples. Had I been born in South America, I might have hated North Americans for their inconsistencies.

The evolutionary law of survival teaches me I must be an integrated personality. I cannot be rent asunder by harboring personal prejudices or racial resentments. I want to spend my time finding the common denominator of mankind, and prejudice or hatred is an emotional waste. I will not vent my hatred for stupid customs and laws upon the individuals or public officials who seek to impose such practices upon me. I seek to destroy an institution, a mores, a disease—not a people. I must look beyond the human factor to the cultural structure, even though it be expressed in human terms. With my eye on the institution, the individuals who shape and are shaped by this institution fall into proper perspective. By every cultural, spiritual, and psychological resource at my disposal I shall seek to destroy the institution of segregation.

I will not submit to segregation myself so long as I am able to speak out fearlessly against it, or so long as my physical strength endures. Where segregation laws exist, of whatever variety, I shall attack the constitutionality of those laws. Where confronted with these laws in person, I shall resist them. If the refusal to abide by segregation statutes means imprisonment, I shall choose prison. If it means death, I can say only that my brothers and cousins are facing death every day. If I am not ready to give my life yet, I will leave the South where I was born and reared and find some spot in regional exile where I may still attack again and again such laws and customs. If my country is finally conquered by a national tide of prejudice which makes it impossible for me to breathe a free air, I will leave my country and find a new asylum, in the best tradition of the pioneers who helped to found America. For me there can be no compromise with segregation and discrimination.

I do not intend to destroy segregation by physical force. That would entail human waste and would not gain my objectives. I hope to see it destroyed by a power greater than all the robot bombs and explosives of human creation—by a power of the spirit, an appeal to the intelligence of man, a laying hold of the creative and dynamic impulses within the minds of men. The great poets and prophets have heralded this method; Christ, Thoreau, and Gandhi have demonstrated it. I intend to do my part through the power of persuasion, by spiritual resistance, by the power of my pen, and by inviting the violence upon my own body. For what is life itself without the freedom to walk proudly before God and man and to glorify creation through the genius of self-expression?

I intend to destroy segregation by positive and embracing methods. When my brothers try to draw a circle to exclude me, I shall draw a larger circle to include them. Where they speak out for the privileges of a puny group, I shall shout for the rights of all mankind. I shall neither supplicate, threaten, nor cajole my country or her people. With humility but with pride I shall offer one small life, whether in foxhole or in wheatfield, for whatever it is worth, to fulfill the prophecy that all men are created equal.

1946–1963

JACKIE ROBINSON'S FIRST MINOR LEAGUE GAME

WENDELL SMITH

It Was a Great Day in Jersey

Pittsburgh Courier, April 27, 1946

JERSEY CITY, N.J.—The sun smiled down brilliantly in picturesque Roosevelt Stadium here Thursday afternoon and an air of excitement prevailed throughout the spacious park, which was jammed to capacity with 25,000 jabbering, chattering opening day fans . . . A seething mass of humanity, representing all segments of the crazy-quilt we call America, poured into the magnificent ball park they named after a man from Hyde Park—Franklin D. Roosevelt—to see Montreal play Jersey City and the first two Negroes in modern baseball history perform, Jackie Robinson and Johnny Wright . . . There was the usual fanfare and color, with Mayor Frank Hague chucking out the first ball, the band music, kids from Jersey City schools putting on an exhibition of running, jumping and acrobatics . . . There was also the hot dogs, peanuts and soda pop . . . And some guys in the distant bleachers whistled merrily: "Take Me Out to the Ball Game" . . . Wendell Willkie's "One World" was right here on the banks of the Passaic River.

The outfield was dressed in a gaudy green, and the infield was as smooth and clean as a new-born babe . . . And everyone sensed the significance of the occasion as Robinson and Wright marched with the Montreal team to deep centerfield for the raising of the Stars and Stripes and the "Star-Spangled Banner" . . . Mayor Hague strutted proudly with his henchmen flanking him on the right and left . . . While the two teams, spread across the field, marched side by side with military precision and the band played on . . . We all stood up—25,000 of us—when the band struck up the National Anthem . . . And we sang lustily and freely, for this was a great day . . . Robinson and Wright stood out there with the rest of the players and dignitaries, clutching their blue-crowned baseball caps, standing erect and as still as West Point cadets on dress parade.

No one will ever know what they were thinking right then, but I have traveled more than 2,000 miles with these courageous pioneers during the past nine weeks—from Sanford, Fla., to Daytona Beach to Jersey City—and I feel that I know them probably better than any newspaperman in the business . . . I know that their hearts throbbed heavily and thumped a steady tempo with the big drum that was pounding out the rhythm as the flag slowly crawled up the centerfield mast.

And then there was a tremendous roar as the flag reached its crest and unfurled gloriously in the brilliant April sunlight . . . The 25,000 fans settled back in their seats, ready for the ball game as the Jersey City Giants jogged out to their positions . . . Robinson was the second batter and as he strolled to the plate the crowd gave him an enthusiastic reception . . . They were for him . . . They all knew how he had overcome many obstacles in the deep South, how he had been barred from playing in Sanford, Fla., Jacksonville, Savannah and Richmond . . . And yet, through it all, he was standing at the plate as the second baseman of the Montreal team . . . The applause they gave so willingly was a salute of appreciation and admiration . . . Robinson then socked a sizzler to the shortstop and was thrown out by an eyelash at first base.

The second time he appeared at the plate marked the beginning of what can develop into a great career. He got his first hit as a member of the Montreal Royals . . . It was a mighty home run over the leftfield fence . . . With two mates on the base paths, he walloped the first pitch that came his way and there was an explosive "crack" as bat and ball met . . . The ball glistened brilliantly in the afternoon sun as it went hurtling high and far over the leftfield fence . . . And, the white flag on the foul-line pole in left fluttered lazily as the ball whistled by.

Robinson jogged around the bases—his heart singing, a broad smile on his beaming bronze face as his two teammates trotted homeward ahead of him . . . When he rounded third, Manager Clay Hopper, who was coaching there, gave him a heavy pat on the back and shouted: "That's the way to hit that ball!" . . . Between third and home-plate he received another ovation from the stands, and then the entire Montreal team stood up and welcomed him to the bench

. . . White hands slapping him on his broad back . . . Deep Southern voices from the bench shouted, "Yo sho' hit 'at one, Robbie, nice goin' kid!" . . . Another said: "Them folks 'at wouldn't let you play down in Jacksonville should be hee'ah now. Whoopee!" . . . And still another: "They cain't stop ya now, Jackie, you're really goin' places, and we're going to be right there with ya!" . . . Jackie Robinson laughed softly and smiled . . . Johnny Wright, wearing a big, blue pitcher's jacket, laughed and smiled . . . And, high up in the press box, Joe Bostic of the Amsterdam News and I looked at each other knowingly, and we, too, laughed and smiled . . . Our hearts beat just a bit faster, and the thrill ran through us like champagne bubbles . . . It was a great day in Jersey . . . It was a great day in baseball!

But he didn't stop there, this whirlwind from California's gold coast . . . He ran the bases like a wild colt from the Western plains. He laid down two perfect bunts and slashed a hit into rightfield . . . He befuddled the pitchers, made them balk when he was roaring up and down the base paths, and demoralized the entire Jersey City team . . . He was a hitting demon and a base-running maniac . . . The crowd gasped in amazement . . . The opposing pitchers shook their heads in helpless agony . . . His understanding teammates cheered him on with unrivaled enthusiasm . . . And Branch Rickey, the man who had the fortitude and courage to sign him, heard the phenomenal news via telephone in the offices of the Brooklyn Dodgers at Ebbetts Field and said admiringly—"He's a wonderful boy, that Jackie Robinson—a wonderful boy!"

When the game ended and Montreal had chalked up a 14 to 1 triumph, Robinson dashed for the club house and the showers . . . But before he could get there he was surrounded by a howling mob of kids, who came streaming out of the bleachers and stands . . . They swept down upon him like a great ocean wave and he was drowned in a sea of adolescent enthusiasm . . . There he was—this Pied Piper of the diamond—perspiration rolling off his bronze brow, idolizing kids swirling all around him, autograph hounds tugging at him . . . And big cops riding prancing steeds trying unsuccessfully to disperse the mob that had cornered the hero of the day . . . One of his own teammates fought his way through the howling mob and finally "saved" Robinson . . . It was Red Durrett, who was a hero in his own right because he had pounded out two prodigious home runs himself, who came to the "rescue." He grabbed Robinson by the arm and pulled him through the crowd. "Come on," Durrett demanded, "you'll be here all night if you don't fight them off. They'll mob you. You can't possibly sign autographs for all those kids."

So, Jackie Robinson, escorted by the red-head outfielder, finally made his way to the dressing room. Bedlam broke loose in there, too . . . Photographers, reporters, kibitzers and hangers-on fenced him in . . . It was a virtual madhouse . . . His teammates, George Shuba, Stan Breard, Herman Franks, Tom Tatum, Marvin Rackley and all the others, were showering congratulations on him . . . They followed him into the showers, back to his locker and all over the dressing room . . . Flash bulbs flashed and reporters fired questions with machine-gun like rapidity . . . And Jackie Robinson smiled through it all.

As he left the park and walked out onto the street, the once-brilliant sun was fading slowly in the distant western skies . . . His petite and dainty little wife greeted him warmly and kindly, "You've had quite a day, little man," she said sweetly.

"Yes," he said softly and pleasantly, "God has been good to us today!"

HARRY RAYMOND

Lynch Try Fails on "Daily" Man and Lawyers in Tenn.

Daily Worker, November 20, 1946

LYNCH TRY FAILS ON "DAILY" MAN AND LAWYERS IN TENN.

NASHVILLE, Tenn., Nov. 19.—I saw the gun toting Ku Klux Klan in action on the outskirts of Columbia, Tenn., last night. They were not wearing white sheets. They were operating as official law enforcement officers of the city, county and state. Cowardly men, they had plotted what they thought would be the perfect frame-up and perhaps a lynching. But they failed.

It all started at seven o'clock last night, when a jury of white men marched into the newly-painted Maury County Courtroom. J. W. Russell, local tire dealer and jury foreman, announced that after an hour and 25 minutes deliberation he and his colleagues had come to the conclusion that William Pillow, 38-year-old Negro stone mason, was not guilty of shooting and wounding a state highway patrolman on Feb. 26, the day after the Columbia Negro community took up arms and stopped the lynching of James Stephenson, navy veteran of major Pacific campaigns.

A few minutes later, Lloyd Kennedy, 21-year-old Negro bootblack, walked out of the courtroom on $5,000 bail. The jury had declared him guilty of firing a shotgun at the patrolman. But they declined to render the verdict demanded by a violent prosecutor, a man called Paul F. Bumpus.

Bumpus had told the jury all law enforcement would break down and wives of jurymen would die at the hands of Negro assassins if Kennedy, as well as Pillow, were not convicted of attempt to commit murder in the first degree and sentenced to 21 years. The jury sentenced Kennedy to serve a five-year maximum term for attempt to commit murder in the second degree. Motion for a new trial set him free on bail.

As I left the courtroom to telegraph the verdict to the Daily Worker, another man, a heavy set Columbian, dashed through the door beside me. He was agitated and declared: "Something must be done," to make up for "failure of the jury system." I recalled that the man called Bumpus a few hours before had suggested that the citizens should organize if the jury failed to impose the maximum sentence against the two Negro defendants.

The atmosphere was tense. I expected something serious, something of a violent nature, to happen. I could have gotten away from it all by returning to Nashville with two Tennessee newspapermen who pleaded with me to ride out of town in their car.

The newspapermen were my friends. But the two Negro lawyers and the white attorney for the defense were also my friends. I knew my job of reporting would not be completed until I personally knew these men, attorneys for the National Association for Advancement of Colored People, were safely out of Columbia.

They had been threatened with lynching. I had heard the threats. I thereupon thanked my newspaper friends for the offer of transportation to Nashville. I told them I would go to Nashville in the automobile owned by Z. Alexander Looby, Nashville Negro attorney and chief defense counsel. Dr. Looby had invited me to ride in the car with him.

We took off from Columbia's "Mink Slide," Negro business district, shortly before eight o'clock in the evening. Thurgood Marshall, brilliant general counsel for the NAACP, was driving the car. I sat next to him in the front seat.

Sitting in the back, amid stacks of law books and typewritten records of the case, sat Looby, owner of the car, and Maurice Weaver of Chattanooga, lone white attorney for the defense. I had warned Weaver I had reason to believe a lynch mob was on the prowl—some of the same gang that tried to hang Stephenson.

We did not have long to wait. Three-quarters of a mile north of the Duck River, on the Nashville Highway, we were hailed to a stop by eight men in three cars. One car, operated by two highway patrolmen, tore past us with siren screaming. It parked in front of us. We were at once pounced upon by the highway patrolmen, several men in civilian clothes and two Columbia policemen.

They approached us with right hands on their pistols and blinding us with flashlights carried in their left hands.

The three lawyers and myself were unarmed. It looked like a lynching. We knew officers of the law had directed and participated in two earlier Maury County lynchings; that they killed two Negroes in the County Jail during the February "trouble." And we had evidence that they were the ones that marked the huge KKK on a casket in a Negro undertaking parlor during the February raid.

Facing guns and glaring flashlights, we piled out of the car, Weaver acting as spokesman and protesting vigorously against the violation of our civil rights. It was an uneven affair. We had nothing but our bare fists. The thugs, who identified themselves as constables, deputy sheriffs, city policemen and highway patrolmen, were heavily armed.

They told us they had a warrant to search the car. We demanded they produce the warrant. They did. And we read it under the flashlights. It was a John Doe warrant, signed by Sam Butts, Columbia deputy sheriff, charging we were transporting liquor in violation of the county local option law. But a search of the car revealed no liquor.

The three lawyers and I returned to the car and Looby took Marshall's place at the wheel. We drove off a short distance, only to be surrounded again by the armed men. This time they charged Marshall had been driving without a license. Marshall produced his license and the gunmen reluctantly told us we could proceed.

We started the car, Looby driving, and were surrounded and halted again. They told me I had been driving the car. I told them they were talking foolishly. There was a short conference. The thugs returned and declared Marshall under arrest for driving while "under the influence of liquor."

The gunmen hustled Marshall into a car, told the rest of us we were free to go. But we feared Marshall was being carried off to be picked up by a lynch mob as had happened in earlier cases. We were more certain of this when the car bearing Marshall turned off the highway and speeded up a back country dirt road.

With our front bumper almost touching the rear of the raiders' car, we trailed them. Looby was at the wheel. The thugs turned back into Columbia. Marshall was taken out of the car and marched into the office of Magistrate J. J. Pogue.

Weaver and I leaped from our car and followed Thurgood and the officers into the building. Looby, driving at top speed, dashed to the Negro district to spread the alarm and secure money and bonds, which we thought would be necessary to get Marshall out of the clutches of the county officers.

Highway patrolmen and city policemen did not enter the Magistrate's office. They circled the area.

Weaver and I immediately confronted the Magistrate. He admitted he had issued the frame-up warrant to search the car. The armed county officers surrounded us. Weaver angrily denounced the county officers as a bunch of "frame-up" artists. He demanded Magistrate Pogue at once examine Marshall, smell his breath and decide whether the Negro lawyer had been drinking. Pogue ordered Marshall to breathe long breaths in his direction.

Pogue turned to the county officers and declared: "This man has not been drinking. I will not sign a warrant for his arrest."

The elderly Magistrate then proceeded to denounce the frame-up. He shook hands with the Negro lawyer, with Weaver and with me. One by one the county officers, their hands on their pistol butts, left the room.

Magistrate Pogue then told us the county officers had come to the wrong man if they wanted to frame-up one of the Negro lawyers. He said he was the one Magistrate in Columbia who refused to sign warrants for the arrest of Negroes during the February raids. "They didn't come to me," Pogue declared. "You can look at my books and there's not a record there of any arrests ordered by me during the February trouble."

But they did come to Magistrate C. Hayes Denton, old-time Maury County lynch mob leader. There might have been another lynching last night if Denton could have been found. That's what we feared. For it has been Denton's tactic to remand the person marked for lynching to jail.

Then a few telephone calls bring the boys out with the rope to storm the jail and to do the job. That has been the pattern of all recent Maury County lynchings.

I am certain such a lynching was planned last night. Thurgood Marshall was the intended victim. But the lynchers failed to carry out their plan because they are cowardly men and they knew we had the entire Columbia Negro community mobilized behind us.

I have not mentioned in this dispatch the names of any of the officers who held us captive on the Nashville highway. But if they think they are unknown, they are badly mistaken.

I have all their names written carefully in my notebook. Marshall, Looby, Weaver and myself demand that each of them be prosecuted to the full extent of the law for their shocking illegal gestapo-like conduct.

ATTORNEY DEMANDS CLARK PROSECUTE TENN. THUGS

NASHVILLE, Tenn., Nov. 19.—The following telegram was sent today to U.S. Attorney General Tom Clark by Thurgood Marshall, general counsel for the National Association for Advancement of Colored People:

"Last night after leaving Columbia, Tenn., where we secured acquittal of one of two Negroes charged with crimes growing out of February disturbances there, lawyers, including myself, were stopped outside Columbia in the night by three carloads of officers, including deputy sheriffs, city policemen, constables and highway patrolmen.

"The alleged purpose was to search the car for whiskey. When no whiskey was found we were stopped by the same officials two more times and on the last occasion I was placed under arrest for driving while drunk and returned to Columbia.

"The magistrate refused to place me in jail after examining me and finding I was completely sober. This type of intimidation of defense lawyers charged with the duty of defending persons charged with crime cannot go unnoticed. Therefore, I demand immediate investigation and criminal charges against the officers participating in last night's outrage. The three lawyers were Z. Alexander Looby, Maurice Weaver and myself."

Maurice Weaver, lone white defense attorney in the Columbia cases, announced he would also demand action against the raiding officers for attempts to illegally intimidate Harry Raymond, Daily Worker correspondent, who was riding in the car with the lawyers bound for Nashville. Weaver charged Raymond, newspaperman assigned to cover the Columbia trial, was held captive by officers on the dark highway along with the lawyers in violation of constitutional rights of freedom of the press.

Commenting on the incident, Weaver declared:

"Mr. Raymond was with us when we were stopped and also went with me when I appeared before Magistrate J. J. Pogue to demand the immediate release of Mr. Marshall. He knows the whole story of the outrageous, un-democratic and tyrannical procedure. Mr. Raymond stood alone by my side, surrounded by armed thugs, in the Magistrate's office outrageously demanding the release of Mr. Marshall."

JOURNAL OF THE NATIONAL MEDICAL ASSOCIATION
Make Lynching a Federal Offense

July 1947

MAKE LYNCHING A FEDERAL OFFENSE

IF THERE WERE NEED of further evidence to prove that a lynch mob cannot be convicted in the civil courts of the South, the recent mock trial in Greenville, S. C., furnished it in the case of the State of South Carolina against the mob of 28 persons charged with lynching Willie Earle for the reputed killing of a white taxicab driver.

For the accused who had committed this shocking crime against the victim, against the commonwealth of South Carolina, against humanity, against the laws of God, the "trial" was hardly more than a holiday experience.

There is one outstanding exception to the above. We believe that those who followed the trial were impressed that the judge interpreted the law intelligently, ruled impartially, and charged the jury legally, and yet that jury returned a unanimous verdict of "not guilty" for that group of confirmed lynchers. The trial proved to be only a farce.

The lynching of Negroes in the South for any offense involving a member of the white race in practically any locality is such a fixed policy that there is only one remedy, and that is for Congress to enact a law making lynching a federal crime to be tried, not before a local jury, but in a United States court, with a change of venue to whatever extent necessary. Even if a Constitutional Amendment is necessary for the purpose, such a step should be taken.

DISCOVERING RACIAL DIFFERENCE

ANNE MOODY

from *Coming of Age in Mississippi*

1947–48

THAT WHITE LADY Mama was working for worked her so hard that she always came home griping about backaches. Every night she'd have to put a red rubber bottle filled with hot water under her back. It got so bad that she finally quit. The white lady was so mad she couldn't get Mama to stay that the next day she told Mama to leave to make room for the new maid.

This time we moved two miles up the same road. Mama had another domestic job. Now she worked from breakfast to supper and still made five dollars a week. But these people didn't work Mama too hard and she wasn't as tired as before when she came home. The people she worked for were nice to us. Mrs. Johnson was a schoolteacher. Mr. Johnson was a rancher who bought and sold cattle. Mr. Johnson's mother, an old lady named Miss Ola, lived with them.

Our house, which was separated from the Johnsons' by a field of clover, was the best two-room house we had been in yet. It was made out of big new planks and it even had a new toilet. We were also once again on paved streets. We just did make those paved streets, though. A few yards past the Johnsons' house was the beginning of the old rock road we had just moved off.

We were the only Negroes in that section, which seemed like some sort of honor. All the whites living around there were well-to-do. They ranged from schoolteachers to doctors and prosperous businessmen. The white family living across the street from us owned a funeral home and the only furniture store in Centreville. They had two children, a boy and a girl. There was another white family living about a quarter of a mile in back of the Johnsons who also had a boy and a girl. The two white girls were about my age and the boys a bit younger. They often rode their bikes or skated down the little hill just in front of our house. Adline, Junior and I would sit and watch them. How we wished Mama could buy us a bike or even a pair of skates to share.

There was a wide trench running from the street alongside our house. It separated our house and the Johnsons' place from a big two-story house up on the hill. A big pecan tree grew on our side of the trench, and we made our playhouse under it so we could sit in the trench and watch those white children without their knowing we were actually out there staring at them. Our playhouse consisted of two apple crates and a tin can that we sat on.

One day when the white children were riding up and down the street on their bikes, we were sitting on the apple crates making Indian noises and beating the tin can with sticks. We sounded so much like Indians that they came over to ask if that was what we were. This was the beginning of our friendship. We taught them how to make sounds and dance like Indians and they showed us how to ride their bikes and skate. Actually, I was the only one who learned. Adline and Junior were too small and too scared, although they got a kick out of watching us. I was seven, Adline five, and Junior three, and this was the first time we had ever had other children to play with. Sometimes, they would take us over to their playhouse. Katie and Bill, the children of the whites that owned the furniture store, had a model playhouse at the side of their parents' house. That little house was just like the big house, painted snow white on the outside, with real furniture in it. I envied their playhouse more than I did their bikes and skates. Here they were playing in a house that was nicer than any house I could have dreamed of living in. They had all this to offer me and I had nothing to offer them but the field of clover in summer and the apple crates under the pecan tree.

The Christmas after we moved there, I thought sure Mama would get us some skates. But she didn't. We didn't get anything but a couple of apples and oranges. I cried a week for those skates, I remember.

Every Saturday evening Mama would take us to the movies. The Negroes sat upstairs in the balcony and the whites sat downstairs. One Saturday we arrived at the movies at the same time as the white children. When we saw each other, we ran and met. Katie walked straight into the downstairs lobby and Adline, Junior, and I followed. Mama was talking to one of the white women and didn't notice that we had walked into the white lobby. I think she thought we were at the side entrance we had always used which led to the balcony. We were standing in the white lobby with our friends, when Mama came in and saw us. "C'mon! C'mon!" she yelled, pushing Adline face on into the door. "Essie Mae, um gonna try my best to kill you when I get you home. I told you 'bout running up in these stores and things like you own 'em!" she shouted, dragging me through the door. When we got outside, we stood there crying, and we could hear the white children crying inside the white lobby. After that, Mama didn't even let us stay at the movies. She carried us right home.

All the way back to our house, Mama kept telling us that we couldn't sit downstairs, we couldn't do this or that with white children. Up until that time I had never really thought about it. After all, we were playing together. I knew that we were going to separate schools and all, but I never knew why.

After the movie incident, the white children stopped playing in front of our house. For about two weeks we didn't see them at all. Then one day they were there again and we started playing. But things were not the same. I had never really thought of them as white before. Now all of a sudden they were white, and their whiteness made them better than me. I now realized that not only were they better than me because they were white, but everything they owned and everything connected with them was better than what was available to me. I hadn't realized before that downstairs in the movies was any better than upstairs. But now I saw that it was. Their whiteness provided them with a pass to downstairs in that nice section and my blackness sent me to the balcony.

Now that I was thinking about it, their schools, homes, and streets were better than mine. They had a large red brick school with nice sidewalks connecting the buildings. Their homes were large and beautiful with indoor toilets and every other convenience that I knew of at the time. Every house I had ever lived in was a one- or two-room shack with an outdoor toilet. It really bothered me that they had all these nice things and we had nothing. "There is a secret to it besides being white," I thought. Then my mind got all wrapped up in trying to uncover that secret.

One day when we were all playing in our playhouse in the ditch under the pecan tree, I got a crazy idea. I thought the secret was their "privates." I had seen everything they had but their privates and it wasn't any different than mine. So I made up a game called "The Doctor." I had never been to a doctor myself. However, Mama had told us that a doctor was the only person that could look at children's naked bodies besides their parents. Then I remembered the time my Grandma Winnie was sick. When I asked her what the doctor had done to her she said, "He examined me." Then I asked her about "examined" and she told me he looked at her teeth, in her ears, checked her heart, blood and privates. Now I was going to be the doctor. I had all of them, Katie, Bill, Sandra, and Paul plus Adline and Junior take off their clothes and stand in line as I sat on one of the apple crates and examined them. I looked in their mouths and ears, put my ear to their hearts to listen for their heartbeats. Then I had them lie down on the leaves and I looked at their privates. I examined each of them about three times, but I didn't see any differences. I still hadn't found that secret.

That night when I was taking my bath, soaping myself all over, I thought about it again. I remembered the day I had seen my two uncles Sam and Walter. They were just as white as Katie them. But Grandma Winnie was darker than Mama, so how could Sam and Walter be white? I must have been thinking about it for a long time because Mama finally called out, "Essie Mae! Stop using up all that soap! And hurry up so Adline and Junior can bathe 'fore that water gits cold."

"Mama," I said, "why ain't Sam and Walter white?"

"'Cause they mama ain't white," she answered.

"But you say a long time ago they daddy is white."

"If the daddy is white and the mama is colored, then that don't make the children white."

"But they got the same hair and color like Bill and Katie them got," I said.

"That still don't make them white! Now git out of that tub!" she snapped.

Every time I tried to talk to Mama about white people she got mad. Now I was more confused than before. If it wasn't the straight hair and the white skin that made you white, then what was it?

“WE ARE 172 YEARS LATE”

HUBERT H. HUMPHREY

Speech to the Democratic National Convention

Philadelphia, July 14, 1948

MR. CHAIRMAN, fellow Democrats, fellow Americans, I realize that in speaking in behalf of the minority report on civil rights as presented by Congressman Biemiller of Wisconsin, that I am dealing with a charged issue, with an issue which has been confused by emotionalism on all sides of the fence. I realize that there are those here—friends and colleagues of mine, many of them who feel just as deeply and keenly as I do about this issue, and who are yet in complete disagreement with me. My respect and admiration for these men and their views was great when I came to this convention. It is now far greater because of the sincerity, the courtesy, and the forthrightness with which many of them have argued in our prolonged discussions in the platform committee. Because of this very great respect, and because of my profound belief that we have a challenging task to do here, because good conscience demands it, decent morality demands it, I feel I must rise at this time to support a report, the minority report, a report that spells out our democracy. A report that the people of this country can and will understand and a report that they will enthusiastically acclaim on the great issue of civil rights.

Now let me say this at the outset, that this proposal is made for no single region, our proposal is made for no single class, for no single racial or religious group in mind. All of the regions of this country, all of the states have shared in our precious heritage of American freedom. All the states and all the regions have seen at least some of the infringements of that freedom. All people, get this, all people, white and black, all groups, all racial groups have been the victims at times in this nation of, let me say, vicious discrimination.

The masterly statement of our keynote speaker, the distinguished United States Senator from Kentucky, Alben Barkley, made that point with great force. Speaking of the founder of our party, Thomas Jefferson, he said this, and I quote;

> He did not proclaim that all the white, or the black, or the red, or the yellow men are equal: that all Christian or Jewish men are equal: that all protestant and catholic men are equal: that all rich and poor men are equal: that all good and bad men are equal. What he declared was that all men are equal; and the equality which he proclaimed was the equality in the right to enjoy the blessings of free government in which they may participate and to which they have given their support.

Now these words of Senator Barkley are appropriate to this convention, appropriate to this convention of the oldest, the most truly progressive political party in America. From the time of Thomas Jefferson, the time when that immortal American doctrine of individual rights, under just and fairly administered laws, the Democratic Party has tried hard to secure expanding freedom for all citizens. Oh yes, I know other political parties may have talked more about civil rights, but the Democratic Party has surely done more about civil rights.

We have made progress, we have made great progress in every part of this country. We have made great progress in the South, we've made it in the West, the North and in the East, but we must now focus the direction of that progress towards the realization of a full program of civil rights for all.

This convention must set out more specifically the direction in which our party efforts are to go. We can be proud that we can be guided by the courageous trail blazing of two great Democratic Presidents. We can be proud of the fact that our great and beloved immortal leader, Franklin Roosevelt gave us guidance. And we can be proud of the fact, we can be proud of the fact that Harry Truman has had the courage to give to the people of America the new emancipation proclamation.

It seems to me, it seems to me that the Democratic Party needs to make definite pledges of the kind suggested in the minority report to maintain the trust and the confidence placed in it by the people of all races and all sections of this country. Sure we are here as Democrats, but my good friends, we're here as Americans. We are here as the believers in the principle and ideology of democracy. And I firmly believe that as men concerned with our country's future, we must specify in our platform the guarantees which we have mentioned in the minority report.

Yes this is far more than a party matter. Every citizen in this country has a stake in the emergence of the United States as a leader of the free world. That world is being challenged by the world of slavery. For us to play our part effectively we must be in a morally sound position. We can't use a double standard. There's no room for double standards in American politics for measuring our own and other people's policies. Our demands for democratic practices in other lands will be no more effective than the guarantee of those practices in our own country.

Friends, delegates, I do not believe that there can be any compromise on the guarantees of the civil rights which we have mentioned in the minority report. In spite of my desire for unanimous agreement on the entire platform, in spite of my desire to see everybody here in honest and unanimous agreement, there are some matters which I think must be stated clearly and without qualification.

There can be no hedging. The newspaper headlines are wrong, there will be no hedging and there will be no watering down if you please of the instruments and the principles of the civil rights program. To those who say that we are rushing this issue of civil rights, I say to them we are 172 years late. To those who say that this civil rights program is an infringement on state's rights, I say this, the time has arrived in America for the Democratic Party to get out of the shadows of state's rights to walk forthrightly into the bright sunshine of human rights. People—people—human beings, this is the issue of the 20th century. People of all kinds, all sorts of people—and these people are looking to America for leadership and they are looking to America for precept and example.

My good friends, my fellow Democrats, I ask you for a calm consideration of our historic opportunity. Let us do forget the evil passions and the blindness of the past. In these times of world, political and spiritual, above all spiritual crisis, we cannot and we must not turn from the path so plainly before us. That path has already led us through many valleys of the shadow of death. And now is the time to recall those who were left on that path of American freedom. For all of us here, for the millions who have sent us, for the whole two billion members of the human family, our land is now more than ever before, the last best hope on earth. And I know that we can, and I know that we shall begin here the fuller and richer realization of that hope. That promise of a land where all men are truly free and equal, and each man uses his freedom and equality wisely and well.

My good friends, I ask my party, I ask the Democratic party to march down the high road of progressive democracy. I ask this convention, I ask this convention to say in unmistakable terms that we proudly hail and we courageously support our President and leader, Harry Truman and his great fight for civil rights in America.

"WE STAND FOR THE SEGREGATION OF THE RACES"

BIRMINGHAM CONVENTION OF STATES' RIGHTS DEMOCRATS

Declaration of Principles

July 17, 1948

BIRMINGHAM, ALABAMA CONVENTION OF STATES' RIGHTS DEMOCRATS, JULY 17, 1948.

DECLARATION OF PRINCIPLES

WE AFFIRM that a political party is an instrumentality for effectuating the principles upon which the party is founded. That a platform of principles is a solemn covenant with the people and with the members of the party. That no leader of the party, in temporary power, has the right or privilege to proceed contrary to the fundamental principles of the party, or the letter or spirit of the Constitution of the United States. That to act contrary to these principles is a breach of faith, a usurpation of power, and a forfeiture of the party name and party leadership.

We believe that racial and religious minorities should be protected in their rights guaranteed by the Constitution, but the bold defiance of the Constitution in selfish appeals to such groups for the sake of political power forges the chains of slavery of such minorities by destroying the only bulwark of protection against tyrannical majorities. The protection of the Constitutional rights of a minority does not justify or require the destruction of Constitutional rights of the majority. The destruction of Constitutional limitations on the power of the central government threatens to create a totalitarian state and to destroy individual liberty in America.

We believe that the protection of the American people against the onward march of totalitarian government requires a faithful observance of Article X of the American Bill of Rights which provides that: "The powers not delegated to the United

States by the Constitution, nor prohibited by it to the States, are reserved to the States respectively, or to the people."

We direct attention to the fact that the first platform of the Democratic Party, adopted in 1840, resolved that: "Congress has no power under the Constitution to interfere with or control the domestic institutions of the several States, and that such States are the sole and proper judges of everything appertaining to their own affairs not prohibited by the Constitution." Such pronouncement is the cornerstone of the Democratic Party.

A long train of abuses and usurpations of power by unfaithful leaders who are alien to the Democratic Parties of the States here represented, has become intolerable to those who believe in the preservation of Constitutional government and individual liberty in America.

The executive department of the Government is promoting the gradual but certain growth of a totalitarian state by domination and control of a politically minded Supreme Court. As examples of the threat to our form of Government, the executive department, with the aid of the Supreme Court, has asserted national dominion and control of submerged oil-bearing lands in California, schools in Oklahoma and Missouri, primary elections in Texas, South Carolina and Louisiana, restrictive covenants in New York, and the D. C., and other jurisdictions, as well as religious instruction in Illinois. By asserting paramount Federal rights in these instances, a totalitarian concept has been promulgated which threatens the integrity of the States and the basic rights of their citizens.

We have repeatedly remonstrated with the leaders of the National organization of our Party but our petitions, entreaties and warnings have been treated with contempt. The latest response to our entreaties was a Democratic Convention in Philadelphia rigged to embarrass and humiliate the South. This alleged Democratic assembly called for a civil rights law that would eliminate segregation of every kind from all American life, prohibit all forms of discrimination in private employment, in public and private instruction and administration and treatment of students; in the operation of public and private health facilities; in all transportation, and require equal access to all places of public accommodation for all persons of all races, colors, creeds and national origin.

This infamous and iniquitous program calls for the reorganization of the civil rights section of the Department of Justice with a substantial increase in a bureaucratic staff to be devoted exclusively to the enforcement of the civil rights program; the establishment within the F. B. I. of a special unit of investigators and a police state in a totalitarian, centralized, bureaucratic government.

This Convention hypocritically denounced totalitarianism abroad but unblushingly proposed and approved it at home. This convention would strengthen the grip of a police state upon a liberty loving people by the imposition of penalties upon local public officers who failed or refused to act in accordance with its ideas in suppressing mob violence.

We point out that if a foreign power undertook to force upon the people of the United States the measures advocated by the Democratic Convention in Philadelphia, with respect to civil rights, it would mean war and the entire Nation would resist such effort.

The Convention that insulted the South in the Party Platform advocated giving the Virgin Islands and other dependencies of the United States "the maximum degree of local self-government." When an effort was made to amend this part of the platform so as to make it read that the Party favored giving the Virgin Islands and the several States the maximum degree of local self-government, the amendment adding the words "these several States" was stricken out and the sovereign states were denied the rights that the Party favors giving the Virgin Islands.

We point out that the South, with clock-like regularity, has furnished the Democratic Party approximately fifty percent of the votes necessary to nominate a President every four years for nearly a century. In 1920 the only states in the Union that went democratic were the eleven southern states.

Notwithstanding this rugged loyalty to the Party, the masters of political intrigue now allow Republican States in which there is scarcely a democratic office holder to dominate and control the Party and fashion its policies.

As Democrats who are irrevocably committed to democracy as defined and expounded by Thomas Jefferson, Andrew Jackson and Woodrow Wilson, and who believe that all necessary steps must be taken for its preservation, we declare to the people of the United States as follows:

1. We believe that the Constitution of the United States is the greatest charter of human liberty ever conceived by the mind of man.

2. We oppose all efforts to invade or destroy the rights vouchsafed by it to every citizen of this Republic.

3. We stand for social and economic justice, which, we believe, can be vouchsafed to all citizens only by a strict adherence to our Constitution and the avoidance of any invasion or destruction of the Constitutional rights of the states and individuals. We oppose the totalitarian, centralized, bureaucratic government and the police state called for by the platforms adopted by the Democratic and Republican Conventions.

4. We stand for the segregation of the races and the racial integrity of each race; the Constitutional right to choose one's associates; to accept private employment without governmental interference, and to earn one's living in any lawful way. We oppose the elimination of segregation, the repeal of miscegenation statutes, the control of private employment by Federal bureaucrats called for by the misnamed civil rights program. We favor home rule, local self-government and a minimum interference with individual rights.

5. We oppose and condemn the action of the Democratic Convention in sponsoring a civil rights program calling for the elimination of segregation, social equality by Federal fiat, regulation of private employment practices, voting and local law enforcement.

6. We affirm that the effective enforcement of such a program would be utterly destructive of the social, economic and political life of the southern people, and of other localities in which there may be differences in race, creed or national origin in appreciable numbers.

7. We stand for the checks and balances provided by the three departments of our Government. We oppose the usurpation of legislative functions by the executive and judicial departments. We unreservedly condemn the effort to establish nation-wide a

police state in this Republic that would destroy the last vestige of liberty enjoyed by a citizen.

8. We demand that there be returned to the people, to whom of right they belong, those powers needed for the preservation of human rights and the discharge of our responsibility as democrats for human welfare. We oppose a denial of those rights by political parties, a barter or sale of those rights by a political convention, as well as any invasion or violation of those rights by the federal government.

We call upon all Democrats and upon all other loyal Americans who are opposed to totalitarianism at home and abroad to unite with us in ignominiously defeating Harry S. Truman and Thomas E. Dewey, and every other candidate for public office who would establish a police state in the United States of America.

"THE SINS AND SORROWS OF THREE HUNDRED YEARS"

LILLIAN SMITH
from *Killers of the Dream*

1949

EVEN its children know that the South is in trouble. No one has to tell them; no words said aloud. To them, it is a vague thing weaving in and out of their play, like a ghost haunting an old graveyard or whispers after the household sleeps—fleeting mystery, vague menace, to which each responds in his own way. Some learn to screen out all except the soft and the soothing; others deny even as they see plainly, and hear. But all know that under quiet words and warmth and laughter, under the slow ease and tender concern about small matters, there is a heavy burden on all of us and as heavy a refusal to confess it. The children know this "trouble" is bigger than they, bigger than their family, bigger than their church, so big that people turn away from its size. They have seen it flash out like lightning and shatter a town's peace, have felt it tear up all they believe in. They have measured its giant strength and they feel weak when they remember.

This haunted childhood belongs to every southerner. Many of us run away from it but we come back like a hurt animal to its wound, or a murderer to the scene of his sin. The human heart dares not stay away too long from that which hurt it most. There is a return journey to anguish that few of us are released from making.

We who were born in the South call this mesh of feeling and memory "loyalty." We think of it sometimes as "love." We identify with the South's trouble as if we, individually, were responsible for all of it. We defend the sins and sorrows of three hundred years as if each sin had been committed by us alone and each sorrow had cut across our heart. We are as hurt at criticism of our region as if our own name were called aloud by the critic. We have known guilt without understanding it, and there is no tie that binds men closer to the past and each other than that.

It is a strange thing, this umbilical cord uncut. In times of ease, we do not feel its pull, but when we are threatened with change, suddenly it draws the whole white South together in a collective fear and fury that wipe our minds clear of reason and we are blocked off from sensible contact with the world we live in.

To keep this resistance strong, wall after wall has been thrown up in the southern mind against criticism from without and within. Imaginations close tight against the hurt of others; a regional armoring takes place to keep out the "enemies" who would make our trouble different—or maybe rid us of it completely. For it is a trouble that we do not want to give up. We are as involved with it as a child who cannot be happy at home and cannot bear to tear himself away, or as a grown-up who has fallen in love with his own disease. We southerners have identified with the long sorrowful past on such deep levels of love and hate and guilt that we do not know how to break old bonds without pulling our lives down. *Change* is the evil word, a shrill clanking that makes us know too well our servitude. *Change* means leaving one's memories, one's sins, one's ancient prison, the room where one was born. How can we do this when we are tied fast!

The white man's burden is his own childhood. Every southerner knows this. Though he may deny it even to himself, yet he drags through life with him the heavy weight of a past that never eases and is rarely understood, of desire never appeased, of dreams that died in his heart.

In this South I was born and now live. Here it was that I began to grow, seeking my way, as do all children, through the honeycomb cells of our life to the bright reality outside. Sometimes it was as if all doors opened inward. . . . Sometimes we children lost even the desire to get outside and tried only to make a comfortable home of the trap of swinging doors that history and religion and a war, man's greed and his guilt had placed us in at birth.

It is not easy to pick out of such a life those strands that have to do only with color, only with Negro-white relationships, only with religion or sex, for they are knit of the same fibers that have gone into the making of the whole fabric, woven into its basic patterns and designs. Religion . . . sex . . . race . . . money . . . avoidance rites . . . malnutrition . . . dreams —no part of these can be looked at and clearly seen without looking at the whole of them. For, as a painter mixes colors and makes of them new colors, so religion is turned into something different by race, and segregation is colored as much by sex as by skin pigment, and money is no longer a coin but a lost wish wandering through a man's whole life.

A child's lessons are blended of these strands however dissonant a design they make. The mother who taught me what I know of tenderness and love and compassion taught me also the bleak rituals of keeping Negroes in their place. The father who rebuked me for an air of superiority toward schoolmates from the mill and rounded out his rebuke by gravely reminding me that "all men are brothers," trained me in the steel-rigid decorums I must demand of every colored male. They who so gravely taught me to split my body from my feelings and both from my "soul," taught me also to split my conscience from my acts and Christianity from southern tradition.

Neither the Negro nor sex was often discussed at length in our home. We were given no formal instruction in these difficult matters but we learned our lessons well. We learned the intricate system of taboos, of renunciations and compensations, of manners, voice modulations, words, feelings, along with our prayers, our toilet habits, and our games. I do not remember how or when, but by the time I had learned that God is love, that Jesus is His Son and came to give us more abundant life, that all men are brothers with a common Father, I also knew that I was better than a Negro, that all black folks have their place and must be kept in it, that sex has its place and must be kept in it, that a terrifying disaster would befall the South if ever I treated a Negro as my social equal and as terrifying a disaster would befall my family if ever I were to have a baby outside of marriage. I had learned that God so loved the world that He gave His only begotten Son so that we might have segregated churches in which it was my duty to worship each Sunday and on Wednesday at evening prayers. I had learned that white southerners are a hospitable, courteous, tactful people who treat those of their own group with consideration and who as carefully segregate from all the richness of life "for their own good and welfare" thirteen million people whose skin is colored a little differently from my own.

I knew by the time I was twelve that a member of my family would always shake hands with old Negro friends, would speak gently and graciously to members of the Negro race unless they forgot their place, in which event icy peremptory tones would draw lines beyond which only the desperate would dare take one step. I knew that to use the word "nigger" was unpardonable and no well-bred southerner was quite so crude as to do so; nor would a well-bred southerner call a Negro "mister" or invite him into the living room or eat with him or sit by him in public places.

I knew that my old nurse who had patiently cared for me through long months of illness, who had given me refuge when a little sister took my place as the baby of the family, who comforted me, soothed, fed me, delighted me with her stories and games, let me fall asleep on her deep warm breast, was not worthy of the passionate love I felt for her but must be given instead a half-smiled-at affection similar to that which one feels for one's dog. I knew but I never believed it, that the deep respect I felt for her, the tenderness, the love, was a childish thing which every normal child outgrows, that such love begins with one's toys and is discarded with them, and that somehow—though it seemed impossible to my agonized heart—I too, must outgrow these feelings. I learned to give presents to this woman I loved, instead of esteem and honor. I learned to use a soft voice to oil my words of superiority. I learned to cheapen with tears and sentimental talk of "my old mammy" one of the profound relationships of my life. I learned the bitterest thing a child can learn: that the human relations I valued most were held cheap by the world I lived in.

From the day I was born, I began to learn my lessons. I was put in a rigid frame too intricate, too complex, too twisting to describe here so briefly, but I learned to conform to its slide-rule measurements. I learned that it is possible to be a Christian and a white southerner simultaneously; to be a gentlewoman and an arrogant callous creature in the same moment; to pray at night and ride a Jim Crow car the next morning and to feel comfortable in doing both. I learned to believe in freedom, to glow when the word *democracy* is used, and to practice slavery from morning to night. I learned it the way all of my southern people learn it: by closing door after door until one's mind and heart and conscience are blocked off from each other and from reality.

I closed the doors. Or perhaps they were closed for me. Then one day they began to open again. Why I had the desire or the strength to open them or what strange accident or circumstance opened them for me would require in the answering an account too long, too particular, too stark to make here. And perhaps I should not have the insight or wisdom that such an analysis would demand of me, nor the will to make it. I know only that the doors opened, a little; that somewhere along that iron corridor we travel from babyhood to maturity, doors swinging inward began to swing outward, showing glimpses of the world beyond, of that clear bright thing we call "reality."

LONNIE E. SMITH AND CHRISTIA V. ADAIR

Message from the NAACP to the Negro Voters of Harris County

August 21, 1950

THE
HOUSTON BRANCH NATIONAL ASSOCIATION
FOR THE ADVANCEMENT OF COLORED PEOPLE
228 Pilgrim Bldg.,
Houston 3, Texas.
August 21, 1950

TO: Every Negro person within Houston, Harris County.
FROM: The Executive Board Houston Branch NAACP.
SUBJECT: The danger of staying at home Saturday August 26, 1950

Attention is called to an article in the Sunday, Aug. 13, edition of the Houston Chronicle, page 13, section "A," column 2, under caption "STRONG SEGREGATION" in which Mr. J.E. Winfree, Sr. speaks for his son, J.E., Jr. who is on the ballot for the Democratic Run Off election to be held Saturday August 26,

NAACP does not endorse or oppose candidates in political campaigns. It is our job to study issues and inform the public concerning same; SEGREGATION AND JIM CROW; both mean injustice and INJUSTICE is the one issue which NAACP takes a stand against, hence, the enclosed copy of the Sunday article will give you the information.

It will be the business of every Negro in Houston, Harris County to see to it that this candidate who does not want the Negro people's vote gets his desire. If you are responsible of any group or if you have the opportunity to come before any group between now and the 26, it is your responsibility to get this information over to that group and insist that they go to the polls and vote on that day. Have them understand that every voter who stays at home is helping JIM CROW get elected because every vote not cast against an issue is for the issue, whether the ballot is put in the box or left unmarked. Do not take for granted that every one in your neighborhood or apartment knows this—You are expected to tell them.

After the Primary Election it was surprising how many Negro people did not go to the polls to vote and if they fail to go for the run-off it will be suicide and murder because if an individual will tell us now while Negro men are dying in Korea, that they mean to press injustices upon us it is time to wake up, get up and do something about it. The only way to do something about it is to go to the polls and vote take your neighbor along.

If it rains, VOTE; If it's hot, VOTE. Better to vote with a headache now than to have one inflicted upon you and your children

Sincerely yours,
Dr. L.E. Smith, Vice President
Mrs. C.V. Adair,
Executive Secretary.

Remember NAACP made it possible for you to vote.

"SEGREGATION IS PER SE INEQUALITY"

JULIUS WATIES WARING

Dissent in Briggs v. Elliott

June 23, 1951

THIS CASE has been brought for the express and declared purpose of determining the right of the State of South Carolina, in its public schools, to practice segregation according to race.

The plaintiffs are all residents of Clarendon County, South Carolina which is situated within the Eastern District of South Carolina and within the jurisdiction of this court. The plaintiffs consist of minors and adults there being forty-six minors who are qualified to attend and are attending the public schools in School District 22 of Clarendon County; and twenty adults who are taxpayers and are either guardians or parents of the minor plaintiffs. The defendants are members of the Board of Trustees of School District 22 and other officials of the educational system of Clarendon County including the superintendent of education. They are the parties in charge of the various schools which are situated within the aforesaid school district and which are affected by the matters set forth in this cause.

The plaintiffs allege that they are discriminated against by the defendants under color of the Constitution and laws of the State of South Carolina whereby they are denied equal educational facilities and opportunities and that this denial is based upon difference in race. And they show that the school system of this particular school district and county (following the general pattern that it is admitted obtains in the State of South Carolina) sets up two classes of schools; one for people said to belong to the white race and the other for people of other races but primarily for those said to belong to the Negro race or of mixed races and either wholly, partially, or faintly alleged to be of African or Negro descent. These plaintiffs bring this action for the enforcement of the rights to which they claim they are entitled and on behalf of many others who are in like plight and condition and the suit is denominated a class suit for the purpose of abrogation of what is claimed to be the enforcement of unfair and discriminatory laws by the defendants. Plaintiffs claim that they are entitled to bring this case and that this court has jurisdiction under the Fourteenth Amendment of the Constitution of the United States and of a number of statutes of the United States, commonly referred to as civil rights statutes.[1] The plaintiffs demand relief under the above referred to sections of the laws of the United States by way of a declaratory judgment and permanent injunction.

It is alleged that the defendants are acting under the authority granted them by the Constitution and laws of the State of South Carolina and that all of these are in contravention of the Constitution and laws of the United States. The particular portions of the laws of South Carolina are as follows:

Article XI, Section 5 is as follows: "Free public schools.—The General Assembly shall provide for a liberal system of free public schools for all children between the ages of six and twenty-one years * * *."

Article XI, Section 7 is as follows: "Separate schools shall be provided for children of the white and colored races, and no child of either race shall ever be permitted to attend a school provided for children of the other race."

Section 5377 of the Code of Laws of South Carolina is as follows: "It shall be unlawful for pupils of one race to attend the schools provided by boards of trustees for persons of another race."

It is further shown that the defendants are acting under the authority of the Constitution and laws of the State of South Carolina providing for the creation of various school districts,[2] and they have strictly separated and segregated the school facilities, both elementary and high school, according to race. There are, in said school district, three schools which are used exclusively by Negroes: to wit, Rambay Elementary School, Liberty Hill Elementary School, and Scotts Branch Union

[1]Fourteenth Amendment of the Constitution of the United States, Section 1; Title 8 U.S.C.A. §§ 41, 43; Title 28, U.S.C.A. § 1343.

[2]Constitution of South Carolina, Article XI, Section 5; Code of Laws, 5301, 5316, 5328, 5404 and 5405; Code of Laws of South Carolina, Sections 5303, 5306, 5343, 5409.

(a combination of elementary and high school). There are in the same school district, two schools maintained for whites, namely, Summerton Elementary School and Summerton High School. The last named serves some of the other school districts in Clarendon County as well as No. 22.

It appears that the plaintiffs filed a petition with the defendants requesting that the defendants cease discrimination against the Negro children of public school age; and the situation complained of not having been remedied or changed, the plaintiffs now ask this court to require the defendants to grant them their rights guaranteed under the Fourteenth Amendment of the Constitution of the United States and they appeal to the equitable power of this court for declaratory and injunctive relief alleging that they are suffering irreparable injuries and that they have no plain adequate or complete remedy to redress the wrongs and illegal acts complained of other than this suit. And they further point out that large numbers of people and persons are and will be affected by the decision of this court in adjudicating and clarifying the rights of Negroes to obtain education in the public school system of the State of South Carolina without discrimination and denial of equal facilities on account of their race.

The defendants appear and by way of answer deny the allegations of the complaint as to discrimination and inequality and allege that not only are they acting within the laws of the State in enforcing segregation but that all facilities afforded the pupils of different races are adequate and equal and that there is no inequality or discrimination practiced against these plaintiffs or any others by reason of race or color. And they allege that the facilities and opportunities furnished to the colored children are substantially the same as those provided for the white children. And they further base their defense upon the statement that the Constitutional and statutory provisions under attack in this case, that is to say, the provisions requiring separate schools because of race, are a reasonable exercise of the State's police power and that all of the same are valid under the powers possessed by the State of South Carolina and the Constitution of the United States and they deny that the same can be held to be unconstitutional by this Court.

The issues being so drawn and calling for a judgment by the United States Court which would require the issuance of an injunction against State and County officials, it became apparent that it would be necessary that the case be heard in accordance with the statute applicable to cases of this type requiring the calling of a three-judge court.[3] Such a court convened and the case was set for a hearing on May 28, 1951.

The case came on for a trial upon the issues as presented in the complaint and answer. But upon the call of the case, defendants' counsel announced that they wished to make a statement on behalf of the defendants making certain admissions and praying that the Court make a finding as to inequalities in respect to buildings, equipment, facilities, curricula and other aspects of the schools provided for children in School District 22 in Clarendon County and giving the public authorities time to formulate plans for ending such inequalities. In this statement defendants claim that they never had intended to discriminate against any of the pupils and although they had filed an answer to the complaint, some five months ago, denying inequalities they now admit that they had found some; but rely upon the fact that subsequent to the institution of this suit, James F. Byrnes, the Governor of South Carolina, had stated in his inaugural address that the State must take steps to provide money for improving educational facilities and that thereafter, the Legislature had adopted certain legislation. They stated that they hoped that in time they would obtain money as a result of the foregoing and improve the school situation.

This statement was allowed to be filed and considered as an amendment to the answer.

By this maneuver, the defendants have endeavored to induce this Court to avoid the primary purpose of the suit. And if the Court should follow this suggestion and fail to meet the issues raised by merely considering this case in the light of another "separate but equal" case, the entire purpose and reason for the institution of the case and the convening of a three-judge court would be voided. The 66 plaintiffs in this cause have brought this suit at what must have cost much in effort and financial expenditures. They are here represented by

[3]Title 28, U.S.C.A. §§ 2281–2284.

6 attorneys, all, save one, practicing lawyers from without the State of South Carolina and coming here from a considerable distance. The plaintiffs have brought a large number of witnesses exclusive of themselves. As a matter of fact, they called and examined 11 witnesses. They said that they had a number more coming who did not arrive in time owing to the shortening of the proceedings and they also stated that they had on hand and had contemplated calling a large number of other witnesses but this became unnecessary by reason of the foregoing admissions by defendants. It certainly appears that large expenses must have been caused by the institution of this case and great efforts expended in gathering data, making a study of the issues involved, interviewing and bringing numerous witnesses, some of whom are foremost scientists in America. And in addition to all of this, these 66 plaintiffs have not merely expended their time and money in order to test this important Constitutional question, but they have shown unexampled courage in bringing and presenting this cause at their own expense in the face of the long established and age-old pattern of the way of life which the State of South Carolina has adopted and practiced and lived in since and as a result of the institution of human slavery.

If a case of this magnitude can be turned aside and a court refused to hear these basic issues by the mere device of admission that some buildings, blackboards, lighting fixtures and toilet facilities are unequal but that they may be remedied by the spending of a few dollars, then, indeed people in the plight in which these plaintiffs are, have no adequate remedy or forum in which to air their wrongs. If this method of judicial evasion be adopted, these very infant plaintiffs now pupils in Clarendon County will probably be bringing suits for their children and grandchildren decades or rather generations hence in an effort to get for their descendants what are today denied to them. If they are entitled to any rights as American citizens, they are entitled to have these rights now and not in the future. And no excuse can be made to deny them these rights which are theirs under the Constitution and laws of America by the use of the false doctrine and patter called "separate but equal" and it is the duty of the Court to meet these issues simply and factually and without fear, sophistry and evasion. If this be the measure of justice to be meted out to them, then, indeed, hundreds, nay thousands, of cases will have to be brought and in each case thousands of dollars will have to be spent for the employment of legal talent and scientific testimony and then the cases will be turned aside, postponed or eliminated by devices such as this.

We should be unwilling to straddle or avoid this issue and if the suggestion made by these defendants is to be adopted as the type of justice to be meted out by this Court, then I want no part of it.

And so we must and do face, without evasion or equivocation, the question as to whether segregation in education in our schools is legal or whether it cannot exist under our American system as particularly enunciated in the Fourteenth Amendment to the Constitution of the United States.

Before the American Civil War, the institution of human slavery had been adopted and was approved in this country. Slavery was nothing new in the world. From the dawn of history we see aggressors enslaving weak and less fortunate neighbors. Back through the days of early civilization man practiced slavery. We read of it in Biblical days; we read of it in the Greek City States and in the great Roman Empire. Throughout medieval Europe, forms of slavery existed and it was widely practiced in Asia Minor and the Eastern countries and perhaps reached its worst form in Nazi Germany. Class and caste have, unfortunately, existed through the ages. But, in time, mankind, through evolution and progress, through ethical and religious concepts, through the study of the teachings of the great philosophers and the great religious teachers, including especially the founder of Christianity—mankind began to revolt against the enslavement of body, mind and soul of one human being by another. And so there came about a great awakening. The British who had indulged in the slave trade, awakened to the fact that it was immoral and against the right thinking ideology of the Christian world. And in this country, also, came about a moral awakening. Unfortunately, this had not been sufficiently advanced at the time of the adoption of the American Constitution for the institution of slavery to be prohibited. But there was a struggle and the better thinking leaders in our Constitutional Convention endeavored to prohibit slavery but unfortunately compromised the issue on the insistent demands of those who were engaged in the slave trade and the purchase and use of slaves. And so as time went on, slavery was perpetuated and eventually became a part of the life and culture of certain of the States of this Union although the rest of the world looked on with shame and abhorrence.

As was so well said, this country could not continue to exist one-half slave and one-half free and long years of war were entered into before the nation was willing to eradicate this system which was, itself, a denial of the brave and fine statements of the Declaration of Independence and a denial of freedom as envisioned and advocated by our Founders.

The United States then adopted the 13th, 14th and 15th Amendments and it cannot be denied that the basic reason for all of these Amendments to the Constitution was to wipe out completely the institution of slavery and to declare that all citizens in this country should be considered as free, equal and entitled to all of the provisions of citizenship.

The Fourteenth Amendment to the Constitution of the United States is as follows: "Section 1. All persons born or naturalized in the United States, and subject to the jurisdiction thereof, are citizens of the United States and of the State wherein they reside. No State shall make or enforce any law which shall abridge the privileges or immunities of citizens of the United States; nor shall any State deprive any person of life, liberty, or property, without due process of law; nor deny to any person within its jurisdiction the equal protection of the laws."

It seems to me that it is unnecessary to pore through voluminous arguments and opinions to ascertain what the foregoing means. And while it is true that we have had hundreds, perhaps thousands, of legal opinions outlining and defining the various effects and overtones on our laws and life brought about by the adoption of this Amendment, one of ordinary ability and understanding of the English language will have no trouble in knowing that when this Amendment was adopted, it was intended to do away with discrimination between our citizens.

The Amendment refers to *all* persons. There is nothing in there that attempts to separate, segregate or discriminate against any persons because of their being of European, Asian or African ancestry. And the plain intendment is that all of these persons are citizens. And then it is provided that no State shall make or enforce any law which shall abridge the privileges of citizens nor shall any state deny "to *any person* within its jurisdiction the equal protection of the laws."

The Amendment was first proposed in 1866 just about a year after the end of the American Civil War and the surrender of the Confederate States government. Within two years, the Amendment was adopted and became part of the Constitution of the United States. It cannot be gainsaid that the Amendment was proposed and adopted wholly and entirely as a result of the great conflict between freedom and slavery. This will be amply substantiated by an examination and appreciation of the proposal and discussion and Congressional debates (see Flack on Adoption of the 14th Amendment) and so it is undeniably true that the three great Amendments were adopted to eliminate not only slavery, itself, but all idea of discrimination and difference between American citizens.

Let us now come to consider whether the Constitution and Laws of the State of South Carolina which we have heretofore quoted are in conflict with the true meaning and intendment of this Fourteenth Amendment. The whole discussion of race and ancestry has been intermingled with sophistry and prejudice. What possible definition can be found for the so-called white race, Negro race or other races? Who is to decide and what is the test? For years, there was much talk of blood and taint of blood. Science tells us that there are but four kinds of blood: A, B, AB and O and these are found in Europeans, Asiatics, Africans, Americans and others. And so we need not further consider the irresponsible and baseless references to preservation of "Caucasian blood." So then, what test are we going to use in opening our school doors and labeling them "white" and "Negro"? The law of South Carolina considers a person of one-eighth African ancestry to be a Negro. Why this proportion? Is it based upon any reason: anthropological, historical or ethical? And how are the trustees to know who are "whites" and who are "Negroes"? If it is dangerous and evil for a white child to be associated with another child, one of whose great-grandparents was of African descent, is it not equally dangerous for one with a one-sixteenth percentage? And if the State has decided that there is danger in contact between the whites and Negroes, isn't it requisite and proper that the State furnish a series of schools one for each of these percentages? If the idea is perfect racial equality in educational systems, why should children of pure African descent be brought in contact with children of one-half, one-fourth, or one-eighth such ancestry? To ask these questions is sufficient answer to them. The whole thing is unreasonable, unscientific and based upon unadulterated prejudice. We see the results of all of this warped thinking in the poor under-privileged and frightened attitude of so many of the Negroes in the southern states; and in the sadistic insistence of the "white supremacists" in declaring that their will must be imposed irrespective of rights of other citizens. This claim of "white supremacy", while fantastic and without foundation, is really believed by them for we have had repeated declarations from leading politicians and governors of this state and other states declaring that "white supremacy" will be endangered by the abolition of segregation. There are present threats, including those of the present Governor of this state, going to the extent of saying that all public education may be abandoned if the courts should grant true equality in educational facilities.

Although some 73 years have passed since the adoption of the Fourteenth Amendment and although it is clearly apparent that its chief purpose, (perhaps we may say its only real purpose) was to remove from Negroes the stigma and status of slavery and to confer upon them full rights as citizens, nevertheless, there has been a long and arduous course of litigation through the years. With some setbacks here and there, the courts have generally and progressively recognized the true meaning of the Fourteenth Amendment and have, from time to time, stricken down the attempts made by state governments (almost entirely those of the former Confederate states) to restrict the Amendment and to keep Negroes in a different classification so far as their rights and privileges as citizens are concerned. A number of cases have reached the Supreme Court of the United States wherein it became necessary for that tribunal to insist that Negroes be treated as citizens in the performance of jury duty. See

Strauder v. West Virginia[4], where the Court says 100 U.S. at page 307, 25 L.Ed. 664; "* * * What is this but declaring that the law in the States shall be the same for the black as for the white; that all persons, whether colored or white, shall stand equal before the laws of the States, and, in regard to the colored race, for whose protection the amendment was primarily designed, that no discrimination shall be made against them by law because of their color? The words of the amendment, it is true, are prohibitory, but they contain a necessary implication of a positive immunity, or right, most valuable to the colored race,—the right to exemption from unfriendly legislation against them distinctively as colored—exemption from legal discriminations, implying inferiority in civil society, lessening the security of their enjoyment of the rights which others enjoy, and discriminations which are steps towards reducing them to the condition of a subject race."

Many subsequent cases have followed and confirmed the right of Negroes to be treated as equals in all jury and grand jury service in the states.

The Supreme Court has stricken down from time to time statutes providing for imprisonment for violation of contracts. These are known as peonage cases and were in regard to statutes primarily aimed at keeping the Negro "in his place."[5]

In the field of transportation the court has now, in effect declared that common carriers engaged in interstate travel must not and cannot segregate and discriminate against passengers by reason of their race or color.[6]

Frequent and repeated instances of prejudice in criminal cases because of the brutal treatment of defendants because of their color have been passed upon in a large number of cases.[7]

[4]100 U.S. 303, 25 L.Ed. 664.

[5]Peonage: Bailey v. Alabama, 219 U.S. 219, 31 S.Ct. 145, 55 L.Ed. 191; U. S. v. Reynolds, 235 U.S. 133, 35 S.Ct. 86, 59 L.Ed. 162.

[6]Transportation: Mitchell v. U. S., 313 U.S. 80, 61 S.Ct. 873, 85 L.Ed. 1201; Morgan v. Virginia, 328 U.S. 373, 66 S.Ct. 1050, 90 L.Ed. 1317; Henderson v. U. S., 339 U.S. 816, 70 S.Ct. 843, 94 L.Ed. 1302; Chance v. Lambeth, 4 Cir., 186 F.2d 879, certiorari denied Atlantic Coast Line R. Co. v. Chance, 341 U.S. 941, 71 S.Ct. 1001, May 28, 1951.

[7]Criminals: Brown v. Mississippi, 297 U.S. 278, 56 S.Ct. 461, 80 L.Ed. 682; Chambers v. Florida, 309 U.S. 227, 60 S.Ct. 472, 84 L.Ed. 716; Shepherd v. Florida, 341 U.S. 50, 71 S.Ct. 549.

Discrimination by segregation of housing facilities and attempts to control the same by covenants have also been outlawed.[8]

In the field of labor employment and particularly the relation of labor unions to the racial problem, discrimination has again been forbidden.[9]

Perhaps the most serious battle for equality of rights has been in the field of exercise of suffrage. For years, certain of the southern states have attempted to prevent the Negro from taking part in elections by various devices. It is unnecessary to enumerate the long list of cases, but from time to time courts have stricken down all of these various devices classed as the "grandfather clause," educational tests and white private clubs.[10]

The foregoing are but a few brief references to some of the major landmarks in the fight by Negroes for equality. We now come to the more specific question, namely, the field of education. The question of the right of the state to practice segregation by race in certain educational facilities has only recently been tested in the courts. The cases of Missouri ex rel. Gaines v. Canada, 305 U.S. 337, 59 S.Ct. 232, 83 L.Ed. 208 and Sipuel v. Board of Regents, 332 U.S. 631, 68 S.Ct. 299, 92 L.Ed. 247, decided that Negroes were entitled to the same type of legal education that whites were given. It was further decided that the equal facilities must be furnished without delay or as was said in the Sipuel case, the state must provide for equality of education for Negroes "as soon as it does for applicants of any other group." But still we have not reached the exact question that is posed in the instant case.

[8]Housing: Buchanan v. Warley, 245 U.S. 60, 38 S.Ct. 16, 62 L.Ed. 149; Shelley v. Kraemer, 334 U.S. 1, 68 S.Ct. 836, 92 L.Ed. 1161.

[9]Labor: Steele v. Louisville & N. R. R. Co., 323 U.S. 192, 65 S.Ct. 226, 89 L.Ed. 173; Tunstall v. Brotherhood of Locomotive Firemen, 323 U.S. 210, 65 S.Ct. 235, 89 L.Ed. 187.

[10]Suffrage: Guinn v. U. S., 238 U.S. 347, 35 S.Ct. 926, 59 L.Ed. 1340; Nixon v. Herndon, 273 U.S. 536, 47 S.Ct. 446, 71 L.Ed. 759; Lane v. Wilson, 307 U.S. 268, 59 S.Ct. 872, 83 L.Ed. 1281; Smith v. Allwright, 321 U.S. 649, 64 S.Ct. 757, 88 L.Ed. 987; Elmore v. Rice, D.C., 72 F.Supp. 516; 4 Cir., 165 F.2d 387; certiorari denied, 333 U.S. 875, 68 S.Ct. 905, 92 L.Ed. 1151; Brown v. Baskin, D.C., 78 F.Supp. 933; Brown v. Baskin, D.C., 80 F.Supp. 1017; 4 Cir., 174 F.2d 391.

We now come to the cases that, in my opinion, definitely and conclusively establish the doctrine that separation and segregation according to race is a violation of the Fourteenth Amendment. I, of course, refer to the cases of Sweatt v. Painter, 339 U.S. 629, 70 S.Ct. 848, 94 L.Ed. 1114, and McLaurin v. Oklahoma State Regents, 339 U.S. 637, 70 S.Ct. 851, 94 L.Ed. 1149. These cases have been followed in a number of lower court decisions so that there is no longer any question as to the rights of Negroes to enjoy all the rights and facilities afforded by the law schools of the States of Virginia, Louisiana, Delaware, North Carolina and Kentucky. So there is no longer any basis for a state to claim the power to separate according to race in graduate schools, universities and colleges.

The real rock on which the defendants base their case is a decision of the Supreme Court of the United States in the case of Plessy v. Ferguson, 163 U.S. 537, 16 S.Ct. 1138, 41 L.Ed. 256. This case arose in Louisiana and was heard on appeal in 1895. The case related to the power of the State of Louisiana to require separate railroad cars for white and colored passengers and the Court sustained the State's action. Much discussion has followed this case and the reasoning and decision has been severely criticized for many years. And the famous dissenting opinion by Mr. Justice Harlan has been quoted throughout the years as a true declaration of the meaning of the Fourteenth Amendment and of the spirit of the American Constitution and the American way of life. It has also been frequently pointed out that when that decision was made, practically all the persons of the colored or Negro race had either been born slaves or were the children of slaves and that as yet due to their circumstances and surroundings and the condition in which they had been kept by their former masters, they were hardly looked upon as equals or as American citizens. The reasoning of the prevailing opinion in the Plessy case stems almost completely from a decision by Chief Justice Shaw of Massachusetts,[11] which decision was made many years before the Civil War and when, of course, the Fourteenth Amendment had not even been dreamed of.

[11]Roberts v. City of Boston, 5 Cush., Mass., 198.

But these arguments are beside the point in the present case. And we are not called upon to argue or discuss the validity of the Plessy case.

Let it be remembered that the Plessy case decided that separate railroad accommodations might be required by a state in intra-state transportation. How similar attempts relating to inter-state transportation have fared have been shown in the foregoing discussion and notes.[12] It has been said and repeated here in argument that the Supreme Court has refused to review the Plessy case in the Sweatt, McLaurin and other cases and this has been pointed to as proof that the Supreme Court retains and approves the validity of Plessy. It is astonishing that such an argument should be presented or used in this or any other court. The Supreme Court in Sweatt and McLaurin was not considering railroad accommodations. It was considering education just as we are considering it here and the Supreme Court distinctly and unequivocally held that the attempt to separate the races in education was violative of the Fourteenth Amendment of the Constitution. Of course, the Supreme Court did not consider overruling Plessy. It was not considering railroad matters, had no arguments in regard to it, had no business or concern with railroad accommodations and should not have even been asked to refer to that case since it had no application or business in the consideration of an educational problem before the court. It seems to me that we have already spent too much time and wasted efforts in attempting to show any similarity between traveling in a railroad coach in the confines of a state and furnishing education to the future citizens of this country.

The instant case which relates to lower school education is based upon exactly the same reasoning followed in the Sweatt and McLaurin decisions. In the Sweatt case, it was clearly recognized that a law school for Negro students had been established and that the Texas courts had found that the privileges, advantages and opportunities offered were substantially equivalent to those offered to white students at the University of Texas. Apparently, the Negro school was adequately

[12]See cases cited in Note 6.

housed, staffed and offered full and complete legal education, but the Supreme Court clearly recognized that education does not alone consist of fine buildings, class room furniture and appliances but that included in education must be all the intangibles that come into play in preparing one for meeting life. As was so well said by the Court: "* * * Few students and no one who has practiced law would choose to study in an academic vacuum, removed from the interplay of ideas and the exchange of views with which the law is concerned." [339 U.S. 629, 70 S.Ct. 850.] And the Court quotes with approval from its opinion in Shelley v. Kramer, supra: "* * * Equal protection of the laws is not achieved through indiscriminate imposition of inequalities." The Court further points out that this right to a proper and equal education is a personal one and that an individual is entitled to the equal protection of the laws. And in closing, the Court, referring to certain cases cited, says: "In accordance with these cases, petitioner may claim his full constitutional right: legal education equivalent to that offered by the State to students of other races. Such education is not available to him in a separate law school as offered by the State."

In the companion case of McLaurin v. Oklahoma State Regents, McLaurin was a student who was allowed to attend the same classes, hear the same lectures, stand the same examinations and eat in the same cafeteria; but he sat in a marked off place and had a separate table assigned to him in the library and another one in the cafeteria. It was said with truth that these facilities were just as good as those afforded to white students. But the Supreme Court says that even though this be so:

"These restrictions were obviously imposed in order to comply, as nearly as could be, with the statutory requirements of Oklahoma. But they signify that the State, in administering the facilities it affords for professional and graduate study, sets McLaurin apart from the other students. The result is that appellant is handicapped in his pursuit of effective graduate instruction. Such restrictions impair and inhibit his ability to study, to engage in discussions and exchange views with other students, and, in general, to learn his profession.

"Our society grows increasingly complex, and our need for trained leaders increases correspondingly. Appellant's case represents, perhaps, the epitome of that need, for he is attempting to obtain an advanced degree in education, to become, by definition, a leader and trainer of others. Those who will come under his guidance and influence must be directly affected by the education he receives. Their own education and development will necessarily suffer to the extent that his training is unequal to that of his classmates. State-imposed restrictions which produce such inequalities cannot be sustained." [339 U.S. 637, 70 S.Ct. 853.]

The recent case of McKissick v. Carmichael, 4 Cir., 187 F.2d 949, 953, wherein the question of admission to the law school of the University of North Carolina was decided follows and amplifies the reasoning of the Sweatt and McLaurin cases. In the McKissick case, officials of the State of North Carolina took the position that they had adopted a fixed and continued purpose to establish and build up separate schools for equality in education and pointed with pride to the large advances that they had made. They showed many actual physical accomplishments and the establishment of a school which they claimed was an equal in many respects and superior in some respects to the school maintained for white students. The Court of Appeals for the 4th Circuit in this case, speaking through Judge Soper, meets this issue without fear or evasion and says: "These circumstances are worthy of consideration by any one who is responsible for the solution of a difficult racial problem; but they do not meet the complainants' case or overcome the deficiencies which it discloses. Indeed the defense seeks in part to avoid the charge of inequality by the paternal suggestion that it would be beneficial to the colored race in North Carolina as a whole, and to the individual plaintiffs in particular, if they would cooperate in promoting the policy adopted by the State rather than seek the best legal education which the State provides. The duty of the federal courts, however, is clear. We must give first place to the rights of the individual citizen, and when and where he seeks only equality of treatment before the law, his suit must prevail. It is for him to decide in which direction his advantage lies."

In the instant case, the plaintiffs produced a large number of witnesses. It is significant that the defendants brought but two. These last two were not trained educators. One was an official of the Clarendon schools who said that the school system needed improvement and that the school officials were hopeful and expectant of obtaining money from State funds to improve all facilities. The other witness, significantly named Crow, has been recently employed by a commission just established which, it is proposed, will supervise educational facilities in the State and will handle monies if, as and when the same are received sometime in the future. Mr. Crow did not testify as an expert on education although he stated flatly that he believed in separation of the races and that he heard a number of other people say so, including some Negroes, but he was unable to mention any of their names. Mr. Crow explained what was likely and liable to happen under the 1951 State Educational Act to which frequent reference was made in argument on behalf of the defense.

It appears that the Governor of this state called upon the legislature to take action in regard to the dearth of educational facilities in South Carolina pointing out the low depth to which the state had sunk. As a result, an act of the legislature was adopted (this is a part of the General Appropriations Act adopted at the recent session of the legislature and referred to as the 1951 School Act). This Act provides for the appointment of a commission which is to generally supervise educational facilities and imposes sales taxes in order to raise money for educational purposes and authorizes the issuance of bonds not to exceed the sum of $75,000,000, for the purpose of making grants to various counties and school districts to defray the cost of capital improvement in schools. The Commission is granted wide power to accept applications for and approve such grants as loans. It is given wide power as to what schools and school districts are to receive monies and it is also provided, that from the taxes there are to be allocated funds to the various schools based upon the enrollment of pupils. Nowhere is it specifically provided that there shall be equality of treatment as between whites and Negroes in the school system. It is openly and frankly admitted by all parties that the present facilities are hopelessly disproportional and no one knows how much money would be required to bring the colored school system up to a parity with the white school system. The estimates as to the cost merely of equalization of physical facilities run anywhere from forty to eighty million dollars. Thus, the position of the defendants is that the rights applied for by the plaintiffs are to be denied now because the State of South Carolina intends (as evidenced by a general appropriations bill enacted by the legislature and a speech made by its Governor) to issue bonds, impose taxes, raise money and to do something about the inadequate schools in the future. There is no guarantee or assurance as to when the money will be available. As yet, no bonds have been printed or sold. No money is in the treasury. No plans have been drawn for school buildings or order issued for materials. No allocation has been made to the Clarendon school district or any other school districts and not even application blanks have, as yet, been printed. But according to Mr. Crow, the Clarendon authorities have requested him to send them blanks for this purpose if, as and when they come into being. Can we seriously consider this a bona-fide attempt to provide equal facilities for our school children?

On the other hand, the plaintiffs brought many witnesses, some of them of national reputation in various educational fields. It is unnecessary for me to review or analyze their testimony. But they who had made studies of education and its effect upon children, starting with the lowest grades and studying them up through and into high school, unequivocally testified that aside from inequality in housing appliances and equipment, the mere fact of segregation, itself, had a deleterious and warping effect upon the minds of children. These witnesses testified as to their study and researches and their actual tests with children of varying ages and they showed that the humiliation and disgrace of being set aside and segregated as unfit to associate with others of different color had an evil and ineradicable effect upon the mental processes of our young which would remain with them and deform their view on life until and throughout their maturity. This applies to white as well as Negro children. These witnesses testified from actual study and tests in various parts of the country, including tests in the actual Clarendon School district under consideration. They showed beyond a doubt that the evils of segregation and color prejudice come from early training. And from their testimony as well as from common experience and knowledge and from our own reasoning, we must unavoidably come to the conclusion that racial prejudice is something that is acquired and that that acquiring is in early childhood. When do we get our first ideas of religion, nationality and the other basic ideologies? The vast number of individuals follow religious and political groups because of their childhood training. And it is difficult and nearly impossible to change and eradicate these early prejudices, however strong may be the appeal to reason. There is absolutely no reasonable explanation for racial prejudice. It is all caused by unreasoning emotional reactions and these are gained in early childhood. Let the little child's mind be poisoned by prejudice of this kind and it is practically impossible to ever remove these impressions however many years he may have of teaching by philosophers, religious leaders or patriotic citizens. If segregation is wrong then the place to stop it is in the first grade and not in graduate colleges.

From their testimony, it was clearly apparent, as it should be to any thoughtful person, irrespective of having such expert testimony, that segregation in education can never produce equality and that it is an evil that must be eradicated. This case presents the matter clearly for adjudication and I am of the opinion that all of the legal guideposts, expert testimony, common sense and reason point unerringly to the conclusion that the system of segregation in education adopted and practiced in the State of South Carolina must go and must go now.

Segregation is per se inequality.

As heretofore shown, the courts of this land have stricken down discrimination in higher education and have declared unequivocally that segregation is not equality. But these decisions have pruned away only the noxious fruits. Here in this case, we are asked to strike its very root. Or rather, to change the metaphor, we are asked to strike at the cause of infection and not merely at the symptoms of disease. And if the courts of this land are to render justice under the laws without fear or favor, justice for all men and all kinds of men, the time to do it is now and the place is in the elementary schools where our future citizens learn their first lesson to respect the dignity of the individual in a democracy.

To me the situation is clear and important, particularly at this time when our national leaders are called upon to show to the world that our democracy means what it says and that it is a true democracy and there is no under-cover suppression of the rights of any of our citizens because of the pigmentation of their skins. And I had hoped that this Court would take this view of the situation and make a clear cut declaration that the State of South Carolina should follow the intendment and meaning of the Constitution of the United States and that it shall not abridge the privileges accorded to or deny equal protection of its laws to any of its citizens. But since the majority of this Court feel otherwise, and since I cannot concur with them or join in the proposed decree, this opinion is filed as a dissent.

"THE CALL OF ALL MY PEOPLE"

CHARLOTTA BASS

Acceptance Speech as Vice Presidential Candidate of the Progressive Party

March 30, 1952

I STAND BEFORE YOU with great pride.

This is a historic moment in American political life.

Historic for myself, for my people, for all women.

For the first time in the history of this nation a political party has chosen a Negro woman for the second highest office in the land.

It is a great honor to be chosen as a pioneer. And a great responsibility. But I am strengthened by thousands on thousands of pioneers who stand by my side and look over my shoulder —those who have led the fight for freedom—those who led the fight for women's rights—those who have been in the front line fighting for peace and justice and equality everywhere. How they must rejoice in this great understanding which here joins the cause of peace and freedom.

These pioneers, the living and the dead, men and women, black and white, give me strength and a new sense of dedication.

I shall tell you how I come to stand here. I am a Negro woman. My people came before the Mayflower. I am more concerned with what is happening to my people in my country than in pouring out money to rebuild a decadent Europe for a new war. We have lived through two wars and seen their promises turn to bitter ashes. Two Negroes were the first Americans to be decorated for bravery in France in World War I, that war that was fought to make the world safe for democracy. But when it ended, we discovered we were making Africa safe for exploitation by the very European powers whose freedom and soil we had defended. And that war was barely over when a Negro soldier, returning to his home in Georgia, was lynched almost before he could take off his uniform. That war was scarcely over before my people were stoned and shot and beaten in a dozen northern cities. The guns were hardly silenced before a reign of terror was unloosed against every minority that fought for a better life.

And then we fought another war. You know Dorie Miller, the spud peeler who came out of his galley to fight while white officers slept at Pearl Harbor. And I think of Robert Brooks, another "first Negro," and of my own nephew. We fought a war to end fascism whose germ is German race superiority and the oppression of other peoples. A Negro soldier returned from that war—he was not even allowed to take off his uniform before he was lynched for daring to exercise his constitutional right to vote in a Democratic primary.

Yes, we fought to end Hitlerism. But less than 7 years after the end of that war, I find men who lead my government paying out my money and your money to support the rebirth of Hitlerism in Germany to make it a willing partner in another war. We thought to destroy Hitlerism—but its germ took root right here. I look about me, at my own people—at all colored peoples all over the world. I see the men who lead my government supporting oppression of the colored peoples of the earth who today reach out for the independence this nation achieved in 1776.

Yes, it is my government that supports the segregation by violence practiced by a Malan in South Africa, sends guns to maintain a bloody French rule in Indo-China, gives money to help the Dutch repress Indonesia, props up Churchill's rule in the Middle East and over the colored peoples of Africa and Malaya. This week Churchill's general in Malaya terrorized a whole village for refusing to act as spies for the British, charging these Malayan and Chinese villagers who enjoyed no rights and no privileges—and I quote him literally—"for failing to shoulder the responsibility of citizenship." But neither the Malayan people—nor the African people who demonstrate on April 6—will take this terror lying down. They are fighting back.

Shall my people support a new war to create new oppressions? We want peace and we shall have freedom. We support the movement for freedom of all peoples everywhere—in Africa, in Asia, in the Middle East, and above all, here in our own country. And we will not be silenced by the rope, the gun, the lynch mob or the lynch judge. We will not be stopped by the reign of terror let loose against all who speak for peace and freedom and share of the world's goods, a reign of terror the like of which this nation has never seen.

For 40 years I have been a working editor and publisher of the oldest Negro newspaper in the West. During those 40 years I stood on a watch tower, watching the tide of racial hatred and bigotry rising against my people and against all people who believe the Constitution is something more than a piece of yellowed paper to be shut off in a glass case in the archives, but a document, a working instrument for freedom.

Yes, during those 40 years, the Eagle stirred her nest, led the struggles of my people, taught them to work with labor as the one group that could help break down racial differences and open the door for Negro people. I have stood watch over a home to protect a Negro family against the outrages of the Ku Klux Klan. And I have fought the brazen attempts to drive Negroes from their homes under restrictive covenants. I have challenged the great corporations which extort huge profits from my people, and forced them to employ Negroes in their plants. I have stormed city councils and state legislatures and the halls of Congress demanding real representation for my people.

I have fought not only for my people. I have fought and will continue to fight unceasingly for the rights and privileges of all people who are oppressed and who are denied their just share of the world's goods their labor produces. I have walked and will continue to walk in picket lines for the right of all men and women, of all races, to organize for their own protection and advancement. I will continue to cry out against police brutality against any people, as I did in the infamous zoot suit riots in Los Angeles in 1944, when I went into dark alleys and reached scared and badly beaten Negro and Mexican American boys, some of them children, from the clubs and knives of city police. Nor have I hesitated in the face of that most unAmerican Un-American Activities Committee—and I am willing to face it again. And so help me God, I shall continue to tell the truth as I know it and believe it as a progressive citizen and a good American.

As I stand here on this platform presenting the cause of the Progressive Party, I cannot help but hark back to the 30 years I spent in the Republican Party as an active member. Often as a member of the Republican Party I was as bewildered and as hopeless for the future as the children of Israel when they marched through the Jordan and failed to envision on the other side. I remember 1940, when I was chosen as Western Regional Director for Wendell Willkie's campaign for the pre-Republican headquarters right here in Chicago, I found two worlds—upstairs was a world for white Republicans and down below was the world for Negro Republicans.

Yes, I could not see the future clear in the Republican Party, as the children of Israel did not see their future. But if you remember, when the liberation came to these victims of Pharoah's hate, as they crossed over, they dragged from the bed of the stream 12 stones and built a monument to commemorate the rolling away of the burdens of their bondage. As a member of the great elephant party, I could not see the light of hope shining in the distance, until one day the news flashed across the nation that a new party was born. In 1948, in the Progressive Party, I found that one political world that could provide a home big enough for Negro and white, for native and foreign born, to live and work together for the same ends—as equals.

Here in this party was the political home for me and for my people. Here no one handed me a ready made program from the back door. Here I could sit at the head of the table as a founding member, write my own program, a program for me and my people, that came from us. In that great founding convention in Philadelphia in 1948 we had crossed the Jordan. There we shared in the labor of building a platform stone by stone, choosing candidates, creating a new political party—as equals.

Now perhaps I could retire. I had helped to found a home for my people. I looked forward to a rest after forty years of struggle.

But how could I retire and where could I retire as long as I saw what Frederick Douglass saw and felt what he did, the need "to stand up for the downtrodden, to open my mouth for the dumb, to remember those in bonds as bound with me."

Could I retire when I saw that slavery had been abolished but not destroyed, that democracy had been won in World War I, World War II, only to take roots in my own country where it blossomed and bloomed and sent forth its fruits to poison the land my people had fought to preserve! Could I retire without thinking of Dorie Miller, of Robert Brooks, of my own nephew John Kinloch who gave up a brilliant career, helped set up the first mixed regiment of white and Negro troops, and then went ahead of them to die in the Battle of the Bulge? I think often of John who was to take over my beloved paper, of John who died that those for whom he fought might enjoy the freedom and liberty for which he lay down his life.

I could not retire and step aside when Rose Lee Ingram and her two boys were railroaded to jail for defending themselves. Could I turn a deaf ear to Rosalie McGee? Where was that Shangri-La in these United States where I could live and breathe in dignity? Where my people enjoyed the rights for which their sons and nephews died? In the North there were the Trenton Six demanding justice; in the Middle West was Cicero. In the South there stood Amy Mallard, the Martinsville Seven, and unnamed hundreds of unavenged deaths that cried out. There was no rest in Florida—there a cross was burning and a bomb killed Harriet Moore and her husband; and white justice sniffed out the life of Samuel Shepherd, threatened Lee Irvin.

No, this new uprising of Terror was not confined to the South. It spread throughout the country, goaded and inflamed by persons in high places who created hysteria every time they opened their mouths. In New York, just a few miles from where I live, they stoned my people at Peekskill—and a governor of a great state defended them. Only last week a Yonkers policeman shot and killed Wyatt and James Blackhall in cold blood—and was held on a minor charge.

Where were the leaders of my nation—yes, my nation, for God knows my whole ambition is to see and make my nation the best in the world—where were these great leaders when these things happened? Why was my President silent when Harriet Moore died? And why did he not call on the Governor of Florida, a fellow Democrat, on his visits to Key West? What did General Eisenhower say or do about mob lynchers and legal lynchers of my people? General MacArthur rode through Georgia in triumph, like another general 85 years ago, but this general drew the applause of the Klan, the Moore dynamiters, the lynchers.

Where were these great leaders who talked so grandly about freedom and spent even more grandly to crush it—what were they doing about my people losing jobs in Detroit while profits were piling up?

To retire meant to leave this world to these people who carried oppression to Africa, to Asia, who made profits from oppression in my own land. To retire meant to leave the field to evil. For there is an evil that stalks in our land, evil that strikes at my people, that would enslave all people, that would send up the world in flames, rob us of our earnings to waste on arms, destroy our living standards, corrupt our youth, silence and enslave us with Smith Acts, McCarran Acts, passed by concentration camp Congressmen.

I believe in a world of good and not of evil. A month ago in New York City, doctors announced the discovery of a new drug that promised a real cure for tuberculosis, that dread killer. Only last week I looked at the pictures of the patients who had offered themselves to try out this new drug. I looked closely at these pictures. I counted the faces. There were ten patients shown. Eight of these ten were Negroes. And seven of these eight were Negro women. Who was it that named tuberculosis the "great white plague"—when three times as many Negroes as whites died from it?

Those pictures symbolize the plight of our people today —yes, and the promise of tomorrow. Tuberculosis is not a disease of race—it is a disease of poverty. It strikes my people hardest because North and South Negro workers earn less than half of what white workers earn. It strikes my people here in Chicago who live 90,000 to the square mile. It strikes my people who live in Harlem 4,000 to the square block, so crowded that all of America could be put into half of New York.

This is what we fight against. We fight to live. We want the $65 billion that goes for death to go to build a new life. Those billions could lift the wages of my people, give them jobs, give education and training and new hope to our youth, free our sharecroppers, build new hospitals and medical centers. The $8 billion being spent to rearm Europe and crush Asia could rehouse all my people living in the ghettos of Chicago and New York and every large city in the nation.

We fight that all people shall live. We fight to send our money to end colonialism for the colored peoples of the world, not to perpetuate it in Malan's South Africa, Churchill's Malaya, French Indo-China and Middle East.

You have called me to lead the fight against evil, the fight for human life and human dignity. I am indeed proud to answer the call of this party of progress. Can you conceive of the party of Taft and Eisenhower and MacArthur and McCarthy and the big corporations, calling a Negro woman to lead the good fight in 1952? Can you see the party of Truman, of Russell of Georgia, of Rankin of Mississippi, of Byrnes of South Carolina, of Acheson, naming a Negro woman to lead the fight against enslavement?

I am stirred by the responsibility that you have put upon me. I am proud that I am the choice of the leaders of my own people and leaders of all those who understand how deeply the fight for peace is one and indivisible with the fight for Negro equality.

And I am impelled to accept this call, for it is the call of all my people and call to my people. Frederick Douglass would rejoice, for he fought not only slavery but the oppression of women. Above all, Douglass would counsel us not to falter, to "continue the struggle while a bondsman in his chains remains to weep." For Douglass had that calm resolution which held fast while others wavered, that steadfastness which helped to shape the party of Abraham Lincoln and held it fast to the fight for abolition.

I make this pledge to my people, the dead and the living —to all Americans, black and white. I will not retire nor will I retreat, not one inch, so long as God gives me vision to see what is happening and strength to fight for the things I know are right. For I know that my kingdom, my peoples of all the world, is not beyond the skies, the moon and the stars, but right here at our feet—acres of diamonds—freedom—peace and justice—for all the peoples if we will but stoop down and get them.

I accept this great honor. I give you as my slogan in this campaign—"Let my people go."

RACIAL TERRORISM IN OREGON

PORTLAND CHALLENGER
Negro Family to Remain Despite Flaming Cross

May 20, 1953

NEGRO FAMILY TO REMAIN DESPITE FLAMING CROSS

COUNTY POLICE are still investigating the Sunday morning cross-burning on the lawn of a Portland Negro family. The cross was burned on the front lawn of Charles Gragg, 11261 NE Knott street, in the Parkrose Heights district.

Earlier, several neighbors had attempted to get Gragg to move elsewhere after it was learned that he was a Negro. The Graggs have lived in the community for three weeks.

Sunday morning Gragg's wife, Joyce, was awakened by a noise. She paid little attention to the noise and only became aroused when a rock was tossed upon the front porch. From the bedroom she and Gragg could see the cross burning on the lawn. Gragg took his family to his mother's home and notified the Portland branch of the National Association for the Advancement of Colored People and the Urban League of Portland.

MANY LETTERS RECEIVED

Gragg said he has received about 100 letters, all in favor of him staying in the neighborhood. One of the letters came from Washington, D. C. "I am determined to stay," said Gragg. "This is a challenge."

Nearby residents told police investigating the burned cross that they did not hear of the cross-burning and none could offer a clue to the officers.

Many Parkrose citizens and neighbors have come forward in behalf of the Graggs. They have expressed a welcome to them, and regret that a few people seem to be fearful of having the Graggs for neighbors.

The NAACP notified the FBI and they too are carrying on an investigation of the burning cross. Sheriff Terry Schrunk feels confident that the guilty party or parties will be apprehended and is making every effort to protect the Graggs.

Oregon's Attorney General, Robert Y. Thornton, has also been notified and is watching the situation.

THE FIGHT FOR DESEGREGATION IN THE CAPITAL

ALICE A. DUNNIGAN

Resents Ike's Taking Credit for Winning DC Restaurant Case

Amsterdam News, June 20, 1953

RESENTS IKE'S TAKING CREDIT FOR WINNING DC RESTAURANT CASE

WASHINGTON—Mrs. Mary Church Terrell, chairman of the Coordinating Committee for the Enforcement of the DC Anti-Discriminating Laws, and one of the complainants who brought suit against the Thompson's restaurant for refusing to serve Negroes, last week blasted the Eisenhower Administration for taking credit for the abolition of segregation in restaurants in the District of Columbia.

"I was as provoked as I could be when I read in the papers this morning that the Eisenhower Administration was taking credit for this victory," said Mrs. Terrell last Friday.

She was referring to a speech which the President made on the previous night naming the abolition of segregation in Washington restaurants as one of the 10 accomplishments which he had achieved since he has been in office.

VISITS RESTAURANT

Mrs. Terrell's statement was made just prior to a visit to Thompson's restaurant Friday, together with four other persons who initiated the case which ended in the Supreme Court's decision last Monday.

The group consisting of Mrs. Terrell, the Rev. W. H. Jernagin, pastor of Mt. Carmel Baptist Church; Mrs. Geneva Brown and Miss Essie Thompson of the United Cafeteria Workers; and David Scull of the Washington Fellowship, visited Thompson's the day after the District Commissioners had declared the law enforceable and were served with the greatest courtesy.

After having lunch Mrs. Terrell said she would ask the Corporation Counsel to withdraw all complaints against the Thompson company and to drop prosecution.

CASE TO BE HEARD

Since the Supreme Court has ruled that the 1873 law is valid, the Thompson case is due to come up for trial in the Municipal Court where, without a doubt, they would be found guilty. The penalty can be as much as $100 fine and the revocation of license for a year.

Mrs. Terrell has asked that the charges be dropped because "the purpose for filing the suit has been served," and too, she said she had discovered, from first hand experience, that the Thompson Company is observing the law.

This case has been a complicated one said Joseph Ferer, attorney for the Coordinating Committee. In relating the history of the case last Thursday, he said that many erroneous reports had gone out through the newspapers.

CASE STARTED 1950

The case actually began on Jan. 27, 1950, when Mrs. Terrell, Rev. D. Jernagin, Mrs. Brown and David Scull, a white Quaker who at that time was president of the Washington Fellowship, visited the Thompson restaurant and were refused service. They filed a complaint with the Municipal Court but were informed by the District Commissioners that they would not prosecute.

The commissioners admitted that they had found no expressed repeal of the old anti-discrimination laws, still they would like to have time to make a further study and to notify the restaurant owners that such laws did exist.

A month later on February 28, 1950, Mrs. Terrell again visited Thompson's. This time she carried a new group because Rev. Dr. Jernagin was in Africa and Mrs. Brown was ill. So the elderly educator, writer and civic leader was accompanied by another member of the Cafeteria Workers Union, Miss Essie Thompson, and another minister, the Rev. Arthur F. Elmes, pastor of the People's Congregational Church.

IN LOWER COURT

When this case reached Municipal Court Judge Myers ruled that the old laws were "repealed by implication" and the Thompson Restaurant Co. was found not guilty.

This decision necessitated a third case. This time Mrs. Terrell, the Rev. Elmes and Miss Jean Joan Williams, a white Quaker member of the Washington Fellowship, again visited the Thompson restaurant on July 27, 1950. Again they were refused service, and the third complaint was filed. This was the case which finally reached the Supreme Court.

In commenting on the Supreme Court decision, Mrs. Terrell said: "I will be 90 years on the 23rd of September and I will die happy to know that the children of my group will not grow up thinking they are inferior because they are deprived of rights which children of other racial groups enjoy."

LEADERS SPEAK

The 84-year-old Rev. Jernagin said "It is a wonderful decision. It will mean so much to the American Negro who has been working so long under a handicap. It is also heartening to the Negro youth of America."

After visiting the restaurant again last week, Rev. Jernagin said:

"We had luncheon there together and were treated very nicely. We have no complaints at all."

When the group visited Thompson's last week and a reporter inquired of David Scull if this was lunch or dinner, the Quaker gentleman replied that it was a "birthday dinner." "Whose birthday?" asked the reporter. "Democracy's," he replied.

SEES DOUBLE HURT

Scull said that his purpose in participating in the suit was to show that the segregation law discriminated as much against the whites as the Negroes. "It discriminates against those white persons who wish to dine with their colored friends," he said.

He expressed his delight at the Supreme Court decision but said, "we have got to go beyond just legal requirements and prove a real sense of brotherhood and cooperative work."

"SEPARATE EDUCATIONAL FACILITIES ARE INHERENTLY UNEQUAL"

EARL WARREN

Opinion in Brown v. Board of Education of Topeka

May 17, 1954

MR. CHIEF JUSTICE WARREN delivered the opinion of the Court.

These cases come to us from the States of Kansas, South Carolina, Virginia, and Delaware. They are premised on different facts and different local conditions, but a common legal question justifies their consideration together in this consolidated opinion.[1]

[1]In the Kansas case, *Brown* v. *Board of Education*, the plaintiffs are Negro children of elementary school age residing in Topeka. They brought this action in the United States District Court for the District of Kansas to enjoin enforcement of a Kansas statute which permits, but does not require, cities of more than 15,000 population to maintain separate school facilities for Negro and white students. Kan. Gen. Stat. § 72–1724 (1949). Pursuant to that authority, the Topeka Board of Education elected to establish segregated elementary schools. Other public schools in the community, however, are operated on a nonsegregated basis. The three-judge District Court, convened under 28 U. S. C. §§ 2281 and 2284, found that segregation in public education has a detrimental effect upon Negro children, but denied relief on the ground that the Negro and white schools were substantially equal with respect to buildings, transportation, curricula, and educational qualifications of teachers. 98 F. Supp. 797. The case is here on direct appeal under 28 U. S. C. § 1253.

In the South Carolina case, *Briggs* v. *Elliott*, the plaintiffs are Negro children of both elementary and high school age residing in Clarendon County. They brought this action in the United States District Court for the Eastern District of South Carolina to enjoin enforcement of provisions in the state constitution and statutory code which require the segregation of Negroes and whites in public schools. S. C. Const., Art. XI, § 7; S. C. Code § 5377 (1942). The three-judge District Court, convened under 28 U. S. C. §§ 2281 and 2284, denied the requested relief. The court found that the Negro schools were inferior to the white schools and ordered the defendants to begin immediately to equalize the facilities. But the court sustained the validity of the contested provisions and denied the plaintiffs admission to the white schools during the equalization program. 98 F. Supp. 529. This Court vacated the District Court's

In each of the cases, minors of the Negro race, through their legal representatives, seek the aid of the courts in obtaining admission to the public schools of their community on a nonsegregated basis. In each instance, they had been denied admission

---

judgment and remanded the case for the purpose of obtaining the court's views on a report filed by the defendants concerning the progress made in the equalization program. 342 U. S. 350. On remand, the District Court found that substantial equality had been achieved except for buildings and that the defendants were proceeding to rectify this inequality as well. 103 F. Supp. 920. The case is again here on direct appeal under 28 U. S. C. § 1253.

In the Virginia case, *Davis* v. *County School Board*, the plaintiffs are Negro children of high school age residing in Prince Edward County. They brought this action in the United States District Court for the Eastern District of Virginia to enjoin enforcement of provisions in the state constitution and statutory code which require the segregation of Negroes and whites in public schools. Va. Const., § 140; Va. Code § 22–221 (1950). The three-judge District Court, convened under 28 U. S. C. §§ 2281 and 2284, denied the requested relief. The court found the Negro school inferior in physical plant, curricula, and transportation, and ordered the defendants forthwith to provide substantially equal curricula and transportation and to "proceed with all reasonable diligence and dispatch to remove" the inequality in physical plant. But, as in the South Carolina case, the court sustained the validity of the contested provisions and denied the plaintiffs' admission to the white schools during the equalization program. 103 F. Supp. 337. The case is here on direct appeal under 28 U. S. C. § 1253.

In the Delaware case, *Gebhart* v. *Belton*, the plaintiffs are Negro children of both elementary and high school age residing in New Castle County. They brought this action in the Delaware Court of Chancery to enjoin enforcement of provisions in the state constitution and statutory code which require the segregation of Negroes and whites in public schools. Del. Const., Art. X, § 2; Del. Rev. Code § 2631 (1935). The Chancellor gave judgment for the plaintiffs and ordered their immediate admission to schools previously attended only by white children, on the ground that the Negro schools were inferior with respect to teacher training, pupil-teacher ratio, extracurricular activities, physical plant, and time and distance involved in travel. 87 A. 2d 862. The Chancellor also found that segregation itself results in an inferior education for Negro children (see note 10, *infra*), but did not rest his decision on that ground. *Id.*, at 865. The Chancellor's decree was affirmed by the Supreme Court of Delaware, which intimated, however, that the defendants might be able to obtain a modification of the decree after equalization of the Negro and white schools had been accomplished. 91 A. 2d 137, 152. The defendants, contending only that the Delaware courts had erred in ordering the immediate admission of the Negro plaintiffs to the white schools, applied to this Court for certiorari. The writ was granted, 344 U. S. 891. The plaintiffs, who were successful below, did not submit a cross-petition.

to schools attended by white children under laws requiring or permitting segregation according to race. This segregation was alleged to deprive the plaintiffs of the equal protection of the laws under the Fourteenth Amendment. In each of the cases other than the Delaware case, a three-judge federal district court denied relief to the plaintiffs on the so-called "separate but equal" doctrine announced by this Court in *Plessy* v. *Ferguson*, 163 U. S. 537. Under that doctrine, equality of treatment is accorded when the races are provided substantially equal facilities, even though these facilities be separate. In the Delaware case, the Supreme Court of Delaware adhered to that doctrine, but ordered that the plaintiffs be admitted to the white schools because of their superiority to the Negro schools.

The plaintiffs contend that segregated public schools are not "equal" and cannot be made "equal," and that hence they are deprived of the equal protection of the laws. Because of the obvious importance of the question presented, the Court took jurisdiction.[2] Argument was heard in the 1952 Term, and reargument was heard this Term on certain questions propounded by the Court.[3]

Reargument was largely devoted to the circumstances surrounding the adoption of the Fourteenth Amendment in 1868. It covered exhaustively consideration of the Amendment in Congress, ratification by the states, then existing practices in racial segregation, and the views of proponents and opponents of the Amendment. This discussion and our own investigation convince us that, although these sources cast some light, it is not enough to resolve the problem with which we are faced. At best, they are inconclusive. The most avid proponents of the post-War Amendments undoubtedly intended them to remove all legal distinctions among "all persons born or naturalized in the United States." Their opponents, just as certainly, were antagonistic to both the letter and the spirit of the Amendments and wished them to have the most limited effect. What others in Congress and the state legislatures had in mind cannot be determined with any degree of certainty.

An additional reason for the inconclusive nature of the

[2]344 U. S. 1, 141, 891.

[3]345 U. S. 972. The Attorney General of the United States participated both Terms as *amicus curiae*.

Amendment's history, with respect to segregated schools, is the status of public education at that time.[4] In the South, the movement toward free common schools, supported by general taxation, had not yet taken hold. Education of white children was largely in the hands of private groups. Education of Negroes was almost nonexistent, and practically all of the race were illiterate. In fact, any education of Negroes was forbidden by law in some states. Today, in contrast, many Negroes have achieved outstanding success in the arts and sciences as well as in the business and professional world. It is true that public school education at the time of the Amendment had advanced further in the North, but the effect of the Amendment on Northern States was generally ignored in the congressional debates. Even in the North, the conditions of public education did not approximate those existing today. The curriculum was usually rudimentary; ungraded schools were common in rural areas; the school term was but three months a year in many states; and compulsory school attendance was virtually unknown. As a consequence, it is not surprising that there should be so little in the history of the Fourteenth Amendment relating to its intended effect on public education.

In the first cases in this Court construing the Fourteenth

[4]For a general study of the development of public education prior to the Amendment, see Butts and Cremin, A History of Education in American Culture (1953), Pts. I, II; Cubberley, Public Education in the United States (1934 ed.), cc. II–XII. School practices current at the time of the adoption of the Fourteenth Amendment are described in Butts and Cremin, *supra*, at 269–275; Cubberley, *supra*, at 288–339, 408–431; Knight, Public Education in the South (1922), cc. VIII, IX. See also H. Ex. Doc. No. 315, 41st Cong., 2d Sess. (1871). Although the demand for free public schools followed substantially the same pattern in both the North and the South, the development in the South did not begin to gain momentum until about 1850, some twenty years after that in the North. The reasons for the somewhat slower development in the South (*e. g.*, the rural character of the South and the different regional attitudes toward state assistance) are well explained in Cubberley, *supra*, at 408–423. In the country as a whole, but particularly in the South, the War virtually stopped all progress in public education. *Id.*, at 427–428. The low status of Negro education in all sections of the country, both before and immediately after the War, is described in Beale, A History of Freedom of Teaching in American Schools (1941), 112–132, 175–195. Compulsory school attendance laws were not generally adopted until after the ratification of the Fourteenth Amendment, and it was not until 1918 that such laws were in force in all the states. Cubberley, *supra*, at 563–565.

Amendment, decided shortly after its adoption, the Court interpreted it as proscribing all state-imposed discriminations against the Negro race.[5] The doctrine of "separate but equal" did not make its appearance in this Court until 1896 in the case of *Plessy* v. *Ferguson*, *supra*, involving not education but transportation.[6] American courts have since labored with the doctrine for over half a century. In this Court, there have been six cases involving the "separate but equal" doctrine in the field of public education.[7] In *Cumming* v. *County Board of Education*, 175 U. S. 528, and *Gong Lum* v. *Rice*, 275 U. S. 78, the validity of the doctrine itself was not challenged.[8] In more recent cases, all on the graduate school level, inequality was found in

[5]*Slaughter-House Cases*, 16 Wall. 36, 67–72 (1873); *Strauder* v. *West Virginia*, 100 U. S. 303, 307–308 (1880):

"It ordains that no State shall deprive any person of life, liberty, or property, without due process of law, or deny to any person within its jurisdiction the equal protection of the laws. What is this but declaring that the law in the States shall be the same for the black as for the white; that all persons, whether colored or white, shall stand equal before the laws of the States, and, in regard to the colored race, for whose protection the amendment was primarily designed, that no discrimination shall be made against them by law because of their color? The words of the amendment, it is true, are prohibitory, but they contain a necessary implication of a positive immunity, or right, most valuable to the colored race,—the right to exemption from unfriendly legislation against them distinctively as colored,—exemption from legal discriminations, implying inferiority in civil society, lessening the security of their enjoyment of the rights which others enjoy, and discriminations which are steps towards reducing them to the condition of a subject race."

See also *Virginia* v. *Rives*, 100 U. S. 313, 318 (1880); *Ex parte Virginia*, 100 U. S. 339, 344–345 (1880).

[6]The doctrine apparently originated in *Roberts* v. *City of Boston*, 59 Mass. 198, 206 (1850), upholding school segregation against attack as being violative of a state constitutional guarantee of equality. Segregation in Boston public schools was eliminated in 1855. Mass. Acts 1855, c. 256. But elsewhere in the North segregation in public education has persisted in some communities until recent years. It is apparent that such segregation has long been a nationwide problem, not merely one of sectional concern.

[7]See also *Berea College* v. *Kentucky*, 211 U. S. 45 (1908).

[8]In the *Cumming* case, Negro taxpayers sought an injunction requiring the defendant school board to discontinue the operation of a high school for white children until the board resumed operation of a high school for Negro children. Similarly, in the *Gong Lum* case, the plaintiff, a child of Chinese descent, contended only that state authorities had misapplied the doctrine by classifying him with Negro children and requiring him to attend a Negro school.

that specific benefits enjoyed by white students were denied to Negro students of the same educational qualifications. *Missouri ex rel. Gaines* v. *Canada*, 305 U. S. 337; *Sipuel* v. *Oklahoma*, 332 U. S. 631; *Sweatt* v. *Painter*, 339 U. S. 629; *McLaurin* v. *Oklahoma State Regents*, 339 U. S. 637. In none of these cases was it necessary to re-examine the doctrine to grant relief to the Negro plaintiff. And in *Sweatt* v. *Painter*, *supra*, the Court expressly reserved decision on the question whether *Plessy* v. *Ferguson* should be held inapplicable to public education.

In the instant cases, that question is directly presented. Here, unlike *Sweatt* v. *Painter*, there are findings below that the Negro and white schools involved have been equalized, or are being equalized, with respect to buildings, curricula, qualifications and salaries of teachers, and other "tangible" factors.[9] "Our decision, therefore, cannot turn on merely a comparison of these tangible factors in the Negro and white schools involved in each of the cases. We must look instead to the effect of segregation itself on public education."

In approaching this problem, we cannot turn the clock back to 1868 when the Amendment was adopted, or even to 1896 when *Plessy* v. *Ferguson* was written. "We must consider public education in the light of its full development and its present place in American life throughout the Nation. Only in this way can it be determined if segregation in public schools deprives these plaintiffs of the equal protection of the laws."

Today, education is perhaps the most important function of state and local governments. Compulsory school attendance laws and the great expenditures for education both demonstrate our recognition of the importance of education to our democratic society. It is required in the performance of our most basic public responsibilities, even service in the armed

[9]In the Kansas case, the court below found substantial equality as to all such factors. 98 F. Supp. 797, 798. In the South Carolina case, the court below found that the defendants were proceeding "promptly and in good faith to comply with the court's decree." 103 F. Supp. 920, 921. In the Virginia case, the court below noted that the equalization program was already "afoot and progressing" (103 F. Supp. 337, 341); since then, we have been advised, in the Virginia Attorney General's brief on reargument, that the program has now been completed. In the Delaware case, the court below similarly noted that the state's equalization program was well under way. 91 A. 2d 137, 149.

forces. It is the very foundation of good citizenship. Today it is a principal instrument in awakening the child to cultural values, in preparing him for later professional training, and in helping him to adjust normally to his environment. In these days, it is doubtful that any child may reasonably be expected to succeed in life if he is denied the opportunity of an education. Such an opportunity, where the state has undertaken to provide it, is a right which must be made available to all on equal terms.

We come then to the question presented: Does segregation of children in public schools solely on the basis of race, even though the physical facilities and other "tangible" factors may be equal, deprive the children of the minority group of equal educational opportunities? We believe that it does.

In *Sweatt* v. *Painter*, *supra*, in finding that a segregated law school for Negroes could not provide them equal educational opportunities, this Court relied in large part on "those qualities which are incapable of objective measurement but which make for greatness in a law school." In *McLaurin* v. *Oklahoma State Regents*, *supra*, the Court, in requiring that a Negro admitted to a white graduate school be treated like all other students, again resorted to intangible considerations: ". . . his ability to study, to engage in discussions and exchange views with other students, and, in general, to learn his profession." Such considerations apply with added force to children in grade and high schools. To separate them from others of similar age and qualifications solely because of their race generates a feeling of inferiority as to their status in the community that may affect their hearts and minds in a way unlikely ever to be undone. The effect of this separation on their educational opportunities was well stated by a finding in the Kansas case by a court which nevertheless felt compelled to rule against the Negro plaintiffs:

> "Segregation of white and colored children in public schools has a detrimental effect upon the colored children. The impact is greater when it has the sanction of the law; for the policy of separating the races is usually interpreted as denoting the inferiority of the negro group. A sense of inferiority affects the motivation of a child to learn. Segregation with the sanction of law, therefore, has a tendency to [retard] the educational and mental development of negro children and to deprive them of

some of the benefits they would receive in a racial[ly] integrated school system."[10]

Whatever may have been the extent of psychological knowledge at the time of *Plessy* v. *Ferguson*, this finding is amply supported by modern authority.[11] Any language in *Plessy* v. *Ferguson* contrary to this finding is rejected.

We conclude that in the field of public education the doctrine of "separate but equal" has no place. Separate educational facilities are inherently unequal. Therefore, we hold that the plaintiffs and others similarly situated for whom the actions have been brought are, by reason of the segregation complained of, deprived of the equal protection of the laws guaranteed by the Fourteenth Amendment. This disposition makes unnecessary any discussion whether such segregation also violates the Due Process Clause of the Fourteenth Amendment.[12]

Because these are class actions, because of the wide applicability of this decision, and because of the great variety of local conditions, the formulation of decrees in these cases presents problems of considerable complexity. On reargument, the consideration of appropriate relief was necessarily subordinated to the primary question—the constitutionality of segregation in public education. We have now announced that such segregation is a denial of the equal protection of the laws. In order that we may have the full assistance of the parties in formulating

[10]A similar finding was made in the Delaware case: "I conclude from the testimony that in our Delaware society, State-imposed segregation in education itself results in the Negro children, as a class, receiving educational opportunities which are substantially inferior to those available to white children otherwise similarly situated." 87 A. 2d 862, 865.

[11]K. B. Clark, Effect of Prejudice and Discrimination on Personality Development (Midcentury White House Conference on Children and Youth, 1950); Witmer and Kotinsky, Personality in the Making (1952), c. VI; Deutscher and Chein, The Psychological Effects of Enforced Segregation: A Survey of Social Science Opinion, 26 J. Psychol. 259 (1948); Chein, What are the Psychological Effects of Segregation Under Conditions of Equal Facilities?, 3 Int. J. Opinion and Attitude Res. 229 (1949); Brameld, Educational Costs, in Discrimination and National Welfare (MacIver, ed., 1949), 44–48; Frazier, The Negro in the United States (1949), 674–681. And see generally Myrdal, An American Dilemma (1944).

[12]See *Bolling* v. *Sharpe*, *post*, p. 497, concerning the Due Process Clause of the Fifth Amendment.

decrees, the cases will be restored to the docket, and the parties are requested to present further argument on Questions 4 and 5 previously propounded by the Court for the reargument this Term.[13] The Attorney General of the United States is again invited to participate. The Attorneys General of the states requiring or permitting segregation in public education will also be permitted to appear as *amici curiae* upon request to do so by September 15, 1954, and submission of briefs by October 1, 1954.[14]

It is so ordered.

[13]"4. Assuming it is decided that segregation in public schools violates the Fourteenth Amendment

"(*a*) would a decree necessarily follow providing that, within the limits set by normal geographic school districting, Negro children should forthwith be admitted to schools of their choice, or

"(*b*) may this Court, in the exercise of its equity powers, permit an effective gradual adjustment to be brought about from existing segregated systems to a system not based on color distinctions?

"5. On the assumption on which questions 4 (*a*) and (*b*) are based, and assuming further that this Court will exercise its equity powers to the end described in question 4 (*b*),

"(*a*) should this Court formulate detailed decrees in these cases;

"(*b*) if so, what specific issues should the decrees reach;

"(*c*) should this Court appoint a special master to hear evidence with a view to recommending specific terms for such decrees;

"(*d*) should this Court remand to the courts of first instance with directions to frame decrees in these cases, and if so what general directions should the decrees of this Court include and what procedures should the courts of first instance follow in arriving at the specific terms of more detailed decrees?"

[14]See Rule 42, Revised Rules of this Court (effective July 1, 1954).

THE WOMEN'S POLITICAL COUNCIL TAKES ACTION

JO ANN GIBSON ROBINSON
from *The Montgomery Bus Boycott and the Women Who Started It*

1953–55

IN 1953, the members of the Women's Political Council (WPC) were confronted with some thirty complaints against the bus company, brought to it by black people in the community.

This organization of black women had been founded in 1946, nine years before the boycott began, by Dr. Mary Fair (Mrs. N. W. or "Frankye") Burks, chairman of the English department at Alabama State College. She became the WPC's first president, and it was she who organized the women who would work together as leaders and followers, giving and taking suggestions, and who would never reveal the secrets of the WPC. Dr. Burks, a profound scholar, highly intelligent and fearless, was a native Alabamian who had suffered from the segregated rules, the hypocrisy of race separation by day only. Pained by the suffering her people would continue to endure if things kept on as they were and had been from the beginning, Dr. Burks *knew* that one day, when human beings had taken all they could digest, the fight would begin. Thus, her thoughts gave birth to the WPC of college women and those who lived in the area.

Historians have written that women—white, black, and in-between—are the men's power structure of the universe. If there had not been women, there would not have been men, and vice versa. And there is the hidden secret that when the curtains of darkness fall, and the sun transports its sunlight into darkness, color is insignificant. Proof of it is in the variegated colors of human beings—white, black, red, yellow, brown—whose physical structures are normally identical.

The WPC was formed for the purpose of inspiring Negroes to live above mediocrity, to elevate their thinking, to fight juvenile and adult delinquency, to register and vote, and in general to improve their status as a group. We were "woman power," organized to cope with any injustice, no matter what, against the darker sect.

In Montgomery in 1955, no one was brazen enough to announce publicly that black people might boycott city buses for the specific purpose of *integrating* those buses. Just to say that minorities wanted "better seating arrangements" was bad enough. That was the term the two sides, white and black, always used later in discussing the boycott. The word "integration" never came up. Certainly all blacks knew not to use that word while riding the bus. To admit that black Americans were seeking to integrate would have been too much; there probably would have been much bloodshed and arrests of those who dared to disclose such an idea! That is why, during the boycott negotiations to come, the Men of Montgomery and other organizations always said that blacks would sit from back toward front, and whites would sit from the front of the bus toward the back, until all seats were taken.

The WPC, however, knew all the time that black Americans were working for integration, pure and simple. No front toward back, or vice versa! We knew we were human beings; that neither whites nor blacks were responsible for their color; that someday those buses, of necessity, had to be integrated; and that after integration neither would be worse off. For both were human; both were clean. And Montgomery, a college town, was capable of integrating, if each side would consider the matter seriously, without prejudice, and decide what was best for all concerned—the bus company, the white population, and the black population. We were, then, bent on integration. There were those afraid to admit it. But, we knew that deep down in the secret minds of all—teachers, students, and community—black Americans wanted integration. That way we would achieve equality. The only way.

The early WPC members all lived in the general neighborhood of the college. Most were professional women. There were competent educators, supervisors, principals, teachers, social workers, other community workers, nurses—women employees from every walk of life. Many of the women from Alabama State College were members; so were many public school teachers. It must be remembered that the women of the WPC were laying their "all" on the line in organizing themselves to defeat segregation in the heart of the Confederacy.

One hundred members was the limit for one group. However, there were so many requests for membership that a second chapter was organized to cover another part of the city. Soon a third group had to be organized, as furious women realized that everybody had to become involved if black Americans were to win their fight, put the bus company out of business, and integrate those carriers or establish a transportation system of their own. By 1955, then, the WPC had three chapters distinguished as Group 1 (the original group), Group 2, and Group 3.

The three divisions that resulted were organized in three different sections of the city and formed one of the best communication systems needed for operation of the boycott. Each group had its own officers—president, secretary, treasurer, telephone coordinators. The three chapter presidents were given all the information of an "expected" boycott, and were kept informed. Each group played a part in the distribution of the notices that called riders off city transportation lines. The three presidents kept in close touch with each other, and each president passed the news on to her group's members.

In the afternoon of Thursday, December 1, a prominent black woman named Mrs. Rosa Parks was arrested for refusing to vacate her seat for a white man. Mrs. Parks was a medium-sized, cultured mulatto woman; a civic and religious worker; quiet, unassuming, and pleasant in manner and appearance; dignified and reserved; of high morals and a strong character. She was—and still is, for she lives to tell the story—respected in all black circles. By trade she was a seamstress, adept and competent in her work.

Tired from work, Mrs. Parks boarded a bus. The "reserved seats" were partially filled, but the seats just behind the reserved section were vacant, and Mrs. Parks sat down in one. It was during the busy evening rush hour. More black and white passengers boarded the bus, and soon all the reserved seats were occupied. The driver demanded that Mrs. Parks get up and surrender her seat to a white man, but she was tired from her work. Besides, she was a woman, and the person waiting was a man. She remained seated. In a few minutes, police summoned by the driver appeared, placed Mrs. Parks under arrest, and took her to jail.

It was the first time the soft-spoken, middle-aged woman had been arrested. She maintained decorum and poise, and the word of her arrest spread. Mr. E. D. Nixon, a longtime stalwart of our NAACP branch, along with liberal white attorney Clifford Durr and his wife Virginia, went to the jail and obtained Mrs. Parks's release on bond. Her trial was scheduled for Monday, December 5, 1955.

The news traveled like wildfire into every black home. Telephones jangled; people congregated on street corners and in homes and talked. But nothing was done. A numbing helplessness seemed to paralyze everyone. Very few stayed off the buses the rest of that day or the next. There was fear, discontent, and uncertainty. Everyone seemed to wait for someone to *do* something, but nobody made a move. For that day and a half, black Americans rode the buses as before, as if nothing had happened. They were sullen and uncommunicative, but they rode the buses. There was a silent tension-filled waiting. For blacks were not talking loudly in public places—they were quiet, sullen, waiting. Just waiting!

Thursday evening came and went. Thursday night was far spent, when, at about 11:30 P.M., I sat alone in my peaceful single-family dwelling on a quiet street. I was thinking about the situation. Lost in thought, I was startled by the telephone's ring. Black attorney Fred Gray, who had been out of town all day, had just gotten back and was returning the phone message I had left for him about Mrs. Parks's arrest. Attorney Gray, though a very young man, had been one of my most active colleagues in our previous meetings with bus company officials and Commissioner Birmingham. A Montgomery native who had attended Alabama State and been one of my students, Fred Gray had gone on to law school in Ohio before returning to his home town to open a practice with the only other black lawyer in Montgomery, Charles Langford.

Fred Gray and his wife Bernice were good friends of mine, and we talked often. In addition to being a lawyer, Gray was a trained, ordained minister of the gospel, actively serving as assistant pastor of Holt Street Church of Christ.

Tonight his voice on the phone was very short and to the point. Fred was shocked by the news of Mrs. Parks's arrest. I informed him that I already was thinking that the WPC should distribute thousands of notices calling for all bus riders to stay off the buses on Monday, the day of Mrs. Parks's trial. "Are you ready?," he asked. Without hesitation, I assured him that we were. With that he hung up, and I went to work.

I made some notes on the back of an envelope: "The Women's Political Council will not wait for Mrs. Parks's consent to call for a boycott of city buses. On Friday, December 2, 1955, the women of Montgomery will call for a boycott to take place on Monday, December 5."

Some of the WPC officers previously had discussed plans for distributing thousands of notices announcing a bus boycott. Now the time had come for me to write just such a notice. I sat down and quickly drafted a message and then called a good friend and colleague, John Cannon, chairman of the business department at the college, who had access to the college's mimeograph equipment. When I told him that the WPC was staging a boycott and needed to run off the notices, he told me that he too had suffered embarrassment on the city buses. Like myself, he had been hurt and angry. He said that he would happily assist me. Along with two of my most trusted senior students, we quickly agreed to meet almost immediately, in the middle of the night, at the college's duplicating room. We were able to get three messages to a page, greatly reducing the number of pages that had to be mimeographed in order to produce the tens of thousands of leaflets we knew would be needed. By 4 A.M. Friday, the sheets had been duplicated, cut in thirds, and bundled. Each leaflet read:

> Another Negro woman has been arrested and thrown in jail because she refused to get up out of her seat on the bus for a white person to sit down. It is the second time since the Claudette Colvin case that a Negro woman has been arrested for the same thing. This has to be stopped. Negroes have rights, too, for if Negroes did not ride the buses, they could not operate. Three-fourths of the riders are Negroes, yet we are arrested, or have to stand over empty seats. If we do not do something to

> stop these arrests, they will continue. The next time it may be you, or your daughter, or mother. This woman's case will come up on Monday. We are, therefore, asking every Negro to stay off the buses Monday in protest of the arrest and trial. Don't ride the buses to work, to town, to school, or anywhere on Monday. You can afford to stay out of school for one day if you have no other way to go except by bus. You can also afford to stay out of town for one day. If you work, take a cab, or walk. But please, children and grown-ups, don't ride the bus at all on Monday. Please stay off of all buses Monday.

Between 4 and 7 A.M., the two students and I mapped out distribution routes for the notices. Some of the WPC officers previously had discussed how and where to deliver thousands of leaflets announcing a boycott, and those plans now stood me in good stead. We outlined our routes, arranged the bundles in sequences, stacked them in our cars, and arrived at my 8 A.M. class, in which both young men were enrolled, with several minutes to spare. We weren't even tired or hungry. Just like me, the two students felt a tremendous sense of satisfaction at being able to contribute to the cause of justice.

After class my two students and I quickly finalized our plans for distributing the thousands of leaflets so that one would reach every black home in Montgomery. I took out the WPC membership roster and called the former president, Dr. Mary Fair Burks, then the Pierces, the Glasses, Mrs. Mary Cross, Mrs. Elizabeth Arrington, Mrs. Josie Lawrence, Mrs. Geraldine Nesbitt, Mrs. H. Councill Trenholm, Mrs. Catherine N. Johnson, and a dozen or more others. I alerted all of them to the forthcoming distribution of the leaflets, and enlisted their aid in speeding and organizing the distribution network. Each would have one person waiting at a certain place to take a package of notices as soon as my car stopped and the young men could hand them a bundle of leaflets.

Then I and my two student helpers set out. Throughout the late morning and early afternoon hours we dropped off tens of thousands of leaflets. Some of our bundles were dropped off at schools, where both students and staff members helped distribute them further and spread the word for people to read the notices and then pass them on to neighbors. Leaflets were also dropped off at business places, storefronts, beauty parlors, beer halls, factories, barber shops, and every other available place. Workers would pass along notices both to other employees as well as to customers.

During those hours of crucial work, nothing went wrong. Suspicion was never raised. The action of all involved was so casual, so unconcerned, so nonchalant, that suspicion was never raised, and neither the city nor its people ever suspected a thing! We never missed a spot. And no one missed a class, a job, or a normal routine. Everything was done by the plan, with perfect timing. By 2 o'clock, thousands of the mimeographed handbills had changed hands many times. Practically every black man, woman, and child in Montgomery knew the plan and was passing the word along. No one knew where the notices had come from or who had arranged for their circulation, and no one cared. Those who passed them on did so efficiently, quietly, and without comment. But deep within the heart of every black person was a joy he or she dared not reveal.

“A BLACK MAN IS A BOY TO A WHITE”

BIG BILL BROONZY

When I Will Get to Be Called a Man

October 1955

When I was born in this world, this is what happened to me:
I was never called a man and now I’m fifty-three

I wonder when will I be called a man
Or do I have to wait ’till I get ninety-three?

When Uncle Sam called me I knew I would be called the real
McCoy
But when I got in the army they called me soldier boy

I wonder when will I be called a man
Or do I have to wait ’till I get ninety-three?

When I got back from overseas, that night we had a ball
I met the boss the next day, he told me “Boy get you some
overall”

I wonder when will I be called a man
Or do I have to wait ’till I get ninety-three?

I worked on a levee camp and a chain gang too
A black man is a boy to a white, don’t care what he can do

I wonder when will I be called a man
Or do I have to wait ’till I get ninety-three?

They said I was undereducated, my clothes was dirty and torn
Now I got a little education, but I’m a boy right on

I wonder when will I be called a man
Or do I have to wait ’till I get ninety-three?

A SOUTHERN MANIFESTO RESISTING "FORCED INTEGRATION"

SOUTHERN SENATORS AND REPRESENTATIVES

Declaration of Constitutional Principles

March 12, 1956

DECLARATION OF CONSTITUTIONAL PRINCIPLES

THE UNWARRANTED decision of the Supreme Court in the public school cases is now bearing the fruit always produced when men substitute naked power for established law.

The Founding Fathers gave us a Constitution of checks and balances because they realized the inescapable lesson of history that no man or group of men can be safely entrusted with unlimited power. They framed this Constitution with its provisions for change by amendment in order to secure the fundamentals of government against the dangers of temporary popular passion or the personal predilections of public officeholders.

We regard the decision of the Supreme Court in the school cases as a clear abuse of judicial power. It climaxes a trend in the Federal Judiciary undertaking to legislate, in derogation of the authority of Congress, and to encroach upon the reserved rights of the States and the people.

The original Constitution does not mention education. Neither does the 14th amendment nor any other amendment. The debates preceding the submission of the 14th amendment clearly show that there was no intent that it should affect the system of education maintained by the States.

The very Congress which proposed the amendment subsequently provided for segregated schools in the District of Columbia.

When the amendment was adopted in 1868, there were 37 States of the Union. Every one of the 26 States that had any substantial racial differences among its people, either approved the operation of segregated schools already in existence or subsequently established such schools by action of the same lawmaking body which considered the 14th amendment.

As admitted by the Supreme Court in the public school case (*Brown* v. *Board of Education*), the doctrine of separate but equal schools "apparently originated in *Roberts* v. *City of Boston* (1849), upholding school segregation against attack as being violative of a State constitutional guarantee of equality." This constitutional doctrine began in the North, not in the South, and it was followed not only in Massachusetts, but in Connecticut, New York, Illinois, Indiana, Michigan, Minnesota, New Jersey, Ohio, Pennsylvania and other northern States until they, exercising their rights as States through the constitutional processes of local self-government, changed their school systems.

In the case of *Plessy* v. *Ferguson* in 1896 the Supreme Court expressly declared that under the 14th amendment no person was denied any of his rights if the States provided separate but equal public facilities. This decision has been followed in many other cases. It is notable that the Supreme Court, speaking through Chief Justice Taft, a former President of the United States, unanimously declared in 1927 in *Lum* v. *Rice* that the "separate but equal" principle is "within the discretion of the State in regulating its public schools and does not conflict with the 14th amendment."

This interpretation, restated time and again, became a part of the life of the people of many of the States and confirmed their habits, customs, traditions, and way of life. It is founded on elemental humanity and commonsense, for parents should not be deprived by Government of the right to direct the lives and education of their own children.

Though there has been no constitutional amendment or act of Congress changing this established legal principle almost a century old, the Supreme Court of the United States, with no legal basis for such action, undertook to exercise their naked judicial power and substituted their personal political and social ideas for the established law of the land.

This unwarranted exercise of power by the Court, contrary to the Constitution, is creating chaos and confusion in the States principally affected. It is destroying the amicable relations between the white and Negro races that have been created through 90 years of patient effort by the good people of both races. It has planted hatred and suspicion where there has been heretofore friendship and understanding.

Without regard to the consent of the governed, outside agitators are threatening immediate and revolutionary changes in our public-school systems. If done, this is certain to destroy the system of public education in some of the States.

With the gravest concern for the explosive and dangerous condition created by this decision and inflamed by outside meddlers:

We reaffirm our reliance on the Constitution as the fundamental law of the land.

We decry the Supreme Court's encroachments on rights reserved to the States and to the people, contrary to established law, and to the Constitution.

We commend the motives of those States which have declared the intention to resist forced integration by any lawful means.

We appeal to the States and people who are not directly affected by these decisions to consider the constitutional principles involved against the time when they too, on issues vital to them, may be the victims of judicial encroachment.

Even though we constitute a minority in the present Congress, we have full faith that a majority of the American people believe in the dual system of government which has enabled us to achieve our greatness and will in time demand that the reserved rights of the States and of the people be made secure against judicial usurpation.

We pledge ourselves to use all lawful means to bring about a reversal of this decision which is contrary to the Constitution and to prevent the use of force in its implementation.

In this trying period, as we all seek to right this wrong, we appeal to our people not to be provoked by the agitators and troublemakers invading our States and to scrupulously refrain from disorder and lawless acts.

Signed by:

MEMBERS OF THE UNITED STATES SENATE

Walter F. George, Richard B. Russell, John Stennis, Sam J. Ervin, Jr., Strom Thurmond, Harry F. Byrd, A. Willis Robertson, John L. McClellan, Allen J. Ellender, Russell B. Long,

Lister Hill, James O. Eastland, W. Kerr Scott, John Sparkman, Olin D. Johnston, Price Daniel, J. W. Fulbright, George A. Smathers, Spessard L. Holland.

MEMBERS OF THE UNITED STATES
HOUSE OF REPRESENTATIVES

ALABAMA: Frank W. Boykin, George M. Grant, George W. Andrews, Kenneth A. Roberts, Albert Rains, Armistead I. Selden, Jr., Carl Elliott, Robert E. Jones, George Huddleston, Jr.

ARKANSAS: E. C. Gathings, Wilbur D. Mills, James W. Trimble, Oren Harris, Brooks Hays, W. F. Norrell.

FLORIDA: Charles E. Bennett, Robert L. F. Sikes, A. S. Herlong, Jr., Paul G. Rogers, James A. Haley, D. R. Matthews.

GEORGIA: Prince H. Preston, John L. Pilcher, E. L. Forrester, John James Flynt, Jr., James C. Davis, Carl Vinson, Henderson Lanham, Iris F. Blitch, Phil M. Landrum, Paul Brown.

LOUISIANA: F. Edward Hébert, Hale Boggs, Edwin E. Willis, Overton Brooks, Otto E. Passman, James H. Morrison, T. Ashton Thompson, George S. Long.

MISSISSIPPI: Thomas G. Abernethy, Jamie L. Whitten, Frank E. Smith, John Bell Williams, Arthur Winstead, William M. Colmer.

NORTH CAROLINA: Herbert C. Bonner, L. H. Fountain, Graham A. Barden, Carl T. Durham, F. Ertel Carlyle, Hugh Q. Alexander, Woodrow W. Jones, George A. Shuford.

SOUTH CAROLINA: L. Mendel Rivers, John J. Riley, W. J. Bryan Dorn, Robert T. Ashmore, James P. Richards, John L. McMillan.

TENNESSEE: James B. Frazier, Jr., Tom Murray, Jere Cooper, Clifford Davis.

TEXAS: Wright Patman, John Dowdy, Walter Rogers, O. C. Fisher.

VIRGINIA: Edward J. Robeson, Jr., Porter Hardy, Jr., J. Vaughan Gary, Watkins M. Abbitt, William M. Tuck, Richard H. Poff, Burr P. Harrison, Howard W. Smith, W. Pat Jennings, Joel T. Broyhill.

THE CHICAGO DEFENDER
Alabama Pickets Rock-Roll Troupe

May 21, 1956

ALABAMA PICKETS ROCK-ROLL TROUPE

BIRMINGHAM, Ala.—(INS)—The North Alabama white citizens council Sunday picketed some of America's top rock and roll recording stars in its campaign against what it terms "Negro music."

Some 50 members of the pro-segregation organization turned up with placards in hand to picket the touring jazz music group, which included Bill Haley, who has made nine recordings to sell over the million mark.

The picketing was orderly. Birmingham police kept council members moving and prohibited them from making cat calls at those attending the white-only Rock and Roll show. There were no incidents.

Most of the audience were teenagers who seemed to consider the picketing a laugh. One young girl, on entering the theater turned to a man carrying a placard which read "Jungle Music Promotes Integration" and said "Bring me my Grapevine."

Other placards read "Be-Bop promotes Communism" and "Communism grows at Be-Bop sessions."

THE "VERTICAL NEGRO PLAN"

HARRY GOLDEN

How to Solve the Segregation Problem

Carolina Israelite, May–June 1956

HOW TO SOLVE THE SEGREGATION PROBLEM

THOSE WHO love North Carolina will jump at the chance to share in the great responsibility now confronting our Governor and the State Legislature. The Special Session of the Legislature, scheduled to open in a few days, will be asked to pass a series of amendments to the State Constitution. These proposals submitted by the Governor and his Advisory Education Committee, include the following—(A) The elimination of the compulsory attendance law, "to prevent any child from being forced to attend a school with a child of another race." (B) The establishment of "Education Expense Grants" for education in a private school, "in the case of a child assigned to a public school attended by a child of another race." (C) A "uniform system of local option" whereby a majority of the folks in a school district may suspend or close a school if the situation becomes "intolerable."

But suppose a Negro child applies for this "Education Expense Grant" and says he wants to go to the private school too? There are fourteen Supreme Court decisions involving the use of public funds; there are only two "decisions" involving the elimination of racial discrimination in the public schools.

The Governor has said that critics of these proposals have not offered any constructive advice or alternatives. Permit me therefore to offer an idea for the consideration of the members of the Special Session. A careful study of my plan, I believe, will show that it will save millions of dollars in tax funds and eliminate forever the danger to our public education system. Before I outline my plan, I would like to give you a little background.

One of the factors involved in our tremendous industrial growth and economic prosperity has been due to the fact that the South, voluntarily, has all but eliminated VERTICAL SEGREGATION. The tremendous buying power of the twelve million Negroes in the South has been based wholly on the *absence of racial segregation*. The white and Negro stand at the same grocery and super-market counters; deposit money at the same bank-teller's window; pay phone and light bills to the same clerk; walk through the same dime and department stores, and stand at the same drug-store counters. It is only when the Negro "*sets*" that the fur begins to fly. Now since we are not even thinking about restoring VERTICAL SEGREGATION, I think my plan would not only comply with the Supreme Court decisions, but would maintain "*sitting down*" segregation. Now here is the GOLDEN VERTICAL NEGRO PLAN. Instead of all those complicated proposals, all the Special Session needs to do is pass one small amendment which would provide ONLY desks in all the public schools of our State; NO SEATS. The desks should be those standing-up jobs, like the old-fashioned bookkeeping desk. Since no one in the South pays the slightest attention to a VERTICAL NEGRO, this will completely solve our problem. And it is not such a terrible inconvenience for young people to stand up during their class-room studies. In fact this may be a blessing in disguise. They are not learning to read sitting down, anyway; maybe "standing up" will help. This will save more MILLIONS of dollars in the cost of our "Remedial English" course when the kids enter college. In whatever direction you look with the GOLDEN VERTICAL NEGRO PLAN, you save MILLIONS of dollars, to say nothing of eliminating forever any danger to our public education system upon which rests the destiny, hopes, and happiness of this society.

"YOU SHOULD ADJOURN THIS FOREVER"

PAUL ROBESON

from *Testimony Before the House Committee on Un-American Activities*

June 12, 1956

Mr. ARENS. Do you know Max Yergan?

Mr. ROBESON. I invoke the fifth amendment.

Mr. ARENS. Max Yergan took an oath before this committee, and testified to tell the truth.

Mr. ROBESON. Why do you not have these people here to be cross-examined, and is this, Mr. Chairman——

Mr. ARENS. Under oath, this man——

Mr. ROBESON. Could I ask whether this is legal.

The CHAIRMAN. This is legal. This is not only legal, but usual. By a unanimous vote this committee has been instructed to perform this very distasteful task.

Mr. ROBESON. It is not distasteful. To whom am I talking to?

The CHAIRMAN. You are speaking to the chairman of this committee.

Mr. ROBESON. Mr. Walter?

The CHAIRMAN. Yes.

Mr. ROBESON. The Pennsylvania Walter?

The CHAIRMAN. That is right.

Mr. ROBESON. Representative of the steelworkers?

The CHAIRMAN. That is right.

Mr. ROBESON. Of the coal mining workers and not United States Steel, by any chance? A great patriot.

The CHAIRMAN. That is right.

Mr. ROBESON. You are the author of all of the bills that are going to keep all kinds of decent people out of the country.

The CHAIRMAN. No, only your kind.

Mr. ROBESON. Colored people like myself, from the West Indies and all kinds, and just the Teutonic Anglo-Saxon stock that you would let come in.

The CHAIRMAN. We are trying to make it easier to get rid of your kind, too.

Mr. ROBESON. You do not want any colored people to come in?

The CHAIRMAN. Proceed.

Mr. ARENS. Under date of December 17, 1948, Dr. Max Yergan testified before this committee under oath as follows:

> Was there a group in the Council on African Affairs of Communist officials, who operated as a sort of leading caucus inside the council?
>
> Dr. YERGAN. Not as such. The relation of Communists to the council was informal, and so far as I know, not organized. Toward the end of my relation to the council it became clear to me that there was a Communist core within the council. This was very clear to me during the last months of my relations to the council.

May I ask you now, was there, to your knowledge, a Communist core in the Council on African Affairs?

Mr. ROBESON. I will take the fifth amendment and could I be allowed to read from my own statement here, while you read this statement just for a moment?

Mr. ARENS. Will you just tell this committee while under oath, Mr. Robeson, the Communists who participated in the preparation of that statement?

Mr. ROBESON. Oh, please.

Mr. ARENS. Now:

> The CHAIRMAN. Could you identify that core clearly? Of whom did it consist?

Mr. ROBESON. Could I read my statement?

Mr. ARENS. As soon as you tell the committee the Communists who participated in the preparation.

> Dr. YERGAN. Dr. Doxey Wilkerson was a member of that core, and took the leading position. Paul Robeson was chairman of the council and certainly a part of that Communist-led core.

Now tell this committee, while you are under oath, was Dr. Yergan lying or was he telling the truth?

Mr. ROBESON. I invoke the fifth amendment. Could I say that for the reason that I am here today, you know, from the mouth of the State Department itself, is because I should not be allowed to travel because I have struggled for years for the independence of the colonial peoples of Africa, and for many years I have so labored and I can say modestly that my name is very much honored in South Africa and all over Africa in my struggles for their independence. That is the kind of independence like Sukarno got in Indonesia. Unless we are double-talking, then these efforts in the interest of Africa would be in the same context. The other reason that I am here today is again from the State Department and from the court record of the court of appeals, that when I am abroad I speak out against the injustices against the Negro people of this land. I sent a message to the Bandung Conference and so forth. That is why I am here. This is the basis and I am not being tried for whether I am a Communist, I am being tried for fighting for the rights of my people who are still second-class citizens in this United States of America. My mother was born in your State, Mr. Walter, and my mother was a Quaker, and my ancestors in the time of Washington baked bread for George Washington's troops when they crossed the Delaware, and my own father was a slave. I stand here struggling for the rights of my people to be full citizens in this country and they are not. They are not in Mississippi and they are not in Montgomery, Ala., and they are not in Washington, and they are nowhere, and that is why I am here today. You want to shut up every Negro who has the courage to stand up and fight for the rights of his people, for the rights of workers and I have been on many a picket line for the steelworkers too. And that is why I am here today.

The CHAIRMAN. Now just a minute.

Mr. ROBESON. All of this is nonsense.

Mr. ARENS. Did you write an article that was subsequently published in the U. S. S. R. Information Bulletin?

Mr. ROBESON. Yes.

Mr. ARENS. In that article, did you say:

> Moscow is very dear to me and very close to my heart. I want to emphasize that only here, in the Soviet Union, did I feel that

> I was a real man with a capital "M." And now after many years I am here again in Moscow, in the country I love more than any other.

Did you say that?

Mr. ROBESON. I would say,——what is your name?

Mr. ARENS. Arens.

Mr. ROBESON. We will take this in context, and I am quite willing to answer the question, and you are reading from a document and it is in context. When I was a singer years ago, and this you have to listen to——

Mr. ARENS. I am listening.

Mr. ROBESON. I am a bass singer, and so for me it was Chaliapin, the great Russian bass, and not Russo the tenor, and so I learned the Russian language and the Russian songs to sing their songs. I wish you would listen now.

Mr. SCHERER. I ask you to direct the witness to answer the question.

Mr. ROBESON. Just be fair to me.

Mr. SCHERER. I ask regular order.

Mr. ROBESON. The great poet of Russia, like Shakespeare of England, is of African blood.

The CHAIRMAN. Let us not go so far afield.

Mr. ROBESON. It is very important. It is very important to explain this. I know what he said.

The CHAIRMAN. You can make an explanation. Did you make that statement?

Mr. ROBESON. When I first went to Russia in 1934——

The CHAIRMAN. Did you make that statement?

Mr. ROBESON. When I first went to Russia in 1934——

The CHAIRMAN. Did you make that statement?

Mr. SCHERER. I ask you to direct the witness to answer the question.

(The witness consulted with his counsel.)

The CHAIRMAN. Did you make that statement?

Mr. ROBESON. I would say in Russia I felt for the first time like a full human being, and no colored prejudice like in Mississippi and no colored prejudice like in Washington and it was the first time I felt like a human being, where I did not feel the pressure of colored as I feel in this committee today.

Mr. SCHERER. Why do you not stay in Russia?

Mr. ROBESON. Because my father was a slave, and my people died to build this country, and I am going to stay here and have a part of it just like you. And no Fascist-minded people will drive me from it. Is that clear? I am for peace with the Soviet Union and I am for peace with China, and I am not for peace or friendship with the Fascist Franco, and I am not for peace with Fascist Nazi Germans, and I am for peace with decent people in the world.

Mr. SCHERER. The reason you are here is because you are promoting the Communist cause in this country.

Mr. ROBESON. I am here because I am opposing the neo-Fascist cause which I see arising in these committees. You are like the Alien Sedition Act, and Jefferson could be sitting here, and Frederick Douglass could be sitting here and Eugene Debs could be here.

The CHAIRMAN. Are you going to answer the questions?

Mr. ROBESON. I am answering them.

The CHAIRMAN. Now, what prejudice are you talking about? You were graduated from Rutgers and you were graduated from the University of Pennsylvania. I remember seeing you play football at Lehigh.

Mr. ROBESON. We beat Lehigh.

The CHAIRMAN. And we had a lot of trouble with you.

Mr. ROBESON. That is right. DeWysocki was playing in my team.

The CHAIRMAN. There was no prejudice against you. Why did you not send your son to Rutgers?

Mr. ROBESON. Just a moment. It all depends a great deal. This is something that I challenge very deeply, and very sincerely, the fact that the success of a few Negroes, including myself or Jackie Robinson can make up—and here is a study from Columbia University—for $700 a year for thousands of Negro families in the South. My father was a slave, and I have cousins who are sharecroppers and I do not see my success in terms of myself. That is the reason, my own success has not meant what it should mean. I have sacrificed literally hundreds of thousands, if not millions, of dollars for what I believe in.

Mr. ARENS. While you were in Moscow, did you make a speech lauding Stalin?

Mr. ROBESON. I do not know.

Mr. ARENS. Did you say in effect that Stalin was a great man and Stalin had done much for the Russian people, for all of the nations of the world, for all working people of the earth? Did you say something to that effect about Stalin when you were in Moscow?

Mr. ROBESON. I cannot remember.

Mr. ARENS. Do you have a recollection of praising Stalin?

Mr. ROBESON. I can certainly know that I said a lot about Soviet people, fighting for the peoples of the earth.

Mr. ARENS. Did you praise Stalin?

Mr. ROBESON. I do not remember.

Mr. ARENS. Have you recently changed your mind about Stalin?

Mr. ROBESON. Whatever has happened to Stalin, gentlemen, is a question for the Soviet Union and I would not argue with a representative of the people who, in building America wasted 60 to 100 million lives of my people, black people drawn from Africa on the plantations. You are responsible and your forebears for 60 million to 100 million black people dying in the slave ships and on the plantations, and don't you ask me about anybody, please.

Mr. ARENS. I am glad you called our attention to that slave problem. While you were in Soviet Russia, did you ask them there to show you the slave labor camps?

The CHAIRMAN. You have been so greatly interested in slaves, I should think that you would want to see that.

Mr. ROBESON. The slaves I see are still as a kind of semiserfdom, and I am interested in the place I am and in the country that can do something about it. As far as I know about the slave camps, they were Fascist prisoners who had murdered millions of the Jewish people and who would have wiped out millions of the Negro people could they have gotten a hold of them. That is all I know about that.

Mr. ARENS. Tell us whether or not you have changed your opinion in the recent past about Stalin.

Mr. ROBESON. I have told you, Mister, that I would not discuss anything with the people who have murdered 60 million of my people, and I will not discuss Stalin with you.

Mr. ARENS. You would not, of course, discuss with us the slave labor camps in Soviet Russia.

Mr. ROBESON. I will discuss Stalin when I may be among the Russian people some day singing for them, and I will discuss it there. It is their problem.

Mr. ARENS. In the summer of 1949, you came back to the United States; is that right?

Mr. ROBESON. In the summer of 1949, yes, that is right.

Mr. ARENS. And when you came back, did you make a speech in New York City, addressing a rally there? Do you recall that?

Mr. ROBESON. I do not.

Mr. ARENS. Let me quote from an article appearing in a paper, and see if you recall this speech:

> I have the greatest contempt for the democratic press and there is something within me which keeps me from breaking your cameras over your heads.

Did you say that to the press people in New York City about the time you were addressing this rally in June of 1949?

Mr. ROBESON. It is sort of out of context.

Mr. ARENS. That was out of context?

Mr. ROBESON. I am afraid it is.

Mr. ARENS. Would you want to refresh your recollection by looking at the article?

Mr. ROBESON. Yes. That was not at a meeting. Why do you not say what it was? When my son married the woman of his choice, some very wild press men were there to make a sensation out of it, and this thing was at his wedding, and I did not say "democratic press," I said "a certain kind of press," and I was reaching for a camera to break it, you are quite right.

Mr. ARENS. That was a misquotation?

Mr. ROBESON. It was not at a meeting. It was when I came out of my son's wedding, and why do you not be honest about this? There is nothing about a meeting, it was a wedding of my son.

Mr. ARENS. Does not this article say, "Paul Robeson Addressing a Welcome Home Rally"?

Mr. ROBESON. I do not care what it says.

Mr. ARENS. That is wrong, too, is it?

Now I would invite your attention, if you please, to the Daily Worker of June 29, 1949, with reference to a get-together with you and Ben Davis. Do you know Ben Davis?

Mr. ROBESON. One of my dearest friends, one of the finest Americans you can imagine, born of a fine family, who went to Amherst and was a great man.

The CHAIRMAN. The answer is "Yes"?

Mr. ROBESON. And a very great friend and nothing could make me prouder than to know him.

The CHAIRMAN. That answers the question.

Mr. ARENS. Did I understand you to laud his patriotism?

Mr. ROBESON. I say that he is as patriotic an American as there can be, and you gentlemen belong with the Alien and Sedition Acts, and you are the nonpatriots, and you are the un-Americans and you ought to be ashamed of yourselves.

The CHAIRMAN. Just a minute, the hearing is now adjourned.

Mr. ROBESON. I should think it would be.

The CHAIRMAN. I have endured all of this that I can.

Mr. ROBESON. Can I read my statement?

The CHAIRMAN. No, you cannot read it. The meeting is adjourned.

Mr. ROBESON. I think it should be and you should adjourn this forever, that is what I would say.

“THIS SECRET OF GOD AND THE DEVIL”

ELIJAH MUHAMMAD

Mr. Muhammad Speaks: Who Is the Original Man?

Pittsburgh Courier, July 28, 1956

MR. MUHAMMAD SPEAKS

EDITOR’S NOTE: *The opinions expressed in this column in no manner reflect the editorial policy or beliefs of The Pittsburgh Courier. The views are the author’s own writings.*

Who Is the Original Man?

THE above question is now answered from the mouth of Allah (God), to us, the so-called Negroes, for the first time since our straying away from our own nation.

This secret of God and the devil has been a mystery to the average one of mankind, to be revealed in all of its clearness to one who was so ignorant that he knew not even himself, born blind, deaf, and dumb in the wilderness of North America.

All praise is due to the Great Mahdi (Allah in Person), Who was to come and has come the Sole Master of the Worlds. I ask myself at time, “What can I do to repay Allah (the Great Mahdi, Fard Muhammad) for His coming, wisdom, knowledge and understanding?

Born in the Southern part of this Wilderness (Wilderness of Sin), where the Man of Sin has always manifested himself to us, the so-called Negroes, that he was really the evil one by the way he treated us. Yet, we were made so dumb that we still couldn’t recognize him.

The truth of him is now being told and taught throughout the world to his anger and sorrow. He is losing no time trying to hinder this truth of the above question, who is the Original man?

He is setting watchers and listeners around me and my followers to see if he can find some other charge to put against us to satisfy his anger of the truth that we preach from the mouth of Allah, Who is with us in Person.

The Original Man, Allah has declared is none other than the Black Man. The first and last, maker and owner of the Universe, from him came all brown, yellow, red and white. By using a special method of birth control law he was able to produce the white race.

The true knowledge of the black and white mankind should be enough to awaken the so-called Negroes, put them on their feet and on the road to self-independence. Yet, they are so afraid of the slavemasters that they even love them to their destruction and wishes that the bearer of truth would not tell the truth even if he knows it.

The time has arrived when it must be told the world over for there are millions who don't know who the Original Man is. Why should this question be put before the world today? Because it is the TIME of judgment between the two (black and white) and without that knowledge of the Original Man, it means to be without knowledge of the rightful owners of the earth.

Allah (to Whom praise is due) is now pointing out to the nations of earth their rightful places and this judgment will bring an end to war over it.

Now it is so easy to recognize the Original man, the real owner of the earth by the history of the two (black and white). We have an unending past history of the black nation, and a limited one of the white race.

We find that history teaches that the earth was populated by the black nation ever since it was created, but the history of the white race doesn't take us beyond 6,000 years.

Everywhere the white race has gone on our planet, he either found the Original Man or a sign that he had been there previously. Allah is proving to the world of black man that the white race actually doesn't own any part of our planet.

The Bible and Holy Qur-an bears witness to the above said, if you are able to understand it. The Holy Qur-an, the beauty of

Scriptures repeatedly challenges them to point out or show the part of the heavens and earth that they created?

It further teaches that they are not even their own creators. We created man (white race) from a small life germ, the soft pronoun "we" used nearly throughout the Holy Qur-an makes the knowledge of the Original Man much clearer and of a more intelligent knowledge of how the white race's creation took place.

In the Bible referring to their creation we have US (Gen. 1:26) creating or rather making the race, the US and WE used show beyond a shadow of a doubt that they came from another people.

A knowledge of the white race removes once and for all times the mistakes that would be made in dealing with them. My followers and I can and are getting along with them in a more understandable way than ever, because we know them.

You can't blame one for the way he or she was born, for they had nothing to do with that. Can we say to them why don't you do righteousness when Nature did not give righteousness to them? Or say to them why are you such a wicked devil? Who is responsible; the made or his maker?

Yet this doesn't excuse us for following and practicing his evil, or accepting him for a righteous guide just because he is not his maker.

MALCOLM X

We Are Rising from the Dead Since We Heard Messenger Muhammad . . .

Pittsburgh Courier, December 15 and 22, 1956

MOSLEM MINISTER EXPLAINS PHILOSOPHY OF ISLAM AND ITS IMPACT ON AMERICA

EDITOR'S NOTE: For the past several years great numbers of Americans have embraced the Moslem faith. On the other hand, the majority of people who are members of Western faiths do not understand the philosophy of Islam and its teachings. Basically, Islam teaches that all men are equal and no color differences exist among Moslems. The author of this article, Malcolm X, is a Moslem minister. He explains his faith from the point of view of a Moslem in the Western world.

By MALCOLM X,
Minister Temple No. 7, New York City

"I am he that liveth, and was dead; and, behold, I am alive forevermore, Amen; and have the keys of hell and of death."

—Revelation 1:18.

BEFORE we heard the teachings of MESSENGER MUHAMMAD, we Americans (so-called Negroes) were in the grave of ignorance. We had been taught by our Christian Slavemaster, as well as by our own ignorant religious leaders that God had cursed us black and sentenced us to a lifetime on earth of servitude to the Christian white race.

The same Slavemaster's Christian religion taught us (or promised us) that we so-called Negroes would sprout wings after death and mount up into the sky where God would have a place especially prepared for us. Since we poor "cursed slaves" were not to get anything on earth while we were alive.

We soon learned to expect it only after death, up in the sky. Therefore, this earth and all its vast riches, which we ourselves originally owned, was left to the deceitful maneuverings of the white race, to build for themselves a heaven on earth while they yet live.

Such religious teachings were designed to make us feel inferior to the white Christian Slavemaster, and he soon was successful in making us fear him, obey him and worship him, instead of Almighty God Allah, the True Supreme Being, the God of our Own Foreparents.

MESSENGER MUHAMMAD has taught us how we so-called Negroes soon became like the beggar, Lazarus, of the Bible: our condition became sickening (very sore). We sat here amid the rubbish of the Western World, at the rich white Christians' feet (or gate) begging for something from their table . . . but from this same Slavemaster whom our own forefathers had made rich, by giving him freely of their slave labor for 400 years, we received only the roughest jobs at the lowest wages, the poorest houses in the slum areas at the highest rent and the worst food and clothing at the highest prices. Our schools were like shacks, and were staffed by teachers who knew and could teach only what the Slavemaster dictated to them.

MESSENGER MUHAMMAD has taught us how we so-called Negroes were KIDNAPPED "from the East" by the white Christian Slavemaster, brought here in chains and robbed of OUR OWN RELIGION, robbed of OUR OWN language, robbed of OUR OWN culture, robbed of OUR OWN God, robbed of OUR OWN flag, robbed of OUR OWN names and robbed even of OUR OWN NATIONALITY . . . and after robbing us of all that we originally could proudly call OUR OWN, then the Slavemaster taught us to call ourselves "Negroes," telling us that this was so because he had brought us from along the banks of the Niger River.

MESSENGER MUHAMMAD asks us today when does one receive one's nationality from a river? The same wicked Slavemaster also taught us that "Negro" means black in Spanish. MESSENGER MUHAMMAD again asks us why then don't all of the dark, Spanish-speaking people of Spain, South and Central America accept it (Negro) as their NATIONALITY, too?

MESSENGER MUHAMMAD says that we too should get

our NATIONALITY from the NATION which our foreparents originated from (as do all other recognized peoples).

MESSENGER MUHAMMAD teaches us how the Bible says we were purposely cut off from OUR OWN KIND after being robbed of our identity by the cruel Christian Slavemaster (Ezekiel 37:11; Psalms 83:4; Psalms 137:1–9). MESSENGER MUHAMMAD says the Slavemaster took our own names, language and religion from us so that we would then have to accept his, obey him and worship him (Daniel 1:6–7).

MESSENGER MUHAMMAD has given us many scriptures to prove that his teachings to us are true and in accord with the prophecies of the Bible. He says it is we so-called Negroes in America who were robbed deaf, dumb and blind to the knowledge of OUR OWN God and OUR OWN SELVES, so that today we are like DRY BONES IN THE VALLEY (spiritually dead, in the GRAVE OF IGNORANCE). We are now only able to speak the Slavemaster's language, and we are even yet called the same slaves names given us by the Slavemaster to our fathers during slaverytime; names such as Jones, Smith, Bunche, Powell, Dawson, Diggs, etc.

NAMES OF the very same Slavemaster who has shown characteristics of his BEASTLIKE nature in his treatment of us (Revelation 15:2). The original names of our FATHERS were cut off from us, kept secret from us by the beast, and thus we knew them not.

All other people have their own religion and believe in a God whom they can associate themselves with, a GOD WHO LOOKS LIKE ONE OF THEIR OWN KIND. But we so-called Negroes, after 400 years of masterful brainwashing by the Slavemaster, pictured our "God" with the same blond hair, pallid skin and cold blue eyes of our murderous Slavemaster.

His Christian religion teaches us that "black" is a curse, thus we who accepted the Slavemaster's religion found ourselves loving and respecting everything and everyone except black and we could picture God as being anything else EXCEPT BLACK. In fact, many of us would rather believe that God is an INVISIBLE (Colorless) SPIRIT than to admit to even the possibility of His being black. Even Daniel saw him with kinky hair (like lamb's wool) in the seventh chapter, ninth verse. How grossly misled and deceived we have been.

MESSENGER MUHAMMAD says that the teachers and religious leaders of our own kind here in America were as blind to the REAL TRUTH as we, therefore, they themselves were not qualified to lead us beyond what the Slavemaster would allow them. How can the blind lead the blind? Thus we remained in the ditch (the grave of spiritual ignorance and mental bondage) which was dug for us to fall into by our white Christian Slavemaster.

Not only did our own preachers and educators here fail to give us the truth, even our darker brothers who were born in the East, came here from the East and neglected to convert us back to the original religion (ISLAM) of our foreparents. Our brothers from the East even failed to recognize us as their long-lost brother who had been kidnapped from the nation of Islam 400 years ago and made to dwell here in this strange land among people not of our own kind or of our own choice (Genesis 15:13).

Our brothers from the East passed us by, and instead tried to lecture on Islam to our Slavemaster, so foolishly thinking they would be successful in turning the Slavemaster into a righteous Moslem . . . knowing all the time that the same slavemaster was the one who has kidnapped, robbed, enslaved and lynched (murdered) their long-lost true brother. Yes. Our brothers from the East came here and seemed to be apologists of Islam, instead of rightly spreading it, or defending it from the sly insults of the unbelieving Slavemaster.

MESSENGER MUHAMMAD teaches us that Almighty God Allah is all-powerful and independent. Allah needs no one to apologize for Him. Islam, His true religion, is not a religion of compromise.

Islam is truth, life itself. It has been kept a secret from us. For 400 years we so-called Negroes were deprived of Islam (life) by our white Slavemaster, who in turn indoctrinated us with his religion of Christianity . . . and like the Biblical Lazarus we soon became so dead mentally and spiritually that our disposition (attitude) became offensive (stunk) in the nostrils of the intelligent and civilized world. Our own kind in the East refused to recognize us as their long-lost brother. They soon forgot us completely, and we too forgot our blood-ties with them.

But Almighty God Allah forgets not. As he predicted in the Old Testament (Malachi 4:5) that He would send Elijah to the lost sheep (so-called Negroes of America) in the "last days" (of the white men's world) to teach us the truth that would free us from our white Slavemaster, and turn our hearts and minds back toward our own kind (our fathers) in the East, and also in that last day the hearts of our people of the East would be turned again toward us (Isaiah 43:5).

We who have been raised by Elijah from the "grave" that had been dug for us by the Slavemaster, bear witness that this same Elijah who was predicted to come has been raised up in our midst today and is even now with us in the person of the Honorable ELIJAH MUHAMMAD. Indeed, he is "the First Begotten" of we so-called Negroes who have long been a dead people. Yes, he is one of the "first fruits" of we who slept, and has been raised from our midst by Almighty God Allah himself.

EXAMINE HIS works among us, for his WORK is sufficient to testify to His IDENTITY. Only a fool, or an envious person would fail to see the greatness of this man after examining his work. We who have ourselves been raised by him, bear witness to his work.

In such short time, MESSENGER MUHAMMAD is accomplishing what our educators and religious leaders here failed to do for 100 years, and what our brothers from the East neglected to do. MESSENGER MUHAMMAD has brought our minds out of the sky (where the ignorant preachers had sent it), and has made us able to face the reality of living. He has restored life (truth) back to our long-lost dead people. Who else other than Almighty Allah could have given this meek and humble little man power to do what all others have failed to do?

". . . and Allah sends down WATER from above, and therewith gives life to the dead earth after its death. Surely there is a SIGN in this for a people who listen . . . (Holy Quran 16:65)."

Praise be to Almighty Allah. Who would have believed it? This little unlearned man, an ex-slave himself (a man like Moses . . . Deut. 18:18) to whom Allah has given sufficient power to stand up and speak the truth so boldly here in the land of our bondage, facing not only the wrath of the wicked Slavemaster (modern Pharoah), but also the wrath of his own kind who are ignorant to the truth and therefore too blind to see what is good for them, plus those who are jealous and envious of his wisdom and his divine mission.

(Conclusion Next Week)

MESSENGER Muhammad's teachings have really inspired us with a thirst in this day for truth. We who follow him actually are filled with a craving to wear the crown of life, the jewels of which are: wisdom, knowledge, understanding, freedom, judgment, equality, food, clothing, shelter, love, peace, happiness. He teaches us that these must be enjoyed while we are living.

These are the very essentials of life, and they adorn the crown of life which we shall wear in Allah's paradise (the Kingdom of God) which will soon be set up on this earth for us to enjoy while we are living. Almighty God Allah has a religion of life (not of death), that teaches us to live and how to live, and the importance of living. Allah is God of the living, not the God of the dead.

All praise is due to Allah. We who once followed foolishly and blindly after the slavemaster's plurality of gods (Trinity), and sought to have our heaven (the necessities of life) up in the sky after we die, are today no longer fooled by the Slavemaster's lie. Today we know that there is but one God. There is no God but Almighty Allah, and we bear witness that the Hon. Elijah Muhammad is His last and greatest messenger to us here in North America. Yes, we who were once dead (spiritually, mentally, politically, socially and economically), lying at the rich white men's feet here in the grave of ignorance, are being raised from this "death" today, being made upright, perpendicular, by the words of this noble messenger of Almighty God, Allah, who has the message of life for 17,000,000 so-called Negroes here in America . . . "The people (so-called Negroes) that walked in darkness (ignorance) have seen a great light (Islam): they that dwell in the land (of bondage) in the shadow of death (the cross), upon them has the light (of Islam) shined . . . (Isaiah 9:2)."

Examine our previous condition, then judge Messenger Muhammad according to his work on us. We who are striving to carry his teachings into practice, today are well on the road to spiritual, intellectual, and economic independence. Thanks to his message we are today well aware of the importance of freedom, justice, equality, wisdom, knowledge, understanding, food, clothing, shelter, love, peace, happiness, in sufficient quantity and quality while we are living. This great teacher has filled us with the desire to rest not until we have our own righteous nation, united together under one God Allah, wherein brotherhood is a living and practiced reality, instead of a "future dream" or a "far away promise" as it is in the religion of our Slavemaster.

Even you must bear witness that this man, Messenger Muhammad, is without question the most fearless and uncompromising representative of Almighty God Allah and his religion of Islam. He does not offer any apology to this wicked race (nor to the fearful and unbelieving Uncle Toms of our own kind) for the condemnation of the wicked that his message from God warns of.

He says (as Noah did) that you can take it or leave it. So you who say you believe in Almighty God Allah, but who hesitate to teach naked truth for fear of hurting the "tender feelings" of this wicked white race . . . since you are filled with fear of the beast (Revelation 21:8) instead of standing in the way holding up progress, hardening your hearts with envy, jealousy and unbelief, step out of His way so that He can prove to the world that indeed there is no God but Allah, and that this great God Allah has come to redeem His long-lost people (the so-called Negroes of America) . . . Revelation 7:2.

You must bear witness that according to the Bible, destruction of the Slavemaster by Almighty God cannot be avoided nor longer delayed. And, oh how well the Slavemaster (modern Pharaoh) is aware of it. Yes, this Government which was founded upon the slavery and sufferings of God's chosen people, is quite upset today because of the teachings of Messenger Muhammad (modern Moses) as was the Bible's Pharaoh.

Government agents have often visited me and questioned me so thoroughly and persistently that I spent many a sleepless night wondering what it is about the presence of this little meek and humble man that has them so terribly concerned and upset.

Yes, they have visited and questioned many of his followers, but the more they visit and question us the more clearly we are able to see and know that this is indeed a divine man, God-sent to us poor slaves (Exodus 3:6 to 10), with truth that frees us from fear forever of this modern Pharaoh.

This little man has not been to college; his formal education in the Slavemaster's school system is very limited, and he is not eloquent in his speech (Exodus 4:10), whereas these Government agents who question us are highly trained and well schooled in all of the modern sciences of life. They are well-learned yet the teachings of this little unlearned man has them confused and upset. The average unlearned person cannot upset a learned person . . . unless he has been given something by the most learned one (the all-knowing one), Almighty God Allah himself.

All praise is due to Allah: How well has He enabled us to see that this little meek and humble man is he of whom the Bible says: "How knoweth this man letters (such great wisdom) having never learned (being unlearned) . . . John 7:15 . . . No man in history has ever fit such prophetic picture more perfectly than this little unlearned man who is teaching us today with such great authority. Yes, he may be unlearned according to the educational standard of the Slavemaster, but he has been well schooled by Almighty God Allah himself . . . and he tells us constantly that his doctrine (message) is not his own but was authored by the one God Allah who sent him (John 7:15).

All praise is due to Allah. Think of this. This man, born in Georgia, mentally blind, deaf and dumb, and as ignorant as all the rest of us. But we see him today upsetting the Slavemaster's health just as Moses did in his day to the Slavemaster of that day, (Exodus 5:2) simply by stating God's plan to give to poor slaves (so-called Negroes) a land of our own wherein we won't have to beg any Slavemaster any more for civil rights, for we shall then have in our own land a righteous government wherein freedom, justice, equality and all the other essentials of life will be natural products flowing to us and for us . . . like milk and honey.

We thank Allah for directing us to this verse in the Holy Quran:

"He it is who raised up from among the illiterates a messenger from among themselves, who writes to them His messages and purifies them, and teaching them the book and the wisdom . . . although they were before in manifest error (62:2).

Also:

"Those who follow the messenger-prophet, the illiterate one, whom they find in the Torah and the Gospel. He enjoins them good, forbids them evil, and makes lawful to them good things and prohibits for them impure things, and removes for them their burden and the shackles which were on them. So those who believe in Him, and help Him . . . these are the successful (7:157)."

I, Myself, being one who was lost and dead, buried here in the rubbish of the West in the thickest darkness of sin and ignorance, am able to stand upright today, on the square with my God and my own kind, able for the first time in 400 years to see and hear. I bear witness that Almighty God Allah is the finder of the lost sheep and life-giver to the dead. He has come in the flesh. He is the only Saviour for the so-called Negroes . . . and I bear witness that Messenger Muhammad has been taught (raised) by this Great God Allah, and in turn today Messenger Muhammad is teaching us (raising us from the dead level of ignorance).

In closing, if you want further knowledge and understanding of his message, visit and hear him every Sunday at 2 P.M., 5335 South Greenwood Ave. (at 54th St.) Chicago, Ill. Or write to him. If you live in New York City vicinity, come to Muhammad's Temple of Islam on Sundays at 2 P.M. We are located at 102 W. 116th St., corner of Lenox, 3rd floor, or visit one of our many other temples in the major cities throughout the land, both in the North and South.

Also, Messenger Muhammad has a weekly column in this paper, The Pittsburgh Courier, each week. Read "Mr. Muhammad Speaks." You who are far from his temples, if you are seeking knowledge, if you crave further light on what you already have "Mr. Muhammad Speaks" will provide you with a wealth of academic as well as religious education.

As-Salaam-Alaikum:
(Peace be unto you).

PAULETTE WILLIAMS GRANT
from *Oral History Interview on Life in Houston in the 1950s and 1960s*

DG: Today is June 30, and we are in the home of Paulette Grant who is being interviewed for the Houston Oral History Project. My name is David Goldstein. How are you today?

PWG: I am fine.

DG: Great. Ms. Grant, let's begin at the beginning. Why don't you tell me about where you were born and your earliest memories?

PWG: O.K. My name is Paulette Williams Grant. I grew up in what is now considered old Freedman's town, Fourth Ward, and I attended Gregory Elementary School from kindergarten to 6th grade. I have often wondered when I pass the school if they were going to do anything with it, if they were going to tear it down like they did so many of the old structures that I was used to seeing there. But Old Freedman's town was such a wonderful place to grow up in because we were so sheltered, we had everything right there although we were right at the end of downtown. We had everything right in the neighborhood, you know, there were stores, your beautician, your school, your music teacher—everybody was right there and it was like just a big, happy family. And I really miss those days now because we are out in the world and people just do not care like that anymore. I loved Gregory. Gregory is the reason I succeeded in life because they gave me the basic foundation from the very beginning. I retired from engineering at Texaco after 33 years, and considering what we had to work with, we had wonderful teachers because the books we had at that time . . . as you know, schools were segregated because this was the early 1950s. The books that we had were the books that the white schools were throwing away, so we never had new books, but surprisingly enough, many of us succeeded and went on to have wonderful careers and wonderful lives. And I attribute that to the teachers. It had to be the teachers.

DG: Where were you born? Where was that first house?

PWG: I was born in Houston, Texas. I was born at the old . . . at that time, it was the Negro Hospital. It is now Riverside. I lived at 1312 Shaw Street and if anyone is familiar with the downtown area, they know that part of the Enron Building parking lot is sitting where my house used to sit. I am a member of the Antioch Missionary Baptist Church. I have been there all of my life. And the church is still the only structure that is still there right now. It is surrounded by tall buildings and it is the only structure still there. This was a beautiful neighborhood. It had the old houses similar to the ones in the Heights with the porches. The porches went all the way around. Little kids . . . you could go under the house because you could actually bend over and just go up under there, but I think that they learned from tearing down those beautiful old homes that we had to preserve the Heights, because the homes were very similar to the ones in the Heights. They were beautiful old homes. My house had like 12 or so steps up to the front porch, a porch all the way across the front. It was just a beautiful neighborhood. Very, very pretty.

DG: What did you do for fun?

PWG: Well, you played with all the kids in the neighborhood. I am an only child but the neighborhood was full of children, and you were safe then. You could go outside and play without having to worry about anybody driving by grabbing you, taking you someplace. So, you were safe. You had all these kids to play with. The neighborhood was full of children, just full of children, and most of the children in the neighborhood went on to be very, very successful people. And they went to the same church. You went to the same school. You went to the same functions, you know, and the teachers at Gregory and even when I went on to graduate from Jack Yates, the teachers, many of them lived in that area, so they also went to the same church. There was nothing you could do because they would tell your parents, you know? I mean, Sunday morning, you would see them, 5 days a week you would see them. The only day you probably did not see them was on a Saturday, and maybe that was what we called our free day!

DG: So, you played with other kids? Did you have favorite stores, favorite theaters? What are your other memories of that time?

PWG: Well, there was a theater on West Dallas called the Rainbow—it was the Rainbow Theater—and we would go there a lot. There was also one downtown. I cannot remember exactly since they have built up downtown so much but there was one also called the Lincoln Theater. As you know, there were very few that we could go to. We could not go to the various theaters around town because they were segregated. I mean, we could not even go to the same restrooms. Usually, the restrooms that we had to go to were way in the back, down some stairs, you had to walk God knows how long before you even got to it, you know, so we did not have a lot of places that we could actually go but we did have our places that we had fun.

DG: Were you aware when you were young and if not . . . I mean, when did you first become aware that there were 2 systems in place and that the other system was maybe a little bit better equipped, a little bit nicer, or was it something you just grew up not even knowing about?

PWG: Well, as I said before, we were very sheltered. Everyone sheltered you. You went to church, you were sheltered. You went to school, you were sheltered. And we were big kids before we actually realized, well, you know, there is a difference. When you grow up with something just being there, you are used to it so you are not really thinking about difference. This was just the way it was, and we just adhered to what was going on. And I don't ever remember not liking it, liking it, disliking it. I never really thought about it at all. We were having a very good time, like I said. We were very sheltered, you know, you didn't know . . . it is like some people say sometimes, "Well, I did not know I was poor until I grew up." You know, you do not realize how much your parents and your teachers actually do to make you comfortable where you do not have this type of isolation feeling. We took part in many, many things. We traveled, we were able to go places and see things. We went to other cities, you know, met other people, so although it was on a segregated basis during that particular time, we still managed to do a lot of things

—very interesting things. It made me very curious. I love to travel. I travel all the time now. But this was instilled in me by these people. My mother always felt like, "Well, if you cannot do one thing, learn to do something else. Don't always have just one thing to fall back on. Always learn." And so, she pushed me. My father pushed me. "Learn this. Nothing you learn is ever wasted."

DG: Let's talk about the Gregory School. That first day when you go over there, I mean everybody remembers that first day of school or their parents do, at least. Can you name some names and tell me about the school, the principal, your teachers and what that school was like?

PWG: I think, if I am not mistaken, I cannot really remember because, like I said, this was kindergarten and I cannot really remember the teacher. Actually, I wrote it down in later years because it has been so long ago. I will be 64 years old in September. So, this has been a long time. But several years ago, I wrote down when I could still remember who the teachers were. I actually wrote it down so that I know who the kindergarten teacher . . . I think, if I am not mistaken, the kindergarten teacher was a Ms. Matthews and some of my friends that were with me during that time, there was Fannie Scott, there was Charles Earl, and Robert Harris. There were just a lot of people that I am still in touch with now. We are still friends. We still socialize together, you know, even after all these years. Like I said, it was just kind of a community. It was almost like a little city within a city. So, we still cling together after all these years. And we have lost friends who died over the years and that is like losing a family member because you were so close growing up.

DG: So, there was no way to compare but what did you learn? What was it like back in those years in elementary school at the Gregory School?

PWG: I would say that it was like school now. I do not think there was a big difference as far as how we were taught.

DG: Heavy discipline?

PWG: Oh, heavy discipline but not abusive discipline. You know, you were not hit, struck, beaten, nothing like that. At that particular time, kids were more afraid of being shamed in front of their friends than the actual hitting, so you could tell me to go . . . if I had done something wrong, you could tell me to go and stand in a corner. My friends are back here in the class looking at me. Oh, this is killing me! You did not need to be abusive to be effective. We had a lot of respect for the teachers. I mean, there was just no way you were going to actually say anything to them wrong, talk back to them, be ugly to them. There was just no way. Oh, you were angry, you did not like it, you know. I mean, what kid does like to be told something that you had done wrong? But, you know, the discipline was just there and it was a different discipline. It was not a child abuse but it made us the people we are now, and every one of us . . . I can think of one or two that maybe kind of fell by the wayside but it was not fell by the wayside in the way you think, you know, where you are in jail or you murdered someone. It is just that they did not go on as far, but they all did very, very well.

DG: When you were a little girl, what did you want to be when you grew up?

PWG: I always have, believe it or not, although I went to work in engineering at Texaco, I always wanted to be a musician. I wanted to be a musician. I am from a family who is very, very, very musically inclined. My grandmother was an organist and I have cousins who are organists at various churches. Even now . . . I had one that started out at Lakewood many, many years ago, and then, in the neighborhood, we had many people in Freedman's Town who were musicians, and one of the promoters, big promoters at the time lived there. So, you got a chance to see a lot of the people and I have always loved music, so I basically wanted to be a musician, but my parents always thought that musicians were kind of not the nice people that they wanted their little girl to be like. And I am kind of happy that it did go the way it went.

DG: Who was the promoter that lived in the neighborhood? Do you remember the name?

PWG: Don Robey. He owned Duke Peacock Records.

DG: So, other than sort of the reading, writing and arithmetic, were there extracurricular activities at Gregory School? Were there electives?

PWG: I would not call them electives but I do remember one thing that we did every year and several times a year. They would take us to the symphony. And I never will forget, to this day, I still remember Leopold Stokowski. They would take us to the symphony every year. And then, we had our parties and May Day programs where, you know, you had the little kids that had their little costumes and they danced. I think they still do the May Day programs, you know, but yes, we had a lot of different functions. But most of the functions were within the community—you've got to realize. They could not take us to the museum or to the . . . maybe they had a special day they could take us, you know, but we could not just go; like I want to take my grandbaby now—I can just go and take her. We had to have special days. And my two grandbabies, Leslie __________, she is 10 right now, and Ms. Adia Marie Grant, she is 7. And the whole world is different for them and I am so happy that it is. I try and expose them to different things. I take them everywhere. I buy things for them to make those minds better, improve those minds. My oldest grandbaby, Leslie, she is at Hipp Preparatory, College Preparatory School and they are very, very strict. But she is doing very well. The younger baby, she attends a school in Sugar Land and she is doing very well. Education has always been very important in my family —very, very important.

DG: When you moved on from the Gregory School, where did you go to school? You said Jack Yates?

PWG: I went to Jack Yates.

DG: What was that like?

PWG: Well, again, the books that we had were the books that the white schools were throwing away, but, again, you have all these people succeed. It kind of puzzles me now . . . when kids have so much, that they seem to fall by the wayside. When we had books, you would start getting your homework, you would turn the page and the page might be torn out, or was scratched over so badly that you could not tell what the lesson was supposed to be. But those teachers made sure that we knew exactly what we were supposed to do. Exactly what we were supposed to do.

DG: Did you expand your horizons? Did you get involved in music when you got to Yates?

PWG: Oh, I have always been . . . I did not go professional or anything like that but I have always sung in choirs and groups and I am in the choir now at my church, you know, so I have always loved music. I have got a very, very vast music collection. I love music. The only type of music, I cannot say I do not like it but I have to kind of be selective with it is jazz. I have not quite figured out jazz, and the jazz I have not figured out is the kind that it just sounds like someone is playing a bunch of chords. There is no melody to it. I do not know what they call that but there is no melody to it. It just sounds like a bunch of people just playing chords and just making up sounds. I like melody. I love country and western, believe it or not. I love gospel, R&B, smooth easy listening. I love music. I have a hobby room in my house and my daughter says all the time, she says, "Oh, you can come out of there with such beautiful things but I put my music on and there is no telling what might come out of that room." I love music. I have always loved it. It is so soothing to my ears.

DG: What year did you graduate from Jack Yates?

PWG: I finished in January of 1963. The reason it was a January class was because at the time, we could start school in September or January and they were considered low and high, like if you went to the first grade from September to January, you were in the low first. Then January to June, you were in the high first. With me, with my birthday being in September, I was just a few days short of being able to start in September, so I had to wait until January. So that is why I finished in January.

DG: O.K., and then what?

PWG: Well, then I went on to college. I went to HCC, I went to University of Houston. I got married. I had two children. My daughter is a field representative with Schweppes Dairy. My son is a pilot. Her name is Kim. My son's name is Leslie. She named her daughter after her brother and her father and her grandfather—all of them were Leslies. I went to work for the City of Houston for about 2 years. It was O.K. but I just do not have the heart for some of the things that I saw. So, I went to work for Texaco in 1969 and I stayed there 33 years. I retired in March of 2002. And I say all the time, "If God made anything better, he kept it." I drive along the freeway every day and say, "Lord, if this is a dream, please, please don't wake me up!" I am having a ball. I am truly enjoying this. I have to give all praises to God because, let me tell you, he just did not have to be this good. Considering where it started, all the things that have gone on and the obstacles that were put in our way, it did not have to be this good, it really did not. I am able to sit here now and do just about anything I want to do. I am not Donald Trump, I am not rich, but I am comfortable and I can do what I want to do. And that truly is a blessing. I think this is what so many of those teachers at Gregory and your parents and the men and women in your neighborhood, I think this is what they were pushing us for. And in the wake of our maybe first black president, I think this is just wonderful. I am standing on the shoulders of many, many great people. I want my children to stand on mine. Mine standing on shoulders, they are standing on shoulders, and all of those shoulders are doing this—pushing, pushing, pushing. Pushing you up. They were taking all type of abuse, misuse, but it was for a reason, and I am sitting here today. That is their reason.

DG: I want to talk about the change. You graduated from high school in 1963. The 1960s—1962, 1963, 1964—I mean, big, tumultuous years in this country's history but you are a high school graduate so you would be forgiven if you were not necessarily aware of all that . . . you know, we graduate from high school, we are worried about what college but what were you aware of and how did things change? Can you just kind of give us the overview of when you sort of became aware of the need for change, how things changed, what your involvement might have been?

PWG: Well, I would say that we realized there was a big difference when we were in high school because I lived in Freedman's Town which is Fourth Ward and I told you on Shaw Street. I passed 2 high schools to get to Jack Yates. Booker T. Washington, at one time, was on old West Dallas but they tore that down and built the Double Tree Hotel, I think, and other things around there. They moved Booker T. Washington to Yale Street, all right? So, that meant there was no high school for us to go to. I rode 3 busses to get to Jack Yates. I rode the Taft bus, I would walk up to West Dallas, I would catch the Taft bus. That would take us to downtown. Going downtown, you walked over 1 block, you went to Main Street, and you could catch just about any bus going down Main Street because they were all going past where we had to get off, which was on Elgin. We would get off on Elgin. Then, we would catch another bus and that bus would take us on to Third Ward within a block of Jack Yates. So, every day, going and coming, I rode 3 busses to school. But it was fun because all your friends are here. You know, you are all doing the same thing so you do not have this isolation or anything. But I think that is when we really became aware that there was a difference because when we would get on the bus on Elgin, there were white children coming from like the Waugh Drive area back there. Well, they had all the front of the bus. We had to sit in the back of the bus and I think Houston Community College now, the central campus, I think that used to be San Jacinto High School. So, when we would get on, the bus would go maybe 2 or 3 blocks and then they would all get off at that high school and then we had the bus to ourselves. But I think that is when it really became evident to us that there was a difference because we could not go to that high school. We had to pass that high school, and there was another one—I cannot really remember now—but we passed high schools to get to Jack Yates, you see. And we should not have had to do that. But we could not go. But, in spite of, we still did what we had to do. We still did it.

A DEMOGRAPHER'S FORECASTS

THE CHICAGO DEFENDER
Predicts End To Housing Bias, Migrations

September 13, 1958

PREDICTS END TO HOUSING BIAS, MIGRATIONS

Taeuber Tells UL Of Changes

OMAHA, Neb.—A population research expert predicts the imminent end of residential segregation of Negroes in large American cities, and at the same time the end of migration of southern Negroes from farm areas to North and South industrial centers.

Dr. Irene B. Taeuber of Princeton University, in a paper read at the 1958 annual conference of the National Urban League here reports:

"The Negro frontier in the movement toward comparability with the general population once was the exodus from the farms and the South.

"Today it is the movement from concentrated settlements into the diversified areas appropriate to the education, incomes, and social status that individuals have achieved."

Dr. Taeuber, author of recent books on the populations of the United States and the Far East, was co-editor of Population Index for 20 years and is a past president of Population Association of America.

Since 1936, she has been research associate, Office of Population Research, Princeton university. A native Missourian, she holds her doctorate from the University of Minnesota.

EDUCATION

The key to future Negro advances, according to Dr. Taeuber, is the improved educational opportunity available in the large cities. Educated urban Negroes, "freed from the drag of continuing increases of the unskilled and uneducated from the rural South," will begin to find acceptance into the general population according to their abilities Dr. Taeuber predicts.

The migration from the farms is stopping, she reports, simply because the numbers of farmer Negroes in the South have dwindled to a hard core that is not likely to migrate.

U. S. Census Bureau figures show that the percentage of non-white workers in agriculture dropped from 21 to 12 per cent from 1948 to 1958. The percentage of non-whites living in rural farm areas in 1956 was only 14 per cent.

Dr. Taeuber compares the process with the migration of foreign-born to the United States in earlier periods.

She predicts that the better-educated "second generation" of urban and northern Negroes will merge more easily into the general population, despite the color barrier, which "makes assimilation for Americans who speak English more difficult than it once was for those whose languages, religions, and cultures were alien, but whose skin was technically white."

ACCEPTANCE

The end of residential segregation is inevitable, Dr. Taeuber reports, because of the increasing acceptance of educated Negroes, and also because of the great increase in fertility among urban Negroes.

"Indefinite continuation of the birth and death rates of 1955," says the report, "would result in a doubling of the non-white population each generation.

"Continually declining white populations and rapidly increasing Negro populations would lead eventually to the transfer of political power in the central cities and so terminate the segregation."

The report makes a number of important points about the movement and characteristics of the Negro population.

1—The Negro migration has not been from South to North but from the fields of the South to the slums of the largest cities in North, South, East, and West.

2—While it has moved from the fields to the cities, the Negro population in the South has remained fairly constant. But the great increases in national Negro population (from 11.0 million in 1930 to 18 million in 1957) have been absorbed by the North and West.

3—The social and economic retardation of the southern Negro was rapidly transferred to those areas into which Negroes were moving.

4—Future redistribution of Negro population must involve primarily those who were born and educated in urban communities rather than the retarded rural South—"an essential change almost revolutionary in its implications for the development of the Negro population and metropolitan America."

Dr. Taeuber points out various areas where Negroes have assimilated well with the general population in the century since the end of slavery:

LITERACY: The percentage of Negro literates rose from practically nothing in 1860 to 90 per cent in 1950.

EDUCATION: By 1950, the school attendance of Negroes approached that of whites at the elementary level, but was considerably lower at the high school and college levels. Grade retardation was more prevalent and more severe among Negroes.

Dr. Taeuber notes that while Negroes in any area tend to have lower educational status than whites in the same area, Negro migrations have been to areas where Negroes and whites alike were on higher levels of achievement. As greater proportions of Negro children grow up in areas of better schooling opportunities, their educational status has progressed rapidly.

ECONOMICS: Because of their low educational level, "Negroes are ill prepared to work in an industrial economy at other than the bottom levels or to provide other than substandard living for their children without major community assistance."

Even with better educations, Negroes have been held back by racial barriers both in the types of job held and their income, the report continues.

LIFE EXPECTANCY: The life expectancy of the Negro has risen from 33 years in 1900 to 63 years in 1956, cutting in half the difference from the life expectancy of the white, which has risen from 47 to 70 years.

While noting that in many areas the disadvantages of the Negro have lessened and his similarities to the whites have increased, Dr. Taeuber shows that in some cases Negroes have carried their rural southern mores to the large cities and resisted change.

Friction with the standards of the general population has resulted from blurred Negro adjustment in the relations of the sexes, the family, and reproduction, the report says.

Dr. Taeuber cites population reports to show that Negro parents have not tended to conform to the urban ideal of small families. Hence, there is the problem of disproportionate numbers of children coming from groups least able to give them adequate background of opportunity.

Negro families have also continued to be less stable, with four times as many "husbands absent" from families for various reasons than among whites.

This disorganized family structure may have been workable in the simple southern rural situation, Dr. Taeuber says, but in complex cities it contributes heavily to problem children and disorganized youth of crowded slums.

The report says Negroes may adapt to the mores of the general society more easily when they are accepted into the middle class.

The fact that residential segregation prevents normal mobility of the Negro population outward geographically and upward economically and socially is also seen as a contributing factor to the problem of the urban Negro and a barrier to his assimilation.

If segregation continues to decline, the report says, the job of Negro assimilation will be easier and more similar to that of earlier immigrant groups.

"A DESTINED DATE WITH FREEDOM"

ELLA BAKER

Bigger Than A Hamburger

Southern Patriot, May 1960

BIGGER THAN A HAMBURGER

(*Miss Baker is executive director of the Southern Christian Leadership Conference, which issued the call for the Student Leadership Conference on Non-violent Resistance to Segregation. This was held at Shaw University, Raleigh, N. C., on Easter weekend with 142 students from the South and 30 from the North in attendance. A sizeable delegation of white students joined the young Negro leaders for the conference. Observations by another participant follow Miss Baker's article.*)

RALEIGH, N. C.—The Student Leadership Conference made it crystal clear that current sit-ins and other demonstrations are concerned with something much bigger than a hamburger or even a giant-sized coke.

Whatever may be the differences in approach to their goal, the Negro and white students, North and South, are seeking to rid America of the scourge of racial segregation and discrimination—not only at lunch counters, but in every aspect of life.

In reports, casual conversations, discussion groups, and speeches, the sense and the spirit of the following statement that appeared in the initial newsletter of the students at Barber-Scotia College, Concord, N. C., were re-echoed time and again:

> "We want the world to know that we no longer accept the inferior position of second-class citizenship. We are willing to go to jail, be ridiculed, spat upon and even suffer physical violence to obtain First Class Citizenship."

By and large, this feeling that they have a destined date with freedom, was not limited to a drive for personal freedom, or even freedom for the Negro in the South. Repeatedly it was emphasized that the movement was concerned with the moral implications of racial discrimination for the "whole world" and the "Human Race."

This universality of approach was linked with a perceptive recognition that "it is important to keep the movement democratic and to avoid struggles for personal leadership."

> It was further evident that desire for supportive cooperation from adult leaders and the adult community was also tempered by apprehension that adults might try to "capture" the student movement. The students showed willingness to be met on the basis of equality, but were intolerant of anything that smacked of manipulation or domination.

This inclination toward *group-centered leadership*, rather than toward a *leader-centered group pattern of organization* was refreshing indeed to those of the older group who bear the scars of the battle, the frustrations and the disillusionment that come when the prophetic leader turns out to have heavy feet of clay.

However hopeful might be the signs in the direction of group-centeredness, the fact that many schools and communities, especially in the South, have not provided adequate experience for young Negroes to assume initiative and think and act independently accentuated the need for guarding the student movement against well-meaning, but nevertheless unhealthy, over-protectiveness.

Here is an opportunity for adult and youth to work together and provide genuine leadership—the development of the individual to his highest potential for the benefit of the group.

> Many adults and youth characterized the Raleigh meeting as the greatest or most significant conference of our period.

Whether it lives up to this high evaluation or not will, in a large measure, be determined by the extent to which there is more effective training in and understanding of non-violent principles and practices, in group dynamics, and in the redirection into creative channels of the normal frustrations and hostilities that result from second-class citizenship.

A CALL FOR ARMED SELF-DEFENSE

ROBERT F. WILLIAMS
from *Negroes with Guns*

1962

WHY do I speak to you from exile?

Because a Negro community in the South took up guns in self-defense against racist violence—and used them. I am held responsible for this action, that for the first time in history American Negroes have armed themselves as a group, to defend their homes, their wives, their children, in a situation where law and order had broken down, where the authorities could not, or rather would not, enforce their duty to protect Americans from a lawless mob. I accept this responsibility and am proud of it. I have asserted the right of Negroes to meet the violence of the Ku Klux Klan by armed self-defense—and have acted on it. It has always been an accepted right of Americans, as the history of our Western states proves, that where the law is unable, or unwilling, to enforce order, the citizens can, and must, act in self-defense against lawless violence. I believe this right holds for black Americans as well as whites.

Many people will remember that in the summer of 1957 the Ku Klux Klan made an armed raid on an Indian community in the South and were met with determined rifle fire from the Indians acting in self-defense. The nation approved of the action and there were widespread expressions of pleasure at the defeat of the Kluxers, who showed their courage by running away despite their armed superiority. What the nation doesn't know, because it has never been told, is that the Negro community in Monroe, North Carolina, had set the example two weeks before when we shot up an armed motorcade of the Ku Klux Klan, *including two police cars*, which had come to attack the home of Dr. Albert E. Perry, vice-president of the Monroe chapter of the National Association for the Advancement of Colored People. The stand taken by our chapter resulted in the official re-affirmation by the NAACP of the right of self-defense. The Preamble to the resolution of the 50th

Convention of the NAACP, New York City, July 1959, states: ". . . we do not deny, but reaffirm, the right of an individual and collective self-defense against unlawful assaults."

Because there has been much distortion of my position, I wish to make it clear that I do not advocate violence for its own sake, or for the sake of reprisals against whites. Nor am I against the passive resistance advocated by the Reverend Martin Luther King and others. My only difference with Dr. King is that I believe in flexibility in the freedom struggle. This means that I believe in non-violent tactics where feasible and the mere fact that I have a Sit-In case pending before the U.S. Supreme Court bears this out. Massive civil disobedience is a powerful weapon under civilized conditions, where the law safeguards the citizens' right of peaceful demonstrations. In civilized society the law serves as a deterrent against lawless forces that would destroy the democratic process. But where there is a breakdown of the law, the individual citizen has a right to protect his person, his family, his home and his property. To me this is so simple and proper that it is self-evident.

When an oppressed people show a willingness to defend themselves, the enemy, who is a moral weakling and coward is more willing to grant concessions and work for a respectable compromise. Psychologically, moreover, racists consider themselves superior beings and they are not willing to exchange their superior lives for our inferior ones. They are most vicious and violent when they can practice violence with impunity. This we have shown in Monroe. Moreover, when because of our self-defense there is a danger that the blood of whites may be spilled, the local authorities in the South suddenly enforce law and order when previously they had been complaisant toward lawless, racist violence. This too we have proven in Monroe. It is remarkable how easily and quickly state and local police control and disperse lawless mobs when the Negro is ready to defend himself with arms.

Furthermore, because of the international situation, the Federal Government does not want racial incidents which draw the attention of the world to the situation in the South. Negro self-defense draws such attention, and the Federal Government will be more willing to enforce law and order if the local authorities don't. When our people become fighters, our leaders will be able to sit at the conference table as equals, not dependent on the whim and the generosity of the oppressors. It will be to the best interests of both sides to negotiate just, honorable and lasting settlements.

The majority of white people in the United States have literally no idea of the violence with which Negroes in the South are treated daily—nay, hourly. This violence is deliberate, conscious, condoned by the authorities. It has gone on for centuries and is going on today, every day, unceasing and unremitting. It is our way of life. Negro existence in the South has been one long travail, steeped in terror and blood—our blood. The incidents which took place in Monroe, which I witnessed and which I suffered, will give some idea of the conditions in the South, such conditions that can no longer be borne. That is why, one hundred years after the Civil War began, we Negroes in Monroe armed ourselves in self-defense and used our weapons. We showed that our policy worked. The lawful authorities of Monroe and North Carolina acted to enforce order *only after, and as a direct result of, our being armed*. Previously they had connived with the Ku Klux Klan in the racist violence against our people. Self-defense prevented bloodshed and forced the law to establish order. This is the meaning of Monroe and I believe it marks a historic change in the life of my people. This is the story of that change.

DISENFRANCHISEMENT PAST AND PRESENT

CONGRESS OF RACIAL EQUALITY

Negro Voting in Louisiana

c. 1962–63

NEGRO VOTING IN LOUISIANA

Prepared by: Baton Rouge
Committee
On
Registration
Education

1st Edition

"... however painful it may be for us to change, not to change will be fatal." James Baldwin

THIS PAMPHLET has been written to present an historical sketch of the Negro's strive to exercise his God-given and constitutional right to vote in our democratic society. The struggle of the Negro in the Southland to secure this right has been one of humiliation and suffering. Police brutality, political and economic intimidations, and other legal and social impediments have been consistently directed against the Negro in an attempt to maintain the status quo and to prevent him from achieving political and social equality.

To eliminate these unjust acts and to secure our just rights, we need more federal legislation and aggressive action in the area of civil rights and liberties, and in voting in particular. But most of all, we need to end fear and apathy among our people and to give them a fighting desire to "register and vote."

It is the sincere hope of those who prepared this pamphlet that, as you read these few pages, you will arrive at a deeper understanding of the necessity of *every* eligible Negro registering and voting. The struggle has not been easy in the past, nor will it be easy in the future. However, struggle we must, each of us, as individuals; for, it is in the individual that the strength and hope of the future lie.

THE HISTORY OF NEGRO SUFFRAGE IN LOUISIANA

THE VOTE IN RECONSTRUCTION

Negro participation in politics began with Reconstruction in 1867. Prior to that time, Negro people in Louisiana had no voice in the policies of their state or of the United States of America. At the beginning of Reconstruction, the registration books were opened to Negroes. Under Federal law, every potential male voter, excluding those disfranchised for their attempts to overthrow the Federal Government during the Civil War, was to be registered. Federal troops were dispersed throughout the South to enforce the law and to guarantee Negroes their right to vote. In Louisiana in 1860, the Negro population was 350,000; and the white, 357,000. In 1867, Negroes began to register, and by the end of the year there were 82,000 Negroes and 44,000 whites registered. At the Constitutional Convention, there were 49 Negroes and 49 whites present. Thus, Negroes held the balance of power.

During the summer and fall of 1867, the Negro masses were stirred into an unparalleled ferment of political activity. At open-air meetings, Negro leaders began to voice their opinions to the masses, demanding civil equality for all. They began to campaign for political offices with a zeal and determination that stunned the white population. The Minority of the South, for the first time, was experiencing the power of the ballot, and with it was making enormous strides toward freedom and equality. Within a few years, Negroes were elected to high offices—governors, sheriffs, mayors, and congressmen—throughout the South. They did not seek to dominate, but to use the power which was rightfully theirs.

These politically starved were pervaded by a spirit of great hope in the future—particularly in education.

Opposition to Negro political power sprang from every corner of the South. The baby had not begun to walk when men sat down to plan his funeral. The Klan, under the leadership of Nathan Bedford Forrest (leader of the Fort Pillow Massacre in which thousands of Negroes were slaughtered), became the epitomy of anti-Negro sentiment. By economic intimidation and political assassination, by whippings and maimings, by the knife, whip, and rope, the Klan, and similar organizations, set out to reduce Negroes to political impotence. All manner of intimidations were raised against the Negro population; but Negro power was deeply entrenched, and nothing short of full-scale revolution could dislodge it. Aware of this, the underground terrorist organizations opened war on the Negro voters. They left the politicians alone, for they knew that the power of the Negro politicians was in the hands of the Negro voters. Negro homes were raided; the occupants were beaten and sometimes killed; roads leading to the polls were blocked by armed mobs; whites came from across the state line to "stack the ballots." With the attack on the individual, the end of Negro voting strength was in sight.

THE FALL OF THE NEGRO VOTE

As Reconstruction came to a close in 1877, there were more registered Negro voters than white. Then came the turning point. The elections of 1878 and 1884 were marked by rioting and violence on the part of whites attempting to overthrow administrations in which Negroes were prominent. By means of threats, physical violence, and roll purges, the feat was soon accomplished. In 1888, there were 127,923 Negroes and 126,884 whites registered. However, by 1898, registered voters had dropped to 74,133 whites and only 12,902 Negroes.

This tremendous drop in white, as well as Negro, registration was a direct result of the 1898 Constitutional Convention. During this Convention, a campaign was initiated to exclude Negroes from the polls. The delegates interpreted their mandate to be: Disenfranchise as many Negroes and as few whites as possible—without violating the Fifteenth Amendment to the Federal Constitution; and do this in such a way that future elections are perfectly "free and fair." To do this, the Convention adopted the now-famous "Section 5" or "Grandfather Clause" of the Louisiana Constitution. By virtue of its provisions, as explained by one delegate, "No man who was a voter on January 1, 1867, or prior thereto, nor his son, nor his grandson, nor any foreigner naturalized prior to January 1, 1898, provided he has resided in Louisiana five years next preceding his application to register, can be denied the right to vote by reason of his failure to possess the educational or property qualifications prescribed by the Constitution." In other words, anyone who was registered before 1867—or whose father or grandfather was so registered—or who was naturalized before 1898, did not have to meet the literacy or property requirements for voting. This, for all practical purposes, limited suffrage in Louisiana to white males; for prior to 1867, Negroes had not been able to register.

Under the new qualifications for voters, Negroes soon constituted only 4.1% of those registered to vote. From 1910 through 1944, the number of registered Negroes never exceeded 1% of the total potential electorate. Toward the close of World War II, Negro registration again began to increase. By 1948, the number of registered Negroes had risen from 1,672 to 28,177. Six years later, the proportion of the voting age Negro population which was registered had risen from 5% to 27%. This increase brought about new and stronger efforts, on the part of the white citizens, to curtail Negro suffrage.

In July, 1954, the State Legislature established the Joint Legislative Committee "to provide ways and means whereby our existing social order shall be preserved and our institutions and ways of life . . . maintained" by a program "to maintain segregation of the races in all phases of our life in accordance with the customs, traditions, and laws of our State." The Committee was empowered to investigate all relevant matters. A series of conferences were held jointly with the State Board of Registration to discuss "uniform enforcement of Louisiana voter qualification laws" (i.e., reducing Negro registration).

Another form which these efforts took was the Citizens' Council movement, which began in Mississippi in 1954—shortly after the Supreme Court handed down its history-making decision on school desegregation in Brown vs. Board of Education. State and local associations quickly sprang up throughout the South. The Association of the Citizens' Council of Louisiana (ACCL) was chartered in early 1956 and worked very closely with the Joint Legislative Committee. The first purpose in its constitution is "to protect and preserve by all legal means our historical Southern Social Institutions in all their aspects . . ."

First, the Council decided upon a "thorough-going cleaning of our registration rolls," and definite steps were taken to remove registered Negroes from the roll books. In September, 1956, the Council purged the registration rolls in Bienville Parish. In the spring of 1959, the Council in Washington Parish undertook a similar inspection of the rolls to challenge "illegally registered" voters. Despite a suit brought by the registrar in the state courts to stop them, the Council succeeded in disenfranchising, as illegally registered, 85% of the Negro and .07% of the white voters in Washington Parish. Federal Courts subsequently ordered the re-registration of these voters.

During the regular session of the 1960 Louisiana Legislature, a series of laws, known as the "Segregation Law Package," were passed. The "package" included an amendment to the Louisiana Constitution which made substantial changes in the voter qualification laws. One of the changes is directed at the character of the prospective voter. Convictions for misdemeanors (other than traffic and game law violations), participation in common law marriage, and parentage of illegitimate children constitute "bad character" and are disqualifiers. Moreover, character disqualifiers "shall not be deemed exclusive . . . but said bad character may be established by any competent evidence."*

The "package" abolished the old provisions that illiterates could register by dictating the information for the LR-1 form. However, illiterates already registered are not, therefore, to be removed from the rolls. Before the passage of the bill, 25,498 white and 16,743 Negro illiterates were registered.

In addition, applicants must now demonstrate that they are "well disposed to the good order and happiness of the State of Louisiana by executing an affidavit affirming that (they) will faithfully and fully abide by all of the laws of the State

*Note: Also in the "package" were new breach of the peace laws, which make it impossible for some persons to legally (as defined by Louisiana) exercise their rights under the U.S. Constitution. For instance, they may be arrested for refusing to move from the premises when so ordered by the owner or manager because of race.

of Louisiana." This, of course, eliminates anyone who actively opposes segregation.

During the 1962 session of the State Legislature, additional laws were passed to prevent or severely limit further Negro registration. The State Board of Registration is to design a literacy test on American citizenship which applicants will now be required to pass. Though the information covered by the test in each parish must be the same, the organization of this information is left to the discretion of the individual registrar. Also, additions and revisions have further complicated the LR-1 registration form.

It is in such a climate of official State opposition that Negroes must attempt to register, and that registrars must perform their duties. Evidence received at the Civil Rights Commission's Louisiana hearing shows that the campaign to disenfranchise Negroes has met with some success in at least 11 parishes: Bossier, Caddo, Claiborne, East Carroll, Jackson, Madison, Ouachita, Plaquemines, Red River, St. Helena, and Webster. An attempted purge in Washington Parish has already been discussed. In Bienville Parish, a Justice Department suit to reinstate purged voters is still pending in the Federal Courts.

REQUIREMENTS FOR REGISTRATION

To register to vote in Louisiana, an applicant must be 21 years of age, a resident of the state for one year, a resident of his parish for six months, and a resident of his precinct for four months. He must, as discussed above, be of "good character," and he must "understand the duties and the obligations of citizenship under a republican form of government. A special form, the LR-1, must be used when registering. On this form, one must give his exact age (in years, months, and days), color, sex, address, occupation, and previous place of registration. A prospective voter must be able to read and interpret, to the satisfaction of the registrar, any clause of the U.S. Constitution or Louisiana Constitution. He must also be able to prove his identity. Under the Constitution, "If the registrar has good reason to believe that he is not the same person, he may require the applicant to produce two credible registered voters of his precinct to make oath to that effect."

TECHNIQUES OF DISCRIMINATION—CASE STUDIES

HIDE AND SEEK

When Negroes wanted to register in Plaquemines, they were unable to find the registrar. As one man put it, "It was something like a game of hide and seek." Only after Negroes filed suit in a Federal Court was a permanent office for registration established in Plaquemines Parish.

A witness before the Civil Rights Commission testified that in Madison Parish (where no Negroes were registered) he and several other Negroes went to the registrar's office in July, 1960. Instead of giving them application forms, the registrar told them to see the sheriff. He made two subsequent trips to the office, but on both occasions found it closed.

THE SILENT TREATMENT

In some parishes, applicants are not even told whether or not they have qualified to register. Negroes Hester and Eugene Williams live on farms 35 miles from the seat of Bossier Parish. Each time they tried to register, they completed an LR-1 form, which was accepted, without comment, by the registrar. Hester made five trips; Eugene, seven. They were never told whether or not they had qualified to register as voters.

IDENTIFICATION

Reverend Philip Brown, formerly registered in New Orleans, was unable to register in Ouachita Parish because he could not identify himself to the satisfaction of the registrar. When, in July of 1960, he presented his driver's license and other papers for identification, he was told that they would not do and that he would have to have two registered voters from his ward and precinct identify him. A voter can only "vouch" once every twelve months, and Reverend Brown was unable to find two eligible vouchers. He found one who had not vouched for 11 months, but he was not acceptable. The registrar told Reverend Brown, "Well, if you will bring in three documents or bills or receipts of letters showing your name and address at this address, then you will be able to register." When he returned and presented three documents to Deputy Registrar Morin, she refused to accept them because she was not the same person who had waited on him before. Again, Reverend Brown was told that he would have to have two registered voters to identify him.

Identification difficulties are frequent in other parishes. In East Carroll, a well-known life-long resident was told that he would have to secure two "vouchers" from his precinct. Since only whites were registered, this was impossible. A friend on the police jury told him that the "voucher" system was expressly designed to prevent Negroes from registering. Once, a white voter in the same parish did agree to "vouch" for a Negro, but later told the man, "I can't fool with that." The registrar of Madison Parish admitted in 1954 that she operated under orders from the sheriff and other public officials, and that she had not yet seen fit to permit Negroes to register and vote.

INTIMIDATION

In St. Helena Parish, Negroes were warned that attempts to vote on their part would result in bloodshed. A Negro testified before the Civil Rights Commission that while he was standing in line to vote in 1952, a white man showed a gun, saying, "Negroes are not going to vote in St. Helena Parish." An FBI investigation remedied the situation and Negroes were allowed to register.

In East Carroll Parish, Negroes were subjected to economic reprisals. Mr. Atlas, a Negro farmer, was not allowed to gin his cotton, market his soybeans, or purchase fuel oil for his home because he attempted to register. Only a federal suit against the firms involved enabled him to resume his farming.

INTERPRETATION

Applicants must be able to interpret any clause of the U.S. Constitution or of the Louisiana Constitution. Whether or not interpretations are correct is left to the discretion of the registrar.

Joe Kirk of Webster Parish had been registered from 1944 to 1957, when he was disenfranchised. Three times after that, he attempted to register but was unable to because of the interpretation requirements. On his fourth try, he was asked whether he had any illegitimate children. When he said no, Registrar Clement said, "You are a damned liar"—and flunked him again.

In Plaquemines Parish, a written interpretation, in accordance with an official set of answers drawn up by segregationist leader Leander Perez, must be submitted. Below is an example of one of Perez' interpretations:

> Art. 1, Sec. 11, La. Const.: No person shall be compelled to give evidence against himself in a criminal case.
>
> Interpretation: No one shall be required to give evidence against himself, nor shall he be required to testify in any case in which he is being prosecuted. The fact that he does not testify shall not be used against him.

In Claiborne and Webster Parishes, oral examinations on the Constitution are given before the applicant is permitted to complete his LR-1 form. This oral interpretation must be to the satisfaction of the registrar.

SLOWDOWNS

In Ouachita Parish, challenge notices were sent to over 5,000 Negro voters. To contest these challenges and to prevent removal of their names from the rolls, these people had to appear before the registrar within 10 days. They went to the courthouse in large numbers, but only a few succeeded in seeing the registrar within the legal time limit. Often, the clerks deliberately wasted time in order to limit the number of Negroes who could be seen. As one witness before the Civil Rights Commission testified, "(there was a line) completely down the corridor, completely down two flights of stairs, onto the lawn. . . . Sometimes people (clerks) would stop and drink a coke or go over to the window and look out, in order to—in my mind, in order to waste a lot of time."

In other parishes, Negroes, after traveling long distances to register, have had to wait in line for hours, while whites were waited on immediately. Frequently, only one Negro may fill out the form at a time.

Civil Rights Violation Complaint
(Note: Send one copy to the U.S. Commission on Civil Rights, 726 Jackson Place, Washington 25, D.C. and send one copy to Civil Rights Division, U.S. Justice Department, Washington 25, D.C.)

My name is ______________________________ and I live in
(Give full name)

____________________________________. I can be reached
(Give full address)

at this phone number: _____________________. I work as a

_____________________________________.
(Give occupation)

I wish to make a formal complaint of the following occurrence: (Give exact details of what happened, giving times, places, names, and all other circumstances, using the back of this sheet and other paper if necessary.)

Signed: ____________________________
(sign here)

(Note: If possible and safe, have complaint notarized. Send air mail as soon as possible after occurrence. If very urgent call the Civil Rights Division of the U.S. Justice Department at RE 7-8200 in Washington, D.C.)

Registration Data

Parish	Potential Registered Whites	Registered Whites	Potential Registered Negroes	Registered Negroes
Acadia	22,399	19,926	4,557	3,780
Allen	8,357	8,169	2,310	1,995
Ascension	10,110	8,401	4,171	2,350
Assumption	5,877	5,022	3,237	1,967
Avoyelles	15,845	13,630	4,717	1,837
Beauregard	8,682	7,969	2,145	1,131
Bienville	5,617	5,184	4,077	26
Bossier	23,696	12,813	6,847	542
Caddo	87,774	58,144	41,749	4,686
Calcasieu	62,987	43,553	14,924	7,364
Caldwell	3,843	4,019	1,161	92
Cameron	3,642	3,184	239	160
Catahoula	4,110	4,117	1,919	377
Claiborne	6,415	5,510	5,032	28
Concordia	5,963	5,323	4,582	383
DeSoto	6,543	5,828	6,753	595
E. Baton Rouge	87,985	66,173	36,908	10,576
East Carroll	2,990	2,845	4,183	0
East Feliciana	7,043	2,448	6,081	82
Evangeline	13,652	13,450	3,342	3,135
Franklin	8,954	8,260	4,433	390
Grant	6,080	6,066	1,553	674
Iberia	20,200	16,662	7,060	2,486
Iberville	8,733	7,236	2,535	484
Jackson	6,607	5,817	14,970	8,563
Jefferson	98,103	77,859	2,881	1,655
Jefferson Davis	12,892	9,599	9,473	5,505
Lafayette	35,513	27,244	3,078	2,039
Lafourche	25,737	22,197	849	220
La Salle	6,799	6,823	5,723	860
Lincoln	9,611	6,927	1,818	1,200
Livingston	12,306	11,814	5,181	0
Madison	3,334	2,714	7,208	301
Morehouse	10,311	7,490	7,444	1,779
Natchitoches	11,328	8,752	125,752	36,283
Orleans	257,495	176,742	16,377	730

Parish	Potential Registered Whites	Registered Whites	Potential Registered Negroes	Registered Negroes
Ouachita	40,185	24,856	2,897	47
Plaquemines	8,633	7,170	5,273	2,313
Pointe Coupee	6,085	5,354	18,141	3,036
Rapides	44,823	30,055	2,181	27
Red River	3,294	3,440	4,608	263
Richland	7,601	6,075	2,143	1,624
Sabine	8,251	8,471	1,105	779
St. Bernard	15,836	14,669	2,621	1,958
St. Charles	8,117	7,451	2,621	1,958
St. Helena	2,363	2,478	2,082	1,243
St. James	4,892	4,447	3,964	2,528
St. John the Baptist	4,982	4,143	4,279	2,967
St. Landry	25,580	21,918	14,982	11,178
St. Martin	9,781	8,449	4,664	2,848
St. Mary	17,991	14,027	7,176	4,077
St. Tammany	16,032	16,878	5,038	2,847
Tangipahoa	22,311	18,631	9,401	3,137
Tonsas	2,287	1,964	3,533	0
Terrebonne	24,393	17,328	5,464	1,796
Union	7,021	5,927	3,006	597
Vermilion	19,710	17,902	2,429	2,065
Vernon	9,279	9,704	1,268	773
Washington	16,804	15,423	6,821	1,729
Webster	15,713	12,217	7,045	130
W. Baton Rouge	3,974	3,323	3,502	1,194
West Carroll	6,171	5,185	1,389	70
W. Feliciana	2,814	1,305	4,553	0
Winn	6,790	6,418	2,590	1,096
State Total	1,289,216	993,118	514,589	159,033

Note: figures for 1960

SOURCES

Ebony Magazine, June, 1962
1961 United States Commission on Civil Rights Report
Margaret Price, *The Negro and the Ballot in the South*

AN ARRAY OF "CITIZENSHIP" QUESTIONS

Louisiana Voter Registration Procedures

c. 1963

REGISTRATION PROCEDURE

THESE ARE THE PRESENT RESIDENCE REQUIREMENTS FOR REGISTRATION IN LOUISIANA:

1 year in the State
6 months in the Parish
3 months in the Precinct
(4 months in the City, to vote in municipal elections)

THIS IS THE PRESENT REGISTRATION PROCEDURE IN LOUISIANA:

1. You are required to register without any help. The Registrar has instructions to exclude all but the applicants from the Registration Office.

2. You are required to identify yourself. Your identification should bear your present address. Acceptable identifications are drivers' licenses, current telephone or electricity and gas bills, school or employment I.D. cards, bank books, rent receipts, time-payment cards, etc.

3. When the Registrar gives you the affidavit form (Form No. 11), you are required to sign it where indicated.

4. On the same Form No. 11, you read a part of the *Preamble of the U. S. Constitution* and write a line from it, as directed by the Registrar.

5. Next, you choose 1 of 10 cards that will be turned face down by the Registrar. He will circle the number of your card on Form No. 11. Each card bears 6 questions, which

are numbered 1, 2, 3, 4, 5, 6. Under each number there are "a," "b," and "c" answers, one of which is the correct answer to the question.

6. You choose your answer, but are not allowed to write on the question card. You circle the letter of the answer you have chosen on Form No. 11. You are required to answer 4 of the 6 questions correctly, but may answer 5 or 6 questions if you prefer.

7. You will have completed Form No. 11 when you have filled in your parish, the date, your signature (according to the Registrar's instructions, if you are a married woman), your Ward and Precinct (which the Registrar will give you), and your address.

8. Now, the Registrar lets you choose 1 of 5 Application Forms. These 5 cards are not different in content; they are different only as to the order in which the information is requested.

9. At the bottom of this Application form and on the back of the card are the 6 character and moral questions. To answer these, you are required to strike out either the "have" or the "have not," either of which may come first on any question.

10. BE SURE TO FILL IN EVERY BLANK.

SAMPLE

AFFIDAVIT **Form No. 11**

Question
Form Selected
Circle one ____________, Louisiana Date ____________

1 6 I do solemnly swear that I will faithfully and fully abide by the laws of this State and that I am well disposed to the good order and
2 7 happiness thereof.

3 8 Sworn to and subscribed before me this

4 9 ____ day of ________, 196 ___ ______________________
Applicant's Signature

____

5 10 (Deputy Registrar)

"Applicant shall demonstrate his ability to read and write from dictation by the Registrar of Voters from the Preamble to the Constitution of the United States of America."

PREAMBLE

We, the people of the United States, in order to form a more perfect union, establish justice, insure domestic tranquility, provide for the common defense, promote the general welfare, and secure the blessings of liberty to ourselves and our posterity, do ordain and establish this Constitution for the United States of America. (Article VIII, 1 (c) (7) La. Constitution)

CITIZEN TEST FOR REGISTRATION

Circle letter indicating your answers to the four numbered questions you have chosen.

1 — a b c	3 — a b c	5 — a b c
2 — a b c	4 — a b c	6 — a b c

(La. Constitution, Article VIII, Sec. 1 (d) and LRS 18:31 (2)

(The above qualification test and a registration application form provided for by Act 63 of 1962, (Form LR-1), were received by me from the

__________________ Parish Registrar of Voters upon my request to register, and I have signed both for acknowledgment and identification with my application to register.)

Date: ________________ 196 ___ ______________________
Applicant for Registration

Ward ______ Precinct ____________ Address ________________

DO NOT WRITE ON THIS CARD **Form No. I**

Applicant must correctly answer any four of the following six questions so as to evidence an elemental knowledge of the Constitution and Government, an attachment thereto, and a simple understanding of the obligations of citizenship under a republican form of government.

1. The church that we attend is chosen—
   a. by the National Government.
   b. by ourselves.
   c. by the Congress.

2. The President must be at least—
   a. twenty-five years old.
   b. thirty years old.
   c. thirty-five years old.

3. It is important for every voter—
   a. to vote as others tell him to vote.
   b. to vote for the most popular candidates.
   c. to vote for the best qualified candidates.

4. The name of our first President was—
   a. John Adams.
   b. George Washington.
   c. Alexander Hamilton.

5. The Constitution of the United States places the final authority in our Nation in the hands of—
   a. the national courts.
   b. the States.
   c. the people.

6. The President of the Senate gets his office—
   a. by election by the people.
   b. by election by the Senate.
   c. by appointment by the President.

Applicant's answers must be provided on Form No. II furnished by the Registrar for permanent records.

This card must be returned to the Registrar

DO NOT WRITE ON THIS CARD **Form No. 2**

Applicant must correctly answer any four of the following six questions so as to evidence an elemental knowledge of the Constitution and Government, an attachment thereto, and a simple understanding of the obligations of citizenship under a republican form of government.

1. The Congress cannot regulate commerce—
   a. between States.
   b. with other countries.
   c. within a state.

2. The general plan of a State government is given—
   a. in the Constitution of the United States.
   b. in the laws of the Congress.
   c. in its own State constitution.

3. The name of our first President was—
   a. John Adams.
   b. George Washington.
   c. Alexander Hamilton.

4. The President gets his authority to carry out laws—
   a. from the Declaration of Independence.
   b. from the Constitution.
   c. from the Congress.

5. Our towns and cities have delegated authority which they get from the—
   a. State.
   b. Congress.
   c. President.

6. A citizen who desires to vote on election day must, before that date, go before the election officers and—
   a. register.
   b. pay all of his bills.
   c. have his picture taken.

Applicant's answers must be provided on Form No. 11 furnished by the Registrar for permanent records.

This card must be returned to the Registrar

DO NOT WRITE ON THIS CARD **Form No. 3**

Applicant must correctly answer any four of the following six questions so as to evidence an elemental knowledge of the Constitution and Government, an attachment thereto, and a simple understanding of the obligations of citizenship under a republican form of government.

1. Limits are placed on the right to vote by the—
   a. National Government.
   b. States.
   c. courts.

2. The Articles of Confederation are—
   a. the Constitution we now have.
   b. a plan for State government.
   c. an early plan of government for the original 13 States.

3. The mail carrier is paid by the—
   a. city.
   b. State.
   c. United States Government.

4. The President is elected—
   a. for four years.
   b. for six years.
   c. for life.

5. The name of our first President was—
   a. John Adams.
   b. George Washington.
   c. Alexander Hamilton.

6. The Congress cannot establish—
   a. churches.
   b. courts.
   c. banks.

Applicant's answers must be provided on Form No. 11 furnished by the Registrar for permanent records.

This card must be returned to the Registrar

DO NOT WRITE ON THIS CARD **Form No. 4**

Applicant must correctly answer any four of the following six questions so as to evidence an elemental knowledge of the Constitution and Government, an attachment thereto, and a simple understanding of the obligations of citizenship under a republican form of government.

1. The name of our first President was—
    a. John Adams.
    b. George Washington.
    c. Alexander Hamilton.

2. The President is elected—
    a. by the Congress.
    b. by the direct vote of the people.
    c. by the people through electors.

3. We usually decide public questions in the United States by a vote of the—
    a. few.
    b. majority.
    c. male citizens.

4. Bad government in a democracy is possible if the people—
    a. make wise votes.
    b. forget to vote.
    c. do not stay at home.

5. A government in which the people delegate authority to chosen officials is—
    a. a totalitarian state.
    b. a republic.
    c. a monarchy.

6. Laws for the District of Columbia are made—
    a. by the State of Maryland.
    b. by the Congress.
    c. by the people who live there.

Applicant's answers must be provided on Form No. 11 furnished by the Registrar for permanent records.

This card must be returned to the Registrar

DO NOT WRITE ON THIS CARD **Form No. 5**

Applicant must correctly answer any four of the following six questions so as to evidence an elemental knowledge of the Constitution and Government, an attachment thereto, and a simple understanding of the obligations of citizenship under a republican form of government.

1. The legislative branch of the State government—
   a. makes the laws for the State.
   b. tries cases in the courts.
   c. explains the laws.

2. Limits are placed on the right to vote by the—
   a. National Government.
   b. States.
   c. courts.

3. The powers granted to the National Government in the Constitution are called—
   a. delegated powers.
   b. denied powers.
   c. the final authority.

4. The name of our first President was—
   a. John Adams.
   b. George Washington.
   c. Alexander Hamilton.

5. The Constitution of the United States places the final authority in our Nation in the hands of—
   a. the national courts.
   b. the States.
   c. the people.

6. Each State has as many Presidential electors as it has—
   a. Senators.
   b. Representatives.
   c. Senators and Representatives.

Applicant's answers must be provided on Form No. 11 furnished by the Registrar for permanent records.

This card must be returned to the Registrar

DO NOT WRITE ON THIS CARD **Form No. 6**

Applicant must correctly answer any four of the following six questions so as to evidence an elemental knowledge of the Constitution and Government, an attachment thereto, and a simple understanding of the obligations of citizenship under a republican form of government.

1. In case of impeachment of the President, the officer who would preside at the trial is—
   a. the Vice President.
   b. the Speaker of the House of Representatives.
   c. Chief Justice of the United States.

2. Money is coined by—
   a. the States.
   b. the people.
   c. the National Government.

3. Our Constitution has been changed—
   a. by the President.
   b. by the Congress and the people.
   c. by the Supreme Court.

4. Limits are placed on the right to vote by the—
   a. National Government.
   b. States.
   c. courts.

5. The Constitution of the United States places the final authority in our Nation in the hands of—
   a. the national courts.
   b. the States.
   c. the people.

6. The name of our first President was—
   a. John Adams.
   b. George Washington.
   c. Alexander Hamilton.

Applicant's answers must be provided on Form No. 11 furnished by the Registrar for permanent records.

This card must be returned to the Registrar

DO NOT WRITE ON THIS CARD **Form No. 7**

Applicant must correctly answer any four of the following six questions so as to evidence an elemental knowledge of the Constitution and Government, an attachment thereto, and a simple understanding of the obligations of citizenship under a republican form of government.

1. The State governments have the authority to—
   a. admit new States into the Union.
   b. set up local governments within the State.
   c. declare war.

2. The Seventeenth Amendment states that Senators shall be elected by—
   a. the State legislatures.
   b. the people of the States.
   c. the Congress.

3. The Constitution of the United States places the final authority in our Nation in the hands of—
   a. the national courts.
   b. the States.
   c. the people.

4. Presidential candidates are nominated—
   a. by State Legislatures.
   b. by National Conventions.
   c. by the people.

5. The written statement of the things for which a political party stands is called the—
   a. ballot.
   b. platform.
   c. candidate.

6. The name of our first President was—
   a. John Adams.
   b. George Washington.
   c. Alexander Hamilton.

Applicant's answers must be provided on Form No. 11 furnished by the Registrar for permanent records.

This card must be returned to the Registrar

DO NOT WRITE ON THIS CARD **Form No. 8**

Applicant must correctly answer any four of the following six questions so as to evidence an elemental knowledge of the Constitution and Government, an attachment thereto, and a simple understanding of the obligations of citizenship under a republican form of government.

1. The number of Representatives from each State depends upon—
   a. the voters.
   b. the population.
   c. the electors.
2. The Senators and Congressmen from my State are elected by the—
   a. State legislature.
   b. voters.
3. The name of our first President was—
   a. John Adams.
   b. George Washington.
   c. Alexander Hamilton.
4. The Constitution of the United States places the final authority in our Nation in the hands of—
   a. the national courts.
   b. the States.
   c. the people.
5. United States judges obtain their offices through—
   a. election by the people of their districts.
   b. appointment by the President without the approval of the Senate.
   c. appointment by the President with the advice and consent of the Senate.
6. A tax on the money a person receives in payment for his labor, or earnings from his property is—
   a. an income tax.
   b. a poll tax.
   c. a sales tax.

Applicant's answers must be provided on Form No. 11 furnished by the Registrar for permanent records.

This card must be returned to the Registrar

DO NOT WRITE ON THIS CARD **Form No. 9**

Applicant must correctly answer any four of the following six questions so as to evidence an elemental knowledge of the Constitution and Government, an attachment thereto, and a simple understanding of the obligations of citizenship under a republican form of government.

1. The name of our first President was—
    a. John Adams.
    b. George Washington.
    c. Alexander Hamilton.

2. The Constitution of the United States places the final authority in our Nation in the hands of—
    a. the national courts.
    b. the States.
    c. the people.

3. All bills of revenue (tax) must begin in—
    a. the Senate.
    b. the Supreme Court.
    c. the House of Representatives.

4. Most States have a lawmaking body made up—
    a. of two houses.
    b. of one house.
    c. of the governor and the department heads.

5. The Members of the House of Representatives are called—
    a. judges.
    b. Congressmen.
    c. Senators.

6. The (U. S.) Supreme Court is made up of—
    a. 9 Justices.
    b. 6 Justices.
    c. 5 Justices.

Applicant's answers must be provided on Form No. 11 furnished by the Registrar for permanent records.

This card must be returned to the Registrar

DO NOT WRITE ON THIS CARD **Form No. 10**

Applicant must correctly answer any four of the following six questions so as to evidence an elemental knowledge of the Constitution and Government, an attachment thereto, and a simple understanding of the obligations of citizenship under a republican form of government.

1. Limits are placed on the right to vote by the—
   a. National Government.
   b. States.
   c. courts.

2. The name of our first President was—
   a. John Adams.
   b. George Washington.
   c. Alexander Hamilton.

3. The judges of the national courts hold office—
   a. for five years.
   b. for life if they obey the laws.
   c. for twenty years.

4. The tax we pay on our property is—
   a. a business tax.
   b. a property tax.
   c. an inheritance tax.

5. The chief work of the Congress is to—
   a. make the laws for the Nation.
   b. explain the laws.
   c. make treaties.

6. The system of courts in a State is called—
   a. the executive branch of the government.
   b. the State judiciary.
   c. the Senate.

Applicant's answers must be provided on Form No. 11 furnished by the Registrar for permanent records.

This card must be returned to the Registrar

ANSWERS TO THE STATE OF LOUISIANA CITIZENSHIP TEST ON OUR CONSTITUTION AND GOVERNMENT

Form No. 1

(The Correct Answers are Underlined)

The applicant must be able to answer any four of the following six questions.

1. The church that we attend is chosen—
   a. by the National Government.
   <u>b. by ourselves.</u>
   c. by the Congress.

2. The President must be at least—
   a. twenty-five years old.
   b. thirty years old.
   <u>c. thirty-five years old.</u>

3. It is important for every voter—
   a. to vote as others tell him to vote.
   b. to vote for the most popular candidates.
   <u>c. to vote for the best qualified candidates.</u>

4. The name of our first President was—
   a. John Adams.
   <u>b. George Washington.</u>
   c. Alexander Hamilton.

5. The Constitution of the United States places the final authority in our Nation in the hands of—
   a. the national courts.
   b. the States.
   <u>c. the people.</u>

6. The President of the Senate gets his office—
   <u>a. by election by the people.</u>
   b. by election by the Senate.
   c. by appointment by the President.

ANSWERS TO CITIZENSHIP TEST ON OUR CONSTITUTION AND GOVERNMENT

Form No. 2

(The Correct Answers are Underlined)

The applicant must be able to answer any four of the following six questions.

1. The Congress cannot regulate commerce—
   a. between States.
   <u>b. within a state.</u>
   c. with other countries.

2. The general plan of a State government is given—
   a. in the Constitution of the United States.
   b. in the laws of the Congress.
   <u>c. in its own State constitution.</u>

3. The name of our first President was—
   a. John Adams.
   <u>b. George Washington.</u>
   c. Alexander Hamilton.

4. The President gets his authority to carry out laws—
   a. from the Declaration of Independence.
   <u>b. from the Constitution.</u>
   c. from the Congress.

5. Our towns and cities have delegated authority which they get from th—
   <u>a. State.</u>
   b. Congress.
   c. President.

6. A citizen who desires to vote on election day must, before that date, go before the election officers and—
   <u>a. register.</u>
   b. pay all of his bills.
   c. have his picture taken.

ANSWERS TO CITIZENSHIP TEST ON OUR CONSTITUTION AND GOVERNMENT

Form No. 3

(The Correct Answers are Underlined)

The applicant must be able to answer any four of the following six questions.

1. Limits are placed on the right to vote by the—
   a. National Government.
   <u>b. States.</u>
   c. Courts.

2. The Articles of Confederation are—
   a. the Constitution we now have.
   b. a plan for State government.
   <u>c. an early plan of government for the original 13 States.</u>

3. The Mail carrier is paid by the—
   a. city.
   b. State.
   <u>c. United States Government.</u>

4. The President is elected—
   <u>a. for four years.</u>
   b. for six years.
   c. for life.

5. The name of our first President was—
   a. John Adams.
   <u>b. George Washington.</u>
   c. Alexander Hamilton.

6. The Congress cannot establish—
   <u>a. churches.</u>
   b. courts.
   c. banks.

ANSWERS TO CITIZENSHIP TEST ON OUR CONSTITUTION AND GOVERNMENT

Form No. 4

(The Correct Answers are Underlined)

The applicant must be able to answer any four of the following six questions.

1. The name of our first President was—
   a. John Adams.
   b. George Washington.
   c. Alexander Hamilton.

2. The President is elected—
   a. by the Congress.
   b. by direct vote of the people.
   c. by the people through electors.

3. We usually decide public questions in the United States by a vote of the—
   a. few.
   b. majority.
   c. male citizens.

4. Bad government in a democracy is possible if the people—
   a. make wise votes.
   b. forget to vote.
   c. don't stay at home.

5. A Government in which the people delegate authority to chosen officials is—
   a. a totalitarian state.
   b. a republic.
   c. a monarchy.

6. Laws for the District of Columbia are made—
   a. by the State of Maryland.
   b. by the Congress.
   c. by the people who live there.

ANSWERS TO CITIZENSHIP TEST ON OUR CONSTITUTION AND GOVERNMENT

Form No. 5

(The Correct Answers are Underlined)

The applicant must be able to answer any four of the following six questions.

1. The legislative branch of the State Government—
   a. makes the laws for the State.
   b. Tries cases in the courts.
   c. explains the laws.

2. Limits are placed on the right to vote by the—
   a. National Government.
   b. States.
   c. courts.

3. The powers granted to the National Government in the Constitution are called—
   a. delegated powers.
   b. denied powers.
   c. the final authority.

4. The name of our first President was—
   a. John Adams.
   b. George Washington.
   c. Alexander Hamilton.

5. The constitution of the United States places the final authority in our Nation in the hands of—
   a. the National courts.
   b. the States.
   c. the people.

6. Each State has as many Presidential electors as it has—
   a. Senators.
   b. Representatives.
   c. Senators and Representatives.

ANSWERS TO CITIZENSHIP TEST ON OUR CONSTITUTION AND GOVERNMENT

Form No. 6

(The Correct Answers are Underlined)

The applicant must be able to answer any four of the following six questions.

1. In case of impeachment of the President, the officer who would preside at the trial is—
   a. the Vice President.
   b. the Speaker of the House of Representatives.
   c. Chief Justice of the United States.

2. Money is coined by—
   a. the States.
   b. the people.
   c. the National Government.

3. Our Constitution has been changed—
   a. by the President.
   b. by the Congress and the people.
   c. by the Supreme Court.

4. Limits are placed on the right to vote by the—
   a. National Government.
   b. States.
   c. courts.

5. The Constitution of the United States places the final authority in our Nation in the hands of—
   a. the national courts.
   b. the States.
   c. the people.

6. The name of our first President was—
   a. John Adams.
   b. George Washington.
   c. Alexander Hamilton.

ANSWERS TO CITIZENSHIP TEST ON OUR CONSTITUTION AND GOVERNMENT

Form No. 7

(The Correct Answers are Underlined)

The applicant must be able to answer any
four of the following six questions.

1. The State governments have the authority to—
   a. admit new States into the Union.
   <u>b. set up local governments within the State.</u>
   c. declare war.

2. The Seventeenth Amendment states that Senators shall be elected by—
   a. the State legislatures.
   <u>b. the people of the States.</u>
   c. the Congress.

3. The Constitution of the United States places the final authority in our Nation in the hands of—
   a. the national courts.
   b. the States.
   <u>c. the people.</u>

4. Presidential candidates are nominated—
   a. by the State Legislatures.
   <u>b. by National Conventions.</u>
   c. by the people.

5. The written statement of the things for which a political party stands is called the—
   a. ballot.
   <u>b. platform.</u>
   c. candidate.

6. The name of our first President was—
   a. John Adams.
   <u>b. George Washington.</u>
   c. Alexander Hamilton.

ANSWERS TO CITIZENSHIP TEST ON OUR CONSTITUTION AND GOVERNMENT

Form No. 8

(The Correct Answers are Underlined)

The applicant must be able to answer any four of the following six questions.

1. The number of Representatives from each State depends upon—
   a. the voters.
   <u>b. the population.</u>
   c. the electors.

2. The Senators and Congressmen from my State are elected by the—
   a. State legislature.
   <u>b. voters.</u>

3. The name of our first President was—
   a. John Adams.
   <u>b. George Washington.</u>
   c. Alexander Hamilton.

4. The Constitution of the United States places the final authority in our Nation in the hands of—
   a. the national courts.
   b. the States.
   <u>c. the people.</u>

5. United States judges obtain their offices through—
   a. election by the people of their districts.
   b. appointment by the President without the approval of the Senate.
   <u>c. appointment by the President with the advice and consent of the Senate.</u>

6. A tax on the money a person receives in payment for his labor, or earnings from his property is—
   <u>a. an income tax.</u>
   b. a poll tax.
   c. a sales tax.

ANSWERS TO CITIZENSHIP TEST ON OUR CONSTITUTION AND GOVERNMENT

Form No. 9

(The Correct Answers are Underlined)

The applicant must be able to answer any four of the following six questions.

1. The name of our first President was—
   a. John Adams.
   <u>b. George Washington.</u>
   c. Alexander Hamilton.

2. The Constitution of the United States places the final authority in our Nation in the hands of—
   a. the national courts.
   b. the States.
   <u>c. the people.</u>

3. All bills of revenue (tax) must begin in—
   a. the Senate.
   b. the Supreme Court.
   <u>c. The House of Representatives.</u>

4. Most States have a lawmaking body made up—
   <u>a. of two houses.</u>
   b. of one house.
   c. of the governor and the department heads.

5. The members of the House of Representatives are called—
   a. Judges.
   <u>b. Congressmen.</u>
   c. Senators.

6. The (U. S.) Supreme Court is made up of—
   <u>a. 9 Justices.</u>
   b. 6 Justices.
   c. 5 Justices.

ANSWERS TO CITIZENSHIP TEST ON OUR CONSTITUTION AND GOVERNMENT

Form No. 10

(The Correct Answers are Underlined)

The applicant must be able to answer any four of the following six questions.

1. Limits are placed on the right to vote by the—
   a. National Government.
   b. States.
   c. courts.

2. The name of our first President was—
   a. John Adams.
   b. George Washington.
   c. Alexander Hamilton.

3. The judges of the national courts hold office—
   a. for five years.
   b. for life if they obey the laws.
   c. for twenty years.

4. The tax we pay on our property is—
   a. a business tax.
   b. a property tax.
   c. an inheritance tax.

5. The chief work of the Congress is to—
   a. make the laws for the Nation.
   b. explain the laws.
   c. make treaties.

6. The system of courts in a State is called—
   a. the executive branch of the government.
   b. the State judiciary.
   c. the Senate.

Ward No. ________
Prect. No. ________
Cert. No. ________

APPLICATION FOR REGISTRATION FORM

OFFICE OF REGISTRAR OF VOTERS
Parish of Orleans, State of Louisiana

I am a citizen of the United States and of the State of Louisiana.

My name is Mr.—Mrs.—Miss ____________________. I was born in the State (or country) of ______________, Parish (or county) of ______________, on the ________ day of ________, in the year ________. I am now ________ years, ________ months and ________ days of age. I have resided in this State since ______________, in this Parish since ______________, and in Precinct No. ________, in Ward No. ________ of this Parish continuously since ______________. I am not disfranchised by any provisions of the Constitution of this State. The name of the householder at my present address is ____________________. My occupation is ____________________. My color is ______. My sex is ______. I am not now registered as a voter in any other Ward or Precinct of this State, except ______________. My last registration was in Ward ________ Precinct ________ Parish ______________. I am now affiliated with the ______________ Party.

In each of the following items the applicant shall mark through the word "have" or the words "have not" so that each item will show a true statement about the applicant:

I have (have not) been convicted of a felony without receiving a full pardon and restoration of franchise.

I have (have not) been convicted of more than one misdemeanor and sentenced to a term of ninety (90) days or more in jail for each such conviction, other than traffic and/or game law violations, within five years before the date of making this application for registration as an elector.

I have (have not) been convicted of any misdemeanor and sentenced to a term of six (6) months or more in jail, other than traffic and/or game law violations, within one year before the date of making this application for registration as an elector.

I have (have not) lived with another in "common law" marriage within five years before the date of making this application for registration as an elector.

TURN CARD OVER

- -

I have (have not) given birth to an illegitimate child within five years before the date of making this application for registration as an elector. (The provisions hereof shall not apply to the birth of any illegitimate child conceived as a consequence of rape or forced carnal knowledge.)

I have (have not) acknowledged myself to be the father of an illegitimate child within five years before the date of making this application for registration as an elector. I do hereby solemnly swear or affirm that I will faithfully and fully abide by all the laws of the State of Louisiana, so help me God.

Signature ______________________

Sworn to and subscribed before me: ______________________
(Deputy) Registrar

CHANGE OF ADDRESS

Date____ Address____ Ward No.____ Prect. No.____ Cert. No.____
Date____ Address____ Ward No.____ Prect. No.____ Cert. No.____
Date____ Address____ Ward No.____ Prect. No.____ Cert. No.____

CHANGE OF NAME

I am now Mr.—Mrs.—Miss __________ Date of change __________
Nature of change ______________________________

REMARKS

____

____

The following information forms no part of the application but is for use of the registration records:
Parish of ______________, State of Louisiana. Date _____, 19 ___.
Address ______________________. Color of eyes __________.
Mother's first or maiden name ______. Name of employer ______.
Property owner ______. Tenant ______. Boarder ______.

A CALL FOR "SEGREGATION FOREVER"

GEORGE WALLACE

Inaugural Address as Governor of Alabama

January 14, 1963

GOVERNOR Patterson, Governor Barnett, from one of the greatest states in this nation, Mississippi, Judge Brown, representing Governor Hollings of South Carolina, members of the Alabama Congressional Delegation, members of the Alabama Legislature, distinguished guests, fellow Alabamians:

Before I begin my talk with you, I want to ask you for a few minutes patience while I say something that is on my heart: I want to thank those home folks of my county who first gave an anxious country boy his opportunity to serve in State politics. I shall always owe a lot to those who gave me that *first* opportunity to serve.

I will never forget the warm support and close loyalty of the folks at Suttons, Haigler's Mill, Eufaula, Beat 6 and Beat 14, Richards Cross Roads and Gammage Beat . . . at Baker Hill, Beat 8, and Comer, Spring Hill, Adams Chapel and Mount Andrew . . . White Oak, Baxter's Station, Clayton, Louisville and Cunningham Place; Horns Crossroads, Texasville and Blue Springs, where the vote was 304 for Wallace and 1 for the opposition . . . and the dear little lady whom I heard had made that one vote against me . . . by mistake . . . because she couldn't see too well . . . and she had pulled the wrong lever. . . . Bless her heart. At Clio, my birthplace, and Elamville. I shall never forget them. May God bless them.

And I shall forever remember that election day morning as I waited . . . and suddenly at ten o'clock that morning the first return of a box was flashed over this state: it carried the message. . . . Wallace 15, opposition zero; and it came from the Hamrick Beat at Putman's Mountain where live the great hill people of our state. May God bless the mountain man . . . his loyalty is unshakable, he'll do to walk down the road with.

I hope you'll forgive me these few moments of remembering . . . but I wanted them . . . and you . . . to know, that I shall never forget.

And I wish I could shake hands and thank all of you in this State who voted for me . . . and those of you who did not . . . for I know you voted your honest convictions . . . and now, we must stand together and move the great State of Alabama forward.

I would be remiss, this day, if I did not thank my wonderful wife and fine family for their patience, support and loyalty . . . and there is no man living who does not owe more to his mother than he can ever repay, and I want my mother to know that I realize my debt to her.

This is the day of my Inauguration as Governor of the State of Alabama. And on this day I feel a deep obligation to renew my pledges, my covenants with you . . . the people of this great state.

General Robert E. Lee said that "duty" is the sublimest word in the English language and I have come, increasingly, to realize what he meant. I SHALL do my duty to you, God helping . . . to every man, to every woman . . . yes, and to every child in this State. I shall fulfill my duty toward honesty and economy in our State government so that no man shall have a part of his livelihood cheated and no child shall have a bit of his future stolen away.

I have said to you that I would eliminate the liquor agents in this state and that the money saved would be returned to our citizens. . . . I am happy to report to you that I am now filling orders for several hundred one-way tickets and stamped on them are these words . . . "for liquor agents . . . destination: . . . out of Alabama." I am happy to report to you that the big-wheeling cocktail-party boys have gotten the word that their free whiskey and boat rides are over . . . that the farmer in the field, the worker in the factory, the businessman in his office, the housewife in her home, have decided that the money can be better spent to help our children's education and our older citizens . . . and they have put a man in office to see that it is done. It shall be done. Let me say one more time . . . no more liquor drinking in your governor's mansion.

I shall fulfill my duty in working hard to bring industry into our state, not only by maintaining an honest, sober and free-enterprise climate of government in which industry can have confidence . . . but in going out and getting it . . . so that our people can have industrial jobs in Alabama and provide a better life for their children.

I shall not forget my duty to our senior citizens . . . so that their lives can be lived in dignity and enrichment of the golden years, nor to our sick, both mental and physical . . . and they will know we have not forsaken them. I want the farmer to feel confident that in this State government he has a partner who will work with him in raising his income and increasing his markets, and I want the laboring man to know he has a friend who is sincerely striving to better his field of endeavor.

I want to assure every child that this State government is not afraid to invest in their future through education, so that they will not be handicapped on the very threshold of their lives.

Today I have stood, where once Jefferson Davis stood, and took an oath to my people. It is very appropriate then that from this Cradle of the Confederacy, this very Heart of the Great Anglo-Saxon Southland, that today we sound the drum for freedom as have our generations of forebears before us done, time and again down through history. Let us rise to the call of freedom-loving blood that is in us and send our answer to the tyranny that clanks its chains upon the South. In the name of the greatest people that have ever trod this earth, I draw the line in the dust and toss the gauntlet before the feet of tyranny . . . and I say . . . segregation now . . . segregation tomorrow . . . segregation forever.

The Washington, D. C. school riot report is disgusting and revealing. We will not sacrifice our children to any such type school system—and you can write that down. The federal troops in Mississippi could better be used guarding the safety of the citizens of Washington, D. C., where it is even unsafe to walk or go to a ball game—and that is the nation's capital. I was safer in a B-29 bomber over Japan during the war in an air raid, than the people of Washington are walking in the White House neighborhood. A closer example is Atlanta. The city officials fawn for political reasons over school integration and

THEN build barricades to stop residential integration—what hypocrisy!

Let us send this message back to Washington by our representatives who are with us today . . . that from this day we are standing up, and the heel of tyranny does not fit the neck of an upright man . . . that we intend to take the offensive and carry our fight for freedom across this nation, wielding the balance of power we know we possess in the Southland . . . that WE, not the insipid bloc voters of some sections . . . will determine in the next election who shall sit in the White House of these United States . . . that from this day . . . from this hour . . . from this minute . . . we give the word of a race of honor that we will tolerate their boot in our face no longer . . . and let those certain judges put *that* in their opium pipes of power and smoke it for what it is worth.

Hear me, Southerners! You sons and daughters who have moved north and west throughout this nation . . . we call on you from your native soil to join with us in national support and vote . . . and we know . . . wherever you are . . . away from the hearths of the Southland . . . that you will respond, for though you may live in the fartherest reaches of this vast country . . . your heart has never left Dixieland.

And you native sons and daughters of old New England's rock-ribbed patriotism . . . and you sturdy natives of the great Mid-West . . . and you descendants of the far West flaming spirit of pioneer freedom . . . we invite you to come and be with us . . . for you are of the Southern mind . . . and the Southern spirit . . . and the Southern philosophy . . . you are Southerners too and brothers with us in our fight.

What I have said about segregation goes double this day . . . and what I have said to or about some federal judges goes TRIPLE this day.

Alabama has been blessed by God as few states in this Union have been blessed. Our state owns ten per cent of all the natural resources of all the states in our country. Our inland waterway system is second to none . . . and has the potential of being the greatest waterway transport system in the entire world. We possess over thirty minerals in usable quantities and our soil is rich and varied, suited to a wide variety of plants. Our native pine and forestry system produces timber faster than we can cut it and yet we have only pricked the surface of the great lumber and pulp potential.

With ample rainfall and rich grasslands our livestock industry is in the infancy of a giant future that can make us a center of the big and growing meat packing and prepared foods marketing. We have the favorable climate, streams, woodlands, beaches, and natural beauty to make us a recreational mecca in the booming tourist and vacation industry. Nestled in the great Tennessee Valley, we possess the Rocket center of the world and the keys to the space frontier.

While the trade with a developing Europe built the great port cities of the east coast, our own fast developing port of Mobile faces as a magnetic gateway to the great continent of South America, well over twice as large and hundreds of times richer in resources, even now awakening to the growing probes of enterprising capital with a potential of growth and wealth beyond any present dream for our port development and corresponding results throughout the connecting waterways that thread our state.

And while the manufacturing industries of free enterprise have been coming to our state in increasing numbers, attracted by our bountiful natural resources, our growing numbers of skilled workers and our favorable conditions, their present rate of settlement here can be increased from the trickle they now represent to a stream of enterprise and endeavor, capital and expansion that can join us in our work of development and enrichment of the educational futures of our children, the opportunities of our citizens and the fulfillment of our talents as God has given them to us. To realize our ambitions and to bring to fruition our dreams, we as Alabamians must take cognizance of the world about us. We must re-define our heritage, re-school our thoughts in the lessons our forefathers knew so well, first hand, in order to function and to grow and to prosper. We can no longer hide our head in the sand and tell ourselves that the ideology of our free fathers is not being attacked and is not being threatened by another idea . . . for it is. We are faced with an idea that if a centralized government assumes enough authority, enough power over its people, that it can provide a utopian life . . . that if given the power to dictate, to forbid, to require, to demand, to distribute, to edict and to judge what is best and enforce that will of judgement upon its citizens from unimpeachable authority . . . then it will produce only "good" . . . and it shall be our father . . . and our God. It is an idea of government that encourages our fears and destroys our faith . . . for where there is faith, there is no fear, and where there is fear, there is no faith. In encouraging our fears of economic insecurity it demands we place that economic management and control with government; in encouraging our fear of educational development it demands we place that education and the minds of our children under management and control of government, and even in feeding our fears of physical infirmities and declining years, it offers and demands to father us through it all and even into the grave. It is a government that claims to us that it is bountiful as it buys its power from us with the fruits of its rapaciousness of the wealth that free men before it have produced and builds on crumbling credit without responsibilities to the debtors . . . our children. It is an ideology of government erected on the encouragement of fear and fails to recognize the basic law of our fathers that governments do not produce wealth . . . people produce wealth . . . free people; and as those people become less free . . . as they learn there is little reward for ambition . . . that it requires faith to risk . . . and they have none . . . as the government must restrict and penalize and tax incentive and endeavor and must increase its expenditures of bounties . . . then this government must assume more and more police powers and we find we are become government-fearing people . . . not God-fearing people. We find we have replaced faith with fear . . . and though we may give lip service to the Almighty . . . in reality, government has become our god. It is, therefore, a basically ungodly government and its appeal to the pseudo-intellectual and the politician is to change their status from servant of the people to master of the people . . . to play at being God . . . without faith in God . . . and without the wisdom of God. It is a system that is the very opposite of Christ for it feeds and encourages everything degenerate and base in our people as it assumes the responsibilities that we ourselves should assume. Its pseudo-liberal spokesmen and some Harvard advocates have never examined the logic of its substitution of what it calls "human rights" for individual rights, for its propaganda play upon words has appeal for the unthinking. Its logic is totally material and irresponsible as it runs the full gamut of human desires . . . including the theory that everyone has voting rights without the spiritual responsibility of preserving freedom. Our founding fathers recognized those rights . . . but only within the frameworks of those spiritual responsibilities. But the strong, simple faith and sane reasoning of our founding fathers has long since been forgotten as the so-called "progressives" tell us that our Constitution was written for "horse and buggy" days . . . so were the Ten Commandments.

Not so long ago men stood in marvel and awe at the cities, the buildings, the schools, the autobahns that the government of Hitler's Germany had built . . . just as centuries before they stood in wonder at Rome's building . . . but it could not stand . . . for the system that built it had rotted the souls of the builders . . . and in turn . . . rotted the foundation of what God meant that men should be. Today that same system on an international scale is sweeping the world. It is the "changing world" of which we are told . . . it is called "new" and "liberal." It is as old as the oldest dictator. It is degenerate and decadent. As the *national* racism of Hitler's Germany persecuted a *national* minority to the whim of a national majority . . . so the *international* racism of the liberals seeks to persecute the *international* white minority to the whim of the *international* colored majority . . . so that we are footballed about according to the favor of the Afro-Asian bloc. But the Belgian survivors of the Congo cannot present their case to a war crimes commission . . . nor the Portuguese of Angola . . . nor the survivors of Castro . . . nor the citizens of Oxford, Mississippi.

It is this theory of international power politic that led a group of men on the Supreme Court for the first time in American history to issue an edict, based not on legal precedent, but upon a volume, the editor of which has said our Constitution is outdated and must be changed and the writers of which, some had admittedly belonged to as many as half a hundred communist-front organizations. It is this theory that led this same group of men to briefly bare the ungodly core of that philosophy in forbidding little school children to say a prayer. And we find the evidence of that ungodliness even in the removal of the words "in God we trust" from some of our dollars, which was placed there as like evidence by our founding fathers as the faith upon which this system of government was built. It is the spirit of power thirst that caused a President in Washington to take up Caesar's pen and with one stroke of it, make a law. A Law which the law making body of Congress refused to pass . . . a law that tells us that we can or cannot buy or sell our very homes, except by his conditions . . . and except at HIS discretion. It is the spirit of power thirst that led that same President to launch a full offensive of twenty-five thousand troops against a university . . . of all places . . . in his own country . . . and against his own people, when this nation maintains only six thousand troops in the beleaguered city of Berlin. We have witnessed such acts of "might makes right" over the world as men yielded to the temptation to play God . . . but we have never before witnessed it in America. We reject such acts as free men. We do not defy, for there is nothing to defy . . . since as free men we do not recognize any government right to give freedom . . . or deny freedom. No government erected by man has that right. As Thomas Jefferson has said, "The God who gave us life, gave us liberty at the same time; no King holds the right of liberty in his hands." Nor does any ruler in American government.

We intend, quite simply, to practice the free heritage as bequeathed to us as sons of free fathers. We intend to re-vitalize the truly new and progressive form of government that is less than two hundred years old . . . a government first founded in this nation simply and purely on faith . . . that there is a personal God who rewards good and punishes evil . . . that hard work will receive its just deserts . . . that ambition and ingenuity and incentiveness . . . and profit of such . . . are admirable traits and goals . . . that the individual is encouraged in his spiritual growth and from that growth arrives at a character that enhances his charity toward others and from that character and that charity so is influenced business, and labor and farmer and government. We intend to renew our faith as God-fearing men . . . *not* government-fearing men nor any other kind of fearing-men. We intend to roll up our sleeves and pitch in to develop this full bounty God has given us . . . to live full and useful lives and in absolute freedom from all fear. Then can we enjoy the full richness of the Great American Dream.

We have placed this sign, "In God We Trust," upon our State Capitol on this Inauguration Day as physical evidence of determination to renew the faith of our fathers and to practice the free heritage they bequeathed to us. We do this with the clear and solemn knowledge that such physical evidence is evidently a direct violation of the logic of that Supreme Court in Washington, D. C., and if they or their spokesmen in this state wish to term this defiance . . . I say . . . then let them make the most of it.

This nation was never meant to be a unit of one . . . but a united of the many . . . that is the exact reason our freedom loving forefathers established the states, so as to divide the rights and powers among the many states, insuring that no central power could gain master government control.

In united effort we were meant to live under this government . . . whether Baptist, Methodist, Presbyterian, Church of Christ, or whatever one's denomination or religious belief . . . each respecting the others' right to a separate denomination . . . each, by working to develop his own, enriching the total of all our lives through united effort. And so it was meant in our political lives . . . whether Republican, Democrat, Prohibition, or whatever political party . . . each striving from his separate political station . . . respecting the rights of others to be separate and work from within their political framework . . . and each separate political station making its contribution to our lives. . . .

And so it was meant in our racial lives . . . each race, within its own framework has the freedom to teach . . . to instruct . . . to develop . . . to ask for and receive deserved help from others of separate racial stations. This is the great freedom of our American founding fathers . . . but if we amalgamate into the one unit as advocated by the communist philosophers . . . then the enrichment of our lives . . . the freedom for our development . . . is gone forever. We become, therefore, a mongrel unit of one under a single all powerful government . . . and we stand for everything . . . and for nothing.

The true brotherhood of America, of respecting the separateness of others . . . and uniting in effort . . . has been so twisted and distorted from its original concept that there is small wonder that communism is winning the world.

We invite the negro citizens of Alabama to work with us from his separate racial station . . . as we will work with him . . . to develop, to grow in individual freedom and enrichment. We want jobs and a good future for BOTH our races. We want to help the physically and mentally sick of BOTH races . . . the tubercular and the infirm. This is the basic heritage of my religion, of which I make full practice . . . for we are all the handiwork of God.

But we warn those, of any group, who would follow the false doctrine of communistic amalgamation that we will not surrender our system of government . . . our freedom of race and religion . . . that freedom was won at a hard price and if it requires a hard price to retain it . . . we are able . . . and quite willing to pay it.

The liberals' theory that poverty, discrimination and lack of opportunity is the cause of communism is a false theory . . . if it were true the South would have been the biggest single communist bloc in the western hemisphere long ago . . . for after the great War Between the States, our people faced a desolate land of burned universities, destroyed crops and homes, with manpower depleted and crippled, and even the mule, which was required to work the land, was so scarce that whole communities shared one animal to make the spring plowing. There were no government hand-outs, no Marshall Plan aid, no coddling to make sure that *our* people would not suffer; instead the South was set upon by the vulturous carpetbagger and federal troops, all loyal Southerners were denied the vote at the point of bayonet, so that the infamous, illegal 14th Amendment might be passed. There was no money, no food and no hope of either. But our grandfathers bent their knee only in church and bowed their head only to God.

Not for one single instant did they ever consider the easy way of federal dictatorship and amalgamation in return for fat bellies. They fought. They dug sweet roots from the ground with their bare hands and boiled them in the old iron pots . . .

they gathered poke salad from the woods and acorns from the ground. They fought. They followed no false doctrine . . . they knew what they wanted . . . and they fought for freedom! They came up from their knees in the greatest display of sheer nerve, grit and guts that has ever been set down in the pages of written history . . . and they won! The great writer, Rudyard Kipling, wrote of them, that: "There in the Southland of the United States of America, lives the greatest fighting breed of man . . . in all the world!"

And that is why today, I stand ashamed of the fat, well-fed whimperers who say that it is inevitable . . . that our cause is lost. I am ashamed *of* them . . . and I am ashamed *for* them. They do not represent the people of the Southland.

And may we take note of one other fact, with all the trouble with communists that some sections of this country have . . . there are not enough native communists in the South to fill up a telephone booth . . . and THAT is a matter of public FBI record.

We remind all within hearing of this Southland that a *Southerner*, Peyton Randolph, presided over the Continental Congress in our nation's beginning . . . that a *Southerner*, Thomas Jefferson, wrote the Declaration of Independence, that a *Southerner*, George Washington, is the Father of our Country . . . that a *Southerner*, James Madison, authored our Constitution, that a *Southerner*, George Mason, authored the Bill of Rights and it was a Southerner who said, "Give me liberty . . . or give me death," Patrick Henry.

Southerners played a most magnificent part in erecting this great divinely inspired system of freedom . . . and as God is our witness, Southerners will save it.

Let us, as Alabamians, grasp the hand of destiny and walk out of the shadow of fear . . . and fill our divine destination. Let us not simply defend . . . but let us assume the leadership of the fight and carry our leadership across this nation. God has placed us here in this crisis . . . let us not fail in this . . . our most historical moment.

You that are here today, present in this audience, and to you over this great state, wherever you are in sound of my voice, I want to humbly and with all sincerity, thank you for your faith in me.

I promise you that I will try to make you a good governor. I promise you that, as God gives me the wisdom and the strength, I will be sincere with you. I will be honest with you.

I will apply the old sound rule of our fathers, that anything worthy of our defense is worthy of one hundred percent of our defense. I have been taught that freedom meant freedom from any threat or fear of government. I was born in that freedom, I was raised in that freedom . . . I intend to live in that freedom . . . and God willing, when I die, I shall leave that freedom to my children . . . as my father left it to me.

My pledge to you . . . to "Stand up for Alabama," is a stronger pledge today than it was the first day I made that pledge. I shall "Stand up for Alabama," as Governor of our State . . . you stand with me . . . and we, together, can give courageous leadership to millions of people throughout this nation who look to the South for their hope in this fight to win and preserve our freedoms and liberties.

So help me God.

And my prayer is that the Father who reigns above us will bless all the people of this great sovereign State and nation, both white and black.

I thank you.

STUDENT NONVIOLENT COORDINATING COMMITTEE

Violence Stalks Voter-Registration Workers in Mississippi

March 12, 1963

Student Nonviolent
Coordinating Committee
5 Beekman Street, Room 1025
New York 38, New York
CO 7-5541

March 12, 1963

VIOLENCE STALKS VOTER-REGISTRATION WORKERS IN MISSISSIPPI

Staff members of the Student Nonviolent Coordinating Committee, working on voter registration in Leflore County, Mississippi, have been the object of a new wave of violence in the past few weeks. The town of Greenwood has been the scene of these recent efforts to terrorize student workers who have also helped to secure food for Negro sharecroppers denied Federal surplus food relief.

On February 25th and 26th, over 150 Negroes attempted to register to vote in Greenwood, Mississippi. This is the largest number of Negroes who have attempted to register in Greenwood or any Black Belt County. Hunger and violence are apparently being used to curtail voter-registration efforts.

SINCE FEBRUARY 20, 1963:

- Four (4) Negro businesses destroyed by fire!
- SNCC Field Secretary sentenced to six months in jail!
- Student worker shot in neck when attacked by passing car!
- Second shooting injures four (4) voter-registration workers!

* * *

BUSINESS PLACES BURNED TO GROUND

FEBRUARY 20:

Four small business places, located on the same street as the Greenwood office of SNCC, were destroyed by fire early Wednesday morning, February 20.

The belief that the real target was the SNCC office finds support in the call reported by Mrs. Nancy Brand, worker in that office. She received an anonymous phone call the morning of the fire from a man who asked if she ever went to the office. When she answered "Yes," the caller said, "You won't be going there any more. That's been taken care of."

The destroyed businesses were Jackson's Garage, George's Cafe, Porter's Pressing Shop, and the Esquire Club.

* * *

SNCC WORKER ARRESTED ON
WASHINGTON'S BIRTHDAY

FEBRUARY 22:

Samuel Block, SNCC field secretary was arrested in front of his office in Greenwood, Mississippi on Friday, February 22. He was taken to an unknown jail and charged with "circulating breach of the peace." When tried on Monday, February 25, the charge was changed to "issuing statements calculated to breach the peace," and Block was sentenced to six months in jail and fined $500.00.

The judge who pronounced sentence told Mr. Block that he would reduce the fine to $250.00 and suspend sentence if he would leave Mississippi for good. Samuel Block was *born* and *reared* in Mississippi.

* * *

STUDENT SHOT AND CRITICALLY WOUNDED

FEBRUARY 28:

James Travis, 20 year old SNCC staff member, narrowly missed death when the car which he was driving was shot into by three white men, seven miles outside Greenwood on Thursday evening, February 28.

Travis was accompanied by Robert Moses, director of SNCC's statewide Mississippi registration program, and Randolph Blackwell, field director of southwide Voter Education Project. An untagged 1962 white Buick passed Travis' car on the highway to Greenville, Mississippi and fired several blasts into his car. Both front windows were demolished, seven bullets pierced the side of the car, and a bullet passed through Travis' shoulder and lodged at the back of his head, behind the spine. He was operated on the next day at University Hospital in Jackson, Mississippi.

* * *

SECOND SHOOTING INJURES FOUR

MARCH 7:

Four voter registration workers were cut by flying glass when the car in which they were sitting was fired into on Wednesday night, March 7. This was the second such shooting in Greenwood in less than ten days.

Those cut by the shattered front window of their car were Sam Block, 23, Willie Peacock, 25, Miss Peggy Marye, 19, and Miss Essie Broome, 24. The four young persons had just left a church meeting dealing with food and clothing needs of the county.

OTHER PERTINENT FACTS:

- There are 19,806 Negroes and 6,881 whites in Leflore County, Mississippi.
- Some 22,000 people were denied Federally supplied surplus commodities. County officials said they could not pay workers to distribute the food; yet no employees were laid off when the 22,000 were deprived of this relief.
- Samuel Block is one of the twenty young Mississippi Negroes working with the Student Nonviolent Coordinating Committee voter-registration program.
- Block has been arrested seven times, beaten twice, and was forced to jump from a second story window last August to flee a lynch mob of white men carrying chains, ropes and iron pipes.

* * *

The STUDENT NONVIOLENT COORDINATING COMMITTEE (SNCC) is an Atlanta-based student movement, with voter-registration programs going on in the hard core rural areas of Alabama, Georgia, and Mississippi. Staff members work for maintenance when it is available.

DEFYING A BAN ON MARCHES IN BIRMINGHAM

FRED SHUTTLESWORTH

Statement on State Court Injunction Against Demonstrations

April 14, 1963

April 14, 1963

STATEMENT BY REV. F. L. SHUTTLESWORTH, AS PRESIDENT OF THE ALABAMA CHRISTIAN MOVEMENT FOR HUMAN RIGHTS, ON REJECTION OF THE STATE COURT INJUNCTION AGAINST DEMONSTRATIONS

THE strange Stars of Segregation have fallen on Alabama, and they seem to have blinded the eyes of its judiciary.

The time to spotlight the Alabama Judicial tyranny is now, for tyranny like hell increases itself. The Alabama City and State Courts are for Segregation; we are for integration and human dignity. They ask us to be lawful, orderly, peaceful, law-abiding, and have respect for the courts. We have done so for more than 7 years in this the worst city and state in the nation.

However the courts do not appear to respect Negroes, nor regard us as persons subject to the same rights and treatment as others. We have as witness the outlawing of the NAACP in 1956, the M/A persecutions in '56, the Tuskegee injunction, the Talladega injunction, the multitude of criminal convictions against Shuttlesworth and many other persons who have committed no crime but that of being born black and having courage to ask for our rights. The unwritten rule in Alabama is: if mobs don't stop Negroes, the police can; and if the police can't, then the courts will.

Despite the harassment by the State, we are comforted by the zeal of Negroes for freedom, the love of our devoted families and Churches, and the hope that America will some day be free. We view this injunction as one of the inevitable torpedoes thrown in our way; but on the road to freedom, justice, and equality, Negroes can have but one slogan: Damn the torpedoes! Full speed ahead!

I, for one, will never cease to try to be free. I will never tell Negroes to quit fighting for freedom in the Land of the Free. And in this undertaking we only ask the consistent judgment of mankind, and the grace of our Heavenly Father.

DALLAS COUNTY CITIZENS COUNCIL

Ask Yourself This Important Question: What Have I Personally Done to Maintain Segregation?

The Selma Times-Journal, June 9, 1963

ASK YOURSELF THIS IMPORTANT QUESTION:

What have I personally done to Maintain Segregation?

If the answer disturbs you, probe deeper and decide what you are willing to do to preserve racial harmony in Selma and Dallas County.

Is it worth four dollars to prevent a "Birmingham" here? That's what it costs to be a member of your Citizens Council, whose efforts are not thwarted by courts which give sit-in demonstrators legal immunity, prevent school boards from expelling students who participate in mob activities and would place federal referees at the board of voter registrars.

Law enforcement can be called only after these things occur, but your Citizens Council prevents them from happening.

Why else did only 350 Negroes attend a so-called mass voter registration meeting that outside agitators worked 60 days to organize in Selma?

Gov. Wallace told a state meeting of the council three weeks ago: "You are doing a wonderful job, but you should speak with the united voice of 100,000 persons. Go back home and get more members."

Gov. Wallace stands in the University doorway next Tuesday facing possible ten years imprisonment for violating a federal injunction.

Is it worth four dollars to you to prevent sit-ins, mob marches and wholesale Negro voter registration efforts in Selma?

If so, prove your dedication by joining and supporting the work of the Dallas County Citizens Council today. Six dollars will make both you and your wife members of an organization which has already given Selma nine years of Racial Harmony since "Black Monday."

Send Your Check To
THE DALLAS COUNTY
Citizens Council
SELMA, ALABAMA
YOUR MEMBERSHIP IS GOOD FOR 12 MONTHS

"WE FACE . . . A MORAL CRISIS"

JOHN F. KENNEDY

Report to the American People on Civil Rights

June 11, 1963

GOOD EVENING, MY FELLOW CITIZENS:

This afternoon, following a series of threats and defiant statements, the presence of Alabama National Guardsmen was required on the University of Alabama to carry out the final and unequivocal order of the United States District Court of the Northern District of Alabama. That order called for the admission of two clearly qualified young Alabama residents who happened to have been born Negro.

That they were admitted peacefully on the campus is due in good measure to the conduct of the students of the University of Alabama, who met their responsibilities in a constructive way.

I hope that every American, regardless of where he lives, will stop and examine his conscience about this and other related incidents. This Nation was founded by men of many nations and backgrounds. It was founded on the principle that all men are created equal, and that the rights of every man are diminished when the rights of one man are threatened.

Today we are committed to a worldwide struggle to promote and protect the rights of all who wish to be free. And when Americans are sent to Viet-Nam or West Berlin, we do not ask for whites only. It ought to be possible, therefore, for American students of any color to attend any public institution they select without having to be backed up by troops.

It ought to be possible for American consumers of any color to receive equal service in places of public accommodation, such as hotels and restaurants and theaters and retail stores, without being forced to resort to demonstrations in the street, and it ought to be possible for American citizens of any color to register and to vote in a free election without interference or fear of reprisal.

It ought to be possible, in short, for every American to enjoy the privileges of being American without regard to his race or his color. In short, every American ought to have the right to be treated as he would wish to be treated, as one would wish his children to be treated. But this is not the case.

The Negro baby born in America today, regardless of the section of the Nation in which he is born, has about one-half as much chance of completing a high school as a white baby born in the same place on the same day, one-third as much chance of completing college, one-third as much chance of becoming a professional man, twice as much chance of becoming unemployed, about one-seventh as much chance of earning $10,000 a year, a life expectancy which is 7 years shorter, and the prospects of earning only half as much.

This is not a sectional issue. Difficulties over segregation and discrimination exist in every city, in every State of the Union, producing in many cities a rising tide of discontent that threatens the public safety. Nor is this a partisan issue. In a time of domestic crisis men of good will and generosity should be able to unite regardless of party or politics. This is not even a legal or legislative issue alone. It is better to settle these matters in the courts than on the streets, and new laws are needed at every level, but law alone cannot make men see right.

We are confronted primarily with a moral issue. It is as old as the scriptures and is as clear as the American Constitution.

The heart of the question is whether all Americans are to be afforded equal rights and equal opportunities, whether we are going to treat our fellow Americans as we want to be treated. If an American, because his skin is dark, cannot eat lunch in a restaurant open to the public, if he cannot send his children to the best public school available, if he cannot vote for the public officials who represent him, if, in short, he cannot enjoy the full and free life which all of us want, then who among us would be content to have the color of his skin changed and stand in his place? Who among us would then be content with the counsels of patience and delay?

One hundred years of delay have passed since President Lincoln freed the slaves, yet their heirs, their grandsons, are not fully free. They are not yet freed from the bonds of injustice.

They are not yet freed from social and economic oppression. And this Nation, for all its hopes and all its boasts, will not be fully free until all its citizens are free.

We preach freedom around the world, and we mean it, and we cherish our freedom here at home, but are we to say to the world, and much more importantly, to each other that this is a land of the free except for the Negroes; that we have no second-class citizens except Negroes; that we have no class or caste system, no ghettoes, no master race except with respect to Negroes?

Now the time has come for this Nation to fulfill its promise. The events in Birmingham and elsewhere have so increased the cries for equality that no city or State or legislative body can prudently choose to ignore them.

The fires of frustration and discord are burning in every city, North and South, where legal remedies are not at hand. Redress is sought in the streets, in demonstrations, parades, and protests which create tensions and threaten violence and threaten lives.

We face, therefore, a moral crisis as a country and as a people. It cannot be met by repressive police action. It cannot be left to increased demonstrations in the streets. It cannot be quieted by token moves or talk. It is a time to act in the Congress, in your State and local legislative body and, above all, in all of our daily lives.

It is not enough to pin the blame on others, to say this is a problem of one section of the country or another, or deplore the fact that we face. A great change is at hand, and our task, our obligation, is to make that revolution, that change, peaceful and constructive for all.

Those who do nothing are inviting shame as well as violence. Those who act boldly are recognizing right as well as reality.

Next week I shall ask the Congress of the United States to act, to make a commitment it has not fully made in this century to the proposition that race has no place in American life or law. The Federal judiciary has upheld that proposition in a series of forthright cases. The executive branch has adopted that proposition in the conduct of its affairs, including the employment of Federal personnel, the use of Federal facilities, and the sale of federally financed housing.

But there are other necessary measures which only the Congress can provide, and they must be provided at this session. The old code of equity law under which we live commands for every wrong a remedy, but in too many communities, in too many parts of the country, wrongs are inflicted on Negro citizens and there are no remedies at law. Unless the Congress acts, their only remedy is in the street.

I am, therefore, asking the Congress to enact legislation giving all Americans the right to be served in facilities which are open to the public—hotels, restaurants, theaters, retail stores, and similar establishments.

This seems to me to be an elementary right. Its denial is an arbitrary indignity that no American in 1963 should have to endure, but many do.

I have recently met with scores of business leaders urging them to take voluntary action to end this discrimination and I have been encouraged by their response, and in the last 2 weeks over 75 cities have seen progress made in desegregating these kinds of facilities. But many are unwilling to act alone, and for this reason, nationwide legislation is needed if we are to move this problem from the streets to the courts.

I am also asking Congress to authorize the Federal Government to participate more fully in lawsuits designed to end segregation in public education. We have succeeded in persuading many districts to desegregate voluntarily. Dozens have admitted Negroes without violence. Today a Negro is attending a State-supported institution in every one of our 50 States, but the pace is very slow.

Too many Negro children entering segregated grade schools at the time of the Supreme Court's decision 9 years ago will enter segregated high schools this fall, having suffered a loss which can never be restored. The lack of an adequate education denies the Negro a chance to get a decent job.

The orderly implementation of the Supreme Court decision, therefore, cannot be left solely to those who may not have the economic resources to carry the legal action or who may be subject to harassment.

Other features will be also requested, including greater protection for the right to vote. But legislation, I repeat, cannot solve this problem alone. It must be solved in the homes of every American in every community across our country.

In this respect, I want to pay tribute to those citizens North and South who have been working in their communities to make life better for all. They are acting not out of a sense of legal duty but out of a sense of human decency.

Like our soldiers and sailors in all parts of the world they are meeting freedom's challenge on the firing line, and I salute them for their honor and their courage.

My fellow Americans, this is a problem which faces us all—in every city of the North as well as the South. Today there are Negroes unemployed, two or three times as many compared to whites, inadequate in education, moving into the large cities, unable to find work, young people particularly out of work without hope, denied equal rights, denied the opportunity to eat at a restaurant or lunch counter or go to a movie theater, denied the right to a decent education, denied almost today the right to attend a State university even though qualified. It seems to me that these are matters which concern us all, not merely Presidents or Congressmen or Governors, but every citizen of the United States.

This is one country. It has become one country because all of us and all the people who came here had an equal chance to develop their talents.

We cannot say to 10 percent of the population that you can't have that right; that your children can't have the chance to develop whatever talents they have; that the only way that they are going to get their rights is to go into the streets and demonstrate. I think we owe them and we owe ourselves a better country than that.

Therefore, I am asking for your help in making it easier for us to move ahead and to provide the kind of equality of treatment which we would want ourselves; to give a chance for every child to be educated to the limit of his talents.

As I have said before, not every child has an equal talent or an equal ability or an equal motivation, but they should have the equal right to develop their talent and their ability and their motivation, to make something of themselves.

We have a right to expect that the Negro community will be

responsible, will uphold the law, but they have a right to expect that the law will be fair, that the Constitution will be color blind, as Justice Harlan said at the turn of the century.

This is what we are talking about and this is a matter which concerns this country and what it stands for, and in meeting it I ask the support of all our citizens.

Thank you very much.

"THE WASHINGTON MARCH IS A LIVING PETITION"

Official Program for the March on Washington

August 28, 1963

MARCH ON WASHINGTON FOR JOBS AND FREEDOM

AUGUST 28, 1963

LINCOLN MEMORIAL PROGRAM

1. The National Anthem	*Led by* Marian Anderson.
2. Invocation	The Very Rev. Patrick O'Boyle, *Archbishop of Washington.*
3. Opening Remarks	A. Philip Randolph, *Director March on Washington for Jobs and Freedom.*
4. Remarks	Dr. Eugene Carson Blake, *Stated Clerk, United Presbyterian Church of the U.S.A.; Vice Chairman, Commission on Race Relations of the National Council of Churches of Christ in America.*
5. Tribute to Negro Women Fighters for Freedom Daisy Bates Diane Nash Bevel Mrs. Medgar Evers Mrs. Herbert Lee Rosa Parks Gloria Richardson	Mrs. Medgar Evers
6. Remarks	John Lewis, *National Chairman, Student Nonviolent Coordinating Committee.*

7. Remarks	Walter Reuther, *President, United Automobile, Aerospace and Agricultural Implement Workers of America, AFL-CIO; Chairman, Industrial Union Department, AFL-CIO.*
8. Remarks	James Farmer, *National Director, Congress of Racial Equality.*
9. Selection	Eva Jessye *Choir*
10. Prayer	Rabbi Uri Miller, *President Synagogue Council of America.*
11. Remarks	Whitney M. Young, Jr., *Executive Director, National Urban League.*
12. Remarks	Mathew Ahmann, *Executive Director, National Catholic Conference for Interracial Justice.*
13. Remarks	Roy Wilkins, *Executive Secretary, National Association for the Advancement of Colored People.*
14. Selection	Miss Mahalia Jackson
15. Remarks	Rabbi Joachim Prinz, *President American Jewish Congress.*
16. Remarks	The Rev. Dr. Martin Luther King, Jr., *President, Southern Christian Leadership Conference.*
17. The Pledge	A. Philip Randolph
18. Benediction	Dr. Benjamin E. Mays, *President, Morehouse College.*

"WE SHALL OVERCOME"

Statement by the heads of the ten organizations calling for discipline in connection with the Washington March of August 28, 1963:

The Washington March of August 28th is more than just a demonstration.

It was conceived as an outpouring of the deep feeling of millions of white and colored American citizens that the time has come for the government of the United States of America, and particularly for the Congress of that government, to grant and guarantee complete equality in citizenship to the Negro minority of our population.

As such, the Washington March is a living petition—in the flesh—of the scores of thousands of citizens of both races who will be present from all parts of our country.

It will be orderly, but not subservient. It will be proud, but not arrogant. It will be non-violent, but not timid. It will be unified in purposes and behavior, not splintered into groups and individual competitors. It will be outspoken, but not raucous.

It will have the dignity befitting a demonstration in behalf of the human rights of twenty millions of people, with the eye and the judgment of the world focused upon Washington, D.C., on August 28, 1963.

In a neighborhood dispute there may be stunts, rough words and even hot insults; but when a whole people speaks to its government, the dialogue and the action must be on a level reflecting the worth of that people and the responsibility of that government.

We, the undersigned, who see the Washington March as wrapping up the dreams, hopes, ambitions, tears, and prayers of millions who have lived for this day, call upon the members, followers and wellwishers of our several organizations to make the March a disciplined and purposeful demonstration.

We call upon them all, black and white, to resist provocations to disorder and to violence.

We ask them to remember that evil persons are determined to smear this March and to discredit the cause of equality by deliberate efforts to stir disorder.

We call for self-discipline, so that no one in our own ranks, however enthusiastic, shall be the spark for disorder.

We call for resistance to the efforts of those who, while not enemies of the March as such, might seek to use it to advance causes not dedicated primarily to civil rights or to the welfare of our country.

We ask each and every one in attendance in Washington or in spiritual attendance back home to place the Cause above all else.

Do not permit a few irresponsible people to hang a new problem around our necks as we return home. Let's do what we came to do—place the national human rights problem squarely on the doorstep of the national Congress and of the Federal Government.

Let's win at Washington.

SIGNED:

Mathew Ahmann, *Executive Director of the National Catholic Conference for Interracial Justice.*

Reverend Eugene Carson Blake, *Vice-Chairman of the Commission on Race Relations of the National Council of Churches of Christ in America.*

James Farmer, *National Director of the Congress of Racial Equality.*

Reverend Martin Luther King, Jr., *President of the Southern Christian Leadership Conference.*

John Lewis, *Chairman of the Student Nonviolent Coordinating Committee.*

Rabbi Joachim Prinz, *President of the American Jewish Congress.*

A. Philip Randolph, *President of the Negro American Labor Council.*

Walter Reuther, *President of the United Automobile, Aerospace and Agricultural Implement Workers of America, AFL-CIO, and Chairman, Industrial Union Department, AFL-CIO.*

Roy Wilkins, *Executive Secretary of the National Association for the Advancement of Colored People.*

Whitney M. Young, Jr., *Executive Director of the National Urban League.*

In addition, the March has been endorsed by major religious, fraternal, labor and civil rights organizations. A full list, too long to include here, will be published.

WHAT WE DEMAND*

1. Comprehensive and effective *civil rights legislation* from the present Congress—without compromise or filibuster—to guarantee all Americans

access to all public accommodations
decent housing
adequate and integrated education
the right to vote

2. Withholding of Federal funds from all programs in which discrimination exists.

3. *Desegregation of all school districts in 1963.*

4. Enforcement of the *Fourteenth Amendment*—reducing Congressional representation of states where citizens are disfranchised.

5. A new *Executive Order* banning discrimination in all housing supported by federal funds.

6. Authority for the Attorney General to institute *injunctive suits* when any constitutional right is violated.

7. A massive federal program to train and place all unemployed workers—Negro and white—on meaningful and dignified jobs at decent wages.

8. A national *minimum wage* act that will give all Americans a decent standard of living. (Government surveys show that anything less than $2.00 an hour fails to do this.)

9. A broadened *Fair Labor Standards Act* to include all areas of employment which are presently excluded.

10. A federal *Fair Employment Practices Act* barring discrimination by federal, state, and municipal governments, and by employers, contractors, employment agencies, and trade unions.

*Support of the March does not necessarily indicate endorsement of every demand listed. Some organizations have not had an opportunity to take an official position on all of the demands advocated here.

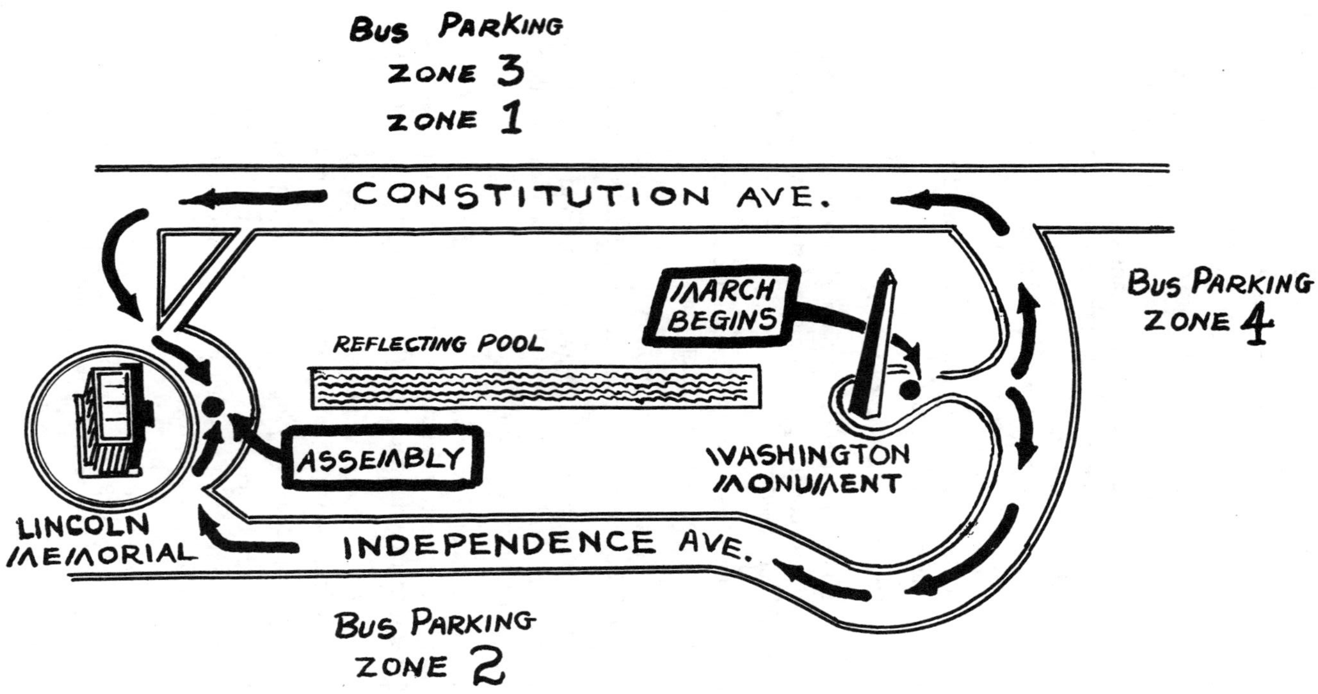

BUS PARKING
ZONE 3
ZONE 1
CONSTITUTION AVE.
BUS PARKING
ZONE 4
MARCH BEGINS
REFLECTING POOL
ASSEMBLY
WASHINGTON MONUMENT
LINCOLN MEMORIAL
INDEPENDENCE AVE.
BUS PARKING
ZONE 2

“THIS GREAT REVOLUTION THAT IS SWEEPING THIS NATION”

JOHN LEWIS

Speech at the March on Washington

August 28, 1963

ORIGINAL TEXT

WE MARCH today for jobs and freedom, but we have nothing to be proud of. For hundreds and thousands of our brothers are not here. They have no money for their transportation, for they are receiving starvation wages . . . or no wages, at all.

In good conscience, we cannot support, wholeheartedly, the administration's civil rights bill, for it is too little, and too late. There's not one thing in the bill that will protect our people from police brutality.

This bill will not protect young children and old women from police dogs and fire hoses, for engaging in peaceful demonstrations. This bill will not protect the citizens in Danville, Virginia, who must live in constant fear in a police state. This bill will not protect the hundreds of people who have been arrested on trumped-up charges. What about the three young men in Americus, Georgia, who face the death penalty for engaging in peaceful protest?

The voting section of this bill will not help thousands of black citizens who want to vote. It will not help the citizens of Mississippi, of Alabama, and Georgia, who are qualified to vote, but lack a 6th Grade education. “One man, one vote,” is the African cry. It is ours, too. (It must be ours.)

People have been forced to leave their homes because they dared to exercise their right to register to vote. What is in the bill that will protect the homeless and starving people of this nation? What is there in this bill to insure the equality of a maid who earns $5 a week in the home of a family whose income is $100,000 a year?

For the first time in 100 years this nation is being awakened to the fact that segregation is evil and that it must be destroyed in all forms. Your presence today proves that you have been aroused to the point of action.

We are now involved in a serious revolution. This nation is still a place of cheap political leaders who build their careers on immoral compromises and ally themselves with open forms of political, economic and social exploitation. What political leader here can stand up and say "My party is the party of principles"? The party of Kennedy is also the party of Eastland. The party of Javits is also the party of Goldwater. Where is *our* party?

In some parts of the South we work in the fields from sun-up to sun-down for $12 a week. In Albany, Georgia, nine of our leaders have been indicted not by Dixiecrats but by the Federal Government for peaceful protest. But what did the Federal Government do when Albany's Deputy Sheriff beat Attorney C.B. King and left him half-dead? What did the Federal Government do when local police officials kicked and assaulted the pregnant wife of Slater King, and she lost her baby?

It seems to me that the Albany indictment is part of a conspiracy on the part of the Federal Government and local politicians in the interest of expediency.

I want to know, which side is the Federal Government on?

The revolution is at hand, and we must free ourselves of the chains of political and economic slavery. The non-violent revolution is saying, "We will not wait for the courts to act, for we have been waiting for hundreds of years. We will not wait for the President, the Justice Department, nor Congress, but we will take matters into our own hands and create a source of power, outside of any national structure that could and would assure us a victory." To those who have said, "Be Patient and Wait," we must say that, "Patience is a dirty and nasty word." We cannot be patient, we do not want to be free gradually, we want our freedom, and we want it now. We cannot depend on any political party, for both the Democrats and the Republicans have betrayed the basic principles of the Declaration of Independence.

We all recognize the fact that if any radical social, political and economic changes are to take place in our society, the people, the masses, must bring them about. In the struggle we must seek more than more civil rights; we must work for the community of love, peace and true brotherhood. Our minds, souls, and hearts cannot rest until freedom and justice exist for *all the people.*

The revolution is a serious one. Mr. Kennedy is trying to take the revolution out of the street and put it into the courts. Listen, Mr. Kennedy, listen Mr. Congressman, listen fellow citizens, the black masses are on the march for jobs and freedom, and we must say to the politicians that there won't be a "cooling-off" period.

All of us must get in the revolution. Get in and stay in the streets of every city, every village and every hamlet of this nation, until true Freedom comes, until the revolution is complete. In the Delta of Mississippi, in southwest Georgia, in Alabama, Harlem, Chicago, Detroit, Philadelphia and all over this nation. The black masses are on the march!

We won't stop now. All of the forces of Eastland, Barnett, Wallace and Thurmond won't stop this revolution. The time will come when we will not confine our marching to Washington. We will march through the South through the Heart of Dixie, the way Sherman did. We shall pursue our own "scorched earth" policy and burn Jim Crow to the ground—non-violently. We shall fragment the South into a thousand pieces and put them back together in the image of democracy. We will make the action of the past few months look petty. And I say to you, WAKE UP AMERICA!!!

SPEECH AS DELIVERED

We march today for jobs and freedom, but we have nothing to be proud of. For hundreds and thousands of our brothers are not here. For they are receiving starvation wages, or no wages at all. While we stand here, there are sharecroppers in the Delta of Mississippi who are out in the fields working for less than three dollars a day, twelve hours a day. While we stand here there are students in jail on trumped-up charges. Our brother James Farmer, along with many others, is also in jail. We come here today with a great sense of misgiving.

It is true that we support the administration's civil rights bill. We support it with great reservations, however. Unless Title III is put in this bill, there is nothing to protect the young children and old women who must face police dogs and fire hoses in the South while they engage in peaceful demonstrations. In its present form, this bill will not protect the citizens of Danville, Virginia, who must live in constant fear of a police state. It will not protect the hundreds and thousands of people that have been arrested on trumped charges. What about the three young men, SNCC field secretaries in Americus, Georgia, who face the death penalty for engaging in peaceful protest?

As it stands now, the voting section of this bill will not help the thousands of black people who want to vote. It will not help the citizens of Mississippi, of Alabama and Georgia, who are qualified to vote, but lack a sixth-grade education. "One man, one vote" is the African cry. It is ours too. It must be ours!

We must have legislation that will protect the Mississippi sharecropper who is put off of his farm because he dares to register to vote. We need a bill that will provide for the homeless and starving people of this nation. We need a bill that will ensure the equality of a maid who earns five dollars a week in a home of a family whose total income is $100,000 a year. We must have a good FEPC bill.

My friends, let us not forget that we are involved in a serious social revolution. By and large, American politics is dominated by politicians who build their careers on immoral compromises and ally themselves with open forms of political, economic, and social exploitation. There are exceptions, of course. We salute those. But what political leader can stand up and say, "My party is the party of principles"? For the party of Kennedy is also the party of Eastland. The party of Javits is also the party of Goldwater. Where is our party? Where is the political party that will make it unnecessary to march on Washington?

Where is the political party that will make it unnecessary to march in the streets of Birmingham? Where is the political party that will protect the citizens of Albany, Georgia? Do you know that in Albany, Georgia, nine of our leaders have been indicted, not by the Dixiecrats, but by the federal government for peaceful protest? But what did the federal government do when Albany's deputy sheriff beat Attorney C.B. King and left him half-dead? What did the federal government do when local police officials kicked and assaulted the pregnant wife of Slater King, and she lost her baby?

To those who have said, "Be patient and wait," we have long said that we cannot be patient. We do not want our freedom gradually, but we want to be free now! We are tired. We are tired of being beaten by policemen. We are tired of seeing our people locked up in jail over and over again. And then you holler, "Be patient." How long can we be patient? We want our freedom and we want it now. We do not want to go to jail. But we will go to jail if this is the price we must pay for love, brotherhood, and true peace.

I appeal to all of you to get into this great revolution that is sweeping this nation. Get in and stay in the streets of every city, every village and hamlet of this nation until true freedom comes, until the revolution of 1776 is complete. We must get in this revolution and complete the revolution. For in the Delta in Mississippi, in southwest Georgia, in the Black Belt of Alabama, in Harlem, in Chicago, Detroit, Philadelphia, and all over this nation, the black masses are on the march for jobs and freedom.

They're talking about slow down and stop. We will not stop. All of the forces of Eastland, Barnett, Wallace, and Thurmond will not stop this revolution. If we do not get meaningful legislation out of this Congress, the time will come when we will not confine our marching to Washington. We will march through the South; through the streets of Jackson, through the streets of Danville, through the streets of Cambridge, through the streets of Birmingham. But we will march with the spirit of love and with the spirit of dignity that we have shown here today. By the force of our demands, our determination, and our numbers, we shall splinter the segregated South into a thousand pieces and put them together in the image of God and democracy. We must say: "Wake up America! Wake up!" For we cannot stop, and we will not and cannot be patient.

1964–1976

DATA FROM THE 1960 CENSUS

SUE CRONK

Labor Report Shows: Negro Women Are Improving Their Status

Washington Post, March 28, 1964

Labor Report Shows:

NEGRO WOMEN ARE IMPROVING THEIR STATUS

NEGRO WOMEN WORKERS are steadily improving their status, the Labor Department Women's Bureau reported Thursday.

Between 1950 and 1960, the number of Negro women employed in such fields as banking, postal service, public administration and some branches of manufacturing more than doubled.

In the same decade, the percentage of Negro women working as domestics dropped from 41 to 36.

However, the Bureau noted, "a significant gap still exists between the incomes of Negro and white women workers."

Only 1 in 10 Negro women earned $3000 or more in 1959, compared to 1 in 4 white women. And the median earnings of nonwhite (Negro, oriental, American Indian and Eskimo) women that year was $1219. While no statistics are available on the 1959 median income of white women alone, that of white and nonwhite combined was $2257.

A detailed study of the gains made by Negro women, as recorded in the 1960 census, will be released today in a booklet, "Negro Women Workers in 1960." It is available for 30 cents from the Superintendent of Documents, U.S. Government Printing Office, Washington, D.C. 20402.

Labor Secretary W. Willard Wirtz said that the major trend in the shift of employment patterns for Negro women workers "is away from the traditional home service types of work" and that it "reflects recent gains in employment and educational status."

The gains have been achieved, the booklet says, "partly because of concerted efforts of (the Negro women's) own and partly because of economic growth, better educational facilities, and various political and social developments."

For example, the median educational level of nonwhite women 25 years and older rose from 7.2 years in 1950 to 8.5 years in 1960.

Another important factor in the Negro woman worker's advancement has been her migration out of rural areas into industrial centers and out of the South into Northern and Western states. Of all nonwhite women of working age (14 years and older), three-fourths lived in cities in 1960.

Nevertheless, higher unemployment "consistently prevailed" among nonwhite women than among white women at the time of the 1960 census. According to Women's Bureau, almost 250,000 nonwhite women—8.5 per cent of all nonwhite women in the labor force—were looking for jobs that year. By comparison, only 4.9 per cent of white women were unemployed at that time.

"In every age group," the Bureau continued, "higher proportions of nonwhite women than white women were seeking work."

Fields in which Negro women have made greatest progress generally have been those which traditionally have hired significant numbers of women, such as the teaching and nursing professions. Yet, occupations which they have entered recently in large numbers include many clerical jobs—secretary, stenographer, typist, cashier, telephone operator and bookkeeper.

The main distinction in 1960, the Women's Bureau says, is that "the majority of Negro women were service workers and the majority of white women were white collar workers."

Although New York State has more nonwhite women workers (more than 282,000) than any other state, the District of Columbia has the largest percentage (53 per cent).

"I SEE AN AMERICAN NIGHTMARE"

MALCOLM X

The Ballot or the Bullet

April 3, 1964

MR. MODERATOR, Brother Lomax, brothers and sisters, friends and enemies: I just can't believe everyone in here is a friend and I don't want to leave anybody out. The question tonight, as I understand it, is "The Negro Revolt, and Where Do We Go From Here?" or "What Next?" In my little humble way of understanding it, it points toward either the ballot or the bullet.

Before we try and explain what is meant by the ballot or the bullet, I would like to clarify something concerning myself. I'm still a Muslim, my religion is still Islam. That's my personal belief. Just as Adam Clayton Powell is a Christian minister who heads the Abyssinian Baptist Church in New York, but at the same time takes part in the political struggles to try and bring about rights to the black people in this country; and Dr. Martin Luther King is a Christian minister down in Atlanta, Georgia, who heads another organization fighting for the civil rights of black people in this country; and Rev. Galamison, I guess you've heard of him, is another Christian minister in New York who has been deeply involved in the school boycotts to eliminate segregated education; well, I myself am a minister, not a Christian minister, but a Muslim minister; and I believe in action on all fronts by whatever means necessary.

Although I'm still a Muslim, I'm not here tonight to discuss my religion. I'm not here to try and change your religion. I'm not here to argue or discuss anything that we differ about, because it's time for us to submerge our differences and realize that it is best for us to first see that we have the same problem, a common problem—a problem that will make you catch hell whether you're a Baptist, or a Methodist, or a Muslim, or a nationalist. Whether you're educated or illiterate, whether you live on the boulevard or in the alley, you're going to catch hell just like I am. We're all in the same boat and we all are going to catch the same hell from the same man. He just happens to be a white man. All of us have suffered here, in this country, political oppression at the hands of the white man, economic exploitation at the hands of the white man, and social degradation at the hands of the white man.

Now in speaking like this, it doesn't mean that we're anti-white, but it does mean we're anti-exploitation, we're anti-degradation, we're anti-oppression. And if the white man doesn't want us to be anti-him, let him stop oppressing and exploiting and degrading us. Whether we are Christians or Muslims or nationalists or agnostics or atheists, we must first learn to forget our differences. If we have differences, let us differ in the closet; when we come out in front, let us not have anything to argue about until we get finished arguing with the man. If the late President Kennedy could get together with Khrushchev and exchange some wheat, we certainly have more in common with each other than Kennedy and Khrushchev had with each other.

If we don't do something real soon, I think you'll have to agree that we're going to be forced either to use the ballot or the bullet. It's one or the other in 1964. It isn't that time is running out—time has run out! 1964 threatens to be the most explosive year America has ever witnessed. The most explosive year. Why? It's also a political year. It's the year when all of the white politicians will be back in the so-called Negro community jiving you and me for some votes. The year when all of the white political crooks will be right back in your and my community with their false promises, building up our hopes for a letdown, with their trickery and their treachery, with their false promises which they don't intend to keep. As they nourish these dissatisfactions, it can only lead to one thing, an explosion; and now we have the type of black man on the scene in America today—I'm sorry, Brother Lomax—who just doesn't intend to turn the other cheek any longer.

Don't let anybody tell you anything about the odds are against you. If they draft you, they send you to Korea and make you face 800 million Chinese. If you can be brave over there, you can be brave right here. These odds aren't as great as those odds. And if you fight here, you will at least know what you're fighting for.

I'm not a politician, not even a student of politics; in fact, I'm not a student of much of anything. I'm not a Democrat, I'm not a Republican, and I don't even consider myself an American. If you and I were Americans, there'd be no problem. Those Hunkies that just got off the boat, they're already Americans; Polacks are already Americans; the Italian refugees are already Americans. Everything that came out of Europe, every blue-eyed thing, is already an American. And as long as you and I have been over here, we aren't Americans yet.

Well, I am one who doesn't believe in deluding myself. I'm not going to sit at your table and watch you eat, with nothing on my plate, and call myself a diner. Sitting at the table doesn't make you a diner, unless you eat some of what's on that plate. Being here in America doesn't make you an American. Being born here in America doesn't make you an American. Why, if birth made you American, you wouldn't need any legislation, you wouldn't need any amendments to the Constitution, you wouldn't be faced with civil-rights filibustering in Washington, D.C., right now. They don't have to pass civil-rights legislation to make a Polack an American.

No, I'm not an American. I'm one of the 22 million black people who are the victims of Americanism. One of the 22 million black people who are the victims of democracy, nothing but disguised hypocrisy. So, I'm not standing here speaking to you as an American, or a patriot, or a flag-saluter, or a flag-waver—no, not I. I'm speaking as a victim of this American system. And I see America through the eyes of the victim. I don't see any American dream; I see an American nightmare.

These 22 million victims are waking up. Their eyes are coming open. They're beginning to see what they used to only look at. They're becoming politically mature. They are realizing that there are new political trends from coast to coast. As they see these new political trends, it's possible for them to see that every time there's an election the races are so close that they have to have a recount. They had to recount in Massachusetts to see who was going to be governor, it was so close. It was the same way in Rhode Island, in Minnesota, and in many other parts of the country. And the same with Kennedy and Nixon when they ran for president. It was so close they had to count all over again. Well, what does this mean? It means that when white people are evenly divided, and black people have a bloc of votes of their own, it is left up to them to determine who's going to sit in the White House and who's going to be in the dog house.

It was the black man's vote that put the present administration in Washington, D.C. Your vote, your dumb vote, your ignorant vote, your wasted vote put in an administration in Washington, D.C., that has seen fit to pass every kind of legislation imaginable, saving you until last, then filibustering on top of that. And your and my leaders have the audacity to run around clapping their hands and talk about how much progress we're making. And what a good president we have. If he wasn't good in Texas, he sure can't be good in Washington, D.C. Because Texas is a lynch state. It is in the same breath as Mississippi, no different; only they lynch you in Texas with a Texas accent and lynch you in Mississippi with a Mississippi accent. And these Negro leaders have the audacity to go and have some coffee in the White House with a Texan, a Southern cracker—that's all he is—and then come out and tell you and me that he's going to be better for us because, since he's from the South, he knows how to deal with the Southerners. What kind of logic is that? Let Eastland be president, he's from the South too. He should be better able to deal with them than Johnson.

In this present administration they have in the House of Representatives 257 Democrats to only 177 Republicans. They control two-thirds of the House vote. Why can't they pass something that will help you and me? In the Senate, there are 67 senators who are of the Democratic Party. Only 33 of them are Republicans. Why, the Democrats have got the government sewed up, and you're the one who sewed it up for them. And what have they given you for it? Four years in office, and just now getting around to some civil-rights legislation. Just now, after everything else is gone, out of the way, they're going to sit down now and play with you all summer long—the same old giant con game that they call filibuster. All those are in cahoots together. Don't you ever think they're not in cahoots together, for the man that is heading the civil-rights filibuster is a man from Georgia named Richard Russell. When Johnson became president, the first man he asked for when he got back to Washington, D.C., was "Dicky"—that's how tight they are. That's his boy, that's his pal, that's his buddy. But they're playing that old con game. One of them makes believe he's for you, and he's got it fixed where the other one is so tight against you, he never has to keep his promise.

So it's time in 1964 to wake up. And when you see them coming up with that kind of conspiracy, let them know your eyes are open. And let them know you got something else that's wide open too. It's got to be the ballot or the bullet. The ballot or the bullet. If you're afraid to use an expression like that, you should get on out of the country, you should get back in the cotton patch, you should get back in the alley. They get all the Negro vote, and after they get it, the Negro gets nothing in return. All they did when they got to Washington was give a few big Negroes big jobs. Those big Negroes didn't need big jobs, they already had jobs. That's camouflage, that's trickery, that's treachery, window-dressing. I'm not trying to knock out the Democrats for the Republicans, we'll get to them in a minute. But it is true—you put the Democrats first and the Democrats put you last.

Look at it the way it is. What alibis do they use, since they control Congress and the Senate? What alibi do they use when you and I ask, "Well, when are you going to keep your promise?" They blame the Dixiecrats. What is a Dixiecrat? A Democrat. A Dixiecrat is nothing but a Democrat in disguise. The titular head of the Democrats is also the head of the Dixiecrats, because the Dixiecrats are a part of the Democratic Party. The Democrats have never kicked the Dixiecrats out of the party. The Dixiecrats bolted themselves once, but the Democrats didn't put them out. Imagine, these lowdown Southern segregationists put the Northern Democrats down. But the Northern Democrats have never put the Dixiecrats down. No, look at that thing the way it is. They have got a con game going on, a political con game, and you and I are in the middle. It's time for you and me to wake up and start looking at it like it is, and trying to understand it like it is; and then we can deal with it like it is.

The Dixiecrats in Washington, D.C., control the key committees that run the government. The only reason the Dixiecrats control these committees is because they have seniority.

The only reason they have seniority is because they come from states where Negroes can't vote. This is not even a government that's based on democracy. It is not a government that is made up of representatives of the people. Half of the people in the South can't even vote. Eastland is not even supposed to be in Washington. Half of the senators and congressmen who occupy these key positions in Washington, D.C., are there illegally, are there unconstitutionally.

I was in Washington, D.C., a week ago Thursday, when they were debating whether or not they should let the bill come onto the floor. And in the back of the room where the Senate meets, there's a huge map of the United States, and on that map it shows the location of Negroes throughout the country. And it shows that the Southern section of the country, the states that are most heavily concentrated with Negroes, are the ones that have senators and congressmen standing up filibustering and doing all other kinds of trickery to keep the Negro from being able to vote. This is pitiful. But it's not pitiful for us any longer; it's actually pitiful for the white man, because soon now, as the Negro awakens a little more and sees the vise that he's in, sees the bag that he's in, sees the real game that he's in, then the Negro's going to develop a new tactic.

These senators and congressmen actually violate the constitutional amendments that guarantee the people of that particular state or county the right to vote. And the Constitution itself has within it the machinery to expel any representative from a state where the voting rights of the people are violated. You don't even need new legislation. Any person in Congress right now, who is there from a state or a district where the voting rights of the people are violated, that particular person should be expelled from Congress. And when you expel him, you've removed one of the obstacles in the path of any real meaningful legislation in this country. In fact, when you expel them, you don't need new legislation, because they will be replaced by black representatives from counties and districts where the black man is in the majority, not in the minority.

If the black man in these Southern states had his full voting rights, the key Dixiecrats in Washington, D.C., which means the key Democrats in Washington, D.C., would lose their seats. The Democratic Party itself would lose its power. It would cease to be powerful as a party. When you see the amount of power that would be lost by the Democratic Party if it were to lose the Dixiecrat wing, or branch, or element, you can see where it's against the interests of the Democrats to give voting rights to Negroes in states where the Democrats have been in complete power and authority, ever since the Civil War. You just can't belong to that party without analyzing it.

I say again, I'm not anti-Democrat, I'm not anti-Republican, I'm not anti-anything. I'm just questioning their sincerity, and some of the strategy that they've been using on our people by promising them promises that they don't intend to keep. When you keep the Democrats in power, you're keeping the Dixiecrats in power. I doubt that my good Brother Lomax will deny that. A vote for a Democrat is a vote for a Dixiecrat. That's why, in 1964, it's time now for you and me to become more politically mature and realize what the ballot is for; what we're supposed to get when we cast a ballot; and that if we don't cast a ballot, it's going to end up in a situation where we're going to have to cast a bullet. It's either a ballot or a bullet.

In the North, they do it a different way. They have a system that's known as gerrymandering, whatever that means. It means when Negroes become too heavily concentrated in a certain area, and begin to gain too much political power, the white man comes along and changes the district lines. You may say, "Why do you keep saying white man?" Because it's the white man who does it. I haven't ever seen any Negro changing any lines. They don't let him get near the line. It's the white man who does this. And usually, it's the white man who grins at you the most, and pats you on the back, and is supposed to be your friend. He may be friendly, but he's not your friend.

So, what I'm trying to impress upon you, in essence, is this: You and I in America are faced not with a segregationist conspiracy, we're faced with a government conspiracy. Everyone who's filibustering is a senator—that's the government. Everyone who's finagling in Washington, D.C., is a congressman—that's the government. You don't have anybody putting blocks in your path but people who are a part of the government. The same government that you go abroad to fight for and die for is the government that is in a conspiracy to deprive you of your voting rights, deprive you of your economic opportunities, deprive you of decent housing, deprive you of decent education. You don't need to go to the employer alone, it is the government itself, the government of America, that is responsible for the oppression and exploitation and degradation of black people in this country. And you should drop it in their lap. This government has failed the Negro. This so-called democracy has failed the Negro. And all these white liberals have definitely failed the Negro.

So, where do we go from here? First, we need some friends. We need some new allies. The entire civil-rights struggle needs a new interpretation, a broader interpretation. We need to look at this civil-rights thing from another angle—from the inside as well as from the outside. To those of us whose philosophy is black nationalism, the only way you can get involved in the civil-rights struggle is give it a new interpretation. That old interpretation excluded us. It kept us out. So, we're giving a new interpretation to the civil-rights struggle, an interpretation that will enable us to come into it, take part in it. And these handkerchief-heads who have been dillydallying and pussyfooting and compromising—we don't intend to let them pussyfoot and dillydally and compromise any longer.

How can you thank a man for giving you what's already yours? How then can you thank him for giving you only part of what's already yours? You haven't even made progress, if what's being given to you, you should have had already. That's not progress. And I love my Brother Lomax, the way he pointed out we're right back where we were in 1954. We're not even as far up as we were in 1954. We're behind where we were in 1954. There's more segregation now than there was in 1954. There's more racial animosity, more racial hatred, more racial violence today in 1964, than there was in 1954. Where is the progress?

And now you're facing a situation where the young Negro's coming up. They don't want to hear that "turn-the-other-cheek" stuff, no. In Jacksonville, those were teenagers, they were throwing Molotov cocktails. Negroes have never done that before. But it shows you there's a new deal coming in. There's new thinking coming in. There's new strategy coming in. It'll be Molotov cocktails this month, hand grenades next month, and something else next month. It'll be ballots, or it'll be bullets. It'll be liberty, or it will be death. The only difference about this kind of death—it'll be reciprocal. You know what is meant by "reciprocal"? That's one of Brother Lomax's words, I stole it from him. I don't usually deal with those big words because I don't usually deal with big people. I deal with small people. I find you can get a whole lot of small people and whip hell out of a whole lot of big people. They haven't got anything to lose, and they've got everything to gain. And they'll let you know in a minute: "It takes two to tango; when I go, you go."

The black nationalists, those whose philosophy is black nationalism, in bringing about this new interpretation of the entire meaning of civil rights, look upon it as meaning, as Brother Lomax has pointed out, equality of opportunity. Well, we're justified in seeking civil rights, if it means equality of opportunity, because all we're doing there is trying to collect for our investment. Our mothers and fathers invested sweat and blood. Three hundred and ten years we worked in this country without a dime in return—I mean without a *dime* in return. You let the white man walk around here talking about how rich this country is, but you never stop to think how it got rich so quick. It got rich because you made it rich.

You take the people who are in this audience right now. They're poor, we're all poor as individuals. Our weekly salary individually amounts to hardly anything. But if you take the salary of everyone in here collectively it'll fill up a whole lot of baskets. It's a lot of wealth. If you can collect the wages of just these people right here for a year, you'll be rich—richer than rich. When you look at it like that, think how rich Uncle Sam had to become, not with this handful, but millions of black people. Your and my mother and father, who didn't work an eight-hour shift, but worked from "can't see" in the morning until "can't see" at night, and worked for nothing, making the white man rich, making Uncle Sam rich.

This is our investment. This is our contribution—our blood. Not only did we give of our free labor, we gave of our blood. Every time he had a call to arms, we were the first ones in uniform. We died on every battlefield the white man had. We have made a greater sacrifice than anybody who's standing up in America today. We have made a greater contribution and have collected less. Civil rights, for those of us whose philosophy is black nationalism, means: "Give it to us now. Don't wait for next year. Give it to us yesterday, and that's not fast enough."

I might stop right here to point out one thing. Whenever you're going after something that belongs to you, anyone who's depriving you of the right to have it is a criminal. Understand that. Whenever you are going after something that is yours, you are within your legal rights to lay claim to it. And anyone who puts forth any effort to deprive you of that which is yours, is breaking the law, is a criminal. And this was pointed out by the Supreme Court decision. It outlawed segregation. Which means segregation is against the law. Which means a segregationist is breaking the law. A segregationist is a criminal. You can't label him as anything other than that. And when you demonstrate against segregation, the law is on your side. The Supreme Court is on your side.

Now, who is it that opposes you in carrying out the law? The police department itself. With police dogs and clubs. Whenever you demonstrate against segregation, whether it is segregated education, segregated housing, or anything else, the law is on your side, and anyone who stands in the way is not the law any longer. They are breaking the law, they are not representatives of the law. Any time you demonstrate against segregation and a man has the audacity to put a police dog on you, kill that dog, kill him, I'm telling you, kill that dog. I say it, if they put me in jail tomorrow, kill—that—dog. Then you'll put a stop to it. Now, if these white people in here don't want to see that kind of action, get down and tell the mayor to tell the police department to pull the dogs in. That's all you have to do. If you don't do it, someone else will.

If you don't take this kind of stand, your little children will grow up and look at you and think "shame." If you don't take an uncompromising stand—I don't mean go out and get violent; but at the same time you should never be nonviolent unless you run into some nonviolence. I'm nonviolent with those who are nonviolent with me. But when you drop that violence on me, then you've made me go insane, and I'm not responsible for what I do. And that's the way every Negro should get. Any time you know you're within the law, within your legal rights, within your moral rights, in accord with justice, then die for what you believe in. But don't die alone. Let your dying be reciprocal. This is what is meant by equality. What's good for the goose is good for the gander.

When we begin to get in this area, we need new friends, we need new allies. We need to expand the civil-rights struggle to a higher level—to the level of human rights. Whenever you are in a civil-rights struggle, whether you know it or not, you are confining yourself to the jurisdiction of Uncle Sam. No one from the outside world can speak out in your behalf as long as your struggle is a civil-rights struggle. Civil rights comes within the domestic affairs of this country. All of our African brothers and our Asian brothers and our Latin-American brothers cannot open their mouths and interfere in the domestic affairs of the United States. And as long as it's civil rights, this comes under the jurisdiction of Uncle Sam.

But the United Nations has what's known as the charter of human rights, it has a committee that deals in human rights. You may wonder why all of the atrocities that have been committed in Africa and in Hungary and in Asia and in Latin America are brought before the UN, and the Negro problem is never brought before the UN. This is part of the conspiracy. This old, tricky, blue-eyed liberal who is supposed to be your and my friend, supposed to be in our corner, supposed to be subsidizing our struggle, and supposed to be acting in the capacity of an adviser, never tells you anything about human rights. They keep you wrapped up in civil rights. And you spend so much time barking up the civil-rights tree, you don't even know there's a human-rights tree on the same floor.

When you expand the civil-rights struggle to the level of human rights, you can then take the case of the black man in this country before the nations in the UN. You can take it before the General Assembly. You can take Uncle Sam before a world court. But the only level you can do it on is the level of human rights. Civil rights keeps you under his restrictions, under his jurisdiction. Civil rights keeps you in his pocket. Civil rights means you're asking Uncle Sam to treat you right. Human rights are something you were born with. Human rights are your God-given rights. Human rights are the rights that are recognized by all nations of this earth. And any time any one violates your human rights, you can take them to the world court. Uncle Sam's hands are dripping with blood, dripping with the blood of the black man in this country. He's the earth's number-one hypocrite. He has the audacity—yes, he has—imagine him posing as the leader of the free world. The free world!—and you over here singing "We Shall Overcome." Expand the civil-rights struggle to the level of human rights, take it into the United Nations, where our African brothers can throw their weight on our side, where our Asian brothers can throw their weight on our side, where our Latin-American brothers can throw their weight on our side, and where 800 million Chinamen are sitting there waiting to throw their weight on our side.

Let the world know how bloody his hands are. Let the world know the hypocrisy that's practiced over here. Let it be the ballot or the bullet. Let him know that it must be the ballot or the bullet.

When you take your case to Washington, D.C., you're taking it to the criminal who's responsible; it's like running from the wolf to the fox. They're all in cahoots together. They all work political chicanery and make you look like a chump before the eyes of the world. Here you are walking around in America, getting ready to be drafted and sent abroad, like a tin soldier, and when you get over there, people ask you what are you fighting for, and you have to stick your tongue in your cheek. No, take Uncle Sam to court, take him before the world.

By ballot I only mean freedom. Don't you know—I disagree with Lomax on this issue—that the ballot is more important than the dollar? Can I prove it? Yes. Look in the UN. There are poor nations in the UN; yet those poor nations can get together with their voting power and keep the rich nations from making a move. They have one nation—one vote, everyone has an equal vote. And when those brothers from Asia, and Africa and the darker parts of this earth get together, their voting power is sufficient to hold Sam in check. Or Russia in check. Or some other section of the earth in check. So, the ballot is most important.

Right now, in this country, if you and I, 22 million African-Americans—that's what we are—Africans who are in America. You're nothing but Africans. Nothing but Africans. In fact, you'd get farther calling yourself African instead of Negro. Africans don't catch hell. You're the only one catching hell. They don't have to pass civil-rights bills for Africans. An African can go anywhere he wants right now. All you've got to do is tie your head up. That's right, go anywhere you want. Just stop being a Negro. Change your name to Hoogagagooba. That'll show you how silly the white man is. You're dealing with a silly man. A friend of mine who's very dark put a turban on his head and went into a restaurant in Atlanta before they called themselves desegregated. He went into a white restaurant, he sat down, they served him, and he said, "What would happen if a Negro came in here?" And there he's sitting, black as night, but because he had his head wrapped up the waitress looked back at him and says, "Why, there wouldn't no nigger dare come in here."

So, you're dealing with a man whose bias and prejudice are making him lose his mind, his intelligence, every day. He's frightened. He looks around and sees what's taking place on this earth, and he sees that the pendulum of time is swinging in your direction. The dark people are waking up. They're losing their fear of the white man. No place where he's fighting right now is he winning. Everywhere he's fighting, he's fighting someone your and my complexion. And they're beating him. He can't win any more. He's won his last battle. He failed to win the Korean War. He couldn't win it. He had to sign a truce. That's a loss. Any time Uncle Sam, with all his machinery for warfare, is held to a draw by some rice-eaters, he's lost the battle. He had to sign a truce. America's not supposed to sign a truce. She's supposed to be bad. But she's not bad any more. She's bad as long as she can use her hydrogen bomb, but she can't use hers for fear Russia might use hers. Russia can't use hers, for fear that Sam might use his. So, both of them are weaponless. They can't use the weapon because each's weapon nullifies the other's. So the only place where action can take place is on the ground. And the white man can't win another war fighting on the ground. Those days are over. The black man knows it, the brown man knows it, the red man knows it, and the yellow man knows it. So they engage him in guerrilla warfare. That's not his style. You've got to have heart to be a guerrilla warrior, and he hasn't got any heart. I'm telling you now.

I just want to give you a little briefing on guerrilla warfare because, before you know it, before you know it— It takes heart to be a guerrilla warrior because you're on your own. In conventional warfare you have tanks and a whole lot of other people with you to back you up, planes over your head and all that kind of stuff. But a guerrilla is on his own. All you have is a rifle, some sneakers and a bowl of rice, and that's all you need —and a lot of heart. The Japanese on some of those islands in the Pacific, when the American soldiers landed, one Japanese sometimes could hold the whole army off. He'd just wait until the sun went down, and when the sun went down they were all equal. He would take his little blade and slip from bush to bush, and from American to American. The white soldiers couldn't cope with that. Whenever you see a white soldier that fought in the Pacific, he has the shakes, he has a nervous condition, because they scared him to death.

The same thing happened to the French up in French Indochina. People who just a few years previously were rice farmers got together and ran the heavily-mechanized French army out of Indochina. You don't need it—modern warfare today won't work. This is the day of the guerrilla. They did the same thing in Algeria. Algerians, who were nothing but Bedouins, took a rifle and sneaked off to the hills, and de Gaulle and all of his highfalutin' war machinery couldn't defeat those guerrillas. Nowhere on this earth does the white man win in a guerrilla warfare. It's not his speed. Just as guerrilla warfare is prevailing in Asia and in parts of Africa and in parts of Latin America, you've got to be mighty naive, or you've got to play the black man cheap, if you don't think someday he's going to wake up and find that it's got to be the ballot or the bullet.

I would like to say, in closing, a few things concerning the Muslim Mosque, Inc., which we established recently in New York City. It's true we're Muslims and our religion is Islam, but we don't mix our religion with our politics and our economics and our social and civil activities—not any more. We keep our religion in our mosque. After our religious services are over, then as Muslims we become involved in political action, economic action and social and civic action. We become involved with anybody, anywhere, any time and in any manner that's designed to eliminate the evils, the political, economic and social evils that are afflicting the people of our community.

The political philosophy of black nationalism means that the black man should control the politics and the politicians in his own community; no more. The black man in the black community has to be re-educated into the science of politics so he will know what politics is supposed to bring him in return. Don't be throwing out any ballots. A ballot is like a bullet. You don't throw your ballots until you see a target, and if that target is not within your reach, keep your ballot in your pocket. The political philosophy of black nationalism is being taught in the Christian church. It's being taught in the NAACP. It's being taught in CORE meetings. It's being taught in SNCC meetings. It's being taught in Muslim meetings. It's being taught where nothing but atheists and agnostics come together. It's being taught everywhere. Black people are fed up with the dillydallying, pussyfooting, compromising approach that we've been using toward getting our freedom. We want freedom *now*, but we're not going to get it saying "We Shall Overcome." We've got to fight until we overcome.

The economic philosophy of black nationalism is pure and simple. It only means that we should control the economy of our community. Why should white people be running all the stores in our community? Why should white people be running the banks of our community? Why should the economy of our community be in the hands of the white man? Why? If a black man can't move his store into a white community, you tell me why a white man should move his store into a black community. The philosophy of black nationalism involves a re-education program in the black community in regards to economics. Our people have to be made to see that any time you take your dollar out of your community and spend it in a community where you don't live, the community where you live will get poorer and poorer, and the community where you spend your money will get richer and richer. Then you wonder why where you live is always a ghetto or a slum area. And where you and I are concerned, not only do we lose it when we spend it out of the community, but the white man has got all our stores in the community tied up; so that though we spend it in the community, at sundown the man who runs the store takes it over across town somewhere. He's got us in a vise.

So the economic philosophy of black nationalism means in every church, in every civic organization, in every fraternal order, it's time now for our people to become conscious of the importance of controlling the economy of our community. If we own the stores, if we operate the businesses, if we try and establish some industry in our own community, then we're developing to the position where we are creating employment for our own kind. Once you gain control of the economy of your own community, then you don't have to picket and boycott and beg some cracker downtown for a job in his business.

The social philosophy of black nationalism only means that we have to get together and remove the evils, the vices, alcoholism, drug addiction, and other evils that are destroying the moral fiber of our community. We ourselves have to lift the level of our community, the standard of our community to a higher level, make our own society beautiful so that we will be satisfied in our own social circles and won't be running around here trying to knock our way into a social circle where we're not wanted.

So I say, in spreading a gospel such as black nationalism, it is not designed to make the black man re-evaluate the white man—you know him already—but to make the black man re-evaluate himself. Don't change the white man's mind—you can't change his mind, and that whole thing about appealing to the moral conscience of America—America's conscience is bankrupt. She lost all conscience a long time ago. Uncle Sam has no conscience. They don't know what morals are. They don't try and eliminate an evil because it's evil, or because it's illegal, or because it's immoral; they eliminate it only when it threatens their existence. So you're wasting your time appealing to the moral conscience of a bankrupt man like Uncle Sam. If he had a conscience, he'd straighten this thing out with no more pressure being put upon him. So it is not necessary to change the white man's mind. We have to change our own mind. You can't change his mind about us. We've got to change our own minds about each other. We have to see each other with new eyes. We have to see each other as brothers and sisters. We have to come together with warmth so we can develop unity and harmony that's necessary to get this problem solved ourselves. How can we do this? How can we avoid jealousy? How can we avoid the suspicion and the divisions that exist in the community? I'll tell you how.

I have watched how Billy Graham comes into a city, spreading what he calls the gospel of Christ, which is only white nationalism. That's what he is. Billy Graham is a white nationalist; I'm a black nationalist. But since it's the natural tendency for leaders to be jealous and look upon a powerful figure like Graham with suspicion and envy, how is it possible for him to come into a city and get all the cooperation of the church leaders? Don't think because they're church leaders that they don't have weaknesses that make them envious and jealous—no, everybody's got it. It's not an accident that when they want to choose a cardinal over there in Rome, they get in a closet so you can't hear them cussing and fighting and carrying on.

Billy Graham comes in preaching the gospel of Christ, he evangelizes the gospel, he stirs everybody up, but he never tries to start a church. If he came in trying to start a church, all the churches would be against him. So, he just comes in talking about Christ and tells everybody who gets Christ to go to any church where Christ is; and in this way the church cooperates with him. So we're going to take a page from his book.

Our gospel is black nationalism. We're not trying to threaten the existence of any organization, but we're spreading the gospel of black nationalism. Anywhere there's a church that is also preaching and practicing the gospel of black nationalism, join that church. If the NAACP is preaching and practicing the gospel of black nationalism, join the NAACP. If CORE is spreading and practicing the gospel of black nationalism, join CORE. Join any organization that has a gospel that's for the uplift of the black man. And when you get into it and see them pussyfooting or compromising, pull out of it because that's not black nationalism. We'll find another one.

And in this manner, the organizations will increase in number and in quantity and in quality, and by August, it is then our intention to have a black nationalist convention which will consist of delegates from all over the country who are interested in the political, economic and social philosophy of black nationalism. After these delegates convene, we will hold a seminar, we will hold discussions, we will listen to everyone. We want to hear new ideas and new solutions and new answers. And at that time, if we see fit then to form a black nationalist party, we'll form a black nationalist party. If it's necessary to form a black nationalist army, we'll form a black nationalist army. It'll be the ballot or the bullet. It'll be liberty or it'll be death.

It's time for you and me to stop sitting in this country, letting some cracker senators, Northern crackers and Southern crackers, sit there in Washington, D.C., and come to a conclusion in their mind that you and I are supposed to have civil rights. There's no white man going to tell me anything about *my* rights. Brothers and sisters, always remember, if it doesn't take senators and congressmen and presidential proclamations to give freedom to the white man, it is not necessary for legislation or proclamation or Supreme Court decisions to give freedom to the black man. You let that white man know, if this is a country of freedom, let it be a country of freedom; and if it's not a country of freedom, change it.

We will work with anybody, anywhere, at any time, who is genuinely interested in tackling the problem head-on, nonviolently as long as the enemy is nonviolent, but violent when the enemy gets violent. We'll work with you on the voter-registration drive, we'll work with you on rent strikes, we'll work with you on school boycotts—I don't believe in any kind of integration; I'm not even worried about it because I know you're not going to get it anyway; you're not going to get it because you're afraid to die; you've got to be ready to die if you try and force yourself on the white man, because he'll get just as violent as those crackers in Mississippi, right here in Cleveland. But we will still work with you on the school boycotts because we're against a segregated school system. A segregated school system produces children who, when they graduate, graduate with crippled minds. But this does not mean that a school is segregated because it's all black. A segregated school means a school that is controlled by people who have no real interest in it whatsoever.

Let me explain what I mean. A segregated district or community is a community in which people live, but outsiders control the politics and the economy of that community. They never refer to the white section as a segregated community.

It's the all-Negro section that's a segregated community. Why? The white man controls his own school, his own bank, his own economy, his own politics, his own everything, his own community—but he also controls yours. When you're under someone else's control, you're segregated. They'll always give you the lowest or the worst that there is to offer, but it doesn't mean you're segregated just because you have your own. You've got to *control* your own. Just like the white man has control of his, you need to control yours.

You know the best way to get rid of segregation? The white man is more afraid of separation than he is of integration. Segregation means that he puts you away from him, but not far enough for you to be out of his jurisdiction; separation means you're gone. And the white man will integrate faster than he'll let you separate. So we will work with you against the segregated school system because it's criminal, because it is absolutely destructive, in every way imaginable, to the minds of the children who have to be exposed to that type of crippling education.

Last but not least, I must say this concerning the great controversy over rifles and shotguns. The only thing that I've ever said is that in areas where the government has proven itself either unwilling or unable to defend the lives and the property of Negroes, it's time for Negroes to defend themselves. Article number two of the constitutional amendments provides you and me the right to own a rifle or a shotgun. It is constitutionally legal to own a shotgun or a rifle. This doesn't mean you're going to get a rifle and form battalions and go out looking for white folks, although you'd be within your rights—I mean, you'd be justified; but that would be illegal and we don't do anything illegal. If the white man doesn't want the black man buying rifles and shotguns, then let the government do its job. That's all. And don't let the white man come to you and ask you what you think about what Malcolm says—why, you old Uncle Tom. He would never ask you if he thought you were going to say, "Amen!" No, he is making a Tom out of you.

So, this doesn't mean forming rifle clubs and going out looking for people, but it is time, in 1964, if you are a man, to let that man know. If he's not going to do his job in running the government and providing you and me with the protection that our taxes are supposed to be for, since he spends all those billions for his defense budget, he certainly can't begrudge you and me spending $12 or $15 for a single-shot, or double-action. I hope you understand. Don't go out shooting people, but any time, brothers and sisters, and especially the men in this audience—some of you wearing Congressional Medals of Honor, with shoulders this wide, chests this big, muscles that big—any time you and I sit around and read where they bomb a church and murder in cold blood, not some grownups, but four little girls while they were praying to the same god the white man taught them to pray to, and you and I see the government go down and can't find who did it.

Why, this man—he can find Eichmann hiding down in Argentina somewhere. Let two or three American soldiers, who are minding somebody else's business way over in South Vietnam, get killed, and he'll send battleships, sticking his nose in their business. He wanted to send troops down to Cuba and make them have what he calls free elections—this old cracker who doesn't have free elections in his own country. No, if you never see me another time in your life, if I die in the morning, I'll die saying one thing: the ballot or the bullet, the ballot or the bullet.

If a Negro in 1964 has to sit around and wait for some cracker senator to filibuster when it comes to the rights of black people, why, you and I should hang our heads in shame. You talk about a march on Washington in 1963, you haven't seen anything. There's some more going down in '64. And this time they're not going like they went last year. They're not going singing "We Shall Overcome." They're not going with white friends. They're not going with placards already painted for them. They're not going with round-trip tickets. They're going with one-way tickets.

And if they don't want that non-nonviolent army going down there, tell them to bring the filibuster to a halt. The black nationalists aren't going to wait. Lyndon B. Johnson is the head of the Democratic Party. If he's for civil rights, let him go into the Senate next week and declare himself. Let him go in there right now and declare himself. Let him go in there and denounce the Southern branch of his party. Let him go in there right now and take a moral stand—right now, not later.

Tell him, don't wait until election time. If he waits too long, brothers and sisters, he will be responsible for letting a condition develop in this country which will create a climate that will bring seeds up out of the ground with vegetation on the end of them looking like something these people never dreamed of. In 1964, it's the ballot or the bullet. Thank you.

CHALLENGING "THE STATE'S POLITICAL POWER-STRUCTURE"

Program of the Mississippi Freedom Democratic Party

c. June 1964

THE MISSISSIPPI FREEDOM DEMOCRATIC PARTY . . .

THREE BASIC considerations underlie the development of the Mississippi Freedom Democratic Party and its plans to challenge the seating of the delegation of the Mississippi Democratic Party at the 1964 National Democratic Convention. They are:

1. The long history of systematic and studied exclusion of Negro citizens from equal participation in the political processes of the state grows more flagrant and intensified daily.

2. The Mississippi Democratic Party has conclusively demonstrated its lack of loyalty to the National Democratic Party, in the past, and currently indicates no intention of supporting the platform of the 1964 National Democratic Convention.

3. The intransigent and fanatical determination of the State's political power-structure to maintain status-quo, clearly demonstrates that the "Mississippi closed society," as Professor James W. Silver of the University of Mississippi asserts, is without leadership or moral resources to reform itself, and hence can only be brought into the mainstream of the twentieth century by forces outside of itself.

A. PARTY DISCRIMINATION:

The Mississippi Democratic Party controls the legislative, executive, and judicial branches of the government of the State. All 49 senators, and all but one of 122 representatives are Democrats. Repeatedly, the State legislature has passed laws and established regulations designed to discriminate against prospective Negro voters. The 1963 gubernatorial campaign was largely directed towards restricting the Negro vote. The state convention is being held in the Jackson Municipal Auditorium and the Heidelburg Hotel, both of which are segregated. In its devotion to racism and suppression and oppression of minority expression, the Mississippi Democratic Party prevents Negro Democrats and white persons who disagree with the party's racist stance to participate in party program and decisions.

B. PARTY DISLOYALTY:

Mississippi citizens who desire to do so cannot support the National Democratic goals by joining the Mississippi Democratic Party. The Mississippi Democratic Party has declared in public speeches and printed matter that it is NOT a part of the National Democratic Party. The campaign literature for the election of Gov. Paul B. Johnson, in 1963 is a case in point, as the following excerpts show: "Our Mississippi Democratic Party is entirely independent and free of the influence of domination of any national party." . . . "The Mississippi Democratic Party which long ago separated itself from the National Democratic Party, and which has fought consistently everything both national parties stand for, . . ."

In 1960 the Mississippi Democratic Party failed to honor its pledge to support the nominees of the National Democratic Convention. Immediately after the convention the Mississippi party convened a convention and voted to support unpledged electors in an effort to defeat the nominees of the Democratic National Convention.

C. THE CLOSED SOCIETY:

"It can be argued that in the history of the United States democracy has produced great leaders in great crises. Sad as it may be, the opposite has been true in Mississippi. As yet there is little evidence that the society of the closed mind will ever possess the moral resources to reform itself, or the capacity for self-examination, or even the tolerance of self-examination."

from "Mississippi: the Closed Society." by James W. Silver

Civil rights groups working in Mississippi are convinced that political and social justice can not be won in Mississippi without massive interest and support of the country as a whole, backed by the authority of the Federal government. As the political leadership of Mississippi feel threatened by the winds of change, they devise new and more extensive legal weapons and police powers. Police preparations are now being made to harass, intimidate and threaten the educational and registration program scheduled to be conducted in Mississippi this summer. Five new bills, prohibiting picketing, banning the distribution of boycott literature, restricting the movement of groups, establishing curfews, authorizing municipalities to pool police manpower and equipment, and increasing penalties that may be assessed by city courts—have been hurriedly signed into law. Other similar bills are still pending.

II. ORGANIZATIONAL STRUCTURE OF THE FREEDOM DEMOCRATIC PARTY

To give Negro citizens of Mississippi an experience in political democracy and to establish a channel through which all citizens, Negro and white, can actively support the principles and programs of the National Democratic Party, the Mississippi Freedom Democratic Party was conceived. The Council of Federated Organizations (COFO), a confederation of all the national and local civil rights and citizenship education groups in Mississippi, is assisting local citizens to develop the Mississippi Freedom Democratic Party. This party is open to all citizens regardless of race. It was officially established at a meeting in Jackson, Mississippi on April 26th; and the approximately 200 delegates present elected a temporary state executive committee, which will be responsible for setting precinct and other state meetings. These meetings will parallel those of the Mississippi Democratic Party, and every effort will be made to comply with all state laws which apply to the formation of political parties. Registered voters in the Freedom Democratic Party will attempt to attend precinct and county meetings of the Mississippi Democratic Party.

The Mississippi Freedom Democratic Party is presently engaged in three major efforts: (1) Freedom Registration; (2) Freedom Candidates; and (3) Convention Challenge.

1. FREEDOM REGISTRATION:

Official registration figures show that only some 20,000 Negroes are registered in Mississippi as compared to 500,000 whites. This represents less than 7% of the 435,000 Negroes 21 years of age in the state. The Freedom Registration is designed to show that thousands of Negroes want to become registered voters. By setting up registrars and deputy registrars in each of the 82 counties of the state, 300,000 persons may be registered in the Freedom Registration. Last November some 83,000 Negroes were registered in a mock gubernatorial race. In the present drive, 75,000 are reported registered, and this will be greatly stepped up when the summer program officially begins at the end of June. This registration will use simplified registration forms based on voting applications used in several Northern States. Any person who registers in the Freedom Registration will be eligible to vote in the Freedom Democratic Party Convention and participate in party work.

2. FREEDOM CANDIDATES:

The four (4) candidates who qualified to run in the June 2 primary in Mississippi were nominees of the Freedom Democratic Party and in addition to their bid in the regular Democratic primary, they will also run in a mock election under the Mississippi Freedom Democratic Party in November. This will help to establish the fact that thousands of Negroes are deprived of citizenship participation because of the racist character of Mississippi's voter registration procedures.

The four candidates are, Mrs. Victoria Gray, opposing Sen. John Stennis; Mrs. Fannie Lou Hamer, opposing Rep. Jamie L. Whitten; the Rev. John Cameron, opposing Rep. William M. Colmer; and Mr. James Houston, opposing Rep. John Bell Williams.

The *Platforms* of the candidates of the Freedom Democratic Party articulate the needs of all the people of Mississippi, such as anti-poverty programs, medicare, aid to education, rural development, urban renewal, and the guarantee of constitutional rights to all. This is in sharp contrast to the lack of real issues in the campaigns of the candidates who won in the primary. Senator Stennis did not even bother to campaign in the state.

3. THE CHALLENGE TO THE DEMOCRATIC NATIONAL CONVENTION:

Delegates from the Freedom Democratic Party will challenge the seating of the "old-line" Mississippi delegation at the Democratic National Convention this August in Atlantic City, N.J. These delegates will have been chosen through precinct meetings, county conventions, caucuses in congressional districts, and at a state wide convention of the Freedom Democratic Party. The State Executive Committee will be ratified and the national Committeeman and Committeewoman will be chosen at this state wide convention.

All steps necessary to preparing and formally presenting the challenge of the Freedom Democratic Party are being taken. *BUT WE NEED YOUR COOPERATION AND HELP!*

*****We need convention delegates to champion the cause of representative government in Mississippi.

*****We need people who will speak out in the credentials committee and on the convention floor.

*****We need hundreds of Democrats—individuals and organizations—to instruct their delegates, petition their representatives, party leaders and the President to face up to the fact that only a renegade democratic party exists in Mississippi which enjoys the benefits of national affiliation but spurns all responsibilities and can only continue to bring disgrace to the National Democratic Party.

"AN IDEA WHOSE TIME HAS COME"

MIKE MANSFIELD, RICHARD RUSSELL, HUBERT H. HUMPHREY, AND EVERETT MCKINLEY DIRKSEN

Remarks in the Senate on the Civil Rights Bill

June 10, 1964

Mr. MANSFIELD. Mr. President, I yield myself 10 minutes.

The ACTING PRESIDENT pro tempore. The Senator from Montana is recognized for 10 minutes.

Mr. MANSFIELD. Mr. President, the calendar of business reads "Legislative day, Monday, March 30, 1964." If my mathematics are correct, that means that the last legislative day the Senate has had was 71 days ago. If my memory is correct, we are now in our third month and first legislative day of debate, in one form or another, of House bill 7152.

The Senate now stands at the crossroads of history, and the time for decision is at hand. I should like, if I may, to read to the Senate a letter:

> DEAR SENATOR MANSFIELD: I am a lifelong resident of Montana, I am 29 years old, and the mother of four children. I am white. In general, I have considered myself a good citizen of my country, I have voted in every election since my 21st year, I have tried to learn the issues and policies of each candidate, of each party, and I voted to the best of my personal judgment. I have formed opinion on various matters, and adopted ideas on specific policies. But through it all, I realize I have been a listener, a receiver, an appreciator, a bystander. A bystander can remain an innocent bystander up to a point, after which he must take part.
>
> How can we, as responsible Americans, continue talking, arguing, bickering over civil rights as though the privileges, responsibilities, and birthrights of a great percentage of our people were favors or rewards to be handed out by a benevolent few?

I am white. By a simple accident of birth, I was allowed to grow up believing in the laws of God and our country. As a child, I learned to recite the Preamble to the Constitution. I learned the Bill of Rights, and memorized the Lincoln Gettysburg Address. I accepted these things as truth. I grew up with the right to feel that I, as an individual, was as good as anyone else, that I had the opportunity to climb as high as my ability, my intelligence, and my ambition would take me. While I did not learn to consider myself as a superior being, I could look upon myself with a lack of inferiority. I did not learn to regard my color with a great sense of pride, but never with guilt or shame.

I was conceived by a pair of good, respectable, hard-working white parents. I was allowed to grow and mature, to have faith in myself and my future, and when I married and gave birth to my lovely children, to have faith in them and their future.

I know that my children may go to the school nearest our home. I know that when I give my children a coin to buy an ice cream cone, that coin is good in any store in town. When we are traveling, we can stop at any hotel or motel of our choice. When we go out to eat, we may do so in any cafe or club we wish and can afford. I can sit in any vacant seat in a bus, I can use a public restroom, and if I am thirsty, I may quench my thirst at any public drinking fountain. These things I consider my rights. I take them for granted and know that no one may deny me these rights.

This morning, the thought occurred to me, that by that same accident of birth, I could have been conceived by a pair of equally good respectable hard-working Negro parents. The process is the same, but what immense differences there would have been in my life and upbringing.

How heartbreaking it must be for a child to have to learn that his future is sharply limited even if his intelligence and his ability is not. How confusing it must be for a child to learn that he may not buy an ice cream cone or a coke in the same shop as a lighter skinned child, even though his dime has the same value as the other. How could my parents have logically explained to me that a dime from a white hand is worth 10 cents, but that same coin in a brown or black hand is "unacceptable"?

Civil rights, Negro rights, is an inflammatory issue everywhere. I hear hate and prejudice and ignorance spouted off in any gathering of people. Everyone has a different reason for feeling that liberties should be denied to colored people. I have heard many, most of them are personal, involving a single bad experience he or she or one of his or her friends or acquaintances once had.

When a person refuses a hamburger on a Friday evening with the statement "I am a Catholic," I accept it. This is a religious belief, and after all, who is harmed by the refusal of a hamburger. When a drink or a dessert is refused with the statement "I am on a diet," I accept that. It is a personal problem, a self-improvement problem. But I cannot accept it when someone refuses to recognize the rights for dignity, pride, education, and decent living to millions of our American people. This is not a religious belief, I don't believe God favors a man's soul simply because of the color of the body it was temporarily housed in. Is it then a matter of self-improvement? Are we white people so insecure and deficient of self-respect that we must hold firm to the inferiority of others so that we may continue to enjoy our superiority?

My opinions were recently brushed aside by an acquaintance when he gently reminded me that I do not know Negro people and so have no personal knowledge of the problem. He was right. I can count the number of Negro people I have known on the fingers of both hands. But does that remove me from this problem?

I did not know a single one of the millions of Jews enslaved and murdered by the Nazis during World War II, but I have the right to deplore and renounce those atrocities. I did not know personally any of the hundreds of men killed during the Japanese attack on Pearl Harbor, but I was entitled to feel the anger and shock of the attack. I had no friends or relatives living in Alaska during the recent disastrous earthquake, but I could have sympathy and a desire to help the stricken people.

I did not personally know President Kennedy, but I experienced a genuine grief and a deep personal sense of loss when he was killed. I have met none of the American astronauts, but I found myself brushing away tears of pride and relief when each of them returned safely to earth. So, while it is true that I know little of Negro people, almost nothing of living among them, I cannot believe that I or anyone must remain immune and removed from the civil rights struggle.

We, as white Americans, may certainly point with pride to our society which produces such personalities as Roosevelt, Eisenhower, MacArthur, Kennedy, Johnson, Henry Ford, Helen Hayes, Jacqueline Kennedy, the Barrymores, Bing Crosby, Will Rogers, Mark Twain, Ernest Hemingway, Babe Ruth, Mickey Mantle and on and on down an endless list of contributors to our country, our arts, our dignity, our basic culture. But this list of fine Americans would not be complete without including George Washington Carver, Dr. Ralph Bunche, Jesse Owens, Jackie Robinson, Frank Yerby, Bill Robinson, Willie Mays, Nat "King" Cole, Louis Armstrong, Sidney Poitier, Marian Anderson, Harry Belafonte.

I am proud of all these people, I am proud to share a heritage with them. I am proud of being an American.

But at night, when I kiss my children good night, I offer a small prayer of thanks to God for making them so perfect, so healthy, so lovely, and I find myself tempted to thank Him for letting them be born white. Then I am not so proud, neither of myself nor of our society which forces such a temptation upon us.

And that is why I don't feel that this is a southern problem, it is a northern problem, a western problem, an eastern problem. It is an American problem, for all Americans. It is my problem.

I am only one person, one woman. I wish there was something I could do in this issue. I want to help. The only way I know how to start is to educate my children that justice and freedom and ambition are not merely privileges, but their birthrights. I must try to impress upon them that these rights must be given, not held tightly unto themselves, for what cannot be given, we do not really have for ourselves.

These are the thoughts of but one of your citizens. I realize that no earth-shaking changes will develop from having written this letter, but it is a beginning. If more can be done by people like me, please tell me what I can do. Thank you for your time.

Sincerely yours,

—— ——.

The ACTING PRESIDENT pro tempore. The Senator from Montana has consumed 12½ minutes.

Mr. RUSSELL. Mr. President——

The ACTING PRESIDENT pro tempore. The Chair recognizes the Senator from Georgia.

FORUM OF FREE DEBATE

Mr. RUSSELL. Mr. President, within the hour, the Senate will decide whether it will abandon its proud position as a forum of free debate by imposing cloture or gag rule upon its Members.

I know the debate has been long and extremely tedious for some Senators. The historic significance of the debate lies, not in the length of time the issue has been before the Senate, not in the number of words spoken on the floor of the Senate, but in the results. Historians will forget the number of hours the Senate has spent in debating the bill. Instead, their concern will be with making their evaluation of the results.

For the true significance of the debate, we must look to the fundamental issues raised by the bill. We must weigh the magnitude of its impact upon our system of government.

Mr. President, at this hour we must decide whether we will proceed, in summary fashion, to gag the Senate; or whether we will proceed, in orderly fashion, to debate comprehensive amendments and to vote upon them, in a conscientious, studied effort to enable the Senate to develop a definitive measure which will not be an unbridled grant of power to appointive officers of the Government.

There is little doubt that the questions involved go to the very heart of our constitutional system. There can be little doubt that if gag rule is imposed and if the bill in its present form is enacted, without giving proper deliberation to amendments, not only will there be a most harmful impact upon our social order, as was stated by the minority leader [Mr. DIRKSEN] in the early days of the debate, but—in addition—the effect upon our economic system and upon what we are proud to call the American way of life will be both far reaching and devastating.

The hours have been long; the discussion has totaled many words. But there are many words in the bill, and many of them are not clear in their meaning, their application, and their significance. The scope of the bill is as wide as our system of government. Within the past few days, the President of the United States stated that this is the most far-reaching, comprehensive bill on this subject ever to be considered by Congress.

Mr. President, a mere totaling of the number of days, the number of hours, the number of speeches, or the number of amendments that may be pending at the desk may seem important today; but they will be completely lost from sight when those who write the history of this period consider and evaluate the impact of the bill upon our governmental system and our economic order.

AMERICAN SYSTEM FINEST

Ours is not a perfect system; the American system of law and order and economy has many defects. But, Mr. President, with all its errors and all its weaknesses, it is the finest system yet devised by man. It has brought more of the good things of life, more happiness, and a greater degree of freedom to more people than have ever before been enjoyed by any other people, under any other governmental system. The American system gives opportunity to those to whom the Senator from Montana referred in such touching terms. The fact that he could call the roll of a long list of Negro citizens who have achieved prominence in so many fields is, of itself, proof that there is no insuperable barrier to those who happen to be members of the Negro race. He referred to religion; but the very fact that the Members of the Senate include Jews, Protestants, Catholics, and Mormons is further proof that our system of government offers unprecedented opportunities to all our people; for if they have the will to achieve, they have the opportunity to do so.

The fact that two Members of the Senate are women, the fact that some of the Members of the House of Representatives are Negroes, and the fact that other Negroes hold high positions in the executive branch of the Government of the United States offers additional clear proof that the American system of government has not failed, but—instead—has extended unparalleled opportunities to all who are willing to strive ceaselessly to make use of them.

O Mr. President, the argument the Senator from Montana made for this bill could also be made for a piece of legislation that would take away from those who have, and give to those who have not.

He spoke of the heartbreak a poor child might experience because he could not go to a certain place. But in this country there are thousands of poor children, of every race, who cannot go to every place to which they may desire to go; and there are poor children who may look on in anguish when they see other children of their own age riding in limousines or other fine cars, whereas the parents of those poor children cannot afford to own such automobiles, or perhaps cannot afford to own automobiles of any sort.

AN EMOTIONAL APPEAL

Mr. President, the argument the Senator from Montana made in behalf of this bill has emotional appeal—but no more emotional appeal than that which could be made for a purely socialistic or communistic system that would divide and distribute among all our people every bit of the property and wealth of the people of these United States.

So, Mr. President, it is evident that the new system that some propose as a remedy, the new laws that some urge upon us, would only pull down those of our people who have been able to climb and to advance—both those who are white and those who are black, both those who are Protestants, those who are Catholics, and those who are Jews. We cannot help any group in our country by taking away or impinging upon the constitutional rights of all; we would only arrive at the lowest common denominator for all our people.

Mr. President, what does equality mean?

It does not mean that a child can stand on the street corner and cry for a car in which he sees another child of his own age riding. That is not equality. Equality does not mean that one person shall be admitted to a club merely because he desires to be, and because to be refused admission would cause him embarrassment or anguish. Our system never contemplated any such "equality" as that. If it had, we would not have achieved our present greatness; instead, we would be wandering in the chaos, the poverty, and the distress that accompany tyrannical government, whether it be Fascist or whether it be Communist.

No, Mr. President, equal rights in this land of ours means that each citizen has an equal opportunity to acquire property through honest means, that once that property has been acquired he has a right to exercise dominion over it. Under our system, many Negroes have accumulated great amounts of property; and the names recounted by the Senator from Montana could have included those of many Negroes of great wealth and who are worth millions of dollars.

There are Negroes in this country who preside over banks with tens of millions of dollars of deposits, who operate insurance companies that have assets running into hundreds of millions of dollars, and who occupy high position in every avenue of life in this land. This, I think, is truly remarkable when we consider that the people this bill is designed to aid are only 100 years removed from slavery, and that most of them, until the last few years, lived in the poorest section of the country—an area that little more than 25 years ago was described by a President of the United States as the Nation's economic problem No. 1, where both whites and blacks were denied opportunities.

Mr. President, the fact that so many Negroes have achieved eminence, and even preeminence, in our society, in our educational, in medical, in cultural, and in literary lines, demonstrates that true equality is the equality to own and control property honestly gained.

UNDERMINING THE FOUNDATION

But we are nibbling away at that cornerstone of our whole system. There will never be a time, Mr. President, when every person in this country will own and control exactly the same amount of property. Should there be such a time it will mean that we are a dead land. It will mean that we have fallen from the eminence that we now enjoy into the very pits of perdition and despair. It will mean that we have destroyed that which the Founding Fathers gave us. It would mean that we have had no appreciation whatever for our heritage, which means the equal right to own and exercise dominion over property. It is not equality to pass laws that give any group, whoever they may be, the right to violate the property rights of another that are guaranteed by the Constitution.

Life, liberty, and property—in that order—are spelled out in the Constitution of the United States as our greatest civil rights. I care not how much politics may be involved, and it matters not how great may be the emotional appeal. We cannot strike down one of those rights without gnawing into the very vitals of constitutional government in this land.

Mr. President, of course this bill would strike down and destroy many rights and powers which, since the foundation of our Government, have properly belonged to the several States. The bill would increase the power of the great national bureaucracy, and thereby would take from our people essential rights.

We often hear the argument that much existing Federal legislation is of a beneficial nature, and that therefore additional

Federal laws to provide other programs that will benefit the people should be enacted. Two examples of programs of that type are the social security program and the school-lunch program.

But, Mr. President, have we now seen the dawn of the day when—in the name of passing a law to help one group of our people—we shall insist upon the destruction of some of the most important rights of all Americans? Would that be equality for all the American people?

PRESSURES FOR BILL

I know that great pressures have been brought to bear on Senators by both political parties and by the President of the United States to vote for this bill. State chairmen and other officials of both parties have been calling and telegraphing Senators since the day when this proposed legislation came before the Senate. The leaders of the great labor organizations also have brought pressure and have threatened disapproval of Senators who vote against the bill.

I have observed with profound sorrow the role that many religious leaders have played in urging passage of the bill, because I cannot make their activities jibe with my concept of the proper place of religious leaders in our national life. During the course of the debate, we have seen cardinals, bishops, elders, stated clerks, common preachers, priests, and rabbis come to Washington to press for the passage of this bill. They have sought to make its passage a great moral issue. But I am at a loss to understand why they are 200 years late in discovering that the right of dominion over private property is a great moral issue. If it is a great moral issue today, it was a great moral issue on the day of the ratification of the Constitution of the United States. Of course, this is not, and cannot be, a moral question; however it may be considered, it is a political question.

Day after day, men of the cloth have been standing on the Mall and urging a favorable vote on the bill. They have encouraged and prompted thousands of good citizens to sign petitions supporting the bill—but all without the knowledge of the effect of what they were demanding of the representatives in the Congress of the United States.

This is the second time in my lifetime an effort has been made by the clergy to make a moral question of a political issue. The other was prohibition. We know something of the results of that.

Mr. President, I realize full well that the authors of the bill have sought, by means of such vast grants of power to the Attorney General, to insure enforcement of the drastic and coercive provisions of the bill, in total disregard of the customs and mores of the people who will be most vitally affected by this bill.

I know, and all other Members of the Senate know, that the bill has been drafted in such a way that its greatest impact will be on the States of the old Confederacy. Some Senators from other sections have sent out newsletters assuring their constituents that the bill does not affect them because their States have statutes dealing with equal accommodations and fair employment, and thus are exempted from the most punitive provisions. But make no mistake about it: If this bill is enacted into law, next year we will be confronted with new demands for enactment of further legislation in this field, such as laws requiring open housing and the "busing" of children.

The country is becoming enmeshed in a philosophy that can only lead to the destruction of our dual system of sovereign States in an indestructible Union. This is the system that has produced the American way of life and has afforded opportunity to all.

Mr. President, our system may have its defects; but, after all, it has brought more benefits to more people than any other system known to mankind. The truth of the matter is that many so-called "impoverished Americans" enjoy a standard of living and opportunities for advancement under our system that make them the envy of most of the other peoples of the world.

CONTRARY TO CONSTITUTION

Mr. President, those of us who have opposed this bill have done so from a profound conviction that the bill not only is contrary to the spirit of the Constitution of the United States, but also violates the letter of the Constitution.

We have opposed it because the broad abdication of power and authority by the legislative branch to the executive branch that it provides would destroy forever the doctrine of separation of powers. This great doctrine was devised by our forefathers as a bulwark against tyranny; and over the years it has protected our liberties and way of life.

But the bill goes even further. It confers upon the Attorney General the power to control many facets in the daily lives and in the private lives of the people of the United States. It greatly broadens Federal supervision and regulation—going into new areas—over the activities of business, commerce, and industry, which are already heavily burdened and hampered by existing law.

One of the saddest aspects of the bill is the general enlargement of the Federal Government over affairs that have heretofore been considered the concern of the States and local governments. I appeal to the Senate to consider the broad aspects of this legislation, and not to be influenced by the frustrations of the hours that have been spent in debate. I appeal to the Senate to vote down this gag rule with assurances that we can proceed to vote upon vital amendments without any lengthy debate. I appeal to Senators to rise above the pressures to which they have been subjected and to reject this legislation that will result in vast changes, not only in our social order, but in our very form of government.

Mr. MANSFIELD. Mr. President, I yield 2 minutes to the distinguished majority whip, the Senator from Minnesota [Mr. HUMPHREY]; and I yield the rest of my time to the distinguished minority leader, the Senator from Illinois [Mr. DIRKSEN].

The ACTING PRESIDENT pro tempore. The Senator from Minnesota is recognized for 2 minutes.

Mr. HUMPHREY. Mr. President, this issue has been burning for many weeks. The moment of great decision is now fast approaching.

In the Senate, the Constitution of the United States is on trial. The question is whether we will have two types of citizenship in this Nation, or first-class citizenship for all. The question is whether there will be two kinds of justice, or equal justice under the law for every American. The question is whether this

Nation will be divided, or as we are taught in our youth in the pledge of allegiance, one Nation, under God, indivisible, with liberty and justice for all.

Mr. President, William Shakespeare in his great drama, "The Life of Henry V," reminds us how the immortal Henry addressed his soldiers before the Battle of Agincourt:

> He that shall live this day, and see old age,
> Will yearly on the vigil feast his neighbours,
> And say, "To-morrow is Saint Crispian:"
>
> * * * * *
>
> This story shall the good man teach his son:
> And Crispin Crispian shall ne'er go by,
> From this day to the ending of the world,
> But we in it shall be remembered: * * *

I say to my colleagues of the Senate that perhaps in your lives you will be able to tell your children's children that you were here for America to make the year 1964 our freedom year. I urge my colleagues to make that dream of full freedom, full justice, and full citizenship for every American a reality by their votes on this day, and it will be remembered until the ending of the world.

The ACTING PRESIDENT pro tempore. The Senator's time has expired.

Mr. DIRKSEN. Mr. President, it is a year ago this month that the late President Kennedy sent his civil rights bill and message to the Congress. For 2 years, we had been chiding him about failure to act in this field. At long last, and after many conferences, it became a reality.

After 9 days of hearings before the Senate Judiciary Committee, it was referred to a subcommittee. There it languished and the administration leadership finally decided to await the House bill.

In the House it traveled an equally tortuous road. But at long last, it reached the House floor for action. It was debated for 64 hours; 155 amendments were offered; 34 were approved. On February 10, 1964, it passed the House by a vote of 290 to 130. That was a 65-percent vote.

It was messaged to the Senate on February 17 and reached the Senate Calendar on February 26. The motion to take up and consider was made on March 9. That motion was debated for 16 days and on March 26 by a vote of 67 to 17 it was adopted.

It is now 4 months since it passed the House. It is 3½ months since it came to the Senate Calendar. Three months have gone by since the motion to consider was made. We have acted on one intervening motion to send the bill back to the Judiciary Committee and a vote on the jury trial amendment. That has been the extent of our action.

Sharp opinions have developed. Incredible allegations have been made. Extreme views have been asserted. The mail volume has been heavy. The bill has provoked many long-distance telephone calls, many of them late at night or in the small hours of the morning. There has been unrestrained criticism about motives. Thousands of people have come to the Capitol to urge immediate action on an unchanged House bill.

For myself, I have had but one purpose and that was the enactment of a good, workable, equitable, practical bill having due regard for the progress made in the civil rights field at the State and local level.

I am no Johnnie-come-lately in this field. Thirty years ago, in the House of Representatives, I voted on antipoll tax and antilynching measures. Since then, I have sponsored or cosponsored scores of bills dealing with civil rights.

At the outset, I contended that the House bill was imperfect and deficient. That fact is now quite generally conceded. But the debate continued. The number of amendments submitted increased. They now number nearly 400. The stalemate continued. A backlog of work piled up. Committees could not function normally. It was an unhappy situation and it was becoming a bit intolerable.

It became increasingly evident that to secure passage of a bill in the Senate would require cloture and a limitation on debate. Senate aversion to cloture is traditional. Only once in 35 years has cloture been voted. But the procedure for cloture is a standing rule of the Senate. It grew out of a filibuster against the armed ship bill in 1917 and has been part of the Standing Rules of the Senate for 47 years. To argue that cloture is unwarranted or unjustified is to assert that in 1917, the Senate adopted a rule which it did not intend to use when circumstances required or that it was placed in the rulebook only as to be repudiated. It was adopted as an instrument for action when all other efforts failed.

Today the Senate is stalemated in its efforts to enact a civil rights bill, one version of which has already been approved by the House by a vote of more than 2 to 1. That the Senate wishes to act on a civil rights bill can be divined from the fact that the motion to take up was adopted by a vote of 67 to 17.

There are many reasons why cloture should be invoked and a good civil rights measure enacted.

First. It is said that on the night he died, Victor Hugo wrote in his diary, substantially this sentiment:

> Stronger than all the armies is an idea whose time has come.

The time has come for equality of opportunity in sharing in government, in education, and in employment. It will not be stayed or denied. It is here.

The problem began when the Constitution makers permitted the importation of persons to continue for another 20 years. That problem was to generate the fury of civil strife 75 years later. Out of it was to come the 13th amendment ending servitude, the 14th amendment to provide equal protection of the laws and dual citizenship, the 15th amendment to prohibit government from abridging the right to vote.

Other factors had an impact. Two and three-quarter million young Negroes served in World Wars I, II, and Korea. Some won the Congressional Medal of Honor and the Distinguished Service Cross. Today they are fathers and grandfathers. They brought back impressions from countries where no discrimination existed. These impressions have been transmitted to children and grandchildren. Meanwhile, hundreds of thousands of colored have become teachers and professors, doctors and dentists, engineers and architects, artists and actors, musicians and technicians. They have become status minded. They have sensed inequality. They are prepared to make the issue. They feel that the time has come for the idea of equal opportunity. To enact the pending measure by invoking cloture is imperative.

Second. Years ago, a professor who thought he had developed an uncontrovertible scientific premise submitted it to his faculty associates. Quickly they picked it apart. In agony he cried out, "Is nothing eternal?" To this one of his associates replied, "Nothing is eternal except change."

Since the act of 1875 on public accommodations and the Supreme Court decision of 1883 which struck it down, America has changed. The population then was 45 million. Today it is 190 million. In the Pledge of Allegiance to the Flag we intone, "One Nation, under God." And so it is. It is an integrated Nation. Air, rail, and highway transportation make it so. A common language makes it so. A tax pattern which applies equally to white and nonwhite makes it so. Literacy makes it so. The mobility provided by 80 million autos makes it so. The accommodations laws in 34 States and the District of Columbia make it so. The fair employment practice laws in 30 States make it so. Yes, our land has changed since the Supreme Court decision of 1883.

As Lincoln once observed:

> The occasion is piled high with difficulty and we must rise with the occasion. As our case is new, so we must think anew and act anew. We must first disenthrall ourselves and then we shall save the Union.

To my friends from the South, I would refresh you on the words of a great Georgian named Henry W. Grady. On December 22, 1886, he was asked to respond to a toast to the new South at the New England society dinner. His words were dramatic and explosive. He began his toast by saying:

> There was a South of slavery and secession—that South is dead. There is a South of union and freedom—that South thank God is living, breathing, growing every hour.

America grows. America changes. And on the civil rights issue we must rise with the occasion. That calls for cloture and for the enactment of a civil rights bill.

Third. There is another reason—our covenant with the people. For many years, each political party has given major consideration to a civil rights plank in its platform. Go back and reexamine our pledges to the country as we sought the suffrage of the people and for a grant of authority to manage and direct their affairs. Were these pledges so much campaign stuff or did we mean it? Were these promises on civil rights but idle words for vote-getting purposes or were they a covenant meant to be kept? If all this was mere pretense, let us confess the sin of hypocrisy now and vow not to delude the people again.

To you, my Republican colleagues, let me refresh you on the words of a great American. His name is Herbert Hoover. In his day he was reviled and maligned. He was castigated and calumniated. But today his views and his judgment stand vindicated at the bar of history. In 1952 he received a volcanic welcome as he appeared before our national convention in Chicago. On that occasion he commented on the Whig Party, predecessor of the Republican Party, and said:

> The Whig Party temporized, compromised upon the issue of freedom for the Negro. That party disappeared. It deserved to disappear. Shall the Republican Party receive or deserve any better fate if it compromises upon the issue of freedom for all men?

To those who have charged me with doing a disservice to my party because of my interest in the enactment of a good civil rights bill—and there have been a good many who have made that charge—I can only say that our party found its faith in the Declaration of Independence in which a great Democrat, Jefferson by name, wrote the flaming words:

> We hold these truths to be self-evident that all men are created equal.

That has been the living faith of our party. Do we forsake this article of faith, now that equality's time has come or do we stand up for it and insure the survival of our party and its ultimate victory. There is no substitute for a basic and righteous idea. We have a duty—a firm duty—to use the instruments at hand—namely, the cloture rule—to bring about the enactment of a good civil rights bill.

Fourth. There is another reason why we dare not temporize with the issue which is before us. It is essentially moral in character. It must be resolved. It will not go away. Its time has come. Nor is it the first time in our history that an issue with moral connotations and implications has swept away the resistance, the fulminations, the legalistic speeches, the ardent but dubious arguments, the lamentations and the thought patterns of an earlier generation and pushed forward to fruition.

More than 60 years ago came the first efforts to secure Federal pure food and drug legislation. The speeches made on this floor against this intrusion of Federal power sound fantastically incredible today. But it would not be stayed. Its time had come and since its enactment, it has been expanded and strengthened in nearly every Congress.

When the first efforts were made to ban the shipment of goods in interstate commerce made with child labor, it was regarded as quite absurd. But all the trenchant editorials, the bitter speeches, the noisy onslaughts were swept aside as this limitation on the shipment of goods made with sweated child labor moved on to fulfillment. Its time had come.

More than 80 years ago came the first efforts to establish a civil service and merit system to cover Federal employees. The proposal was ridiculed and drenched with sarcasm. Some of the sharpest attacks on the proposal were made on this very Senate floor. But the bullet fired by a disappointed office seeker in 1881 which took President Garfield's life was the instrument of destiny which placed the Pendleton Act on the Federal statute books in 1883. It was an idea whose time had come.

When the New York Legislature placed a limit of 10 hours per day and 6 days per week upon the bakery workers in that State, this act was struck down by the U.S. Supreme Court. But in due time came the 8-hour day and the 40-hour week and how broadly accepted this concept is today. Its time had come.

More than 60 years ago, the elder La Follette thundered against the election of U.S. Senators by the State legislatures. The cry was to get back to the people and to first principles. On this Senate floor, Senators sneered at his efforts and even left the Chamber to show their contempt. But 50 years ago, the Constitution was amended to provide for the direct election of Senators. Its time had come.

Ninety-five years ago came the first endeavor to remove the limitation on sex in the exercise of the franchise. The comments made in those early days sound unbelievably ludicrous. But on and on went the effort and became the 19th amendment to the Constitution. Its time had come.

When the eminent Joseph Choate appeared before the Supreme Court to assert that a Federal income tax statute was unconstitutional and communistic, the Court struck down the work of Congress. Just 20 years later in 1913 the power of Congress to lay and collect taxes on incomes became the 16th amendment to the Constitution itself.

These are but some of the things touching closely the affairs of the people which were met with stout resistance, with shrill and strident cries of radicalism, with strained legalisms, with anguished entreaties that the foundations of the Republic were being rocked. But an inexorable moral force which operates in the domain of human affairs swept these efforts aside and today they are accepted as parts of the social, economic and political fabric of America.

Pending before us is another moral issue. Basically it deals with equality of opportunity in exercising the franchise, in securing an education, in making a livelihood, in enjoying the mantle of protection of the law. It has been a long, hard furrow and each generation must plow its share. Progress was made in 1957 and 1960. But the furrow does not end there. It requires the implementation provided by the substitute measure which is before us. And to secure that implementation requires cloture.

Let me add one thought to these observations. Today is an anniversary. It is in fact the 100th anniversary of the nomination of Abraham Lincoln for a second term for the Presidency on the Republican ticket. Two documents became the blueprints for his life and his conduct. The first was the Declaration of Independence which proclaimed the doctrine that all men are created equal. The second was the Constitution, the preamble to which began with the words:

> We, the people * * * do ordain and establish this Constitution for the United States of America.

These were the articles of his superb and unquenchable faith. Nowhere and at no time did he more nobly reaffirm that faith than at Gettysburg 101 years ago when he spoke of "a new nation, conceived in liberty and dedicated to the proposition that all men are created equal."

It is to take us further down that road that a bill is pending before us. We have a duty to get that job done. To do it will require cloture and a limitation on debate as provided by a standing rule of the Senate which has been in being for nearly 50 years. I trust we shall not fail in that duty.

That, from a great Republican, thinking in the frame of equality of opportunity—and that is all that is involved in this bill.

To those who have charged me with doing a disservice to my party—and there have been many—I can only say that our party found its faith in the Declaration of Independence, which was penned by a great Democrat, Thomas Jefferson by name. There he wrote the great words:

> We hold these truths to be self-evident, that all men are created equal.

That has been the living faith of our party. Do we forsake this article of faith, now that the time for our decision has come?

There is no substitute for a basic ideal. We have a firm duty to use the instrument at hand; namely, the cloture rule, to bring about the enactment of a good civil rights bill.

I appeal to all Senators. We are confronted with a moral issue. Today let us not be found wanting in whatever it takes by way of moral and spiritual substance to face up to the issue and to vote cloture.

"IS THIS AMERICA, THE LAND OF THE FREE?"

FANNIE LOU HAMER

Testimony to the Credentials Committee, Democratic National Convention

August 22, 1964

Mr. Chairman, and to the Credentials Committee, my name is Mrs. Fannie Lou Hamer, and I live at 626 East Lafayette Street, Ruleville, Mississippi, Sunflower County, the home of Senator James O. Eastland and Senator Stennis.

It was the thirty-first of August in 1962, that eighteen of us traveled twenty-six miles to the county courthouse in Indianola to try to register to become first-class citizens. We was met in Indianola by policemen, highway patrolmen, and they only allowed two of us in to take the literacy test at the time. After we had taken this test and started back to Ruleville, we was held up by the city police and the state highway patrolmen and carried back to Indianola where the bus driver was charged that day with driving a bus the wrong color.

After we paid the fine among us, we continued on to Ruleville, and Reverend Jeff Sunny carried me four miles in the rural area where I had worked as a timekeeper and sharecropper for eighteen years. I was met there by my children, who told me that the plantation owner was angry because I had gone down, tried to register. After they told me, my husband came, and said the plantation owner was raising Cain because I had tried to register. And before he quit talking the plantation owner came and said, "Fannie Lou, do you know—did Pap tell you what I said?"

And I said, "Yes, sir."

He said, "Well, I mean that." Said, "If you don't go down and withdraw your registration, you will have to leave." Said, "Then if you go down and withdraw, then you still might have to go because we are not ready for that in Mississippi."

And I addressed him and told him and said, "I didn't try to register for you. I tried to register for myself." I had to leave that same night.

On the tenth of September 1962, sixteen bullets was fired into the home of Mr. and Mrs. Robert Tucker for me. That same night two girls was shot in Ruleville, Mississippi. Also, Mr. Joe McDonald's house was shot in.

And June the ninth, 1963, I had attended a voter registration workshop—was returning back to Mississippi. Ten of us was traveling by the Continental Trailways bus. When we got to Winona, Mississippi, which is in Montgomery County, four of the people got off to use the washroom, and two of the people —to use the restaurant—two of the people wanted to use the washroom. The four people that had gone in to use the restaurant was ordered out. During this time I was on the bus. But when I looked through the window and saw they had rushed out, I got off of the bus to see what had happened. And one of the ladies said, "It was a state highway patrolman and a chief of police ordered us out."

I got back on the bus and one of the persons had used the washroom got back on the bus, too. As soon as I was seated on the bus, I saw when they began to get the five people in a highway patrolman's car. I stepped off of the bus to see what was happening and somebody screamed from the car that the five workers was in and said, "Get that one there." And when I went to get in the car, when the man told me I was under arrest, he kicked me.

I was carried to the county jail and put in the booking room. They left some of the people in the booking room and began to place us in cells. I was placed in a cell with a young woman called Miss Euvester Simpson. After I was placed in the cell, I began to hear sounds of licks and screams. I could hear the sounds of licks and horrible screams. And I could hear somebody say, "Can you say, 'yes, sir,' nigger? Can you say 'yes, sir'?" And they would say other horrible names.

She would say, "Yes, I can say 'yes, sir.'"

"So, well, say it."

She said, "I don't know you well enough." They beat her, I don't know how long. And after a while she began to pray, and asked God to have mercy on those people.

And it wasn't too long before three white men came to my cell. One of these men was a state highway patrolman and he asked me where I was from. And I told him Ruleville and he said, "We are going to check this." And they left my cell and it wasn't too long before they came back. He said, "You's from Ruleville all right," and he used a curse word. And he said, "We are going to make you wish you was dead."

I was carried out of that cell into another cell where they had two Negro prisoners. The state highway patrolmen ordered the first Negro to take the blackjack. The first Negro prisoner ordered me, by orders from the state highway patrolman, for me to lay down on a bunk bed on my face.

And I laid on my face and the first Negro began to beat. And I was beat by the first Negro until he was exhausted. I was holding my hands behind me at that time on my left side, because I suffered from polio when I was six years old. After the first Negro had beat until he was exhausted, the state highway patrolman ordered the second Negro to take the blackjack. The second Negro began to beat and I began to work my feet, and the state highway patrolman ordered the first Negro had beat me to sit on my feet—to keep me from working my feet. I began to scream and one white man got up and began to beat me in my head and tell me to hush. One white man—my dress had worked up high—he walked over and pulled my dress, I pulled my dress down and he pulled my dress back up.

I was in jail when Medgar Evers was murdered.

All of this is on account of we want to register, to become first-class citizens. And if the Freedom Democratic Party is not seated now, I question America. Is this America, the land of the free and the home of the brave, where we have to sleep with our telephones off of the hooks because our lives be threatened daily, because we want to live as decent human beings, in America? Thank you.

UNDERSTANDING "THE THREE STAGES OF A RIOT"

ROBERT PENN WARREN AND BAYARD RUSTIN

An Exchange on Urban Riots and Policing

1964

RPW: Let me turn to the riots this summer, which you know a great deal about and I know were deeply involved in emotionally. (interruption). We were talking about the riots. Now, of course there are many questions around and about the riots. Let's take one question—we know these things are socially conditioned—the participants are conditioned by society in a certain way. Now, what do we make of that fact? Is that—recognizing that, then where do other responsibilities come in, on the part of police, on the part of the City Fathers, on the part of the Negroes in influence—taking these various factors, you relate them to the fact that social condition—

BR: Well, I think, sir, it's most important to understand the three stages of a riot first. Number one, I think that the rioting was the result of pent-up frustration, pent-up frustration that grew from the economic conditions, the absence of hope, and the confusion that one finds in ghettoes, the inability to sleep at nights in the summer because you sleep in shifts, and the inability to sleep because the trash is not collected at proper hours, and garbage collectors come in the middle of the night—all kinds of filthy dirt in addition to the conditions outside. Now, there was a second stage, and that is the stage that all criminal elements use. When they see something going on, regardless of what caused it, they then move in because they're criminals, black criminals or white criminals, whatever it happens to be. The third stage is the stage where certain political groups for their own objectives try to keep the situation stirred up. Now I would say, therefore, if one goes back to stage number one, the responsibility on the part of black and white people of good will is as rapidly as possible to relieve these frustrations by working for jobs, for decent housing, and for quality educated schools. If one comes to point number two, one is then in a very difficult position in regard to police. They have to maintain some degree of law and order. The problem that I think made a number of people in Harlem angry, was the police used force far beyond that which was necessary. Now, I don't think the police did this because they got into a back room and said, let's be nasty. I think it is because they are afraid of the ghetto, they are frightened men and they do what all men do when frightened, behave as if the truth were not true. This is the ticklish part. I think what we were trying to get the police to do in New York was to recognize that until we can deal with these fundamental questions, no matter how well they behave it is never good enough, and that if they had set up a board it could review cases of so-called brutality, and if we had some responsible Negro on that board that people knew, this would be a bow and would make this kind of thing less possible. So far as the third stage is concerned, where the political folks come in to make hay, as when they attempted the progressive labor people for their own means to keep a parade going on Lenox Avenue when they knew there would be problems, that has to be dealt with as we attempted to deal with it, by the Negro community's intelligent leadership itself. It was not the police put an end to this, it was those of us who went into the streets and got people off the streets, who organized the youth to keep them off the streets to make that parade absolutely impossible to take place. They had finally thirty people. So I—this is the opening statement I would—

RPW: Yes. Let me raise the question about Philadelphia, where there was a police board of review. Now, was that an effective board, or was that just not enough?

BR: Well, I know Clarence Pickett, who is the former head of the American Friends Service Committee, who was the chairman of that board, and I had quite a long talk with him afterwards and I would trust his judgment. His judgment was that if it had not been for the police review board, the likelihood is that they would have had trouble earlier and to a greater degree, that it was in fact helpful. But you will note that I said earlier, even if police behaved ideally there would be frustrations. You must think of the police as jailers, that is to say, if you have a ghetto, which is like a cell, which people are to be kept in, they end up looking upon the police because he maintains order there, as the man who is finally responsible for keeping them there. Furthermore, he's the white man they see every day, or the Negro man they see taking orders from a white superior, and therefore the Negro police becomes an Uncle Tom. Now, I don't agree to all this, but I am trying to get you to feel what people feel.

RPW: Let me ask you this—Negro police were the first targets of the riot in Philadelphia I understand from the papers.

BR: This may be—I—

RPW: —men following their natural course of duty as far as I know violence.

BR: Well, they may be—I don't know the Philadelphia story—I've not studied it. I can say two things. I do know Negro policemen in New York who are amongst the most brutal police, and I think that here again an explanation is needed. The Negro has all of his life been told whatever field he goes into he's got to be better at it than anybody else. Therefore the Negro policeman is out to do two things, to prove he's a good policeman, which given the nature of our society and vengeance toward criminals, etc., very often means mistreatment, and secondly, he is trying to prove to the people downtown that he is not being soft because they are Negro like himself. So I can well understand this, being—the place in the given situation.

RPW: Now, what about the relation between say the—we'll say white riots, like they had in New Hampshire, like the English riots, of—quotes—unoppressed young people, what kind of psychological ground do they have in common between the—if any—between that and the Harlem, Rochester, Philadelphia riots? How much is a world question and non-racial question?

BR: Myrdal once pointed out in the American Dilemma that wherever you find Negroes of whatever class they are exaggerated Americans, they will be more of that in their effort to become a part. I think we're talking about two different things that have a common root. I would call the poverty in Harlem physical poverty which comes from the absence of plenty. There is another form of violence which comes from the poverty of plenty. Now at the root of both of these is the same thing, the feeling on the part of young people that they don't belong, they don't know what their place in society is, that somehow they are a sub-class which has nowhere to go, and there is a great deal of frustration among white youngsters, even rich ones, children who tear up a house in Long Island and who take dope in Westchester, and it springs from the basic fact that we don't have hope, we don't have a future, we don't know who we are. And I think there is less excuse for their doing that, because in addition to everything that they've got, the Negro also has physical discomfort—it's a plus matter. But I think it springs mainly from the same thing.

RPW: You tie both the disorder among the privileged white young and the underprivileged Negro young to a common ground in a lack of direction and a lack of a direct sense of identity, is that right?

BR: Yes, sir.

RPW: Both these counts?

BR: And I use the term "poverty of plenty" advisedly.

RPW: It's a good term. How much of the general feeling of a crisis of identity do you accept in terms of the Negro movement or the Negro revolution? How do you interpret it?

BR: I interpret it quite seriously from my experience with great numbers of young people who are forced to say, who am I, black man? out of the conditions that they face. But who would have to ask that question if they weren't white in this society? Now therefore the thing which I think is wrong is not the posing of the question but the answer.

JOHN HERBERS

Dr. King Rebuts Hoover Charges

The New York Times, November 20, 1964

DR. KING REBUTS HOOVER CHARGES

Offers to Discuss Criticisms—He Is
Supported by Negro Rights Leaders

Special to The New York Times

ATLANTA, Nov. 19—The Rev. Dr. Martin Luther King Jr. said in a statement today that J. Edgar Hoover "has apparently faltered under the awesome burden, complexities and responsibilities of his office."

Mr. Hoover, director of the Federal Bureau of Investigation, said in an interview with a group of women reporters in Washington yesterday that Dr. King was "the most notorious liar in the country" for saying that F.B.I. agents in Albany, Ga., had failed to act on Negroes' civil rights complaints because they were Southerners.

Today Dr. King wired Mr. Hoover that he would make himself available at any time for a discussion of the bureau's work on civil rights cases.

DISAGREE ON ORIGINS

Dr. King's statement and telegram were released here by the Southern Christian Leadership Conference, of which he is president. He prepared them at Bimini, in the Bahamas, where he is writing his acceptance speech for the Nobel Peace Prize, to be awarded in Oslo next month.

In yesterday's interview, Mr. Hoover said that four of the five agents working in the Albany area at the time referred to were from the North, and that when he had attempted to confer with Dr. King on the matter, the Negro leader had ignored his telephone calls.

In the same interview, Mr. Hoover said the Warren Commission "was unfair and unjust" in criticizing the bureau for failure to notify the Secret Service that Lee Harvey Oswald, President Kennedy's assassin, was in Dallas.

Dr. King issued this statement regarding Mr. Hoover's charge:

"I cannot conceive of Mr. Hoover making a statement like this without being under extreme pressure. He has apparently faltered under the awesome burden, complexities and responsibilities of his office. Therefore, I cannot engage in a public debate with him. I have nothing but sympathy for this man who has served his country so well."

Dr. King's telegram to Mr. Hoover said:

"I was appalled and surprised at your reported statement maligning my integrity. What motivated such an irresponsible accusation is a mystery to me.

QUESTIONS EFFECTIVENESS

"I have sincerely questioned the effectiveness of the F.B.I. in racial incidents, particularly where bombings and brutalities against Negroes are at issue. But I have never attributed this merely to the presence of Southerners in the F.B.I.

"This is part of a broader question of Federal involvement in the protection of Negroes in the South and the seeming inability to gain convictions in even the most heinous crimes perpetuated against civil rights workers.

"It remains a fact that not a single arrest was made in Albany, Ga. during the many brutalities against Negroes. Neither has a single arrest been made in connection with the tragic murder of the four children in Birmingham nor in the case of the three murdered civil rights workers in Mississippi.

"Moreover, all F.B.I. agents inevitably work with local law enforcement officers in car thefts, bank robberies and other interstate violations. This makes it more difficult to function effectively in cases where the rights and safety of Negro citizens are being threatened by these same [local] law enforcement officers.

"I will be happy to discuss this question with you at length in the near future. Although your statement said you have attempted to meet with me, I have sought in vain for any record of such a request.

"I have always made myself available to all F.B.I. agents of the Atlanta office and encouraged our staff and affiliates to cooperate with them in spite of the fact that many of our people have suspicions and distrust of the F.B.I. as a result of the slow pace of justice in the South."

NUMBER OF ARRESTS

Several arrests have been made recently in racial crimes in Mississippi on information gathered by the F.B.I.

Two white men were arrested on charges of murdering two Negroes in Meadville, Miss. last May and about 20 whites have been arrested in connection with bombings, church burnings and beating of civil rights workers in the McComb and Natchez areas.

A Federal grand jury has indicted law enforcement authorities of Philadelphia, Miss., for alleged beatings of Negro prisoners.

In the interview, Mr. Hoover also was critical of "red neck sheriffs" and other authorities in Mississippi reported to have participated in racial crimes.

Most civil rights leaders in the South have been critical of the F.B.I. for not providing more protection from racial violence. The bureau maintains it is an investigative agency only and tries to work where possible with local authorities.

In Albany, where Dr. King conducted a campaign against segregation in 1962, civil rights groups charged there had been a "complete breakdown of law enforcement" and asked the F.B.I. to intervene. James E. McMahon, then agent in charge of the bureau's Atlanta office, said there had been no such breakdown.

Leslie W. Dunbar, executive director of the Southern Regional Council, said it was difficult for the agents to "act contrary to the interests of the local law people."

"It is not altogether accurate to single out the F.B.I. for criticism," he said. "The F.B.I. works for the Department of Justice. In civil rights situations it's pretty much restricted to carrying out the assignments which it receives from the Department."

In Albany, Mr. Dunbar said, "the record of the whole Justice Department was poor. Just as the Kennedy Administration had its Bay of Pigs, it also had Albany, where it did everything wrong."

Mrs. Ruby Hurley, southeastern regional director for the National Association for the Advancement of Colored People, said she had found agents in charge of the major F.B.I. offices "very cooperative" in investigating civil rights cases.

"The difficulty is with the agents who go out to investigate," she said. "They tend to take on the coloration of the community."

Mrs. Hurley said in many instances the agents talked with the white people but "never talk with the Negroes—the people who are being oppressed.

"In some other instances," she said, "I have been pleased with the work of the F.B.I."

She said she was "a little appalled at the bluntness" of Mr. Hoover's statement.

The Student Nonviolent Coordinating Committee referred to the F.B.I.'s "historic failure to make concrete advances in assuring that Southern Negroes can exercise the simplest rights that most Americans take for granted."

Julian Bond, who heads the committee's communication staff, released a statement saying:

"Let Director Hoover prove that King is a liar by having his agents personally escort to the courthouse any Mississippi Negro who wants to register to vote but who knows any policeman or any white man may beat and jail him while the F.B.I. stands by taking notes."

DR. KING GIVES VIEWS

BIMINI, the Bahamas, Nov. 19 (AP)—The Rev. Dr. Martin Luther King Jr. said today the Federal Bureau of Investigation under the direction of J. Edgar Hoover was "following the path of appeasement of political powers in the South."

The Negro integration leader said in an interview:

"If this continues, the reign of terror in Mississippi, Alabama and Georgia will increase rather than subside."

Dr. King, referring to Mr. Hoover's attack on him yesterday, said he was certain the F.B.I. chief "would not have made such a vicious accusation without being under extreme pressure."

"This pressure," he continued, "has come on the racial front and from the Warren Report, raising serious questions about the effectiveness of the F.B.I."

Mr. Hoover, in his news conference yesterday, said Dr. King had advised Negroes not to report civil rights violations to the F.B.I. office in Albany, Ga., because the staff members were Southerners.

DENIES ACCUSATION

"I never advised Negroes in Albany not to report to the F.B.I.," Dr. King said today. "On the contrary, we reported every incident. But we were dismayed by the fact that nothing was ever done.

"The fact that no arrests have been made in the brutalities at Albany, the murder of three civil rights workers in Mississippi and the bombing of a church in Birmingham, Ala., has left us all discouraged.

"This has encouraged individuals on the lunatic fringe to feel that they are aided and abetted by Federal agents."

Dr. King said he had never made a blanket criticism of the F.B.I. and its agents. He said he believed a Southerner dedicated to his job could be as effective as one from the North.

"Rather than criticize the F.B.I.," Dr. King said, "I have acted as a mediator, urging Negroes to keep faith with the F.B.I. and to not lose hope.

"But you can't explain to a Negro why a plane can be bombed and its pieces scattered for miles and the crime can be solved, but they can't find out who bombed a church."

Sample Alabama Literacy Test Questions

c. 1964–65

SAMPLE SAMPLE

(35)

"B"

1. Has the following part of the U. S. Constitution been changed? "Representatives shall be apportioned among the several states according to their respective numbers, counting the whole number of persons in each state, excluding Indians not taxed." <u>No</u>
2. Which of the following is one of the duties of the United States Internal Revenue Service?
   _____ passing legislation
   __X__ collection of income taxes
   _____ giving welfare checks
3. There are three main types of city government in Alabama. Name one. <u>Mayor Council</u>
4. Law requires that "In God we trust" be placed on all money issued in the United States. <u>True</u>

- -

"C"

1. Does the population of the state affect the amount of individual or corporate income taxes which may be levied on its citizens? <u>No</u>
2. Who pays members of Congress for their services, their home states or the United States? <u>United States</u>
3. How many senators are elected from each state? <u>Two</u>
4. If the United States is a party in a suit can the case be heard in a federal court? <u>Yes</u>

SAMPLE SAMPLE

(38)

"B"

1. What body can try impeachments of the president of the United States? Senate
2. Check the applicable definition for responsibility:
   __X__ a duty
   _____ a speech
   _____ failure
3. Name the (acting) attorney general of the United States. Nicholas Katzenbach
4. Women may now serve on juries in Alabama State courts. True

---

"C"

1. If a person charged with treason denies his guilt, how many persons must testify against him before he can be convicted? Two
2. At what time of day on January 20 each four years does the term of the president of the United States end? 12 noon
3. If the president does not wish to sign a bill, how many days is he allowed in which to return it to Congress for reconsideration? Ten
4. If a bill is passed by Congress and the President refuses to sign it and does not send it back to Congress in session within the specified period of time, is the bill defeated or does it become law? It becomes law unless Congress adjourns before the expiration of 10 days

SAMPLE SAMPLE

(41)

"B"

1. Can the president of the United States be removed from office for conviction of bribery? Yes
2. Check the applicable definition for "treaty":

   __X__ agreement between nations

   _____ a tax

   _____ a written oration
3. Name the man who is nationally known for heading the Federal Bureau of Investigation for many years. Hoover
4. What officer is designated by the Constitution to be president of the Senate of the United States? Vice President

---

"C"

1. Can the state coin money with the consent of Congress? No
2. Name one area of authority over state militia reserved exclusively to the states. The appointment of officers
3. The power of granting patents, that is, of securing to inventors the exclusive right to their discoveries, is given to the Congress for the purpose of promoting progress.
4. The only legal tender which may be authorized by states for payment of debts is U. S. Currency.

SAMPLE SAMPLE

(46)

"B"

1. Can you be imprisoned, under Alabama law, for a debt? No
2. In addition to becoming a U. S. citizen by birth, a person may become a citizen by:
   _____ immigration
   __X__ naturalization
   _____ voting
3. Name one person by name or title who is part of the judicial branch of government in Alabama. Chief Justice Livingston
4. The first sentence of the United States Constitution is called the Preamble. True

---

"C"

1. In what year did the Congress gain the right to prohibit the migration of persons to the states? 1808
2. Who is the commander-in-chief of the army and navy of the United States? The President
3. Which of the Parts above, of the United States Constitution, deals with the federal government's authority to call the state militia into federal service? Part I
4. The president is forbidden to exercise his authority of pardon in cases of impeachment.

“THE AMERICAN DREAM IS AT THE EXPENSE OF THE AMERICAN NEGRO”

JAMES BALDWIN AND WILLIAM F. BUCKLEY

Debate at the Cambridge Union

February 18, 1965

Union president Fullerton, other Union officers, student debaters Heycock and Burford, and guest debaters Baldwin and Buckley enter the Union debating hall to applause.

FULLERTON: The motion before the house tonight is: the American dream is at the expense of the American Negro, your proposer Mr. David Heycock of Pembroke College, and opposer Mr. Jeremy Burford of Emmanuel College. Mr. James Baldwin will speak third; Mr. William F. Buckley Jr. will speak fourth. Mr. Heycock has the ear of the house.

FULLERTON: It is now with very great pleasure and a very great sense of honor that I call up Mr. James Baldwin to speak third to this motion.

[*Applause.*]

BALDWIN: Good evening. I find myself, not for the first time, in the position of a kind of Jeremiah. For example, I don’t disagree with Mr. Burford that the inequalities suffered by the American Negro population of the United States has hindered the American dream. Indeed it has. I quarrel with some other things he has to say. The other, deeper element of a certain awfulness I feel has to do with one’s point of view. I have to put it that way. One’s sense, one’s system of reality. It would seem to me the proposition before the house, when I put it that way, *is* the American dream *at* the expense of the American Negro, or the American dream *is* at the expense of the American Negro—is a question, hideously loaded—and that one's response to that question, one's reaction to that question, has to depend in effect—in effect on where you find yourself in the world. What your sense of reality is, what your system of reality is. That is, it depends on assumptions which we hold, so deeply, as to be scarcely aware of them.

A white South African, or a Mississippi sharecropper, or a Mississippi sheriff, or a Frenchman driven out of Algeria, all have, at bottom, a system of reality which compels them to —for example, in the case of the French exiled from Algeria, to defend French reasons for having ruled Algeria. The Mississippi, or the Alabama, sheriff, who really does believe when he's facing a Negro, a boy or a girl, that this woman, this man, this child, must be insane to attack the system to which he owes his entire identity. Of course, for such a person, the proposition of which . . . which we are trying to discuss here tonight, does not exist.

And on the other hand, *I* have to speak as one of the people who have been most attacked by what we must now here call the Western, or the European, system of reality. What white people in the world . . . the doctrine of white supremacy, I hate to say it here, comes from Europe. That's how it got to America. Beneath then, what everyone's reaction to this proposition is, has to be the question of whether or not civilizations can be considered as such equal, or whether one civilization has the right to overtake and subjugate, and in fact to destroy, another.

Now what happens when that happens? Leaving aside all the physical facts which one can quote, leaving aside rape, or murder, leaving aside the bloody catalog of oppression—which we are, in one way, too familiar with already—what this does to the subjugated, the most private, the most serious thing this does to the subjugated, is to destroy his sense of reality. It destroys, for example, his father's authority over him. His father can no longer tell him anything because the past had disappeared, and his father has no power in the world.

This means, in the case of an American Negro born in that glittering republic, and in the moment you are born—since you don't know any better—every stick and stone, and every face, is white, and since you have not yet seen a mirror, you suppose that you are too. It comes as a great shock around the age of five or six or seven to discover the flag to which you have pledged allegiance, along with everybody else, has not pledged allegiance to you. It comes as a great shock to discover that Gary Cooper killing off the Indians, when you were rooting for Gary Cooper, that the Indians were you! [*Audience laughter*]

It comes as a great shock to discover the country which is your birthplace, and to which you owe your life and your identity, has not in its whole system of reality evolved any place for you. The disaffection, the demoralization, and the gap between one person and another only on the basis of the color of their skin begins there, and accelerates, accelerates throughout a whole lifetime, so at present that you realize you're thirty and are having a terrible time managing to trust your countrymen. By the time you are thirty, you have been through a certain kind of mill, and the most serious effect of the mill you have been through is, again, not the catalog of disaster—the policemen, the taxi drivers, the waiters, the landlady, the landlord, the banks, the insurance companies, the millions of details twenty-four hours of every day which spell out to you that you are a worthless human being—it is not that! It is by that time that you have begun to see it happening in your daughter, or your son, or your niece, or your nephew. You are thirty by now, and nothing you have done has helped you escape the trap. But what is worse than that, is that nothing you have done, and as far as you can tell, nothing you can do, will save your son or your daughter from meeting the same disaster and not impossibly coming to the same end.

Now we're speaking about expense. I suppose there are several ways to address oneself to . . . some attempt to find what that word means here. Let me put it this way, that from a very literal point of view, the harbors and the ports and the railroads of the country, the economy, especially of the southern states, could not conceivably be what it has become if they had not had—and do not still have, indeed—and for so long, so many generations, cheap labor. I am stating very seriously, and this is not an overstatement, *I* picked the cotton, and *I* carried it to market, and *I* built the railroads, under someone else's whip, for nothing. For nothing.

The southern oligarchy, which has until today so much power in Washington, and therefore some power in the world, was created by my labor and my sweat, and the violation of my women, and the murder of my children. This, in the land of the free and the home of the brave, and no one can challenge that statement, it is a matter of historical record.

In another way, this dream—and we'll get to the dream in a moment—is at the expense of the American Negro. You watch this in the deep South in great relief, but not only in the deep South. In the deep South you are dealing with a sheriff, or a landlord, or a landlady, or the girl of the Western Union desk. And she doesn't know quite who she's dealing with. By which I mean that if you're not a part of the town, and if you are a northern nigger, it shows in millions of ways. So she simply knows that it's an unknown quantity and she wants [to] have nothing to do with it so she won't talk to you, you have to wait for a while to get your telegram, OK, we all know this, we've been through it, and by the time you get to be a man it's very easy to deal with.

But what is happening in the poor woman, the poor man's mind, is this: they have been raised to believe, and by now they helplessly believe, that no matter how terrible their lives may be, and their lives have been quite terrible, and no matter how far they fall, no matter what disaster overtakes them, they have one enormous knowledge and consolation which is like a heavenly revelation: at least they are not black. Now I suggest that of all the terrible things that can happen to a human being, that is one of the worst. I suggest that what has happened to white southerners is in some ways, after all, much worse than what has happened to Negroes there.

Because, Sheriff Clark in Selma, Alabama, cannot be considered, you know, no one is . . . can be dismissed as a total monster. I'm sure he loves his wife, his children [*audience laughter*]. I am sure that, you know, he likes to get drunk. You know, he's, after all, one's got to assume, and is he visibly a man like me. But he doesn't know what drives him to use the club, to menace with a gun, and to use a cattle prod. Something awful must have happened to a human being to be able to put a cattle prod against a woman's breast, for example. What happens to the woman is ghastly. What happens to the man who does it, is, in some ways, much, much worse.

This is being done, after all, not a hundred years ago but in 1965, in a country which is blessed with what we call prosperity—a word we won't examine too closely—with a certain kind of social coherence, which calls itself a civilized nation, which espouses the notion of the freedom of the world. And it is perfectly true from the point of view now, simply of an American Negro, any American Negro watching this, no matter where he is, from the vantage point of Harlem—which is another terrible place—has to say to himself, in spite of what the government says—the government says, "We can't do anything about it"—but if those are white people being murdered in Mississippi work farms, being carried off to jail, if those are white children running up and down the streets, the government would find some way of doing something about it. We have a civil rights bill now. We had an amendment, the Fifteenth Amendment, nearly a hundred years ago. I hate to sound again like an Old Testament prophet, but if the amendment was not honored then, I don't have any reason to believe that the civil rights bill will be honored now.

And after all, one's been there since before, you know, a lot of other people got there. If one has got to prove one's title to the land, isn't four hundred years enough? Four hundred years, at least three wars. The American soil is full of the corpses of my ancestors. Why is my freedom, or my citizenship, or my right to live there, how is it conceivably a question now? And I suggest further that in the same way the moral life of Alabama sheriffs, and poor Alabama ladies—white ladies—that their moral lives have been destroyed by the plague called color, that the American sense of reality has been corrupted by it.

At the risk of sounding excessive, what I always felt when I finally left the country and found myself abroad in other places, and watched Americans abroad, and these are my countrymen, and I do care about them. And even if I didn't, there is something between us. We have the same shorthand. I know when I look at a girl or a boy from Tennessee where they came from in Tennessee, and what that means. No Englishman knows that, no Frenchman, no one in the world knows that except another black man who comes from the same place. One watches these lonely people denying the only kin they have. We talk about integration in America as though it were some great, new conundrum. The problem in America is that we have been integrated for a very long time. Put me next to any African and you will see what I mean. And my grandmother was not a rapist.

What we are not facing is the results of what we've done. What one begs the American people to do for all our sakes is simply to accept our history. I was there not only as a slave but also as a concubine. One knows the power after all which can be used against another person if you've got absolute power over that person.

It seemed to me when I watched Americans in Europe that what they didn't know about Europeans was what they didn't know about me. They weren't trying, for example, to be nasty to the French girl, or rude to the French waiter; they didn't know they hurt their feelings. They didn't have any sense that this particular woman, this particular man, though they spoke another language, and had different manners and ways, was a human being. And they walked over them with the same kind of bland ignorance and condescension—charming and cheerful—with which they have always patted me on the head and called me "Shine," and were upset when I was upset.

What is relevant about this is that whereas forty years ago when I was born, the question of having to deal with what is unspoken by the subjugated, what is never said to the master, of having to deal with this reality, was a very remote, very remote possibility; it was in no one's mind. When I was growing up, I was taught in American history books that Africa had no history and neither did I. That I was a savage, about whom the less said the better, who had been saved by Europe and brought to America. And of course, I believed it. I didn't have much choice, those were the only books there were. Everyone else seemed to agree if you walk out of Harlem, ride out of Harlem, downtown, the world agrees what you see is much bigger, cleaner, whiter, richer, safer than where you are. They collect the garbage, people obviously can pay their life insurance, the children look happy, safe; you're not. And you go back home and it would seem that, of course, that it's an act of God that this *is* true, that you belong where white people have put you.

It is only since the Second World War that there's been a counterimage in the world, and that image had not come about through any legislation on the part of any American government, but through the fact that Africa was suddenly on the stage of the world and Africans had to be dealt with in a way they had never been dealt with before. This gave an American Negro, for the first time, a sense of himself beyond a savage or a clown. It has created, and will create, a great many conundrums.

One of the great things that the white world does not know, but I think I do know, is that black people are just like everybody else. One has used the myth of Negro and the myth of color to pretend and to assume that you are dealing, essentially, with something exotic, bizarre, and practically, according to human laws, unknown. Alas, that is not true. We are also mercenaries, dictators, murderers, liars. We are human too. What is crucial here, is that unless we can manage to establish some kind of dialogue between those people whom I pretend have paid for the American dream, and those other people who have not achieved it, we will be in terrible trouble.

I want to say at the end, at the last, is that that is what concerns me most. We are sitting in this room and we are all—at least we like to think we are—relatively civilized, and we can talk to each other at least on certain levels, so that we could walk out of here assuming that the measure of our enlightenment, or at least our politeness, has some effect on the world. It may not.

I remember, for example, when the ex attorney general Mr. Robert Kennedy said that it was conceivable that in forty years in America, we might have a Negro president. And that sounded like a very emancipated statement, I suppose, to white people. They were not in Harlem when this statement was first heard, and did not hear, and possibly will never hear, the laughter and the bitterness and the scorn with which this statement was greeted. From the point of view of the man in the Harlem barbershop, Bobby Kennedy only got here yesterday, and now he's already on his way to the presidency. We've been here for four hundred years, and now he tells us that maybe in forty years, if you're good [*audience laughter*], we may let you become president.

What is dangerous here is a turning away from, the turning away from anything any white American says. The reason for the political hesitation, in spite of the Johnson landslide, is that one has been betrayed by American politicians for so long. And I am a grown man, and perhaps I can be reasoned with, I certainly hope I can be. But I don't know, and neither does Martin Luther King, none of us know, how to deal with those other people whom the white world has so long ignored who don't believe anything the white world says, and don't entirely believe anything I or Martin say. And one can't blame them; you watch what has happened to them in less than twenty years.

It seems to me that the city of New York, for example—this is my last point—has had Negroes in it for a very long time. If the city of New York were able, as it has indeed been able for the last fifteen years, to reconstruct itself, tear down buildings and raise great new ones, downtown and for money, and has done nothing whatever except build housing projects in the ghetto for the Negroes. And of course the Negroes hate it. Presently the property does indeed deteriorate because it surely cannot bear it; they want to get out of the ghetto. If the American pretensions were based on more solid, a more honest assessment of life and of themselves, it would not mean for Negroes when someone may . . . says "urban renewal" that Negroes simply are going to be thrown out in the street, which is what it does mean now. It is not an act of God; we are dealing with a society made and ruled by men. If the American Negro had not been present in America, I am convinced that the history of the American labor movement would be much more edifying than it is.

It is a terrible thing for an entire people to surrender to the notion that one-ninth of its population is beneath them. And until that moment, until the moment comes, when we, the Americans, we the American people, are able to accept the fact that I have to accept, for example, that my ancestors are both white and black, that on that continent we are trying to forge a new identity for which we need each other, and that I am not a ward of America, I am not an object of missionary charity, I am one of the people who built the country. Until this moment there is scarcely any hope for the American dream because the people who are denied participation in it, by their very presence, will wreck it.

And if that happens, it's a very grave moment for the West. Thank you.

[*Applause that develops into standing ovation for Baldwin. The ovation lasts for just over one minute.*]

FULLERTON: I am now very grateful and very pleased to be able to call on Mr. William F. Buckley Jr. to speak forth to this motion.

[*Applause.*]

BUCKLEY: Thank you, Mr. President, Mr. Heycock, Mr. Burford, Mr. Baldwin, gentlemen. It seems to me that of all the indictments Mr. Baldwin has made of America here tonight and in his copious literature of protest, the one that is the most striking involves, in effect, the refusal of the American community to treat him other than as a Negro. The American community has refused to do this. The American community, almost everywhere he goes, treats him with a kind of unction, a kind of satisfaction at posturing carefully before his flagellations of our civilization, that indeed quite properly commands the contempt which he so eloquently showers upon it.

It is impossible, in my judgment, to deal with the indictment of Mr. Baldwin unless one is prepared to deal with him as a white man. Unless one is prepared to say to him, "The fact that your skin is black is utterly irrelevant to the arguments that you raise." The fact that you sit here as is your rhetorical device and lay the entire weight of the Negro ordeal on your own shoulders is irrelevant to the argument that we are here to discuss.

The gravamen of Mr. Baldwin's charges against America are not so much that our civilization has failed him and his people, that our ideals are insufficient, but that we have no ideals, that our ideals rather are some sort of a superficial coating which we come up with at any given moment in order to justify whatever commercial and noxious experiment we are engaged in. Thus Mr. Baldwin can write his book *The Fire Next Time* in which he threatens America . . . he didn't, in writing that book, speak with the British accents that he used exclusively tonight in which he threatened America with the necessity for us . . .

[*Coughing, scattered laughter, and a shout of "shame!" Fullerton admonishes the crowd to permit Buckley to speak.*]

BUCKLEY: . . . for us to jettison our entire civilization. "The only thing that the white man has that the Negro should want," he said, "is power." And he is treated from coast to coast of the United States with a kind of unctuous servitude which, in point of fact, goes beyond anything that was ever expected from the most servile Negro creature by a southern family.

I'm proposing to pay him the honor this night of saying to him, Mr. Baldwin, I'm going to speak to you without any reference whatever to those surrounding protections which you are used to in virtue of the fact that you are a Negro, and in virtue of the fact that your race has dreadfully suffered at the hands of my race. I am treating you as a fellow American, as a person whose indictments of our civilization are unjustified. As a person who—if his counsels are listened to—would be cursed by all of his grandchildren's grandchildren in virtue of what he actually seeks to bring down upon America in pursuit of his neurotic mission.

Ladies and gentlemen, we may or may not as you like spend as much of the balance of this evening as you like in reciting these luridities of oppression. One hundred and twenty-five years ago this house was bitterly divided over the question of whether or not the same people in England who practiced the faith of Erasmus, your most distinguished graduate, should be allowed to vote. By a slim margin it was condescended that they ought to be allowed to do so. In other parts of this country, there are people who in virtue of their having been invited into the United Nations, we are now told, are not savages or clowns who, for instance, in the case of the Watusi are responsible for—according to statistics, I know statistics seem to disturb some of you—but according to these statistics, some 10,000 or 12,000 of them were killed over a six-week period. We know that class antagonism and even [*unintelligible*] are responsible for—to take the figures of the American federation of labor and CIO—are responsible for 22 million deaths over a period of two and a half years in Red China. We know that British Guyana, in which there are very few white people, has been engaged in an internecine war between Indians and Africans. We know that the [*unintelligible*] don't get on with the [*unintelligible*] and we know that the untouchables have a hard life in India. We know that there was more blood shed trying to bring emancipation to the Irish here in the British Isles than has been shed by all of the people, ten times the number of people who have been lynched as a result of the delirium of race consciousness, race supremacy, in the United States in the days since the Reconstruction.

Shall we devote the night to these luridities? Shall we devote the evening to examining the sociological facts of human nature? There is an endogamous instinct in the average person whether he be Irish or whether he be German, or whether he be French or whether English. Shall we discuss these class antagonisms in terms of race, in terms of economic standing? Shall we discuss the fate of the oiks in Eton College? Shall we discuss in effect the existential dilemma of humankind? That people do, in fact, group together, and that when they amass power, they often tend to ascertain that the English had done as the Irish had done. Let us ask the questions, sir . . .

[*Buckley calls on a questioner in the audience.*]

AUDIENCE MEMBER: Point of information, sir. Why don't we discuss the motion?

[*Laughter, applause, and shouts of "hear, hear!"*]

BUCKLEY: To respond to your question, I was not given your instructions on how to comport myself before being invited here.

[*Laughter and applause.*]

It is a fact, and let us stipulate, that the situation in America is as it is, that the situation in Africa is as it is, that the situation in India is as it is. The question before the house, as I understand it, is not ought we to have purchased slaves generations ago, or as we may be permitted to put it another way, ought the blacks who sold us these slaves, ought they to have sold them to us, but rather is there anything in the American dream, which intrinsically argues against some kind of a deliverance from a system that we all recognize as evil, as unsatisfactory, as arguing against the best impulses of a civilized society.

And here we need to ask the question, What in fact shall we do about it, Mr. President? What shall we, in America, try to do, for instance, to eliminate those psychic humiliations which I join Mr. Baldwin in believing are the very worst aspects of this discrimination? You found it a source of considerable mirth to laugh away the statistics of my colleague Mr. Burford. I don't think they are insignificant; they are certainly not insignificant in a world which attaches a considerable importance to material progress. It is in fact the case that seven-tenths of the white income of the United States is equal to the income that is made by the average Negro. I don't think that this is an irrelevant statistic, ladies and gentlemen, but it takes the capitalization of fifteen, sixteen, seventeen thousand dollars per job in the United States. This was the capitalization that . . . that was not created exclusively as a result of Negro travail. My great-grandparents worked too; presumably yours worked also. I don't know of anything that has ever been created without the expense of something. All of you who hope for a diploma here are going to do that at the expense of a considerable amount of effort and I would thank you . . . [*audience laughter*] please not to deny the fact that a considerable amount of effort went into the production of a system which grants a greater degree of material well-being to the American Negro and that that is enjoyed by 95 percent of the other peoples of the human race. But even so, to the extent that your withering laughter suggested here, that you found this a contemptible observation, I agree! I don't think it matters that there are 35 millionaires among the Negro community, if there were 35, if there were 20 million millionaires among the Negro community of the United States, I would still agree with you, that we have a dastardly situation, but I am asking you not to make politics "as the crow flies," to use the fleeted phrase of Professor Oakeshott, but rather to consider what in fact is it that we Americans ought to do? What are your instructions that I am to take back to the United States, my friends? [*audience laughter*] I want to know what it is that we should do, and especially I want to know whether it is time, in fact, to abandon the American dream as it has been defined by Mr. Heycock and Mr. Burford.

What in fact is it that we ought to do, for instance, to avoid due humiliations mentioned by Mr. Baldwin as being a part of his own experience during his lifetime. At the age of twelve, you will find on reading his book, he trespassed outside the ghetto of Harlem and was taken by the scruff of the neck by a policeman on Forty-Second Street and Madison Avenue, and said, "Here you nigger, go back to where you belong." Fifteen, twenty years later he goes in and asks for a scotch whiskey at the airport at Chicago, and is told by the white barman that he is obviously underage and under the circumstances cannot be served. I know! I know from your faces that you share with me the feeling of compassion and the feeling of outrage that this kind of thing should have happened. What in fact are we going to do to this policeman and what in fact are we going to do to this barman? How are we going to avoid the kind of humiliations that are perpetually visited on members of a minority race?

Obviously the first element is concern. We've got to care that it happens, we have got to do what we can to change the warp and woof of moral thought in society in such fashion as to try to make it happen less and less. But the proposition before us tonight, as elaborated by Mr. Baldwin in his book *The Fire Next Time*, is we ought precisely to recognize that because the American civilization, and indeed the Western civilization, has failed him and his people, we ought to throw it over. He tells us that our civilization rests on the rantings of the Hebrew, sunbaked fanatic called Jesus—not, says he—reaching the depths of historical knowledge—truly the founder of the Christian religion. The founder of the Christian religion was actually Paul, whom he describes as a merciless fanatic. And as a result of the teachings of these people and notice, please, the soritic leap from that moment until this, we have Dachau. And Dachau forever foreclosed the notion and possibility that Christianity was a viable civilization. What is it appropriate for us to do under the circumstances if we assume that Dachau was the natural consequence of the teachings of Saint Paul and Jesus? What shall we do with the library around here to begin with? Shall we descend on it and uproot all the literature that depends in any way on the teachings of Plato and Aristotle because they justified slavery? Or shall we rather make the point, shall we . . . sir . . .

[*Buckley calls on a questioner in the audience.*]

AUDIENCE MEMBER: You keep asking what we should do and then you are telling us what we should *not* do.

BUCKLEY: I'll tell you in due course. The primary question before the house, as posed by the larger attitude taken by Mr. Baldwin, sir, is whether or not our civilization has shown itself so flawed as the result of the failure of its response to the Negro problem of the United States that it ought to be jettisoned. Now I suggest that anybody who argued, as indeed it may have been argued in this very house, for all I know, in this very chamber, 125 years ago, the very fact that Jews and Catholics were not given the vote, were not allowed to vote in England as late as 1828, suggested English civilization ought to have been jettisoned. I suggest that the other possibility ought to be considered: that precisely the reason they *did* get the vote was because English civilization was *not* jettisoned. That the whole point of our philosophical concern ought never to be to make that terrible fault that is made so frequently by the positivists, that we should so immanentize our own misgivings as to rush forward to jettison and to overthrow our civilization because we do not live up to its higher ideals.

Let me urge this point to you which I can do with authority, my friends, the only thing that I can tonight [*scattered laughter*], and that is to tell you that in the United States, there is a concern for the Negro problem. Now if you get up to me and say . . . [*audience laughter*] if you get up to me and say, "Well now, is it the kind of concern that we, the students of Cambridge, would show if the problem were our own?" all I can say is I don't know. It may very well be that there has been some sort of a sunburst of moral enlightenment that has hit this community so as to make it predictable that if you were the governors of the United States, the situation would change overnight. I'm prepared to grant this as a form of courtesy, Mr. President [*audience laughter*].

But meanwhile I am saying to you that the engines of concern in the United States are working. The presence of Mr. Baldwin here tonight is in part a reflection of that concern [*scattered audience mumbling and shouting*]. You cannot go to a university in the United States, a university in the United States, presumably also governed by the Lord's spiritual as you are, in which Mr. Baldwin is not the toast of the town. You cannot go to a university of the United States in which practically all other problems of public policy are preempted by the primary policy of concern for the Negro. I challenge you to name another civilization anytime, anywhere, in the history of the world in which the problems of a minority which have been showing considerable material and political advancement is as much a subject of dramatic concern as it is in the United States.

There is one thing that Americans are not willing to do. They are not willing, as a result of the exasperation of Mr. Baldwin to say that the whole American proposition was an unfortunate experiment. They are not willing to say that as a result of the fact that we have not accelerated faster the progress of the Negroes, we are going to desert the constitutional system, we are going to desert the idea of the rule of law, we are going to desert the idea of the individual rights of the American citizen, that we are going to burn all the Bibles, and turn our backs on Europe, and tell them that we want to reject our entire Judeo-Christian civilization and our entire Hellenic background because of the continuous persistence of the kind of evil that is so carefully and eloquently described by Mr. Baldwin.

[*Buckley calls on a questioner in the audience.*]

AUDIENCE MEMBER: I wonder if you can point out to me any one of Mr. Baldwin's writings in which he actually said he wants to get rid of civilization [*applause*]?

BUCKLEY: I don't know your rules intimately enough to know whether or not I should have been forbidden from reading Mr. Baldwin's books before arriving here. I understand it is part of the purpose of this program to promote the reading of those books [*audience laughter and applause*]. I quote you exactly a passage from Mr. Baldwin—which I would have thought would have traversed the Atlantic Ocean—in which he says, "The only thing that the whites have that the Negroes should want is power." If Mr. Baldwin chooses this electric occasion to renounce his own renunciation of civilization then I would think that you would have had a historic debate on your hands, Mr. President, and I do urge you to give Mr. Baldwin that opportunity and I hope he takes it.

Let me just say finally, ladies and gentlemen, this: there is no instant cure for the race problem in America, and anybody who tells you that there is, is a charlatan and ultimately a boring man. Boring . . . [*audience laughter and coughing*] precisely because he is then speaking in the kind of abstractions that do not relate to the human experience. The trouble in America where the Negro community is concerned is a very complicated one. I urge those of you who have an actual rather than a purely ideologized interest in the problem to read the book *Beyond the Melting Pot* by Professor Glazer, also coauthor of *The Lonely Crowd*, a prominent Jewish intellectual, who points to the fact that the situation in America where the Negroes are concerned is extremely complex as a result of an unfortunate conjunction of two factors. One is the dreadful efforts to perpetuate discrimination by many individual American citizens as a result of their lack of that final and ultimate concern which some people are truly trying to agitate. The other is as a result of the failure of the Negro community itself to make certain exertions, which were made by other minority groups during the American experience. If you can stand a statistic not of my own making, let me give you one which Professor Glazer considers as relevant; he says, for instance, "In 1900, there were 3,500 Negro doctors in America; in 1960, there were 3,900, an increase in 400." Is this because there were no opportunities, as has been suggested by Mr. Heycock and also by Mr. Baldwin, implicitly? No, says Professor Glazer, there are a great many medical schools, who by no means practice discrimination, who are anxious to receive . . . to train Negro doctors; there are scholarships available to put them through. But in fact that particular energy, which he remarks was so noticeable in the Jewish community, and to a certain and lesser extent, in the Italian, Irish community, for some reason is not there.

We should focus on the necessity to animate this particular energy, but he comes to the conclusion which strikes me as plausible, that the people who can best do it, who can do it most effectively, are Negroes themselves. And what should James Baldwin be doing rather than telling us that we should renounce our civilization. Rather in my judgment he should be addressing his own people, and urging them to take at least the advantage of those opportunities that exist, and urging us, as he has been doing, to make those opportunities wider and better than those that exist. Says Mr. Glazer: in relative terms, the Chinese community derives forty-five times as much income from the patronage of its own people as the Negroes do from the patronage of their own people. In fact, these problems do exist, and let us so sentimentalize the question as to assume they don't exist, because to do so is hardly to render any kind of creative fervor to the Negro problem.

Let me conclude by reminding you, ladies and gentlemen, that where the Negro is concerned, the danger as far as I can see at this moment is that they will seek to reach out for some sort of radical solutions on the basis of which the true problem is obscured. They have done a great deal to focus on the fact of white discrimination against Negroes. They have great . . . done a great deal to agitate a moral concern, but where, in fact, do they go now? They seem to be slipping, if you will read carefully, for instance, the words of Mr. Bayard Rustin, towards some sort of a procrustean formulation which ends up less urging the advancement of the Negro than the regression of the white people. Fourteen times as many people in New York City born of Negroes are illegitimate as of whites. This is a problem. How shall we address it? By seeking out laws that encourage illegitimacy in white people? This, unfortunately, tends to be the rhetorical momentum that some of the arguments are taking.

[*Buckley calls on a questioner in the audience.*]

AUDIENCE MEMBER: One thing you might do, Mr. Buckley, is let them vote in Mississippi [*audience applause and shouts of "here, here!"*]!

BUCKLEY: I agree, I agree [*applause continues*]. I couldn't agree with you more. And for . . . [*audience laughter*]. Except, lest I appear too ingratiating, which is hardly my objective here tonight, I think actually what is wrong in Mississippi, sir, is not that not enough Negroes are voting but that too many white people are voting [*audience laughter and applause*].

Booker T. Washington said that the important thing where Negroes are concerned is not that they hold public office but that they be prepared to hold public office, not that they vote but that they be prepared to vote. What ought we to do with the Negroes having taught the Negroes in Mississippi to despise Ross Barnett? Shall we then teach them to emulate their cousins in Harlem and adore Adam Clayton Powell Jr.? It is much more complicated, sir, than simply the question of giving them the vote. If I were myself a constituent of the community of Mississippi at this moment, what I would do is vote to lift the standards of the vote so as to disqualify 65 percent of the white people . . . [*audience laughter*] who are presently voting [*audience laughter and applause*].

I say, then, that what we need is a considerable amount of frankness that acknowledges that there are two sets of difficulties: the difficulties of the white person who acts as white people and brown people and black people do all over the world to protect their own vested interests who have, as all of the races in the entire world have and suffer from a kind of a racial narcissism, which tends always to convert every contingency into such a way as to maximize their own power, that yes, we must do. But we must also reach through to the Negro people and tell them that their best chances are in a mobile society, and the most mobile society in the world today, my friends, is the United States of America.

AUDIENCE MEMBER: "Hear, hear!"

BUCKLEY: The most mobile society in the world is the United States of America, and it is precisely that mobility which will give opportunities to the Negroes which they must be encouraged to take, but they must not, in the course of their ordeal, be encouraged to adopt the kind of cynicism, the kind of despair, the kind of iconoclasm that is urged upon them by

Mr. Baldwin in his recent works. Because of one thing I can tell you I believe with absolute authority, that where the United States is concerned, if it ever becomes a confrontation between a continuation of our own sort of idealism, the private stock of which, granted, like most people in the world we tend to lavish only every now and then on public enterprises, reserving it so often for our own irritations and pleasures, but the fundamental friend of the Negro people in the United States is the good nature and is the generosity, and is the good wishes, is the decency, the fundamental decency that do lie at the reserves of the spirit of the American people.

These must not be laughed at, under no circumstances must they be laughed at, and under no circumstances must America be addressed and told that the only alternative to the status quo is to overthrow that civilization which we consider to be the faith of our fathers, the faith indeed of your fathers. This is what must animate whatever meliorism must come because if it does finally come to a confrontation, a radical confrontation, between giving up what we understand to be the best features of the American way of life, which at that level is indistinguishable, so far as I can see, from the European way of life, then we will fight the issue, and we will fight the issue not only in the Cambridge Union, but we will fight it as you were once recently called to do on beaches and on hills, on mountains and on landing grounds. And we will be convinced that just as you won the war against a particular threat to civilization, you were nevertheless waging a war in favor of and for the benefit of Germans, your own enemies, just as we are convinced that if it should ever come to that kind of a confrontation, our own determination to win the struggle will be a determination to wage a war not only for whites but also for Negroes.

[*Audience applause and scattered shouting for about half a minute.*]

FULLERTON: Will the tellers take their places, please?

[*Members of the Union cast their votes by walking through the "aye" or "nay" door. After the votes are tallied, Fullerton rises to announce the results.*]

FULLERTON: Those voted in favor of the motion, the motion being that the American dream is at the expense of the Negro, those voted in favor of that motion 544 persons and against 164 persons. The motion is therefore carried by 380 votes. I declare the house to stand adjourned.

[*Applause.*]

“A MEASURE . . . VITALLY NEEDED AND LONG OVERDUE”

JOHN CONYERS

Speech in Congress on the Voting Rights Act

July 8, 1965

MR. CONYERS. Mr. Chairman, this Congress is now demonstrating its determination finally to guarantee to all Americans the right to vote and finally enforce the 15th amendment of the Constitution, incidentally 95 years after its passage. For this reason it will be an everlasting source of pride to me that I was a Member of this 89th Congress, for it is a Congress marked for greatness by the historic measures it has passed. I was particularly honored to be chosen by my colleagues to serve on the Judiciary Committee which has toiled these last few months to fashion fully effective legislation securing the right to vote. What we do today could, for the first time in American history, guarantee the right of all Americans to fully and fairly participate in the democratic process.

President Johnson's speech on March 15 was the most explicit and far reaching ever made by an American President concerning the right to vote. Can Congress do any less than fulfill its own responsibility in this area? The overwhelming national support given the President's speech showed it reflected the sentiments of the great majority of the American people. We have seen thousands of American citizens from all walks of life journey to Selma, Ala., and other places in this country to make personal witness of their determination to support equal rights for all Americans. The great majority of this House, I feel sure, will approve the strongest bill necessary to finally guarantee the right to vote because we know such a measure is vitally needed and long overdue. The American people have clearly shown that they fully support the proposition that “we must overcome the crippling legacy of bigotry and injustice—and we shall overcome.”

Over the last 8 years Congress has passed three different laws designed to guarantee the right to vote which primarily relied on the Federal courts for enforcement. However, that method has been painfully slow and woefully inadequate. It is only after this discouraging record of obstructions and delays that we have resorted to more far-reaching remedies.

The committee bill establishes a Federal system of administrative enforcement. I readily admit that such a procedure goes against all the normal instincts of the American governmental system which prefers local and judicial instead of Federal and administrative enforcement. However, we have no other choice if we are to pass effective legislation. Surely there can be no doubt, at this late date, about the continuous refusal of local officials in so many areas of our country to enforce the constitutional guarantees of the right to vote.

My concern is that this bill must be fully effective if we are to meet our responsibility to deal with the moral and political crisis facing the country. Even with the 1957, 1960, and 1964 Civil Rights Acts millions of Americans are still denied the right to vote by means both devious and blatant. After three unsuccessful attempts, if our fourth try at drafting legislation guaranteeing the right to vote is not successful, I fear we risk creating a feeling of cynicism and frustration among many Americans regarding the effectiveness and justice of our system of Government.

May I quote to you an example of that deep feeling of cynicism and frustration expressed by one of America's great Negro statesmen, Frederick Douglass, a number of years ago. He said:

> So far as the colored people of the country are concerned, the Constitution is but a stupendous sham, a rope of sand, a dead sea apple, fair without and foul within, keeping the promise to the eye and breaking it to the heart. The Federal Constitution, so far as we are concerned, has abdicated its functions and abandoned the objects for which the Constitution was framed and adopted, and for this I arraign it at the bar of public opinion, both of our country and that of the civilized world. I am here to tell the truth, and tell it without fear or favor, and the truth is that neither the Republican Party nor the Democratic Party has yet complied with the solemn oath, taken by their prospective

> representatives, to support the Constitution and execute the laws enacted under its provisions. They have promised us law, and abandoned us to anarchy; they have promised protection and given us violence.

Such was Frederick Douglass' cry of accusation against the Federal Government in 1886. Today we are assembled to answer and refute this cry of outrage.

CONSTITUTIONAL BASIS OF VOTING RIGHTS BILL

Now much has been said to the effect that we are overreaching the limits of the 15th amendment. I believe that this is not the case. I have no doubt about the firm constitutional basis upon which H.R. 6400 rests. In the year 1939 the Supreme Court indicated the very wide scope of the 15th amendment, in its decision striking down the Oklahoma constitution's grandfather clause:

> The reach of the 15th amendment against contrivances by a State to thwart equality in the enjoyment of the right to vote by citizens of the United States regardless of race or color has been amply expounded by prior decisions. The amendment nullifies sophisticated as well as simple-minded modes of discrimination. It hits onerous procedural requirements which effectively handicap exercise of the franchise by the colored race although the abstract right to vote may remain unrestricted as to race.

But if for any reason it may be unclear that the 15th amendment empowered Congress to guarantee the right to all Americans equal access to the ballot in State and local elections, we need only remember the special responsibility of the Federal Government under article IV, section 4, which has been discussed very little in this debate, for there it says that:

> The United States shall guarantee to every State in this Union a republican form of government.

Surely the essence of a republican form of government is that every citizen is allowed and even encouraged to select his representatives. Otherwise our claim that governments derive "their just powers from the consent of the governed" would be the most despicable form of legal and political sophistry imaginable.

But more than any particular section of the Constitution, my colleagues, this bill implements the promise of the Constitution as stated in the preamble. "We, the people of the United States, in order to form a more perfect union"—this country will never have the unity it so desperately craves and so vitally needs in this troubled modern world in my judgment if any group in America is denied their constitutional rights and the equal protection of the laws; "establish justice"—at that point let me say the Founding Fathers knew so well that in the final analysis the vote is the best guarantee of our concept of equal justice; "insure domestic tranquility"—the outraged sense of justice of so many Americans, both black and white, will never allow us to enjoy domestic peace until the promise of America is fulfilled, "provide for the common defense"—we are weak before our enemies if our goals abroad are so shamelessly ignored and subverted here at home, "promote the general welfare"—to build a great and prosperous nation which will provide a good life for all of our citizens, to do this we must begin essentially by guaranteeing every American equal justice under law; "and finally to secure the blessings of liberty to ourselves and our posterity"—for no person, or for that matter any group, can be secure in their inalienable rights unless all Americans are.

But as we all know, this bill will not end racial discrimination as it is practiced or as it lies dormant in the hearts and minds of all too many Americans in every part of this great Nation.

The CHAIRMAN. The time of the gentleman from Michigan has expired.

Mr. RODINO. Mr. Chairman, I yield the gentleman 3 additional minutes.

Mr. CONYERS. However, a firm and enforced declaration by Congress that Negro-Americans are to be treated equally by guaranteeing that most basic democratic right—the right to vote—will go a long way toward dispelling the whole complex of prejudices which form the psychological base for racial discrimination in this country.

Modern science has shown us that it is only a belief in the prejudiced stereotypes of the Negro depicting him as somewhat less than human which allows otherwise compassionate human beings to be unmoved when Americans commit barbarous acts of cruelty and violence against their fellow countrymen. To do these things a person apparently must believe that Negroes, as such, with only few exceptions, are essentially different from whites. This person must nourish and preserve a stereotype depicting Negroes as relatively unteachable, and therefore ignorant; as insensitive to the demands of abstract ideals, and therefore less troubled by discrimination than the white man; as devoid of moral fibers and therefore predisposed to crime; as scornful of cleanliness and personal fitness and therefore susceptible to disease; and as motivated solely by bodily appetites.

H.R. 6400 will not end this kind of prejudice. Indeed, no law, in and of itself, can or ever will. But H.R. 6400 is a beginning, a very crucial, vital, and important beginning, if we are to achieve the promise of "the last best hope of the world."

Throughout this debate runs the theme of recognition by the majority of the heroic role Negro-Americans have played in their country's history. Negro-Americans have fought valiantly and shed their blood in every American war from the Revolutionary War down to the present. Members of this great body —from both sides of the aisle and representing various regions of the country—have spoken eloquently of how, within the brief span of a few generations, Negro-Americans have overcome the crippling legacy of slavery.

This petition for redress of grievances—the greatest ever presented in American history—is, thank God, being heard, understood, and supported overwhelmingly by the American people. And what is sought? Nothing more than freedom in its most elementary political sense—the right to vote. This, then, is what brings us here today. And I for one, my colleagues, am confident that we will acquit ourselves in these deliberations with great distinction.

CORE Voter Registration Training Materials for Louisiana

c. 1965

PREFACE

It has been my experience to find that CORE staff is just as ignorant about the political structure of Louisiana as the people in the community in which they are working. This is not a reflection on anyone, it's just that the people in the community have been denied the right to vote and the majority of staff were either too young to vote or were concentrating on other programs and had no interest or time for politics. Now, with the passage of the voting bill, it is imperative that there be a political awareness among the people and staff alike.

A serious shortage of paper (and money) in this office prevents us from supplying you with more than one booklet, but if you have need of a booklet of this type in your political education program, I would strongly urge that you cut the stencils and run them off on your project.

These booklets may be used as you see fit, but it is my suggestion that only one page be issued to your class or group at a time. This has a twofold purpose, first, it allows the teacher to stay ahead of the class, thus, any local person can teach, which would be a tremendous step towards community organization in some areas. Secondly, if you have a shortage of stencils and paper, as most projects do, you won't have to use your complete supply all at once and it will give you more time to hustle up more supplies.

After page "one" has been issued to the "class" or "discussion group" (or whatever you prefer to call it), it is then read and thoroughly discussed before the quiz sheets are distributed. After the questions have been answered, there should be another discussion and a question and answer period.

They are then given the next lesson, (not the questions) to take home and study. The answers to some of the questions cannot be found in the text of this booklet. This was done deliberately to stimulate the interest of the group and start them to asking questions and doing their own research into the political structure of their parish. Classes should be held at least once a week but preferably twice a week, possibly on Tuesdays, since these are relatively uncluttered days as far as the community is concerned.

This is the first of four booklets designed as a teaching aid for political education classes. I sincerely welcome all criticisms and comments and if there are any suggestions for improvement, please don't hesitate to write or otherwise contact me.

FREEDOM,
RICHARD TINSLEY

REGISTRATION

After qualifications for voting have been determined, some procedure must be set up so that a record may be compiled of those eligible to vote. This is known as registration, a procedure the purpose of which is to assure the public that only those qualified will be permitted to cast their ballots. This is but one of many safeguards against such corrupt practices as stuffing the ballot boxes, padding the rolls, voting the names of deceased or fictitious persons, repeating, or voting by nonresidents or floaters. For example, a 1958 Act of the Louisiana Legislature on this subject makes it unlawful to buy the registration of any voter, to offer money or anything of value or the promise of anything of value to induce him to register, and also makes it unlawful for any person to receive money or anything of value, or the promise thereof, for his registration.

Registration in Louisiana is required of all voters throughout the state, both urban and rural, for both primary and general elections. The registrar of voters, who is elected by the governing body of the parish, (except in Orleans parish, where the Governor makes the appointment), conducts registration. The State Board of Registration, composed of the Governor, Lieutenant Governor, and Speaker of the House of Representatives, can remove any registrar at will. The board appoints a State Director of Registration.

Louisiana uses both periodic and permanent registration. The former plan lies in effect in all parishes in which permanent registration has not been adopted. The period of periodic registration is four years, with the current registration running from January 1, 1965 through December 31, 1968. Under permanent registration a voter must register only once, providing he does not move or his name is not in some other authorized manner stricken from the records as unqualified. If the voter resides in a parish having a population exceeding 300,000 and he fails to vote during a two-year period, in cases in which he has registered a party affiliation (four years if he is not affiliated with "a party holding a primary in parishes containing cities having a population exceeding 100,000") his name is taken off the rolls and he must re-register to become eligible to vote. In all other parishes the names of all voters who fail to vote at least once in every four years are removed from the rolls, and a new registration is then necessary prior to again exercising the right to vote.

Permanent registration is mandatory in all parishes with municipalities of over 100,000 population (Orleans, Caddo, East Baton Rouge). Other parishes have an option to come under the plan through the action of the governing body of the parish. By January 31, 1959, a total of 38 of Louisiana's 64 parishes had adopted permanent registration. Well over one-half of the state's total population live in these parishes.

REGISTRATION

1. NAME THREE METHODS OF CHEATING AT THE POLLS:
   1. ______
   2. ______
   3. ______
2. EXPLAIN IN YOUR OWN WORDS THE 1958 ACT OF THE LOUISIANA LEGISLATURE. ______
   ______
   ______
   ______
3. WHO CONDUCTS REGISTRATION? ______
   ______
4. WHAT OFFICIALS COMPOSE THE STATE BOARD OF REGISTRATION? ______
   ______
   GIVE THEIR NAMES AND TITLES:
   ______
   ______
   ______
5. HOW MANY TYPES OF REGISTRATION ARE THERE IN LOUISIANA? ______
   NAME THEM: ______
6. WHAT TYPE OF REGISTRATION IS IN EFFECT IN YOUR PARISH? ______
7. WHAT HAPPENS IF YOU FAIL TO VOTE WITHIN A FOUR-YEAR PERIOD? ______
   ______
8. WHO HAS THE AUTHORITY TO STATE WHAT TYPE OF REGISTRATION THAT A PARISH WILL HAVE? ______
9. IF A PERSON IS REMOVED FROM THE ROLLS FOR NOT VOTING DURING A CERTAIN PERIOD OF TIME, CAN HE EVER BE ELIGIBLE TO VOTE AGAIN? ______
   EXPLAIN: ______
   ______
10. HOW DOES THE STATE DIRECTOR GET INTO OFFICE? ______
    ______

QUALIFICATIONS FOR VOTING IN LOUISIANA

AGE

Twenty-one years

RESIDENCE

1. State; One year
2. Parish; One year
3. Precinct: Three months
4. Municipalities: Four months

CITIZENSHIP

United States Citizenship

LITERACY

No literacy requirements

DISQUALIFICATIONS

1. Conviction for crime without pardon and express restoration of suffrage.* (*The right to vote)
2. Confinement in public prison at the time of elections.
3. Inmates of charitable homes except the Soldiers Home and the United States Hospital at Carville.
4. Interdicted persons, as well as those not interdicted who are obviously insane or idiotic.
5. Deserters from the military service who have not served out their time of enlistment.
6. Dishonorable discharge from the Louisiana National Guard or from the military service of the United States, where not reinstated.

ABSENTEE VOTING

Permitted, by mail, for members of the armed services, United States Merchant Marine, civilian employees of the United States serving outside the United States, members of religious groups and welfare agencies officially attached to and serving with the armed forces, and spouses and dependents of any of these; also for persons required to be outside the United States for more than 15 days. All other qualified voters not in the parish on election day must vote in person at the clerk of courts office, (civil sheriff in Orleans Parish) from two to ten days prior to the election

QUALIFICATIONS FOR VOTING

1. HOW LONG MUST ONE RESIDE IN THE CITY TO BE ELIBIBLE TO VOTE? ____________________
IN THE PARISH? ____________________
IN THE STATE? ____________________
2. IF A PERSON IS INSANE BUT NOT COMMITTED TO AN ASYLUM, CAN HE QUALIFY TO VOTE? ________
3. IF A PERSON IS IN THE ARMED FORCES OVERSEAS, CAN HE VOTE IN HIS HOME PARISH? ____________ IF SO HOW MAY THIS BE DONE?
____
____
4. WHAT ARE THE LITERACY REQUIREMENTS FOR A POTENTIAL VOTER? ____________________
____
5. IF YOU ARE A QUALIFIED VOTER AND PLAN TO BE OUT OF THE PARISH ON ELECTION DAY, CAN YOU STILL CAST YOUR VOTE? ________________
HOW? ____________________________________
6. HOW LONG MUST YOU RESIDE IN A PRECINCT BEFORE YOU CAN VOTE IN THAT PRECINCT?
____

PARISH OFFICIALS

THE SHERIFF is elected in the state general election for a four-year term. He serves as the chief law enforcement officer and appoints his own deputies. It is the duty of the sheriff to enforce the laws, maintain peace and order, keep the jail, and act as an officer of the district court in preserving order and executing the court's writs. He collects state, parish, and if a city desires it, municipal property taxes.

THE CLERK OF THE DISTRICT COURT is the recorder of the court proceedings and custodian of the records of the court and other important parish records. He is elected for a four-year term at the state general election.

THE ASSESSOR is also elected at the state general election for four years. He assesses the value of property for the purpose of taxation.

THE CORONER should be a qualified physician. He is responsible for investigating cases of death where the cause is unknown. He acts as sheriff when there is a vacancy in that office, or when the sheriff is an interested party in a case. He may also be appointed parish health officer by the police jury. The coroner is elected for a four-year term at the state general election.

THE PARISH SCHOOL BOARD is in charge of administration of the schools on the parish level, and is independent of the other local governmental operations. In all parishes members of the parish school boards serve for overlapping six-year terms; Bogalusa (Washington Parish), Monroe (Ouachita Parish), and Lake Charles (Calcasieu Parish) have independent city school systems with separate school boards. Each of these boards consists of five members who are elected at large.

(For more detailed information on school boards see "Education")

PARISH OFFICIALS

1. WHO ACTS AS SHERIFF WHEN THERE IS A VACANCY IN THAT OFFICE? ________________
2. WHO DETERMINES THE VALUE OF YOUR PROPERTY FOR TAXATION PURPOSES?
____
3. WHAT ARE THE DUTIES OF THE CLERK OF THE DISTRICT COURT? ________________
____
4. WHO COLLECTS STATE AND PARISH TAXES?
____
5. HOW MANY CITIES IN LOUISIANA HAVE INDEPENDENT CITY SCHOOL SYSTEMS? __________
NAME THEM. ________________________
ARE THEIR SCHOOL BOARDS SEPARATE? _______
6. HOW LONG IS THE TERM IN OFFICE FOR A SHERIFF? ________________________
7. HOW LONG DOES A SCHOOL BOARD MEMBER SERVE IN OFFICE? ____________________
8. THE ____________________ MAY BE APPOINTED PARISH HEALTH OFFICER BY ________________
________________________________.

TRUE OR FALSE

9. DEPUTY SHERIFFS ARE ELECTED BY THE PEOPLE. TRUE ______ FALSE ______
10. THE DISTRICT ATTORNEY INVESTIGATES CASES OF DEATH WHERE THE CAUSE IS UNKNOWN. TRUE ______ FALSE ______

POLITICAL PARTIES AND ELECTIONS

GOVERNMENT by the people cannot exist in reality unless there is some adequate method by which the people can express their will concerning how and by whom they shall be governed. One way in which the people may effect changes in Government personnel is by revolution but for more than 150 years now the American people for the most part have spurned the resort to arms as a method of political action. They have been content to use the free popular election as a device for indicating officially their wishes for or against current public policies and practices and whether they want A, B, or C for President and X, Y, or Z for Governor.

REGISTRATION:

The first step in any electoral process is the establishing of those qualifications which must be met by the potential voters. Those requirements vary to some extent from state to state but usually include provisions relating to age, residence, citizenship, disqualifications and registration. After the qualifications to vote have been determined, then some procedure must be devised so that a record may be compiled of those eligible to vote. THIS IS KNOWN AS REGISTRATION. An adequate and effective registration procedure will go far toward assuring honesty and fairness in the conduct of elections. Upon the honest and faithful maintenance of the registration books depends the purity of the ballot box, and upon the purity of the ballot box depends in large measure the success or failure of our democratic form of government. A delegate to the Constitutional Convention of 1845 stated this point well when he said: "The abuse of suffrage (right to vote) was certainly one of the greatest evils that threatened the durability of a representative system of government."

ELECTIONS:

There are two types of elections—the primary election, at which party candidates for the various offices to be filled are nominated, and the general election or inter-party election. If either of these types of elections is to be honestly and fairly conducted, three conditions must exist: first, it must be assured that only those persons who are qualified by law to exercise the suffrage shall be permitted to cast their ballots; second, that only the ballots cast by qualified voters shall be counted; third, that votes cast by qualified voters shall be counted correctly and the totals certified without fraud or deceit.

POLITICAL PARTIES AND ELECTIONS

1. THERE ARE TWO TYPES OF ELECTIONS, THEY ARE ________________ AND ________________
2. WHAT IS SUFFRAGE? ________________
3. WHAT IS THE FIRST STEP IN ANY ELECTORAL PROCESS? ________________
4. THE COMPILING OF RECORDS OF THOSE WHO ARE ELIGIBLE TO VOTE IS KNOWN AS ________________
5. THERE ARE TWO WAYS FOR A DISSATISFIED PEOPLE TO CHANGE GOVERNMENT PERSONNEL. THEY ARE ________________ AND ________________
6. TO CONDUCT AN HONEST AND FAIR ELECTION, THREE CONDITIONS MUST EXIST; NAME THEM:
   1. ________________
   2. ________________
   3. ________________

PALM SPRINGS DESERT SUN

School Trustees Set Talk on Negro Hiring and *Greater Effort Pledged on Hiring of Negro Teachers*

September 30 and October 1, 1965

SCHOOL TRUSTEES SET TALK ON NEGRO HIRING

NEGRO LEADERS and trustees of the Palm Springs Unified School District will meet tonight to discuss school practices which the Negroes have questioned in recent weeks.

Top item on the four-point agenda is the issue of hiring more Negro teachers in the Palm Springs district.

Local Negroes say they want at least one Negro teacher in each grade level. Presently the district employs two full-time Negro teachers and one Negro substitute.

Tonight's meeting was scheduled after Negroes appeared at last week's regular board meeting and asked to discuss problems with the trustees. The meeting is at 7:30 in the administration-education center at 333 S. Farrell Drive.

The second item on the agenda is a discussion of school practices on discipline. Many Negro parents say school officials have been tougher on Negro students if trouble occurs. School officials have denied the accusations.

The discussion also will review administrative procedures in working with students, not only in discipline but in counseling.

Negroes also are expected to ask the board to expand the social studies curriculum to include the teaching of Negro history. Local leaders say they would like this area to be handled by Negro teachers or persons thoroughly familiar with Negro background.

The fourth point will be a discussion of the policy, practice and facilities for bus service to the Negro community at the north end of Palm Springs.

GREATER EFFORT PLEDGED ON HIRING OF NEGRO TEACHERS

By TOM WATSON
Managing Editor

DELIBERATE EFFORTS to hire Negro teachers for the Palm Springs Unified School District have been largely unsuccessful, but a greater effort will be made, school officials said last night.

The promise was made to a group of about 100 persons, evenly divided between Negroes and Caucasians, at a special meeting of the board of education.

"In all my trips around the state last year, from San Diego to Chico and elsewhere, I was not scheduled to see one Negro," said Dr. James Runge, assistant superintendent for instruction.

Runge, who conducts teacher recruiting for the district, said the number of Negro students in teacher training programs is not very high.

"Those who are, largely tend to remain in the same general area where they go to school," he said. "This is a problem with others, not just Negroes.

"When we set up interviews, we ask specifically to talk to Negroes who are interested in Palm Springs."

Runge indicated that a general shortage of teachers in California will make it necessary to recruit persons from other states. He said this may be a problem because of a new requirement that California elementary teachers must have five years of college training to obtain a life credential.

"Some we contact from out of state will not be qualified without additional course work, and this may discourage many from coming to California," Runge said.

Last night's meeting was the result of a request by the Negro community to discuss with the school board the problem of hiring more Negro teachers.

Ernest Moore, one of the Negro spokesmen, told the board the community would like to see at least one Negro teacher at each grade level.

"Our children are not getting the education they should be getting," Moore said. "Some of our children can not pass simple tests for the most minute jobs. The question is how did he graduate in the first place—just because he put in four years in high school?

"Many of our children are highly qualified, but some problems arise that they must go to one of their own people to discuss. If there is no one that he feels will understand his problem, then he may do the only other thing he knows and punch it out.

"I can't emphasize the need too strongly. We must have some Negro teachers, especially in elementary schools and in the headstart age level (preschoolers)."

Dr. Austin Sellery, district superintendent, told the group the administration's intentions were in keeping with the group's desires.

"It is generally recognized we are not doing as good a job of recruiting Negroes as we might," Sellery said. "It will be necessary for us to discover other means of contacting qualified Negroes, because they just have not been available to us through our normal methods."

Runge said several Negroes had applied for teaching jobs this year, but they did not meet the competition. He said the district always has the best qualified candidates available at the time openings occur.

Several speakers said the problems of interesting teachers in coming to Palm Springs are the living conditions for Negroes and the community image.

One speaker, Joseph Zwerdling, suggested the community provide good housing at low cost as an incentive to Negro teachers.

"When we have disease in the community," he said, "we make sure we get the doctors and specialists to cure it. When we need a golf course or airport terminal, we provide them. We should provide low-cost housing and other favors as incentives."

Another speaker, Wardell Ward, chairman of the local chapter of the Congress of Racial Equality, said the resort image of Palm Springs is blown up so big that it scares prospective workers.

"Negro teachers look at our millionaire's paradise and wonder how they can live here on a teacher's salary," Ward said. "Let's show them they can make it here."

Moore disagreed that special privileges are necessary but he said the Negro teachers need a chance and they would prove themselves as competent as anyone.

Dr. Cecil Jones, a board member, said he did feel it was a community problem to create an atmosphere and conditions that would attract Negro teachers and make them feel they can live as well as other teachers.

Negro leaders themselves agreed to help contact possible teacher candidates.

One woman charged that even if district standards for teachers are so high that Negroes could not meet the competition, the teachers here are not taking an interest in Negro children.

Several persons echoed Moore's statement that despite highly qualified teachers, very few local youngsters attend and finish college and that Negro youngsters are being neglected in the primary grades.

Another major request by the group was for the teaching of Negro history in the social studies curriculum.

"Part of the problem of prejudice comes from a lack of knowledge about races," Moore said. "Many persons do not realize there are many Negroes who have distinguished themselves. Many of our own children need to realize this."

Ward urged that Negro history be made a part of the regular instruction in American history. "A separate class will be a segregated class," he said.

It was noted that textbooks still have to be developed to cover the problem of Negro history.

"The role of the Negro in our nation should be taught because it is part of the truth," Sellery said.

He said the district could begin laying the groundwork by acquiring suitable books for school libraries. He said the district also could borrow materials now being developed by other districts that have the resources and qualified personnel to develop such a program.

Rev. Jeff Rollins, one of the Negro spokesmen, called on the board and the Negro community to work together to solve the problems.

"We are disturbed," he said, "but we are here to unite, not fight. Matters continue to arise daily, and we must work together and share in solving the problems. If calamities come, we all will share the consequences."

"AN ALL-BLACK PROJECT IS NEEDED"

VINE CITY PROJECT

Statement on Black Power

Spring 1966

PREFACE

IN ATTEMPTING to analyze where the movement is going, certain questions have arisen as to the future roles played by white personnel. In order to make this issue clearer, we have written a few paragraphs, stemming from our observations and experiences, which serve as a preview to a broader study on the subject.

The answers to these questions lead us to believe that the form of white participation, as practiced in the past, is now obsolete. Some of the reasons are as follows:

The inability of whites to relate to the cultural aspects of Black society; attitudes that whites, consciously or unconsciously, bring to Black communities about themselves (western superiority) and about Black people (paternalism); inability to shatter white-sponsored community myths of Black inferiority and self-negation; inability to combat the views of the Black community that white organizers, being "white," control Black organizers as puppets; insensitivity of both Black and white workers towards the hostility of the Black community on the issue of interracial "relationships" (sex); the unwillingness of whites to deal with the *roots* of racism which lie within the white community; whites, though individual "liberals," are symbols of oppression to the Black community—due to the *collective* power that whites have over Black lives.

Because of these reasons, which force us to view America through the eyes of victims, we advocate a conscious change in the role of whites, which will be in tune with the developing self-consciousness and self-assertion of the Afro-American people.

In concluding, we state that our position does *not* stem from "hatred" or "racism" against white people, but from a conscientious effort to develop the best methods of solving our national problem.

I

The myth that the Negro is somehow incapable of liberating himself, is lazy, etc., came out of the American experience. In the books that children read, whites are always "good" (good symbols are white), Blacks are "evil," are seen as "savages" in movies, their language is referred to as a "dialect," and Black people in this country are supposedly descended from savages.

Any white person who comes into the Movement has these concepts in his mind about Black people, if only subconsciously. He cannot escape them because the whole society has geared his subconscious in that direction.

Miss America coming from Mississippi has a chance to represent all of America, but a Black person from neither Mississippi nor New York will never represent America. So that white people coming into the Movement cannot relate to the "Nitty Gritty," cannot relate to the experience that brought such a word into being, cannot relate to chitterlings, hog's head cheese, pig feet, ham hocks, and cannot relate to slavery, because these things are not a part of their experience. They also cannot relate to the Black religious experience, nor to the Black church unless, of course, this church has taken on white manifestations.

Negroes in this country have never been allowed to organize themselves because of white interference. As a result of this, the stereotype has been reinforced that Blacks cannot organize themselves. The white psychology that Blacks have to be watched, also reinforces this stereotype. Blacks, in fact, feel intimidated by the presence of whites, because of their knowledge of the power that whites have over their lives. One white person can come into a meeting of Black people and change the complexion of that meeting, whereas one Black person would not change the complexion of that meeting unless he was an obvious Uncle Tom. People would immediately start talking about "brotherhood," "love," etc.; race would not be discussed.

If people must express themselves freely, there has to be a climate in which they can do this. If Blacks feel intimidated by whites, then they are not liable to vent the rage that they feel about whites in the presence of whites—especially not that one is anti-white, but because the efforts that one is trying to achieve cannot succeed because whites have an intimidating effect in direct proportion to the amount of degradation that Black people have suffered at the hands of white people.

It must be offered that white people who desire change in this country should go, where that problem (of racism) is most manifest. That problem is not in the Black community. The white people should go into white communities where the whites have created power for the express purpose of denying Blacks human dignity and self-determination. Whites who come into the Black community with ideas of change seem to want to absolve the power structure of its responsibility for what it is doing, and saying that change can only come through Black unity, which is only the worst kind of paternalism. This is not to say that whites have not had an important role in the Movement. In the case of Mississippi, their role was very key in that they helped give Blacks the right to organize, but that role is now over, and it should be. People now have the right to picket, the right to give out leaflets, the right to vote, the right to demonstrate, the right to print.

These things which revolve around the right to organize have been accomplished mainly because of the entrance of white people into Mississippi, in the summer of '64. Since these goals have now been accomplished, their (whites') role in the Movement has now ended. What does it mean if Black people, once having the right to organize, are not allowed to organize themselves? It means that Blacks' ideas about inferiority are being reinforced. Shouldn't people be able to organize themselves? Blacks should be given this right. Further (white participation) means in the eyes of the Black community that whites are the "brains" behind the Movement and Blacks cannot function without whites. This only serves to perpetuate existing attitude within the existing society, i.e., Blacks are "dumb," "unable to take care of business," etc. Whites are "smart," the "brains" behind everything.

How do Blacks relate to other Blacks as such? How do we react to Willie Mays as against Mickey Mantle? What is our response to Mays hitting a home-run against Mantle performing the same deed? Is our interest in baseball ordered by our appreciation of the artistry of the game, or is it ordered by the participation of Negroes in baseball? One has to come to the conclusion that it is because of Black participation in baseball. Negroes still identify with the Dodgers because of Jackie Robinson's efforts with the Dodgers. Negroes would instinctively champion all-Black teams if they opposed all-white or predominately white teams. The same principle operates for the Movement as it does for baseball: a mystique must be created whereby Negroes can identify with the Movement.

Thus an all-Black project is needed in order for the people to free themselves. This has to exist from the beginning. This relates to what can be called "coalition politics." There is no doubt in our minds that some whites are just as disgusted with this system as we are. But it is meaningless to talk about coalition if there is no one to align ourselves with, because of the lack of organization in the white communities. There can be no talk of "hooking-up" unless Black people organize Blacks and white people organize whites. If these conditions are met, then perhaps at some later date—and if we are going in the same direction—talks about exchange of personnel, coalition, and other meaningful alliances can be discussed.

In the beginning of the Movement, we had fallen into a trap whereby we thought that our problems revolved around the right to eat at certain lunch counters or the right to vote, or to organize our communities. We have seen, however, that the problem is much deeper. The problem of this country, as we had seen it, concerned old Blacks and old whites (and therefore) if decisions were left to the young people, then solutions would be arrived at. But this negates the history of Black people and whites. We have dealt stringently with the problem of "Uncle Tom," but we have not yet gotten around to Simon Legree. We must ask ourselves who is the real villain? Uncle Tom or Simon Legree? Everybody knows Uncle Tom, but who knows Simon Legree?

So what we have now (in SNCC) is a closed society. A clique. Black people cannot relate to SNCC, because of its unrealistic, nonracial atmosphere; denying their experiences of America as a racist society. In contrast, SCLC has a staff that at least maintains a Black facade. The front office is virtually all-Black, but nobody accuses SCLC of being "racist."

If we are to proceed towards true liberation, we must cut ourselves off from white people . . . We must form our own institutions, credit unions, co-ops, political parties, write our own histories. One illustrating example, is the SNCC "Freedom Primer." Blacks cannot relate to that book psychologically, because white people wrote it and, therefore it presents a white viewpoint.

To proceed further, let us make some comparisons between the Black Movement of the (early) 1900s and the Movement of the 1960s—the NAACP with SNCC. Whites subverted the Niagara Movement which, at the outset, was an all-Black Movement. The name of the new organization was also very revealing, in that it presupposed that Blacks have to be advanced to the level of whites. We are now aware that the NAACP has grown reactionary, is controlled by the power-structure itself, and stands as one of the main roadblocks to Black freedom. SNCC, by allowing the whites to remain in the organization, can have its efforts subverted in the same manner, i.e., through having them play important roles such as community organizers, etc. Indigenous leadership cannot be built with whites in the positions they now hold.

These facts do not mean that whites cannot help. They can participate on a voluntary basis. We can contract work out to them, but in no way can they participate on a policy-making level.

The charge may be made that we are "racists," but whites who are sensitive to our problems will realize that we must determine our own destiny. We, as Black people, must re-evaluate our history, our ideas of self, the world, Africa and her contributions to mankind. We must take the credit for our contributions to this society and to the world. Credit will be given to white people where it is due, but surely our contributions must be given credit. These myths (of inferiority and "savagery") must be broken by Black people, so that no mistake can be made about who is accomplishing what for whom. This is one way to break the myths.

As to the charge of "Black racism," as against white supremacy: we can say that the racial makeup of any organization does not make it racist, i.e., supreme court makeup of all white judges, Black churches and Black businesses being all Black.

The naming of the newspaper, "Nitty-Gritty," which served to polarize the feelings of race, illustrated in a very graphic manner the attitudes that whites have towards cultural aspects of our society. The whites were opposed to the name and Blacks were affirmative on the issue. The alternative was the "Atlanta Voice"; surely such a name could not speak to the needs of grass-roots Black people.

Black people can say to the "Nitty-Gritty": I can see myself there. Can say to Mays hitting a home run: I see myself there. Can say to the Atlanta Project: I see myself there!

II

In an attempt to resolve an internal crises that is now confronting SNCC, the Black-White issue (which is causing eruptions that are seriously hampering our struggle for self-determination) must now be dealt with.

In an analysis of our history in this country, we have been forced to come to the conclusion that 400 years of oppression and slavery suffered in this country by our Black forebears parallels in a very graphic way the oppression and colonization suffered by the African people. The questions can be rightfully asked, what part did the white colonizers play in the liberation of independent African Nations; who were the agitators for African independence? Answers to those questions compel us to believe that our struggle for liberation and self-determination can only be carried out effectively by Black people.

The necessity of dealing with the question of identity is of prime importance in our own struggle. The systematic destruction of our links to Africa, the cultural cut-off of Blacks in this country from Blacks in Africa are not situations that conscious Black people in this country are willing to accept. Nor are conscious Black people in this country willing to accept an educational system that teaches all aspects of western civilization and dismisses our Afro-American contribution with one week of inadequate information (Negro History Week) and deals with Africa not at all. Black people are not willing to align themselves with a western culture that daily emasculates our beauty, our pride and our manhood. It follows that white people, being part of western civilization in a way that Black people could never be, are totally inadequate to deal with Black identity which is key to our struggle for self-determination.

When it comes to the question of organizing Black people, we must insist that the people who come in contact with the Black masses are not white people who, no matter what their liberal leanings are, are not equipped to dispel the myths of western superiority. White people only serve to perpetuate these myths; rather, organizing must be done by Black people who are able to see the beauty of themselves, are able to see the important cultural contributions of Afro-Americans, are able to see that this country was built upon the blood and backs of our Black ancestors.

In an attempt to find a solution to our dilemma we propose that our organization (SNCC) should be Black staffed, Black controlled and Black financed. We do not want to fall into a similar dilemma that other Civil Rights organizations have fallen. If we continue to rely upon white financial support we will find ourselves entwined in the tentacles of the white power complex that controls this country. It is also important that a Black organization (devoid of cultism) be projected to our people so that it can be demonstrated that such organizations are viable.

More and more we see Black people in this country being used as a tool of the white liberal establishment. Liberal whites have not begun to address themselves to the real problems of Black people in this country; witness their bewilderment, fear and anxiety when Nationalism is mentioned concerning Black people. An analysis of their (white liberal) reaction to the word alone (Nationalism) reveals a very meaningful attitude of whites of any ideological persuasion towards Blacks in this country. It means that previous solutions to Black problems in this country have been made in the interests of those whites dealing with those problems and not in the best interests of Black people in this country. Whites can only subvert our true search and struggle for self-determination, self-identification, and liberation in this country. Re-evaluation of the white and Black roles must NOW take place so that whites no longer designate roles that Black people play but rather Black people define white people's roles.

Too long have we allowed white people to interpret the importance and meaning of the cultural aspects of our society. We have allowed them to tell us what was good about our Afro-American music, art and literature. How many Black critics do we have on the "jazz" scene? How can a white person who is not a part of the Black psyche (except in the oppressor's role) interpret the meaning of the Blues to us who are manifestations of the songs themselves?

It must also be pointed out that on whatever level of contact that Blacks and whites come together, that meeting or confrontation is not on the level of the Blacks but always on the level of whites. This only means that our everyday contact with whites is a reinforcement of the myth of white supremacy. Whites are the ones who must try to raise themselves to our humanistic level. We are not, after all, the ones who are responsible for a genocidal war in Vietnam; we are not the ones who are responsible for Neo-Colonialism in Africa and Latin America; we are not the ones who held a people in animalistic bondage over 400 years.

We reject the American Dream as defined by white people and must work to construct an American reality defined by Afro-Americans.

III

One point we would like to emphasize is the failure on the part of conscious whites and Blacks in dealing with the American reality in terms of differences. We are beginning to emphasize the analysis of the differences between Black and white people.

There has been an escapist attitude on the part of SNCC of looking at the problem as if race did not matter. This negates the special history of Black people in this country, mainly the slavery period and the inhuman forms of segregation we have been forced to suffer. Another important point is that most Blacks and whites tend to view Blacks in the light of the myth that the power structure has created and perpetrated in this country. Black people are considered as "citizens" along the same lines as white people in this country, when in reality, Black people are a semi-colonialized people, victims of a domestic colonialism. Our introduction into this country occurred during the same time as the partition of Africa and Asia by the European powers, so that the American institution of slavery was, too, a form of Western Colonialism. Therefore Black people in this country react in the same way as do other colonial peoples to their environment and experience; but the myths of America label them citizens, which is an unreal attitude.

Also, one of the main blocks in terms of Black self-recognition and self-identification in this country has been interference from the dominant white society. From the 1900s to the present time Afro-American writers and thinkers have had to contend with the encroachment of white intellectuals upon their culture and upon their thoughts. Not only did the white intellectuals encroach upon their thought and culture but they brought to it their whole American background of racism and paternalism so that Black culture was portrayed as something being base, second-rate or below the culture of the United States, which was considered "serious" or "real." One graphic example of this is modern Afro-American music. This music which is rooted in the whole experience of our people in this country was not even named by Black people. Modern Afro-American music is named "jazz," which is a term that is derived from white American society. It is white slang for sexual intercourse; so that our music which may be called the mainstream of our culture was looked upon as being base and second-rate or dirty and containing sensuousness, sexuality and other eroticisms. This however says more about the white American psyche than it does about aspects of Afro-American culture.

One of the criticisms of white militants and radicals is that when we view the masses of white people we view the overall reality of America. We view the racism, the bigotry, and distortion of personality; we view man's inhumanity to man; we view in reality 180 million racists. The sensitive white intellectual and radical who is fighting to bring about change is conscious of this fact, but does not have the courage to admit this. When he admits this reality, then he must also admit his involvement because he is a part of the collective white America. It is only to the extent that he recognizes this that he will be able to change this reality. Another concern is how does the white radical view the Black Community and how does he view the poor white community in terms of organizing. So far, we have found that most white radicals have sought to escape the horrible reality of America by going into the Black Community and attempting to organize Black people while neglecting the organization of their own people's racist communities. How can one clean up someone else's yard when one's own yard is untidy? Again we feel that SNCC and the civil rights movement in general are in many aspects similar to the anti-colonial situations in the African and Asian countries. We have the whites in the Movement corresponding to the white civil servants and missionaries in the colonial countries who have worked with the colonial people for a long period of time and have developed a paternalistic attitude toward them. The reality of the colonial people taking over their own lives and controlling their own destiny must be faced. Having to move aside and letting this natural process of growth and development take place must be faced. These views should not be equated with outside influence or outside agitation but should be viewed as the natural process of growth and development within a movement; so that the move by the Black militants in SNCC in this direction should be viewed as a turn towards self-determination.

It is very ironic and curious how aware whites in this country can champion anti-colonialism in other countries in Africa, Asia, and Latin America, but when Black people move towards similar goals of self-determination in this country they are viewed as racists and anti-white by these same progressive whites. In proceeding further, it can be said that this attitude derives from the overall point of view of the white psyche as it concerns the Black people. This attitude stems from the era of the slave revolts when every white man was a potential deputy or sheriff or guardian of the State. Because when Black people got together among themselves to work out their problems, it became a threat to white people, because such meetings were potential slave revolts. It can be maintained that this attitude or way of thinking has perpetuated itself to this current period and that it is part of the psyche of white people in this country whatever their political persuasion might be. It is part of the white fear-guilt complex resulting from the slave revolts. There have been examples of whites who stated that they can deal with Black fellows on an individual basis but become threatened or menaced by the presence of groups of Blacks. It can be maintained that this attitude is held by the majority of progressive whites in this country.

It is a very grave error to mistake Black self-assertion for racism or Black supremacy. Black people in this country more so than the colonial peoples of the world know what it means to be victims of racism, bigotry, and slavery. Realizing our predicament, from these inhuman attitudes it would be ridiculous for us to turn around and perpetuate the same reactionary outlook on other people. We more than anyone else realize the importance of achieving the type of society, the type of world, whereby people can be viewed as human beings. The means of reaching these goals must be, however, from the point of view of respecting the differences between peoples and cultures and not pretending that everyone is the same. The refusal to respect differences is one of the reasons that the world is exploding today. Also expanding upon the differences among peoples and the respect it should be accorded: if one looks at "integration" as progress then one is really perpetuating the myth of white supremacy. One is saying that Blacks have nothing to contribute, and should be willing to assimilate into the mainstream of Great white civilization, i.e., the west.

A thorough re-examination must be made by Black people concerning the contributions that we have made in shaping this country. If this re-examination and re-evaluation is not made, and Black people are not given their proper due and respect, then the antagonisms and contradictions are going to become more and more glaring, more and more intense until a national explosion may result.

When people attempt to move from these conclusions it would be faulty reasoning to say they are ordered by racism, because, in this country and in the west, Racism has functioned as a type of white nationalism when dealing with Black people. We all know the havoc that this has created throughout the world and particularly among non-white people in this country.

Therefore any re-evaluation that we must make will, for the most part, deal with identification. Who are Black people; what are Black people; what is their relationship to America and the World?

It must be repeated that the whole myth of "Negro Citizenship," perpetuated by the White Power Elite, has confused the thinking of radical and progressive Blacks and whites in this country. The broad masses of Black people react to American Society in the same manner as colonial peoples react to the west in Africa and Latin America, and have the same relationship—that of the colonized towards the colonizer.

THE LOWNDES COUNTY FREEDOM ORGANIZATION

JOHN HULETT

How the Black Panther Party Was Organized

Los Angeles, May 22, 1966

HOW THE BLACK PANTHER PARTY WAS ORGANIZED

John Hulett is Chairman of the Lowndes County Freedom Organization. He gave this speech in Los Angeles on May 22, 1966 at a meeting on the Vietnam war. The meeting was sponsored by nine different antiwar committees.

I'M HAPPY to have the opportunity to come and share this evening with you. I'd like to give you a general idea of what's happening in the state of Alabama and in Lowndes County. This county, as far as I'm concerned, is one of the worst counties in the state of Alabama, and not only that, it is one of the poorest counties in the nation.

Lowndes County consists of a population of about 15,000 people. Out of these 15,000 people, 80 percent are Negroes, 20 percent white. The entire county is controlled entirely by whites. It has always been this way . . .

Last year in March, some 30 people assembled at the courthouse in Hayneville to make an attempt to get registered. They were talked about and many people were sitting by their radios that day and their televisions, waiting to see what would happen in Lowndes County. We made the attempt and two weeks later, two people became registered voters. Today we have at least 2,500 registered Negro voters.

According to the 1960 statistics, there are only 1,900 possible white registered voters in the county. Today, all of these people are registered. Two years ago, 118 percent of these white people voted. In the general elections this year for governor, I learned that there will be even more white people voting.

Last year, we started a group in Lowndes County known as the Lowndes County Christian Movement for Human

Rights. This was a civil rights group. We fought for integration in this county. We fought that Negroes might have a right to get registered to vote. We protested at the school so that all the people could have education—and for this we got nothing . . .

We sat down together and discussed our problems. We thought about what we were going to do with these 2,500 registered voters in the county, whether or not we were going to join Lyndon Baines Johnson's party. Then we thought about the other people in the state of Alabama who were working in this party. We thought of the city commissioner of Birmingham, Eugene Bull Conner; George Wallace who is now the governor of the state of Alabama; Al Lingo, who gave orders to those who beat the people when they got ready to make the march from Selma to Montgomery; the sheriff of Dallas County, known as Jim Clark—these people control the Democratic Party in the state of Alabama.

So the Negroes in Lowndes County decided that it's useless to stay in the Democratic Party or the Republican Party in the state of Alabama. Through the years, these are the people who kept Negroes from voting in the South and in the state of Alabama. Why join the Democratic Party?

A POLITICAL GROUP OF OUR OWN

Some time ago, we organized a political group of our own known as the Lowndes County Freedom Organization, whose emblem is the Black Panther.

We were criticized, we were called communists, we were called everything else, black nationalists and what not, because we did this. Any group which starts at a time like this to speak out for what is right—they are going to be ridiculed. The people of Lowndes County realized this. Today we are moving further . . .

Too long Negroes have been begging, especially in the South, for things they should be working for. So the people in Lowndes County decided to organize themselves—to go out and work for the things we wanted in life—not only for the people in Lowndes County, but for every county in the state of Alabama, in the Southern states, and even in California.

You cannot become free in California while there are slaves

in Lowndes County. And no person can be free while other people are still slaves, nobody.

In Lowndes County, there is a committee in the Democratic Party. This committee not only controls the courthouse, it controls the entire county. When they found out that the Negroes were going to run candidates in the primary of the Democratic Party on May 3, they assembled themselves together and began to talk about what they were going to do. Knowing this is one of the poorest counties in the nation, what they decided to do was change the registration fees in the county.

Two years ago, if a person wanted to run for sheriff, tax collector or tax assessor, all he had to do was pay $50 and then he qualified to be the candidate. This year, the entrance fee is about $900. If a person wants to run, he has to pay $500 to run for office. In the primary, when they get through cheating and stealing, then the candidate is eliminated. So we decided that we wouldn't get into such a primary because we were tired of being tricked by the Southern whites. After forming our own political group today, we feel real strong. We feel that we are doing the right thing in Lowndes County.

We have listened to everybody who wanted to talk, we listened to them speak, but one thing we had to learn for ourselves. As a group of people, we must think for ourselves and act on our own accord. And this we have done.

Through the years, Negroes in the South have been going for the bones while whites have been going for the meat. The Negroes of Lowndes County today are tired of the bones—we are going to have some of the meat too.

FIGHTING THE "TRICKS" OF THE RACISTS

At the present time, we have our own candidates which have been nominated by the Lowndes County Freedom Organization. And we fear that this might not be enough to avoid the tricks that are going to be used in Lowndes County against us . . .

In Lowndes County, the sheriff is the custodian of the courthouse. This is a liberal sheriff, too, who is "integrated," who walks around and pats you on the shoulder, who does not carry a gun. But at the same time, in the county where there are only 800 white men, there are 550 of them who walk around with a gun on them. They are deputies. This is true; it might sound like a fairy tale to most people, but this is true.

After talking to the sheriff about having the use of the courthouse lawn for our mass nominating meeting, not the courthouse but just the lawn, he refused to give the Negroes permission. We reminded him that last year in August, that one of the biggest Klan rallies that has ever been held in the state of Alabama was held on this lawn of this courthouse. And he gave them permission. A few weeks ago an individual who was campaigning for governor—he got permission to use it. He used all types of loud speakers and anything that he wanted.

But he would not permit Negroes to have the use of the courthouse. For one thing he realized that we would build a party—and if he could keep us from forming our own political group then we would always stand at the feet of the Southern whites and of the Democratic Party. So we told him that we were going to have this meeting, we were going to have it here, on the courthouse lawn. And we wouldn't let anybody scare us off. We told him, we won't expect you to protect us, and if you don't, Negroes will protect themselves.

Then we asked him a second time to be sure he understood what we were saying. We repeated it to him the second time. And then we said to him, sheriff, if you come out against the people, then we are going to arrest you.

And he said, I will not give you permission to have this meeting here. I can't protect you from the community.

Then we reminded him that according to the law of the state of Alabama, that this mass meeting which was set up to nominate our candidates must be held in or around a voters' polling place. And if we decide to hold it a half a mile away from the courthouse, some individual would come up and protest our mass meeting. And our election would be thrown out.

So we wrote the Justice Department and told them what was going to happen in Lowndes County.

All of a sudden the Justice Department started coming in fast into the county. They said to me, John, what is going to happen next Tuesday at the courthouse?

I said, We are going to have our mass meeting. And he wanted to know where. And I said on the lawn of the courthouse.

He said, I thought the sheriff had told you you couldn't come there. And I said, Yes, but we are going to be there.

Then he wanted to know, if shooting takes place, what are we going to do. And I said, that we are going to stay out here and everybody die together.

And then he began to get worried, and I said, Don't worry. You're going to have to be here to see it out and there's no place to hide, so whatever happens, you can be a part of it.

And then he began to really panic. And he said, There's nothing I can do.

And I said, I'm not asking you to do anything. All I want you to know is we are going to have a mass meeting. If the sheriff cannot protect us, then we are going to protect ourselves. And I said to him, through the years in the South, Negroes have never had any protection, and today we aren't looking to anybody to protect us. We are going to protect ourselves.

That was on Saturday. On Sunday, at about 2 o'clock, we were having a meeting, and we decided among ourselves that we were going to start collecting petitions for our candidates to be sure that they got on the ballot. The state laws require at least 25 signatures of qualified electors and so we decided to get at least 100 for fear somebody might come up and find fault. And we decided to still have our mass meeting and nominate our candidates.

About 2:30, here comes the Justice Department again, and he was really worried. And he said he wasn't satisfied. He said to me, John, I've done all I can do, and I don't know what else I can do, and now it looks like you'll have to call this meeting off at the courthouse.

And I said, we're going to have it.

He stayed around for awhile and then got in his car and drove off, saying, I'll see you tomorrow, maybe. And we stayed at this meeting from 2:30 until about 11:30 that night. About 11:15, the Justice Department came walking up the aisle of the church and said to me, Listen. I've talked to the Attorney General of the state of Alabama, and he said that you can go ahead and have a mass meeting at the church and it will be legal.

Then we asked him, Do you have any papers that say that's true, that are signed by the Governor or the Attorney General?

And he said no. And we said to him, Go back and get it legalized, and bring it back here to us and we will accept it.

And sure enough, on Monday at 3 o'clock, I went to the courthouse and there in the sheriff's office were the papers all legalized and fixed up, saying that we could go to the church to have our mass meeting.

To me, this showed strength. When people are together, they can do a lot of things, but when you are alone you cannot do anything . . .

There are 600 Negroes in the county who did not trust in themselves and who joined the Democratic Party. We warned the entire state of Alabama that running on the Democratic ticket could not do them any good, because this party is controlled by people like Wallace; and whoever won would have to do what these people said to do . . .

Now, to me, the Democratic Party primaries and the Democratic Party is something like an integrated gambler who carries a card around in his pocket and every now and then he has to let somebody win to keep the game going. To me, this is what the Democratic Party means to the people in Alabama. It's a gambling game. And somebody's got to win to keep the game going every now and then.

There is another guy who was running on the ticket calling himself a liberal, the Attorney General of the state of Alabama, Richmond Flowers. Most of you have heard about him. When he started campaigning to the people of Alabama, especially the Negro people, he assembled all their leaders and he made all kinds of promises to them—if you elect me for your governor, I'll do everything in the world for you.

And at the same time, he never made a decent campaign speech to the white people of this state. We kept warning our people in the state of Alabama that this was a trick and many Negroes listened to their so-called leaders, who profess to speak for the state of Alabama, and they got caught in the trap too.

I would like to say here, and this is one thing I am proud of, the people in Lowndes County stood together, and the 600 people who voted in the Democratic primary have realized one thing, that they were tricked by the Democratic Party. And now they too are ready to join us with the Lowndes County Freedom Organization whose emblem is the black panther.

We have seven people who are running for office this year in our county; namely, the coroner, three members of the board of education—and if we win those three, we will control the board of education—tax collector, tax assessor, and the individual who carries a gun at his side, the sheriff.

Let me say this—that a lot of persons tonight asked me, Do you really think if you win that you will be able to take it all over, and live?

I say to the people here tonight—yes, we're going to do it. If we have to do like the present sheriff, if we have to deputize every man in Lowndes County 21 and over, to protect people, we're going to do it.

There was something in Alabama a few months ago they called fear. Negroes were afraid to move on their own, they waited until the man, the people whose place they lived on, told them they could get registered. They told many people, don't you move until I tell you to move and when I give you an order, don't you go down and get registered. . . .

EVICTIONS AND THREATS

Then all the people were being evicted at the same time and even today in Lowndes County, there are at least 75 families that have been evicted, some now are living in tents while some are living in one-room houses—with 8 or 9 in a family. Others have split their families up and are living together with their relatives or their friends. But they are determined to stay in Lowndes County, until justice rolls down like water.

Evicting the families wasn't all—there were other people who live on their own places who owe large debts, so they decided to foreclose on these debts to run Negroes off the place. People made threats—but we're going to stay there, we aren't going anywhere.

I would like to let the people here tonight know why we chose this black panther as our emblem. Many people have been asking this question for a long time. Our political group is open to whoever wants to come in, who would like to work with us. But we aren't begging anyone to come in. It's open, you come, at your own free will and accord.

But this black panther is a vicious animal as you know. He never bothers anything, but when you start pushing him, he moves backwards, backwards, and backwards into his corner, and then he comes out to destroy everything that's before him.

Negroes in Lowndes County have been pushed back through the years. We have been deprived of our rights to speak, to move, and to do whatever we want to do at all times. And now we are going to start moving. On November 8 of this year, we plan to take over the courthouse in Hayneville. And whatever it takes to do it, we're going to do it.

We've decided to stop begging. We've decided to stop asking for integration. Once we control the courthouse, once we control the board of education, we can build our school system where our boys and girls can get an education in Lowndes County. There are 89 prominent families in this county who own 90 percent of the land. These people will be taxed. And we will collect these taxes. And if they don't pay them, we'll take their property and sell it to whoever wants to buy it. And we know there will be people who will buy land where at the present time they cannot buy it. This is what it's going to take.

We aren't asking any longer for protection—we won't need it—or for anyone to come from the outside to speak for us, because we're going to speak for ourselves now and from now on. And I think not only in Lowndes County, not only in the state of Alabama, not only in the South, but in the North—I hope they too will start thinking for themselves. And that they will move and join us in this fight for freedom . . . Thank you and good night.

“MOVE ON OVER, OR WE’RE GOING TO MOVE ON OVER YOU”

STOKELY CARMICHAEL

Speech on Black Power

Berkeley, October 29, 1966

IT’S A PRIVILEGE and an honor to be in the white intellectual ghetto of the West. This is a student conference, as it should be, held on a campus, and we’ll never be caught up in intellectual masturbation on the question of Black Power. That’s a function of the people who are advertisers but call themselves reporters. Incidentally, for my friends and members of the press, my self-appointed white critics, I was reading Mr. Bernard Shaw two days ago, and I came across a very important quote that I think is most apropos to you. He says, “All criticism is an autobiography.” Dig yourself. OK.

The philosophers Camus and Sartre raise the question of whether or not a man can condemn himself. The black existentialist philosopher who is pragmatic, Frantz Fanon, answered the question. He said that man could not. Camus and Sartre don’t answer the question. We in SNCC tend to agree with Fanon—a man cannot condemn himself. If he did, he would then have to inflict punishment upon himself. An example is the Nazis. Any of the Nazi prisoners who, after he was caught and incarcerated, admitted that he committed crimes, that he killed all the many people he killed, had to commit suicide. The only ones able to stay alive were the ones who never admitted that they committed a crime against people—that is, the ones who rationalized that Jews were not human beings and deserved to be killed, or that they were only following orders. There’s another, more recent example provided by the officials and the population—the white population—of Neshoba County, Mississippi (that’s where Philadelphia is). They could not condemn Sheriff Rainey, his deputies, and the other fourteen men who killed three human beings. They could not because they elected Mr. Rainey to do precisely what he did; and condemning him would be condemning themselves.

In a much larger view, SNCC says that white America cannot condemn herself for her criminal acts against black America. So black people have done it—you stand condemned. The institutions that function in this country are clearly racist; they're built upon racism. The questions to be dealt with then are: How can black people inside this country move? How can white people who say they're not part of those institutions begin to move? And how then do we begin to clear away the obstacles that we have in this society, to make us live like human beings?

Several people have been upset because we've said that integration was irrelevant when initiated by blacks, and that in fact it was an insidious subterfuge for the maintenance of white supremacy. In the past six years or so, this country has been feeding us a "thalidomide drug of integration," and some Negroes have been walking down a dream street talking about sitting next to white people. That does not begin to solve the problem. We didn't go to Mississippi to sit next to Ross Barnett, we did not go to sit next to Jim Clark, we went to get them out of our way. People ought to understand that; we were never fighting for the right to integrate, *we were fighting against white supremacy.* In order to understand white supremacy we must dismiss the fallacious notion that white people can give anybody his freedom. A man is born free. You may enslave a man after he is born free, and that is in fact what this country does. It enslaves blacks after they're born. The only thing white people can do *is stop denying black people their freedom.*

I maintain that every civil rights bill in this country was passed for white people, not for black people. For example, I am black. I know that. I also know that while I am black I am a human being. Therefore I have the right to go into any public place. White people didn't know that. Every time I tried to go into a public place they stopped me. So some boys had to write a bill to tell that white man, "He's a human being; don't stop him." That bill was for the white man, not for me. I knew I could vote all the time and that it wasn't a privilege but my right. Every time I tried I was shot, killed or jailed, beaten or economically deprived. So somebody had to write a bill to tell white people, "When a black man comes to vote, don't bother him." That bill was for white people. I know I can live anyplace I want to live. It is white people across this country who are incapable of allowing me to live where I want. You need a civil rights bill, not me. The failure of the civil rights bill isn't because of Black Power or because of the Student Nonviolent Coordinating Committee or because of the rebellions that are occurring in the major cities. That failure is due to the whites' incapacity to deal with their own problems inside their own communities.

And so in a sense we must ask, How is it that black people move? And what do we do? But the question in a much greater sense is, How can white people who are the majority, and who are responsible for making democracy work, make it work? They have failed miserably on this point. They have never made democracy work, be it inside the United States, Vietnam, South Africa, the Philippines, South America, Puerto Rico, or wherever America has been. We not only condemn the country for what it has done internally, but we must condemn it for what it does externally. We see this country trying to rule the world, and someone must stand up and start articulating that this country is not God, and that it cannot rule the world.

The white supremacist attitude, which you have either consciously or subconsciously, is running rampant through society today. For example, missionaries were sent to Africa with the attitude that blacks were automatically inferior. As a matter of fact, the first act the missionaries did when they got to Africa was to make us cover up our bodies, because they said it got them excited. We couldn't go bare-breasted any more because they got excited! When the missionaries came to civilize us because we were uncivilized, to educate us because we were uneducated, and to give us some literate studies because we were illiterate, they charged a price. The missionaries came with the Bible, and we had the land; when they left, they had the land, and we still have the Bible. That's been the rationalization for Western civilization as it moves across the world —stealing, plundering and raping everybody in its path. Their one rationalization is that the rest of the world is uncivilized and they are in fact civilized. But the West is un-civ-i-lized. And that still runs on today, you see, because now we have "modern-day missionaries," and they come into our ghettos— they Head Start, Upward Lift, Bootstrap, and Upward Bound us into white society. They don't want to face the real problem.

A man is poor for one reason and one reason only—he does not have money. If you want to get rid of poverty, you give people money. And you ought not to tell me about people who don't work, and that you can't give people money if they don't work, because if that were true, you'd have to start stopping Rockefeller, Kennedy, Lyndon Baines Johnson, Lady Bird Johnson, the whole of Standard Oil, the Gulf Corporation, all of them, including probably a large number of the board of trustees of this university. The question, then, is not whether or not one can work; it's *Who has power to make his or her acts legitimate?* That is all. In this country that power is invested in the hands of white people, and it makes their acts legitimate.

We are now engaged in a psychological struggle in this country about whether or not black people have the right to use the words they want to use without white people giving their sanction. We maintain the use of the words Black Power—let them address themselves to that. We are not going to wait for white people to sanction Black Power. We're tired of waiting; every time black people try to move in this country, they're forced to defend their position beforehand. It's time that white people do that. They ought to start defending themselves as to why they have oppressed and exploited us. A man was picked as a slave for one reason—the color of his skin. Black was automatically inferior, inhuman, and therefore fit for slavery, so the question of whether or not we are individually suppressed is nonsensical, and it's a downright lie. We are oppressed as a group because we are black, not because we are lazy or apathetic, not because we're stupid or we stink, not because we eat watermelon or have good rhythm. We are oppressed because we are black.

In order to escape that oppression we must wield the group power we have, not the individual power that this country sets as the criterion under which a man may come into it. That's what is called integration. "You do what I tell you to do and we'll let you sit at the table with us." Well, if you believe in integration, you can come live in Watts, send your children to the ghetto schools. Let's talk about that. If you believe in integration, then we're going to start adopting us some white people to live in our neighborhoods. So it is clear that this question is not one of integration or segregation. We cannot afford to be concerned about the 6 per cent of black children in this country whom you allow to enter white schools. We are going to be concerned about the 94 per cent. You ought to be concerned about them too. But are we willing to be concerned about the black people who will never get to Berkeley, never get to Harvard, and cannot get an education, the ones you'll never get a chance to rub shoulders with and say, "Why, he's almost as good as we are; he's not like the others"? The question is, How can white society begin to move to see black people as human beings? I am black, therefore I am. Not: I am black and I must go to college to prove myself. I am black, therefore I am. And don't deprive me of anything and say to me that you must go to college before you gain access to X, Y, and Z. That's only a rationalization for suppression.

The political parties of this country do not meet the needs of the people on a day-to-day basis. How can we build new political institutions that will become the political expressions of people? How can you build political institutions that will begin to meet the needs of Oakland, California? The need of Oakland, California, is not 1,000 policemen with submachine guns. They need that least of all. How can we build institutions that will allow those people to function on a day-to-day basis, so that they can get decent jobs and have decent houses, and they can begin to participate in the policy and make the decisions that affect their lives? That's what they need, not Gestapo troops, because this is not 1942, and if you play like Nazis, we're not going to play Jew this time around. Get hip to that. Can white people move inside their own community and start tearing down racism where in fact it exists? It is you who live in Cicero and stopped us from living there. White people stopped us from moving into Grenada, Miss. White people make sure that we live in the ghettos of this country. White institutions do that. They must change. In order for America to really live on a basic principle of human relationships, a new society must be born. Racism must die. The economic exploitation by this country of non-white people around the world must also die.

There are several programs in the South where whites are trying to organize poor whites so they can begin to move around the question of economic exploitation and political disfranchisement. We've all heard the theory several times. But few people are willing to go into it. The question is, Can the white activist stop trying to be a Pepsi generation who comes alive in the black community, and be a man who's willing to move into the white community and start organizing where the organization is needed? Can he do that? Can the white activist disassociate himself from the clowns who waste time parrying with each other and start talking about the problems that are facing people in this state? You must start inside the white community. Our political position is that we don't think the Democratic Party represents the needs of black people. We know that it does not. If, in fact, white people believe that they're going to move inside that structure, how are they going to organize around a concept of whiteness based on true brotherhood and on stopping economic exploitation in order to form a coalition base for black people to hook up with? You cannot build a coalition based on national sentiment. If you want a coalition to address itself to real changes in this country, white people must start building those institutions inside the white community. And that's the real question facing the white activists today. Can they tear down the institutions that have put us all in the trick bag we've been into for the last hundreds of years? Frederick Douglass said that the youth should fight to be leaders today. God knows we need to be leaders today, because the men who run this country are sick. We must begin to start building those institutions and to fight to articulate our position, to fight to be able to control our universities (we need to be able to do that), to fight to control the basic institutions that perpetuate racism by destroying them and building new ones. That's the real question that faces us today, and it is a dilemma because most of us don't know how to work.

Most white activists run into the black community as an excuse. We cannot have white people working in the black community—on psychological grounds. The fact is that all black people question whether or not they are equal to whites, since every time they start to do something, white people are around showing them how to do it. If we are going to eliminate that for the generation that comes after us, then black people must be in positions of power, doing and articulating for themselves. That's not reverse racism; it is moving onto healthy ground: it is becoming what the philosopher Sartre says, an "antiracist racist." And this country can't understand that. What we have in SNCC is antiracist racism. We are against racists. If everybody who's white sees himself as racist and sees us against him, he's speaking from his own guilt.

We do not have the power in our hands to change the institution of war in this country—to begin to re-create it so that they learn to leave the Vietnamese people alone. The only power we have is the power to say, "Hell, no!" to the draft.

The war in Vietnam is illegal and immoral. The question is, What can we do to stop that war? What can we do to stop the people who, in the name of America, are killing babies, women, and children? We have to say to ourselves that there's a higher law than the law of a fool named Rusk; there's a higher law than the law of a buffoon named Johnson. It's the law of each of us. We will not murder anybody who they say kill, and if we decide to kill, *we're* going to decide who it shall be. This country will only stop the war in Vietnam when the young men who are made to fight it begin to say, "Hell, no, we ain't going."

The peace movement has been a failure because it hasn't gotten off the college campuses where everybody has a 2S and is not afraid of being drafted anyway. The problem is how you can move out of that into the white ghettos of this country and articulate a position for those white youth who do not want to go. You cannot do that. It is sometimes ironic that many of the peace groups have begun to call SNCC violent and say they can no longer support us, when we are in fact the most militant organization for peace or civil rights or human rights against the war in Vietnam in this country today. There isn't one organization that has begun to meet our stand on the war in Vietnam. We not only say we are against the war in Vietnam; we are against the draft. No man has the right to take a man for two years and train him to be a killer. Any black man fighting in the war in Vietnam is nothing but a black mercenary. Any time a black man leaves the country where he can't vote to supposedly deliver the vote to somebody else, he's a black mercenary. Any time a black man leaves this country, gets shot in Vietnam on foreign ground, and returns home and you won't give him a burial place in his own homeland, he's a black mercenary. Even if I believed the lies of Johnson, that we're fighting to give democracy to the people in Vietnam, as a black man living in this country I wouldn't fight to give this to anybody. We have to use our bodies and our minds in the only way that we see fit. We must begin, as the philosopher Camus says, to come alive by saying "No." This country is a nation of thieves. It stole everything it has, beginning with black people. The U.S. cannot justify its existence as the policeman of the world any longer. The marines are at ready disposal to bring democracy, and if the Vietnamese don't want democracy, well then, "We'll just wipe them out, because they don't deserve to live if they won't have our way of life."

There is a more immediate question: What do you do on your campus? Do you raise questions about the hundred black students who were kicked off campus a couple of weeks ago? Eight hundred? And how does that question begin to move? Do you begin to relate to people outside the ivory tower and university walls? Do you think you're capable of building those human relationships as the country now stands? You're fooling yourself. It is impossible for white and black people to talk about building a relationship based on humanity when the country is the way it is, when the institutions are clearly against us.

We have found all the myths of the country to be nothing but downright lies. We were told that if we worked hard we would succeed, and if that were true we would own this country lock, stock, and barrel. We have picked the cotton for nothing; we are the maids in the kitchens of liberal white people; we are the janitors, the porters, the elevator men; we sweep up your college floors. We are the hardest workers and the lowest paid. It is nonsensical for people to talk about human relationships until they are willing to build new institutions. Black people are economically insecure. White liberals are economically secure. Can you begin to build an economic coalition? Are the liberals willing to share their salaries with the economically insecure black people they so much love? Then if you're not, are you willing to start building new institutions that will provide economic security for black people? That's the question *we* want to deal with!

American students are perhaps the most politically unsophisticated students in the world. Across every country of the world, while we were growing up, students were leading the major revolutions of their countries. We have not been able to do that. They have been politically aware of their existence. In South America our neighbors have one every 24 hours just to remind us that they are politically aware. But we have been unable to grasp it because we've always moved in the field of morality and love while people have been politically jiving with our lives. You can't move morally against men like Brown and Reagan. You can't move morally against Lyndon Baines Johnson because he is an immoral man. He doesn't know what it's all about. So you've got to move politically. We have to develop a political sophistication that doesn't parrot ("The two-party system is the best system in the world"). We have to raise questions about whether we need new types of political institutions in this country, and we in SNCC maintain that we need them now. Any time Lyndon Baines Johnson can head a party that has in it Bobby Kennedy, Wayne Morse, Eastland, Wallace, and all those other supposed-to-be-liberal cats, there's something wrong with that party. They're moving politically, not morally. If that party refuses to seat black people from Mississippi and goes ahead and seats racists like Eastland and his clique, it's clear to me that they're moving politically, and that one cannot begin to talk morality to people like that.

We must question the values of this society, and I maintain that black people are the best people to do that since we have been excluded from that society. We ought to think whether or not we want to become a part of that society. That's precisely what the Student Nonviolent Coordinating Committee is doing. We are raising questions about this country. I do not want to be a part of the American pie. The American pie means raping South Africa, beating Vietnam, beating South America, raping the Philippines, raping every country you've been in. I don't want any of your blood money. I don't want to be part of that system. We are the generation who has found this country to be a world power and the wealthiest country in the world. We must question whether or not we want this country to continue being the wealthiest country in the world at the price of raping everybody else. And because black people are saying we do not now want to become a part of you, we are called reverse racists. Ain't that a gas?

White society has caused the failure of nonviolence. I was always surprised at Quakers who came to Alabama and counseled me to be nonviolent, but didn't have the guts to tell James Clark to be nonviolent. That's where nonviolence needs to be preached—to Jim Clark, not to black people. White people should conduct their nonviolent schools in Cicero where they are needed, not among black people in Mississippi. Six-foot-two men kick little black children in Grenada—can you conduct nonviolent schools there? Can you name one black man today who has killed anybody white and is still alive? Even after a rebellion, when some black brothers throw bricks and bottles, ten thousand of them have to pay the price. When the white policeman comes in, anybody who's black is arrested because we all look alike.

The youth of this country must begin to raise those questions. We are going to have to change the foreign policy of this country. One of the problems with the peace movement is that it is too caught up in Vietnam, and if America pulled out the troops from Vietnam this week, next week you'd have to get another peace movement for Santo Domingo. *We have to hook up with black people around the world; and that hookup must not only be psychological, but real.* If South America were to rebel today, and black people were to shoot the hell out of all the white people there, as they should, Standard Oil would crumble tomorrow. If South Africa were to go today, Chase Manhattan Bank would crumble tomorrow. If Zimbabwe, which is called Rhodesia by white people, were to go tomorrow, General Electric would cave in on the East Coast. How do we stop those institutions that are so willing to fight against "Communist aggression" but close their eyes against racist oppression? We're not talking about a policy of aid or sending Peace Corps people in to teach people how to read and write and build houses while we steal their raw materials from them. Because that's all this country does. What underdeveloped countries need is information about how to become industrialized, so they can keep their raw materials where they have them, produce goods, sell them to this country for the price it's supposed to pay. Instead, America keeps selling goods back to them for a profit and keeps sending our modern-day missionaries there, calling them the sons of Kennedy. And if the youth are going to participate in that program, how do you begin to control the Peace Corps?

This country assumes that if someone is poor, they are poor because of their own individual blight, or because they weren't born on the right side of town, or they had too many children, or went in the army too early, or because their father was a drunk, or they didn't care about school—they made a mistake. That's a lot of nonsense. Poverty is well calculated in this country, and the reason why the poverty program won't work is because the calculators of poverty are administering it.

How can you, as the youth in this country, move to start carrying those things out? Move into the white community. We have developed a movement in the black community. The white activist has miserably failed to develop the movement inside of his community. Will white people have the courage to go into white communities and start organizing them? That's the question for the white activist. We won't get caught up in questions about power. This country knows what power is. It knows what Black Power is because it deprived black people of it for over four hundred years. White people associate Black Power with violence because of their own inability to deal with blackness. If we had said "Negro power" nobody would get scared. Everybody would support it. If we said power for colored people, everybody'd be for that, but it is the word "black" that bothers people in this country, and that's their problem, not mine. That's the lie that says anything black is bad.

You're all a college and university crowd. You've taken your basic logic course. You know about major premise, minor premise. People have been telling you anything all black is bad. Let's make that our major premise.

Major premise: Anything all black is bad.

Minor premise or particular premise: I am all black.

Therefore . . . I'm never going to be put in that bag; I'm all black and I'm all good. Anything all black is not necessarily bad. Anything all black is only bad when you use force to keep whites out. Now that's what white people have done in this country, and they're projecting their same fears and guilt on us, and we won't have it. Let them handle their own affairs and their own guilt. Let them find their own psychologists. We refuse to be the therapy for white society any longer. We have gone stark, raving mad trying to do it.

I look at Dr. King on television every single day, and I say to myself: "Now there is a man who's desperately needed in this country. There is a man full of love. There is a man full of mercy. There is a man full of compassion." But every time I see Lyndon on television, I say, "Martin, baby, you got a long way to go."

If we were to be real and honest, we would have to admit that most people in this country see things black and white. We live in a country that's geared that way. White people would have to admit that they are afraid to go into a black ghetto at night. They're afraid because they'd be "beat up," "lynched," "looted," "cut up," etc. It happens to black people inside the ghetto every day, incidentally. Since white people are afraid of that, they get a man to do it for them—a policeman. Figure his mentality. The first time a black man jumps, that white man's going to shoot him. Police brutality is going to exist on that level. The only time I hear people talk about nonviolence is when black people move to defend themselves against white people. Black people cut themselves every night in the ghetto—nobody talks about nonviolence. Lyndon Baines Johnson is busy bombing the hell out of Vietnam—nobody talks about nonviolence. White people beat up black people every day—nobody talks about nonviolence. But as soon as black people start to move, the double standard comes into being. You can't defend yourself. You show me a black man who advocates aggressive violence who would be able to live in this country. Show him to me. Isn't it hypocritical for Lyndon to talk about how you can't accomplish anything by looting and you must accomplish it by the legal ways? What does he know about legality? Ask Ho Chi Minh.

We must wage a psychological battle on the right for black people to define themselves as they see fit, and organize themselves as they see fit. We don't know whether the white community will allow for that organizing, because once they do they must also allow for the organizing inside their own community. It doesn't make a difference, though—we're going to organize our way. The question is how we're going to facilitate those matters, whether it's going to be done with a thousand policemen with submachine guns, or whether it's going to be done in a context where it's allowed by white people warding off those policemen. Are white people who call themselves activists ready to move into the white communities on two counts, on building new political institutions to destroy the old ones that we have, and to move around the concept of white youth refusing to go into the army? If so, then we can start to build a new world. We must urge you to fight now to be the leaders of today, not tomorrow. This country is a nation of thieves. It stands on the brink of becoming a nation of murderers. We must stop it. We must stop it. We must stop it.

We are on the move for our liberation. We're tired of trying to prove things to white people. We are tired of trying to explain to white people that we're not going to hurt them. We are concerned with getting the things we want, the things we have to have to be able to function. The question is, Will white people overcome their racism and allow for that to happen in this country? If not, we have no choice but to say very clearly, "Move on over, or we're going to move on over you."

“WHAT WE WANT NOW!”

Ten-Point Program of the Black Panther Party for Self Defense

May 15, 1967

WHAT WE WANT NOW!
WHAT WE BELIEVE

TO THOSE POOR SOULS WHO DON’T KNOW BLACK HISTORY, THE BELIEFS AND DESIRES OF THE BLACK PANTHER PARTY FOR SELF DEFENSE MAY SEEM UNREASONABLE. TO BLACK PEOPLE, THE TEN POINTS COVERED ARE ABSOLUTELY ESSENTIAL TO SURVIVAL. WE HAVE LISTENED TO THE RIOT PRODUCING WORDS “THESE THINGS TAKE TIME” FOR 400 YEARS. THE BLACK PANTHER PARTY KNOWS WHAT BLACK PEOPLE WANT AND NEED. BLACK UNITY AND SELF DEFENSE WILL MAKE THESE DEMANDS A REALITY.

WHAT WE WANT

1. WE WANT FREEDOM. WE WANT POWER TO DETERMINE THE DESTINY OF OUR BLACK COMMUNITY.

2. WE WANT FULL EMPLOYMENT FOR OUR PEOPLE.

3. WE WANT AN END TO THE ROBBERY BY THE WHITE MAN OF OUR BLACK COMMUNITY.

4. WE WANT DECENT HOUSING, FIT FOR SHELTER HUMAN BEINGS.

5. WE WANT EDUCATION FOR OUR PEOPLE THAT EXPOSES THE TRUE NATURE OF THIS DECADENT AMERICAN SOCIETY. WE WANT EDUCATION THAT TEACHES US OUR TRUE HISTORY AND OUR ROLE IN THE PRESENT DAY SOCIETY.

6. WE WANT ALL BLACK MEN TO BE EXEMPT FROM MILITARY SERVICE.

7. WE WANT AN IMMEDIATE END TO POLICE BRUTALITY AND MURDER OF BLACK PEOPLE.

8. WE WANT FREEDOM FOR ALL BLACK MEN HELD IN FEDERAL, STATE, COUNTY, AND CITY PRISONS AND JAILS.

9. WE WANT ALL BLACK PEOPLE WHEN BROUGHT TO TRIAL TO BE TRIED IN COURT BY A JURY OF THEIR PEER GROUP OR PEOPLE FROM THEIR BLACK COMMUNITIES. AS DEFINED BY THE CONSTITUTION OF THE UNITED STATES.

10. WE WANT LAND, BREAD, HOUSING, EDUCATION, CLOTHING, JUSTICE AND PEACE.

WHAT WE BELIEVE

1. WE BELIEVE THAT BLACK PEOPLE WILL NOT BE FREE UNTIL WE ARE ABLE TO DETERMINE OUR DESTINY.

2. WE BELIEVE THAT THE FEDERAL GOVERNMENT IS RESPONSIBLE AND OBLIGATED TO GIVE EVERY MAN EMPLOYMENT OR A GUARANTEED INCOME. WE BELIEVE THAT IF THE WHITE AMERICAN BUSINESS MEN WILL NOT GIVE FULL EMPLOYMENT, THEN THE MEANS OF PRODUCTION SHOULD BE TAKEN FROM THE BUSINESS MEN AND PLACED IN THE COMMUNITY SO THAT THE PEOPLE OF THE COMMUNITY CAN ORGANIZE AND EMPLOY ALL OF ITS PEOPLE AND GIVE A HIGH STANDARD OF LIVING.

3. WE BELIEVE THAT THIS RACIST GOVERNMENT HAS ROBBED US AND NOW WE ARE DEMANDING THE OVERDUE DEBT OF FORTY ACRES AND TWO MULES. FORTY ACRES AND TWO MULES WAS PROMISED 100 YEARS AGO AS RETRIBUTION FOR SLAVE LABOR AND MASS MURDER OF BLACK PEOPLE. WE WILL ACCEPT THE PAYMENT IN CURRENCY WHICH WILL BE DISTRIBUTED TO OUR MANY COMMUNITIES. THE GERMANS ARE NOW AIDING THE JEWS IN ISRAEL FOR THE GENOCIDE OF THE JEWISH PEOPLE. THE GERMANS MURDERED 6,000,000 JEWS. THE AMERICAN RACIST HAS TAKEN PART IN THE SLAUGHTER OF OVER 50,000,000 BLACK PEOPLE; THEREFORE, WE FEEL THAT THIS IS A MODEST DEMAND THAT WE MAKE.

4. WE BELIEVE THAT IF THE WHITE LANDLORDS WILL NOT GIVE DECENT HOUSING TO OUR BLACK COMMUNITY, THEN THE HOUSING AND THE LAND SHOULD BE MADE INTO CO-OPERATIVES SO THAT OUR COMMUNITY, WITH GOVERNMENT AID, CAN BUILD AND MAKE DECENT HOUSING FOR ITS PEOPLE.

5. WE BELIEVE IN AN EDUCATIONAL SYSTEM THAT WILL GIVE TO OUR PEOPLE A KNOWLEDGE OF SELF. IF A MAN DOES NOT HAVE KNOWLEDGE OF HIMSELF AND HIS POSITION IN SOCIETY AND THE WORLD, THEN HE HAS LITTLE CHANCE TO RELATE TO ANYTHING ELSE.

6. WE BELIEVE THAT BLACK PEOPLE SHOULD NOT BE FORCED TO FIGHT IN THE MILITARY SERVICE TO DEFEND A RACIST GOVERNMENT THAT DOES NOT PROTECT US. WE WILL NOT FIGHT AND KILL OTHER PEOPLE OF COLOR IN THE WORLD WHO, LIKE BLACK PEOPLE, ARE BEING VICTIMIZED BY THE WHITE RACIST GOVERNMENT OF AMERICA. WE WILL PROTECT OURSELVES FROM THE FORCE AND VIOLENCE OF THE RACIST POLICE AND THE RACIST MILITARY, BY WHATEVER MEANS NECESSARY.

7. WE BELIEVE WE CAN END POLICE BRUTALITY IN OUR BLACK COMMUNITY BY ORGANIZING BLACK SELF DEFENSE GROUPS THAT ARE DEDICATED TO DEFENDING OUR BLACK COMMUNITY FROM RACIST POLICE OPPRESSION AND BRUTALITY. THE SECOND AMENDMENT OF THE CONSTITUTION OF THE UNITED STATES GIVES US A RIGHT TO BEAR ARMS. WE THEREFORE BELIEVE THAT ALL BLACK PEOPLE SHOULD ARM THEMSELVES FOR SELF DEFENSE.

8. WE BELIEVE THAT ALL BLACK PEOPLE SHOULD BE RELEASED FROM THE MANY JAILS AND PRISONS BECAUSE THEY HAVE NOT RECEIVED A FAIR AND IMPARTIAL TRIAL.

9. WE BELIEVE THAT THE COURTS SHOULD FOLLOW THE UNITED STATES CONSTITUTION SO THAT BLACK PEOPLE WILL RECEIVE FAIR TRIALS. THE 14TH AMENDMENT OF THE U.S.

CONSTITUTION GIVES A MAN A RIGHT TO BE TRIED BY HIS PEER GROUP. A PEER IS A PERSON FROM A SIMILAR ECONOMIC, SOCIAL, RELIGIOUS, GEOGRAPHICAL, ENVIRONMENTAL, HISTORICAL AND RACIAL BACKGROUND. TO DO THIS THE COURT WILL BE FORCED TO SELECT A JURY FROM THE BLACK COMMUNITY FROM WHICH THE BLACK DEFENDANT CAME. WE HAVE BEEN, AND ARE BEING TRIED BY ALL WHITE JURIES THAT HAVE NO UNDERSTANDING OF THE "AVERAGE REASONING MAN" OF THE BLACK COMMUNITY.

10. WHEN IN THE COURSE OF HUMAN EVENTS, IT BECOMES NECESSARY FOR ONE PEOPLE TO DISSOLVE THE POLITICAL BONDS WHICH HAVE CONNECTED THEM WITH ANOTHER, AND TO ASSUME AMONG THE POWERS OF THE EARTH, THE SEPARATE AND EQUAL STATION TO WHICH THE LAWS OF NATURE AND NATURE'S GOD ENTITLE THEM, A DECENT RESPECT TO THE OPINIONS OF MANKIND REQUIRES THAT THEY SHOULD DECLARE THE CAUSES WHICH IMPEL THEM TO SEPARATION. WE HOLD THESE TRUTHS TO BE SELF-EVIDENT, THAT ALL MEN ARE CREATED EQUAL, THAT THEY ARE ENDOWED BY THEIR CREATOR WITH CERTAIN INALIENABLE RIGHTS, THAT AMONG THESE ARE LIFE, LIBERTY AND THE PURSUIT OF HAPPINESS. THAT TO SECURE THESE RIGHTS, GOVERNMENTS ARE INSTITUTED AMONG MEN, DERIVING THEIR JUST POWERS FROM THE CONSENT OF THE GOVERNED,—THAT WHENEVER ANY FORM OF GOVERNMENT BECOMES DESTRUCTIVE OF THESE ENDS, IT IS THE RIGHT OF PEOPLE TO ALTER OR TO ABOLISH IT, AND TO INSTITUTE NEW GOVERNMENT, LAYING ITS FOUNDATION ON SUCH PRINCIPLES AND ORGANIZING ITS POWERS IN SUCH FORM AS TO THEM SHALL SEEM MOST LIKELY TO EFFECT THEIR SAFETY AND HAPPINESS.

PRUDENCE, INDEED, WILL DICTATE THAT GOVERNMENTS LONG ESTABLISHED SHOULD NOT BE CHANGED FOR LIGHT AND TRANSIENT CAUSES; AND ACCORDINGLY ALL EXPERIENCE HATH SHEWN, THAT MANKIND ARE MORE DISPOSED TO SUFFER, WHILE EVILS ARE SUFFERABLE, THAN TO RIGHT THEMSELVES BY ABOLISHING THE FORMS TO WHICH THEY ARE ACCUSTOMED. BUT WHEN A LONG TRAIN OF ABUSES

AND USURPATIONS, PURSUING INVARIABLY THE SAME OBJECT, EVINCES A DESIGN TO REDUCE THEM UNDER ABSOLUTE DESPOTISM, IT IS THEIR RIGHT, IT IS THEIR DUTY, TO THROW OFF SUCH GOVERNMENT, AND TO PROVIDE NEW GUARDS FOR THEIR FUTURE SECURITY.

THE RIGHT TO INTERRACIAL MARRIAGE

EARL WARREN

Opinion in Loving v. Virginia

June 12, 1967

MR. CHIEF JUSTICE WARREN delivered the opinion of the Court.

This case presents a constitutional question never addressed by this Court: whether a statutory scheme adopted by the State of Virginia to prevent marriages between persons solely on the basis of racial classifications violates the Equal Protection and Due Process Clauses of the Fourteenth Amendment.[1] For reasons which seem to us to reflect the central meaning of those constitutional commands, we conclude that these statutes cannot stand consistently with the Fourteenth Amendment.

In June 1958, two residents of Virginia, Mildred Jeter, a Negro woman, and Richard Loving, a white man, were married in the District of Columbia pursuant to its laws. Shortly after their marriage, the Lovings returned to Virginia and established their marital abode in Caroline County. At the October Term, 1958, of the Circuit Court of Caroline County, a grand jury issued an indictment charging the Lovings with violating Virginia's ban on interracial marriages. On January 6, 1959, the Lovings pleaded guilty to the charge and were sentenced to one year in jail; however, the trial judge suspended the sentence for a period of 25 years on the condition that the Lovings leave the State and not return to Virginia together for 25 years. He stated in an opinion that:

> "Almighty God created the races white, black, yellow, malay and red, and he placed them on separate continents. And but

[1]Section 1 of the Fourteenth Amendment provides:

"All persons born or naturalized in the United States and subject to the jurisdiction thereof, are citizens of the United States and of the State wherein they reside. No State shall make or enforce any law which shall abridge the privileges or immunities of citizens of the United States; nor shall any State deprive any person of life, liberty, or property, without due process of law; nor deny to any person within its jurisdiction the equal protection of the laws."

> for the interference with his arrangement there would be no cause for such marriages. The fact that he separated the races shows that he did not intend for the races to mix."

After their convictions, the Lovings took up residence in the District of Columbia. On November 6, 1963, they filed a motion in the state trial court to vacate the judgment and set aside the sentence on the ground that the statutes which they had violated were repugnant to the Fourteenth Amendment. The motion not having been decided by October 28, 1964, the Lovings instituted a class action in the United States District Court for the Eastern District of Virginia requesting that a three-judge court be convened to declare the Virginia antimiscegenation statutes unconstitutional and to enjoin state officials from enforcing their convictions. On January 22, 1965, the state trial judge denied the motion to vacate the sentences, and the Lovings perfected an appeal to the Supreme Court of Appeals of Virginia. On February 11, 1965, the three-judge District Court continued the case to allow the Lovings to present their constitutional claims to the highest state court.

The Supreme Court of Appeals upheld the constitutionality of the antimiscegenation statutes and, after modifying the sentence, affirmed the convictions.[2] The Lovings appealed this decision, and we noted probable jurisdiction on December 12, 1966, 385 U. S. 986.

The two statutes under which appellants were convicted and sentenced are part of a comprehensive statutory scheme aimed at prohibiting and punishing interracial marriages. The Lovings were convicted of violating § 20–58 of the Virginia Code:

> "*Leaving State to evade law.*—If any white person and colored person shall go out of this State, for the purpose of being married, and with the intention of returning, and be married out of it, and afterwards return to and reside in it, cohabiting as man and wife, they shall be punished as provided in § 20–59, and the marriage shall be governed by the same law as if it had been solemnized in this State. The fact of their cohabitation here as man and wife shall be evidence of their marriage."

[2] 206 Va. 924, 147 S. E. 2d 78 (1966).

Section 20–59, which defines the penalty for miscegenation, provides:

> "*Punishment for marriage.*—If any white person intermarry with a colored person, or any colored person intermarry with a white person, he shall be guilty of a felony and shall be punished by confinement in the penitentiary for not less than one nor more than five years."

Other central provisions in the Virginia statutory scheme are § 20–57, which automatically voids all marriages between "a white person and a colored person" without any judicial proceeding,[3] and §§ 20–54 and 1–14 which, respectively, define "white persons" and "colored persons and Indians" for purposes of the statutory prohibitions.[4] The Lovings have

[3]Section 20–57 of the Virginia Code provides:

"*Marriages void without decree.*—All marriages between a white person and a colored person shall be absolutely void without any decree of divorce or other legal process." Va. Code Ann. § 20–57 (1960 Repl. Vol.).

[4]Section 20–54 of the Virginia Code provides:

"*Intermarriage prohibited; meaning of term 'white persons.'*—It shall hereafter be unlawful for any white person in this State to marry any save a white person, or a person with no other admixture of blood than white and American Indian. For the purpose of this chapter, the term 'white person' shall apply only to such person as has no trace whatever of any blood other than Caucasian; but persons who have one-sixteenth or less of the blood of the American Indian and have no other non-Caucasic blood shall be deemed to be white persons. All laws heretofore passed and now in effect regarding the intermarriage of white and colored persons shall apply to marriages prohibited by this chapter." Va. Code Ann. § 20–54 (1960 Repl. Vol.).

The exception for persons with less than one-sixteenth "of the blood of the American Indian" is apparently accounted for, in the words of a tract issued by the Registrar of the State Bureau of Vital Statistics, by "the desire of all to recognize as an integral and honored part of the white race the descendants of John Rolfe and Pocahontas. . . ." Plecker, The New Family and Race Improvement, 17 Va. Health Bull., Extra No. 12, at 25–26 (New Family Series No. 5, 1925), cited in Wadlington, The *Loving* Case: Virginia's Anti-Miscegenation Statute in Historical Perspective, 52 Va. L. Rev. 1189, 1202, n. 93 (1966).

Section 1–14 of the Virginia Code provides:

"*Colored persons and Indians defined.*—Every person in whom there is ascertainable any Negro blood shall be deemed and taken to be a colored person, and every person not a colored person having one fourth or more of American Indian blood shall be deemed an American Indian; except that members of Indian tribes existing in this Commonwealth having one fourth or more of Indian blood and less than one sixteenth of Negro blood shall be deemed tribal Indians." Va. Code Ann. § 1–14 (1960 Repl. Vol.).

never disputed in the course of this litigation that Mrs. Loving is a "colored person" or that Mr. Loving is a "white person" within the meanings given those terms by the Virginia statutes.

Virginia is now one of 16 States which prohibit and punish marriages on the basis of racial classifications.[5] Penalties for miscegenation arose as an incident to slavery and have been common in Virginia since the colonial period.[6] The present statutory scheme dates from the adoption of the Racial Integrity Act of 1924, passed during the period of extreme nativism which followed the end of the First World War. The central features of this Act, and current Virginia law, are the absolute prohibition of a "white person" marrying other than another "white person,"[7] a prohibition against issuing marriage licenses until the issuing official is satisfied that the applicants' statements as to their race are correct,[8] certificates

[5]After the initiation of this litigation, Maryland repealed its prohibitions against interracial marriage, Md. Laws 1967, c. 6, leaving Virginia and 15 other States with statutes outlawing interracial marriage: Alabama, Ala. Const., Art. 4, § 102, Ala. Code, Tit. 14, § 360 (1958); Arkansas, Ark. Stat. Ann. § 55–104 (1947); Delaware, Del. Code Ann., Tit. 13, § 101 (1953); Florida, Fla. Const., Art. 16, § 24, Fla. Stat. § 741.11 (1965); Georgia, Ga. Code Ann. § 53–106 (1961); Kentucky, Ky. Rev. Stat. Ann. § 402.020 (Supp. 1966); Louisiana, La. Rev. Stat. § 14:79 (1950); Mississippi, Miss. Const., Art. 14, § 263, Miss. Code Ann. § 459 (1956); Missouri, Mo. Rev. Stat. § 451.020 (Supp. 1966); North Carolina, N. C. Const., Art. XIV, § 8, N. C. Gen. Stat. § 14–181 (1953); Oklahoma, Okla. Stat., Tit. 43, § 12 (Supp. 1965); South Carolina, S. C. Const., Art. 3, § 33, S. C. Code Ann. § 20–7 (1962); Tennessee, Tenn. Const., Art. 11, § 14, Tenn. Code Ann. § 36–402 (1955); Texas, Tex. Pen. Code, Art. 492 (1952); West Virginia, W. Va. Code Ann. § 4697 (1961).

Over the past 15 years, 14 States have repealed laws outlawing interracial marriages: Arizona, California, Colorado, Idaho, Indiana, Maryland, Montana, Nebraska, Nevada, North Dakota, Oregon, South Dakota, Utah, and Wyoming.

The first state court to recognize that miscegenation statutes violate the Equal Protection Clause was the Supreme Court of California. *Perez* v. *Sharp*, 32 Cal. 2d 711, 198 P. 2d 17 (1948).

[6]For a historical discussion of Virginia's miscegenation statutes, see Wadlington, *supra*, n. 4.

[7]Va. Code Ann. § 20–54 (1960 Repl. Vol.).

[8]Va. Code Ann. § 20–53 (1960 Repl. Vol.).

of "racial composition" to be kept by both local and state registrars,[9] and the carrying forward of earlier prohibitions against racial intermarriage.[10]

I.

In upholding the constitutionality of these provisions in the decision below, the Supreme Court of Appeals of Virginia referred to its 1955 decision in *Naim* v. *Naim*, 197 Va. 80, 87 S. E. 2d 749, as stating the reasons supporting the validity of these laws. In *Naim*, the state court concluded that the State's legitimate purposes were "to preserve the racial integrity of its citizens," and to prevent "the corruption of blood," "a mongrel breed of citizens," and "the obliteration of racial pride," obviously an endorsement of the doctrine of White Supremacy. *Id.*, at 90, 87 S. E. 2d, at 756. The court also reasoned that marriage has traditionally been subject to state regulation without federal intervention, and, consequently, the regulation of marriage should be left to exclusive state control by the Tenth Amendment.

While the state court is no doubt correct in asserting that marriage is a social relation subject to the State's police power, *Maynard* v. *Hill*, 125 U. S. 190 (1888), the State does not contend in its argument before this Court that its powers to regulate marriage are unlimited notwithstanding the commands of the Fourteenth Amendment. Nor could it do so in light of *Meyer* v. *Nebraska*, 262 U. S. 390 (1923), and *Skinner* v. *Oklahoma*, 316 U. S. 535 (1942). Instead, the State argues that the meaning of the Equal Protection Clause, as illuminated by the statements of the Framers, is only that state penal laws containing an interracial element as part of the definition of the offense must apply equally to whites and Negroes in the sense that members of each race are punished to the same degree. Thus, the State contends that, because its miscegenation statutes punish equally both the white and the Negro participants in an interracial marriage, these statutes, despite their reliance on racial classifications, do not constitute an

[9]Va. Code Ann. § 20–50 (1960 Repl. Vol.).
[10]Va. Code Ann. § 20–54 (1960 Repl. Vol.).

invidious discrimination based upon race. The second argument advanced by the State assumes the validity of its equal application theory. The argument is that, if the Equal Protection Clause does not outlaw miscegenation statutes because of their reliance on racial classifications, the question of constitutionality would thus become whether there was any rational basis for a State to treat interracial marriages differently from other marriages. On this question, the State argues, the scientific evidence is substantially in doubt and, consequently, this Court should defer to the wisdom of the state legislature in adopting its policy of discouraging interracial marriages.

Because we reject the notion that the mere "equal application" of a statute containing racial classifications is enough to remove the classifications from the Fourteenth Amendment's proscription of all invidious racial discriminations, we do not accept the State's contention that these statutes should be upheld if there is any possible basis for concluding that they serve a rational purpose. The mere fact of equal application does not mean that our analysis of these statutes should follow the approach we have taken in cases involving no racial discrimination where the Equal Protection Clause has been arrayed against a statute discriminating between the kinds of advertising which may be displayed on trucks in New York City, *Railway Express Agency, Inc.* v. *New York*, 336 U. S. 106 (1949), or an exemption in Ohio's ad valorem tax for merchandise owned by a nonresident in a storage warehouse, *Allied Stores of Ohio, Inc.* v. *Bowers*, 358 U. S. 522 (1959). In these cases, involving distinctions not drawn according to race, the Court has merely asked whether there is any rational foundation for the discriminations, and has deferred to the wisdom of the state legislatures. In the case at bar, however, we deal with statutes containing racial classifications, and the fact of equal application does not immunize the statute from the very heavy burden of justification which the Fourteenth Amendment has traditionally required of state statutes drawn according to race.

The State argues that statements in the Thirty-ninth Congress about the time of the passage of the Fourteenth Amendment indicate that the Framers did not intend the Amendment to make unconstitutional state miscegenation laws. Many of the statements alluded to by the State concern the debates over the Freedmen's Bureau Bill, which President Johnson vetoed, and the Civil Rights Act of 1866, 14 Stat. 27, enacted over his veto. While these statements have some relevance to the intention of Congress in submitting the Fourteenth Amendment, it must be understood that they pertained to the passage of specific statutes and not to the broader, organic purpose of a constitutional amendment. As for the various statements directly concerning the Fourteenth Amendment, we have said in connection with a related problem, that although these historical sources "cast some light" they are not sufficient to resolve the problem; "[a]t best, they are inconclusive. The most avid proponents of the post-War Amendments undoubtedly intended them to remove all legal distinctions among 'all persons born or naturalized in the United States.' Their opponents, just as certainly, were antagonistic to both the letter and the spirit of the Amendments and wished them to have the most limited effect." *Brown* v. *Board of Education*, 347 U. S. 483, 489 (1954). See also *Strauder* v. *West Virginia*, 100 U. S. 303, 310 (1880). We have rejected the proposition that the debates in the Thirty-ninth Congress or in the state legislatures which ratified the Fourteenth Amendment supported the theory advanced by the State, that the requirement of equal protection of the laws is satisfied by penal laws defining offenses based on racial classifications so long as white and Negro participants in the offense were similarly punished. *McLaughlin* v. *Florida*, 379 U. S. 184 (1964).

The State finds support for its "equal application" theory in the decision of the Court in *Pace* v. *Alabama*, 106 U. S. 583 (1883). In that case, the Court upheld a conviction under an Alabama statute forbidding adultery or fornication between a white person and a Negro which imposed a greater penalty than that of a statute proscribing similar conduct by members of the same race. The Court reasoned that the statute could not be said to discriminate against Negroes because the punishment for each participant in the offense was the same. However, as recently as the 1964 Term, in rejecting the reasoning of that case, we stated "*Pace* represents a limited view of the Equal Protection Clause which has not withstood analysis in the subsequent decisions of this Court." *McLaughlin* v. *Florida*, *supra*, at 188. As we there demonstrated, the Equal Protection Clause requires the consideration of whether the classifications drawn by any statute constitute an arbitrary and invidious discrimination. The clear and central purpose of the Fourteenth Amendment was to eliminate all official state sources of invidious racial discrimination in the States. *Slaughter-House Cases*, 16 Wall. 36, 71 (1873); *Strauder* v. *West Virginia*, 100 U. S. 303, 307–308 (1880); *Ex parte Virginia*, 100 U. S. 339, 344–345 (1880); *Shelley* v. *Kraemer*, 334 U. S. 1 (1948); *Burton* v. *Wilmington Parking Authority*, 365 U. S. 715 (1961).

There can be no question but that Virginia's miscegenation statutes rest solely upon distinctions drawn according to race. The statutes proscribe generally accepted conduct if engaged in by members of different races. Over the years, this Court has consistently repudiated "[d]istinctions between citizens solely because of their ancestry" as being "odious to a free people whose institutions are founded upon the doctrine of equality." *Hirabayashi* v. *United States*, 320 U. S. 81, 100 (1943). At the very least, the Equal Protection Clause demands that racial classifications, especially suspect in criminal statutes, be subjected to the "most rigid scrutiny," *Korematsu* v. *United States*, 323 U. S. 214, 216 (1944), and, if they are ever to be upheld, they must be shown to be necessary to the accomplishment of some permissible state objective, independent of the racial discrimination which it was the object of the Fourteenth Amendment to eliminate. Indeed, two members of this Court have already stated that they "cannot conceive of a valid legislative purpose . . . which makes the color of a person's skin the test of whether his conduct is a criminal offense." *McLaughlin* v. *Florida*, *supra*, at 198 (Stewart, J., joined by Douglas, J., concurring).

There is patently no legitimate overriding purpose independent of invidious racial discrimination which justifies this classification. The fact that Virginia prohibits only interracial marriages involving white persons demonstrates that the racial classifications must stand on their own justification, as measures designed to maintain White Supremacy.[11] We have consistently denied the constitutionality of measures which restrict the rights of citizens on account of race. There can be no doubt that restricting the freedom to marry solely because of racial classifications violates the central meaning of the Equal Protection Clause.

II.

These statutes also deprive the Lovings of liberty without due process of law in violation of the Due Process Clause of the Fourteenth Amendment. The freedom to marry has long been recognized as one of the vital personal rights essential to the orderly pursuit of happiness by free men.

Marriage is one of the "basic civil rights of man," fundamental to our very existence and survival. *Skinner* v. *Oklahoma*, 316 U. S. 535, 541 (1942). See also *Maynard* v. *Hill*, 125 U. S. 190 (1888). To deny this fundamental freedom on so unsupportable a basis as the racial classifications embodied in these statutes, classifications so directly subversive of the principle of equality at the heart of the Fourteenth Amendment, is surely to deprive all the State's citizens of liberty without due process of law. The Fourteenth Amendment requires that the freedom of choice to marry not be restricted by invidious racial discriminations. Under our Constitution, the freedom to marry, or not marry, a person of another race resides with the individual and cannot be infringed by the State.

These convictions must be reversed.

It is so ordered.

[11]Appellants point out that the State's concern in these statutes, as expressed in the words of the 1924 Act's title, "An Act to Preserve Racial Integrity," extends only to the integrity of the white race. While Virginia prohibits whites from marrying any nonwhite (subject to the exception for the descendants of Pocahontas), Negroes, Orientals, and any other racial class may intermarry without statutory interference. Appellants contend that this distinction renders Virginia's miscegenation statutes arbitrary and unreasonable even assuming the constitutional validity of an official purpose to preserve "racial integrity." We need not reach this contention because we find the racial classifications in these statutes repugnant to the Fourteenth Amendment, even assuming an even-handed state purpose to protect the "integrity" of all races.

A PRESIDENT WITHOUT EQUAL ON CIVIL RIGHTS

THURGOOD MARSHALL
from *Oral History Interview on Lyndon B. Johnson*

1941–67

INTERVIEWEE: THURGOOD MARSHALL

INTERVIEWER: T. H. BAKER

B: This is the interview with Thurgood Marshall. Sir, to begin in the beginning, did you have any knowledge of Mr. Johnson back when he was a congressman or senator?

M: I knew of him when he was a congressman, and I knew of him directly through Aubrey Williams and people like that in the Youth Administration. The first I became interested was when he ran for the Senate.

B: Was this in the '48—?

M: Yes, in Texas. I was in Texas working on the primary cases, and all of our people of the NAACP in that area were enthusiastically behind him.

B: Excuse me, sir, this must have been in '41 then, when Mr. Johnson first ran for the Senate and didn't get elected.

M: It *was* '41 when he first ran. It was '41, because that's when the primary cases started. If I remember correctly, in the runoff the labor support dwindled away but the Negro support stuck with him. But when he became a senator, he was not among the liberals.

B: I was going to ask you about that. You said that the NAACP people in Texas were favorably inclined toward Mr. Johnson in those days?

M: Solidly. So was the national office.

B: Did they have any real basis for this?

M: Yes. Well, they knew him. The Negroes down there, they know each other pretty well. They were a pretty hard bunch. We followed their judgment. I didn't know him. But we couldn't engage in politics. All we could do was to talk about it. But Walter White, the head of the NAACP, did meet with him, as I remember, and did say that he was all right.

B: Did Mr. Johnson have any direct connection with what became the primary cases?

M: No, none at all. He had no connection with them one way or the other. I never saw him, so he could not have had any connection. I ran the case and I didn't—

B: You certainly would have seen him.

M: I would have known it, yes.

B: Then after 1948—after he became a senator—was there any change in this feeling?

M: Well, Walter White, who handled the legislative matters in Congress, got very angry with him and stayed angry until he died, as a matter of fact.

B: On what basis?

M: He just wouldn't support any of the legislation the NAACP was after. Walter White chalked it up to his great admiration for Sam Rayburn. He thought Sam Rayburn was calling the turn. Now whether that's true or not I don't know. But on our records he was not a liberal senator.

B: Incidentally, did Mr. Johnson have any connection with your other Texas case in the '50's?

M: None.

B: Sweatt versus Painter at the University—?

M: None. Not one way or the other. We never knew what happened.

B: How about, I guess what is *the* case, the school integration case—Brown versus the Board of Education?

M: Nothing. He had nothing to do with it at all.

B: This attitude you mentioned that Walter White had—did Mr. Johnson's activity in connection with the '57 civil rights bill change that any?

M: Walter was dead in '57; Walter died in '55.

B: That's right. Roy Wilkins—

M: Roy Wilkins took over then. No. Roy did not have the same opinion of him. Roy had a better opinion of him. He felt that he was the type of man in the Senate who could get things done, but he didn't. But he could have. He just chalked it up to politics. But he didn't have any—. As a matter of fact, Roy had very good thoughts about him. I know that as then and as of now.

B: What was the general opinion among civil rights leaders like yourself, of the '57 bill? Did you feel it was progress?

M: Nothing. It wasn't doing any good. It was just barely progress because it had been a hundred years—eighty years—since we'd had one. The smallest slice was good rather than the whole loaf of bread. But it was understandable in my book because it was a strictly political move of getting something done. But when we'd been fighting since 1909 for something, it was good. Then when we looked at it, we had a different feeling.

B: Mostly I guess because of the elimination of the Part 3?

M: Sure. Oh, yes, we fought to the bitter end on that. Yet as you look back, it was great progress, it seems to me, to get them to move at all. I don't know, and I guess nobody would know, just what was sold in there and how it was sold. Whether we could have gotten more or not I don't know. Nobody will know except—well, Lyndon Johnson would know and those people that were running that inner core of the Senate in those days.

You see, as I looked at him as a senator and leader, they always said he was a great compromiser, but I've always thought that he had the compromise in his pocket when the thing started each time. He just waited for the right time to take it out.

B: You mean he had already figured out what was going to happen?

M: Sure. He always won. Well, that all changed when he became President, anyhow.

B: In those years before Mr. Johnson left the Senate, did you ever talk to him about this problem of compliance with the '54 decision?

M: I never talked to him. I don't remember having ever talked to him until I came down as Solicitor General; I don't believe. I might have, but I don't remember.

B: Incidentally, I would like to ask one question here that's not directly related to Mr. Johnson. What happened in '55 that caused the NAACP Legal Defense Fund and the NAACP to end their directorate connection—to split almost entirely?

M: The United States Treasury Department, specifically the Internal Revenue Service—they decided that they were going to take away the exemption of the Legal Defense Fund.

B: Because the directorate was—?

M: No, no. They then got reasons afterwards. But as soon as the Eisenhower Administration took over, they came after us. I think they're still under investigation. We've been under investigation all the way up to the Kennedy Administration. We found out that if they took away our tax exemption, it would be two years before we could litigate it—complete the litigation. With a reserve fund of about twenty or thirty thousand dollars, we couldn't take that chance. So we ended up with three or four specific things. One was the Board of Directors had to be entirely separate. The staff had to be entirely separate. The books were always separate. And the fourth one was we had to take NAACP out of the name.

Well, we agreed to the first two and we had already agreed to the third. We refused to take the name out; that's why we split. That's the only reason we split—to save it.

B: Was that a general tone of the Eisenhower Administration, or was there any one particular—?

M: Well, it just happened at that time. I don't blame anybody. It could be efficiency. Up until that time the charitable organizations group was run by very inefficient bureaucrats. The reason was it meant nothing to the government because if you knock out the exemption of one charity, the people will give it to another charity. The government doesn't make any money out of it. And the Eisenhower Administration, bent on efficiency, it could be that. But I do also know that Internal Revenue and the Secretary of Treasury got repeated letters from the southern Senators and Congressmen, "How come they're tax exempt?" What did it I don't know. But I do know we were under—. I know of one time when they had two men in my office and two men in the NAACP office for six months, going through every single check, trying to find something. Well, they didn't find anything.

B: Actually the two have been practically separate for a good many years.

M: We only had the interlocking Board; that's all we had. We have separate buildings; separate bank accounts; separate books; and we were very careful about it.

B: To get back to Mr. Johnson, was there any dismay among civil rights leaders like yourself when he showed up on the '60 ticket for the Democratic party?

M: It wasn't dismay; it was great surprise! If I remember correctly, some of them were dismayed. I was not. I have a funny feeling of giving the people a chance. And I remember before Averell Harriman went to the convention, in his house he talked to me about Johnson being Vice President and was positive he was going to be, and asked me what was my impression.

B: This was *before* the convention?

M: Before the convention.

B: Harriman must have been one of the very few people who was seriously considering that.

M: Before the convention. I told him I thought there was no problem at all. I said, "Because in my book Texas is not South; it's Southwest," and that his record wasn't that bad. But I do remember that other people in NAACP hit the ceiling.

B: Surely not Mr. Wilkins himself?

M: Yeah, oh he did hit the ceiling! He bounced off the ceiling.

B: But I believe he calmed down or endorsed—

M: Very shortly thereafter—it wasn't long.

B: Did anyone have to talk to him to—?

M: At that stage they were all talking to the Kennedys. I don't know how many times Roy must have been in there with the Kennedys. Once I talked to Bobby—that's all—just once. Roy ran the show, I mean. Being in Legal Defense I had to stay out of anything that looked like politics, so I did. But once I talked to—I had a very unsatisfactory conference with Bobby about the civil rights movement.

B: When was that?

M: Shortly after they took over—about the first of the year, I guess.

B: After President Kennedy was inaugurated?

M: Yes.

B: It was an unsatisfactory conference?

M: Yes.

B: In what way?
M: He spent all this time telling us what we should do.
B: What sort of suggestions did he have for you?
M: Well, that we ought to concentrate on this and concentrate on that and what have you. I told him that so far as I was concerned we had been in the civil rights business since 1909, and he'd been in the President business a year. Well, I mean, that's the way—. But Roy used to have many conferences with the President, very rewarding ones.
B: People have said that the intensity of the civil rights movement kind of caught the Kennedy Administration by surprise when they came in.
M: It should have. I don't know. I did have a conference with the President about three months before he announced his candidacy, when he was a senator, about just what was cooking. I'm sure I didn't pull any punches with him. I don't remember. It was a lunch and we spent about two hours together. But he got the story. He knew what it was. But I don't think the President realized the urgency of it.
B: You're referring to President Kennedy now?
M: Yes. I don't think he realized.
B: Apparently, the activity in the South—Dr. King's activities and others—pushed the Kennedy Administration.
M: Somebody pushed them.
B: Then in that first year President Kennedy appointed you to the Circuit Judgeship.
M: Yes. That was when—'61. Congress held it up for a year —eleven months.
B: Did you have any doubts about leaving your work with the Legal and Defense Fund to—?
M: No. I thought it was time for younger people to take over, as a matter of fact. It was a good possibility I might have gone into private practice in about five years from then. I mean, I had to look forward to taking care of a family.
B: You mean after the circuit judgeship, retire and go into—?
M: No.
B: You mean you had been contemplating retirement?
M: Yes.
B: Incidentally, sir, at that time in '61, was there any serious debate about you being replaced by a white man?
M: No. It was strict seniority.

B: Mr. Greenberg was just next in line?

M: By, believe it or not, it was only a month or so over Connie Motley. I called Connie in and told her that this was the score. She said, "Of course." If there was anything she was for, it was the seniority. She just didn't like that two months business because it was sort of a gamble one way or the other. Then I got them both together, and that's all there was to it. But I thought we'd reached the stage where it was unimportant. But this Black Power business and all now—

B:That's why I asked. Probably now it would be a real issue.

M: No, Connie Motley would be just as rough as anybody else —or rougher. She doesn't believe in that stuff.

B: Did you see anything of Mr. Johnson in those years while you were on the circuit court while he was Vice President —socially or otherwise?

M: No way, not until he called. That's the first time I knew about it.

B: That would be in '65 when he called you about the—

M: '61.

B: I'm talking about Mr. Johnson now.

M: That's right, '65.

B: When he called you about the Solicitor Generalship.

M: He called one day, around this time I think, and I was up in the judges' dining room at the courthouse. My bailiff came up and tapped me on the shoulder. I said, "Fred, what in the world is wrong?" I mean, he's not supposed to bother us at lunch. He was as red as a beet. I said, "What's wrong, Fred?" He said, "The President wants to speak to you. He's on the phone!" I said, "The President of what?" "The President of the United States!" So he had held an elevator, and I went down. Sure enough he was on there. We chatted for about two or three minutes, and he said, "I want you to be my Solicitor General." I said, "Sir?" We chatted about it, and I said, "Well, Mr. President, I'll have to think this over." He said, "Well, go ahead, but don't tell a living soul." I said, "I assume that means nobody but my wife?" He said, "Yes, that's what I mean by nobody." He said, "Take all the time you want." I said, "Very well, sir." He hung up, and I hung up.

I went home and talked to my wife and we discussed the problems, because one was a lifetime job to trade in for a job at the beckoning of one person. Secondly, it was a $4500 cut in salary. Third, the living expenses in Washington would be twice what I was paying in New York. So she said okay. We kept thinking about it, and the next day the phone rang. He was on the phone again. I said, "Well, Mr. President, you said I had all the time I needed." He said, "You had it." I said, "Okay."

I went down the next morning, and I started telling him these things. He said, "You don't have to tell me. I can tell you everything including what you've got in your bank account. I'm still asking you to make the sacrifice." We talked for quite a while, and I said, "Okay with me."

B: Did he explain to you why he wanted you as opposed to just somebody else?

M: He said he wanted, number one, he wanted me in his Administration. Number two, he wanted me in that spot for two reasons. One, he thought I could handle it. Secondly, he wanted people—young people—of both races to come into the Supreme Court Room, as they all do by the hundreds and thousands, and somebody to say, "Who is that man up there with that swallow tail coat on arguing," and somebody to say, "He's the Solicitor General of the United States." Somebody will say, "But he's a Negro!" He wanted that image, number one.

Number two, he thought that he would like to have me as his representative before the Court. The other thing which goes through every conversation we had from then on—he would say at least three or four times, "You know this has nothing to do with any Supreme Court appointment. I want that distinctly understood. There's no quid pro here at all. You do your job. If you don't do it, you go out. If you do it, you stay here. And that's all there is to it."

B: He made it clear this did not mean that you would eventually get a Supreme Court appointment?

M: Over and over again. He made the announcement in the East Room, and it was very funny when I went in. The press knew nothing about any of this. When I went in he first said that I would come behind Mrs. Johnson, and then he said, "You come and go in right side-by-side with me at the door." We went in together. A murmur went around the press boys, and I found out afterwards that the question they were asking was, "Who has resigned from the Supreme Court?" He made the announcement and then we had the swearing in, and that was that.

B: During those conversations, did either of you discuss what would happen before Congress with your confirmation?

M: No, he said he could take care of that—that it would be hard, would be tough. He said, "If you can stand the gaff, I can." That time and every other time I've talked to him, the thing I was impressed with was what he intended to do with this country.

B: Could you elaborate on that, sir?

M: Well, he intended to wipe as much of it out as he could.

B: You mean white discrimination?

M: He intended to be to this century what Abraham Lincoln was to the last century, and he was going to do it. I frankly believe if he had had four more years, he just about would have done it. I mean, he rebelled at the discrimination against women—women judges. He always did. He said he wanted to leave the presidency in a position that there was no government job with a race tag on it—none! That's what he was driving at. He would constantly say, "If you've got any ideas, let me have them. If you don't want to bother with me, give them to Ramsey or Nick or somebody like that. But if there's any way we can break through, let me know."

B: Did you do that, sir?

M: Only once or twice. I couldn't give him any ideas. I mean, he had most of them himself. And then he was pushing them like mad.

B: While you were Solicitor General, did you, in addition to the work of the Solicitor Generalship itself, serve Mr. Johnson or the White House as an advisor on civil rights generally or appointments or things?

M: No, sir. Any ideas I'd have I would funnel them through the Attorney General which I thought was proper. It was particularly true, because I knew they got through. I mean, I know both Nick Katzenbach and Ramsey. I know if I made a suggestion they would pass it on.

He didn't welcome too much suggestion. If he wanted your advice, he would ask you for it. On some occasions he did, and I always gave it to him. I would go up there sometimes, especially on Saturday afternoon. It was the best time to get in that joint, and not be seen going in, because everybody was gone on Saturday afternoon.

B: What kind of things would he ask your advice on?

M: It was just problems about the Department, or my job, or the whole race problem, in general. But in absolute general terms, nothing specific. Then when I came on the Court, that was cut off completely. I didn't have to worry about it. He said the same thing, so that was cut off.

B: Within the Justice Department in those years, were there any serious debates over the speed of prosecution, particularly in the civil rights area?

M: Oh, yes, we didn't have to worry too much in the civil rights area because John Doar, who was running it, he was about as dedicated as anybody in government. We would sit down. We had these Wednesday night meetings with all department heads, but we'd have earlier ones with John and people like that. The whole trouble in those days was it was just completely understaffed. He just didn't have the staff, and he would borrow sometimes one or two of my men to help him out. But I would say that the entire Department of Justice had been geared to it. They could get preference over any other Department. But it was tough.

B: Did you ever think in those days about moving efforts into the North as opposed to the southern small towns?

M: We've always been looking at the North. We were always looking at the North. But you couldn't get any complaints. Nobody would complain.

B: Surely the Urban League or the NAACP could have lent a hand there.

M: Only on labor cases. That's all they seemed to be interested in. They just didn't do it. I think that after—well, from after '55 on, I think we sort of laid down a little.

B: You mean after '65 on—after the passage of the voting laws? Or were you referring to the NAACP?

M: No, I'm talking about '65. I think we thought that was the *sine qua non*. That was it—we're here! You see, we tended to do that in '55. Then we got out of that with Martin

Luther King, etc. Then '65, I think, it moved in again. You know, everybody fighting in the civil rights fight has always been a little inclined to just sit down and take a breather. We found out you can't take a breather. If you do, that other guy will run you ragged.

Let me tell you about my appointment to the Supreme Court. I was sitting in my office, and it was about, I guess, ten o'clock in the morning. Ramsey Clark called Mrs. Lavery, who is the same secretary I have with me now, and said, "Is the Judge in?" She said, "Yes." "Well, tell him I'm on my way." He was right there in that same hall on the fifth floor. He came on down and shut the door. He said, "What are you up to this morning?" I said, "Well, I've got to go up to the White House and talk to some students," one of these student groups, I've forgotten what it was, maybe with the Fellows, I don't know, "over in the Executive Building." He said, "What time are you due up there?" I said, "Eleven o'clock." He said, "You got a car?" I said, "Well, I know Mrs. Lavery well enough to be sure she's called for a car, and there'll be a car down there waiting for me." He said, "Well, instead of getting there at eleven, you get there at a quarter of eleven. Instead of going over across the street, you go in the main—. The boss wants to see you." I said, "About what?" He said, "I don't know." Ramsey, I mean, he won't tell you anything about anybody anyhow. I kept trying. He said, "I actually don't know." So I said, "Well, which way shall I go in?" There are three different ways you can go in without being seen. And he told me which way to go, and I went up there and went in and waited a few minutes. Marvin Watson came out and said, "Come on." And I went in and we chatted—the President and I. He said, "You know something, Thurgood, I'm going to put you on the Supreme Court." I said, "Well, thank you, sir." We talked a little while. We went out to the press and he announced it. We came back in the room and I said, "Now, Mr. President, if it's all right with you I'd like to call my wife. It would be better than for her to hear it on the radio." He said, "You mean you haven't called Cissy yet?" I said, "No, how could I? I've been talking to you." So we got her on the phone and I told her to sit down. She said, "Well, I'm standing." I said, "Well, sit down." She sat down and he said, "Cissy—Lyndon Johnson." She said, "Yes, Mr. President." "I've just put your husband on the Supreme Court." She said, "I'm sure glad I'm sitting down."

B: Didn't you have a little bit of a suspicion that it might be coming?

M: I had a hope. Any lawyer has a hope, but no suspicion. We had a party the night before for Tom Clark because he resigned that day. All of us were chatting around, and nobody suspected—and nobody said a word to me. A lot of people think it was discussed. I didn't know about it. I imagine it was. I know Clark must have known, and I know Ramsey knew. But they just don't pass out any information.

B: Did Mr. Johnson ever, then or later before you were actually on the bench, talk to you about what he thought a Supreme Court Justice ought to be?

M: Yes, his own man, and I told him that. He said, "Like what?" I said, "Just like the steel decision. When President Truman's, one of his very closest friends, Justice Tom C. Clark, not only voted against him but wrote the opinion against him." He said, "You mean you'd do that to me?" I said, "Exactly." He said, "Well, that's the kind I'm looking for." No, he dwelled on independence. The same way with Solicitor General. He said, "If you and Katzenbach can't make a decision, come up here and I'll make it for you. But you are your own boss." I said, "Well, the statute doesn't say that." He says, "I do." But he insisted on that. I found with him that, while I was Solicitor General, several times I didn't agree fully with the Attorney General. He had no trouble with me. I didn't win every time.

B: What sort of disagreements would you have?

M: About technical things.

B: Tactics in a case?

M: No, about whether we should take a case or not or what have you—certain things in there which I wouldn't discuss because that story won't be told, I'm sure, by anybody.

B: Well, that's the problem. If you don't tell it here, it won't be, except when you write your memoirs.

M: I can guarantee you that the three people involved, not a one of them is going to tell it. I'll bet you money on it.

B: I guess we'll leave it at that. In that case, that's a story that's lost.

Did you also discuss with the President whether or not you would have trouble with Congress this time?

M: No, he said he would get it through. I remember the day that it cleared the Senate. I got a call in the afternoon shortly after it cleared, and he was upstairs in his living quarters. He said, "Well, you made it." I said, "Yes, sir. Thank you again," etc. etc. He said, "You know, you sure got me into a lot of trouble." I said, "Who got who into it? You did it, I didn't do it. I didn't do it." He just laughed! But I still don't see how he got it through, but he did.

You also realize that when he took me off the Court of Appeals he put Connie Motley on the district court. Everybody was saying, "The first Negro woman!" To me that wasn't important! She was the first woman on the Second Circuit District Court. She was the first woman, not the first Negro woman—the first woman! He had that in his mind for quite awhile.

B: And you did have a rough time before that committee.

M: Oh, that first one. Well, the second one, I knew what was coming because Senator [Strom] Thurmond had as his adviser a lawyer who is a law professor now down at Memphis Law School. He writes articles on the Fourteenth Amendment, and law schools won't publish them. When I saw him advising him, I said, "Well, I don't have too much to worry about." The questions he asked I expected. I wasn't going to answer them in the first place, because he wanted to know what was in the minds of the committee that drafted the Fourteenth Amendment. I don't know how you're going to find that out. I said I didn't know because I'm not a person that goes around lying. But you see I had already been through eleven months before, so I mean this few days—

B: You mentioned this earlier, but I think it would be appropriate to repeat it. After the accession to the bench here, no more contact with Mr. Johnson?

M: Except at dinners and receptions—that's all.

B: Did he ever try to seek your advice?

M: No. A couple of times I wanted to volunteer,—but I decided not—and I didn't.

B: I know you've got another appointment coming up here. Is there anything else you would like to add?

M: No. I just think Lyndon Johnson, insofar as minorities, civil rights, people in general, the inherent dignity of *the* individual human being—I don't believe there has ever been a President to equal Lyndon Johnson—bar none!

B: That's high praise indeed, sir. Do you see any faults—?

M: Well, Lincoln, for example—Lincoln had a lot of politics involved with what he was doing.

B: There are those who would say, "So does Lyndon Johnson!"

M: I don't think so. That's the difference when you talk to him man-to-man. He's talking from his heart. When he does things, it doesn't seem so, but when you actually talk to him, the basic instincts that come out, I mean, he has no reason to persuade me about it—no. I've got one solid vote. That's all I've got. I don't even control my wife's vote. A guy tends to let it out. He was just frustrated at times. But, of course, he had to use his political acumen to get these things through Congress. There is no other way to do it. I don't know how he got my nomination through. I don't know until this day. It took some doing, I'm sure.

B: It must have.

M: I'm sure it took some doing.

B: All that's high praise, sir. Do you see any faults—any bad side to the man?

M: I don't. I don't even think he was intemperate. I don't think he shot from the hip ever. I don't think he did. I think he gave the impression of shooting from the hip after planning six months where to shoot.

B: These frustrations you mention, would these be frustrations over the progress of civil rights and anti-discrimination?

M: Yes.

B: Is there anything else you would like to add?

M: No, that's about it.

B: Thank you very much, sir.

MADISON CAPITAL TIMES

Mob Violence in Milwaukee

August 30, 1967

MILWAUKEE RIGHTS OFFICE FIREBOMBED

Marchers Attacked by Whites

45 Arrested in South Side Melee

By KEN HARTNETT

MILWAUKEE (*AP*)—Negro open-housing demonstrators, saved by a barrage of police tear gas from surging walls of screaming, rock-throwing whites, returned to their headquarters Tuesday night and watched it ravaged by flames.

Fire officials said the fire that destroyed the headquarters of the Milwaukee Youth Council of the National Association for the Advancement of Colored People was caused by an arsonist.

The blaze erupted less than an hour after council members, led by their adviser, the Rev. James E. Groppi, a white Roman Catholic priest, escaped from a white throng police estimated at 13,000.

The hecklers spilled over sidewalks along the 22-block route that took the marchers deep into the predominantly Polish South Side.

The mob, chanting "kill, kill, kill," hurled insults, bottles and rocks at the 200 marchers protected by a thin line of policemen.

Police said 45 persons were arrested.

Twenty-two persons were injured, 11 of them policemen.

A similar demonstration along the same route Monday night resulted in 16 arrests and two injuries.

Less than an hour after the marchers groped their way through a protective screen of tear gas toward a viaduct leading out of the South Side Tuesday night, they were caught up in a new crisis.

It developed as their bus pulled up outside council headquarters in the Inner Core, the Negro section that was the scene of rioting July 30.

Police and Negro witnesses gave conflicting versions of what happened.

Sgt. Frank Miller said the council members began protesting what they called lack of police protection as they began moving out of the bus. Bottles smashed the windshield of a police car, he said, and shots rang out from a vacant building alongside council headquarters.

Miller said police fired tear gas to disperse the Negroes and fired shotguns into the air.

During the melee, he said, an automobile drove by and a firebomb was thrown through the window of the council headquarters building.

Firemen were kept out of the area for 15 minutes while police sought a sniper. None was found.

Negroes, who clustered on the street corner near the burning building, denied there was any sniper or melee and insisted police did all the shooting.

They said that police fired tear gas canisters into the building —a claim Miller denied.

No one was injured and no arrests were reported at the fire. No description was obtained of the occupants of the auto, police said.

Milwaukee, with a Negro population of 86,000, has only six Negro families living on the South Side, a traditionally conservative community of factories, small businesses and lower middle class homes.

About 88 per cent of the city's Negroes live in the Inner Core, a belt of largely dilapidated houses stretching toward the northwest from the central city.

Civil rights criticism of housing patterns was stepped up this summer after the Common Council refused for a fourth time—each time by an 18–1 vote—to adopt an open-housing ordinance.

Milwaukee Mayor Henry Maier declined to reimpose a strict

curfew he clamped on the city during rioting in its inner core section four weeks ago. He asked for a voluntary curfew, but it was ignored.

Maier planned to stay at city hall during the night to keep Gov. Warren Knowles abreast of the activities, but early today when it appeared the situation in the trouble spots had returned to normal, he ended his vigil.

Maier also criticized Fr. Groppi. He said the situation was made more tense by "provocateurs."

"We know there are known communists in there," Maier said of the marchers. "Groppi achieved what he wanted. He's got the white backlash out in the open."

Maier said the persons he referred to as communists were not members of the youth council.

5-Year-Old Negro Struck by Chunk of Concrete

NOT TOO YOUNG TO BE HATED

MILWAUKEE (*AP*)—The child was no more than five but he was borne aloft by a Negro marcher as the tight wedge of 200 demonstrators moved through the ranks of whites ranged along the sidewalk Tuesday night.

A chunk of concrete slab flew from the darkness and struck him.

The line kept moving under the prod of police anxious to get the marchers out of the virtually all-white South Side and end a second straight night of racial crisis.

The child moaned. It was not possible to see where he was hit. Soon the adult with him had him wrapped in a jacket and was trying to force his way back through the marchers toward a police car.

"The strength of being black today is knowing one is never too young to die," said the white priest at the head of the line, the Rev. James E. Groppi, adviser to the Milwaukee Youth Council of the National Association for the Advancement of Colored People. "The impoverishment," he said, "the despair."

"We're willing," he said, "to shed our blood if that's what's needed here to get our rights."

An hour earlier, while the open housing marchers were advancing into the South Side, three policemen, their riot guns serving as night sticks, pushed back a mass of whites spilling out from a street corner.

—

A little white girl cried. A white man in a blue hat rushed over to her, "Did they hit you?" he shouted. The child sobbed but said nothing. "Why did you hit that little girl?" he screamed at the police.

Near the same corner stood the Rev. John Maurice, a Roman Catholic priest. He listened as white men shouted, "Don't bring the rats to the South Side. Leave the rats on the North Side." Another man, in his fifties, his face mild, joined in the shouting, which grew increasingly more threatening.

"Is that a Christian way to act?" the priest asked him. "Are you a Christian?"

"I used to be until that guy Groppi came along," the man answered. "They ought to throw him out of the church."

Father Maurice was one of 30 clergymen that circulated through the white crowd in an attempt to keep it calm.

As firecrackers and bottles flew through the heavy air, cries of delight went up from the white masses estimated by police at 13,000.

Occasionally, white youths would press close to the line of march and invite Negroes to step out. The Negroes would invite the whites in. On at least two occasions, the challenges were accepted and brief scuffles, which police quickly ended, would break out.

Police Chief Harold Breier stood to the rear of the marchers, directing tactics. He responded to greetings from the white masses with smiles, but turned cold toward onlookers who left the sidewalk to chat with him.

—

Cries of "Kill, Kill, Kill" resounded in the night.

"We're citizens of another country," said Father Groppi. "We're strangers in our own country."

"Eee-ui, Ee-yi, ee-yi, oh . . .

"Father Groppi's got to go," the mob chanted.

"We've been saying 'love' for over 400 years," said a chubby Negro teen-age girl, "But we ain't gonna say it no more, baby."

Cheer as Marchers Hurt

"KILL, KILL, KILL," THE MOB CHANTED

By WILLIAM SCHULZ

MILWAUKEE (*AP*)—"I'm all right. I'm just scared," the blonde teenager said to the priest who was comforting her. Then she saw the blood streaming from her burned hand.

She had been sitting with about 200 open housing demonstrators in a South Side Milwaukee park when a large firecracker exploded in her lap. She rolled on the ground, clutching her ears, as others beat out the sparks from her charred slacks and shredded straw handbag.

The priest and a police officer got her to a car and to a hospital.

—

But there was no letup for the rest of the group.

Surrounded by thousands of whites yelling "kill, kill, kill," they fled through billowing tear gas from the predominantly Polish area.

The demonstration had started off almost like a picnic with marchers flowing down one sidewalk and hecklers across the street. A cordon of police separated them.

—

"Give me an F, give me an R, give me an E," the marchers shouted. "What does it spell—Freedom."

A blue convertible with more than a dozen youths standing in it and clinging to the trunk drove by, carrying an effigy of the group's leader, the Rev. James Groppi, a white Catholic priest.

Signs proclaiming "White Power" and "Polish Power" appeared as the white crowd got larger, soon outnumbering the marchers 10 to one.

A newsman told a policeman the officers were doing a good job. "Yea, but for how long," he answered.

Beer bottles were thrown, spraying their contents as they fell among the marchers.

A large crowd, waiting for the marchers, blocked the street and the police opened up with tear gas and fired shots into the air.

"Shoot the niggers," a balding white man yelled as police pushed both groups back. "We live here."

Police opened the street and the marchers continued, down the center of the street now, while whites lined both curbs.

More bottles, firecrackers and eggs were thrown as they sat in Kosciuszko Park. Two white girls among the marchers were injured and carried off by police. The crowd cheered.

"Keep cool, walk fast, girls in the middle," Father Groppi yelled. "Don't be afraid. If we were afraid we wouldn't have come here, we would not be good Christians."

"Why did they come here? Why aren't they working, doing an honest job?" a woman complained.

—

The fleeing marchers nearly had reached the bridge toward downtown and safety when a barrage of bottles, rocks and firecrackers rained out of a used car lot. Police lobbed a volley of tear gas among the used cars.

More than 20 of the marchers had been hit by debris by the time they got to their headquarters, "Freedom House," and began to disperse. Then a firebomb, police said, was thrown through the front window.

About 30 youths fled as the yellow frame building was destroyed.

—

"Someone out there threw a bottle and the cops started firing tear gas," said Richard Green, who was inside. Police denied they fired at the Freedom House.

"We huddled on the floor, we didn't know who was shooting," said Prentice McKinney, "We didn't know if it was some punks from the South Side or what."

Several members of the neighborhood Youth Corps live in the building. When it was over they were looking for a place to sleep.

Fr. Groppi Raps Maier

MAYOR TRIES TO HEAD OFF MORE MILWAUKEE MARCHES

By LEE A. MEYERPETER

MILWAUKEE (*UPI*)—Mayor Henry Maier sought today by legal means and moral persuasion to bring an end to open housing demonstrations which forced police Tuesday night to use tear gas to keep order.

Meantime, the Rev. James Groppi, a white Roman Catholic priest, who is leading the marchers, criticized the mayor for inactivity, and said it could have been the police who burned down the headquarters of his civil rights group.

Groppi said he wouldn't know until later today whether he would lead a third night of marching into the city's Polish south side.

The priest, holding a news conference in front of the charred Freedom House headquarters of the Milwaukee Youth Council of the National Association for the Advancement of Colored People, said police could have started the fire with a tear gas bomb Tuesday night at the conclusion of the march.

"They were throwing tear gas all around here," the priest said. "No one could have gotten in to throw a fire bomb as they say, because they had the area sealed off."

Deputy Fire Chief Edward Canavan, whose firemen were kept away briefly by sporadic gunfire while trying to save the house, said the fire could have been started only with a fire bomb. "A tear gas bomb would have to smolder for about a half hour, and then be near some combustible material."

Groppi produced a spent tear gas shell, which he said had been found in the house.

The mayor, who said Father Groppi had proved his point that "people can and do hate," sought to get Archbishop William E. Cousins to intercede with the priest to stop the demonstrations.

Father Groppi also criticized police for "firing shotguns around here" Tuesday night, saying they could "have killed some innocent people." He said he was "very concerned" about Mayor Maier's decision not to impose a curfew such as he did during racial troubles on the north side early this month.

"If the blood of one black child is spilled, it's on the hands of the mayor," Groppi said.

FORSAKING "THE CAUCASIAN RACE"
FOR "DOWN DEEP AFRICA"

A Teacher to Father James Groppi

August 30, 1967

Milwaukee
8/30/67

TO the
REV. JAMES GROPPI,
1122 W. CLARKE ST.,
MILWAUKEE, WISCONSIN.

YOU an ORDAINED MINISTER of the GOSPEL of JESUS CHRIST, professing your FAITH in the GOD-GIVEN RULINGS of YOUR RACE: no—FORSAKING THAT RACE in the LEADERSHIP of ELEMENTS of DOWN DEEP AFRICA, from whence their FOREFATHERS MIGRATED to these UNITED STATES; today their OFFSPRING TOGETHER WITH YOUR PRAYERS to their GOD, aiming for destruction of CIVILIZATION and ALL CONTENTS where THEY have been NURTURED, GIVEN HOMAGE for THESE PAST MANY YEARS.

DO YOU—as a MEMBER of the CAUCASIAN RACE of your FOREFATHERS, forsake that privilege BESTOWED UPON YOU IN YOUR BIRTHRIGHT?

LECTURES to YOUR DARKENED FRIENDS, EXPRESSING the EVIL of DESTRUCTION of PROPERTIES and GOD*GIVEN RIGHTS for FREEDOM in EVERY-DAY LIVING, and PRIVILEGES, that could be theirs, OBEYING the LAWS of our LAND and COUNTRY.

For SHAME FATHER GROPPI, FOREVER MAY YOUR PATHS BE ROUGHENED IN AS MANY WAYS as YOU ARE TREATING with INDIGNITY, CONTEMPT, ABUSE or AFFRONT YOUR GOD-GIVEN BIRTHRIGHT.

A TEACHER.

THE MAYOR OF MILWAUKEE
RESPONDS TO A RIOT

HENRY MAIER

Statement at a Press Conference

August 31, 1967

STATEMENT BY MAYOR HENRY W. MAIER AT PRESS CONFERENCE ON AUGUST 31, 1967

THESE ARE agonizing days. In many ways, the situation is more difficult to handle than was the recent civil disorder.

Yesterday I was overwhelmed with charges of police brutality in the handling of the ugly elements in the crowds on the South Side. Specifically, the people said police manhandled them and there was too much tear gas.

Today, charges are reaching me that police were too tough in handling events last night at the Freedom House.

I have no control of individual police judgments.

However, I am in deep sympathy with the typical police officer.

In my opinion, his job is the toughest in urban America.

I agree with what the *Milwaukee Journal* said in an editorial yesterday afternoon. It said this:

"One of the few things Milwaukee has to be proud about over the last two nights is its police force. Firmly, courageously and with great restraint the police kept a dangerous situation under control in the face of surging passions and unthinking hate."

We are trying our best to keep the peace and to prevent anyone from throwing a lighted match into a gas tank, even working, as we are, "in the face of surging passions and unthinking hate," even so, we are not prohibiting peaceful assembly on private property.

I specifically stated that yesterday and I want to re-emphasize that today.

I have double checked with the Chief of Police and the City

Attorney and they assure me that the proclamation protects the right of peaceful assembly.

Our target is not people who want to meet peacefully.

We are seeking to relieve tensions.

We are seeking this objective so that the people of good will in this city, so that the majority in this city, can bring its influence into play.

We must try to keep the extremists, who seem to want a civil war, from tearing at each other.

We are trying to do all this without abridging entirely the rights to speak, to march and to parade and to demonstrate.

But, people who throw bricks and bottles anywhere in this city will be arrested.

I don't care if they are white or Negro.

I don't care if they support open housing or oppose it.

I don't care if they are for Father Groppi or against him.

I don't care if they live on the North Side or the South Side or the West Side.

Against this background, I believe that the most significant event in the last 24 hours was the stand taken by the Archbishop against any further demonstrations by Father Groppi.

I agree entirely with the Archbishop's statement that another demonstration serves little or no purposes.

And, I wholeheartedly agree with the Archbishop that future violence must be avoided at all costs.

This means we must have a time free of tensions, a time for reason.

We are in a sick time, a time when little children are made pawns in a revolution.

One side—with bottles and bricks flying—holds up a five year old child to be smacked by stones.

The other side—knowing for a certainty that danger lurks—takes its children to the curbs to hear obscenity and racism.

Therefore, I do not intend to answer anybody's wild charges.

Instead I intend to keep working with as many citizens of this community as I can find who want to weld our community.

I have had encouraging meetings and pledges of constructive support from:

Negro tavernowners, barbers, union stewards and businessmen, from Negro clergymen, from the Common View group, from clergymen in all walks of life, from the Conference on Religion and Race, from citizens in all walks of life.

It is this story of men of good will which I wish could be told, particularly by our television media.

The goodwill is there. I know it because I have seen and heard it myself.

Somehow we must get our Milwaukee Marshall Plan into focus, into attention, and begin working on the 39 Points.

"HERE IN VIETNAM THERE IS NO SKIN COLOR"

Leonard D. Mills to Father James Groppi

November 4, 1967

Nov. 4, 1967
Danang, RVN

Dear Father Groppi,

I am writing this letter mainly for myself, but also for several Marines who want to express their feelings on the racial situation at home.

I suppose I should begin by telling you a little about myself. I am twenty and a corporal in the Marines. I was brought up in a town in Texas. My father is English and my mother is Polish. I had lived on the South Side of Milwaukee for seven years before joining the Marines. I went to high school at Pulaski and college at the University of Wisconsin in Milwaukee.

Up until now I have always been very proud of my nationality and of my city. But now because of a few prejudiced immature individuals I have become ashamed of my city. I had always considered my neighbors and relatives to be just, honest, and fine Catholics, now after reading in magazines and newspapers about the troubles that have occurred I doubt their honesty, and their sense of justice, and their love of God and their fellow man.

When I was young, I lived in the South where everything and everyone was prejudiced. I guess I was too young to realize the sin in it all. But after moving to Milwaukee and growing older I have become aware of the injustice that is occurring in the South. But I really was not aware that the same things are happening in my own neighborhood.

Why Father, can't these prejudiced people see that they need one another. Why don't they realize that this hatred and bigotry is a sin against themselves as well as against their fellow man.

Here in Vietnam there is no skin color, we are all brothers-in-arms, fighting for the principles that make our country the greatest on earth. The greatest of these principles is freedom, and equality of man. We need one another here. For without that guy next to you, no matter what his skin color happens to be you just might not be around the next day. We all eat in the same mess halls, smoke the same kind of cigarette, drink from one another's canteens, and even share each other's soap. No one ever thinks of asking whose canteen they are drinking from, or thinks about who sleeps next to them, or who they are going to be eating with.

Many of my best friends, and I mean best, are "soul brothers" from all parts of the country, and we have been in many long discussions on the race problem. Most of my buddies say all they want to have is respect. But I know alot of people don't respect themselves so they don't respect others.

My buddies have done alot for me. They have taught me many things and have made me open my eyes to what's going on. I owe them more than I can repay, but I want to start. I want to show everyone that when I talk about brotherly love I am sincere.

That is why I am proud of you Father, and for the wonderful job you are doing. That is the purpose of this letter, to tell you that I and several white Milwaukeeans respect you and support you.

I have several ideas I want to express, but perhaps I can discuss them in another letter. But for now God bless you and please keep up the work.

Sincerely yours,
Leonard D. Mills
CPL. U.S. MARINE CORPS

"TWO SOCIETIES, ONE BLACK, ONE WHITE—SEPARATE AND UNEQUAL"

REPORT OF THE NATIONAL ADVISORY COMMISSION ON CIVIL DISORDERS

from the *Summary*

February 29, 1968

INTRODUCTION

The summer of 1967 again brought racial disorders to American cities, and with them shock, fear, and bewilderment to the Nation.

The worst came during a 2-week period in July, first in Newark and then in Detroit. Each set off a chain reaction in neighboring communities.

On July 28, 1967, the President of the United States established this Commission and directed us to answer three basic questions:

What happened?

Why did it happen?

What can be done to prevent it from happening again?

To respond to these questions, we have undertaken a broad range of studies and investigations. We have visited the riot cities; we have heard many witnesses; we have sought the counsel of experts across the country.

This is our basic conclusion: Our Nation is moving toward two societies, one black, one white—separate and unequal.

Reaction to last summer's disorders has quickened the movement and deepened the division. Discrimination and segregation have long permeated much of American life; they now threaten the future of every American.

This deepening racial division is not inevitable. The movement apart can be reversed. Choice is still possible. Our principal task is to define that choice and to press for a national resolution.

To pursue our present course will involve the continuing polarization of the American community and, ultimately, the destruction of basic democratic values.

The alternative is not blind repression or capitulation to lawlessness. It is the realization of common opportunities for all within a single society.

This alternative will require a commitment to national action—compassionate, massive, and sustained, backed by the resources of the most powerful and the richest nation on this earth. From every American it will require new attitudes, new understanding, and, above all, new will.

The vital needs of the Nation must be met; hard choices must be made, and, if necessary, new taxes enacted.

Violence cannot build a better society. Disruption and disorder nourish repression, not justice. They strike at the freedom of every citizen. The community cannot—it will not—tolerate coercion and mob rule.

Violence and destruction must be ended—in the streets of the ghetto and in the lives of people.

Segregation and poverty have created in the racial ghetto a destructive environment totally unknown to most white Americans.

What white Americans have never fully understood—but what the Negro can never forget—is that white society is deeply implicated in the ghetto. White institutions created it, white institutions maintain it, and white society condones it.

It is time now to turn with all the purpose at our command to the major unfinished business of this Nation. It is time to adopt strategies for action that will produce quick and visible progress. It is time to make good the promises of American democracy to all citizens—urban and rural, white and black, Spanish-surname, American Indian, and every minority group.

Our recommendations embrace three basic principles:

- To mount programs on a scale equal to the dimension of the problems;
- To aim these programs for high impact in the immediate future in order to close the gap between promise and performance;
- To undertake new initiatives and experiments that can change the system of failure and frustration that now dominates the ghetto and weakens our society.

These programs will require unprecedented levels of funding and performance, but they neither probe deeper nor demand more than the problems which called them forth. There can be no higher priority for national action and no higher claim on the Nation's conscience.

We issue this report now, 5 months before the date called for by the President. Much remains that can be learned. Continued study is essential.

As Commissioners we have worked together with a sense of the greatest urgency and have sought to compose whatever differences exist among us. Some differences remain. But the gravity of the problem and the pressing need for action are too clear to allow further delay in the issuance of this report.

CHAPTER 4.—THE BASIC CAUSES

In addressing the question "Why did it happen?" we shift our focus from the local to the national scene, from the particular events of the summer of 1967 to the factors within the society at large that created a mood of violence among many urban Negroes.

These factors arc complex and interacting; they vary significantly in their effect from city to city and from year to year; and the consequences of one disorder, generating new grievances and new demands, become the causes of the next. Thus was created the "thicket of tension, conflicting evidence, and extreme opinions" cited by the President.

Despite these complexities, certain fundamental matters are clear. Of these, the most fundamental is the racial attitude and behavior of white Americans toward black Americans.

Race prejudice has shaped our history decisively; it now threatens to affect our future.

White racism is essentially responsible for the explosive mixture which has been accumulating in our cities since the end of World War II. Among the ingredients of this mixture are:

- *Pervasive discrimination and segregation* in employment, education, and housing, which have resulted in the continuing exclusion of great numbers of Negroes from the benefits of economic progress.

- *Black in-migration and white exodus*, which have produced the massive and growing concentrations of impoverished Negroes in our major cities, creating a growing crisis of deteriorating facilities and services and unmet human needs.
- *The black ghettos*, where segregation and poverty converge on the young to destroy opportunity and enforce failure. Crime, drug addiction, dependency on welfare, and bitterness and resentment against society in general and white society in particular are the result.

At the same time, most whites and some Negroes outside the ghetto have prospered to a degree unparalleled in the history of civilization. Through television and other media, this affluence has been flaunted before the eyes of the Negro poor and the jobless ghetto youth.

Yet these facts alone cannot be said to have caused the disorders. Recently, other powerful ingredients have begun to catalyze the mixture:

- *Frustrated hopes* are the residue of the unfulfilled expectations aroused by the great judicial and legislative victories of the civil rights movement and the dramatic struggle for equal rights in the South.
- *A climate that tends toward approval and encouragement of violence* as a form of protest has been created by white terrorism directed against nonviolent protest; by the open defiance of law and Federal authority by state and local officials resisting desegregation; and by some protest groups engaging in civil disobedience who turn their backs on nonviolence, go beyond the constitutionally protected rights of petition and free assembly, and resort to violence to attempt to compel alteration of laws and policies with which they disagree.
- *The frustrations of powerlessness* have led some Negroes to the conviction that there is no effective alternative to violence as a means of achieving redress of grievances, and of "moving the system." These frustrations are reflected in alienation and hostility toward the institutions of law and government and the white society which controls them, and in the reach toward racial consciousness and solidarity reflected in the slogan "Black Power."
- *A new mood* has sprung up among Negroes, particularly among the young, in which self-esteem and enhanced racial pride are replacing apathy and submission to "the system."

• *The police are not merely a "spark" factor.* To some Negroes police have come to symbolize white power, white racism, and white repression. And the fact is that many police do reflect and express these white attitudes. The atmosphere of hostility and cynicism is reinforced by a widespread belief among Negroes in the existence of police brutality and in a "double standard" of justice and protection—one for Negroes and one for whites.

* * * * *

To this point, we have attempted only to identify the prime components of the "explosive mixture." In the chapters that follow we seek to analyze them in the perspective of history. Their meaning, however, is clear:

In the summer of 1967, we have seen in our cities a chain reaction of racial violence. If we are heedless, none of us shall escape the consequences.

"THE POLICEMAN IN THE GHETTO IS A SYMBOL"

REPORT OF THE NATIONAL ADVISORY COMMISSION ON CIVIL DISORDERS

Police and the Community

February 29, 1968

INTRODUCTION

WE HAVE cited deep hostility between police and ghetto communities as a primary cause of the disorders surveyed by the Commission. In Newark, Detroit, Watts, and Harlem—in practically every city that has experienced racial disruption since the summer of 1964, abrasive relationships between police and Negroes and other minority groups have been a major source of grievance, tension and, ultimately, disorder.

In a fundamental sense, however, it is wrong to define the problem solely as hostility to police. In many ways, the policeman only symbolizes much deeper problems.

The policeman in the ghetto is a symbol not only of law, but of the entire system of law enforcement and criminal justice.

As such, he becomes the tangible target for grievances against shortcomings throughout that system: Against assembly-line justice in teeming lower courts; against wide disparities in sentences; against antiquated correctional facilities; against the basic inequities imposed by the system on the poor—to whom, for example, the option of bail means only jail.

The policeman in the ghetto is a symbol of increasingly bitter social debate over law enforcement.

One side, disturbed and perplexed by sharp rises in crime and urban violence, exerts extreme pressure on police for tougher law enforcement. Another group, inflamed against police as agents of repression, tends toward defiance of what it regards as order maintained at the expense of justice.

The policeman in the ghetto is the most visible symbol, finally, of a society from which many ghetto Negroes are increasingly alienated.

At the same time, police responsibilities in the ghetto are even greater than elsewhere in the community since the other institutions of social control have so little authority: The schools, because so many are segregated, old and inferior; religion, which has become irrelevant to those who have lost faith as they lost hope; career aspirations, which for many young Negroes are totally lacking; the family, because its bonds are so often snapped. It is the policeman who must deal with the consequences of this institutional vacuum and is then resented for the presence and the measures this effort demands.

Alone, the policeman in the ghetto cannot solve these problems. His role is already one of the most difficult in our society. He must deal daily with a range of problems and people that test his patience, ingenuity, character, and courage in ways that few of us are ever tested. Without positive leadership, goals, operational guidance, and public support, the individual policeman can only feel victimized. Nor are these problems the responsibility only of police administrators; they are deep enough to tax the courage, intelligence and leadership of mayors, city officials, and community leaders. As Dr. Kenneth B. Clark told the Commission:

> This society knows * * * that if human beings are confined in ghetto compounds of our cities and are subjected to criminally inferior education, pervasive economic and job discrimination, committed to houses unfit for human habitation, subjected to unspeakable conditions of municipal services, such as sanitation, that such human beings are not likely to be responsive to appeals to be lawful, to be respectful, to be concerned with property of others.

And yet, precisely because the policeman in the ghetto is a symbol—precisely because he symbolizes so much—it is of critical importance that the police and society take every possible step to allay grievances that flow from a sense of injustice and increased tension and turmoil.

In this work, the police bear a major responsibility for making needed changes. In the first instance, they have the prime responsibility for safeguarding the minimum goal of any civilized society: Security of life and property. To do so, they are given society's maximum power: Discretion in the use of force.

Second, it is axiomatic that effective law enforcement requires the support of the community. Such support will not be present when a substantial segment of the community feels threatened by the police and regards the police as an occupying force.

At the same time, public officials also have a clear duty to help the police make any necessary changes to minimize so far as possible the risk of further disorders.

We see five basic problem areas:

- The need for change in police operations in the ghetto, to insure proper conduct by individual officers and to eliminate abrasive practices.
- The need for more adequate police protection of ghetto residents, to eliminate the present high sense of insecurity to person and property.
- The need for effective mechanisms for resolving citizen grievances against the police.
- The need for policy guidelines to assist police in areas where police conduct can create tension.
- The need to develop community support for law enforcement.

Our discussion of each of these problem areas is followed by specific recommendations which relate directly to achieving more effective law enforcement and to the prevention and control of civil disorders.[1]

POLICE CONDUCT AND PATROL PRACTICES

In an earlier era, third-degree interrogations were widespread, indiscriminate arrests on suspicion were generally accepted and "alley justice" dispensed with the nightstick was common.

Today, many disturbances studied by the Commission began with a police incident. But these incidents were not, for the most part, the crude acts of an earlier time. They were routine

[1]We wish to acknowledge our indebtedness to and reliance upon the extensive work done by the President's Commission on Law Enforcement and Administration of Justice (the "Crime Commission"). The reports, studies, surveys, and analyses of the Crime Commission have contributed to many of our conclusions and recommendations.

police actions such as stopping a motorist or raiding an illegal business. Indeed, many of the serious disturbances took place in cities whose police are among the best led, best organized, best trained and most professional in the country.

Yet some activities of even the most professional police department may heighten tension and enhance the potential for civil disorder. An increase in complaints of police misconduct, for example, may in fact be a reflection of professionalism; the department may simply be using law enforcement methods which increase the total volume of police contacts with the public. The number of charges of police misconduct may be greater simply because the volume of police-citizen contacts is higher.

Here we examine two aspects of police activities that have great tension-creating potential. Our objective is to provide recommendations to assist city and police officials in developing practices which can allay rather than contribute to tension.

POLICE CONDUCT

Negroes firmly believe that police brutality and harassment occur repeatedly in Negro neighborhoods. This belief is unquestionably one of the major reasons for intense Negro resentment against the police.

The extent of this belief is suggested by attitude surveys. In 1964, a New York Times study of Harlem showed that 43 percent of those questioned believed in the existence of police "brutality."[2] In 1965, a nationwide Gallup poll found that 35 percent of Negro men believed there was police brutality in their areas; 7 percent of white men thought so. In 1966, a survey conducted for the Senate Subcommittee on Executive Reorganization found that 60 percent of Watts Negroes aged 15 to 19 believed there was some police brutality. Half said they had witnessed such conduct. A University of California at Los Angeles study of the Watts area found that 79 percent of the Negro males believed police lack respect for, or use insulting language to, Negroes, and 74 percent believed police use

[2]The "brutality" referred to in this and other surveys is often not precisely defined and covers conduct ranging from use of insulting language to excessive and unjustified use of force.

unnecessary force in making arrests. In 1967, an Urban League study of the Detroit riot area found that 82 percent believed there was some form of police brutality.

The true extent of excessive and unjustified use of force is difficult to determine. One survey done for the Crime Commission suggests that when police-citizen contacts are systematically observed, the vast majority are handled without antagonism or incident. Of 5,339 police-citizen contacts observed in slum precincts in three large cities, in the opinion of the observer only 20—about three-tenths of 1 percent—involved excessive or unnecessary force. And although almost all of those subjected to such force were poor, more than half were white. Verbal discourtesy was more common—15 percent of all such contacts began with a "brusque or nasty command" on the part of the officer. Again, however, the objects of such commands were more likely to be white than Negro.

Such "observer" surveys may not fully reflect the normal pattern of police conduct. The Crime Commission Task Force concluded that although the study gave "no basis for stating the extent to which police officers used force, it did confirm that such conduct still exists in the cities where observations were made." Our investigations confirm this conclusion.

Physical abuse is only one source of aggravation in the ghetto. In nearly every city surveyed, the Commission heard complaints of harassment of interracial couples, dispersal of social street gatherings and the stopping of Negroes on foot or in cars without objective basis. These, together with contemptuous and degrading verbal abuse, have great impact in the ghetto. As one Commission witness said, these strip the Negro of the one thing that he may have left—his dignity, "the question of being a man."

Some conduct—breaking up of street groups, indiscriminate stops and searches—is frequently directed at youths, creating special tensions in the ghetto where the average age is generally under 21. Ghetto youths, often without work and with homes that may be nearly uninhabitable, particularly in the summer, commonly spend much time on the street. Characteristically, they are not only hostile to police but eager to demonstrate their own masculinity and courage. The police, therefore, are often subject to taunts and provocations, testing their self-control and, probably, for some, reinforcing their hostility to Negroes in general. Because youths commit a large and increasing proportion of crime, police are under growing pressure from their supervisors—and from the community—to deal with them forcefully. "Harassment of youths" may therefore be viewed by some police departments—and members even of the Negro community—as a proper crime prevention technique.

In a number of cities, the Commission heard complaints of abuse from Negro adults of all social and economic classes. Particular resentment is aroused by harassing Negro men in the company of white women—often their light-skinned Negro wives.

"Harassment" or discourtesy may not be the result of malicious or discriminatory intent of police officers. Many officers simply fail to understand the effects of their actions because of their limited knowledge of the Negro community. Calling a Negro teenager by his first name may arose resentment because many whites still refuse to extend to adult Negroes the courtesy of the title, "Mister." A patrolman may take the arm of a person he is leading to the police car. Negroes are more likely to resent this than whites because the action implies that they are on the verge of flight and may degrade them in the eyes of friends or onlookers.

In assessing the impact of police misconduct, we emphasize that the improper acts of a relatively few officers may create severe tensions between the department and the entire Negro community. Whatever the actual extent of such conduct, we concur in the Crime Commission's conclusion that:

> * * * all such behavior is obviously and totally reprehensible, and when it is directed against minority-group citizens, it is particularly likely to lead, for quite obvious reasons, to bitterness in the community.

POLICE PATROL PRACTICES

Although police administrators may take steps to eliminate misconduct by individual police officers, many departments have adopted patrol practices which in the words of one commentator, have "* * * replaced harassment by individual patrolmen with harassment by entire departments."

These practices, sometimes known as "aggressive preventive patrol," take a number of forms, but invariably they involve a large number of police-citizen contacts initiated by police rather than in response to a call for help or service. One such practice utilizes a roving task force which moves into high-crime districts without prior notice and conducts intensive, often indiscriminate, street stops and searches. A number of obviously suspicious persons are stopped. But so also are persons whom the beat patrolman would know are respected members of the community. Such task forces are often deliberately moved from place to place making it impossible for its members to know the people with whom they come in contact.

In some cities, aggressive patrol is not limited to special task forces. The beat patrolman himself is expected to participate and to file a minimum number of "stop-and-frisk" or field interrogation reports for each tour of duty. This pressure to produce, or a lack of familiarity with the neighborhood and its people, may lead to widespread use of these techniques without adequate differentiation between genuinely suspicious behavior and behavior which is suspicious to a particular officer merely because it is unfamiliar.

Police administrators, pressed by public concern about crime, have instituted such patrol practices often without weighing their tension-creating effects and the resulting relationship to civil disorder.

Motorization of police is another aspect of patrol that has affected law enforcement in the ghetto. The patrolman comes to see the city through a windshield and hear about it over a police radio. To him, the area increasingly comes to consist only of lawbreakers. To the ghetto resident, the policeman comes increasingly to be only an enforcer.

Loss of contact between the police officer and the community he serves adversely affects law enforcement. If an officer has never met, does not know and cannot understand the language and habits of the people in the area he patrols, he cannot do an effective police job. His ability to detect truly suspicious behavior is impaired. He deprives himself of important sources of information. He fails to know those persons with an "equity" in the community—homeowners, small businessmen, professional men, persons who are anxious to support proper law enforcement—and thus sacrifices the contributions they can make to maintaining community order.

RECOMMENDATIONS

Police misconduct—whether described as brutality, harassment, verbal abuse or discourtesy—cannot be tolerated even if it is infrequent. It contributes directly to the risk of civil disorder. It is inconsistent with the basic responsibility and function of a police force in a democracy. Police departments must have rules prohibiting such misconduct and enforce them vigorously. Police commanders must be aware of what takes place in the field and take firm steps to correct abuses. We consider this matter further in the section on policy guidelines.

Elimination of misconduct also requires care in selecting police for ghetto areas, for there the police responsibility is particularly sensitive, demanding and often dangerous. The highest caliber of personnel is required if police are to overcome feelings within the ghetto community of inadequate protection and unfair, discriminatory treatment. Despite this need, data from Commission investigators and from the Crime Commission disclose that often a department's worst, not its best, are assigned to minority group neighborhoods. As Prof. Albert Reiss, director of the Center for Research on Social Organization, University of Michigan, testified before the Commission:

> I think we confront in modern urban police departments in large cities much of what we encounter in our schools in these cities. The slum police precinct is like the slum schools. It gets, with few exceptions, the worst in the system.

Referring to extensive studies in one city, Professor Reiss concluded:

> In predominantly Negro precincts, over three-fourths of the white policemen expressed prejudice or highly prejudiced attitudes towards Negroes. Only one percent of the officers expressed attitudes which could be described as sympathetic towards Negroes. Indeed, close to one-half of all the police officers in predominantly Negro high-crime-rate areas showed extreme prejudice against Negroes. What do I mean by extreme

> racial prejudice? I mean that they describe Negroes in terms that are not people terms. They describe them in terms of the animal kingdom. * * *

Although some prejudice was displayed in only 8 percent of police-citizen encounters:

> The cost of such prejudiced behavior I suggest is much higher than my statistics suggest. Over a period of time, a substantial proportion of citizens, particularly in high-crime-rate areas, may experience at least one encounter with a police officer where prejudice is shown.

To insure assignment of well-qualified police to ghetto areas, the Commission recommends:

- Officers with bad reputations among residents in minority areas should be immediately reassigned to other areas. This will serve the interests of both the police and the community.
- Screening procedures should be developed to ensure that officers with superior ability, sensitivity and the common sense necessary for enlightened law enforcement are assigned to minority group areas. We believe that, with proper training in ghetto problems and conditions, and with proper standards for recruitment of new officers, in the long run most policemen can meet these standards.
- Incentives, such as bonuses or credits for promotion, should be developed wherever necessary to attract outstanding officers for ghetto positions.

The recommendations we have proposed are designed to help insure proper police conduct in minority areas. Yet there is another facet of the problem: Negro perceptions of police misconduct. Even if those perceptions are exaggerated, they do exist. If outstanding officers are assigned to ghetto areas, if acts of misconduct, however infrequent, result in proper—and visible—disciplinary action and if these corrective practices are made part of known policy, we believe the community will soon learn to reject unfounded claims of misconduct.

Problems stemming from police patrol cannot, perhaps, be so easily resolved. But there are two considerations which can help to allay such problems. The first relates to law enforcement philosophy behind the use of techniques like aggressive patrol. Many police officials believe strongly that there are law enforcement gains from such techniques. However, these techniques also have law enforcement liabilities. Their employment therefore should not be merely automatic but the product of a deliberate balancing of pluses and minuses by command personnel.

We know that advice of this sort is easier to give than to act on. The factors involved are difficult to weigh. Gains cannot be measured solely in the number of arrests. Losses in police protection cannot be accepted solely because of some vague gain in diminished community tension. The kind of thorough, objective assessment of patrol practices and search for innovation we need will require the best efforts of research and development units within police departments, augmented if necessary by outside research assistance. The Federal Government can also play a major role in funding and conducting such research.

The second consideration concerning patrol is execution. There is more crime in the ghetto than in other areas. If the aggressive patrol clearly relates to the control of crime, the residents of the ghetto are likely to endorse the practice. What may arouse hostility is not the fact of aggressive patrol but its indiscriminate use so that it comes to be regarded not as crime control but as a new method of racial harassment. All patrol practices must be carefully reviewed to insure they are properly carried out by individual officers.

New patrol practices must be designed to increase the patrolman's knowledge of the ghetto. Although motorized patrols are essential, means should be devised to get the patrolman out of the car and into the neighborhood and keeping him on the same beat long enough to get to know the people and understand the conditions. This will require training the patrolman to convince him of the desirability of such practices. There must be continuing administrative supervision. In practice as well as theory, all aspects of patrol must be lawful and conform to policy guidelines. Unless carried out with courtesy and with understanding of the community, even the most enlightened patrol practices may degenerate into what residents will come to regard as harassment. Finally, this concept of patrol should be publicly explained so that ghetto residents understand it and know what to expect.

THE PROBLEM OF POLICE PROTECTION

The strength of ghetto feelings about hostile police conduct may even be exceeded by the conviction that ghetto neighborhoods are not given adequate police protection.

This belief is founded on two basic types of complaint. The first is that the police maintain a much less rigorous standard of law enforcement in the ghetto, tolerating there illegal activities like drug addiction, prostitution, and street violence that they would not tolerate elsewhere. The second is that police treat complaints and calls for help from Negro areas much less urgently than from white areas. These perceptions are widespread. As David Hardy, of the staff of the *New York Daily News*, testified:

> To put it simply, for decades little if any law enforcement has prevailed among Negroes in America, particularly those in the ghettos. If a black man kills another black man, the law is generally enforced at its minimum. Violence of every type runs rampant in a ghetto.

A Crime Commission study found that Negroes in Philadelphia and San Diego are convinced that the police apply a different standard of law enforcement in the ghettos. Another Crime Commission study found that about one white person in two believes police provide very good protection in his community; for Negroes, the figure is one in five. Other surveys have reported that Negroes in Harlem and south central Los Angeles mention inadequate protection more often than brutality or harassment as a reason for their resentment toward the police.

The report of a New Haven community group summarizes the complaints:

> The problem of the adequacy of current police protection ranked with "police misconduct" as the most serious sore points in police-community relations. * * * When calls for help are registered, it is all too frequent that police respond too slowly or not at all. * * * When they do come, [they] arrive with many more men and cars than are necessary * * * brandishing guns and adding to the confusion.[3]

[3]"In Search of Fair and Adequate Law Enforcement," report of the Hill-Dwight Citizens Commission on Police Community Relations, June 1967, pp. 12–13.

There is evidence to suggest that the lack of protection does not necessarily result from different basic police attitudes but rather from a relative lack of police personnel for ghetto areas, considering the volume of calls for police. As a consequence, the police work according to priorities. Because of the need for attention to major crimes, little, if any, attention can be accorded to reports of a suspicious person, for example, or a noisy party or a drunk. And attention even to major crimes may sometimes be routine or skeptical.

Ghetto residents, however, see a dual standard of law enforcement. Particularly because many work in other areas of the city and have seen the nature of police responsiveness there, they are keenly aware of the difference. They come to believe that an assault on a white victim produces one reaction and an assault on a Negro quite another. The police, heavily engaged in the ghetto, might assert that they cannot cover serious offenses and minor complaints at the same time—that they cannot be two places at once. The ghetto resident, however, often concludes that the police respond neither to serious offenses nor to minor complaints.

Recent studies have documented the inadequacies of police response in some ghetto areas. A Yale Law Journal study of Hartford, Conn., found that:

> [T]he residents of a large area in the center of the Negro ghetto are victims of over one-third of the daylight residential burglaries in the city. Yet during the daytime, only one of Hartford's 18 patrol cars and none of its 11 foot patrolmen is assigned to this area. Sections in the white part of town about the same size as the central ghetto area receive slightly more intensive daytime patrol even though the citizens in the ghetto area summon the police about six times as often because of criminal acts.[4]

In a United States Commission on Civil Rights study, a review of police communications records in Cleveland disclosed that police took almost four times as long to respond to calls concerning robbery from the Negro district as for the district where response was next slowest. The response time for some other crimes was at least twice as long.

[4] "Program Budgeting for Police Departments," 76 Yale L.J. 822 (1967).

The Commission recommends:

- Police departments should have a clear and enforced policy that the standard of law enforcement in ghetto areas is the same as in other communities; complaints and appeals from the ghetto should be treated with the same urgency and importance as those from white neighborhoods.
- Because a basic problem in furnishing protection to the ghetto is the shortage of manpower, police departments should review existing deployment of field personnel to ensure the most efficient use of manpower. The Police Task Force of the Crime Commission stressed the need "to distribute patrol officers in accordance with the actual need for their presence." Communities may have to pay for more and better policing for the entire community as well as for the ghetto.

In allocating manpower to the ghetto, enforcement emphasis should be given to crimes that threaten life and property. Stress on social gambling or loitering, when more serious crimes are neglected, not only diverts manpower but fosters distrust and tension in the ghetto community.

THE PROBLEM OF GRIEVANCE MECHANISMS

A third source of Negro hostility to police is the almost total lack of effective channels for redress of complaints against police conduct. In Milwaukee, Wis., and Plainfield, N.J., for example, ghetto residents complained that police reject complaints out of hand. In New Haven, a Negro citizens' group characterized a police review board as worthless. In Detroit, the Michigan Civil Rights Commission found that, despite well-intentioned leadership, no real sanctions are imposed on offending officers. In Newark, the mayor referred complaints to the FBI, which had very limited jurisdiction over them. In many of the cities surveyed by the Commission, Negro complaints focused on the continued presence in the ghetto of officers regarded as notorious for prejudice and brutality.

The 1967 Report of the Civil Rights Commission also states that a major issue in the Negro community is inadequate investigation of complaints against the police. It even reports threats of criminal actions designed to discourage complainants. A survey for the Crime Commission found substantial evidence that policemen in some cities have little fear of punishment for using unnecessary force because they appear to have a degree of immunity from their departments.

RECOMMENDATIONS

Objective evaluation, analysis and innovation on this subject are vitally necessary. Yet attention has been largely and, unfortunately, diverted by protracted debate over the desirability of "civilian review boards." Research conducted by the Crime Commission and others shows that the benefits and liabilities of such boards have probably both been exaggerated.

In the context of civil disorder, appearances and reality are of almost equal importance in the handling of citizen complaints against the police. It is not enough that there are adequate machinery and procedures for handling complaints; it is also necessary that citizens believe these procedures are adequate. Some citizens will never trust an agency against which they have a grievance. Some irresponsible citizens will attempt to provoke distrust of every agency. Hence, some police administrators have been tempted to throw up their hands and do nothing on the ground that whatever they do will be misunderstood. These sentiments may be understandable, but the police should appreciate that Negro citizens also want to throw up their hands. For they believe that the "police stick together," that they will cover up for each other, that no officer ever receives more than token punishment for misconduct and that even such expensive legal steps as false arrest or civil damage suits are foredoomed because "it is the officer's word against mine."

We believe that an internal review board—in which the police department itself receives and acts on complaints—regardless of its efficiency and fairness, can rarely generate the necessary community confidence or protect the police against unfounded charges. We also believe, as did the Crime Commission, that police should not be the only municipal agency subject to outside scrutiny and review. Incompetence and mistreatment by any public servant should be equally subject to review by an independent agency.

The Crime Commission Police Task Force reviewed the various external grievance procedures attempted or suggested in this country and abroad. Without attempting to recommend a specific procedure, our Commission believes that police departments should be subject to external review. We discussed this problem in Chapter 10, The Community Response. Here, we highlight what we believe to be the basic elements of an effective system.

The Commission recommends:

- Making a complaint should be easy. It should be possible to file a grievance without excessive formality. If forms are used, they should be easily available and their use explained in widely distributed pamphlets. In large cities, it should not be necessary to go to a central headquarters office to file a complaint, but it should also be possible to file a complaint at neighborhood locations. Police officers on the beat, community service aides or other municipal employees in the community should be empowered to receive complaints.
- A specialized agency, with adequate funds and staff, should be created separate from other municipal agencies, to handle, investigate and to make recommendations on citizen complaints.
- The procedure should have a built-in conciliation process to attempt to resolve complaints without the need for full investigation and processing.
- The complaining party should be able to participate in the investigation and in any hearings, with right of representation by counsel, so that the complaint is fully investigated and findings made on the merits. He should be promptly and fully informed of the outcome. The results of the investigation should be made public.
- Since many citizen complaints concern departmental policies rather than individual conduct, information concerning complaints of this sort should be forwarded to the departmental unit which formulates or reviews policy and procedures. Information concerning all complaints should be forwarded to appropriate training units so that any deficiencies correctable by training can be eliminated.

Although we advocate an external agency as a means of resolving grievances, we believe that the basic need is to adopt procedures which will gain the respect and confidence of the entire community. This need can, in the end, be met only by sustained direction through the line of command, thorough investigation of complaints, and prompt, visible disciplinary action where justified.

THE NEED FOR POLICY GUIDELINES

How a policeman handles day-to-day contacts with citizens will, to a large extent, shape the relationships between the police and the community. These contacts involve considerable discretion. Improper exercise of such discretion can needlessly create tension and contribute to community grievances.

Formally, the police officer has no discretion; his task is to enforce all laws at all times. Formally, the officer's only basic enforcement option is to make an arrest or to do nothing. Formally, when a citizen resists arrest, the officer's only recourse is to apply such reasonable force as he can bring with his hands, nightstick and revolver.

Informally—and in reality—the officer faces an entirely different situation. He has and must have a great deal of discretion; there are not enough police or jails to permit the levels of surveillance that would be necessary to enforce all laws all the time—levels which the public would, in any event, regard as intolerable.

Patrick V. Murphy, now Director of Public Safety in the District of Columbia, told the Commission:

> The police, of course, exercise very broad discretion, and although in many states the law says or implies that all laws must be enforced and although the manuals of many police departments state every officer is responsible for the enforcement of all laws, as a practical matter it is impossible for the police to enforce all laws and, as a result, they exercise very broad discretion. * * * [B]y failing to understand the fact that they do exercise important discretion every day, some police do not perceive just how they maintain the peace in different ways in different sections of a city.

The formal remedies of law, further, are inappropriate for many common problems. A family quarrel or a street fight, followed by an arrest, would give the parties a record and, typically, a suspended sentence; it would not solve the problem. And the appropriate legal grounds for making an arrest are often not present, for the officer has not witnessed the incident nor does he have a sworn complaint from someone who has. Pacifying the dispute may well be the best approach, but many officers lack the training or experience to do so effectively. If the parties resist pacification or arrest, the officer, alone on the street, must either back down or use force—sometimes lethal.

Crime Commission studies and our police survey show that guidance for the exercise of discretion in many situations is often not available to the policeman. There are guidelines for wearing uniforms—but not for how to intervene in a domestic dispute; for the cleaning of a revolver—but not for when to fire it; for use of departmental property—but not for whether to break up a sidewalk gathering; for handling stray dogs—but not for handling field interrogations.

RECOMMENDATIONS

Contacts between citizens and the police in the ghetto require discretion and judgment which should be based upon carefully-drawn, written departmental policy. The Report of the Crime Commission and the Police Task Force Report considered this problem in detail and recommended subjects for policy guidelines.

The Commission recommends the establishment of guidelines covering, at a minimum:

- The issuance of orders to citizens regarding their movements or activities—for example, when, if ever, should a policeman order a social street gathering to break up or move on.
- The handling of minor disputes—between husband and wife, merchant and customer or landlord and tenant. Guidelines should cover resources available in the community—family courts, probation departments, counseling services, welfare agencies—to which citizens can be referred.
- The decision whether to arrest in a specific situation involving a specific crime—for example, when police should arrest persons engaged in crimes such as social gambling, vagrancy and loitering and other crimes which do not involve victims. The use of alternatives to arrest, such as a summons, should also be considered.

- The selection and use of investigating methods. Problems concerning use of field interrogations and "stop-and-frisk" techniques are especially critical. Crime Commission studies and evidence before this Commission demonstrate that these techniques have the potential for becoming a major source of friction between police and minority groups. Their constitutionality is presently under review in the United States Supreme Court. We also recognize that police regard them as important methods of preventing and investigating crime. Although we do not advocate use or adoption of any particular investigative method, we believe that any such method should be covered by guidelines drafted to minimize friction with the community.
- Safeguarding the constitutional right of free expression, such as rights of persons engaging in lawful demonstrations, the need to protect lawful demonstrators and how to handle spontaneous demonstrations.
- The circumstances under which the various forms of physical force—including lethal force—can and should be applied. Recognition of this need was demonstrated by the regulations recently adopted by the City of New York further implementing the state law governing police use of firearms.
- The proper manner of address for contacts with any citizen.

The drafting of guidelines should not be solely a police responsibility. It is the duty of mayors and other elected and appointed executive officials to take the initiative, to participate fully in the drafting and to ensure that the guidelines are carried out in practice.

Police research and planning units should be fully used in identifying problem areas, performing the necessary studies and in resolving problems. Their product should be reviewed by the chief of police and city executives, and by representatives of the prosecution, courts, correction agencies and other criminal-justice agencies. Views of ghetto residents should be obtained, perhaps through police-community relations programs or human relations agencies. Once promulgated, the guidelines should be disseminated clearly and forcefully to all operational personnel. Concise, simply worded and, if necessary, foreign language summaries of police powers and individual rights should be distributed to the public. Training the police to perform according to the guidelines is essential. Although conventional instruction is a minimum requirement, full understanding can only be achieved by intensive small-group training, involving simulation.

Guidelines, no matter how carefully drafted, will have little effect unless the department enforces them. This primarily requires command supervision and commitment to the guidelines. It also requires:

- A strong internal investigative unit to enforce compliance. Such a unit should not only enforce the guidelines on a case-by-case basis against individual officers but should also develop procedures to deter and prevent violations. The Crime Commission discussed the various methods available.
- A fair and effective means to handle citizen complaints.

Finally, provision should be made for periodic review of the guidelines, to ensure that changes are made to take account of current court rulings and new laws.

COMMUNITY SUPPORT FOR LAW ENFORCEMENT

A fifth major reason for police-community hostility—particularly obvious since the recent disorders—is the general breakdown of communication between police and the ghetto. The contacts that do occur are primarily adversary contacts.

In the section on police patrol practices, we discussed one basic aspect of this problem. Here we consider how police forces have tried, with varying degrees of success, to deal with three issues underlying relations with ghetto communities.

RECRUITMENT, ASSIGNMENT, AND PROMOTION OF NEGROES

The Crime Commission Police Task Force found that for police in a Negro community, to be predominantly white can serve as a dangerous irritant; a feeling may develop that the community is not being policed to maintain civil peace but to maintain the status quo. It further found that contact with Negro officers can help to avoid stereotypes and prejudices in the minds of white officers. Negro officers also can increase departmental insight into ghetto problems and provide information necessary for early anticipation of the tensions and grievances that can lead to disorders. Commission witnesses confirm these conclusions.

There is evidence that Negro officers also can be particularly effective in controlling any disorders that do break out. In studying the relative performance of Army and National Guard forces in the Detroit disorder, we concluded that the higher percentage of Negroes in the Army forces contributed substantially to their better performance. As a result, last August, we recommended an increase in the percentage of Negroes in the National Guard. The need for increased Negro participation in police departments is equally acute.

Despite this need—and despite recent efforts to hire more Negro police, the proportion of Negroes on police forces still falls far below the proportion of Negroes in the total population. Of 28 departments which reported information of this kind in a Commission survey of police departments, the percentage of Negro sworn personnel ranged from less than 1 percent to 21 percent. The median figure for Negro sworn personnel on the force was 6 percent; the median figures for the Negro population was approximately 24 percent. In no case was the proportion of Negroes in the police department equal to the proportion in the population.[5] A 1962 survey of the United States Civil Rights Commission, as reported in the Crime Commission Police Task Force Report, shows correspondingly low figures for other cities.

There are even more marked disproportions of Negro supervisory personnel. Our survey showed the following ratios:

- One in every 26 Negroes is a sergeant; the white ratio is one in 12.
- One in every 114 Negroes is a lieutenant; the white ratio is one in 26.
- One in every 235 Negroes is a captain or above; the white ratio is one in 53.

[5]The data from this survey can be found in Table A at the end of this chapter, p. 169.

Public Safety Director Murphy, testifying before the Commission, described the problem and at least one of its causes:

> I think one of the serious problems facing the police in the nation today is the lack of adequate representation of Negroes in police departments. I think the police have not recruited enough Negroes in the past and are not recruiting enough of them today. I think we would be less than honest if we didn't admit that Negroes have been kept out of police departments in the past for reasons of racial discrimination.

In a number of cities, particularly larger ones, police officials are not only willing but anxious to appoint Negro officers. There are obstacles other than discrimination. While these obstacles cannot readily be measured, they can be identified. One is the relatively high standards for police employment. Another is pay; better qualified Negroes are often more attracted by other, better paying positions. Another obstacle is the bad image of police in the Negro community. There also are obstacles to promotion apart from discrimination, such as the more limited educational background of some Negro officers.

RECOMMENDATIONS

The Commission recommends:

- Police departments should intensify their efforts to recruit more Negroes. The Police Task Force of the Crime Commission discussed a number of ways to do this and the problems involved. The Department of Defense program to help police departments recruit returning servicemen should be fully utilized. An Army report of Negro participation in the National Guard and Army reserves may also provide useful information.
- In order to increase the number of Negroes in supervisory positions, police departments should review promotion policies to ensure that Negroes have full opportunity to be rapidly and fairly promoted.
- Negro officers should be so assigned as to ensure that the police department is fully and visibly integrated. Some cities have adopted a policy of assigning one white and one Negro officer to patrol cars, especially in ghetto areas. These assignments result in better understanding, tempered judgment and increased ability to separate the truly suspect from the unfamiliar.

Recruiting more Negro officers, alone, will not solve the problems of lack of communication and hostility toward police. A Negro's understanding of the ghetto is not enough to make him a good officer. He must also meet the same high standards as white officers and pass the same screening process. These requirements help create a dilemma noted by the Crime Commission. The need to develop better relations with minority group communities requires recruitment of police from these groups—groups handicapped by lack of educational opportunities and achievement. To require that police recruits have a high school diploma sets a standard too low in terms of the need for recruiting college graduates and perhaps too high in terms of the need for recruiting members of minority groups.

To meet this problem, the Crime Commission recommended creation of a new type of uniformed "community service officer." This officer would typically be a young man between 17 and 21 with the "aptitude, integrity and stability necessary to perform police work." He would perform a variety of duties short of exercising full law enforcement powers, with primary emphasis on community service work. While so serving, he would continue his studies in order to be promoted as quickly as possible to the status of a police officer.

The Commission recommends:

- The community service officer program should be adopted. Use of this program to increase the number of Negroes in police departments will help to establish needed channels of communication with the Negro community; will permit the police to perform better their community service functions, especially in the minority group neighborhoods; and will also create a number of badly needed jobs for Negro youths.

The standards of selection for such community service officers or aides should be drawn to insure that the great majority of young Negro males are eligible to participate in the program. As stated in the Crime Commission Task Force Report, selection should not be based on inflexible educational requirements, but instead "* * * should be made on an individual basis with priority being given to applicants with promising aspirations, honesty, intelligence, a desire and a tested capacity to advance his education and an understanding of the neighborhood and its problems." An arrest record or a minor conviction record should not in itself be a bar to employment.

The Commission recommends:

- The Federal Government should launch a program to establish community service officers or aides in cities with populations over 50,000. Eligible police departments should be reimbursed for 90 percent of the costs of employing one aide for every 10 full-time police officers.

We emphasize, however, that recruitment of community service aides must complement, not replace, efforts to recruit more Negroes as police officers.

COMMUNITY SERVICE FUNCTIONS

Because police run almost the only 24-hour-a-day, 7-day-a-week emergency service, they find it very hard not to become involved in a host of nonpolice services. Complaints about a wide range of matters, from noisy neighbors and deteriorated streets to building code violations, at best are only peripheral to police work. Because these are often not police matters and because police increasingly face serious shortages of manpower and money, police administrators have resisted becoming involved in such matters. This resistance, coupled with centralization and motorization of the police, has resulted in the police becoming more distant from the people they serve.

RECOMMENDATIONS

The Commission believes that police cannot, and should not, resist becoming involved in community service matters.[6] There will be benefits for law enforcement no less than for public order.

First, police, because of their "front line position" in dealing with ghetto problems, will be better able to identify problems in the community that may lead to disorder. Second, they will be better able to handle incidents requiring police intervention,

[6]We join in the Crime Commission's caveat that police should not become involved in service tasks which involve neither policing nor community help (such as tax collection, licensing, and dog-pound duties).

particularly marital disputes that have a potential for violence. How well the police handle domestic disturbances affects the incidence of serious crimes, including assaults and homicides. Third, willing performance of such work can gain police the respect and support of the community. Finally, development of nonadversary contacts can provide the police with a vital source of information and intelligence concerning the communities they serve.

A variety of methods have been devised to improve police performance of this service function. We comment on two of special interest. The first is the New York Police Department's experimental "Family Crisis Intervention" program to develop better police response to marital disputes; if results develop as expected, this may serve as a model for other departments.

Second, neighborhood service centers have been opened in some cities. These centers typically are established in tense, high-crime areas, in easily accessible locations such as storefronts or public housing projects. Staffed by a civilian city employee as well as a police officer, their task is to provide information and service—putting a citizen in touch with the right agency, furnishing general advice. This gives the beat patrolman somewhere to refer a marital dispute. It gives the local resident a clear, simple contact with official advice. It gives the police in general the opportunity to provide services, not merely to enforce the law. The needed additional manpower for such centers could be provided by the community service aides recommended earlier or by continuing to employ experienced policemen who have reached the age of retirement.

COMMUNITY RELATIONS PROGRAMS

Many police departments have established programs to deal specifically with police-community relations. The Crime Commission recommended a number of such programs, and Federal funds have been made available for putting them into operation. Although of great potential benefit, the results thus far have been disappointing. This is true partly because the changes in attitude sought by such programs can only be achieved over time. But there are other reasons, as was shown by Detroit's experience with police-community meetings: Minimum participation by ghetto residents; infrequent meetings;

lack of patrolmen involvement; lack of attention to youth programs; lack of coordination by police leadership, either within the department or with other city programs.

More significantly, both the Detroit evaluation and studies carried on for the Commission show that too often these are not community-relations programs but public-relations programs, designed to improve the department's image in the community. In one major city covered by the Commission's study, the department's plan for citizen observers of police work failed because people believed that the citizen observer was allowed to see only what the police thought he should see. Similarly, the police chief's "open house," an opportunity for discussion, was considered useless by many who regarded him as unsympathetic and unresponsive.

Moreover, it is clear that these programs have little support among rank and file officers. In Detroit, more than a year after instructions were sent out to establish such programs, several precincts still had failed to do so. Other cities have had similar experiences. On the command level, there is often little interest. Programs are not integrated into the departments; units do not receive adequate budgetary support.

Nevertheless, some programs have been successful. In Atlanta, a Crime Prevention Bureau has within 2 years established a good relationship with the community, particularly with the young people. It has concentrated on social services, persuading almost 600 dropouts to return to school, assisting some 250 hardship cases with food and work, arranging for dances and hydrant showers during the summer, working quickly and closely with families of missing persons. The result is a close rapport with the community—and recruits for the department. Baltimore and Winston-Salem are reported to have equally successful programs.

RECOMMENDATIONS

Community relations programs and training can be important in increasing communication and decreasing hostility between the police and the ghetto. Community relations programs can also be used by police to explain new patrol practices, law enforcement programs, and other police efforts to reduce crime. Police have a right to expect ghetto leaders to work responsibly to reduce crime. Community relations programs offer a way to create and foster these efforts.

We believe that community relations is an integral part of all law enforcement. But it cannot be made so by part-time effort, peripheral status or cliche methods.

One way to bolster community relations is to expand police department award systems. Traditionally, special awards, promotional credit, bonuses, and selection for special assignments are based on heroic acts and arrest activity. Award systems should take equal cognizance of the work of officers who improve relations with alienated members of the community and by so doing minimize the potential for disorder.

However, we see no easy solution to police-community relations and misunderstandings, and we are aware that no single procedure or program will suffice. Improving community relations is a full-time assignment for every commander and every officer—an assignment that must include the development of an attitude, a tone, throughout the force that conforms with the ultimate responsibility of every policeman: Public service.

COMMUNITY ON THE MOVE FOR EQUALITY

Have Sanitation Workers A Future?

Spring 1968

HAVE SANITATION WORKERS A FUTURE?

Yes, If You Will Help To Build It!
How? That's Simple—

WE NEED YOU!

1. Do not shop downtown, or with the downtown branch stores anywhere in the city or any enterprise named Loeb.
2. Stop your subscriptions to the daily newspapers. Get news about the Movement from the radio or television or by joining the mass meetings. Be sure to pay your newspaper carrier his commission.
3. Do not buy new things for Easter. Let our Lent be one of sacrifices. What better way to remember Jesus' work for us and the world?
4. Support the workers with letters and telegrams to the Mayor and the City Council.
5. Join us in the daily marches downtown.
6. Call others each day and remind them of the movement.
7. Attend the nightly mass meetings Monday through Friday.
8. Do not place your garbage at the curb. Handle it the best way you can without helping the city and the Mayor's effort to break the strike.
9. Whenever you associate with white people, let them know what the issues are and why you support this cause.
10. Support the relief efforts for the workers and their families with gifts of money and food. Checks can be made out to "C.O.M.E." and food taken to Clayborn Temple A.M.E. Church, 280 Hernando.

- -

Community On the Move for Equality
WORK CARD

Name ______________________ Phone ____________
Address ______________________
I will march _______ I will picket _______
I can answer phone or do clerical work _______
I can serve on a committee:

Work Committee	_______
Telephone Committee	_______
Transportation Committee	_______

Hours I can best serve:

9:00am–11:00am	_____	11:00am–1:00pm	_____
1:00pm–3:00pm	_____	3:00pm–6:00pm	_____
6:00pm–8:00pm	_____	8:00pm–10:00pm	_____
10:00pm–12:00pm	_____		

Signature ______________________________________

WHITNEY M. YOUNG

Oral History Interview on Lyndon B. Johnson

1955–68

INTERVIEWEE: WHITNEY YOUNG, JR.

INTERVIEWER: THOMAS HARRISON BAKER

B: This is the interview with Whitney M. Young, Jr. of the Urban League. Mr. Young, do you recall when you first met or knew anything about Lyndon Johnson?

Y: I first met Mr. Johnson when he was in the Senate as the Majority Leader. I had occasion to appear for testimony on several bills at which he was present and to talk with him about various legislation.

B: Would that have included the '57 Civil Rights Bill?

Y: That's right.

B: Had you formed an opinion of Mr. Johnson then, or had you classified him in regard to Civil Rights?

Y: No, I still was a little bit in doubt. I had some clues that Mr. Johnson was a man who had a feeling tone and some understanding of the problems of the poor. His style, his language, and some of his review of his own experiences led me to believe that basically he was a man with compassion, and with a concern. At that point I must confess though, I felt that I was dealing with him as a mass group, as one had learned to expect Southerners to respond to civil rights issues.

B: Did your opinion change any by his activity in supporting the '57 Bill?

Y: Not so much. That was not the occasion upon which I really began to know that we had a strong supporter in Lyndon Johnson for civil rights. At that point, I still felt he was rising to the leadership role of the Senate. In that role he was making certain compromises and concessions in order to facilitate legislation. So, I saw it more as a manifestation of his skill in trying to process legislation than I did as a manifestation of any real conviction on the issue of civil rights.

B: Did it bother you any that Mr. Johnson was on the Democratic ticket in 1960?

Y: That really came as quite a surprise, particularly after the rather competitive and sometimes heated dialogue with John Kennedy, and the fact that I thought that Lyndon Johnson, himself, would feel that he had a more powerful and persuasive role to play as the Senate leader, and that this in fact would probably be a step down in terms of power—which I always felt that Mr. Johnson didn't particularly retreat from wanting power. I wasn't overly disturbed about it however, because I have always—well, I've made the statement many times that some of the best liberals I know are reconstructed Southerners. I'm a Southerner myself, and I know that Southerners—I have yet to see a single Southerner who didn't have the capacity to like, if not love, and feel very close to individual black people, though the problem of acceptance of the group was difficult.

I've also observed that people, when their base, their constituency, changes they can sometimes be honest with their own feelings when they aren't concerned about running from a particular geographic area. I suppose we'll always recall the experience of Hugo Black. All of us in civil rights were greatly distressed at his proposed appointment, particularly when it was revealed that he was formerly a member of the Klan. And yet he went on, as is now well known, to become one of the great liberals and fighters for civil rights. And there have been many other cases of people Judge Waties Waring and Ralph McGill, *Ivan Allen* at the present time, who one time was a rigid segregationist, turned out to be not just a great Southern mayor but one of the greatest mayors of the land.

B: Sir, you became Executive Director of the Urban League at the same time Mr. Johnson became Vice President. Did this throw you closer together—particularly his position on the Commission on Equal Employment Opportunities?

Y: There were three things that happened right away to sort of endear Mr. Johnson to me. Upon my appointment a few weeks afterwards, Roy Wilkins, of the NAACP, had a reception for me in the hotel here, and Lyndon Johnson heard about it, was in town, and personally came over to welcome me in my new job.

Secondly, we had several meetings very early, just the two of us, and then with others around his responsibilities heading the President's Commission. I was impressed with what he said and the kind of people he was getting around him and the determination that he exhibited to make this a much more effective Commission and to really do something. He immediately put a black man on, if you recall—a fellow named Hobart Taylor—as the chief staff person for that Commission.

Now the third thing was, I came on the job in October and in November I was having our most important event, our Equal Opportunity Day Dinner, and I asked Mr. Johnson to come and speak and he agreed. This was a meeting at the Waldorf with some 1500 people, the biggest businessmen in the country and labor leaders, black people and church people and what have you. And he came and he made a speech that made mine sound like the moderate!

B: I guess it might be appropriate to mention here that in the last year of his Presidency, Mr. Johnson surprised everyone and showed up at that dinner, too, in '68.

Y: That's right. And it was really a beautiful gesture on his part, and it gave us a chance to say—and the people really said it by their spontaneous enthusiastic reception. There was a room of 2000 people and there was hardly a dry eye in the place; there were no boos; there was nothing but enthusiastic cheers. It gave us a real opportunity to say "Thanks" to what we all feel has been the greatest leadership job in civil rights done by any President.

B: Back in the Vice Presidential years, did Mr. Johnson really ask you for your advice on things to do? I know that the Urban League was beginning then under your direction, the new thrust, the new ideas. Did you really share ideas?

Y: Yes. I suppose we visited on the phone at least once a week and in person at least once a month. He did share with me some of his frustrations that I think have been generally assumed at being more or less under reins and under check, not having as much say-so as he would like to have in the general policy making of the country. He was scrupulously ethical and loyal to John Kennedy in any kind of group meeting, but you sort of sensed it in individual meetings when he was pressed to do certain things that he would sort of indicate that, after all, he was not the President of the United States. For a man who had had great power and had great energy, I did sense in him a bit of restlessness and some annoyance at what he felt was failure to make maximum use of his skills and his energies by the Administration.

B: Was his frustration directed particularly at President Kennedy or more at, say, Attorney General Robert Kennedy or some of the other staff members?

Y: I would say they were sort of lumped together. You sort of thought of them as the clique or the clan, the Eastern Establishment. I guess the more unkind characterizations have been the Mafia group that they were called by many of the press. So he really felt, I think, that he was boxed in by a whole lot of individuals whose style and whose accents he felt, I think, that President Kennedy felt more comfortable with and did not really make maximum use of his. I think also there was—he became philosophical about it, President Johnson—and it was directed more at the system, that historically the role of the Vice President had not been one of major influence. I think he did feel that it would be changed under John Kennedy, especially since he had been such a strong influence within the Senate, that he would be used more.

B: Did Mr. Johnson play a major role in drafting civil rights proposals in '63?

Y: Yes. He played a very key role and was actually more supportive of some of the measures than some of the Administration, the other Kennedy people, were. Initially we had seven or eight titles, and there were any number of the members of the Administration who were trying very hard to get us to cut down the number and take out certain ones like, oh, the Public Accommodations Bill, and Title VI particularly, dealing with withholding of federal funds. It was their opinion, even after the March on Washington, that this was just impossible and it would hurt our chances of getting some other titles if we didn't drop those.

Mr. Johnson didn't feel that way.

B: This was one of the frustrations you mentioned?

Y: Yes. I think Mr. Johnson had a little more confidence in the mood of the country than did Mr. Kennedy at that point. And being a Southerner, and I think being probably a little closer to the people, put him in a position to be a little more accurate about that mood.

B: Did you and Mr. Johnson discuss in these years the events in the South, particularly what Dr. King and the Southern Christian Leadership Conference were doing?

Y: I don't recall a great deal of discussion on specifics. I do know that we discussed the possibility of certain methods resulting in a counter kind of reaction, and I can remember on many occasions pointing out that the old, old methods had been used for so long and had proven ineffective that people who found the newer methods of confrontation distasteful had only themselves to blame for not going along with the more polite and more reasonable kinds of appeals that organizations like the Urban League and people like myself had made. So I was in no position to criticize the methods as long as they were not violent, as long as my methods hadn't worked.

B: Was Mr. Johnson then reluctant to encourage you in planning the March on Washington in '63?

Y: No. I think we were able to convince Mr. Johnson—and he saw it—and we convinced him before we did Mr. Kennedy—that this would be a very healthy sort of way of expressing the pent-up emotions and that the alternative to letting people have this kind of collective display of their feelings would be engaging in much more undisciplined kinds of activities around the country.

B: I know that many members of the Administration feared that it would get out of control, the March would get out of control.

Y: That's right. I never could understand this. I tried to point out to the Administration then that if black people were violent people inherently, then we would have been violent long before now—or else we have the longest time fuse known to man. We certainly have had the provocations, but the whole history of violence in this country, black people have usually been the victims and they've not been the prosecutors of it, and that we are by nature a people whose leadership has come from the churches and who have a great faith in ourselves and in our system. Given the way we were organizing it, at no point did I feel the panic and anxiety that members of the Administration seemed to feel.

B: That same year, indeed about the same time, you announced your concept of a domestic Marshall Plan. Had you discussed this in advance with Mr. Johnson?

Y: Yes—not in too specific details. I did share with him the memorandum that our Board worked on for almost six or eight months leading up to the announcement and then later there was a magazine article on it in the New York Times and then later in my book, *To Be Equal*, which went into it more in detail. Mr. Johnson is mentioned in the book as a person who seemed to understand the concept. I think Mr. Johnson understood this—I've always felt that when he talked about the Great Society he was serious. But there were two reasons for it.

I think he saw the Great Society as sort of a monument. In a way it would be going a step beyond what his great hero Franklin Roosevelt did. I've always felt that if it hadn't been for the Viet Nam war—which is one of the ironical bits of fate—that Mr. Johnson would have made America the Great Society. He had all of the skills and the conviction, the dedication, the motivation that was needed in the domestic area, that could have mobilized the people, could have gotten the resources, could have made them see this as an investment. So he understood that we were talking about an investment and not an expenditure and a way of tapping great potential.

B: Is there a direct connection between your ideas and Mr. Johnson's anti-poverty plans, which are very similar? Is this the kind of thing that you had discussed?

Y: Yes. I was involved in the Poverty Program, the planning of it, from the very start—even when John Kennedy was in, and more so when President Johnson came in. I'd say a lot of our ideas really constituted some of the same concepts of the Marshall Plan. It was programmed, by this point, 1969, it was supposed to be around eight billion dollars. And I think it would have been, but here again I think the war intervened.

B: Right after the assassination of President Kennedy, I know you had a conference very shortly with Mr. Johnson. I gather you did not need any reassuring on his stand on, say, the Civil Rights Bill. But what did you discuss there?

Y: The press got to me immediately after the assassination, and I remember my first comment when asked about how did I feel about Lyndon Johnson as the President. I said, "I had always felt that if ever I turned on the radio and heard the President of the United States speaking with a deep Southern accent that I would panic. But I did not feel that way at all." In fact I felt, by that time, that Lyndon Johnson would do exactly what he did, but the next day he did call me and we talked at some length on the phone and then two or three days later I met with him. He was not, at that point, trying to get unity as much as he was saying, "I need your help." And he was giving full recognition to the shock of the country and the possible anxiety people might have about a Southerner being President. He wanted very much to convey that not only did we not have to worry but he wanted to do far more than any other President.

B: Did he offer you a position in the Administration then or anytime fairly soon? It was rumored, for example, that you were offered the Deputy Directorship of the War on Poverty.

Y: I was offered several jobs by Mr. Johnson. He's talked to me—his people have—about cabinet positions, about heading OEO, on a variety of occasions. On every occasion I was only able to resist his arm-twisting by reminding him that I felt and was able to prove to him that I was better able to serve both his own objectives and the country's objectives in my present spot, that it was a unique position and one from which I could exercise a maximum influence and control, and I thought it would be unwise if all of the black leadership that had talent or abilities were to leave and go with the Administration. That some of us needed to be outside.

B: There aren't many people that have been able to resist that kind of pressure.

Y: I know! He's a very persuasive man.

B: There are some ideas of yours which have not shown up in the anti-poverty plans. For example I believe at one time you advocated a kind of public works for employment and in your most recent book *Beyond Racism*, you have some ideas like the Neighborhood Development Corporation and the Council of Social Advisers and the Executive Vice President for Domestic Development. Had you discussed this kind of thing with Mr. Johnson?

Y: Yes, some of these had been discussed. I remember on any number of occasions we used to mutually deplore what we felt was the lack of coordination of all of the efforts, first just within the federal government—how each department had its own poverty operation. Labor was doing something for the hardcore, and Agriculture, and OEO, and Health Education and Welfare. But there was nobody coordinating this so as to avoid duplication and overlap and competitiveness. As a result you not only had lack of coordination that he wanted so much, but you also had much duplication and many people who were not being served. We talked about how could such a position be established. I think he really had hoped that the OEO director would be able to do it, but this was a little unrealistic. He didn't have cabinet status and you can't expect other cabinet members to be coordinated by their peers. This is what has led me to believe that there has to be either the Vice President, or somebody so designated, has to be given that kind of authority.

B: For a time Mr. Humphrey, under Mr. Johnson, seemed to have, at least in theory, that authority.

Y: Yes he did, but I think here again Mr. Johnson, after smarting under the restrictions of being a Vice President, because of his own personality and drive, found himself probably doing some of the same things to Mr. Humphrey because he was a man who wanted to stay on top of everything and who had a fantastic memory and ability to absorb facts about so many things. I just never felt he really unleashed the authority for domestic planning to Mr. Humphrey, and by the time he was forced to by the pressures of international events there wasn't any resources.

B: Sir, did Mr. Johnson's opinion on this kind of thing change toward the end of his Presidency? For example, you praised the Kerner Report highly and Mr. Johnson's public response to it was cool, to put it as mildly as possible.

Y: I think that was a mistake on the part of Mr. Johnson. I think it was a spontaneous thing. I've always felt that what he was really reacting to was not so much what the Kerner Commission Report said but how it failed to acknowledge the many things he had done, that had been accomplished, under his administration in the domestic area. The Kerner Commission on that point, and probably consciously, because they wanted to concentrate on what was still missing rather than what we had. But I think Mr. Johnson took it personally. I think that was a part of his lack of enthusiasm for the Report.

But the other thing was, I think the term racism sort of shook him up as it has practically everybody. The reason being as I tried to explain in my book, *Beyond Racism*, that they misinterpreted it. They thought of it as meaning a vile, vulgar, bigot type who wanted to go around lynching black people, which most white people certainly don't want to do. But that really wasn't the meaning of it. It had to do with how institutions had historically ignored or discriminated against, or people had conducted themselves in a way that suggested they felt superiority over other people.

But I think Mr. Johnson, with his natural political and public relations instincts, felt that this term—this kind of indictment—just wasn't the best way to sell something. He couldn't have disagreed with the findings because in his own speeches many, many times he has pointed out that the real agitators are not Communist-trained infiltrators, but they are rats and poverty and all of this. He had said most of the things that are in that report.

B: Was Mr. Johnson discouraged and frustrated by the increase in black militancy, and black separatism?

Y: Initially he was, and I think he always took it rather personally if he himself were attacked. I know that he was greatly concerned and curious about Dr. King particularly, and some of Dr. King's remarks, because he had a great deal of respect for Dr. King. I don't think he clearly understood how strongly Dr. King felt about Viet Nam, for example.

B: Did you find yourself having to explain Dr. King to Mr. Johnson?

Y: Yes, I did.

B: I assume when you were in Atlanta you were close with Dr. King?

Y: That's right, Dr. King and I were good friends. We have had our differences on to what extent should the civil rights movement become involved in the international affairs, particularly Viet Nam. I must confess I have changed somewhat in my own thinking now and feel maybe Dr. King was more right than probably I was, because it is hard to separate the war from the domestic problems in terms of resources of the country and of manpower and all this. But I used to have to keep telling President Johnson, whether it was Dr. King or whether he was booed or any black person said something, that he was not to take it personally. He seemed to feel you know what man has ever done more and that why doesn't everybody know this and why aren't they appreciative? I had to remind him that black people were like any other ethnic group, we ran the spectrum. We have as much right to have our crackpots as anybody else and if he could get rid of all the white crackpots, the Klan and the White Citizens Council, the John Birchers and the Minute Men, that I could get rid of the Black Panthers. But I felt if we believed in equality then we're going to have to give black people the right to have crackpots just like white people.

B: Is the Viet Nam war one of the keys to this, too? Did this attitude of his increase when the war stand began to be criticized?

Y: Yes, that was really the only thing that black people ever really became very critical of President Johnson on. Nobody could make a substantial argument that he hadn't done more until it got to the point that the monies were not forthcoming because of it. But I think President Johnson's attitude with regard to the war was first one of he felt he had been poorly advised. He had gotten into something that he was not an acknowledged expert on, that he had relied upon the advice largely of President Kennedy's appointees. Then to have some of that same camp become the most violent antagonists on it, I think was deeply disturbing to him because by the time those advisers were out of the picture, the number had escalated to the point where he was just sort of caught in the middle of this thing.

B: Did he discuss this with you, in about those words that you just used?

Y: No, not—well, you know, President Johnson was a very unusual fellow in a conversation. You'd go in with a specific item for the agenda but, depending on his most recent encounter or telephone call or something, you'd find yourself sort of listening.

B: I suppose toward the end that was mostly Viet Nam?

Y: That's right, it really was. And the very thought that anybody wanted peace more than he did was just terribly repulsive to him. The very thought that he didn't want to take that money and put it in the domestic program distressed him no end. I think it's now clear that he began to have real doubts about the war. I thought it took a tremendously big man to acknowledge—in part he really did acknowledge his failures.

B: Sir, the time is just about up here. Is there anything else that stands out that you feel should be said.

Y: I mentioned once before I think the innate compassionate nature of Mr. Johnson. It goes back to a point I was making earlier, the average Southerner, almost without exception, has had contacts with black people. And they know black people. They know the whole range of black people from principals of high schools and businessmen and college presidents right down to the more illiterate. So there is a response based upon feeling tone through actual contact.

The average Northerner—many of them never have contacts with black people, and when they do they are usually not their peers but people who are in very menial jobs. So their reaction to race is ofttimes academic and intellectual and not emotional.

Mr. Johnson brought this quality of emotion to the problem of race relations and was able to translate it to the group situation. I think this is responsible for his success and developed some real conviction and real sincerity. I now begin to feel that President Johnson has always been a liberal, but he was also a politician and he had to be elected from Texas. But the moment he was placed in the position of being President of all the people, I don't know anybody who exhibited a greater respect for the Constitution and the Bill of Rights as far as black people are concerned than did President Johnson. He was not always an easy man to talk to because, as I said, he was often filled with many things he wanted to talk about, but he was a down-to-earth person. I thought in many ways. I never had any trouble getting him. I never abused that, but he seemed appreciative. He did twist my arm on several occasions. He sent me to Viet Nam when I didn't want to go for the inspection trip. He put me on five Presidential Commissions, many of which I didn't want.

B: You went to Viet Nam twice, didn't you?

Y: Yes.

B: Both times at—

Y: No, the first time was privately supported by the Urban League, but the President—I did talk to him before I went and he made all the arrangements for security and made possible for me to see all the people I needed to see. The Ambassador had a luncheon for me, and I met with General Westmoreland, so I got all the courtesies.

B: Anything else, sir?

Y: I think that'll do it.

B: Thank you very much.

ANNETTE CHANDLER

Father Groppi: A Modern Priest Looks at a Racist Society

Denver Center Fourth Estate, March 5, 1969

FATHER GROPPI: A MODERN PRIEST LOOKS AT A RACIST SOCIETY

"We live in a society that says it is wrong for you to stand up for your God-given rights," stated Father James E. Groppi, polemical crusader for human rights, in a February 26 talk at Denver's Crusade for Justice Center.

Groppi, a white Roman Catholic priest, has been a target for abuse concerning his activities with black militants in his role as advisor to the Milwaukee Youth Council of the National Association for the Advancement of Colored People.

During the summer of 1967, the city of Milwaukee experienced racial unrest over a fair housing ordinance. Mrs. Vel Phillips, the city's lone black alderman, had proposed five times that the issue be debated by the 19 member council and each time was defeated.

Throughout the week of August 28, blacks marching in protest of the treatment given the ordinance clashed with white hecklers. As a result of these clashes, Mayor Henry Maier imposed a ban on demonstrations.

On August 31, in defiance of the mayor's edict, Father Groppi led Negro youths in a march on the city hall. Milwaukee police broke up the march and arrested numerous individuals, including Groppi, who was carried bodily to a patrol wagon. The priest was charged with resisting arrest, disorderly conduct, and other similar offenses.

As snowfall blanketed the Denver streets, Groppi fired the capacity crowd by urging Mexicans, blacks, and poor whites to confront the system that is exploiting human beings. He said, "We've reached our breaking point. The man will not listen."

Groppi justified the use of violent tactics by the statement,

"Nothing else has worked. One gets tired of walking picket lines, attending school board meetings, and being carried in paddy wagons to face racist white juries."

He feels white America and the church have no business preaching to him about tactics as long as they remain silent while the government continues to burn up Vietnamese children. Referring to outbursts in Milwaukee, Groppi said, "Our people who participated in that violence did not feel any guilt whatsoever." He continued by saying, "We don't talk about the morality of tactics, we talk about the effectiveness of tactics."

Groppi compared the Milwaukee militants' reaction to seeing "smoke coming up 3rd St." to "the same feeling white America gets when it reads about the Boston Tea Party."

Speaking about education, Groppi said Mexican and black children are being psychologically harmed because "white America teaches our children they are inferior." Groppi believes we live in a system that has accepted a class etiquette and he strongly advocates teaching black culture and black pride to combat the American myth that to be beautiful one must have blue eyes and blonde hair.

When asked his attitude toward cross-bussing in the Denver Public Schools, Groppi replied, "Are you people still talking about that? We fought for that years ago in Milwaukee." He added that integration can be harmful if the system is attempting to transform minority members into white Americans.

Moving next to the subject of police racism, Father Groppi stated, "Police brutality is a reality." He exemplified this statement by relating an experience he witnessed from the back of a Milwaukee paddy wagon. As a group of black children began throwing rocks at the passing vehicle, the verbal reaction of the police in the vehicle was, "Shoot those dirty black bastards, kill those niggers."

Groppi expressed his conception of justice as it exists in America by referring to 15 Milwaukee judges as being members of the Eagles Club, an organization which prohibits black membership. Groppi feels, "If you belong to a racist club, you are a racist."

"When Nixon talks about law and order, he means he's going to keep those niggers in place." Groppi believes President Nixon made his attitudes quite apparent when he failed to appoint a single minority member to the Cabinet. Further illustrating his lack of confidence in Nixon, Father Groppi declared, "A recent Nixon appointee to the Civil Rights Commission once belonged to the Eagle's Club."

The Three-M system of missionaries, money, and marines accompanies government money, said Groppi. He has never been involved in any type of poverty program because "such money comes with conditions attached."

The essence of Father Groppi's philosophy is the Christian belief which ordains all men must love one another. Groppi stated minority members need the dynamic type of leadership exhibited by Christ. "Christ was a revolutionist and was put to death because he dared to confront the system."

Groppi accuses society of crippling people by teaching them to accept injustice, rather than teaching individuals to stand up for their rights. Groppi says one can learn to endure the pain of injustice if it results in involvement. He feels, "Christians should learn to endure the pain of sitting in jail."

Groppi expresses bitter disgust for those who are pretentious about Christianity. He states, "I do not believe in a superfluous and gymnastic performance of rituals that teach a doctrine of escapism. One must stand up for his God-given rights."

Father Groppi's appearance before approximately 500 individuals representing various ethnic and social backgrounds was sponsored by the Crusade for Justice and prefaced with a talk by Corky Gonzales, leader of the Mexican organization. Groppi and Gonzales became acquainted while working in Washington D.C. with the Poor People's Campaign and share similar views on the injustices of society.

Gonzales was followed by entertainment in the form of songs and dances performed by youth involved in the Crusade for Justice organization.

"I INTEND TO STAY HERE AND FIGHT"

SHIRLEY CHISHOLM

Speech at Howard University

Washington, D.C., April 21, 1969

GOOD AFTERNOON, STUDENTS. I usually speak extemporaneously because I like to see what is happening as I try to bring a message to you. But there's so many things that I have on my mind this afternoon, and in the interest of time, as well as to give you the opportunity to ask me any kind of questions you desire, I'm going to read my speech today. At another time, when I'm not so pressured, I will speak extemporaneously on many, many things that I want to bring to you from time to time.

While nothing is easy for the black man in America, neither is anything impossible. Like old man river, we are moving along, and we will continue to move resolutely until our goal of unequivocal equality is attained. We must not be docile, we must not be resigned, nor must we be inwardly bitter. We must see ourselves in an entirely new perspective, and we cannot sit in our homes waiting for someone to reach out and do things for us.

Every tomorrow has two handles. We can take hold of the handle of anxiety or the handle of faith. And the first battle is won, my brothers and sisters, when we fight for belief in ourselves and find that it has come to us while we are still battling. We must not allow petty things to color our lives and stimulate them into vast proportions of evil. To dwell on every slight and clutch it close to our breast and nourish it will corrode our thinking. We're on the move now, and as Frederick Douglass said, "Power concedes nothing without a struggle." It never has, and it never will.

The United States can no longer afford the luxury of costly morally, religiously, and ethically wrong racial discrimination. For America needs all of her citizens with their abilities developed to make a fuller contribution to the future. Many problems scream loudly in this country: the thousands of black citizens disenfranchised, living under degrading conditions; the millions of poor throughout this nation, white and black, who lack the bare rudiments for fruitful living; the rapidly growing numbers of children caught in a web of disillusionment which destroys their will to learn; the increasing numbers of aged who do not even look forward to rest or retirement.

And despite the historic legislation in our cities and our states, nearly eleven million black citizens today still live in basic ghetto communities of our cities. From decades of nonparticipation or only modest participation, the black man has within the last two years shifted his goal to full political participation for full American citizenship. And while on the picket line, at the lunch counter, and in the bus and the store boycott, the black man came face to face with the full breadth and weight of the power and influence exercised by local and state governments, intertwining and often stifling the protests.

Indeed, a principal by-product of the American civil rights movement has been the awakening of the black citizen to his awesome political potential. And just as the picket line and the lunch counter demonstrations and the boycotts were dramatic and effective weapons of protest for the civil rights movement, the polling place is the new phase in the new thrust of the black man's bid for equality of opportunity. "Power concedes nothing." How else can any man rise to power, and hold sway over millions or tens of thousands, except by smothering dissenting voices?

Freedom is an endless horizon, and there are many roads that lead to it. We must walk arm in arm with other men, and we must struggle toward goals which are commonly desired and sound. We must give and lend to the youth a stronger voice and encourage their individuality. We must look to the schools and constantly work for their improvement, because that is where the future leadership of the country will be coming from, to a large extent—particularly in the black communities.

The leaders of today in the black communities must be able to place the goal of freedom ahead of personal ambition. The truly dedicated leader follows what his conscience tells him is best for his people. For whatever else the black man is, he is American. Or whatever he is to become—integrated, unintegrated, or disintegrated—he will become it in America. Only a minority of black people have ever succumbed to the temptation to seek greener pastures of another country or another ideology.

You know, so often nowadays we hear people say that we should go back to Africa, we should establish ourselves in Africa, or we should do a lot of other things. Well, if people want to go back to Africa, or people want to go to Africa just like people want to go to Europe, that's their own personal business. And you do it voluntarily. I don't intend to go to Africa. I intend to stay here and fight, because the blood, sweat, and tears of our forefathers are rooted in the soil of this country. And the reason that Wall Street is the great financial center that it is today is because of the blood, sweat, and tears of your forefathers who worked in the tobacco and the cotton fields. And now because this nation is a mercantile nation, and is enjoying the efforts and the labor of many of our forefathers, many of us want to escape and many of us want to run away. We didn't ask to be brought here in the first place. We came here shackled in chains at our ankles and our wrists, and we were a cheap supply of labor, and we worked. We did many, many things.

And now that the problem is becoming a little bit too hot, everybody has all kinds of solutions for us. If you want to go to Africa willingly, you can go, just like other people in this country go to Europe, willingly. Nobody has to tell you or create something special for you. Our roots are here. Our blood and our sweat and our tears are here. And we're going to stay here. And we're going to fight.

For years, thousands of people from the European shores have been coming to this land. They came here hardly able to speak the English language. But they came here and acquired the technological know-how, and they acquired the necessary skills that enabled them to become assimilated in the American culture, and to move out and up into the American middle class. Hardly speakin' English.

But we who have been born here, we who have been citizens by birth, have not been able to become fully assimilated in the American culture because of an unmistakable and almost insurmountable barrier, that just will not disappear, because color doesn't disappear. And so, it behooves us to stay here and to fight. We have made this land, even though we have not been given the recognition, and nobody has to create any little nation or any little group, and send us scuttling off. We want to go, we go. Freedom of choice.

The black man's total commitment to America indicates that the prospect ahead does seem bright. It is true that we are angry about our present plight, for we measure this country not by her achievements but by her potential.

"Black Power." Oh how that phrase upsets so many people. Let me give you my definition of Black Power. Black Power is no different from any other kind of power in this country. Just as I told you a few moments ago, the people from European countries came here and found their way in the American scheme of things, after they were able to get a certain kind of economic and financial security. The next thing that they became interested in was to achieve power to control their own destinies. And so, for example, in New York City you had, at one time, the Germans in ascendency, then you had the Italians, then you had the Jewish people and the Irish—every other group moving out to get power to control their destinies.

But nobody had to label that as "White Power," because it was understood and assumed that it would always be White Power. Now that we are beginning to do what they have been telling us to do for a long time—take ourselves up by our bootstraps and begin to consolidate our efforts and move out like every other group has moved out in America—everybody is so hysterical and panic stricken because of the adjective that precedes the word power—"black." You know it would have been hoped in this country that we would never have to use the word "black" before the word "power," because America has been built on a series of immigrants coming into this land, rising up and moving out in terms of achieving power to control their lives.

But you see, they made one mistake. They thought that, because we had been relegated for such a long time to a subservient position, and that we had accepted, rather docilely, the position of second-class citizenship, that we would never rise up, that we would never speak out. And so, when we began to say to the world, in our own way, that we too know and understand what other groups have been doing for a long time in this country. Consolidating and using our power and our efforts to move up—and we want the world to know that it is Black Power, because we have learned what other groups have been learning and doing for a long time in this country. And people just have to get used to that word, "Black Power."

It is, indeed, a reality that is gaining in emotional intensity, if not always rational clarity. The harnessing and the solidification of Afro-American power, however, is constantly being dissipated with factionalism. Internal struggle for power by one group over another. This behavior is no different from that of the whites. But we as a people cannot afford the luxury of fighting among ourselves if we are going to make real progress.

And black people will gain only as much as they can through their ability to organize independent bases of economic and political power—through boycotts, electoral activity, rent strikes, et cetera. Black power is concerned with organizing the rage of black people. Organizing the rage. And it's putting new hard questions and demands to white America. We will build a new sense of community among our people. We will foster a bond between those who have made it and those on the bottom.

As Charles Hamilton says, "Alienation will be overcome, and trust will be restored." And let us remember that a great people are not affected by each puff of wind that blows ill. We must fight, constantly, for belief in ourselves. And above all we must harken back to the days of darkness, when Frederick Douglass, the great abolitionist, even in those times, echoed the famous phrase that has come realistically to haunt the black people today in America, as they fight to enter the political, economic, and social mainstream of these United States, the land of their birth. And that phrase is, "Power concedes nothing."

Let me say to you, my brothers and sisters, that until we can organize to create black unity with an economic base, until we can develop a plan for action to achieve the goals to make us totally independent, and not have to look to the Man in order to live, we're not liberated. We must become doers, and producers, in the system, in order to be able to control our own destinies. We have the potential, but we must consolidate all of our strength for eventual liberation.

And the black man's responsibility today is to establish his own values and his own goals. In doing so, he will be affecting the larger American society, of which he's a part. The black man and the black woman cannot, however, act alone. They must act within a community or family, job, and neighborhood. Let us not kid ourselves into thinking that the white man is suddenly going to make the choice readily available. The new day will come with honest black pride, and unified black action and education, politics, and economics. Why it has taken us so long to discover this simple approach is one of the mysteries of the twentieth century. The Jews, the Poles, and the Slovaks discovered this phenomenon years ago. Compassion and understanding may moralize the system periodically, but it will never make it honest, just, and decent for us. Only the application of real economic and political power can achieve that goal.

"Black is beautiful." You hear that phrase a great deal. Black is beautiful in what you do to contribute to the building of a strong black community throughout this country. The time, now, is to counteract the poison that has inflicted ignorance and hatred in the American social and political body. In seeking your identity, you can explore your African heritage, not simply by adopting the outward manifestations of African dress and appearance, but by going beyond the roots of that superficial type of thing, that many of us might be doing, to learn about contemporary Africa and its people.

I talk with so many people who affect these manifestations, and they don't know anything about Africa. Learn about contemporary Africa and its people. And appreciate that you and they have tremendous historical and cultural links, that there is much that we can offer to each other's growth. Nineteen sixty-eight has clearly and painfully demonstrated the degree of stress and alienation that afflicts all of our institutions. Our young people have questioned the validity of traditional university education. They and many of their elders have fought against the tragic depletion of human and material resources in a complex Asian conflict that seems only to attract simple answers. The fabric of our incomplete nationhood has been torn down the seam of black/white confrontation in this country.

We need a liberated and developing black community in America that, once it has fully discovered its inherent worth and power, turns to the even greater task of protecting and enlarging upon its triumphs by further enriching an American culture that already has drawn so much from the black life stream. We need black businessmen who can rise beyond the local tax-and-spend, and make dollars as well as sense for a black community that plays a full part in all levels of government. And there can be no understanding of the recent rioting in northern black ghettos, or any realistic analysis of its impact upon the civil rights movement in the nation, without the realization that black citizens have just, pressing, and long-neglected grievances.

We do not erupt simply for exercise. We do not curse imaginary obstacles and procedures. Our resentments are not the product of a momentary flare-up but of years of postponement, denial, insult, and abuse. The conscience of political democracy cries out for an end to false democracy. It is just and inevitable that black Americans are tired of being governed by laws they had no part in making and by officials in whose choice they have no voice. It is idiotic to labor under the old white-supremacist supposition that a white man knows what's good for the black man. The nonwhite American is saying we no longer want tokens which will only take us on a subway ride. We want some bread, some meat, and a slice—not a sliver—of the pie, the same ways any other ethnic group receives under this system.

In humanitarian terms, the war on poverty must be fought wherever it is found. Part of the battle must be fought with the establishment of the hundred-dollar-per-week minimum for all Americans, so that subsidization by welfare authorities is drastically reduced and a man is paid a decent, living wage in today's automated society. In today's most affluent society, if you please. The goal must be $2.50 per hour—a national minimum for all Americans. This reduces poverty.

More crassly put, we will be able to get more people off welfare and relief rolls and on to tax rolls. We can get them out of the alleys of society and into the mainstream of productive society, and productive employment, where they can support themselves and their dependents, with dignity and pride. Where they can contribute to the growth and strength of the nation's economy.

The war on poverty must be fought with the inalienable right of every working American. The right to collective bargaining to protect themselves from human exploitation and human abuse. The grape worker in California, the migrant farm worker in New York, the rural blacks working in the South, the nonprofessional service workers in institutions are examples of the system which, year in and year out, relegates these people to the most shameful, subservient conditions as part of the labor force—the most important force, which keeps American business moving in this country. Our job is not to make poverty more endurable but to get rid of it!

The poor whites and the hungry blacks in the rural South —there's a serious question of the capacity of the American system itself to provide a decent living for the unfavored. And I think we can, if we will move forward in the way of plain justice, just plain justice, and decency, for the low man on the totem pole in America. It does no good to have the right to sit in the front of a bus if you don't have the bus fare. Or the right to sit down at a lunch counter and buy a cup of coffee if you don't have the dime to pay for it. As one leader said, "A mouth full of civil rights and an empty stomach, or a banner reading 'We shall overcome' on a wall that is full of holes or a floor where the rats are playing games with each other [inaudible] . . ."

Yes, the revolution of 1968–69 is about freedom, my friends. It's activists who speak to ghetto towns and tell it like it is. It's about parents who refuse to go on having their children programmed to deny their black identity in order to enter a society where the basic color scheme is white. It is about manhood and the assertion of self. The keys to the new mood in black America are the feelings that the nation does not really wish to do away with its dual society. Well, blacks then must have the dominant role in determining their own destiny. The nonviolent tactic has not always prevented the brutalization of the inhabitants of the ghetto, where the black people resisted, or the brutality of the Bull Connors, the dogs and the cattle prods, the murderers and the church bombings, as they insisted upon their rights as free men. Or as they demanded for their children a human dignity which American racism sought to deny all black people.

These are all testimonies that we will not turn back. This nation, if it desires to grow, if it wants to continue to remain among the leading nations of this world, it is going to have to make sure that it utilizes the fullest of all the capacities of all of its citizens. There is no more time. Time's running out. There is no more time for debate in the Congress on civil rights bills. No more time for rich bishops to keep the church doors closed. No more time for unions to discriminate against black and Puerto Rican workers, both overtly and covertly.

We are living in an epoch of liberation of oppressed and deprived people in this country, which has always said it wants to make the world safe for democracy. Charity begins at home first. And the reality of the two Americas—one white, comfortable, and free; and the other black, fettered, and poor—must now become in reality the dream that the late Dr. Martin Luther King gave his life for. This greatest man, this saint must not be permitted to have died in vain. We've seen fit to introduce a bill in Congress to make his birth a national holiday, when every American will cease to work on this day to take stock of himself and the concept of human brotherhood. And every American shall see that a nation of men of different origins can abide together in peace, democracy, and equality.

In conclusion, let me say that the hour is late. Jargon is of no use any longer. We have been analyzed, surveyed, graphed, depicted. We have loads of documents and information on us as a people, on the shelves of the different departments of this country. Everyone knows about us. We don't need that anymore. The time now is for action.

Young people, I believe in you. I truly believe in you. I happen to feel that, although I'm approaching middle age—I'm now forty-four, and they say that in four years I'll be called a middle-aged woman—I don't feel like that. I happen to feel this community is going to be ultimately saved by the students, the young people. We may not always approve of some of your methods, because we realize that youth is often in a hurry and wants to get things done. But we know that you are tuned in to what's wrong with a country that has been talking about democracy but has not been practicing it. So allow me, as one of those who are moving into the middle-age category, to give you some ideas and suggestions. I know from time to time we will disagree, but healthy disagreement is all right. I know that you are going to be the inheritors of this country. And so we've got to depend on you even though you may not always agree with everything that we say. Thank you for giving me the opportunity to bring you this message.

NICK KOTZ

Future of Civil Rights Worries Old Guard as Gains Are Noted

Washington Post, December 25, 1972

FUTURE OF CIVIL RIGHTS WORRIES OLD GUARD AS GAINS ARE NOTED

AUSTIN, Tex.—The old guard of the civil rights movement gathered recently around Lyndon Johnson and Earl Warren to recall nostalgically the historic progress won for minorities in the 1960s. But the meeting represented less a victory celebration of the past than a worried questioning about the future.

The dominant theme of the two-day symposium, which marked the public opening of Lyndon Johnson's civil rights papers, was a questioning of whether the legal victories over segregation and discrimination can now be translated into economic betterment for the lives of millions of still poor blacks, Mexican Americans, Indians and Puerto Ricans.

If the civil rights movement is to have a future, most of the conferees agreed, it must now deal with problems of economic and political power, with jobs, housing, health care and welfare.

The hard-won right to sit at a lunch counter is not worth much, it was agreed, unless you have the money to buy a hamburger.

This switching from legal to economic issues in the name of "civil rights" is a transition that some have not made. Burke Marshall, deputy dean of the Yale Law School, sought to draw clear distinctions between old civil rights legal victories involving discrimination and segregation and present economic issues which he said "involve distribution of wealth."

ISSUES MERGED

But these issues have merged, even in the minds of such pragmatic establishment leaders as Clarence Mitchell, Washington lobbyist for the NAACP. Economic and civil rights problems cannot be separated, he said, if there are not enough good jobs available for all. Mitchell said an inadequate job supply inflames old civil rights passions because it pits blacks seeking a first opportunity against whites who also need work.

If there is impatience with progress made, the conferees suggested, it is partly because few young blacks remember the tumultuous events of the 1950s and 1960s which finally tore down segregation in the South and brought marked economic gains as well.

The income of blacks rose at a faster rate than that of whites in the 1960s and young black couples in the North earned as much as young white couples. Against those marks of progress, blacks point out that the dollar spread between the income of blacks and whites actually increased, and that young black couples kept pace with their white peers only because more black wives worked. And statistical economic gains do not brighten the deteriorating central city slums.

There was general agreement that racial minorities will achieve adequate material gains relative to the white majority only if the nation creates millions of new public service jobs, raises the minimum wage, redistributes wealth and tax burdens through tax reform, and invests more in health care, education and a reformed welfare system.

WARNING SOUNDED

Every speaker, ranging from former President Johnson and former Supreme Court Justice Warren to young black leaders Julian Bond and Vernon Jordan warned ominously that if the civil rights revolution dies without further concrete economic gains for the minority poor, then death will come with a bang, and not a whimper.

But discussions about means to further progress produced fewer answers than problem areas—how to create a new American coalition to support government programs to help the poor, how to stop bitter fighting between minority groups for economic and political gains, how to reconcile the sometimes conflicting aims of integration and black power, how to find leaders who can inspire both the poor and a frightened, angry middle class.

Julian Bond, the young black legislator from Georgia, said

blacks must depend increasingly on achieving their goals by organizing themselves for political action.

Blacks then must seek coalitions, said Bond, "but the question is with whom?" He said the 1972 election showed that coalition is possible "with no one, at least for now," since blacks were isolated as the only group to vote strongly for the losing candidate, George McGovern.

HUMPHREY'S VIEW

Bond did not note, however, that an effective coalition had elected black minister Andrew Young to Congress from an Atlanta district which is only 38 per cent black. And Sen. Hubert Humphrey (D-Minn.) held out hope for further black political gains, pointing to polls showing most whites now willing to vote for black candidates.

Humphrey said that a majority coalition in Congress and the nation can be created only by broadening the entire concept of civil rights to include the needs of most Americans for better health care, education and more jobs.

Yet Bond questioned how emphasis can be shifted to color blind economic issues when President Nixon successfully pursued a political strategy in which those economic problems were interpreted in racial terms. As a result, he said, Mr. Nixon "recruited a frightened constituency against the forgotten."

Charting a future course for civil rights is more difficult today, several leaders said, because it is far more difficult to identify the enemy.

SIMPLER BATTLE

The battle was in some ways simpler, said Urban League director Jordan, "when the President was a friend of the movement and the villains were clearly identifiable sheriffs whose snapping police dogs and vicious cattle prods won us headlines and friends."

"Woolworth's (lunch counter) was the enemy in the 1960s," said Bond, "but who is the enemy today? Is it the local manager who won't give you a job as an assistant manager, is it the corporate structure in New York or is it the stockholders?"

And there was remembrance by the civil rights leaders that despite their occasional bitter disagreements with the volatile

President Johnson, they then had the access to White House power which they now lack with President Richard Nixon.

"Oh my God, how I wish he was in the White House now," said Bond, who described the White House under Richard Nixon as having become "Uncle Strom's Cabin."

Interestingly, the two most prestigious conferees, former Chief Justice Warren and Mr. Johnson, stressed the past and present problems of a national history of white racism.

Warren emphasized that the U.S. Supreme Court, in "racist construction of our Constitution," had erased the victory of the Civil War and brought black people in the American South "close to a condition of apartheid in the 20s and 30s of this 20th century."

Progress came in the 1960s, Warren said, when the court, the Congress and the President pursued common goals. He implied that such joint leadership is lacking today.

Mr. Johnson concentrated his entire speech on the theme that being "black in a white society" has given the black masses such an "unequal history" that compensatory measures must be initiated by white America to now ensure that blacks get into college, overcome educational handicaps to become professionals, and gain promotions up the job ladder, not just a precarious perch on the bottom rung.

But Mr. Johnson's analysis suggests the use of some sort of quotas, written or understood, and the quota issue simmered in the private conversations at this conference of liberals. Many of the lawyers and activists, particularly Jewish ones, who fought for civil rights gains in the 1960s, stated quietly and privately their flat opposition to quotas.

The conference presented an historic record of the past and a possible preview of the future in civil rights. Glimpses of the past could be found in the collection of Lyndon Johnson's civil rights papers which are contained in the giant library that is a monument to Mr. Johnson's out-sized Texas ego and to his accomplishments.

Although the civil rights papers are filled with heaps of congratulatory letters to LBJ, one can also find memoranda among them representing the tedious work that went into passage of the 1964, 1965 and 1968 Civil Rights Acts.

The voices of the future came from two articulate black women who have just been elected to Congress—Barbara Jordan from Houston, Texas, and Yvonne Brathwaite Burke from California. Lyndon Johnson said their victories gave him the greatest pleasure since he has left the presidency. The conferees agreed that the election of these two women and of other blacks to public office provides new hope with which to face the uncertain future of civil rights in America.

RON HUTSON

Common Fear, Safety for Students, Ripples through North Dorchester, Roxbury as Busing Becomes Real

Boston Globe, June 27, 1974

"I want to go to high school, but I'll quit before I go to South Boston and get killed. I'll get a job, I guess. Hell, I don't know what I'll do. But I'd rather get a job than have to swim across the river everyday."

. . . Ernest Hurd, English High student.

COMMON FEAR, SAFETY FOR STUDENTS, RIPPLES THROUGH NORTH DORCHESTER, ROXBURY AS BUSING BECOMES REAL

Ernest, Patricia and Kenneth Hurd, who live with their mother in the predominantly black Columbia Point housing project in North Dorchester, have been assigned to South Boston High school next fall under the state's racial imbalance plan.

Fifteen-year-old Ernest, serious and articulate, vows he won't go, although he has done well at the 90 percent black English High school and plans to go to college.

"I want to go to high school, but I'll quit before I go to South Boston and get killed," said the lean, dark-skinned youth the other day as he balanced himself on his elbows on the kitchen table and stared blankly out of the window at the dingy brown brick buildings.

"I'll get a job, I guess. Hell, I don't know what I'll do. But I'd rather get a job than have to swim across the river everyday."

Patricia, also an English High sophomore, and Kenneth, an eighth grader at the McCormack intermediate school on Columbia Point, also are afraid of traveling to South Boston. But Patricia will probably attend school there anyway.

"I'll probably go to school if I have to," said 16-year-old Patricia. "But we should be allowed to go to school where we want to go. Isn't that what public school means?"

Kenneth, at 14 less certain of his options, added: "I haven't made up my mind about it yet. I'm really mixed up about this thing."

The split in the Hurd family is characteristic of the way in which the racial imbalance plan and busing have divided blacks and whites, politicians and constituents, parents and children in North Dorchester and Roxbury—the two communities with the largest concentration of blacks in Greater Boston.

Blacks in the two communities have given the strongest support for the nine-year-old Racial Imbalance Law, while white parents in both areas have been outspoken in their opposition to the law.

The division and much of the confusion over the racial imbalance plan and busing persists, though Federal Judge W. Arthur Garrity Jr. has ruled the Boston School system is unconstitutionally segregated and has ordered implementation of the state's racial imbalance plan.

Two weeks before the ruling a school department employee who has worked closely with the imbalance plan and who asked not to be named said: "I really don't think the parents really believe this plan is for real."

BELIEVE NOW

Judge Garrity's ruling has apparently made believers out of most parents, but it has not changed their thinking about the plan.

"Just because the judge ruled . . . that doesn't mean I have to agree with what he says," said Mrs. Maude Hurd, mother of Ernest, Patricia and Kenneth. "I haven't changed my feelings. I'm still against busing my children into South Boston."

Although both Roxbury and North Dorchester have sizable black populations, basically they are different. North Dorchester is a racially mixed community that includes everything from affluent white sections to poor black and Spanish-speaking neighborhoods. Roxbury is almost exclusively poor and black.

But behind the apprehension and confusion in both communities is a common fear by both black and white parents for the safety of their children if they are sent to schools where they will be in a minority.

Mrs. Barbara Halliday is a white mother of two small children who attend the racially balanced Holland elementary school near their home in the Mount Bowdoin area of North Dorchester.

"All my life we have heard that blacks are lazy and they are all on welfare," she said. "Blacks and whites both have stereotypes of each other. But to put my son in a classroom with people who will yell 'whitey' and 'pig' at him . . . well, I think that is unfair."

To residents of the Columbia Point section of North Dorchester, the problem is similar perhaps, but more pressing.

It is no secret that few Columbia Point residents ever travel to South Boston and few South Boston residents ever go into the Columbia Point housing project. While South Boston and black Columbia Point may be the two most racially antagonistic neighborhoods in Boston.

Yet, under the state's controversial racial imbalance plan, high school, intermediate and elementary school students from "The Point" and other North Dorchester neighborhoods and Roxbury will attend school with South Boston youths.

Of the two neighborhoods, perhaps North Dorchester is most affected by the racial imbalance plan.

North Dorchester is a changing community that defies characterization. Its exclusively white, affluent neighborhoods, like the stately old Jones Hill section and parts of Meeting House Hill, abut its poorer neighborhoods like Upham's corner and Codman Square and Columbia Point.

For the most part, its narrow and congested streets are lined with two-to-four unit wood frame homes built during the late 1800's. While there are pockets of carefully kept two-family homes, increasingly vacant and abandoned homes are becoming the community's number one menace, as absentee landlords replace the old homeowners.

WORKINGMAN'S AREA

Basically, then, North Dorchester is a middle to lower income workingman's neighborhood, extending

North Dorchester registered the greatest increase in the city in nonwhite population between 1960 and 1970, according to a survey prepared by the United Community Planning Corp., research division of the Massachusetts Bay United Way.

Some 43,541 of the community's 101,386 residents are nonwhite.

During the past five years black and Spanish-speaking families have settled mostly in the poorer housing along the Blue Hill avenue and Dudley street spurs out of predominantly black Roxbury.

Increasingly, North Dorchester is becoming racially tense, as more black families move in to become homeowners and renters, and white families watch the rapid change in what was formerly their neighborhood.

In fact, many whites, too poor or too attached to their neighborhood to follow their neighbors' flight to the suburbs, have watched themselves become minorities in neighborhoods that were once all white.

They don't like to admit it, but many whites are afraid of becoming white minorities. The busing issue is a natural in their desperate battle to hold the neighborhood line.

One apprehensive Dorchester white in a minority is Mrs. Sharon Linteris, a young housewife who moved onto Bowdoin street in North Dorchester from Virginia seven years ago. Then, the neighborhood was all white. Now it is nearly all black.

Mrs. Linteris has two children, four and two years old. "I've become a minority in my own neighborhood. Now I know how black people feel when they are in a minority," she said.

"My four-year-old girl asked me the other day 'Gee, mommy, I want to be brown too. Why am I not brown like my friends?' I told her we live in a brown neighborhood, honey."

Mrs. Linteris, a graduate of a Southern university and admittedly a liberal on racial issues, is apprehensive about her child attending a predominantly black school, though she says she does not mind living close to blacks.

"I just don't want my child to be a minority," she declared. She and her husband plan to purchase a home in Boston's Roxbury Crossing section later this year, she said.

But many other white North Dorchester parents, like Mrs. Dorothy Flint, of Mount Everett street, take a more traditional line.

"I don't mind my children going to school with black

children. But nobody is going to tell me where I have to send my children. The state has no right to tell me where my child goes to school," she said.

Saturday, after Judge Garrity ordered implementation of the state's racial imbalance plan Mrs. Flint said: "I guess I always knew there would be busing. I knew because the people of Boston just didn't have a chance."

Two of her five children attend the Holland elementary school. Barring any last minute changes in the imbalance plan, which school department officials hint may be forthcoming, Mrs. Flint's children will remain in the Holland school next year.

Unlike North Dorchester, Roxbury is almost exclusively poor and black. Roxbury, the core of Boston, suffers from many of the same problems as North Dorchester, but the problems are more severe.

For decades, Roxbury neighborhoods have been marked by vacant and abandoned housing, congested streets, absentee landlords, and a crippling inability to draw investors to the area.

Some 63,000 persons make Roxbury home; 41,000 are black. Median annual income is $6588 for Roxbury's 20,676 households, the lowest in Boston except for the South End.

Like most inner city neighborhoods on the decline, Roxbury lost 26 percent of its population between 1960 and 1970. But statistics from a survey by the United Community Planning Corp. show Roxbury's nonwhite population rose by some 12 percent in the same period.

Parents in Roxbury have been curiously quiet on the racial imbalance plan and the issue of forced busing. Black leaders attribute the relative silence to the fact that the state Board of Education's plan affects few elementary and intermediate schools in central Roxbury.

Other sources say Roxbury parents have been silent because they feel their children have little to lose with busing.

Isaac Graves, 26, a Roxbury resident and newly appointed Roxbury Little City Hall manager, explained: "It's part of the traditional education that we (blacks) got from being in the South. Black people are willing to get on a bus and get a good education. But black parents are saying to the Boston School

Committee, 'Show me that my kid will be safe. If the kid sitting next to my kid isn't going to grab him off the bus, then this busing thing is cool.'"

But while some Roxbury residents apparently feel busing may improve their children's education, there are others who feel the racial imbalance plan is part of an effort to force black children to quit school.

One of those persons is Mrs. Eta Edlow, of 131 Eustis st., Roxbury. Her 17-year-old nephew, Jesse James, a sophomore at English High, lives with her. Jesse has been assigned to South Boston High. He, too, says he will not be bused to South Boston next fall.

"If our black children do quit school rather than let themselves be bused, then some brain out there will say 'Ah Ha! That's just what we want.' Then those people (white students and school administrators) will have a fistful of dollars that the black kids won't benefit from," said Mrs. Edlow.

English High opened last September with a nearly all black student population. The school department projects an enrollment for next year of about 2070 students, of which about 42 percent will be black.

"If the school department forces these kids to go to schools where they don't want to go, they will quit. English is a brand new school. Eventually there won't be any black kids in that school," Mrs. Edlow said.

Nevertheless, it is from Roxbury and North Dorchester that the main supporters of the Racial Imbalance Law have been elected and re-elected.

And it is men and women like State Rep. Doris Bunte (D-Boston), Royal L. Bolling Sr., (D-Boston), Royal L. Bolling Jr., (D-Dorchester), Melvin H. King (D-Boston) and William Owens (D-Mattapan) who have worked to block repeal of the Imbalance Law and insisted on implementation of busing.

SPLIT SLOWLY SURFACING

Other black leaders and parents in North Dorchester and Roxbury are beginning to question the stand their elected representatives have taken. As more mothers realize that busing may come and the fear for their children's safety becomes a reality, the split is slowly coming to the surface.

Mrs. Sandra Young is the education coordinator for the Columbia Point Area Planning Action Council (APAC) and a spokesman for angry Columbia Point mothers.

"Black politicians are pushing for busing. But how can you as a black politician push for busing black kids into South Boston. It just doesn't make sense," Mrs. Young said.

"Tell me why . . . why are the two most racially tense areas in this city like South Boston and Columbia Point being put one against another in this imbalance plan?

"The real question is when are people going to start taking into consideration the education at the end of the bus ride. We (Columbia Point parents) fought damned hard to get good education at the McCormack and Dever Schools (on Columbia Point). Do you think we'll be able to go over to South Boston to make sure our kids are getting a quality education? Not without a suit of armor," Mrs. Young said.

But the politicians reply that most black parents will send their children on the bus because they feel white schools, even though in equally disadvantaged neighborhoods, offer a better education.

"They (black parents) don't dig that South Boston thing at all," said the senior Bolling: "It's going to be very touchy if anything goes wrong over there. But they'll even go to Southie (South Boston High). Very reluctantly. But they'll go."

Ernest Hurd and other students who live in the Columbia Point projects are less certain. They have heard about the graffiti painted in bold black letters on the rear wall of South Boston High. It reads: "Kill Niggers."

The fact that the school department has announced that parents will be hired to ride the buses to South Boston and monitor the halls to insure safety is no comfort to him, Ernest says.

"I don't see why they have to take me out of English. We (blacks) fought damned hard for that school. There is going to be a lot of people ending up in the hospital. That's all I can say."

“A GIANT STEP BACKWARDS” ON SCHOOL DESEGREGATION

THURGOOD MARSHALL
from *Dissent in* Milliken v. Bradley

July 25, 1974

MR. JUSTICE MARSHALL, with whom MR. JUSTICE DOUGLAS, MR. JUSTICE BRENNAN, and MR. JUSTICE WHITE join, dissenting.

In *Brown* v. *Board of Education*, 347 U. S. 483 (1954), this Court held that segregation of children in public schools on the basis of race deprives minority group children of equal educational opportunities and therefore denies them the equal protection of the laws under the Fourteenth Amendment. This Court recognized then that remedying decades of segregation in public education would not be an easy task. Subsequent events, unfortunately, have seen that prediction bear bitter fruit. But however imbedded old ways, however ingrained old prejudices, this Court has not been diverted from its appointed task of making “a living truth” of our constitutional ideal of equal justice under law. *Cooper* v. *Aaron*, 358 U. S. 1, 20 (1958).

After 20 years of small, often difficult steps toward that great end, the Court today takes a giant step backwards. Notwithstanding a record showing widespread and pervasive racial segregation in the educational system provided by the State of Michigan for children in Detroit, this Court holds that the District Court was powerless to require the State to remedy its constitutional violation in any meaningful fashion. Ironically purporting to base its result on the principle that the scope of the remedy in a desegregation case should be determined by the nature and the extent of the constitutional violation, the Court’s answer is to provide no remedy at all for the violation proved in this case, thereby guaranteeing that Negro children in Detroit will receive the same separate and inherently unequal education in the future as they have been unconstitutionally afforded in the past.

I cannot subscribe to this emasculation of our constitutional guarantee of equal protection of the laws and must respectfully dissent. Our precedents, in my view, firmly establish that where, as here, state-imposed segregation has been demonstrated, it becomes the duty of the State to eliminate root and branch all vestiges of racial discrimination and to achieve the greatest possible degree of actual desegregation. I agree with both the District Court and the Court of Appeals that, under the facts of this case, this duty cannot be fulfilled unless the State of Michigan involves outlying metropolitan area school districts in its desegregation remedy. Furthermore, I perceive no basis either in law or in the practicalities of the situation justifying the State's interposition of school district boundaries as absolute barriers to the implementation of an effective desegregation remedy. Under established and frequently used Michigan procedures, school district lines are both flexible and permeable for a wide variety of purposes, and there is no reason why they must now stand in the way of meaningful desegregation relief.

The rights at issue in this case are too fundamental to be abridged on grounds as superficial as those relied on by the majority today. We deal here with the right of all of our children, whatever their race, to an equal start in life and to an equal opportunity to reach their full potential as citizens. Those children who have been denied that right in the past deserve better than to see fences thrown up to deny them that right in the future. Our Nation, I fear, will be ill served by the Court's refusal to remedy separate and unequal education, for unless our children begin to learn together, there is little hope that our people will ever learn to live together.

Desegregation is not and was never expected to be an easy task. Racial attitudes ingrained in our Nation's childhood and adolescence are not quickly thrown aside in its middle years. But just as the inconvenience of some cannot be allowed to stand in the way of the rights of others, so public opposition, no matter how strident, cannot be permitted to divert this Court from the enforcement of the constitutional principles at issue in this case. Today's holding, I fear, is more a reflection of a perceived public mood that we have gone far enough in enforcing the Constitution's guarantee of equal justice than it is the product of neutral principles of law. In the short run, it may seem to be the easier course to allow our great metropolitan areas to be divided up each into two cities—one white, the other black—but it is a course, I predict, our people will ultimately regret. I dissent.

"THE WHOLE TRAGIC AFFAIR"

THOMAS PETTIGREW

Race, Schools and Riots in Boston

New Society, November 1974

RACE, SCHOOLS AND RIOTS IN BOSTON

This autumn's riots against school busing are nationally significant for Americans. They reflect the weakened drive for racial justice, which Ford inherits from Nixon.

THE HEADLINES of strife this autumn over the racial desegregation of Boston's schools recall similar stories emanating from the American south over a decade ago. But race relations in the United States have changed sharply over these years; and the Boston events accurately reflect the political climate that now prevails after a half-decade of negative national leadership.

The drama began to take shape last June. Federal District Court Judge W. Arthur Garrity ruled that Boston had deliberately maintained a racially segregated public school system. He ordered that a desegregation plan, already devised by the state of Massachusetts, be carried out in September as a first step. This decision came after a long, intense, but little-publicised trial initiated by black parents and the local branch of the National Association for the Advancement of Coloured People. The evidence of intentional apartheid was even more blatant than usual in such cases. Judge Garrity found that both teachers and students had been segregated through a variety of attendance and grading patterns. Consequently, the plaintiffs were entitled in his view to every legal means of relief, no matter how "distasteful." Garrity's opinion was crisp and pointed but hardly a surprise. He followed almost to the letter the legal precedents established by the federal judiciary over the last two decades.

The choice of the state plan as an interim solution, however, was unfortunate. It had been drawn up under a state law for "racial balance," and had been subject to severe restrictions that do not apply under federal law. Thus, the plan is modest, reducing majority-black schools only from 68 to 40 and transporting just 6,000 out of the system's 94,000 pupils. It is also inefficient in its use of transport and it pairs some schools that lack middle class students. The state plan, then, raised cries of "throwing poor blacks together with poor whites, while sparing the affluent suburbs."

The summer was tense. City police and the mass media planned their strategy; an information telephone centre was established to dispel rumours; and segregationist forces organised under the banner of an ad hoc group called ROAR (Restore Our Alienated Rights). Many of ROAR's leaders were officers in the Boston Home and School Association, a parental organisation with units in each school. This link gave ROAR what resistance groups in other American cities have lacked: an established organisation that provides both legitimation and lists of names. Such a base is a sociological necessity for the sustained opposition that ROAR has managed to mount throughout the autumn.

As September approached, ROAR called for a massive boycott of the schools by white students. Three days before the schools opened, a large "anti-busing" march and rally was held. Before this gathering, Senator Edward Kennedy bravely but foolishly attempted to speak in favor of obeying the federal court order. He was greeted by an angry mob that refused to let him speak, pelted him with refuse, and jeered him with some of the vilest, most personal taunts experienced in American politics.

When schools opened on 12 September, the pupil boycott was partially successful and violence predictably erupted. System-wide attendance stood at 65 per cent and the majority of schools operated normally. But trouble centred at South Boston High School, where fewer than 100 students attended out of the 1,500 expected. White crowds, composed largely of women, shouted "Animals!" and worse at the black students as they arrived by bus. Later several buses were badly stoned by white teenage gangs, and numerous black children were seriously cut by the flying window glass. The crisis caused the black community to re-evaluate its position; but after a mass meeting with Mayor Kevin White the community agreed to push on with the effort to desegregate the schools despite the dangers. White, for his part, agreed to order motorcycle police escorts for the buses. The determination of black Bostonians went largely unreported by the press, though it represents a remarkable phenomenon in this time of racial disillusionment in America. It apparently derived as much from a proud resolve not to be "turned around" by naked white force as from support for interracial education.

Attendance by the following week slowly climbed to 75 per cent as more parents judged the schools to be safe for their children. But during the remainder of September, racial conflict spread to three other high schools with more middle class student bodies. By 4 October, the segregationists staged a protest march of about 5,000 through South Boston that cut school attendance for that day almost in half. Marching at the head of this demonstration were state legislators, school committee members, and all but one member of the city council.

Inevitably, such tension produced (four days later) the most severe violence to date. In South Boston, a lone black driver caught in traffic was pulled from his car and injured by a white mob. The police throughout the period were fairer than expected, considering their ties to the white resisters; but on this day they overreacted against black students at English High School. This triggered black retaliation, and hundreds of black students poured out of the school and on to the streets. They pulled fire alarms and severely stoned passing cars driven by whites. The final toll for 8 October was 38 injured persons, 24 white and 14 black. The following day 300 state police and 100 metropolitan police were added to Boston's weary constabulary. But Judge Garrity refused the mayor's request for 125 federal marshals. Tensions began to cool slightly. By November, attendance had risen to over 80 per cent, though truancy laws had yet to be enforced. Sporadic incidents at various high schools continued to flare up; and only a handful of white students were coming to South Boston High. The ugly potential for further violence remained.

The local and national mass media tended to handle these events differently. Boston's press, television and radio reported the "bad" news but took pains to balance it with reports of the success of desegregation in most of the schools. The local media were still accused of extreme bias by the segregationists, and a boycott was initiated of the liberal *Boston Globe*. The national media, with a few notable exceptions, did "their thing." They focused heavily on the violence and gave white America yet another excuse for slowing down racial change. "If you all in 'liberal' Boston can't do it without trouble," questioned one reporter openly, "why should we be ordered to desegregate our schools here in Kansas City?" Virtually no national media attention was paid to the many cities—from Springfield, Massachusetts, to Minneapolis and Denver—that *were* successfully desegregating their public schools this fall without conflict.

Equally significant were the many speculative "social theories" used by the media to "explain" Boston's problems. In general, these explanations were far more sympathetic to the protesters than those advanced for white southern segregationists in the 1960s. Much was made of South Boston being a tight-knit, low-income Irish-American community, whose integrity had been somehow violated by racial desegregation. Ignored was the fact that the area is predominantly lower middle class (high-level blue-collar and low-level white-collar), not lower class; and that this class segment of industrial societies throughout the world is typically, and understandably, the most threatened by intergroup change. Some media stories stressed the ethnic factor and even compared the Irish segregationists of Boston to the IRA in Belfast. Ignored again was the fact that national opinion surveys have consistently shown Irish-Americans in general to be *less* anti-black than most white groups.

Boston's demography and geography hold advantages for the desegregation process. On the plus side, only about a fifth of the city's population is black, a modest proportion by urban American standards. And the black community has a relatively large and established middle class with roots going back to the American revolution. Moreover, the shape of the predominantly-black residential area is long and narrow, a far easier shape with which to design a desegregation plan than the enormous black areas of New York, Chicago and Los Angeles.

On the minus side, however, the central city constitutes only a fourth of the metropolitan population. This, in turn, means that Boston itself is comparable to Pittsburgh as a predominantly working class city. "Making it" up the social mobility ladder from an area such as South Boston has long entailed moving to the suburbs. Boston is also distinctive for its dominance by one ethnic group. The Boston Irish still comprise a majority of all voters, even though there is a great diversity of other ethnic groups from Italian to Scots-Canadian. The fact has important implications. It has meant that the Boston Irish have not been required to exercise the special genius that the Irish in other American cities have repeatedly demonstrated for leading ethnic coalitions. It has also led to an insulated parochialism, not common to Irish-Americans elsewhere. Adding to this phenomenon are the deep scars that persist from the bruising encounters during the last century between the newly-arrived Irish immigrants and the entrenched "Yankees" (largely English descendants who long ago departed for the suburbs).

These Irish-Yankee scars are most evident in the school system itself. It is without question one of the worst public school systems of any American city, poor for white as well as black children. This is true in part because of the bitter struggle at the turn of the century when the Boston Irish wrested control of the schools. When they finally succeeded, they rigidly maintained the old 19th century patterns and treated the system as a source of political patronage. Another result of this struggle is a large Roman Catholic parochial school system that takes middle class whites out of the public schools and reduces civic interest in the quality of public education. Almost two out of every five white children of school age attend parochial schools; this proportion is exceeded by only Philadelphia and St Louis and increases the black penetration in the public schools to 38 per cent. Out of the old Irish-Yankee conflict, too, came a school committee that is politically powerful and virtually free of control from the mayor's office. Elected "at large" throughout the city, no black has ever been on the committee.

The school committee has long been highly politicised. As part of the patronage system, virtually all school issues are treated as political. Committee members generally see their positions as stepping stones to higher political office, and rarely have either interest or expertise in education. Into this charged setting, racial desegregation arose as an issue eleven years ago. Almost by accident, the committee chairwoman in 1963, Mrs Louise Day Hicks, discovered that resistance to racial change in the schools was political gold. She has shrewdly exploited it ever since to further a political career that has included six years on the school committee, two years in the United States House of Representatives, two unsuccessful bids for mayor, and at present a second term as a city councillor. She has become a national figure, the personification of northern urban resistance to racial desegregation.

Mrs Hicks's role in the present crisis is considerable. She has served as a political model for many young and ambitious politicians who now gather at the head of every mob and demonstration. More important, she initially established the belief that school desegregation would *never* come to Boston. This factor is critical. Racial violence throughout the United States over the past two decades has not been wild, random, and spontaneous. Rather it has been quite rational—in the sense that it has occurred in those situations where white segregationists sensed that the process was not inevitable, and that a bit of publicised violence might well turn back the racial clock.

In fairness to Mrs Hicks, it must be said that she has received abundant help in restraining the development of this needed sense of inevitability. Not only the many political hacks who followed her stance, but the many "liberal" leaders of the city and state crumbled one by one as the autumn approached. Mayor White, ever mindful that some view him as a possibility for the Democratic Party's 1976 national ticket, has wavered throughout. He seldom fails to add a dependent clause to his every public sentence that reiterates his personal distaste for "forced busing" for desegregation. The liberal Republican state governor for the past six years, Francis Sargent, did well in maintaining his principles until June when he, too, caved into the Hicks-led pressure. Most surprising was the failure of the just-elected Democratic governor, Michael Dukakis. Dukakis, who was long the hope of the Massachusetts left, did not even wait for pressure to mount. Last spring, a half-year before the 5 November election, he advocated an ingenious way to reorganise Boston's schools so as to assure continued segregation. The only exceptions to this failure to counter Mrs Hicks's leadership were provided by the state's two members of the United States Senate. But Washington, DC, is almost 500 miles away. Save for Kennedy's abortive attempt to address the "anti-busers" in September and several statements by Edward Brooke, a black Republican, the two senators have not played a prominent public role.

The culminating act in this sad political drama came from the White House itself. On a bright warm 9 October, President Gerald Ford held a televised press conference in the rose garden. When asked about Boston, Ford deplored the violence but felt compelled to declare his opposition to racial change. He "respectfully disagreed" with the court decision which he did not consider "the best solution to quality education in Boston." The president took the opportunity to remind the American people that he had "consistently opposed forced busing to achieve racial balance. . . ." Not even Richard Nixon, in his wildest anti-black moments, had ever as president spoken out against a specific court decision for desegregation precisely when street violence was taking place over the decision. The message to black Americans was unambiguous: the highest official of their country had no concern for their legal rights. The message for Boston's white segregationists was equally loud and clear: "their president" was with them in their efforts to obstruct the court order. President Ford appeared to be for "law and order" only if he personally approved of the law in question.

"Anti-busing" leaders were overjoyed. "I was so happy when I heard his statement," said one, "I felt like screaming." "I love him," said another; "he said what we've been saying all along." Ford's "leadership," said a harrassed Mayor White angrily, "encouraged false hopes and fanned the flames of resistance that will almost inevitably lead to further disruption in Boston." In response to similar widespread criticism, Ford later made—at Senator Brooke's request—a vapid tape for use in Boston concerning the paramount importance of children's safety. It had no demonstrable effect, but it apparently represented the best that could be expected from an American president elected only by Grand Rapids, Michigan, and by Richard Nixon.

Two concerns loom large as the year closes. First, resistance to the court order is still in full force, flushed with a sense of triumph and political protection. Yet the organised nature of much of the violence, inside and outside the schools, strongly suggests that this resistance has gone far beyond the rights of free speech and protest guaranteed by America's Bill of Rights. Many legal observers now believe that the possibility of a clear case of a "conspiracy to obstruct justice" exists. But the US Justice Department would normally have to move for such action. It would surely alter the situation dramatically and reduce the disruption. But the Justice Department has shown no inclination to go in this direction; after all, its lawyers heard President Ford's rose garden wisdom, too. President Dwight Eisenhower sent in troops into Little Rock, Arkansas in 1957; President John Kennedy sent in marshals and troops into Oxford, Mississippi, in 1962; but President Gerald Ford now seems unwilling even to send government lawyers into court in 1974.

Second, a whole new legal round opens on 16 December. On that date, the school committee is under court order to submit a plan for full city-wide school desegregation to begin in the fall of 1975. The committee is not likely to meet this court order satisfactorily. It is almost as if Adolf Hitler had been ordered in 1937 to draw up a plan for world peace, for neither political motivation nor demonstrated competence are present. Probably Massachusetts educational officials, joined perhaps by the mayor's staff and a planner for the plaintiffs, will eventually have to design the comprehensive plan. Whoever constructs it, this plan for 1975 will almost surely involve more "busing" and fewer predominantly-black schools. Several working class areas of the city (East Boston and Charlestown) are already protesting against desegregation in anticipation of this *next* plan, for they are not currently affected.

The whole tragic affair has so far followed the descriptions of social science textbooks as if it were a simulated experiment. Hence, the textbook prediction for the future, given the present situation, seems likely to be borne out. If no Justice Department action is brought against unlawful disruption and if no political counter is made to Mrs Hicks and her followers, violent attempts to overthrow the court orders will continue unabated. Now that the November elections have passed, chances for some degree of affirmative political leadership appear somewhat brighter. But the Boston episode in any event will remain as harsh evidence of what happened to the American civil rights thrust of the 1960s—after six years of the Nixon and Ford administrations.

"TO CREATE AND SUSTAIN A SOCIETY IN WHICH ALL OF US ARE EQUAL"

BARBARA JORDAN

Keynote Address at the Democratic National Convention

New York City, July 12, 1976

THANK YOU, ladies and gentlemen, for a very warm reception.

It was one hundred and forty-four years ago that members of the Democratic Party first met in convention to select a presidential candidate. Since that time, Democrats have continued to convene once every four years and draft a party platform and nominate a presidential candidate. And our meeting this week is a continuation of that tradition.

But there is something different about tonight. There is something special about tonight. What is different? What is special? I, Barbara Jordan, am a keynote speaker.

A lot of years have passed since 1832, and during that time it would have been most unusual for any national political party to ask a Barbara Jordan to deliver a keynote address. But tonight, here I am. And I feel that notwithstanding the past that my presence here is one additional bit of evidence that the American Dream need not forever be deferred.

Now that I have this grand distinction, what in the world am I supposed to say?

I could easily spend this time praising the accomplishments of this party and attacking the Republicans.

But I don't choose to do that.

I could list the many problems which Americans have. I could list the problems which cause people to feel cynical, angry, frustrated: problems which include lack of integrity in government; the feeling that the individual no longer counts; the reality of material and spiritual poverty; the feeling that the grand American experiment is failing or has failed. I could recite these problems, and then I could sit down and offer no solutions. But I don't choose to do that either.

The citizens of America expect more. They deserve and they want more than a recital of problems.

We are a people in a quandary about the present. We are a people in search of our future. We are a people in search of a national community.

We are a people trying not only to solve the problems of the present: unemployment, inflation—but we are attempting on a larger scale to fulfill the promise of America. We are attempting to fulfill our national purpose, to create and sustain a society in which all of us are equal.

Throughout our history, when people have looked for new ways to solve their problems, and to uphold the principles of this nation, many times they have turned to political parties. They have often turned to the Democratic Party.

What is it, what is it about the Democratic Party that makes it the instrument the people use when they search for ways to shape their future? Well, I believe the answer to that question lies in our concept of governing. Our concept of governing is derived from our view of people. It is a concept deeply rooted in a set of beliefs firmly etched in the national conscience of all of us.

Now what are these beliefs?

First, we believe in equality for all and privileges for none. This is a belief that each American, regardless of background, has equal standing in the public forum, all of us. Because we believe this idea so firmly, we are an inclusive rather than an exclusive party. Let everybody come.

I think it no accident that most of those immigrating to America in the nineteenth century identified with the Democratic Party. We are a heterogeneous party made up of Americans of diverse backgrounds.

We believe that the people are the source of all governmental power; that the authority of the people is to be extended, not restricted. This can be accomplished only by providing each citizen with every opportunity to participate in the management of the government. They must have that.

We believe that the government which represents the authority of all the people, not just one interest group, but all the people, has an obligation to actively underscore, actively seek to remove those obstacles which would block, *individual achievement*, obstacles emanating from race, sex, economic condition. The government must remove them. Seek to remove them.

We are a party of innovation. We do not reject our traditions, but we are willing to adapt to changing circumstances, when change we must. We are willing to suffer the discomfort of change in order to achieve a better future.

We have a positive vision of the future founded on the belief that the gap between the promise and reality of America can one day be finally closed. We believe that.

This, my friends, is the bedrock of our concept of governing. This is a part of the reason why Americans have turned to the Democratic Party. These are the foundations upon which a national community can be built.

Let all understand that these guiding principles cannot be discarded for short-term political gains. They represent what this country is all about. They are indigenous to the American idea. And these are principles which are not negotiable.

In other times, I could stand here and give this kind of exposition on the beliefs of the Democratic Party and that would be enough. But today that is not enough. People want more. That is not sufficient reason for the majority of the people of this country to decide to vote Democratic. We have made mistakes. We have made mistakes. We realize that. We admit our mistakes. In our haste to do all things for all people, we did not foresee the full consequences of our actions. And when the people raised their voices, we didn't hear. But our deafness was only a temporary condition, and not an irreversible condition.

Even as I stand here and admit that we have made mistakes, I still believe that as the people of America sit in judgment on each party, they will recognize that our mistakes were mistakes of the heart. They'll recognize that.

And now we must look to the future. Let us heed the voice of the people and recognize their common sense. If we do not, we not only blaspheme our political heritage, we ignore the common ties that bind all Americans.

Many fear the future. Many are distrustful of their leaders, and believe that their voices are never heard. Many seek only to satisfy their private work wants. To satisfy their private interest.

But this is the great danger America faces. That we will cease to be one nation and become instead a collection of interest groups: city against suburb, region against region, individual against individual. Each seeking to satisfy private wants.

If that happens, who then will speak for America? Who then will speak for the common good? This is the question which must be answered in 1976.

Are we to be one people bound together by common spirit sharing in a common endeavor, or will we become a divided nation?

For all of its uncertainty, we cannot flee the future. We must not become the new Puritans and reject our society. We must address and master the future together. It can be done if we restore the belief that we share a sense of national community, that we share a common national endeavor. It can be done.

There is no executive order, there is no law, that can require the American people to form a national community. This we must do as individuals and if we do it as individuals, there is no president of the United States who can veto that decision.

As a first step, we must restore our belief in ourselves. We are a generous people, so why can't we be generous with each other? We need to take to heart the words spoken by Thomas Jefferson:

> Let us restore to social intercourse that harmony and that affection without which liberty and even life are but dreary things.

A nation is formed by the willingness of each of us to share in the responsibility for upholding the common good.

A government is invigorated when each one of us is willing to participate in shaping the future of this nation.

In this election year, we must define the common good and begin again to shape a common future. Let each person do his or her part. If one citizen is unwilling to participate, all of us are going to suffer. For the American ideal, though it is shared by all of us, is realized in each one of us.

And now, what are those of us who are elected public officials supposed to do? We call ourselves public servants, but I'll tell you this: we as public servants must set an example for the rest of the nation. It is hypocritical for the public official to admonish and exhort the people to uphold the common good if we are derelict in upholding the common good. More is required of public officials than slogans and handshakes and press releases. More is required. We must hold ourselves strictly accountable. We must provide the people with a vision of the future.

If we promise as public officials, we must deliver. If we, as public officials, propose, we must produce. If we say to the American people, "it is time for you to be sacrificial," sacrifice. If the public official says that, we must be the first to give. We must be. And again, if we make mistakes, we must be willing to admit them. We have to do that. What we have to do is strike a balance between the idea that government should do everything, and the idea, the belief, that government ought to do nothing. Strike a balance.

Let there be no illusions about the difficulty of forming this kind of a national community. It's tough, difficult, not easy. But a spirit of harmony will survive in America only if each of us remembers that we share a common destiny.

If each of us remembers when self-interest and bitterness seem to prevail, that we share a common destiny, I have confidence that we can form this kind of national community.

I have confidence that the Democratic Party can lead the way. I have that confidence. We cannot improve on the system of government handed down to us by the founders of the republic; there is no way to improve upon that. But what we can do is to find new ways to implement that system and realize our destiny.

Now, I began this speech by commenting to you on the uniqueness of a Barbara Jordan making a keynote address. Well, I am going to close my speech by quoting a Republican president, and I ask you that as you listen to these words of Abraham Lincoln, relate them to the concept of national community in which every last one of us participates: "As I would not be a slave, so I would not be a master."

This expresses my idea of democracy. Whatever differs from this, to the extent of the difference, is no democracy.

CHRONOLOGY

NOTE ON THE TEXTS

NOTES

INDEX

Chronology

1919 The 369th Infantry Regiment ("Harlem Hellfighters") marches in victory parade down Fifth Avenue in New York City on February 17. Racially motivated mob violence erupts in at least twenty-five U.S. cities and towns during the "Red Summer." At least four black and three white persons are killed in Washington, D.C., July 18–22, and twenty-three black and fifteen white persons are killed in Chicago, July 27–31. Tuskegee Institute archives record the lynching of 534 black persons from 1910 to 1919. Cyril Briggs founds the African Blood Brotherhood for African Liberation and Redemption (ABB), headquartered in Harlem. White mobs and U.S. troops kill more than 100 persons in Phillips County, Arkansas, September 30–October 4, in response to false reports of an uprising by black sharecroppers; five white men are also killed during the violence. Organized self-defense of black neighborhoods during Washington and Chicago riots leads to commentary in the black press about the emergence of the "New Negro." In November twelve black sharecroppers who survived the massacre in Arkansas are tried and sentenced to death for murder.

1920 Second Ku Klux Klan, founded in 1915 in Georgia, begins expanding nationwide. Parade and rally held in New York City by the Universal Negro Improvement Association on August 2 draws 25,000 people as UNIA founder Marcus Garvey is proclaimed "provisional president" of Africa. Ratification of the Nineteenth Amendment, forbidding the denial of suffrage on account of sex, is completed on August 18. Republican Warren G. Harding wins the presidential election, November 2, defeating James M. Cox 404–127 in the electoral voting and carrying one southern state (Tennessee). Two members of a white posse and at least six black persons are killed in election day violence in Ococee, Florida, that causes almost all of the black population to flee the town. James Weldon Johnson is named executive secretary of the National Association for the Advancement of Colored People (NAACP), the first black person to hold the position. Census shows 77 percent of the black population lives in the eleven southern (former Confederate) states.

1921 Newspaper in Tulsa, Oklahoma, reports on May 31 that a black man has been arrested for allegedly attempting to assault a white woman in an office elevator. That night shooting begins when a large white mob gathers at the county courthouse and confronts a smaller group of armed black men attempting to prevent a possible lynching. As many as two thousand armed white men invade the Greenwood neighborhood in the early hours of June 1, destroying the business district known as "the Negro Wall Street" and burning thirty-five city blocks. Riot ends later in the day when the Oklahoma National Guard imposes martial law in Tulsa. Officials report that twenty-six black and ten white persons were killed in the violence, while unofficial estimates of the dead range from fifty-five to more than 150.

1922 Dyer federal anti-lynching bill, first introduced in 1918, passes Republican-controlled House of Representatives, 230–119, on January 26. Bill is filibustered by southern Democrats in the Senate and withdrawn in December.

1923 Manhunt for an alleged rapist leads to violence in the black town of Rosewood, Florida, in early January in which six black persons and two white persons are killed and the town is burned. In a case arising from the 1919 massacre in Arkansas, the U.S. Supreme Court rules 6–2 in *Moore v. Dempsey* that the "mob domination" of the trial of six black defendants violated the due process clause of the Fourteenth Amendment. Decision is a legal victory for the NAACP and a significant precedent in the federal judicial review of state criminal trials. Texas passes law excluding black voters from Democratic primary elections. Marcus Garvey is convicted of mail fraud in connection with the Black Star Line and sentenced to five years in prison (will begin serving his sentence in 1925). Harding dies on August 2 and Vice President Calvin Coolidge becomes president.

1924 Virginia Democratic Party establishes white primary paid for by state funds. Both the Republican and Democratic national conventions reject proposals to condemn the Ku Klux Klan in their platforms. Coolidge wins the presidential election, November 4, defeating John W. Davis

382–136 in the electoral voting without carrying any southern states.

1925 A. Philip Randolph, Socialist co-editor of *The Messenger*, begins organizing union of Pullman Company sleeping car porters. About 30,000 robed members of the Ku Klux Klan parade down Pennsylvania Avenue in Washington, D.C., on August 8. In Detroit Dr. Ossian Sweet moves his family into a house in a white neighborhood. On September 9 a crowd gathers, rocks are thrown at the Sweet home, and a white man is killed by shots fired from the house. Sweet, his wife and two brothers, and seven family friends are arrested and charged with first-degree murder. NAACP hires Clarence Darrow and Arthur Garfield Hays to represent the defendants, who are tried together. Mistrial is declared on November 27 after the jury is unable to reach a verdict.

1926 Henry Sweet, Ossian's brother, is retried separately and found not guilty on May 13 (charges against the remaining defendants are eventually dropped). Supreme Court unanimously rules in *Corrigan v. Buckley* that racially restrictive real estate covenants are private actions that do not violate the Fourteenth Amendment.

1927 Supreme Court unanimously rules in *Nixon v. Herndon* that the Texas law prohibiting black voters from participating in the Democratic primary violates the equal protection clause of the Fourteenth Amendment. Texas enacts a new law giving the Democratic state committee power to exclude black voters from its primaries. Marcus Garvey's sentence is commuted, and he is deported to Jamaica.

1928 Herbert Hoover wins presidential election on November 6, defeating Al Smith in the electoral voting 444–87 and carrying Texas, Tennessee, Florida, North Carolina, and Virginia. Oscar De Priest, a Republican, wins House seat in Chicago, becoming the first black congressman to be elected since 1898 and the first from outside the South.

1929 Federal district judge rules that the Democratic white primary in Virginia violates the Fourteenth and Fifteenth Amendments. Tuskegee Institute records the lynching of 281 black persons from 1920 to 1929.

1930 Nomination to the Supreme Court of John Parker, a federal appellate judge from North Carolina, is opposed by the NAACP and the American Federation of Labor and rejected by the Senate, 39–41. Wallace Fard founds the Allah Temple of Islam (later the Nation of Islam) in Detroit. Jessie Daniel Ames, a suffragist from Texas, founds Association of Southern Women for the Prevention of Lynching, a group of white women who campaign against mob violence. James Weldon Johnson resigns as NAACP executive secretary and is succeeded by Walter White.

1931 Nine black youths, aged thirteen to twenty, are accused on March 25 of raping two young white women on board a freight train in northern Alabama. They are tried in Scottsboro, Alabama, April 6–9, and eight of the defendants are sentenced to death (the case of Roy Wright, the youngest accused, ends in a mistrial when the jury deadlocks over whether to impose the death penalty). The Communist Party USA (CPUSA) denounces the trials as a legal lynching, while International Labor Defense (ILD), the party's legal arm, engages in a successful struggle with the NAACP over which organization would represent the defendants on appeal. Black sharecroppers and tenant farmers work with Communist organizers to form the Alabama Sharecroppers Union.

1932 Supreme Court rules 5–4 in *Nixon v. Condon* that the Texas law permitting the Democratic Party to exclude black voters from its primaries violates the equal protection clause of the Fourteenth Amendment. James W. Ford, a leading black Communist, is nominated as the CPUSA candidate for vice president (Ford will also be on the party ticket in 1936 and 1940). In *Powell v. Alabama* the Supreme Court overturns the convictions of the Scottsboro defendants, ruling 7–2 that the failure to effectively appoint defense counsel in a capital case violates the due process clause of the Fourteenth Amendment. Franklin D. Roosevelt wins presidential election on November 8, defeating Hoover in the electoral voting 472–59 and carrying all of the southern states. Three members of the Sharecroppers Union are killed in Tallapoosa County, Alabama, during confrontation with sheriff's posse seeking to seize a farmer's livestock.

1933 Angelo Herndon, a young black Communist organizer, is convicted of inciting insurrection in Georgia and sentenced to eighteen to twenty years on a chain gang. Scottsboro defendants Haywood Patterson and Clarence Norris are retried and sentenced to death.

1934 W.E.B. Du Bois, a founding member of the NAACP and editor of its magazine *The Crisis*, resigns from the organization in dispute over his advocacy of separate black institutions and voluntary segregation. Wallace Fard disappears, and Elijah (Poole) Muhammad becomes the leader of the Nation of Islam. Arthur Mitchell defeats Oscar De Priest, becoming the first black Democrat elected to Congress.

1935 Supreme Court overturns the 1933 convictions in the Scottsboro case, ruling 8–0 in *Norris v. Alabama* that the systemic exclusion of blacks from the juries that indicted and tried the defendants violated the equal protection clause of the Fourteenth Amendment. In *Grovey v. Townsend* the court rejects 9–0 the latest challenge to the Texas white Democratic primary, holding that the exclusion of black voters by the state party does not violate the Constitution because it is the private act of a voluntary association and not the result of government action. Charles Houston, the former dean of Howard Law School, becomes special counsel to the NAACP and begins planning a long-term legal campaign against segregation. (Houston returns to private practice in 1938 but will continue to advise the NAACP.) Brotherhood of Sleeping Car Porters and Maids wins recognition from the Pullman Company and is granted an international charter by the American Federation of Labor.

1936 Haywood Patterson is again retried and sentenced to seventy-five years in prison. In *Brown v. Mississippi* the Supreme Court overturns the convictions of three black tenant farmers sentenced to death for the murder of a white planter, ruling 9–0 that the use of confessions obtained by torture violates the due process clause of the Fourteenth Amendment. (The defendants later pled no contest to manslaughter charges.) Roosevelt is reelected on November 3, defeating Alf Landon 523–8 in the electoral voting and carrying all eleven southern states while becoming the first Democratic candidate to win a majority of the black vote nationwide.

1937 House passes federal anti-lynching bill 276–119 on April 15. In *Herndon v. Lowry* the Supreme Court overturns Angelo Herndon's conviction, ruling 5–4 that the "vague and indeterminate" Georgia insurrection law violates the Fourteenth Amendment. Clarence Norris is retried and sentenced to death, two other defendants are sentenced to ninety-nine- and seventy-five-year prison terms, a fourth defendant receives twenty years for assaulting a deputy while in custody, while charges against the remaining four "Scottsboro Boys" are dropped. (Norris's death sentence is commuted to life in 1938, and all the imprisoned men are either paroled or escape custody from 1943 to 1950.)

1938 Vote to end Senate filibuster of anti-lynching bill fails 42–46 on February 16. Supreme Court hears *Missouri ex rel. Gaines v. Canada*, case brought by the NAACP arguing that the refusal of the University of Missouri to admit a black applicant to its all-white law school violates the equal protection clause of the Fourteenth Amendment. Court rules 6–2 for the plaintiff, rejecting state's claim that providing tuition for black students to attend law school in other states constitutes equal treatment.

1939 Contralto Marian Anderson gives concert at the Lincoln Memorial for integrated audience of 75,000 on April 9, Easter Sunday, after the Daughters of the American Revolution bar her from performing at Constitution Hall. Supreme Court rules 6–2 in *Lane v. Wilson* that highly restrictive Oklahoma voter registration law violates the Fifteenth Amendment. Tuskegee Institute records the lynching of 119 black persons from 1930 to 1939.

1940 In *Chambers v. Florida* the Supreme Court overturns 8–0 the conviction of four black tenant farmers sentenced to death for the murder of a white man, ruling that their confessions, made after several days of constant questioning while they were held incommunicado, violate the due process clause of the Fourteenth Amendment. (Three of the defendants will be acquitted by a judge at retrial, while the fourth is committed to the state mental hospital.) Thurgood Marshall becomes executive director of the NAACP Legal Defense Fund (will serve until 1961). Roosevelt signs bill on September 16 establishing the first peacetime draft in American history. White House announces in October that the armed services will remain segregated. Roosevelt wins reelection on November 5, defeating Wendell Willkie 449–82 in the electoral voting and carrying all the southern states while winning a majority of the black vote.

Census shows 69 percent of the black population living in southern states.

1941 A. Philip Randolph, president of the Brotherhood of Sleeping Car Porters, calls for 10,000 black Americans to march on Washington, D.C., on July 1 to demand an end to segregation in the armed forces and racial discrimination in defense industries. Randolph and Walter White meet with President Roosevelt, who attempts to forestall the march, but Randolph insists on presidential action against hiring discrimination. Roosevelt issues Executive Order 8802 on June 25, prohibiting racial discrimination in hiring by federal departments and defense contractors and establishing a Fair Employment Practice Committee (FEPC) to monitor compliance. Randolph announces postponement of the march on June 28. Armed forces remain segregated, and most black servicemen will serve in supply and service units, although the army will form two black infantry divisions, as well as black artillery, tank, and tank destroyer battalions. In July 1941 the army begins training its first black pilots; the first black marines are recruited in 1942; and the navy commissions its first black officers in 1944. Japanese attack Pearl Harbor, December 7, bringing the United States into World War II.

1942 Members of the Fellowship of Reconciliation, a pacifist organization, form Chicago Committee of Racial Equality to undertake "nonviolent direct action" against discrimination. March on Washington Movement holds large public rallies in New York, June 16, and Chicago, June 26, as part of continuing campaign against job discrimination. House of Representatives votes 252–84 on October 13 to abolish poll taxes in federal elections. Democrat William Dawson is elected to the House of Representatives from Chicago, succeeding the retiring Arthur Mitchell as the sole black member of Congress. Senate votes 41–37 against ending debate on the poll tax bill. (Legislation to abolish poll taxes in federal elections is passed by the House in 1943, 1945, 1947, and 1949, but is blocked in the Senate.)

1943 Committee of Racial Equality conducts sit-in protests in Chicago restaurants. (Organization is renamed Congress of Racial Equality [CORE] in 1944.) Fighting between black and white residents in a city park in Detroit leads to rioting, June 20–23, in which twenty-five black and nine white persons are killed. Confrontation between a white police officer and a black soldier in Harlem section of New York City results in riot, August 1–2, in which six black persons are killed.

1944 In *Smith v. Allwright* the Supreme Court reverses *Grovey v. Townsend*, ruling 8–1 that the exclusion of black voters from the Texas Democratic primary is a violation of the Fifteenth Amendment. Roosevelt is reelected on November 7, defeating Thomas Dewey 432–99 in the electoral voting and carrying all eleven southern states. Adam Clayton Powell Jr, a Democrat, is elected to Congress from a district in Harlem and becomes the second black representative serving in the House of Representatives.

1945 Poll tax is abolished in Georgia. Roosevelt dies on April 12 and Vice President Harry S. Truman becomes president. Congress votes to end funding for the FEPC after June 30, 1946. Japan surrenders on August 14, ending World War II.

1946 Black army veteran Isaac Woodard is left blind after he is beaten by two police officers in Batesburg, South Carolina, on February 13. In *Morgan v. Virginia* the Supreme Court rules 7–1 that Virginia law requiring segregated seating on interstate buses is an unconstitutional burden on interstate commerce. (Decision does not address intrastate travel or segregation on interstate lines that is the result of bus company policy.) Roger and Dorothy Malcolm and George and Mae Dorsey are shot to death by a white mob at Moore's Ford, near Monroe, Georgia, on July 25 after Roger Malcolm wounded a white man in a scuffle. Murders attract widespread public attention, along with the torture, mutilation, and murder of army veteran John Jones by a mob in Minden, Louisiana, on August 8. (Despite an extensive federal investigation, no one is ever charged in the Moore's Ford murders; one man is acquitted of federal charges in the assault on Woodard, and five men, including two deputy sheriffs, are acquitted of federal charges in the murder of Jones.) Truman appoints fifteen-member presidential committee on civil rights on December 5, with Charles Wilson, president of General Electric, serving as its chairman.

1947 Fellowship of Reconciliation organizes "Journey of Reconciliation" in which integrated group of sixteen activists ride interstate buses in Virginia, North Carolina, Tennessee, and Kentucky to test compliance with the *Morgan* decision. Four of the riders are arrested in Chapel Hill, North Carolina, and later sentenced to serve thirty-day terms on a chain gang. Jackie Robinson plays his first game for the Brooklyn Dodgers on April 15, becoming the first black player in major league baseball since the 1880s. Presidential committee on civil rights submits its report on October 29; its recommendations include the creation of a civil rights division in the Department of Justice, a national civil rights commission, and a new FEPC with enforcement powers; ending segregation in the armed forces; and federal legislation to punish lynching, secure voting rights, and abolish segregation in interstate transport.

1948 Truman endorses many of the recommendations of the civil rights committee but, in the face of strong southern opposition, does not submit civil rights legislation to Congress. Randolph warns Truman at White House meeting that he will lead a civil disobedience campaign against the draft unless the armed forces are integrated. In *Shelley v. Kraemer*, Supreme Court rules 6–0 that judicial enforcement of racially restrictive property covenants is a violation of the equal protection clause of the Fourteenth Amendment. After liberals force a floor fight, Democratic national convention adopts platform plank on civil rights, July 14, that calls for a federal anti-lynching law, a new FEPC, the abolition of poll taxes, and desegregation of the armed forces. Adoption of plank causes partial southern walkout from the convention, and on July 17 southern "Dixiecrats" hold a States' Rights convention and nominate Governor Strom Thurmond of South Carolina for president. Truman issues executive orders 9980, establishing a Fair Employment Board to promote nondiscriminatory employment practices in the federal civil service, and 9981, declaring "equality of treatment and opportunity" in the armed services to be presidential policy. Randolph ends call for civil disobedience. Truman names seven-member committee to oversee integration of the armed forces and appoints Charles Fahy, a former solicitor general, as its chairman. In the presidential election, November 2, Truman wins 303 electoral votes, Thomas Dewey 189, and Thurmond 39. Thurmond carries Louisiana, Mississippi, Alabama, and South Carolina, while Truman wins the other seven southern states and also carries key states of Ohio, Illinois, and California with strong support from black voters.

1949 Senate votes 63–23 on March 17 to increase the majority needed for cloture from two-thirds of the senators present and voting to two-thirds of the Senate. Administration proposes legislation to make lynching a federal crime, create a new FEPC, abolish poll taxes in national elections, and end segregation in interstate transportation, but none of the bills are brought to a vote in the Senate. Fahy Committee approves integration plans of the air force and navy but encounters resistance to desegregation from the army. William Hastie, former dean of the Howard Law School and a leading civil rights lawyer, is appointed by Truman to the Third Circuit Court of Appeals, becoming the first black federal appellate judge. Tuskegee Institute records the lynching of thirty-one black persons from 1940 to 1949.

1950 Fahy Committee accepts army integration plan. Supreme Court decides three civil rights cases on June 5, all by 9–0 votes: in *Sweatt v. Painter*, the court rules that separate law school established by the University of Texas does not provide equal educational opportunity and orders the university to desegregate its previously all-white law school; in *McLaurin v. Oklahoma State Regents*, it rules that the University of Oklahoma could not impose segregated seating arrangements on a black graduate student; and in *Henderson v. United States*, it rules that segregated seating on railroad dining cars denies the equal access to public accommodations guaranteed by the Interstate Commerce Act. Although the NAACP attorneys arguing *Sweatt* and *McLaurin* had asked the court to overturn the 1896 *Plessy v. Ferguson* decision establishing the "separate but equal" doctrine of constitutionally permissible segregation, the decisions do not rule on its continuing validity. Korean War begins June 25. Thurgood Marshall decides to litigate against segregation in the public schools in direct challenge to *Plessy*. (Public schools are segregated by law in all eleven southern states as well as Delaware, Maryland, West Virginia, Kentucky, Missouri, Oklahoma, and the District of Columbia; laws in Kansas, New Mexico, and Arizona allow individual school districts to segregate.)

1951 Poll tax is abolished in South Carolina. NAACP attorneys argue school segregation cases in federal and state courts in South Carolina, Kansas, and Delaware. Harry and

Harriette Moore, NAACP activists in Florida who campaigned against police violence and led voter registration drives, are killed when their home in Mims is bombed on December 25.

1952 Fourth school case is argued in federal court in Virginia. Charlotta Bass, former editor of the black newspaper *The California Eagle*, is nominated for vice president by the Progressive Party. Republican Dwight D. Eisenhower wins presidential election, November 4, defeating Adlai Stevenson 442–89 in the electoral vote and carrying Texas, Tennessee, Florida, and Virginia. In December Supreme Court hears arguments on appeal in the four school cases, now consolidated as *Brown v. Board of Education of Topeka*, as well as *Bolling v. Sharpe*, case challenging school segregation in the District of Columbia.

1953 Divided Supreme Court orders reargument in *Brown*. Armistice is signed in Korea on July 27. Frederick Vinson, chief justice of Supreme Court since 1946, dies on September 8. Eisenhower appoints California governor Earl Warren as chief justice. Poll tax is abolished in Tennessee in November, while poll taxes remain in Texas, Arkansas, Mississippi, Alabama, and Virginia. *Brown* and *Bolling* are reargued in December. Warren begins working with other justices to bring about unanimous decision.

1954 On May 17 the Supreme Court rules 9–0 in *Brown* that public school segregation violates the equal protection clause of the Fourteenth Amendment. Writing for the court, Warren declares that the "separate but equal" doctrine has no place in public education and requests further argument concerning implementation. In companion case of *Bolling*, the court rules 9–0 that school segregation in the District of Columbia violates the due process clause of the Fifth Amendment. *Brown* decision is denounced by many southern elected officials. "Citizens' Council" is organized in Indianola, Mississippi, in July to oppose desegregation by political, legal, and economic means; by the end of the year chapters of the organization are founded in Texas, Louisiana, Alabama, Georgia, and Virginia, as well as throughout Mississippi. Desegregation begins in District of Columbia and Baltimore schools. Malcolm X (born Malcolm Little) becomes minister of Temple No. 7 of the Nation of Islam in Harlem. Department of Defense announces on October 30 that the armed forces have been fully desegregated.

1955 Desegregation begins in St. Louis schools in February. In *Brown II* Supreme Court rules 9–0 on May 31 that school cases should be remanded to lower federal courts and instructs them to issue desegregation orders "with all deliberate speed" without setting a deadline for compliance. Implementation of school desegregation decisions is obstructed by resistance and delay by school authorities and state governments, and by reluctance of some federal judges to issue effective desegregation orders. Emmett Till, a fourteen-year-old boy visiting from Chicago, is beaten and shot to death in Tallahatchie County, Mississippi, on August 28 after he allegedly acts disrespectfully to a white woman. Till's murder and the acquittal on September 23 of the two white men charged with killing him attract widespread public attention. Interstate Commerce Commission rules that segregated seating on interstate buses and trains is a violation of the Interstate Commerce Act. Supreme Court rules in *Baltimore v. Dawson* and *Holmes v. Atlanta* that municipal recreation facilities cannot be racially segregated. Rosa Parks, an active member of the NAACP, is arrested in Montgomery, Alabama, on December 1 for violating the municipal bus segregation ordinance. Montgomery Improvement Association is organized at mass meeting held on December 5 to conduct boycott of city buses, and Martin Luther King Jr., the pastor of the Dexter Avenue Baptist Church, is elected as its president.

1956 University of Alabama admits Autherine Lucy as its first black student after prolonged litigation in federal court. White students and Tuscaloosa residents riot on February 6, and Lucy is suspended, allegedly for her own safety; she is later expelled for criticizing the university. "Declaration of Constitutional Principles," also known as the "Southern Manifesto," is introduced in Congress on March 12. Signed by nineteen senators and seventy-seven representatives, it denounces *Brown* as an "abuse of judicial power" and endorses resistance to integration by "any lawful means." Bus boycott begins in Tallahassee, Florida, on May 26. Alabama attorney general John Patterson obtains injunction against the NAACP in state court for failing to comply with state corporate registration laws and obtains order directing the

NAACP to turn over its membership lists. (Several other southern states also undertake legal campaigns to restrict the operations of the NAACP and the Legal Defense Fund.) Virginia legislature adopts program of "massive resistance" to school desegregation calling for the closing of schools under desegregation orders. Eisenhower wins reelection on November 6, defeating Adlai Stevenson in the electoral voting 457–73 and carrying Texas, Louisiana, Tennessee, Virginia, and Florida. Supreme Court affirms ruling of lower federal court in *Browder v. Gayle* declaring segregation on Alabama intrastate buses to be unconstitutional. Montgomery boycott ends on December 21 as municipal buses begin operating on a desegregated basis.

1957 Southern Negro Leadership Conference on Transportation and Nonviolent Integration (later known as the Southern Christian Leadership Conference) is organized in Atlanta with King as its chairman. Ghana becomes independent nation, March 6, beginning period of decolonization in sub-Saharan Africa. First federal civil rights bill since 1875 is passed on August 29 after it is significantly weakened in the Senate to avoid a filibuster. The act creates a federal civil rights commission with investigatory powers; replaces the existing civil rights section of the Department of Justice with a division headed by an assistant attorney general; makes conspiring to deny citizens their right to vote in federal elections a federal crime; and gives federal prosecutors the power to obtain injunctions against discriminatory practices used to deny citizens their voting rights. Federal district court orders nine black students admitted to Central High School in Little Rock, Arkansas, on September 3, but Governor Orval Faubus uses the National Guard to prevent them from entering the school. After the district court orders Faubus to end his interference, the governor withdraws the Guard, and on September 23 the students are attacked by a large mob. Eisenhower sends more than 1,000 paratroopers of the 101st Airborne Division to Little Rock and places the Arkansas National Guard under federal control. Students are escorted to class by armed soldiers on September 25. Airborne troops are withdrawn from Little Rock, November 27, as federalized Guard continues to protect the students.

1958 Buses in Tallahassee begin desegregated service in May. In *NAACP v. Alabama* Supreme Court upholds 9–0 on

First Amendment grounds the refusal of the organization to turn its membership lists over to the Alabama authorities (injunction against the Alabama NAACP remains in effect). On September 12 the court decides *Cooper v. Aaron*, unanimously overturning a district court decision allowing the Little Rock school board to postpone desegregation until 1960 because of the threat of continued violence. In opinion signed by all nine justices, Warren writes that governors and state legislators are bound by the Constitution to uphold Supreme Court decisions. In response to decision, Little Rock high schools are closed for most of the 1958–59 school year, then reopen with token desegregation. Schools under desegregation orders are closed in Norfolk, Charlottesville, and Warren County, Virginia.

1959 Virginia supreme court rules that school closing law passed in 1956 violates the state constitution. Mack Charles Parker, a black man accused of raping a white woman, is taken from jail in Poplarville, Mississippi, and lynched by a mob on April 25. After Virginia legislature repeals its compulsory school attendance laws, Prince Edward County closes its schools to avoid desegregation. *The Hate That Hate Produced*, television documentary on the Nation of Islam, airs in July and brings Malcolm X to wider public attention.

1960 King moves to Atlanta, where the SCLC has its headquarters, and becomes copastor with his father at the Ebenezer Baptist Church. Four black students stage sit-in at segregated lunch counter in Greensboro, North Carolina, on February 1. Sit-in movement spreads rapidly, and by the end of the month thirty-one lunch counter sit-ins are held in North Carolina, Maryland, Virginia, South Carolina, Georgia, Florida, Tennessee, Louisiana, and Texas, resulting in hundreds of arrests. Student Nonviolent Coordinating Committee (SNCC) is founded at conference in Raleigh, North Carolina, organized by Ella Baker, executive director of the SCLC. Civil rights act is passed by Congress, April 21; it provides criminal penalties for forcibly obstructing federal court orders; makes interstate flight after committing a bombing or arson a federal crime; and allows federal courts to appoint referees to register voters in cases where a pattern or practice of voting discrimination has been proven at trial. Lunch counters are desegregated in San Antonio, Texas, Nashville, Tennessee, and Winston-Salem, Charlotte, and Greensboro, North Carolina, by July. Survey of school desegregation records substantial desegregation efforts in the District of Columbia, West Virginia, Delaware, Kentucky, Maryland, Missouri, Oklahoma, and Texas; token desegregation in Arkansas, Florida, North Carolina, Tennessee, and Virginia; and no desegregation in Alabama, Georgia, Louisiana, Mississippi, and South Carolina. King is arrested during an Atlanta sit-in on October 19 and sentenced to four months in state prison for violating his probation on a traffic charge. Democratic presidential nominee Senator John F. Kennedy calls Coretta Scott King to express concern, and his brother, Robert F. Kennedy, calls the judge handling the case. King is released on bond and his father publicly endorses Kennedy. On November 8 Kennedy narrowly defeats Richard M. Nixon with crucial support from black voters in key states of Illinois and Texas. Kennedy wins 303 electoral votes and Nixon 219, while fifteen electors vote for Senator Harry Byrd, a leading segregationist. Nixon carries Virginia, Tennessee, and Florida, while Kennedy wins the remainder of the southern states with the exception of Mississippi and Alabama, whose unpledged electors vote mostly for Byrd. Limited school desegregation begins in New Orleans under federal court order as federal marshals escort black elementary school pupils past hostile crowds. Supreme Court rules 9–0 in *Gomillion v. Lightfoot* that the redrawing of the Tuskegee, Alabama, city boundaries in order to exclude black voters violates the Fifteenth Amendment; in *Boynton v. Virginia* it rules 7–2 that segregation of facilities in interstate bus terminals violates the Interstate Commerce Act.

1961 Federal district court orders University of Georgia to admit Hamilton Holmes and Charlayne Hunter. They are suspended after a riot on campus by white students but are reinstated by court order. James Farmer becomes national director of CORE and begins planning "Freedom Rides" to test compliance with the *Boynton* decision. President Kennedy issues Executive Order 10925 establishing Committee on Equal Employment Opportunity to investigate racial discrimination by government contractors and recommend action by the Justice Department. First group of Freedom Riders leaves Washington May 4 and travels through Virginia, North Carolina, South Carolina, and Georgia to Atlanta. On May 14 they leave Atlanta for Birmingham on two buses, one of which is attacked by a mob and firebombed outside Anniston, Alabama; when the other bus arrives in Birmingham, the Freedom Riders are beaten by Klansmen. Second group of Freedom Riders organized by SNCC leaves Birmingham on May 20 and is attacked by a mob in the Montgomery bus station. Attorney General Robert F. Kennedy sends federal marshals to Montgomery to protect Freedom Riders while urging an end to the protest. Marshals use tear gas against mob surrounding a church where civil rights meeting is being held. In attempt to avoid further federal involvement, Robert Kennedy arranges for Alabama and Mississippi National Guard to escort twenty-seven Freedom Riders from Montgomery to Jackson, Mississippi, where they are arrested at the bus station. Despite opposition from the Kennedy administration, Freedom Rides continue during the summer, with at least 1,000 people participating throughout the South and more than 300 people arrested in Jackson alone. (Many of the protestors arrested in Mississippi receive sixty-day sentences on state prison farms.) Interstate Commerce Commission issues new rules forbidding interstate carriers to use segregated terminals. Herbert Lee, a farmer working with Robert Moses of SNCC to register black voters, is killed in Liberty, Mississippi, on September 25 by E. H. Hurst, a state representative. Coroner's jury rules the killing to be self-defense, though Louis Allen, a witness, later tells the FBI Lee did not attack Hurst; Allen will be murdered in 1964. Coalition of civil rights groups and local black organizations in Albany, Georgia, forms Albany Movement to conduct protest campaign against segregation. More than 700 people are arrested in December before demonstrations are suspended to allow for negotiations with the city government.

1962 Boycott of city buses begins in Albany after negotiations fail. Council of Federated Organizations (COFO) is organized in Mississippi in February by coalition of civil rights groups, including NAACP, CORE, and SNCC, to register black voters. In March Robert Kennedy approves FBI wiretapping of Stanley Levison, a close adviser to King who had been identified by FBI informers as a major clandestine fundraiser for the Communist Party from 1952 to

1957. Justice Department officials warn King against associating with Levison, but he continues the relationship. Voter Education Project, new effort by coalition of groups including CORE, SNCC, NAACP, and SCLC to register blacks in the South, is launched in April. (In 1962 approximately 29 percent of the eligible black population in the South is registered to vote.) Fifth Circuit Court of Appeals orders James Meredith admitted to the University of Mississippi. Mass demonstrations resume in Albany in late July but are suspended in August when local leadership decides to concentrate on voter registration. Congress submits Twenty-fourth Amendment to the Constitution, abolishing poll taxes in federal elections, to the states for ratification on August 27. Mississippi governor Ross Barnett gives televised address vowing to resist any federal attempt to integrate the university and personally blocks attempts by Meredith to register. Meredith, Deputy Attorney General Nicholas Katzenbach, and 400 federal marshals arrive on Oxford campus of the university on September 30 after President Kennedy federalizes the Mississippi National Guard. During the night a mob of more than 2,000 people repeatedly attacks the marshals, who are reinforced by the Guard; two people are killed and more than 300 injured during the riot. Violence ends on October 1 as U.S. Army troops arrive from Memphis and Meredith registers. (U.S. Army deploys 12,000 men to Oxford area by October 2; the last troops will be withdrawn on July 24, 1963.) Kennedy issues Executive Order 11063 prohibiting racial discrimination in federally owned housing, in public housing built with federal funds, and in new housing built with loans from federal agencies.

1963 SCLC begins major campaign against segregation in Birmingham, Alabama, on April 3. King is arrested and writes "Letter from Birmingham Jail," justifying disobedience to unjust laws, before being released on bail. Mass marches by black high school students begin on May 2. Birmingham public safety commissioner Eugene (Bull) Connor orders police dogs and fire hoses used on the marchers and the police make more than 2,400 arrests. Demonstrations are suspended on May 8 for negotiations mediated by Justice Department officials, and an agreement is reached that establishes timetable for desegregation of downtown department stores, the creation of a biracial civic committee, and the release on bond of jailed protestors. After Klansmen set off two bombs in Birmingham on the night of May 11, rioting breaks out despite pleas of movement leaders for continued nonviolence. Supreme Court reverses convictions of sit-in protestors on May 20, ruling that state enforcement of restaurant segregation is a violation of the Fourteenth Amendment. Campaign of sit-ins and demonstrations begins in Jackson, Mississippi, led by Medgar Evers, the state field secretary of the NAACP since 1954. Two black students register at the University of Alabama at Tuscaloosa on June 11 after confrontation outside of administration building in which Katzenbach orders Governor George Wallace to cease his obstruction of the court order admitting the students. On the evening of June 11 President Kennedy gives televised address in which he calls racial discrimination "a moral crisis" and proposes passage of a new civil rights bill. Medgar Evers is assassinated outside his home early on June 12. National Guard is sent to Cambridge, Maryland, after rioting breaks out during protest campaign against segregation. Administration submits civil rights bill to Congress prohibiting racial discrimination in public accommodations. Demonstrations are suspended in Jackson, June 20, after the city agrees to hire black police officers, promote black sanitation workers, and desegregate municipal facilities. Agreement is mediated by Justice Department in Cambridge calling for limited school desegregation, the creation of a biracial committee, and holding a referendum on desegregating public accommodations. (During spring and summer of 1963, campaigns against segregation are also organized in Gadsden, Alabama; Savannah, Georgia; Plaquemine, Louisiana; Danville, Virginia; Raleigh, Greensboro, and Durham, North Carolina; and Charleston, South Carolina.) More than 200,000 people attend March for Jobs and Freedom in Washington, August 28, during which King delivers "I Have a Dream" speech. Klansmen bomb church in Birmingham on September 15, killing Denise McNair, age eleven, Cynthia Wesley, fourteen, Carole Robertson, fourteen, and Addie Mae Collins, fourteen. After learning that King is continuing to communicate with Stanley Levison, Robert Kennedy authorizes FBI wiretapping of King in October. (Wiretapping continues until June 1966; the FBI will also repeatedly place microphones in King's hotel rooms.) President Kennedy is assassinated in Dallas on

November 22 and Vice President Lyndon B. Johnson becomes president. Johnson begins intensive effort to move civil rights bill through Congress.

1964 In January COFO leadership approves SNCC plan to bring hundreds of volunteers, mostly white northern college students, to Mississippi during the summer. Ratification of the Twenty-fourth Amendment is completed on January 23. House of Representatives passes civil rights bill, 290–130, on February 10, and the Senate begins debate on the bill, March 9. Malcolm X resigns from the Nation of Islam. George Wallace enters three Democratic presidential primaries and receives 34 percent of the vote in Wisconsin, 30 percent in Indiana, and 43 percent in Maryland. Supreme Court rules 9–0 on May 25 that Prince Edward County, Virginia, must reopen its public school system, which has been closed since 1959. (In 1964, ten years after *Brown* decision, 55 percent of black students in the District of Columbia, Delaware, Kentucky, Maryland, Missouri, Oklahoma, and West Virginia attend integrated schools, while only 1.2 percent of black students in the eleven southern states attend school with whites.) Supreme Court unanimously overturns Alabama ban on the NAACP, allowing the organization to operate in the state for the first time since 1956. Senate votes 71–29 on June 10 to limit further debate on the civil rights bill, ending the longest filibuster in Senate history, and passes revised civil rights bill, 73–27, on June 19. First of approximately 950 "Freedom Summer" volunteers begin arriving in Mississippi to register voters, work in community centers, and teach in "Freedom Schools." Civil rights workers Andrew Goodman, Michael Schwerner, and James Chaney are murdered near Philadelphia, Mississippi, June 21, by Klansmen who bury their bodies under an earthen dam. Malcolm X announces formation of the Organization of Afro-American Unity on June 28. House passes final version of civil rights bill on July 2 and Johnson signs it the same day. The act strengthens federal power to protect voting rights; prohibits discrimination in public accommodations; authorizes the attorney general to file suits for the desegregation of schools and public facilities; bars discrimination in federally assisted programs; prohibits discrimination by employers and unions; and establishes an Equal Employment Opportunity Commission with investigative and mediative powers. Senator Barry Goldwater, who voted against the civil rights bill, wins the Republican presidential nomination. Fatal shooting of a black youth by a police officer in New York City leads to rioting in Harlem, July 18–21, in which one person is killed. The bodies of the three missing civil rights workers are discovered by the FBI on August 4. Newly founded Mississippi Freedom Democratic Party selects delegates to attend the Democratic national convention and challenge the seating of the all-white regular Democrats. Convention credentials committee votes on August 25 to seat regular Democrats who pledge their loyalty to the national party while offering Freedom Democrats two at-large seats. Freedom Democrats reject offer, and all but three of the regular Mississippi Democrats walk out of the convention. King is awarded the Nobel Peace Prize on October 14. Johnson wins election on November 3, defeating Goldwater 486–52 in the electoral voting; Goldwater carries Louisiana, Mississippi, Alabama, Georgia, and South Carolina. FBI mails tape compiled from potentially compromising hotel room recordings to King on November 21, along with an anonymous letter in which he is urged to commit suicide in order to avoid public disgrace. FBI agents arrest nineteen people on federal civil rights charges in the murders of Goodman, Schwerner, and Chaney (seven defendants, including a deputy sheriff, are convicted by an all-white jury in 1967). In *Katzenbach v. McClung* and *Heart of Atlanta Motel v. United States*, both decided 9–0, the Supreme Court upholds the constitutionality of the public accommodations sections of the 1964 Civil Rights Act, which are based on the power of Congress to regulate interstate commerce.

1965 SCLC begins voter registration campaign in Selma, Alabama, where more than 700 people are arrested during a march on February 1. Jimmie Lee Jackson, a church deacon and woodcutter, is fatally wounded by a state trooper during a demonstration in nearby Marion, Alabama. Malcolm X is assassinated in New York by members of the Nation of Islam on February 21. United States begins sustained bombing of North Vietnam on March 2. SCLC leaders organize fifty-four-mile march from Selma to Montgomery, the state capital. Several hundred marchers are beaten and tear-gassed by state police and sheriff's deputies as they cross the Edmund Pettus Bridge in Selma on "Bloody Sunday," March 7. James Reeb, a Unitarian minister from Boston, is fatally beaten in Selma on the evening of March 9. Johnson addresses Congress on March 15 and calls for the passage of a new voting rights bill. Civil rights march leaves Selma on March 21 under federal military protection and ends with mass rally outside of the state capitol in Montgomery on March 25. Viola Liuzzo, a civil rights volunteer from Detroit, is shot and killed by Klansmen in Lowndes County, Alabama. Senate votes 70–30 to end debate on voting rights bill, May 25, and passes the bill 77–19 on May 26. House of Representatives passes its version of the bill, 333–85, on July 9, and the final version is signed by Johnson on August 6. The Voting Rights Act prohibits the use of literacy tests in jurisdictions where less than 50 percent of the eligible population either was registered to vote on November 1, 1964, or voted in the 1964 presidential election (Alabama, Georgia, Louisiana, Mississippi, South Carolina, Virginia, and parts of North Carolina); gives the federal government the power to register voters in these jurisdictions; and prohibits changes in voting procedures in the covered jurisdictions without approval from either the attorney general or a federal court panel. (Proportion of eligible black voters registered in the South increases from 43 percent in 1964 to 62 percent in 1968.) Traffic stop by police leads to rioting in the Watts section of Los Angeles, August 11–16, in which thirty-four persons, most of them black, are killed. Johnson issues Executive Order 11246 requiring all federal contractors and subcontractors to take "affirmative action" to hire and promote persons without regard to race.

1966 Floyd McKissick succeeds James Farmer as national director of CORE. Civil rights activist Vernon Dahmer dies after his home is fire-bombed by Klansmen in Hattiesburg, Mississippi, on January 10. (At least thirty-five persons are killed by white supremacist terrorism in the South from 1954 to 1967.) Robert C. Weaver becomes the first black cabinet member when he is sworn in as the first secretary of housing and urban development. In *South Carolina v. Katzenbach*, the Supreme Court upholds 8–1 the constitutionality of the Voting Rights Act, and in *Harper v. Virginia State Board of Elections* it rules 6–3 that the imposition of poll taxes in state and local elections violates the Fourteenth Amendment. (In 2013 the court will overturn

5–4 the section in the Voting Rights Act requiring covered jurisdictions to obtain prior approval before changing their voting laws.) Johnson submits new civil rights bill to Congress on April 28 that provides enforcement powers to the EEOC, expands federal protection for civil rights workers, prohibits discrimination in the sale, rental, or financing of housing, and seeks to prevent discrimination in jury selection. Lowndes County Freedom Organization, an independent political party organized in Alabama by Stokely Carmichael and other SNCC activists, nominates all-black slate of candidates for county offices. John Lewis, national chairman of SNCC since 1963, is defeated for reelection by Carmichael, who announces that SNCC will no longer send white organizers into black communities. James Meredith begins one-man "walk against fear" through Mississippi and is wounded in an ambush on June 6. King, McKissick, and Carmichael agree to lead march along Meredith's intended route during which Carmichael gives speech calling for "black power." SCLC and Chicago civil rights groups begin campaign against housing discrimination, organizing series of marches through white neighborhoods that are often met with violence from mobs. House of Representatives passes civil rights bill with weakened open housing provision 259–157 on August 9. Attempt to end debate on civil rights bill fails in the Senate, where the open housing provision is opposed by Everett Dirksen, Republican minority leader whose support was crucial in the passage of 1964 and 1965 bills. Black Panther Party for Self-Defense is founded by Huey Newton and Bobby Seale in Oakland, California, on October 15. Edward Brooke, the Republican attorney general of Massachusetts, is elected to the Senate on November 8, becoming the first black senator since 1881 (six black representatives are reelected in 1966).

1967 King gives speech strongly condemning American involvement in Vietnam on April 4. H. Rap Brown succeeds Stokely Carmichael as chairman of SNCC and continues its commitment to "Black Power." Supreme Court rules 5–4 in *Reitman v. Mulkey* that a California state constitutional amendment allowing racial discrimination by property owners violates the Fourteenth Amendment, while in *Loving v. Virginia* the court rules 9–0 that laws prohibiting interracial marriage violate the Fourteenth Amendment.

Johnson appoints Thurgood Marshall to be the first black justice on the Supreme Court, June 13. Traffic arrest by police in Newark, New Jersey, leads to riot, July 12–17, in which twenty-six persons, most of them black, are killed. Police raid on after-hours club in Detroit, July 23, leads to widespread rioting, and on July 25 Johnson sends 4,700 army paratroopers to reinforce the National Guard. Riot ends July 27 after thirty-three black and ten white persons are killed. Johnson appoints commission headed by Illinois governor Otto Kerner to investigate recent civil disorders. House of Representatives passes bill extending protection for civil rights workers 326–93 on August 16. FBI director J. Edgar Hoover approves counterintelligence program (COINTELPRO) intended to disrupt black nationalist groups. Marches against housing discrimination in Milwaukee are met with violence from white mobs, August 28–31. Black Panther leader Huey Newton is charged in the shooting death of an Oakland police officer, the first in series of violent encounters between Black Panthers and the police. Carl Stokes wins election in Cleveland, Ohio, and Richard Hatcher is elected in Gary, Indiana, November 7, becoming the first black mayors of major American cities.

1968 Three black students are shot to death by state highway patrolmen on campus of South Carolina State College in Orangeburg, February 8, after series of demonstrations protesting segregation of a local bowling alley. Senate adds provision prohibiting racial discrimination in the sale, rental, or financing of housing to the civil rights bill passed by the House in 1967. Kerner Commission delivers report on February 29 warning that "the nation is moving toward two societies, one black, one white—separate and unequal." Senate votes to end debate on civil rights bill, March 4, after Dirksen reverses his earlier opposition to fair housing legislation and passes the bill 71–20 on March 11. Johnson announces on March 31 that he will not seek reelection. King is assassinated in Memphis on April 4. Rioting in Washington, Chicago, Baltimore, Kansas City, and other cities, April 5–9, results in forty-six deaths. House of Representatives passes Senate version of civil rights bill 250–172, and Johnson signs it on April 11. Abernathy succeeds King as president of the SCLC and leads Poor People's March to Washington, where protestors build "Resurrection City," plywood shantytown near the Washington Monument, in May. In *Green v. County School Board of New Kent County* the Supreme Court rejects 9–0 the "freedom of choice" desegregation plan adopted by a Virginia school district and orders it to end its dual school system. Senator Robert Kennedy is assassinated in Los Angeles on June 5 while campaigning for the Democratic presidential nomination. Supreme Court rules 7–2 in *Jones v. Alfred H. Mayer Co.* that racial discrimination in housing sales violates the 1866 Civil Rights Act. Police evict remaining protestors from Resurrection City on June 24. Huey Newton is convicted of voluntary manslaughter. Richard M. Nixon wins presidential election on November 5, defeating Vice President Hubert H. Humphrey and George Wallace, who ran as an independent. Nixon wins 301 electoral votes and carries Virginia, North Carolina, South Carolina, Florida, and Tennessee; Humphrey wins 191 electoral votes and carries Texas; and Wallace wins 46 electoral votes and carries Louisiana, Arkansas, Mississippi, Alabama, and Georgia. Shirley Chisholm wins election in Brooklyn and becomes the first black woman to serve in Congress. Black Panther leader Eldridge Cleaver flees the country to avoid imprisonment for a parole violation and goes into exile in Algeria.

1969 Federal appellate judge Warren Burger succeeds Earl Warren as chief justice on June 23. Department of Labor announces "Philadelphia Plan," requiring federal building contractors in Philadelphia to meet specific goals for hiring minority workers. Plan is criticized for establishing racial quotas, which are prohibited by the 1964 Civil Rights Act, but it withstands challenge in the federal courts and is later extended to several other cities. Nixon issues Executive Order 11478 requiring all federal agencies to adopt "affirmative programs for equal employment opportunity." Nomination of federal appellate judge Clement Haynsworth Jr. to the Supreme Court is opposed by civil rights groups and labor unions. In *Alexander v. Holmes County Board of Education*, decided 8–0, the Supreme Court declares the "all deliberate speed" standard is no longer constitutionally permissible and orders the immediate desegregation of thirty-three Mississippi school districts. Haynsworth nomination is rejected by the Senate 55–45 on November 21, becoming the first Supreme Court appointment defeated in a confirmation vote since 1930.

1970 Nomination of federal appellate judge G. Harrold Carswell to the Supreme Court meets with strong opposition from civil rights groups and is rejected by the Senate, 51–45, on April 8. Huey Newton is released from prison after his manslaughter conviction is overturned on appeal. Federal census shows 45 percent of the black population living in the southern states.

1971 Congressional Black Caucus is founded, February 2, with thirteen members (twelve representatives and one nonvoting delegate from the District of Columbia). Black Panther party splits into bitterly opposed factions headed by Newton and Cleaver. In *Griggs v. Duke Power Company* the Supreme Court rules 8–0 in favor of black employees who challenged the use of standardized tests by an employer with a past history of discrimination. Decision makes it easier to bring suits under the employment provisions of the 1964 Civil Rights Act in cases where there is no evidence of discriminatory intent. On April 20 the court rules 9–0 in *Swann v. Charlotte-Mecklenburg Board of Education*, upholding a court-ordered busing plan designed to achieve racial balance in a de jure segregated school system. (By close of the 1970–71 school year 33 percent of black students in the South attend white-majority schools.) Nomination of Assistant Attorney General William Rehnquist to the Supreme Court is approved 68–26 on December 10 despite opposition from civil rights groups.

1972 Congress passes Equal Employment Opportunity Act, March 24, giving the Equal Employment Opportunity Commission the power to file class-action lawsuits and extending its jurisdiction to cover state and local governments and educational institutions. Nixon wins reelection on November 7, defeating George McGovern 520–17 in the electoral voting and carrying all eleven southern states. Andrew Young, a former aide to King, is elected to the House of Representatives from Georgia, and Barbara Jordan is elected to the House from Texas; they are the first blacks elected to Congress from the South since 1898.

1973 Last American troops are withdrawn from South Vietnam on March 29. Tom Bradley becomes the first black mayor of Los Angeles. In *Keyes v. Denver School District No. 1*, decided June 21, the Supreme Court upholds 7–1 desegregation order involving busing in Denver, Colorado, ruling that decisions by school officials had reinforced de facto segregation. Maynard Jackson wins election in Atlanta on October 16 and becomes the first black mayor of a major southern city.

1974 Federal district judge rules that the Boston public schools are unconstitutionally segregated and orders the implementation of a busing plan. In *Milliken v. Bradley* the Supreme Court overturns 5–4 lower court decision ordering desegregation plan involving Detroit and fifty-three suburban school districts, ruling that the suburban districts had not engaged in discrimination. Nixon resigns the presidency on August 9 and is succeeded by Vice President Gerald Ford. School year begins in Boston on September 12 as white mobs attack buses carrying black students into South Boston. Protests and incidents of violence continue as school attendance drops.

1975 Elijah Muhammad dies on February 25. His death leads to a split in the Nation of Islam between members continuing to adhere to the Nation's separatist doctrines and those moving toward mainstream Sunni Islam.

1976 Photograph of white anti-busing protestor using an American flag to attack a black attorney outside Boston City Hall is widely printed in the press. Barbara Jordan delivers keynote address at the Democratic National Convention in New York City. Boston school year begins without major incidents as white enrollment in the public school system declines. Jimmy Carter wins presidential election on November 2, defeating Ford 297–240 in the electoral voting and carrying every southern state except Virginia, while seventeen black representatives win reelection to Congress.

Note on the Texts

This volume collects American writing about the political, legal, social, economic, and cultural aspects of the system of racial discrimination, segregation, disenfranchisement, and violence known as "Jim Crow." It brings together speeches, pamphlets, manifestos, essays, debates, newspaper and magazine articles, literary sketches, public and private letters, public testimony, judicial opinions and legal briefs, interviews, songs, memoranda, government documents, training materials prepared by civil rights activists, and excerpts from narratives and memoirs written by participants and observers and dealing with events in the period from 1919 to 1976. Some of these documents were not written for publication, and some of them existed only in manuscript or typescript during the lifetimes of their creators. With twenty-five exceptions, the texts presented in this volume are taken from printed sources. In cases where there is only one printed source for a document, the text offered here comes from that source. Where there is more than one printed source for a document, the text printed in this volume is taken from the source that appears to contain the fewest editorial alterations in the spelling, capitalization, paragraphing, and punctuation of the original. In the twenty-five instances where no printed source was available, the text in this volume is printed from a typescript or online transcription.

This volume prints texts as they appear in the sources listed below, but with a few alterations in editorial procedure. The text of the membership appeal by Marcus Garvey addressed to "the Negro Citizens of New York" in July 1921 is presented in *The Marcus Garvey and Universal Negro Improvement Association Papers* from a typed document in the National Archives. The bracketed conjectural readings offered by the editors of *The Marcus Garvey and Universal Negro Improvement Association Papers* in places where the document was mutilated are accepted without brackets in this volume when these readings seem to be the only possible ones, but when they do not, the missing word or words are indicated by a bracketed two-em space, i.e., [   ]. In one instance the editors indicated a damaged passage by printing an ellipsis followed by "[*words mutilated*]"; the present volume omits the ellipsis and prints a bracketed two-em space at 67.10. The bracketed correction used by the editors of *The Marcus Garvey and Universal Negro Improvement Association Papers* to supply the missing number in an address is accepted and printed without brackets in this volume at 69.35.

In *Mary McLeod Bethune: Building a Better World* (1999), edited by Audrey Thomas McCluskey and Elaine Smith, bracketed editorial insertions were used to identify government organizations and to supply the first names of individuals in the text of the letter to Franklin D. Roosevelt drafted by Bethune on November 27, 1939. This volume omits the bracketed insertions.

Four errors that appeared in the printed source texts are corrected in this volume: at 77.36, "two witnesses" becomes "three witnesses," at 142.33, "D. A. Sweet" becomes "D. A. Stewart," at 186.18–20, the sentence "He states . . . Jackson and Morgan counties," which was repeated in *The Daily Worker*, is printed only once, and at 270.1, "sailors" becomes "soldiers." Two errors that appeared in typescript sources are also corrected: at 587.7, "effect is in" becomes "effect in," and at 701.4, "were closely" becomes "were close."

In presenting the text of the oral history interview with Otis Clark conducted by the Voices of Oklahoma project in 2009, this volume corrects eleven errors in the online transcript by reference to the audio recording of the interview: at 51.31 "were" becomes "or," at 51.40 "(inaudible)" becomes "talkies," at 52.1–2 and 59.14 "(inaudible)" becomes "Stepin Fetchit," at 52.25 "until said" becomes "in Tulsa," at 55.23 "done" becomes "down," at 55.36–37 "garage store" becomes "garage door," at 56.36 "week loss cross" becomes "we crossed," at 57.39 "law (rights)" becomes "law," at 58.4 "years in" becomes "years and," and at 63.18 "you are" becomes "your." Two transcription errors in the oral history interview of Thurgood Marshall conducted by the Lyndon Baines Johnson Library in 1969 are also corrected by reference to the audio recording: at 634.13 "elimination of Part 3 divisions" becomes "elimination of the Part 3" and at 634.20 "inner corps" becomes "inner core."

An error in the online transcription of the speech by Charlotta Bass accepting the vice-presidential nomination of the Progressive Party on March 30, 1952, has been corrected in this volume by reference to the excerpts from the speech printed in the April 2, 1952, number of the *National Guardian*: at 332.18–19 "the great corporations which Negroes" becomes "the great corporations which extort huge profits from my people, and forced them to employ Negroes."

The following is a list of the documents included in this volume, in the order of their appearance, giving the source of each text:

1919–1945

Walter White: The Race Conflict in Arkansas. *The Survey*, December 13, 1919.

Ida B. Wells-Barnett: Condemned Arkansas Rioters Look to Chicago for Help. *The Chicago Defender*, December 13, 1919.

Archibald H. Grimké: The Shame of America, December 29, 1919. Archibald H. Grimké, *The Shame of America, or, The Negro's Case Against the Republic* (Washington, D.C.: American Negro Academy, 1924).

Military Intelligence Division: Memorandum on Marcus Garvey, May 5, 1921. *The Marcus Garvey and Universal Negro Improvement Association Papers*, vol. III, *September 1920–August 1921*, ed. Robert A. Hill (Berkeley: University of California Press, 1984), 387–88. Copyright © 1984 by the Regents of the University of California. Reprinted by permission.

Mary E. Jones Parrish: from *Events of the Tulsa Disaster*. Mary E. Jones Parrish, *Events of the Tulsa Disaster* (Privately printed, 1922), 7–13, 41–42.

B. C. Franklin: The Tulsa Race Riot and Three of Its Victims. Collection of the Smithsonian National Museum of African American History and Culture. Gift from Tulsa Friends and John W. and Karen R. Franklin.

Otis Clark: Oral History Interview on the Tulsa Race Massacre. Interview with John Erling, November 23, 2009, Voices of Oklahoma, Oklahoma Historical Society. Used by permission of John Erling.

Marcus Garvey: Membership Appeal to the Negro Citizens of New York, July 1921. *The Marcus Garvey and Universal Negro Improvement Association Papers*, vol. III, *September 1920–August 1921*, ed. Robert A. Hill (Berkeley: University of California Press, 1984), 560–64. Copyright © 1984 by the Regents of the University of California. Reprinted by permission.

Scipio Africanus Jones: Petition for Writ of Habeas Corpus in *Moore v. Dempsey*, September 21, 1921. *The Crisis*, December 1921 to January 1922.

Warren G. Harding: Address in Birmingham, Alabama, October 26, 1921. *Address of the President of the United States at the celebration of the semicentennial of the founding of the city of Birmingham, Alabama, October 26, 1921* (Washington, D.C., 1921).

Raymond Clapper: Timely Talk on Race Issue. *Riverside Daily Press*, October 26, 1921.

James Weldon Johnson: The Passage of the Dyer Bill. *New York Age*, February 4, 1922.

Colonel Mayfield's Weekly: Negro Porter Whipped by Masked Citizens of Abilene. *Colonel Mayfield's Weekly*, February 18, 1922.

W. P. Evans: To the Editor of *The Observer*. *The Charlotte Observer*, May 20 and June 3, 1923.

George Brooks: Far Away Blues. Angela Y. Davis, *Blues Legacies and Black Feminism* (New York: Pantheon, 1998), 278.

Walter White: Report on the Lynching of Sammie Smith, December 1924. Typescript, NAACP Records, Manuscript Division (053.00.09), Library of Congress. Courtesy of the National Association for the Advancement of Colored People.

The Rocky Mountain News: Decision Rendered in Students' Row. *The Rocky Mountain News*, January 8, 1925.

Alain Locke: Enter the New Negro. *The Survey Graphic*, March 1925.

W.E.B. Du Bois: The Challenge of Detroit. *The Crisis*, November 1925.

The New York Amsterdam News: We Must Fight if We Would Survive. *The New York Amsterdam News*, November 18, 1925.

Nettie George Speedy: "Not Guilty," Dr. Sweet Tells Jury. *The Chicago Defender*, November 28, 1925.

Clifton F. Richardson: Why I Stay in Texas and Fight. *Pittsburgh Courier*, September 24, 1927.

Ned Cobb: from *All God's Dangers: The Life of Nate Shaw*. Theodore Rosengarten, *All God's Dangers: The Life of Nate Shaw* (New York: Alfred A. Knopf, 1974), 101–8, 188–190. Copyright © 1974 by Theodore Rosengarten and the Estate of Ned Cobb. Used by permission of Alfred A. Knopf, an imprint of the Knopf Doubleday Publishing Group, a division of Penguin Random House LLC. All rights reserved.

Elizabeth Lawson: *They Shall Not Die! Stop the Legal Lynching: The Story of Scottsboro in Pictures*. Elizabeth Lawson, *They Shall Not Die! Stop the Legal Lynching: The Story of Scottsboro in Pictures* (New York: Workers' Library Publishers, 1932).

The Advocate: Calls Negro Masses to Unite. *The Advocate*, June 19, 1932.

The Chicago Defender: What Do You Say About It? *The Chicago Defender*, September 10, 1932.

Baltimore Afro-American: The Lynching of George Armwood. *Baltimore Afro-American*, October 28, 1933. Courtesy of the AFRO American Newspaper Archives.

California Eagle: Scottsboro Youths in Greatest Danger; Organizations Asked to Send Delegates to Congress. *California Eagle*, July 20, 1934.

Ben Davis, Jr.: Scottsboro Attorneys in Higher Court. *The Daily Worker*, February 16, 1935. Used by permission of *People's World*.

Marguerite Young: Knight Has No Answer to the Scottsboro Defense. *The Daily Worker*, February 19, 1935. Used by permission of *People's World*.

Baltimore Afro-American: Watching the Scottsboro Case in Supreme Court. *Baltimore Afro-American*, February 23, 1935. Courtesy of the AFRO American Newspaper Archives.

Louis R. Lautier: Highest Court Hears Scottsboro Case. *Baltimore Afro-American*, February 23, 1935. Courtesy of the AFRO American Newspaper Archives.

Grace Mott Johnson: Draft Letter to the Editor on the Scottsboro Case, April 6, 1936. Typescript, NAACP Records, Group I, Box D-74, correspondence folder April 1–27, 1936, Manuscript Division, Library of Congress. Used by permission of The National Association for The Advancement of Colored People.

Haywood Patterson to Anna Damon, October 12, 1937. *The Scottsboro Boys in Their Own Words: Selected Letters, 1931–1950*, ed. Kwando M. Kinshasa (Jefferson, NC: McFarland & Company, Inc., 2014), 187–88. Copyright © 2014 by Kwando M. Kinshasa. Used by permission of McFarland Company, Inc., Box 611, Jefferson, NC 28640.

Mary McLeod Bethune: Draft Letter to Franklin D. Roosevelt, November 27, 1939. *Mary McLeod Bethune: Building a Better World*, ed. Audrey Thomas McCluskey and Elaine Smith (Bloomington: Indiana University Press, 1999), 236–40. Copyright © 1999 by Indiana University Press.

Walter White: It's Our Country, Too. *Saturday Evening Post*, December 14, 1940. Licensed by Curtis Licensing, Indianapolis. All rights reserved.

James G. Thompson: Should I Sacrifice To Live "Half-American"? *Pittsburgh Courier*, January 31, 1942. Used by permission of the Pittsburgh Courier Archives.

March on Washington Movement: Why Should We March? Leaflet, Box 26, A. Philip Randolph Papers, Manuscript Division, Library of Congress.

Thurgood Marshall: The Gestapo in Detroit. *The Crisis*, August 1943. Copyright © 1943 by The Crisis Publishing Company Inc. Used by permission of the publisher of *The Crisis*, The National Association for the Advancement of Colored People.

Deton J. Brooks, Jr.: Morale Sags at Camp Forrest as Jim Crow Rules. *The Chicago Defender*, November 6, 1943.

James Agee: *The Negro Soldier*. *Time*, March 27, 1944. Copyright © 1944 TIME USA LLC. All rights reserved. Used under license.

Fletcher P. Martin: Negro Marines Win Admiration Of Vets in Southwest Pacific. *The Apache Sentinel*, April 7, 1944.

Committee for Equal Justice for Mrs. Recy Taylor: The Woman Next Door: A Story of Unequal Justice. Brochure, NAACP Records, Manuscript Division (018.00.00), Library of Congress. Used by permission of The National Association for the Advancement of Colored People.

Earl Conrad, Eugene Gordon, and Henrietta Buckmaster: Equal Justice Under Law. Earl Conrad and Eugene Gordon, *Equal Justice*

Under Law, foreword by Henrietta Buckmaster (New York: Committee for Equal Justice for Mrs. Recy Taylor, n.d.).

Raymond and Rosa Parks to Chauncey Sparks, March 16, 1945. Typescript, SG12505, Folder 8, Alabama Department of Archives and History.

Theodore Stanford: Reporting from Europe. 784th Wins Battle Honors In Capturing German Towns, *Pittsburgh Courier*, March 31, 1945; Democracy Goal of Tan Yanks Abroad, *Pittsburgh Courier*, May 19, 1945; German Women See Tan Yanks as Men Only, *Pittsburgh Courier*, June 9, 1945. Used by permission of the Pittsburgh Courier Archives.

Pauli Murray: An American Credo. *Common Ground*, Winter 1945. Copyright 1945 by the Common Council for American Unity.

1946–1963

Wendell Smith: It Was a Great Day in Jersey. *Pittsburgh Courier*, April 27, 1946. Courtesy of the National Baseball Hall of Fame and Museum, Cooperstown, NY, Wendell Smith papers, BA MSS 001.

Harry Raymond: Lynch Try Fails on "Daily" Man and Lawyers in Tenn. *Daily Worker*, November 20, 1946. Used by permission of *People's World*.

Journal of the National Medical Association: Make Lynching a Federal Offense. *Journal of the National Medical Association*, July 1947. Used by permission of Elsevier.

Anne Moody: from *Coming of Age in Mississippi*. Anne Moody, *Coming of Age in Mississippi* (New York: Dial Press, 1968), 36–40. Copyright © 1968 by Anne Moody. Used by permission of Doubleday, an imprint of the Knopf Doubleday Publishing Group, a division of Penguin Random House LLC. All rights reserved.

Hubert H. Humphrey: Speech to the Democratic National Convention, July 14, 1948. *The Civil Rights Rhetoric of Hubert H. Humphrey, 1948–1968*, ed. Paula Wilson (Lanham MD: University Press of America, 1996), 3–5. Copyright © 1996 by University Press of America. Reprinted by permission of the Minnesota Historical Society.

Birmingham Convention of States' Rights Democrats: Declaration of Principles, July 17, 1948. Strom Thurmond Collection, Mss 100.355, Clemson University Libraries. Used by permission.

Lillian Smith: from *Killers of the Dream*. Lillian Smith, *Killers of the Dream* (New York: W. W. Norton, 1949), 15–20. Copyright © 1949, 1961 by Lillian Smith. Used by permission of W. W. Norton & Company, Inc.

Lonnie E. Smith and Christia V. Adair: Message from the NAACP to the Negro Voters of Harris County, August 21, 1950. Christia V. Adair Collection, MSS109, Houston Metropolitan Research Center, Houston Public Library. Used by permission of the The National Association for the Advancement of Colored People.

Julius Waties Waring: Dissent in *Briggs v. Elliott*, June 23, 1951. 98 Federal Supplement 529 (E.D.S.C. 1951), 538–48.

Charlotta Bass: Acceptance Speech as Vice Presidential Candidate of the Progressive Party, March 30, 1952. BlackPast.org, accessed January 28, 2025, https://www.blackpast.org/african-american-history/1952-charlotta-bass-acceptance-speech-vice-presidential-candidate-progressive-party.

Portland Challenger: Negro Family to Remain Despite Flaming Cross. *Portland Challenger*, May 20, 1953. Used by permission of Dian Hilliard.

Alice A. Dunnigan: Resents Ike's Taking Credit for Winning DC Restaurant Case. *New York Amsterdam News*, June 20, 1953. Used by permission.

Earl Warren: Opinion in *Brown v. Board of Education of Topeka*, May 17, 1954. U.S. Reports: 347 U.S. 483 (1954), 486–96.

Jo Ann Gibson Robinson: from *The Montgomery Bus Boycott and the Women Who Started It: The Memoir of Jo Ann Gibson Robinson. The Montgomery Bus Boycott and the Women Who Started It: The Memoir of Jo Ann Gibson Robinson*, ed. David J. Garrow (Knoxville: University of Tennessee Press, 1987), 22–24, 43–47. Copyright © 1987 by The University of Tennessee Press/Knoxville. Used by permission of The University of Tennessee Press.

Big Bill Broonzy: When Will I Get to Be Called a Man. William Broonzy as told to Yannick Bruynoghe, *Big Bill Blues* (London: Cassell, 1955), 70. Copyright © 1955 by Yannick Bruynoghe.

Southern Senators and Representatives: Declaration of Constitutional Principles, March 12, 1956. *Congressional Record*, 84th Congress, 2nd Session, 4460–4461.

The Chicago Defender: Alabama Pickets Rock-Roll Troupe. *The Chicago Defender*, May 21, 1956. Used by permission of United Press International.

Harry Golden: How to Solve the Segregation Problem. *The Carolina Israelite*, May–June 1956. Reprinted by permission of the Estate of Harry L. Golden.

Paul Robeson: from Testimony Before the House Committee on Un-American Activities, June 12, 1956. *Investigation of the Unauthorized Use of United States Passports—Part 3*, Hearing before the House Committee on Un-American Activities, 84th Congress, 2nd

Session (Washington, D.C.: Government Printing Office, 1956), 4498–99, 4503–5, 4505–6, 4508–9.

Elijah Muhammad: Mr. Muhammad Speaks: Who Is the Original Man?, *The Pittsburgh Courier*, July 28, 1956. Used by permission of the Pittsburgh Courier Archives.

Malcolm X: We Are Rising from the Dead Since We Heard Messenger Muhammad . . . *The Pittsburgh Courier*, December 15 and 22, 1956. Used by permission of the Pittsburgh Courier Archives.

Paulette Williams Grant: Oral History Interview on Life in Houston in the 1950s and 1960s. Interview by David Goldstein, Houston Oral History Project, Houston Public Library, OHE 0239, June 30, 2008. Used by permission of Houston History Research Center.

The Chicago Defender: Predicts End To Housing Bias, Migrations. *The Chicago Defender*, September 13, 1958.

Ella Baker: Bigger Than A Hamburger. *The Southern Patriot*, May 1960.

Robert F. Williams: from *Negroes with Guns*. Robert F. Williams, *Negroes with Guns*, ed. Marc Schleifer (New York: Marzani & Munsell, Inc., 1962), 39–41. Copyright © 1962 Marzani & Munsell, Inc.

Congress of Racial Equality: Negro Voting in Louisiana, c. 1962–63. Typescript, Wisconsin Historical Society Mss 85, Congress of Racial Equality, Southern Regional Office Records, box 17, folder 4.

Louisiana Voter Registration Procedures, c. 1963. Veterans of the Civil Rights Movement—Louisiana Voter Literacy Test, accessed January 28, 2025, https://www.crmvet.org/info/la-test.htm.

George Wallace: Inaugural Address as Governor of Alabama, January 14, 1963. *The Inaugural Address of Governor George Wallace, January 14, 1963, Montgomery, Alabama*. Pamphlet, SG 030847, Alabama Department of Archives and History. Used by permission of the Alabama Department of Archives and History.

Student Nonviolent Coordination Committee: Violence Stalks Voter-Registration Workers in Mississippi, March 12, 1963. Typescript, Wisconsin Historical Society, Ella Baker Papers, 1959–65, SC 628.

Fred Shuttlesworth: Statement on State Court Injunction Against Demonstrations, April 14, 1963. Typescript, Shuttlesworth Collection, Birmingham Civil Rights Institute.

Dallas County Citizens Council: Ask Yourself This Important Question: What Have I Personally Done to Maintain Segregation? *The Selma Times-Journal*, June 9, 1963.

John F. Kennedy: Report to the American People on Civil Rights, June 11, 1963. *Public Papers of the Presidents of the United States: John F. Kennedy, 1963* (Washington, D.C.: Government Printing Office, 1964), 468–71.

Official Program for the March on Washington, August 28, 1963. March on Washington (Program), 08/28/1963; Bayard Rustin Papers, John F. Kennedy Library, National Archives and Records Administration.

John Lewis: Speech at the March on Washington, Original Text and Speech as Delivered, August 28, 1963. Original text: Typescript, Wisconsin Historical Society, Hank Werner Papers, Z. Accessions, M71-358, box 2, folder 5. Speech as delivered: Voices of Democracy, the U.S. Oratory Project, accessed January 28, 2025, https://voicesofdemocracy.umd.edu/lewis-speech-at-the-march-on-washington-speech-text/.

1964–1976

Sue Cronk: Labor Report Shows: Negro Women Are Improving Their Status. *The Washington Post*, March 28, 1964. Copyright © 1964 *The Washington Post*. All rights reserved. Used under license.

Malcolm X: The Ballot or the Bullet, April 3, 1964. *Malcolm X Speaks: Selected Speeches and Statements*, ed. George Breitman (New York: Grove Press, 1966), 23–44. Copyright © 1965 by Merit Publishers and Betty Shabazz.

Program of the Mississippi Freedom Democratic Party, c. June 1964. Typescript, Wisconsin Historical Society, Ella Baker Papers, Archives Main Stacks, SC 628.

Mike Mansfield, Richard Russell, Hubert H. Humphrey, and Everett McKinley Dirksen: Remarks in the Senate on the Civil Rights Bill, June 10, 1964. *Congressional Record*, 88th Congress, 2nd Session, 13307–10, 13319–20.

Fannie Lou Hamer: Testimony to the Credentials Committee, Democratic National Convention, August 22, 1964. *The Speeches of Fannie Lou Hamer: To Tell It Like It Is*, ed. Maegan Parker Brooks and David W. Houck (Jackson: University Press of Mississippi, 2011). Copyright © 2011 University Press of Mississippi. Used by permission of The Family of Fannie Lou Hamer.

Robert Penn Warren and Bayard Rustin: An Exchange on Urban Riots and Policing, 1964. Typescript, Robert Penn Warren Center for the Humanities, Vanderbilt University. Used by permission of John Burt.

John Herbers: Dr. King Rebuts Hoover Charges. *The New York Times*, November 20, 1964. Copyright © 1964 *The New York Times*. All rights reserved. Used under license.

Sample Alabama Literacy Questions, c. 1964–65. Veterans of the Civil Rights Movement—Alabama Voter Literacy Test, Parts "B" and

"C," accessed January 28, 2025, https://www.crmvet.org/info/litques.pdf.

James Baldwin and William F. Buckley: Debate at the Cambridge Union, February 18, 1965. Nicholas Buccola, *The Fire Is Upon Us: James Baldwin, William F. Buckley Jr., and the Debate over Race in America* (Princeton, NJ: Princeton University Press, 2019), 374, 379–99. Copyright © 2019 by Princeton University Press. Reprinted by permission of Princeton University Press.

John Conyers: Speech in Congress on the Voting Rights Act, July 8, 1965. *Congressional Record*, 89th Congress, 1st Session, 15999–16000.

CORE Voter Registration Training Materials for Louisiana, c. 1965. Veterans of the Civil Rights Movement—Louisiana Voter Application and Literacy Tests, accessed January 28, 2025, https://www.crmvet.org/info/la-vr-training.pdf.

Palm Springs Desert Sun: School Trustees Set Talk on Negro Hiring, September 30, 1965, and Greater Effort Pledged on Hiring Negro Teachers, October 1, 1965. *Palm Springs Desert Sun*, September 30 and October 1, 1965. Used by permission of *The Desert Sun*.

Vine City Project: Statement on Black Power, Spring 1966. "Black Power: A Reprint of a Position Paper for the SNCC Vine City Project," United States National Student Association, accessed January 28, 2025, https://freedomarchives.org/Documents/Finder/DOC513_scans/SNCC/513.SNCC.black.power.summer.1966.pdf.

John Hulett: How the Black Panther Party Was Organized, May 22, 1966. *The Black Panther Party* (New York: Merit Publishers, 1968), 7–15. Copyright 1966 by John Hulett.

Stokely Carmichael: Speech on Black Power, October 29, 1966. Stokely Carmichael, *Stokely Speaks: Black Power Back to Pan-Africanism* (New York: Random House, 1971), 45–60. Copyright © 1965, 1971 by Stokely Carmichael.

Ten-Point Program of the Black Panther Party for Self-Defense. *The Black Panther*, May 15, 1967.

Earl Warren: Opinion in *Loving v. Virginia*, June 12, 1967. U.S. Reports: 388 U.S. 1 (1967), 2–12.

Thurgood Marshall: from Oral History Interview on Lyndon B. Johnson, 1941–67. Transcript, Thurgood Marshall Oral History Interview I, 7/10/69, by T. H. Baker, Internet Copy, LBJ Library.

Madison Capital Times: Mob Violence in Milwaukee. Ken Hartnett: Milwaukee Rights Office Firebombed, August 30, 1967; Not Too Young To Be Hated, August 30, 1967; William Schulz: Cheer as Marchers Hurt: "Kill, Kill, Kill," the Mob Chanted,

August 30, 1967. Used by permission of the Associated Press.
Lee A. Meyerpeter: Mayor Tries to Head Off More Milwaukee Marches, August 30, 1967. Used by permission of United Press International.

A Teacher to Father James Groppi, August 30, 1967. Typescript, Wisconsin Historical Society, James Groppi Papers, box 8, folders 3–6, Correspondence, Hate Mail, 1967.

Henry Maier: Statement at a Press Conference, August 31, 1967. Typescript, Wisconsin Historical Society, Maier Administration, box 170, folder 23, Speeches, 1967.

Leonard D. Mills to Father James Groppi, November 4, 1967. Typescript, Wisconsin Historical Society, James Groppi Papers, box 4, folder 3, Correspondence, Support Mail, 1966–67.

Report of the National Advisory Commission on Civil Disorders: from the Summary: Introduction, The Basic Causes, February 29, 1968. *Report* (Washington, D.C.: Government Printing Office, 1968), 1–2, 5.

Report of the National Advisory Commission on Civil Disorders: Police and the Community, February 29, 1968. *Report* (Washington, D.C.: Government Printing Office, 1968), 157–68.

Community on the Move for Equality: Have Sanitation Workers a Future?, Spring 1968. Leaflet, Veterans of the Civil Rights Movement—1968 Organizing & Political Materials, accessed January 28, 2025, crmvet.org/docs/6803_memphis1.pdf.

Whitney Young: from Oral History Interview on Lyndon B. Johnson, 1955–68. Transcript, Whitney M. Young, Jr., Oral History Interview I, 6/18/69, by Thomas Harrison Baker, Internet Copy, LBJ Library.

Annette Chandler: Father Groppi: A Modern Priest Looks at a Racist Society. *Denver Center Fourth Estate*, March 5, 1969. Used by permission of University of Colorado Denver.

Shirley Chisholm: Speech at Howard University, April 21, 1969. *Say It Loud!: Great Speeches on Civil Rights and African American Identity*, ed. Catherine Ellis and Stephen Drury Smith (New York: The New Press, 2010), 104–11. Copyright © 2010 by Catherine Ellis and Stephen Drury Smith.

Nick Kotz: Future of Civil Rights Worries Old Guard as Gains Are Noted. *The Washington Post*, December 25, 1972. Copyright © 1972 *The Washington Post*. All rights reserved. Used under license.

Ron Hutson: Common Fear, Safety for Students, Ripples through North Dorchester, Roxbury as Busing Becomes Real. *The Boston Globe*, June 27, 1974. Copyright © 1974 Boston Globe Media Partners. All rights reserved. Used under license.

Thurgood Marshall: from Dissent in *Milliken v. Bradley*, July 25, 1974. U.S. Reports: 433 U.S. 267 (1967), 781–83, 814–15.

Thomas Pettigrew: Race, Schools and Riots in Boston. *New Society*, November 1974.

Barbara Jordan: Keynote Address at the Democratic National Convention, July 12, 1976. Barbara Jordan, *Speaking the Truth with Eloquent Thunder*, ed. Max Sherman (Austin: University of Texas Press, 2007), 35–40. Copyright © 2007 by the University of Texas Press. Used by permission of the Barbara Jordan Foundation.

This volume presents the texts of the printings, typescripts, and online transcriptions chosen as sources here but does not attempt to reproduce features of their typographic design or physical layout. The texts are printed without alteration except for the changes previously discussed and for the correction of typographical errors. Spelling, punctuation, and capitalization are often expressive features, and they are not altered, even when inconsistent or irregular. The text of "Race, Schools and Riots in Boston" by Thomas Pettigrew is taken from the November 1974 number of *New Society*, an English publication, and retains the English spellings (e.g., "rumours" for "rumors") and punctuation (e.g., the use of "Mrs" without a period) in that printing. The following is a list of typographical errors corrected, cited by page and line number: 13.30, Declaraton; 17.23, oxydized; 26.39, villanous; 29.14, bedriven; 30.1–2, if were were; 30.25, it is; 33.27, granay; 33.35, lead; 34.21, though; 35.6–7, spmpathy; 35.22, oftimes; 36.2, victum; 38.6, he said.; 51.32, 802 were; 55.29, sisters; 56.34, where; 58.35, little-old, shack; 66.11, this an; 73.6, Straus; 73.7, E. M. A. Lien; 73.7, J. E. Horner; 73.8, T. W. Keese; 75.2, meeting:; 75.28, W. W. Keese; 77.36, Wards; 85.21, titantic; 101.11, for: he; 101.24, dellapidated; 102.4, that its; 102.14, exodous; 102.15, probition; 102.15, imigration; 102.24, Poto; 102.37, by he; 103.12, remoltest; 103.19, statement find; 104.36, flood if; 106.27, do) Inquire; 106.38, that it; 127.23, revaluaation; 140.29, missles; 142.33, Bistol; 143.27, automolble; 147.3, spheriod; 160.35, Boaz; 168.6, brass-band; 171.9, meetngs; 171.11, Is this; 177.18–19, an dwhatever; 178.20, Easter nShore; 178.24, 'good boy"; 182.37, with his; 183.2, fnished; 183.10, suposed; 185.23, Callohan; 186.25, Derventer; 187.4 and 5, Deventer; 189.36, didnt; 206.10, that six; 229.16, record; Many; 229.19, kill by; 230.28, things; 233.35, Y.M.C.A. put; 243.9, Island; 253.8, threasher.; 264.8, platoon's; 266.31, averaged; 267.17, peoples'; 267.20, home.; 270.6, Completly; 271.33, Ayran; 280.2, with their; 284.6, before and; 288.2, corespondent; 288.10, Pouge; 293.32, "'Essie; 300.2, people.; 301.10, hypocratically; 303.12, ignominously; 310.8, its; 318.28, Europens; 325.10, Charmichael; 333.5,

Wilkie's; 337.28, inestigating; 339.9, Co-Ordinating; 341.24, at all.; 341.32, and the; 347.25, laws.; 363.20, sarrying; 365.16, need; 370.15, Douglas; 376.2, an earth; 378.23, KIDNAPED; 380.7, bondage which; 380.14 and 22, kidnaped; 382.37, (Isaiah 9:2); 384.12–13, Almight; 390.32, happy than; 396.23, of the; 396.29, segregation.; 397.7, for he; 397.25, ECONOMICS.; 398.21, as contributing; 406.37–38, preceeding; 410.36, register. When; 417.11, instructons; 430.27, from President.; 431.7, places; 434.29, names; 436.32, of; 443.36, capitol.; 446.33 and 39, pseudo-; 447.24, seek; 448.15, beleagured; 448.32, desserts; 449.22, others; 523.16, makes; 525.1, resolved It; 525.24, 1880; 536.29, dicuss; 537.13, conection; 538.16, F.B.I.; 539.24, F.B.I,"; 548.20, have don't have; 565.5, resorted more; 565.18, 1965; 583.23, problem; 584.32, personel; 586.8, will ever; 617.8, than; 622.22, DISPOSE; 647.33, dellapidated; 649.18, clerymen; 692.20, figures; 698.12, possibly; 698.26, and and control; 719.30, villans; 720.27, particulary; 722.29, then; 723.4, havent'; 725.25, chilren; 725.33, shcool; 727.26, is is; 728.31, montiter; 736.4, ethonic; 737.29, Sergeant.

Notes

In the notes below, the reference numbers denote page and line of this volume (the line count includes headings but not rule lines). No note is made for material included in the eleventh edition of *Merriam-Webster's Collegiate Dictionary*. Biblical references are keyed to the King James Version. Quotations from Shakespeare are keyed to *The Riverside Shakespeare*, ed. G. Blakemore Evans (Boston: Houghton Mifflin, 1974). Footnotes and bracketed editorial notes within the text were in the originals. For further historical background and references to other studies, see David M. Kennedy, *Freedom from Fear: The American People in Depression and War, 1929–1945* (New York: Oxford University Press, 1999); James T. Patterson, *Grand Expectations: The United States, 1945–1974* (New York: Oxford University Press, 1996); Grace Elizabeth Hale, *Making Whiteness: The Culture of Segregation in the South, 1890–1940* (New York: Pantheon Books, 1998); *Encyclopedia of African-American Civil Rights, From Emancipation to the Present*, ed. Charles D. Lowery and John F. Marszalek (Westport, CT: Greenwood Press, 1992); Ralph E. Luker, *Historical Dictionary of the Civil Rights Movement* (Lanham, MD: The Scarecrow Press, 1997); Tera Hunter, *To 'Joy My Freedom: Black Women's Lives and Labors after the Civil War* (Cambridge, MA: Harvard University Press, 1997); Robin D.G. Kelley, *Freedom Dreams: The Black Radical Imagination* (Boston: Beacon Press, 2002); Danielle McGuire, *At the Dark End of the Street: Black Women, Rape, and Resistance—A New History of the Civil Rights Movement from Rosa Parks to the Rise of Black Power* (New York: Alfred A. Knopf, 2010); and Barbara Ransby, *Ella Baker and the Black Freedom Movement: A Radical Democratic Vision* (Chapel Hill: The University of North Carolina Press, 2003).

1919–1945

3.2 WALTER WHITE] Born in Atlanta, Walter White (1893–1955) graduated from Atlanta University in 1916. White became assistant executive secretary of the NAACP in 1918 and its executive secretary in 1930, serving until his death. He published two novels, *The Fire in the Flint* (1924) and *Flint* (1926), a study of lynching, *Rope and Faggot* (1929), and an autobiography, *A Man Called White* (1948).

7.2 IDA B. WELLS-BARNETT] Born in Holly Springs, Mississippi, Ida B. Wells-Barnett (1862–1931) published a newspaper in Memphis, Tennessee, until its offices were destroyed by a white mob in 1892. Wells began a campaign against lynching, lecturing in the United States and Great Britain and publishing the pamphlets *Southern Horrors* (1892) and *A Red Record* (1895). She married Ferdinand Barnett, a Chicago lawyer and newspaper editor, in 1895. A founder of the NAACP, Wells-Barnett continued to write about racial violence in the pamphlets *Lynch Law in Georgia* (1899), *Mob Rule in New Orleans* (1900), *The East St. Louis Massacre* (1917), and *The Arkansas Race Riot* (1920).

7.14 Governor Brough] Charles Hillman Brough (1876–1935), a former professor of economics and sociology at the University of Arkansas, was the Democratic governor of Arkansas, 1917–21.

7.29–30 Equal Rights League . . . Fellowship League] Originally founded in 1864, the National Equal Rights League was revived in 1908 by the militant black leader William Monroe Trotter (1872–1934). The People's Movement Club was an independent black political organization in Chicago founded by Oscar De Priest (1871–1951), who later served as a Republican congressman, 1929–35. Wells-Barnett founded the Negro Fellowship League in 1908. The League opened a settlement house in Chicago in 1910 that closed in 1920 due to a lack of funds.

8.3 Governor Brough to call a meeting] Brough met with four hundred white and black leaders in Little Rock on November 24, 1919, to "promote more harmony between the two races, and to prevent further race troubles." The conference adopted a resolution expressing its "willingness" to have the twelve condemned men appeal their sentences to the Arkansas Supreme Court.

8.4–5 electrocute eleven of our Race] Eleven of the twelve condemned men were convicted in trials held from November 3 to November 4, 1919, and sentenced on November 11, while the twelfth man was convicted on November 17 and sentenced two days later.

8.11–12 Governor Brough . . . State Baptist Association] In his remarks to the black State Baptist Convention on November 19, 1919, Brough criticized the *Chicago Defender* for printing "outrageously false stories of the Phillips county troubles and race conditions in Arkansas." Earlier in the month Brough had written to the postmaster general, asking that the "incendiary and misleading" *Defender* be banned from the U.S. mails.

10.2–4 ARCHIBALD H. GRIMKÉ . . . *the Republic*] Archibald H. Grimké (1849–1930) was born in South Carolina, the son of a white father and an enslaved mother, and the nephew of the abolitionists Angelina Grimké Weld and Sarah Grimké. He graduated from Harvard Law School in 1874 and served as the American consul in Santo Domingo, 1894–98, as president of the American Negro Academy, and as a member of the NAACP board of directors, 1913–23. Grimké gave this address to a meeting of the American Negro Academy in Washington, D.C.

10.6–8 THE AUTHOR . . . God was just.] Thomas Jefferson, *Notes on the State of Virginia* (1785), query XVIII.

12.1–2 side of Warren . . . Savannah.] Joseph Warren (1741–1775), the president of the Massachusetts Provincial Congress, was killed at the battle of Bunker Hill, June 17, 1775. Casimir Pulaski, a Polish cavalry officer serving as a volunteer with the Continental Army, was fatally wounded in the unsuccessful American assault on Savannah, Georgia, October 9, 1779.

15.6–26 Said Jackson . . . noblest reward."] "Address to the Men of Color," printed in *Niles' Weekly Register*, January 28, 1815.

16.7 Dred Scott Decision] *Scott v. Sandford*, decided March 6, 1857.

17.35 Hartford Convention] A meeting held in Hartford, Connecticut, from December 15, 1814, to January 5, 1815, by twenty-six Federalists from New Hampshire, Vermont, Massachusetts, Rhode Island, and Connecticut. The delegates condemned the War of 1812 and the policies of the Jefferson and Madison administrations and proposed the adoption of several constitutional amendments, including limiting the president to a single term, excluding enslaved persons from the apportionment of representatives and direct taxes, prohibiting naturalized citizens from serving in Congress or holding federal office, and requiring a two-thirds majority in both the Senate and the House of Representatives to admit new states, restrict commerce with foreign nations, or declare an offensive war. Their proposals failed to win support in the aftermath of the American victory at New Orleans and the signing of the peace treaty with Great Britain.

17.39–18.1 explosions of 1850 and 1854] In the aftermath of the U.S.-Mexican War Congress passed a series of acts that later became known as "the compromise of 1850." The legislation admitted California into the Union as a free state, organized territorial governments for New Mexico and Utah without a congressional prohibition of slavery in those territories, settled the Texas–New Mexico boundary dispute, assumed $10 million of the debt of the Texas republic, abolished the slave trade in the District of Columbia, and replaced the 1793 Fugitive Slave Act with a stronger law that denied alleged fugitives legal protection and compelled northern authorities to cooperate in returning escaped people. In 1854 Congress passed legislation for organizing Kansas and Nebraska as federal territories that repealed the Missouri Compromise prohibition against slavery in federal territory north of 36°30' and allowed the question of whether slavery would be permitted in the new territories to be decided by their elected legislatures.

18.38–39 "What fools these mortals be!"] *A Midsummer's Night Dream*, III.ii.115.

20.3 Henry Wilson] A successful shoe manufacturer, Wilson (1812–1875) served in the Massachusetts Senate as an antislavery Whig, 1845–47 and 1851–53, in the U.S. Senate as a Republican, 1855–73, and as vice president of the United States from 1873 until his death.

20.10–17 "Future generations . . . admitted to freedom."] From Charles Sumner's speech in the U.S. Senate, January 5, 1865.

20.21–23 fought and died . . . Milliken's Bend?] Black troops played major roles in the Union assaults on Port Hudson, Louisiana, May 27, 1863, and Fort Wagner, South Carolina, July 18, 1863; in the Battle of the Crater, fought near Petersburg, Virginia, on July 30, 1864, and in the battle of Honey Hill, fought near Ridgeland, South Carolina, November 30, 1864; and in the defense of Milliken's Bend, Louisiana, June 7, 1863.

21.18–19 "Oh! Justice thou . . . their gratitude."] Cf. *Julius Caesar*, III. ii.104–5: "O judgment! thou art fled to brutish beasts, / And men have lost their reason."

23.22 "Let us have peace," said Grant] Ulysses S. Grant used this phrase at the conclusion of his letter of May 29, 1868, accepting the Republican nomination for president, and it became the main slogan of the party's campaign.

26.11–12 decision of the Supreme Court in 1917] In a case brought by the NAACP, the U.S. Supreme Court ruled 9–0 in *Buchanan v. Warley* that a Louisville, Kentucky, ordinance prohibiting black people from living in white-majority neighborhoods violated the Fourteenth Amendment.

28.10–12 Boston Commons . . . Shaw and his black regiment.] The memorial to Colonel Robert Gould Shaw (1837–1863) and the men of the 54th Massachusetts Infantry was sculpted by Augustus Saint-Gaudens (1848–1907) and dedicated in 1897.

29.4 *Marcus Garvey*] Born in Jamaica, Garvey (1887–1940) founded the Universal Negro Improvement Association in 1914. He emigrated to New York City in 1916 and founded the Black Star Line in 1919 to promote travel between the Western Hemisphere and Africa. Garvey was convicted of mail fraud in 1923 and deported to Jamaica in 1927.

30.2 MARY E. JONES PARRISH] Mary Elizabeth Jones Parrish (c. 1890–c. 1972) was born in Mississippi and moved to Tulsa around 1919 to teach typing and shorthand. After the massacre in 1921 she wrote a narrative of her experiences and collected accounts from more than fifteen other survivors. *Events of the Tulsa Disaster* was privately printed in 1922, sometime before Parrish left the city and moved to Muskogee, Oklahoma, where she taught commercial subjects in high school.

30.6 Rochester] In New York State.

30.18 Frisco] The St. Louis and San Francisco Railway Company.

30.32 "Tulsa, Then and Now . . . G. A. Gregg] George Archibald Gregg (1873–1940) was the executive secretary of the Hunton Branch of the Tulsa YMCA. He left the city on May 26 to visit his family in Kansas and returned on June 5. In an account published in the *Kansas City Sun*, July 2, 1921, Gregg wrote: "I left a happy, hopeful, progressive people. I found a crushed, humiliated, discouraged humanity. I left a praying people; I found them wondering if God is just."

31.5–7 A Colored boy . . . "Lynching is feared] On May 31, 1921, the *Tulsa Tribune* reported that a black youth identified as Dick Rowland had been arrested the previous day for "attempting to assault" a white elevator operator in a downtown office building. It is uncertain whether any edition of the newspaper that day printed an editorial predicting or calling for a lynching.

31.9 the lynching of a White boy in Tulsa] Roy Belton, age nineteen, was taken from the courthouse on August 28, 1920, and hanged from an advertising billboard. Belton had been accused of fatally shooting a taxi driver.

31.14–15 he was brought to trial . . . appear against him.] The charges against Rowland were dismissed in September 1921 after Sarah Page, the elevator operator, informed the county attorney that she did not wish to have the case prosecuted.

32.3 Chicago Riot . . . Washington trouble] See Chronology, 1919.

33.25 dufold] Folding bed.

39.2–3 B. C. FRANKLIN . . . *Its Victims*] Buck Colbert Franklin (1879–1960) was admitted to the Oklahoma bar in 1907 and practiced law in Ardmore and Rentiesville before moving to Tulsa early in 1921. After the massacre he successfully sued the city to overturn a zoning ordinance that would have prevented the rebuilding of the Greenwood district. Franklin's typescript is dated August 22, 1931, and appears to have been written for publication, although it was not printed during his lifetime. His autobiography *My Life and An Era* was published in 1997, co-edited by his son, the historian John Hope Franklin (1915–2009).

42.6–7 lynching of that white man] See note 31.9.

44.36–37 dry bones in the valley] See Ezekiel 37.

44.38–39 "He saved others . . . cannot save."] Matthew 27:42.

48.24–25 The Last Days . . . Bulwer Lytton] Novel (1834) by the British writer Edward Bulwer-Lytton (1803–1873).

50.2 OTIS CLARK] Clark was interviewed on November 23, 2009. He died in 2012 at the age of 109.

62.10–11 Bishop Mason] Charles Harrison Mason (1866–1961) founded the Pentecostal Church of God in Christ in Memphis, Tennessee, in 1907.

71.2 SCIPIO AFRICANUS JONES] The son of an enslaved mother, Jones (1863–1943) was admitted to the Arkansas bar in 1889 and practiced law in Little Rock. A leader in the Arkansas black community, Jones agreed in late November 1919 to argue the appeals of the black men convicted in the trials held after the Phillips County massacre.

72.34 Governor of the State] See note 7.14.

82.28–30 greatest case . . . the highest court] On February 19, 1923, the U.S. Supreme Court ruled 6–2 in *Moore v. Dempsey* that the "mob domination" of the trials of six of the Phillips County defendants violated the due process clause of the Fourteenth Amendment and ordered the case remanded to federal district court. Through a series of legal maneuvers and political negotiations, Scipio Africanus Jones succeeded in freeing all twelve of the condemned men, as well as the twenty-one still serving prison terms, by January 1925.

83.2–3 HARDING . . . *Birmingham, Alabama*] Harding spoke at a celebration of the founding of the city in 1871.

87.24–25 Mr. Lothrop Stoddard's . . . Tide of Color] *The Rising Tide of Color Against White World-Supremacy* (1920) by the American historian and journalist Lothrop Stoddard (1883–1950). In his book Stoddard wrote: "The grim truth of the matter is this: The whole white race is exposed, immediately or ultimately, to the possibility of social sterilization and final replacement or absorption by the teeming colored races."

87.26–27 Mr. F. D. Lugard . . . recent Edinburgh Review] Sir Frederick Lugard (1858–1945) was a British soldier, explorer, and colonial administrator who served as the governor of Hong Kong, 1907–12, and as governor-general of Nigeria, 1914–19. In the April 1921 number of *The Edinburgh Review*, Lugard discussed five books: Stoddard's *The Rising Tide of Color*; *Children of the Slaves* (1920), by the British journalist and travel writer Stephen Graham (1884–1975); *Finding a Way Out* by Robert Russa Moton (1867–1940), principal of the Tuskegee Institute, 1915–35; *The Backwards Peoples and Our Relations with Them* (1920), by the British explorer and colonial administrator Sir Henry (Harry) Johnston (1858–1927); and *The Souls of Black Folk* (1903) by W.E.B. Du Bois.

94.2 RAYMOND CLAPPER] Clapper (1892–1944) was a Washington correspondent for the United Press agency, 1917–33. He later became a columnist for Scripps-Howard and was killed in a midair collision while covering the war in the Central Pacific.

96.2 JAMES WELDON JOHNSON] A poet, songwriter, novelist, journalist, and diplomat, Johnson (1871–1938) wrote for *The New York Age*, 1914–23, and served as a field secretary for the NAACP, 1916–1920, and as its executive secretary, 1920–30.

96.3 *the Dyer Bill*] A federal anti-lynching bill first introduced in the House of Representatives in 1918 by Leonidas C. Dyer (1871–1957), who served as a Republican from Missouri, 1911–33.

96.14 the Speaker's] Frederick H. Gillett (1851–1935) was a Republican congressman from Massachusetts, 1893–1925, and a senator, 1925–31. He served as Speaker of the House of Representatives, 1919–25.

96.26 Mr. Mondell] Frank Mondell (1860–1939) was a Republican congressman from Wyoming, 1895–97 and 1899–1923, who served as the House majority leader, 1919–23.

96.30–31 Mr. Sissoms . . . Mr. Cooper] Thomas Sisson (1869–1923), a Democratic congressman from Mississippi, 1909–23, and Henry Cooper (1850–1931), a Republican congressman from Wisconsin, 1893–1919 and 1921–31.

97.9 Chairman Campbell] The House was sitting as a Committee of the Whole to debate the Dyer bill, with Philip Campbell (1862–1941), a Republican congressman from Kansas, 1903–23, as chairman.

97.24–25 Blanton of Texas] Thomas Blanton (1872–1957) was a Democratic congressman from Texas, 1917–37.

98.27 Dyer Anti-Lynching Bill . . . Senate.] The bill was filibustered in the Senate and withdrawn from consideration in December 1922.

99.2 *COLONEL MAYFIELD'S WEEKLY*] A Ku Klux Klan newspaper published in Houston from 1921 to 1924 by "Billie" Mayfield, a former officer in the Texas National Guard.

100.2 W. P. EVANS] Walter Parsley Evans (1865–1937) was a merchant who owned a successful department store and a wood, brick, coal, and ice yard in Laurinburg, North Carolina.

100.21 "Ruth to Naomi."] See the book of Ruth.

102.28–29 Booker T. Washington . . . where you are."] From Washington's address at the Atlanta Exposition, September 18, 1895.

107.1 the com- him and his] A line was omitted in the text printed in *The Charlotte Observer* on June 3, 1923.

108.3 *Far Away Blues*] The song was recorded as a duet by blues singers Bessie Smith (1894–1937) and Clara Smith (1894–1935) and was released as a 78 rpm single on October 4, 1927. (The two singers were not related.)

109.3 *Report . . . Sammie Smith*] The text printed here is taken from the typescript in the NAACP archives. White wrote a story about Sammie Smith's lynching that appeared in the *New York World* on January 4, 1925.

111.20 Governor Austin Peay] Peay (1876–1927), a lawyer, was the Democratic governor of Tennessee from 1923 until his death.

111.23 Hilary E. Howse] A Democrat, Howse (1866–1938) served as mayor of Nashville, 1909–15 and from 1923 until his death.

114.1 Lem Motlow . . . Jack Daniel Distillery] Lem Motlow (1869–1947) inherited the distillery from his maternal uncle Jack Daniel (1849–1911) in 1907.

114.8 M. R. Patterson] Malcolm R. Patterson (1861–1935) was the Democratic governor of Tennessee, 1907–11.

114.11 Motlow was acquitted] Motlow fatally shot Clarence Pullis (1879–1924), a white Pullman conductor, on March 17, 1924. At Motlow's trial in St. Louis, Ed Wallis, a black Pullman porter, testified that Motlow had racially insulted him while drunk and denied striking him. Motlow testified that he had fired in self-defense after Wallis began choking him and had struck Pullis by accident, a version of events contradicted by the testimony of two white passengers. In his closing arguments Frank Bond, one of Motlow's defense attorneys, described Wallis as "insolent" and said: "There are two classes of Negroes in this country. One is the kind who knows his place. . . . The other class demands racial and social equality. They want to intermarry with your daughters and mine." The all-white, all-male jury acquitted Motlow on December 10, 1924.

115.19–21 four young white men . . . names and addresses] No one was ever charged in connection with the lynching of Sammie Smith.

118.2 ALAIN LOCKE] Born in Philadelphia, Alain Locke (1885–1954) graduated from Harvard and became the first black American to be named a Rhodes Scholar. Locke was a professor of philosophy at Howard University, 1912–25 and 1928–53. In 1925 he edited the anthology *The New Negro: An Interpretation*, a collection of essays, poetry, and fiction that included contributions by Countee Cullen, W.E.B. Du Bois, Jessie Fauset, Langston Hughes, Zora Neale Hurston, Claude McKay, Jean Toomer, and Walter White.

120.3–8 We have tomorrow . . . We march!] Langston Hughes (1901–1967), "Youth," first published in *The Crisis*, August 1924.

125.3–8 Mine is the . . . crumbling shore.] Claude McKay (1890–1948), "To the Intrenched Classes" (1922).

125.11–14 O Southland useless thing.] James Weldon Johnson (1871–1938), "O Southland!" (1917).

125.19–26 How would you . . . your feet?] James Weldon Johnson, "To America" (1917).

126.27–28 A Negro newspaper . . . English, French and Spanish] *The Negro World*, published by the Universal Negro Improvement Association, 1918–33.

126.30 Two important magazines] *The Crisis*, founded in 1910 by the NAACP and edited by W.E.B. Du Bois, and *Opportunity: A Journal of Negro Life*, founded in 1923 by the National Urban League and edited by the sociologist Charles Spurgeon Johnson (1893–1956).

126.33 three pan-African congresses] The congresses were held in Paris, 1919, in London, Brussels, and Paris, 1921, and in London, Paris, and Lisbon, 1923.

129.13–14 Mayor of Detroit] John W. Smith (1882–1942) was mayor of Detroit, 1924–28. In November 1924 Smith had won the nonpartisan election for mayor with strong support from Catholic, black, and immigrant voters, narrowly defeating a write-in candidate backed by the Ku Klux Klan.

131.1 "Tenderloin"] Manhattan district extending from 23rd to 42nd Streets and from Fifth to Seventh Avenues.

131.5 Clarence Kelsey] Kelsey (1856–1930), a prominent New York real estate financier, was a leading fundraiser for Hampton and Tuskegee Institutes.

132.10 "Anglo-Saxon" . . . agitation in Virgina] In 1924 the Virginia legislature passed a Racial Integrity Act that was supported by the recently formed Anglo-Saxon Clubs of America. The act prohibited interracial marriages and defined a "white person" as a "person who has no trace whatsoever of any blood other than Caucasian," although "persons who have one-sixteenth or less of the blood of the American Indian and have no other non-Caucasic blood" were also deemed to be white.

133.4–7 a physician . . . Negro folk songs] Dr. Alexander Turner (1882–1944), a surgeon, was one of the founders of Dunbar Memorial, a small hospital established in 1918 to serve Detroit's black community. Leota Henson Turner (1866–1955), his wife, was a pianist who had studied in Germany and the niece of baritone Frederick Loudin (1836–1904), a member, and later director, of the Fisk Jubilee Singers.

133.8–11 He moved in . . . gave up his home] The Turners moved into a house on Spokane Avenue on June 23, 1925, but within hours were forced to flee and sign the deed to their home over to a local homeowners' association.

136.2 NETTIE GEORGE SPEEDY] Speedy (1878–1957) was a journalist for the *Chicago Defender* and the *Metropolitan Post*. She was one of the first black women to play golf in the United States.

136.7 Dr. Ossian H. Sweet] Born in Florida, Ossian Sweet (1895–1960) graduated from Wilberforce University and the Howard University medical school. He began practicing in Detroit in 1921.

136.8 Prosecutor Robert Toms] Toms (1886–1960) was chief prosecutor of Wayne County, 1925–29, and a Michigan circuit judge, 1929–59. Toms also served as the presiding judge at the 1947 Nuremberg trials of Luftwaffe general Erhard Milch and of eighteen SS concentration camp officials.

136.10 Arthur Garfield Hayes] A New York City attorney with a successful private practice, Hays (1881–1954) was general counsel of the American Civil Liberties Union, 1921–54, and had appeared along with Clarence Darrow for the defense in the 1925 Scopes evolution trial in Tennessee.

136.11 Mrs. Gladys Sweet] Born in Pittsburgh, Gladys Mitchell Sweet (1901–1928) moved to Detroit at age seven and married Ossian Sweet in 1922. She died of tuberculosis that may have been contracted while she was being held in the Wayne County jail.

136.12 Otis and Henry] Otis Sweet (b. 1899) was a dentist with a practice in Detroit. Henry Sweet (1904–1940) was a student at Wilberforce. He later graduated from the Howard University law school and became an attorney in Detroit.

136.16–17 Dr. Sweet . . . to commit murder.] The trial ended on November 27, 1925, when Judge Frank Murphy declared a mistrial after the jury was unable to reach a verdict. Murphy granted bail to the jailed defendants and agreed that they would be retried individually. After Henry Sweet was acquitted on May 13, 1926, the charges against the remaining defendants were dismissed.

136.19 Judge Frank Murphy] Murphy (1890–1949) was a trial judge in Detroit, 1924–30, mayor of Detroit, 1930–33, governor-general of the Philippines, 1933–35, high commissioner to the Philippines, 1935–36, Democratic governor of Michigan, 1937–38, attorney general of the United States, 1939–40, and an associate justice of the U.S. Supreme Court from 1940 until his death.

136.22–29 "When I opened . . . my people before,"] The *Detroit Free Press* of November 19, 1925, reported that Dr. Sweet said: "When I opened the door and saw the mob I realized I was facing the same mob that had hounded my people throughout its entire history. In my mind I was pretty confident of what I was up against, with my back against the wall. I was filled with a peculiar fear—the kind no one could feel unless they had known the history of our race."

138.32 Mr. Darrow] Defense attorney Clarence Darrow (1857–1938).

142.22 John W. Fletcher . . . "To jail."] John W. Fletcher, a waiter, moved with his wife and two sons into a house at 9428 Stoepel Avenue on July 9, 1925. The following night a white mob bombarded the house with chunks of coal until Fletcher opened fire and wounded a fifteen-year-old boy. He was taken to police headquarters and charged with assault, then released on bail and permitted to remove his belongings from the house. The assault charge was later dismissed.

142.27–32 Wellington Bristol . . . police protection] Vollington and Agnes Bristol owned and operated a funeral home in Detroit. They were unable to find satisfactory white tenants for their property on American Avenue and were unable to rent to black tenants because of threats. On July 7, 1925, the day after they moved into the house, a white mob attacked their home but were driven back by police.

143.38–40 the report . . . 30 years of lynchings] *Thirty Years of Lynching in the United States, 1889–1918*, published by the NAACP as a pamphlet in April 1919.

144.7–8 Judge Ira W. Jayne . . . J. J. Crowley] Ira W. Jayne (1882–1961), Wayne County circuit judge, 1919–56; Edsel Ford (1893–1943), son of Henry Ford and president of the Ford Motor Company, 1919–43; Joseph J. Crowley (1862–1925), one of the founders of Crowley's, a large department store in downtown Detroit.

145.2 CLIFTON F. RICHARDSON] Richardson (1892–1939) was managing editor of the *Houston Observer*, 1916–19, editor of the *Houston Informer*, 1919–30, and editor and publisher of the *Houston Defender* from 1930 until his death.

145.29–30 "fight it out . . . all summer."] In a message sent to Secretary of War Edwin M. Stanton from Spotsylvania Court House, Virginia, on May 11, 1864, Ulysses S. Grant wrote, "I propose to fight it out on this line if it takes all summer."

148.12–15 "For right is right . . . be sin."] From "The Right Must Win," hymn (1849) by English cleric Frederick William Faber (1814–1863).

149.2–4 NED COBB . . . *Nate Shaw*] Ned Cobb (1885–1973) was a black tenant farmer in Tallapoosa County, Alabama, who joined the newly formed Alabama Sharecroppers Union in 1931 because "I heard about it bein an organization for the poor class of people." Believing that "when trouble comes, stand up for one another," in December 1932 Cobb and several other union members confronted a deputy sheriff's posse sent to seize an indebted black farmer's livestock. In an exchange of gunfire one black man was killed while Cobb and four deputies were wounded; two other black sharecroppers later died from their wounds. Cobb was convicted in 1933 of assault with the intent to kill and served twelve years in prison before returning to farming in Tallapoosa County. In 1969 he met Theodore Rosengarten (b. 1944), a Harvard graduate student researching the history of the Sharecroppers Union. Rosengarten recorded Cobb telling his life story and used the tapes to write *All God's Dangers: The Life of Nate Shaw* (1974). In later printings of the book Rosengarten acknowledged that "Nate Shaw" was a pseudonym for Ned Cobb.

149.6 MAYNARD CURTIS . . . Jim Curtis's son] In a prefatory note to *All God's Dangers*, Theodore Rosengarten wrote: "The characters in this book are real. Their names, except for historical figures, are fictitious. The names of most places and landmarks have also been changed."

160.2 ELIZABETH LAWSON . . . *Scottsboro in Pictures*] "Elizabeth Lawson" was a pseudonym for Elsa Block, a white Communist activist who later edited the Party's regional newspaper *The Southern Worker* from 1933 to 1937 under the name "Jim Mallory." *They Shall Not Die!* was printed by the Workers' Library, the publishing arm of the Communist Party of the United States.

161.1–3 Leo Tolstoi . . . Floyd Dell] Aleksey Tolstoy (1883–1945), Soviet novelist known for works of historical and science fiction; Eugene Gordon

(1891–1974), black journalist and short story writer who edited *The Saturday Evening Quill*, 1928–30, and joined the Communist Party in 1931; Waldo Frank (1889–1967), novelist and essayist whose works included *Our America* (1919) and *Virgin Spain* (1926); Mary Heaton Vorse (1874–1967), a suffragist, journalist, and novelist known for writing about labor organizing and strikes; Michael Gold (1893–1967), Communist journalist and author of the autobiographical novel *Jews Without Money* (1930); Charles R. Walker (1893–1974), journalist and author of *Steel: The Diary of a Furnace Worker* (1922); Floyd Dell (1887–1969), novelist, playwright, poet, essayist, and editor.

161.10–11 National Association . . . International Ministers Alliance] The Interdenominational Colored Ministers' Alliance of Chattanooga, Tennessee, hired Stephen Roddy (1890–1934), a white attorney from their city, to defend the Scottsboro defendants at their trial in April 1931. Roddy and his cocounsel Milo Moody (1861–1948) were later retained by the NAACP to appeal the verdicts but left the case when the defendants chose to be represented by attorneys working for International Labor Defense.

161.13–15 League of Struggle . . . International Labor Defense] The League of Struggle for Negro Rights was founded by the Communist Party in 1930 and dissolved in 1936. International Labor Defense was the legal arm of the Communist Party of the United States, 1925–46.

162.13 A. Refregier . . . John Reed Club] Russian American artist Anton Refregier (1905–1979), later known as a painter of murals, including the *History of San Francisco* series (1940–48) in the Rincon Annex Post Office in San Francisco. The John Reed Club was an organization of artists and writers aligned with the Communist Party, founded in 1929 and dissolved in 1935.

162.24 B. D. AMIS] Benjamin DeWayne Amis (1896–1993) was general secretary of the League of Struggle for Negro Rights and editor of its newspaper, *The Liberator.*

163.7–12 Haywood Patterson . . . Willie Roberson] At the time of their arrest on March 25, 1931, Patterson was eighteen, Williams was thirteen, Roy Wright was either twelve or fourteen, Andy Wright was eighteen, Clarence Norris was eighteen, Charlie Weems was twenty, Ozie Powell was probably fourteen, Olen Montgomery was sixteen, and Willie Roberson was seventeen.

170.22–23 Gov. B. M. Miller] Benjamin M. Miller (1864–1944) was the Democratic governor of Alabama, 1931–35.

172.5–6 new trial . . . Alabama Supreme Court] The Alabama Supreme Court heard arguments in the case, January 21–22, 1932. In a 6–1 ruling on March 24, it upheld the convictions of Patterson, Norris, Weems, Powell, Montgomery, Roberson, and Andy Wright, but overturned the conviction of Eugene Williams on the grounds that he was a juvenile under state law. (Both Williams and Roy Wright remained in jail awaiting retrial.)

174.9 James W. Ford] Born in Alabama, James W. Ford (1893–1957) attended Fisk University, served in the army in France in World War I, and worked for the post office in Chicago after the war. Ford joined the Communist Party in 1926 and was its vice-presidential candidate in 1932, running with William Z. Foster, and in 1936 and 1940, running with Earl Browder. The Communist ticket received about 103,000 votes in 1932 out of more than thirty-nine million cast.

177.9 lynching of George Armwood] George Armwood was arrested in Somerset County, Maryland, on October 16, 1933, and accused of assaulting an elderly white woman. He was taken by the state police to the Baltimore City jail, but at the insistence of local authorities was returned to the Eastern Shore, where he was lynched on the night of October 18. Although nine members of the lynch mob were identified by officers of the state police, a grand jury issued no indictments in the case.

177.15 the state troops] Maryland state police.

178.18 CLARENCE MITCHELL] A native of Baltimore, Clarence Mitchell (1911–1984) was a reporter and columnist for the *Afro-American*, 1933–37, before working for the National Urban League and the Fair Employment Practice Committee. He later served as the labor director of the NAACP, 1946–50, and as its Washington chief lobbyist, 1950–78.

178.24 LEVI JOLLEY] Levi Jolley (1907–1970) was a reporter for the *Baltimore Afro-American*, 1926–37, city editor of the *Philadelphia Afro-American*, 1937–45, city editor of the *Baltimore Afro-American*, 1945–49, and Washington correspondent for the *Pittsburgh Courier*, 1954–61.

184.8–11 the 1931 mob orgy . . . Matthew Williams] On December 4, 1931, Matthew Williams, age twenty-three, allegedly killed the owner of the box factory in Salisbury where he worked and then was shot by the owner's son. A mob abducted him from the hospital and hanged him from a tree on the courthouse lawn, then tied his body to a lamppost and set it on fire. A grand jury found that Williams had died "at the hands of persons unknown" and issued no indictments.

184.15 George Davis] George Davis, a twenty-seven-year-old farm laborer, was arrested on November 23, 1931, for allegedly assaulting a white woman in Kent County, Maryland, and was taken to the Baltimore City jail while lynch mobs searched for him in several counties on the Eastern Shore. He was convicted of attempted rape in January 1932 and sentenced to sixteen years in prison.

184.19 Euel Lee] Euel Lee, a fifty-eight-year-old farm laborer also known as Orphan Jones, was arrested in Worcester County, Maryland, on October 12, 1931, and charged with murdering a white farmer, his wife, and their two daughters. The next day he was taken to the Baltimore City jail to prevent a possible lynching. His attorney Bernard Ades (1903–1986), a member of

International Labor Defense, succeeded in having Lee's trial venue changed to Towson, Maryland, where he was convicted in January 1932. The verdict was overturned by the Maryland Court of Appeals because of the long-standing exclusion of blacks from Baltimore County jury panels. Lee was retried in Towson and was again convicted. After a series of unsuccessful appeals, Euel Lee was hanged in Baltimore on October 28, 1933.

185.10–11 Scottsboro Boys . . . original trial] On November 7, 1932, the U.S. Supreme Court overturned the 1931 convictions in the Scottsboro case, ruling 7–2 in *Powell v. Alabama* that the inadequate counsel provided to the accused at their trial violated their right to due process under the Fourteenth Amendment. Haywood Patterson was retried, convicted, and again sentenced to death in April 1933 despite the recantation by Ruby Bates, one of the alleged victims, of her previous testimony. James Horton (1878–1973), the judge in Patterson's second trial, set aside his conviction in June 1933, but was then removed from the case. In December 1933 Patterson and Clarence Norris were convicted in separate trials and again sentenced to death. Their convictions were upheld by the Alabama Supreme Court on June 28, 1934. (The trials of the remaining defendants, who all remained imprisoned, were postponed pending appeal of the new convictions).

185.15 at 3015 South San Pedro street] In Los Angeles, California.

185.23 Judge W. W. Callahan] William Washington Callahan (1863–1947) had presided over the trials of Haywood Patterson and Clarence Norris in the fall of 1933. His rulings and instructions to the jury were highly favorable to the prosecution.

185.29–30 Angelo Herndon . . . 20 years] Angelo Herndon (1913–1997) was a black Communist labor organizer who was convicted in January 1933 of inciting insurrection against the state of Georgia and sentenced to 18–20 years in prison. Herndon was released on bail in August 1934 and published his autobiography, *Let Me Live*, in March 1937. In *Herndon v. Lowry*, decided April 26, 1937, the U.S. Supreme Court overturned his conviction in a 5–4 decision, ruling that the "vague and indeterminate" Georgia insurrection statute "violates the guarantees of liberty embodied in the Fourteenth Amendment."

186.2 BEN DAVIS, JR.] The son of a black newspaper publisher in Atlanta, Benjamin Davis (1903–1964) graduated from Harvard Law School and helped defend Angelo Herndon at his trial in 1933. Davis joined the Communist Party and moved in 1935 to New York City, where he became an editor at *The Daily Worker* and served as a city councilman, 1943–49. He was one of eleven Communist leaders convicted under the Smith Act in 1949 for advocating the violent overthrow of the U.S. government and served almost four years of a five-year sentence.

186.16 Attorney Leibowitz] A highly successful New York criminal defense attorney, Samuel Leibowitz (1893–1978) was engaged by International Labor Defense in January 1933 to represent the Scottsboro defendants. Leibowitz was the lead defense counsel for Haywood Patterson and Clarence Norris when they were retried in 1933.

186.20 Jackson and Morgan counties] Patterson and Norris had been indicted by a grand jury sitting in Scottsboro, the seat of Jackson County, but were retried in Decatur, the seat of Morgan County.

186.24–25 Justice Van Devanter] Willis Van Devanter (1859–1941) served as an attorney in the Department of the Interior, 1897–1903, as a federal circuit judge, 1903–10, and as an associate justice of the U.S. Supreme Court, 1911–37.

187.8 Chief Justice Hughes] Charles Evans Hughes (1862–1948) was the Republican governor of New York, 1907–10, and an associate justice of the U.S. Supreme Court from 1910 to 1916, when he resigned after receiving the Republican nomination for president. He then served as secretary of state, 1921–25, and as chief justice of the Supreme Court, 1930–41.

187.12 Justice Stone] Harlan Fiske Stone (1862–1946) was dean of Columbia Law School, 1910–23, attorney general of the United States, 1924–25, an associate justice of the U.S. Supreme Court, 1925–41, and chief justice of the Supreme Court from 1941 until his death.

187.14 Mr. Pollak] Walter H. Pollak (1887–1940), a prominent constitutional lawyer who had successfully argued *Powell v. Alabama* before the U.S. Supreme Court in 1932 (see note 185.10–11).

187.15 Justice Butler] Pierce Butler (1866–1939) was an associate justice of the U.S. Supreme Court from 1923 until his death. He wrote the dissenting opinion in *Powell v. Alabama*.

187.26 Mr. Frankel . . . Tom Knight] Osmond Fraenkel (1888–1983) was a New York civil liberties lawyer who joined the Scottsboro defense team in 1933. Thomas E. Knight, Jr. (1898–1937), was the Democratic attorney general of Alabama, 1931–35, and its lieutenant governor from 1935 until his death. Knight had argued *Powell v. Alabama* before the U.S. Supreme Court in 1932 and prosecuted Patterson and Norris at their trials in 1933.

188.2 MARGUERITE YOUNG] A former reporter for the Associated Press and the *New York World-Telegram*, Young (1905–1995) was a Washington correspondent for *The Daily Worker*, 1934–36. She later wrote for *New Masses* and the *New York Herald Tribune*.

192.17 Brandeis] Louis Brandeis (1856–1941), an associate justice of the U.S. Supreme Court, 1916–39.

192.32 Dean Charles Houston] A graduate of Harvard Law School, Charles Hamilton Houston (1895–1950) was the dean of Howard Law School, 1929–35. Houston became general counsel of the NAACP in 1935 and served until 1938, when he returned to his law practice in Washington, D.C. Houston continued to be involved in civil rights litigation until his death as an advisor to his successor as NAACP legal counsel, his former student Thurgood Marshall.

194.2 LOUIS R. LAUTIER] Louis R. Lautier (1897–1962) began reporting for the *Baltimore Afro-American* from Washington in 1924 and was the Washington correspondent for the National Negro Publishers Association, 1945–61. In 1955 he became the first black correspondent admitted to membership in the National Press Club.

195.22 Owen J. Roberts] Owen J. Roberts (1875–1955) served as the special prosecutor in the Teapot Dome oil lease scandal, 1924–30, and as an associate justice of the U.S. Supreme Court, 1930–45.

196.34 Neal against Delaware] In 1881 the Supreme Court overturned, 4–2, the conviction of William Neal, a black man who had been sentenced to death for the rape of a white woman after being indicted and tried by all-white juries. Justice John Marshall Harlan (1833–1911) wrote in his opinion for the court that the prosecution had conceded that no black citizen had ever served as a juror in Delaware, and quoted the assertion by the state's chief justice that "the great body of black men residing in this State are utterly unqualified by want of intelligence, experience, or moral integrity to sit on juries." Neal was retried and acquitted.

197.6 decision in the gold clause cases] On February 18, 1935, the U.S. Supreme Court decided three cases arising from the joint resolution passed by Congress in June 1933 abrogating clauses in private and public contracts requiring payments in gold. The court upheld 5–4 the power of Congress to void private contracts in the interest of regulating currency and ruled, by the same majority, that affected government bondholders were entitled only to minimal damages.

197.7–8 the striking . . . bill of exceptions] Patterson's motion for a new trial and his bill of exceptions (objections to the trial court's rulings) had been rejected by the Alabama Supreme Court on the grounds that they had been filed past the deadlines mandated by state law. As a consequence, Knight had argued that the U.S. Supreme Court lacked jurisdiction to hear Patterson's appeal.

198.1 James C. McReynolds] McReynolds (1862–1946) was attorney general of the United States, 1913–14, and an associate justice of the U.S. Supreme Court, 1914–41. He took no part in the Scottsboro cases heard by the court in 1935.

198.12–13 the cases . . . Supreme Court] The court unanimously decided *Norris v. Alabama* and *Patterson v. Alabama* on April 1, 1935, with Chief Justice Hughes writing the opinion in both cases. In *Norris* the court ruled that the consistent exclusions of blacks from jury panels in Jackson and Morgan Counties violated the equal protection clause of the Fourteenth Amendment and reversed the plaintiff's conviction. Because of the technicalities involved in Patterson's appeal the court did not overturn his conviction but instead remanded the case to the Alabama Supreme Court for further proceedings consistent with the *Norris* decision.

199.2–4 GRACE MOTT JOHNSON . . . *Case*] An active member of the NAACP, Grace Mott Johnson (1882–1967) was an artist best known for her sculptures of animals. The copy of the draft in the NAACP archives does not indicate whether her letter was published.

199.8 The "Scottsboro Case" is now] In May 1935 the Alabama Supreme Court quashed the indictments of the Scottsboro defendants, but they were all reindicted in November, and in January 1936 Haywood Patterson was found guilty for the fourth time and sentenced by the jury to seventy-five years in prison. Two days after Patterson's conviction Ozie Powell slashed a deputy during an altercation and was seriously wounded by a gunshot to the head.

200.2 *Anna Damon*] A leading Communist activist, Anna Damon, born Anna Cohen (c. 1898–1944), was national secretary of International Labor Defense from 1934 until her death.

200.19–21 the boys hav deserted . . . sort of Show] In a series of trials held in July 1937 Clarence Norris was sentenced to death, Andy Wright to ninety-nine years, and Charlie Weems to seventy-five years. Ozie Powell pled guilty to assaulting the deputy in 1936 and was sentenced to twenty years after the rape charge against him was dropped. The prosecution then dismissed the charges against Olen Montgomery, Roy Wright, Willie Roberson, and Eugene Williams. They quickly left the state and went to New York City, where they broke with Samuel Leibowitz, accusing him of "making a million" off their case, and briefly appeared onstage at the Apollo Theater.

200.34–35 After we are all freed] Charlie Weems was paroled in 1943, Ozzie Powell in 1946, and Andy Wright in 1950. Haywood Patterson (1912–1952) escaped from Kilby prison in 1948 and fled to Detroit. While in hiding he collaborated with the journalist Earl Conrad on his autobiography, *Scottsboro Boy* (1950). Within weeks of its publication Patterson was arrested by the FBI on a fugitive warrant, but Michigan governor G. Mennen Williams refused extradition and Alabama dropped its request. In 1951 Patterson was convicted of manslaughter for stabbing a man to death in a barroom brawl and was sentenced to six to fifteen years. He died in prison of cancer the following year. Clarence Norris (1912–1989) had his death sentence commuted to life imprisonment in 1938 and was paroled in 1946. He violated his parole by leaving Alabama for Cleveland and then New York City. In 1976 Norris was pardoned by Alabama governor George Wallace. It was believed that at the time he was the last living Scottsboro defendant.

201.5 the Committee] The Scottsboro Defense Committee, formed in December 1935 by the ILD, the NAACP, the American Civil Liberties Union, the League for Industrial Democracy, and the Methodist Federation for Social Service. Its creation was a result of the Communist Party's newly adopted Popular Front strategy of forging alliances with non-Communist groups.

202.2 MARY MCLEOD BETHUNE] Born in South Carolina, Mary McLeod Bethune (1875–1955) was the founding president of Bethune-Cookman

College, 1923–42, president of the National Association of Colored Women's Clubs, 1924–28, and the founding president of the National Council of Negro Women, 1935–1949. As director of the Division of Negro Affairs of the National Youth Administration, 1938–43, she was the first black woman to serve as a division head in a federal agency.

202.23–24 Senators Connally . . . Bilbo] Thomas Connally (1877–1963) was a Democratic congressman from Texas, 1917–29, and a senator, 1929–53; James Byrnes (1882–1972) was a Democratic congressman from South Carolina, 1911–25, a senator, 1931–41, an associate justice of the U.S. Supreme Court, 1941–42, director of the Office of Economic Stabilization, 1942–43, director of the Office of Wartime Mobilization, 1943–45, and secretary of state, 1945–47; Carter Glass (1858–1946) was a Democratic congressman from Virginia, 1902–18, secretary of the treasury, 1918–20, and a senator from 1920 until his death; Ellison Smith (1864–1944) was a Democratic senator from South Carolina from 1909 until his death; Walter George (1878–1957) was a Democratic senator from Georgia, 1921–57; Pat Harrison (1881–1941) was a Democratic congressman from Mississippi, 1911–19, and a senator from 1919 until his death; Theodore Bilbo (1877–1947) was the Democratic governor of Mississippi, 1916–20 and 1928–32, and a senator from 1935 until his death.

202.26–27 filibuster . . . Anti-Lynching Bill] An anti-lynching bill was passed by the House of Representatives, 276–119, on April 15, 1937, but was filibustered when it was brought up in the Senate on January 6, 1938. A motion for cloture was defeated, 42–46, on February 16, and the Senate then voted 58–22 on February 21 to take up other business.

203.16 Prof. Ralph J. Bunche] Bunche (1903–1971) was professor of political science at Howard University, 1928–41. He later served as an analyst with the Office of Strategic Services, 1942–43, an official at the State Department, 1944–46, and a senior member of the UN Secretariat from 1946 until his death. In 1950 Bunche became the first person of color to receive the Nobel Peace Prize, which he was awarded for mediating the 1949 Arab-Israeli armistice agreements.

203.20 Senator Taft . . . Perry W. Howard] Robert A. Taft (1889–1953) was a Republican senator from Ohio from 1939 until his death. Perry W. Howard (1877–1961) practiced law in Jackson, Mississippi, before moving to Washington, D.C., where he became a partner in one of the city's leading black law firms. He served as the Republican national committeeman from Mississippi, 1924–60.

203.22–23 Thomas E. Dewey] Dewey (1902–1971) was an assistant U.S. attorney, 1931–32, acting U.S. attorney for the Southern District of New York, 1932–33, a special prosecutor investigating organized crime and corruption in Manhattan, 1935–37, Manhattan district attorney, 1938–41, Republican governor of New York, 1943–54, and the Republican nominee for president, 1944 and 1948.

203.31–32 Discharge Petition . . . Anti-Lynching Bill] In January 1939 Joseph Gavagan (1892–1968), a Democratic congressman from New York, 1929–43, introduced an anti-lynching bill in the House that was supported by the NAACP. On July 28 it was discharged from the Rules Committee after 218 members signed a petition for it to be sent to the floor. The House passed the bill, 252–131, on January 10, 1940, but it was never taken up by the Senate.

203.33 Emmett J. Scott] A journalist from Texas, Scott (1873–1957) was personal secretary to Booker T. Washington, 1897–1912, secretary of Tuskegee Institute, 1912–19, special assistant to the secretary of war, 1917–19, secretary-treasurer and then secretary of Howard University, 1919–38, and assistant publicity director of the Republican National Committee, 1939–42.

204.1 Arthur Krock] Krock (1886–1974) was the Washington bureau chief of *The New York Times*, 1932–53, and a political columnist for the newspaper, 1933–66.

204.13–16 a Negro . . . Federal judges] William H. Hastie (1904–1976) became the first black federal judge in 1937 when he was appointed to a renewable ten-year term as a judge of the territorial district court in the Virgin Islands. Hastie resigned in 1939 to become dean of Howard Law School. He later served as governor of the Virgin Islands, 1946–49, before becoming the first black judge to sit on a federal circuit court, serving from 1950 until his death.

204.30–31 Mr. Ickes . . . Mr. Straus] Harold Ickes (1874–1952) was secretary of the interior, 1933–46; Nathan Straus (1889–1961) was administrator of the U.S. Housing Authority, 1937–42.

205.15–17 Charles H. Houston . . . Supreme Court bench.] For Houston, see note 192.33. Justice Pierce Butler (see note 187.14) had died on November 16, 1939. President Roosevelt appointed Frank Murphy (see note 136.19) to his seat on the court on January 4, 1940.

208.25 Burke-Wadsworth Conscription Bill] Also known as the Selective Training and Service Act, the bill was signed into law by President Roosevelt on September 16, 1940, establishing the first peacetime draft in American history. It required all men age twenty-one to thirty-five to register with local draft boards, and those men chosen by lottery to serve for twelve months. The bill was sponsored by Edward Burke (1880–1968), a Democratic congressman from Nebraska, 1933–35, and a senator, 1935–41, and James Wadsworth (1877–1952), a Republican senator from New York, 1915–27, and a congressman, 1933–51.

208.28–29 senators Wagner and Barbour] Robert F. Wagner (1877–1953), a Democratic senator from New York, 1927–49, and William W. Barbour (1881–1943), a Republican senator from New Jersey, 1931–37 and from 1938 until his death.

212.18–19 Brig. Gen. Benjamin O. Davis] Benjamin O. Davis Sr. (1877–1970) enlisted in 1898 and was commissioned in the black Ninth U.S. Cavalry Regiment in 1901. In World War II he served as an inspector of black army units in the U.S. and Europe.

212.22 Lt. Benjamin O. Davis, Jr.] Benjamin O. Davis, Jr. (1912–2002), was the first black graduate of West Point in the twentieth century. In World War II Davis commanded the 99th Pursuit Squadron and the 332nd Fighter Group in North Africa and Italy. He retired from the U.S. Air Force as a lieutenant general in 1970.

213.9–10 Herbert H. Lehman . . . William N. Haskell] Lehman (1878–1963) was the Democratic governor of New York, 1933–42, director of the United Nations Relief and Rehabilitation Administration, 1943–46, and senator from New York, 1949–57. Haskell (1878–1952) was commander of the New York National Guard, 1926–40.

213.16–17 the 369th New York Antiaircraft Regiment] The regiment was sent in 1942 to Hawaii, where the following year it was broken up into smaller units, one of which, the 870th Anti-Aircraft Artillery Automatic Weapons Battalion, fought in the Okinawa campaign in 1945.

213.19–20 William H. Hastie . . . civilian aide] Hastie (see note 204.13–16) resigned from his position in the War Department in January 1943 in protest against the segregation of training facilities by the Army Air Forces.

213.21–22 Campbell Johnson . . . Clarence Dykstra] Johnson (1895–1968), an attorney and social worker, continued to serve with the Selective Service Administration during and after World War II. Dykstra (1883–1950), president of the University of Wisconsin, 1937–45, was director of the Selective Service Administration from October 1940 to April 1941, when he was succeeded by his deputy, General Lewis Hershey.

214.14 Henry L. Stimson] Stimson (1867–1950) was secretary of war, 1911–13, secretary of state, 1929–33, and secretary of war, July 1940–September 1945.

215.28–29 "After many years . . . Secretary of the Navy] From a letter sent to the NAACP, August 2, 1940, by Captain Francis Whiting (1891–1978), director of recruiting in the Bureau of Navigation (later renamed the Bureau of Personnel). Frank Knox (1874–1944), publisher of the *Chicago Daily News* and the Republican nominee for vice president in 1936, served as secretary of the navy from July 1940 until his death in April 1944.

216.26 WPA . . . NYA] The Works Progress Administration (renamed the Works Projects Administration in 1939) and the National Youth Administration, New Deal agencies founded in 1935 and abolished in 1943.

217.33 chippers] Workers who used compressed air hammers to cut the edges off metal.

218.34 William Green . . . AFL] A member of the United Mine Workers of America, Green (1873–1952) was president of the American Federation of Labor from 1924 until his death.

220.19–20 Glenn L. Martin Company] An aircraft manufacturing company.

220.37–38 Sidney Hillman . . . Dr. Robert C. Weaver] Hillman (1887–1946) was the founding president of the Amalgamated Clothing Workers of America, 1914–46, and one of the founders of the Committee for Industrial Organization (later the Congress of Industrial Organizations) in 1935. Weaver (1907–1997) was an economist who had worked for the Department of the Interior and the U.S. Housing Authority. He later served as administrator of the federal Housing and Home Finance Agency, 1961–66, and as the first secretary of housing and urban development, 1966–68, becoming the first black American to serve in the cabinet.

222.2 JAMES G. THOMPSON] Thompson (1915–1999) wrote from his hometown of Wichita, Kansas, where he worked in the cafeteria at Cessna Aircraft, a company that refused to employ blacks on the production floor. He left Cessna in March 1942 and directed the *Courier*'s campaign promoting the "Double V" slogan until February 1943, when he enlisted in the army. Thompson served in the India-Burma theater with the 2257th Quartermaster Truck Company (Aviation) and returned to civilian life in 1946.

224.2–3 MARCH ON WASHINGTON MOVEMENT] On January 15, 1941, A. Philip Randolph (1889–1979), the president of the Brotherhood of Sleeping Car Porters, called for 10,000 black Americans to march on Washington, D.C., and demand an end to segregation in the armed forces and to racial discrimination in hiring for defense industries. The March on Washington Committee was formed with Randolph as its director, and on May 1 it called for the march to be held July 1. When Randolph and Walter White met with President Roosevelt on June 18, Roosevelt attempted to forestall the march, but Randolph insisted that action be taken against hiring discrimination. On June 25 Roosevelt issued Executive Order 8802 prohibiting racial discrimination in hiring by federal departments and defense contractors and establishing a Fair Employment Practice Committee (FEPC) to monitor compliance. Randolph announced the postponement of the march on June 28 but maintained the committee (later renamed the March on Washington Movement) to exert pressure on the administration.

224.7–9 St. Louis . . . New York City] In 1942 the March on Washington Movement held rallies in St. Louis, August 14, Chicago, June 26, and New York City, June 16.

226.16 assemble . . . May, 1943] The meeting was held in Chicago, June 30–July 4, 1943. Randolph later turned his attention to a new organization founded in 1943, the National Committee for a Permanent FEPC, and the March on Washington Movement held its final meeting in October 1946.

228.2 THURGOOD MARSHALL] A native of Baltimore, Marshall (1908–1993) graduated from Howard Law School in 1933. He was a counsel for the NAACP, 1934–38, its special counsel, 1938–40, director of the NAACP Legal Defense Fund, 1940–61, a federal circuit judge, 1961–65, solicitor general of the United States, 1965–67, and an associate justice of the U.S. Supreme Court, 1967–91.

229.24 Commissioner Witherspoon] John H. Witherspoon (1903–1977) was police commissioner of Detroit, June 1942–December 1943, and later served as city controller, 1950–58.

230.13 Roxy is an all night theater] A movie theater open twenty-four hours a day to accommodate patrons working the evening and night shifts in defense plants.

231.24 Mayor Jeffries] Edward Jeffries (1900–1950) served on the Detroit city council, 1932–40, and as mayor, 1940–48. (Under the 1918 Detroit city charter, municipal elections are held on a nonpartisan basis.)

237.2 DETON J. BROOKS, JR.] Brooks (1909–1975) would report for the *Chicago Defender* from India, Burma, China, and occupied Japan, 1944–45, and later served as research director of the Cook County welfare department, 1958–64, and as commissioner of human resources for Chicago, 1969–75.

237.31 the 931st Field Artillery Battalion] The Eighth Illinois Infantry, a National Guard unit that fought in the Spanish-American War and (as the 370th Infantry) in World War I, was the first regiment in the U.S. Army to have all black officers. In 1940 the Eighth Illinois was converted into the 148th Field Artillery Regiment, and in 1943 the regiment was broken up into smaller units, including the 931st Field Artillery Battalion. The 931st was converted in 1944 into the 1698th Engineer Combat Battalion, which served in Germany in 1945.

238.34 Illinois 33rd division] The 33rd Infantry Division was an Illinois National Guard formation called into federal service in 1941. It fought in New Guinea and the Philippines, 1944–45.

240.2 JAMES AGEE] From 1942 to 1948 the novelist, journalist, and critic James Agee (1909–1955) reviewed films for both *Time* and *The Nation*. In the March 11, 1943, number of *The Nation*, Agee wrote: "The Army Orientation film *The Negro Soldier* is straight and decent as far as it goes, and means a good deal, I gather, to most of the Negro soldiers who have seen it. It is also pitifully, painfully mild; but neither the film nor those who actually made it should be criticized for that. The mildness is, rather, a cruel measure of the utmost that the War Department dares or is willing to have said on the subject. The same mildness makes the film amenable to very broad public distribution, without wholly obviating its almost certain good effect upon a massive white audience which needs to be reached and influenced, however tamely. . . . I believe that to many people the screen presentation of the Negro as some thing other than a clown, a burnt-cork job, or a plain imbecile, will be more startling and more instructive than we are likely to imagine."

240.17 Carlton Moss] Moss (1909–1997) wrote radio dramas in the 1930s and was a director-producer with the New York Negro Unit of the Federal Theatre Project, 1936–39. He later directed industrial training films and educational documentaries, including *Frederick Douglass: The House on Cedar Hill* (1953), *George Washington Carver* (1959), and *Black Genesis: The Art of Tribal Africa* (1970).

240.35 the Hall Johnson Choir] Hall Johnson (1888–1970) was a black composer, arranger, and choral director who formed the Hall Johnson Choir in 1926. The choir performed onstage, on the radio, and in films such as *Lost Horizon* (1937), *Dumbo* (1941), and *Cabin in the Sky* (1943).

242.2 FLETCHER P. MARTIN] Martin (1916–2005) joined the *Louisville Defender*, a weekly newspaper, in 1942 and reported from the South Pacific for the Negro Newspaper Publishers Association, 1943–45. After his return from overseas he became the city editor of the *Defender* and in 1946 was the first black journalist to be awarded a Nieman fellowship at Harvard. Martin became the first black reporter at the *Chicago Sun-Times* in 1952 and later worked for the U.S. Information Agency in Ethiopia, Ghana, and Kenya.

242.3 *Negro Marines*] The U.S. Marine Corps was opened to black enlistees on June 1, 1942.

245.30–31 Gov. Chauncey M. Sparks] Sparks (1884–1968) was the Democratic governor of Alabama, 1943–47.

249.2–4 EARL CONRAD . . . HENRIETTA BUCKMASTER] Conrad (1906–1986), a white journalist who wrote for the liberal New York tabloid *PM*, reported on the case of Recy Taylor for the *Chicago Defender*. He later collaborated with Haywood Patterson on his autobiography (see note 200.34–35). Eugene Gordon (see note 161.1–3) reported on the Recy Taylor case for *The Daily Worker*. Henrietta Buckmaster (1909–1983), the pen name of Henrietta Henkle, was a white novelist, journalist, and historian whose works included *Let My People Go* (1941), a history of the antislavery movement.

252.15 Benny Corbett] The family name is spelled "Corbitt" in Danielle L. McGuire, *At the Dark End of the Street* (2010), a recent history of the Recy Taylor case.

252.17–18 Louis Corbett] Spelled "Lewey Corbitt" in *At the Dark End of the Street*. The deputy was not related to Benny Corbitt.

253.19–22 In Quincy, Florida . . . two short months] James Williams, age twenty-six, Fred Lane, twenty, and James Davis, sixteen, were arrested on July 30, 1944, and sentenced to death on August 31. They were electrocuted on October 9 after the Florida Supreme Court dismissed their appeal, which claimed their confessions had been obtained through torture.

254.19–20 Little Amanda Baker] The body of Amanda Baker, age thirteen, was found on October 11, 1944.

254.32–39 three white youths . . . to allow bail] Berry and his companion were attacked on December 24, 1944. The three men charged in the case, Ralph New, Ralph Goza, and Harold Morgan, were acquitted by all-white juries in 1945.

255.14 Wesley Johnson] Johnson, age eighteen, was accused of rape and lynched in Henry County, Alabama, on February 2, 1937.

255.15 Bibb Graves] Graves (1873–1942) was the Democratic governor of Alabama, 1927–31 and 1935–39.

255.16–17 impeach . . . J. L. Corbitt] The impeachment of Corbitt for negligence in allowing Johnson to be lynched was tried before the Alabama Supreme Court, which voted 4–2 for acquittal on June 5, 1937.

259.2 RAYMOND AND ROSA PARKS] Rosa Parks (1913–2005), the secretary of the Montgomery branch of the NAACP since 1943, went to Abbeville in September 1944 to investigate the rape of Recy Taylor and helped organize the Alabama Committee for Equal Justice. Raymond Parks (1903–1977), her husband, worked as a barber and was a charter member of the Montgomery NAACP branch.

259.23 indictments will be returned] No indictments were ever issued. In 2011 the Alabama legislature passed a resolution expressing "profound regret" for the failure to prosecute the offenders. Recy Taylor died in 2017 at age ninety-seven.

261.3 THEODORE STANFORD] Stanford (1914–1955) was a correspondent in western Europe for the *Pittsburgh Courier* in 1945 and later reported for the paper from New York. He was the managing editor of the *Philadelphia Independent* at the time of his death in an automobile accident.

261.8–9 The 784th Tank Battalion] The battalion, along with the 758th and 761st, was one of three black tank battalions that fought in Europe.

262.11 battle for Sevelen] Troops of the 784th Tank Battalion and the 35th Infantry Division captured the Rhineland town of Sevelen in an eighteen-hour battle, March 3–4, 1945.

262.21 battle for Rheinburg] The town was captured on March 5, 1945.

263.22 our 37-mm. and small calibre guns] The 784th Tank Battalion was equipped with M4 medium and M5 light tanks; the M5 had a four-man crew and was armed with a 37 mm gun and three .30-caliber machine guns.

264.23 T./4] Technician fourth grade, a rank equivalent to sergeant.

264.24–25 action in Straelen] The town was captured on March 2, 1945.

272.2 PAULI MURRAY] Murray (1910–1985) graduated from Howard Law School in 1944, did postgraduate legal study at Berkeley, and was admitted to the California bar in 1945. She would later edit *States' Laws on Race and Color* (1950), a compilation that Thurgood Marshall called a "bible" for civil rights lawyers, and co-author the influential law review article "Jane Crow and the Law: Sex Discrimination and Title VII" (1965). Murray helped found the National Organization for Women in 1966 and in 1977 became the first black woman to be ordained as an Episcopal priest.

272.33–34 Claude McKay . . . my strength."] Cf. Claude McKay (1889–1948), "America" (1921): "I will confess I love this cultured hell that tests my youth."

274.25 Mr. Bilbo] See note 202.23–24.

1946–1963

279.2 WENDELL SMITH] Smith (1914–1972) was a black sportswriter who began his career with the *Pittsburgh Courier* in 1937. He covered Robinson's games for that paper in 1946 and 1947 and later collaborated with him in the writing of his autobiography, *Jackie Robinson: My Own Story* (1948).

279.20–21 Wendell Willkie's "One World"] A 1943 best seller, *One World* argued for international cooperation and racial equality.

281.24 Branch Rickey] Rickey (1881–1965) was general manager of the Brooklyn Dodgers, 1943–50, and owned 25 percent of the team. He was a key strategist in the effort to desegregate Major League Baseball.

283.2 HARRY RAYMOND] A pen name of Philadelphia native Harold J. Lightcap (1896–1959), who reported for *The Daily Worker* on civil rights and other subjects for twenty-seven years.

290.2 ANNE MOODY] Moody (1940–2015) grew up in Centreville, Mississippi, and graduated from Tougaloo College, where she became increasingly active in the civil rights movement. In May 1963 she was attacked by a white mob during a sit-in at a Jackson, Mississippi, segregated lunch counter. She later moved to New York City, where she wrote *Coming of Age in Mississippi* (1968) and *Mr. Death: Four Stories* (1975).

295.2 HUBERT H. HUMPHREY] Humphrey (1911–1978) was the Democratic-Farmer-Labor mayor of Minneapolis, 1945–48, a senator from Minnesota, 1949–64 and 1971–78, vice president of the United States, 1965–69, and the Democratic nominee for president in 1968.

297.38–39 valleys of the shadow of death] See Psalm 23:4.

304.2 LILLIAN SMITH] Smith (1897–1966), a white southern critic of segregation, is most often remembered for her best-selling novel *Strange Fruit* (1944), which concerns an interracial romance. She also wrote poetry and nonfiction.

309.2–3 LONNIE E. SMITH AND CHRISTIA V. ADAIR] Smith (1901–1971), a Houston dentist, was prevented from voting in the 1940 Democratic primary in Houston because of his race; he challenged his exclusion and with *Smith v. Allwright* (1944) was later allowed to cast ballots. Adair (1893–1989) was executive secretary of the Houston NAACP while *Smith v. Allwright* was proceeding through the courts; she later campaigned for the desegregation of city libraries, hospitals, airports, and other facilities.

311.2 JULIUS WATIES WARING] Born in Charleston, Waring (1880–1968) graduated from the College of Charleston, passed the South Carolina bar, and then practiced law in Charleston from 1902 to 1942. Waring served as a judge of the U.S. District Court for the Eastern District of South Carolina, 1942–52, and was the chief judge of the court, 1948–52. In *Duvall v. School Board* (1944) Waring ruled that equally qualified teachers should receive equal pay regardless of race, and in *Elmore v. Rice* (1947) and *Brown v. Baskin* (1948) he struck down the South Carolina white primary. These decisions caused him to be ostracized by Charleston society, and a cross was burned on his lawn. In 1952 Waring retired from the bench and moved to New York City.

311.3 Briggs v. Elliot] The case was consolidated on appeal with *Brown v. Board of Education of Topeka*; see pp. 342–50.

317.7–8 As was so well said . . . one-half free] An allusion to Abraham Lincoln's "House Divided" speech, delivered at the Illinois State Capitol on June 16, 1858.

318.14 see Flack] Horace E. Flack, *The Adoption of the Fourteenth Amendment* (1908).

330.2 CHARLOTTA BASS] Born in South Carolina, Bass (c. 1880–1969) moved to Los Angeles in 1910. She was the publisher and editor of *The California Eagle* from 1912 to 1951.

330.27–29 Two Negroes . . . in France in World War I] Henry Johnson (1892–1929) and Needham Roberts (1901–1949) of the 369th Infantry Regiment (the "Harlem Hellfighters") received the Croix de Guerre for their bravery during a May 14, 1918, encounter with a German patrol. Johnson was posthumously awarded the Medal of Honor in 2015.

331.3 Dorie Miller] Doris (Dorie) Miller (1919–1943), a mess attendant on the battleship *West Virginia*, was awarded the Navy Cross for aiding wounded sailors and manning an anti-aircraft gun during the attack on Pearl Harbor. Promoted to cook, Miller was killed on November 24, 1943, when a Japanese submarine sank the escort carrier *Liscome Bay* off Makin Atoll.

331.5–6 Robert Brooks, another "first Negro,"] Brooks (1915–1941), a private serving with the 192nd Tank Battalion, was killed on December 8, 1941, in a Japanese air raid on Luzon in the Philippines. After his death the army discovered that Brooks, who was light-skinned, had been assigned to an all-white unit (his race had been recorded as "white" when he was drafted). He was the first Armored Force soldier killed in World War II, and on December 23, 1941, the main parade ground at Fort Knox, Kentucky, was named Brooks Field in his honor.

331.6 my own nephew] John Kinloch (1921–1945), the former managing editor of *The California Eagle*, was drafted into the army in 1943 and served as a public relations specialist in England and France before volunteering for combat duty. Kinloch was killed in action in Germany on April 3, 1945, while serving with the 9th Infantry Division. (In early 1945 a shortage of infantry replacements in western Europe caused the army to organize and train platoons of black volunteers from service units and assign them to reinforce white rifle companies in various infantry divisions.)

331.23 a Malan] D. F. Malan (1874–1959), prime minister of South Africa from 1948 to 1952; under his leadership the National Party began the apartheid system that institutionalized racial segregation.

331.27 Churchill's general in Malaya] Sir Gerald Templer (1898–1979) commanded British forces in Malaya, 1952–54, while also directing the civil government.

331.32–33 the African people . . . April 6] Members of the African National Congress and the South African Indian Congress held rallies against apartheid on April 6, 1952, boycotting state-sponsored celebrations of the three-hundredth anniversary of the arrival of the Dutch in Cape Town.

333.11–13 when the liberation came . . . a monument] Joshua 4:1–11.

333.34–37 what Frederick Douglass . . . with me."] From "The Black Man's Future in the Southern States," an address Douglass delivered in Boston on February 5, 1862; at the conclusion of the address Douglass quotes Hebrews 13:3.

334.9 Rose Lee Ingram] Ingram (1902–1980), a Georgia sharecropper, was sentenced to death in January 1948 along with her teenaged sons Wallace and Sammie Lee for the murder of her white neighbor John Ed Stratford. The prosecution described the case as a dispute over livestock, while the defense claimed that her sons had been defending her against sexual assault. The case prompted widespread protests, and in April 1948 the death sentences were commuted to life imprisonment. The Ingrams were eventually paroled in August 1959.

334.11 Rosalie McGee] Willie McGee (c. 1916–1951), a black grocery worker from Hattiesburg, Mississippi, was sentenced to death in December 1945 for raping a white woman and executed in May 1951. In the interim the Civil Rights Congress, the successor to International Labor Defense (see note 161.13–15), and numerous public figures made great efforts to exonerate him, believing him to be innocent or the case against him unproven. Rosalie McGee, also spelled Rosalee, toured the country on his behalf as his wife and the mother of his children. In *The Eyes of Willie McGee: A Tragedy of Race, Sex, and Secrets in the Jim Crow South* (2010), Alex Heard argues that McGee's wife Eliza Patton divorced him in 1946, and that Rosalee McGee was actually Rosalee Saffold (b. 1919), who probably met McGee after he was jailed.

334.15 Trenton Six] Six young black men who were sentenced to death in 1948 for the murder of an elderly white shopkeeper in Trenton, New Jersey. Their convictions were overturned by the New Jersey Supreme Court on the grounds of improper jury instructions. Four of the defendants were acquitted on retrial in 1951, while the remaining two were sentenced to life in prison. Their convictions were again overturned on appeal; one of the men died in prison in 1952, while the other pled guilty and was paroled in 1954.

334.16–7 Cicero . . . Martinsville Seven] When a black family moved into an apartment in Cicero, Illinois, several thousand white residents rioted on the night of July 11, 1951, and severely damaged their building. On November 20, 1948, Amy Mallard (1905–1990), an elementary school teacher in Lyons, Georgia, witnessed the murder of her husband by a white mob. After his funeral she was arrested and accused of her husband's murder, then released without bond. A grand jury subsequently indicted two men; one was acquitted after twenty minutes of jury deliberations, and the other had the charges against him dismissed. The Mallards' home was destroyed by arson, and the family fled to Buffalo, New York. Seven young black men from Martinsville, Virginia, were sentenced to death in 1949 for the rape of a white woman. Despite the legal and political efforts of the NAACP and the Civil Rights Congress, the Martinsville Seven were electrocuted in February 1951. Virginia governor Ralph Northam pardoned all seven in 2021 as an official acknowledgment of a lack of due process in their convictions.

334.19–21 Harriet Moore . . . Lee Irvin] Harriette Moore (1902–1952) and her husband Harry T. Moore (1905–1951) were NAACP activists in Brevard County, Florida. They were murdered in December 1951 when a bomb exploded under their home in Mims. In July 1949 the "Groveland Four," Ernest Thomas, age twenty-five, Samuel Shepherd, twenty-two, Walter Irvin, twenty-two, and Charles Greenlee, sixteen, were accused of the rape of a white woman in Lake County, Florida. Thomas fled and was killed by a posse, Shepherd and Irvin were sentenced to death, and Greenlee was given a life sentence. In April 1951 the U.S. Supreme Court unanimously overturned the convictions of Shepherd and Irvin on the grounds that inflammatory pretrial publicity had deprived them of a fair trial. Shepherd was killed and Irvin seriously wounded in November 1951 when they were shot by the Lake County sheriff while allegedly trying to escape. Irvin was retried in February 1952 and again sentenced to death, but his sentence was commuted to life imprisonment. He was paroled in 1968 and died the following year. Greenlee was paroled in 1960 and died in 2012. It is believed that the assassination of the Moores was linked to their involvement in the Groveland case.

334.25–27 In New York . . . defended them.] Plans for Paul Robeson to sing at a benefit concert for the Civil Rights Congress near Peekskill, New York, on August 27, 1949, were interrupted when concertgoers were attacked by a mob armed with rocks and baseball bats. Additional violence followed on September 4 after Robeson performed at the rescheduled concert. New York governor Thomas Dewey refused to meet with a large delegation that traveled to Albany to protest the attacks, claiming that Communists had provoked the violence.

334.27–28 Yonkers policeman . . . James Blackhall] Samuel Labensky, a former Westchester County Parkway police officer, killed Wyatt Blacknall, thirty-five, and his brother James, twenty-two, outside a Yonkers tavern on March 19, 1952, after complaining to the bartender about his serving black customers. Labensky pled self-defense and temporary insanity and was acquitted of murder and manslaughter charges on June 11, 1952.

334.34–35 Governor of Florida] Fuller Warren (1905–1973) was governor of Florida, 1949–53.

335.12 Smith Acts, McCarran Acts] The Smith Act, also known as the Alien Registration Act (1940), criminalized those who called for the overthrow of the government by force. It was used in 1949 to prosecute the leadership of the Communist Party of the United States. The McCarran Act, also known as the Internal Security Act (1950), required Communist groups to register with authorities and authorized the president to order the preventive detention of possible spies and saboteurs in case of war, invasion, or foreign-supported insurrection.

336.8 Taft . . . McCarthy] Republican senator Robert A. Taft (1889–1953), General Dwight D. Eisenhower (1890–1963), General Douglas MacArthur (1880–1964), and Senator Joseph McCarthy (1908–1957). At the time of Bass's speech Taft, Eisenhower, and MacArthur were all considered possible Republican presidential nominees in 1952.

336.10–12 Russell . . . Acheson] Richard Russell (1897–1971), Democratic senator from Georgia, 1931–71; John E. Rankin (1882–1960), Democratic congressman from Mississippi, 1921–53; James F. Byrnes, see note 202.23–24; Dean Acheson (1893–1971), secretary of state, 1949–53.

336.22–24 Douglass . . . remains to weep."] From Douglass's 1855 lecture "The Nature, Character, and History of the Anti-slavery Movement."

339.2 ALICE A. DUNNIGAN] Born near Russellville, Kentucky, Dunnigan (1906–1983) began her career as a Kentucky history teacher. In 1947, having worked briefly as a reporter for the *Chicago Defender*, she became the Washington bureau chief for the Associated Negro Press, in which capacity she was the first black woman accredited as a White House correspondent. In 1960 she joined Lyndon B. Johnson's campaign staff. Her autobiography, *A Black Woman's Experience: From Schoolhouse to White House*, appeared in 1974.

339.25–26 Supreme Court's decision] On June 8, 1953, the U.S. Supreme Court ruled 8–0 in *District of Columbia v. Thompson* that an 1873 statute prohibiting racial discrimination in public accommodations within the District was still in effect.

342.3 EARL WARREN] Warren (1891–1974) was district attorney of Alameda County, California, 1925–38, attorney general of California, 1938–42, governor of California, 1942–53, Republican nominee for vice president in 1948, and chief justice of the U.S. Supreme Court, 1953–69.

351.2 JO ANN GIBSON ROBINSON] Robinson (1912–1992) taught English at Alabama State College in Montgomery, Alabama, and was a leading organizer of the Montgomery bus boycott; she was arrested on several occasions and threatened with violence for her role in the boycott. She left Montgomery in 1960, eventually settling in Los Angeles, where she worked as a public schoolteacher. Her memoir, *The Montgomery Bus Boycott and the Women Who Started It*, appeared in 1987.

355.35–36 the Claudette Colvin case] Colvin (b. 1939) was arrested on March 2, 1955, for refusing to relinquish her seat to a white woman on a Montgomery bus. She was subsequently one of the plaintiffs in *Browder v. Gale* (1956), which resulted in a federal district court ruling that segregation on Alabama intrastate buses was unconstitutional.

358.2 BIG BILL BROONZY] Broonzy, born Lee Conley Bradley (1903?–1958), was a blues singer, songwriter, and guitarist. He moved to Chicago from Arkansas in 1920, made his first record in 1927, and eventually recorded over 200 songs, including "Key to the Highway" (1941).

363.7–8 America's top . . . recording stars] An advertisement in the *Birmingham News*, May 17, 1956, announced that "2 Big Shows" would be held at the Birmingham Auditorium on May 20, one "For Whites" at 3:30 P.M. and one "For Colored" at 8:30 P.M. The performers were listed as Bill Haley and His Comets, The Platters, Clyde McPhatter, LaVern Baker, Big Joe Turner, The Teenagers, the Teen Queens, Bo Diddley, The Drifters, The Flamingos, The Colts, and Red Prysock and his Rock N' Roll Orchestra.

363.12 Bill Haley] Haley (1925–1981) led Bill Haley and His Comets, whose hits included "Rock Around the Clock" (1954) and "Shake, Rattle and Roll" (1954).

364.2 HARRY GOLDEN] Golden (1902–1981), born Herschel Goldhirsch in what is now western Ukraine and raised in New York City, moved to Charlotte, North Carolina, in 1941; from 1942 to 1968 he published a one-man newspaper, *The Carolina Israelite*. *Only in America* (1958), a compilation of his *Israelite* columns, became a best seller, and he subsequently published more than a dozen books.

366.2 PAUL ROBESON] Robeson (1898–1976), a former All-American football player and Rutgers valedictorian who graduated from Columbia law school in 1923, became internationally famous in the 1920s and 1930s as a concert performer and actor on stage and screen. In 1950 the State Department revoked his passport over his overseas criticism of American race policies; he published the newspaper *Freedom* from Harlem from 1950 to 1955 and *Here I Stand*, an autobiography, in 1958.

366.6 Mr. ARENS . . . Max Yergan] Richard Arens (1913–1969) served as counsel to the House Un-American Activities Committee and later as its permanent secretary. Yergan (1892–1975), who worked as a YMCA missionary in India and South Africa from 1916 to 1936, cofounded the International Committee on African Affairs (later the Council on African Affairs) with Robeson in 1937, and in 1940 became president of the National Negro Congress. In 1948 he broke with the Communist Party and began providing information to the FBI and testifying before investigatory committees.

366.20 Mr. Walter] Francis E. Walter (1894–1963), a Democratic congressman from Pennsylvania, 1933–63, who was chairman of the House Un-American Activities Committee, 1955–63.

367.30 Dr. Doxey Wilkerson] Wilkerson (1905–1993), a professor of education, joined the Communist Party of the United States in 1943, and edited *The People's Voice* in Harlem from 1944 to 1948; he publicly resigned from the party in 1957.

368.7 Sukarno] Sukarno, born Koesno Sosrodihardjo (1901–1970), was a leader in the Indonesian struggle to secure independence from Dutch colonial rule, and served as Indonesia's first president from 1945 to 1966.

368.13 the Bandung Conference] A meeting held in Bandung, Indonesia, in 1955 of representatives from twenty-nine Asian and African nations, organized to foster economic cooperation and to oppose colonial rule.

368.32–369.3 an article . . . any other] See "Robeson Weighs Equal Rights Practices of US and the Soviet Union," *USSR Information Bulletin*, July 15, 1949.

369.12–13 Chaliapin . . . Russo the tenor] Feodor Chaliapin (1873–1938) and Domenico Russo (1874–1932).

369.16 SCHERER] Gordon H. Scherer (1906–1988), a Republican congressman from Ohio from 1953 to 1963.

369.21–22 The great poet of Russia . . . blood.] Alexander Pushkin (1799–1837) had an African great-grandfather whose life he described in his unfinished novel *The Moor of Peter the Great*, first published posthumously in 1837.

370.7 Fascist Franco] Generalissimo Francisco Franco (1892–1975), who ruled Spain from 1939 to 1975.

370.14 the Alien Sedition Act] The Alien and Sedition Acts of 1798 made it more difficult to seek U.S. citizenship, enabled the detention and deportation of noncitizens, and imposed criminal penalties for antigovernment speech.

370.25 deWysocki] Victor deWysocki II (1896–1962), a fullback, was captain of the Lehigh team.

372.12–16 an article . . . over your heads.] Robeson made these remarks in front of a group of reporters, and they were widely quoted. See, for example, Henry Lee, "Robeson Jr. Marries Campus Friend," *Daily News* (New York), June 29, 1949.

373.4 Ben Davis] See note 186.2.

373.20 read my statement?] Robeson's statement of more than 1,300 words was first printed as an appendix to *Thirty Years of Treason: Excerpts from Hearings before the House Committee on Un-American Activities, 1938–1968* (1971), edited by Eric Bentley. Robeson's passport was returned to him in 1958 after the Supreme Court ruled 5–4 that American citizens could not be denied passports because of their political beliefs.

374.2 ELIJAH MUHAMMAD] Muhammad, born Elijah Robert Poole (1897–1975) in Sandersville, Georgia, joined the Nation of Islam after hearing Wallace Fard Muhammad lecture about Islam and black empowerment in Detroit in 1931. He led the organization from 1934 until his death, by which time it had grown to include tens of thousands of members.

377.2 MALCOLM X] Born Malcolm Little in Omaha, Nebraska, Malcolm (1925–1965) joined the Nation of Islam while in prison for burglary, taking the name "X" in 1950 to replace the "slave name" he inherited. Paroled in 1952 he took on increasing responsibilities within the Nation of Islam, attracting new followers. In 1964 he broke with the NOI, founding his own group, Muslim Mosque, Inc., and becoming an adherent of Sunni Islam. An increasingly prominent public figure, he traveled worldwide and began work, with Alex Haley, on *The Autobiography of Malcolm X*, published posthumously in 1965. He was assassinated in New York City in February 1965 by members of the Nation of Islam.

391.2 Leopold Stokowski] Born in London, Stokowski (1882–1977) immigrated to the United States in 1905 and became a prominent conductor; he directed the Philadelphia Orchestra from 1912 to 1941.

401.2 ROBERT F. WILLIAMS] Williams (1925–1996) led the Monroe, North Carolina, branch of the NAACP from 1951 to 1959, and worked to integrate public libraries and pools; he was dismissed from this position in 1959 over his advocacy of violent self-defense. In 1961, after a warrant was issued for his arrest on kidnapping charges, he fled to Cuba where he became the voice of Radio Free Dixie for several years, broadcasting to the continental United States. At the invitation of Mao Zedong, he moved to China in 1965, and then on to Tanzania, returning to the U.S. in 1969. Charges against him were eventually dropped.

405.36–37 the Fort Pillow Massacre] At the end of the battle of Fort Pillow, in Henning, Tennessee, on April 12, 1864, Confederate troops under

Nathan Bedford Forrest (1821–1877) massacred more than 200 Union soldiers who were attempting to surrender, most of them from two black artillery regiments.

441.2 GEORGE WALLACE] Born in Clio, Alabama, and educated at the University of Alabama law school, Wallace (1919–1998) was Alabama governor from 1963 to 1967, 1971 to 1979, and 1983 to 1987. He ran for president in 1964, 1968, and 1972; in 1968, as a candidate of the American Independent Party, he carried five states: Alabama, Arkansas, Georgia, Louisiana, and Mississippi.

441.5 GOVERNOR Patterson] John M. Patterson (1921–2021), governor of Alabama from 1959 to 1963.

443.19 where once Jefferson Davis stood] Davis (1808–1889), president of the Confederate States of America from 1861 to 1865, was inaugurated on February 18, 1861, on the steps of the Alabama Capitol in Montgomery.

443.31 school riot report] In January 1963, a Special Committee on Group Activities appointed by the superintendent of the District of Columbia public schools and led by Shane MacCarthy (1908–1983), issued a report on the 1962 Thanksgiving Day riots, in which violence erupted at a high school championship football game in Washington, D.C.

447.31 the survivors of Castro] Approximately 250,000 Cubans emigrated to the United States in the four years following January 1959, when Fidel Castro (1925–2016) took power in Cuba.

448.12–13 a full offensive . . . a university] President Kennedy sent 12,000 troops to Oxford, Mississippi, in September–October 1962 to control riots that followed attempts by James Meredith (b. 1933), a black student, to enroll at the University of Mississippi.

448.22–24 As Thomas Jefferson . . . his hands."] The first half of this quotation, before the semicolon, comes from Jefferson's tract *A Summary View of the Rights of British America* (1774); no source has been discovered for its second half.

451.1 poke] Pokeweed (*Phytolacca americana*), the leaves and shoots of which are edible after boiling (but potentially fatal without proper preparation).

451.7–9 Rudyard Kipling . . . the world!"] Quoted from "The Southerner," an editorial by Asa ("Ace") Carter and Jesse Mabry published in *The Southerner* in March 1956, where Kipling is loosely paraphrased. Carter (1925–1979) worked as a speechwriter for Wallace and is credited as co-author of his 1963 inaugural address.

457.23–24 the outlawing of the NAACP . . . the Talladega injunction] In 1956, in the wake of the Montgomery bus boycott and other protests, the Alabama attorney general tried to compel the NAACP to reveal its membership lists, effectively outlawing the organization when they refused to do so; MIA refers to Montgomery Improvement Association (see Chronology, 1955). A state judge issued an injunction in 1957 against a boycott of white merchants in Tuskegee, Alabama. In April 1962, following student civil rights protests in Talladega, an Alabama circuit court judge issued an injunction against such protests.

460.17–18 "Black Monday."] May 17, 1954, the date of the U.S. Supreme Court's decision in *Brown v. Board of Education.* John Bell Williams (1918–1983), a Democratic congressman from Mississippi, is said to have first used the phrase in reference to *Brown* in a speech to the House of Representatives.

466.2–3 the Constitution . . . Harlan] See Harlan's dissenting opinion in *Plessy v. Ferguson* (1896).

473.3 JOHN LEWIS] Born in Troy, Alabama, Lewis (1940–2020) led the Student Nonviolent Coordinating Committee from 1963 to 1966. In 1965 he was attacked by police on the Edmund Pettus Bridge in Selma, Alabama, while leading a march from Selma to Montgomery. Elected to Congress from Georgia's fifth district in 1986, he served until his death in 2020. He was awarded the Presidential Medal of Freedom in 2012.

473.4 *Speech at the March on Washington*] Lewis revised his speech under pressure from the organizers of the march, who felt his original text was too critical of the Kennedy administration.

473.20–22 the three young men . . . peaceful protest?] On August 8, 1963, Ralph Allen (1941–2005), Don Harris (b. 1941?), and John W. Perdew (1941–2014), all members of the Student Nonviolent Coordinating Committee, were arrested for organizing a large student protest at a segregated theater in Americus, Georgia. They were charged with insurrection, then a capital offense in Georgia, but in October 1963 Georgia's insurrection law was declared unconstitutional and charges against them were overturned.

473.26 "One man . . . African cry.] The phrase was a slogan of the African National Congress and of other southern African political movements. In May 1961, following a stay-at-home strike, Nelson Mandela (1918–2013) called for "One man, one vote" as "the key to our future."

474.16–18 C.B. King . . . Slater King] C. B. King (1923–1988), a native of Albany, Georgia, helped to found the Albany Movement civil rights coalition in 1961 and supported it as an attorney; in July 1962, while attempting to visit a jailed demonstrator, he was beaten with a cane by the county sheriff. His brother Slater King (1927–1969) and his sister-in-law Marion King (1931–1995) were also active in the movement. Marion was beaten unconscious by a Camilla, Georgia, police officer in July 1962 while attempting to deliver food and clothing to demonstrators. She lost her unborn child a month later as a result of the attack.

475.16–17 Eastland . . . Thurmond] Southern defenders of segregation: James Eastland (1904–1986), senator from Mississippi; Ross Barnett (1898–1987), governor of Mississippi; George Wallace (1919–1998), Alabama governor; and Strom Thurmond (1902–2003), South Carolina senator.

475.36 James Farmer] Farmer (1920–1999), a cofounder in 1942 of what became the Congress of Racial Equality, co-organizer in 1961 of Freedom Rides through the South, in a test of equality in interstate transportation, and co-organizer in 1963 of the March on Washington, was arrested in Plaquemine, Louisiana, in August 1963 during a peaceful protest march.

476.21 FEPC] Fair Employment Practice Commission.

1964–1976

481.30 W. Willard Wirtz] Wirtz (1912–2010) served as secretary of labor, 1962–69, in the cabinets of John Kennedy and Lyndon Johnson.

483.2 MALCOLM X] See note 377.2.

483.3 *The Ballot or the Bullet*] Malcolm X gave this speech at a symposium sponsored by the Congress of Racial Equality (CORE), a civil rights organization founded in 1942.

483.5 Brother Lomax] Louis Lomax (1922–1970) was a freelance journalist whose books include *The Negro Revolt* (1962) and *When the Word Is Given: A Report on Elijah Muhammad, Malcolm X, and the Black Muslim World* (1963).

483.15 Adam Clayton Powell] Powell (1908–1972) was a Democratic congressman from New York, 1945–67 and 1969–71.

483.18–19 Dr. Martin Luther King] Atlanta-born King (1929–1968) was a Baptist minister and civil rights activist from 1955 until his assassination. He oversaw the Montgomery bus boycott, led the Southern Christian Leadership Conference, and was an organizer of the 1963 March on Washington. Dr. King was awarded the Nobel Peace Prize in 1964.

483.21 Rev. Galamison] Milton A. Galamison (1923–1988) was pastor of the Siloam Presbyterian Church in the Bedford-Stuyvesant section of Brooklyn, 1948–68. Galamison organized successful one-day school boycotts in February and March 1964 to protest de facto segregation in the New York City public school system.

484.15–16 President Kennedy . . . with Khrushchev] President Kennedy announced in October 1963 that the U.S. would begin selling wheat to the Soviet Union.

485.38–39 the same with Kennedy . . . president] In the presidential election of 1960 Democratic senator John Kennedy won 303 electoral votes to Republican vice president Richard Nixon's 219. The popular vote was much tighter, with Kennedy receiving 34,220,984 votes (49.7 percent), Nixon 34,108,157 (49.5 percent).

486.9–10 filibustering on top of that] Southern senators began a filibuster against the civil rights bill on March 30 that lasted until June 10, 1964, when the Senate voted 71–29 to end the debate.

486.22 Eastland] James O. Eastland (1904–1986) was a Democratic senator from Mississippi, 1943–78, and chairman of the Senate Judiciary Committee, 1956–78.

486.39 Richard Russell] Russell (1897–1971) was a Democratic senator from Georgia, 1933–71.

487.29 Dixiecrats bolted themselves once] The adoption by the Democratic convention in 1948 of a minority report calling for a federal anti-lynching law, the establishment of a Fair Employment Practices Commission, the abolition of poll taxes, and the desegregation of the armed forces led to a walkout by southern "Dixiecrats" who held a States' Rights convention on July 17 and nominated South Carolina governor Strom Thurmond (1902–2003) for president.

488.9 I was in Washington . . . Thursday] During his visit to the Capitol on March 26 Malcolm X had his only encounter with Martin Luther King, Jr., when the two men met and shook hands in a Senate corridor.

488.12–13 huge map . . . location of Negroes] The map had been introduced as an exhibit by Senator Richard Russell when he proposed equalizing racial proportions throughout all fifty states by relocating black families from the South.

488.23–25 the constitutional amendments . . . right to vote.] The Fifteenth Amendment established that the right to vote for all adult male citizens could not be denied based on race, ethnicity, or prior status as an enslaved person.

490.35 Jacksonville] Rioting began in Jacksonville, Florida, on March 23, 1964, when the police dispersed an anti-segregation march by hundreds of black youths and continued the following day. During the violence a black housekeeper, Johnnie Mae Chappell, was fatally shot in a racially motivated attack.

493.16–17 United Nations . . . charter of human rights] The Universal Declaration of Human Rights, a key tenet of the United Nations Charter, was approved without dissent by the fifty-eight members of the General Assembly in 1948.

493.19 Hungary] In October 1956 the Soviet Union successfully deployed tanks and troops to suppress a popular revolt against the Communist government in Hungary.

494.5 "We Shall Overcome."] A gospel song, origins unclear, possibly based on "I'll Overcome Some Day" by Charles Albert Tindley. The modern civil rights version of the song appeared during a Charleston, South Carolina, cigar factory strike in 1946–47.

496.21–25 They did the same thing . . . defeat those guerrillas.] Widespread revolt against French colonial rule in Algeria reignited in 1954 and concluded in 1962 with the nation's independence. When Charles de Gaulle returned to power in 1958, he actively sought an end to the conflict.

496.32 Muslim Mosque, Inc.] Malcolm X incorporated the organization on March 16, 1964.

497.13 SNCC] Student Nonviolent Coordinating Committee, a civil rights organization founded in 1960.

499.5 Billy Graham] William Franklin Graham, Jr. (1918–2018), was an ordained Baptist minister and a popular evangelist.

502.8–10 bomb a church . . . four little girls] Klansmen bombed the Sixteenth Street Baptist Church in Birmingham, Alabama, on September 15, 1963, killing Denise McNair, age eleven, Cynthia Wesley, fourteen, Carole Robertson, fourteen, and Addie Mae Collins, fourteen.

502.11–12 the government . . . find who did it.] In September 1963 the FBI launched an investigation into the Birmingham church bombing. A memorandum submitted to FBI director J. Edgar Hoover in 1965 identified four Klansmen—Robert Chambliss, Herman Cash, Thomas Blanton, Jr., and Bobby Frank Cherry—as suspects in the case. Hoover did not inform prosecutors of the findings, and the FBI closed the investigation in 1968. Alabama attorney general Bill Baxley reopened the investigation in 1971, and Chambliss was convicted of murder on November 18, 1977; he died in prison in 1985. Cash died in 1994 without ever having been charged. In 2000 Blanton and Cherry were charged with murder. Blanton was convicted on May 1, 2001, and Cherry was found guilty on May 22, 2002; both men were sentenced to life imprisonment. Cherry died in prison in 2004; Blanton died in prison in 2020.

502.13 Eichmann . . . Argentina] Adolf Eichmann (1906–1962) was captured in Argentina by Israeli agents on May 11, 1960, and taken to Israel, where he was tried in 1961 and hanged on May 31, 1962. An officer in the SS, Eichmann headed the Jewish Department of the Reich Main Security Office, 1939–45, and played a major role in the Nazi deportation of European Jews to extermination camps.

502.26 march on Washington in 1963] The March on Washington for Jobs and Freedom occurred on August 28, 1963. At the event Dr. Martin Luther King, Jr., delivered his "I Have a Dream" speech standing in front of the Lincoln Memorial.

504.3–4 *Mississippi Freedom Democratic Party*] Founded in Jackson, Mississippi, in 1964 by James W. Wright, Fannie Lou Hamer, Ella Baker, and Bob Moses, the party remained in existence until the Democratic National Convention in 1968.

504.23 James W. Silver] Silver (1907–1988) was the author of *Mississippi: The Closed Society* (1964).

505.15 Paul B. Johnson] Johnson (1916–1985) was Democratic governor of Mississippi, 1964–68.

507.27–31 The four candidates . . . John Bell Williams.] All four incumbents were members of the segregated Mississippi Democratic Party. Stennis (1901–1995) was a senator, 1947–89; Whitten (1910–1995) was a congressman, 1941–95; Colmer (1890–1980) was a congressman, 1937–73; and Williams (1918–1983) was a congressman, 1947–68, who then served as the state's governor, 1968–72.

509.2–5 MIKE MANSFIELD . . . EVERETT MCKINLEY DIRKSEN] Mansfield (1903–2001) was a Democratic senator from Montana, 1953–77, then U.S. ambassador to Japan, 1977–88. For Russell see note 486.39. For Humphrey see note 295.2. Dirksen (1896–1969) was a Republican senator from Illinois, 1951–69.

512.3–6 George Washington Carver . . . Harry Belafonte] Carver (c. 1864–1943) was an agricultural scientist. Bunche (1904–71), see note 203.16. Owens (1913–1980), a track-and-field athlete, won four gold medals at the 1936 Olympic Games in Berlin. Jackie Robinson (1919–1972) was the first black baseball player in the major leagues. Yerby (1916–1991) was a novelist best known for *The Foxes of Harrow* (1946). Bill Robinson (1878–1949), "Bojangles," was an American tap dancer and actor. Mays (1931–2024), the "Say Hey Kid," was a major league baseball player. Cole (1919–1965) was a jazz pianist and singer. Armstrong (1901–1971), "Satchmo," was a jazz trumpet player, singer, and actor. Poitier (1927–2022) received the Academy Award for Best Actor in 1963 for his performance in *Lilies of the Field*. Anderson (1897–1993) performed before the Lincoln Memorial in 1939 after the Daughters of the American Revolution would not allow her to sing at their concert. Belafonte (1927–2023) was a calypso singer and actor.

522.13 Victor Hugo] French poet, novelist, and politician (1802–1885).

523.6–7 the act of 1875 . . . struck it down] The Civil Rights Act of 1875 prohibited racial discrimination in public accommodations, public transportation, and service on juries. The act did not provide for federal enforcement. In 1883 the U.S. Supreme Court (in the *Civil Rights Cases*) declared the act unconstitutional because it exceeded the authority of Congress to regulate private individuals.

523.19 As Lincoln once observed] From his Annual Message to Congress, December 1, 1862.

523.25 Henry W. Grady] Grady (1850–1889) was an orator and journalist. He promoted southern industrialization and coined the term "The New South."

525.7–8 to secure Federal pure food and drug legislation] The Pure Food and Drug Act was signed into law by President Theodore Roosevelt in June 1906.

525.19–20 to establish a civil service] The Pendleton Civil Service Reform Act was signed into law by President Chester Arthur in January 1883.

525.23–24 The bullet fired . . . Garfield's life] James A. Garfield was shot by Charles J. Guiteau on July 2, 1881, and died from massive infection on September 19.

525.28–30 New York legislature . . . bakery workers in that State] In *Lochner v. New York* (1905) the U.S. Supreme Court struck down the 1895 New York Bakeshop Act on the grounds that it violated an employee's right to contract with an employer.

525.34 La Follette] Robert M. La Follette (1855–1925) represented Wisconsin in both houses of Congress and served as the state's governor, 1901–6. He was the Progressive Party candidate for president in 1924. The Seventeenth Amendment (ratified in 1913) established the direct election of U.S. senators.

528.2 FANNIE LOU HAMER] Hamer (1917–1977) was a voting rights activist and the cofounder (with Gloria Steinem, Shirley Chisholm, Betty Friedan, and Bella Abzug) of the National Women's Political Caucus in 1971.

528.9 James O. Eastland] See note 486.22.

528.9 Stennis] See note 507.27–31.

530.23 Medgar Evers] Evers (1925–1963) was a civil rights activist killed outside his home in Jackson, Mississippi, by Byron De La Beckwith, a member of the White Citizens' Council. His death occurred just hours after President Kennedy delivered a major civil rights address. Both his murder and the resulting trials received national attention and spurred civil rights protests.

530.25 Freedom Democratic Party] See note 504.3–4.

531.2–3 ROBERT PENN WARREN AND BAYARD RUSTIN] Warren (1905–1989) won the Pulitzer Prize in fiction for *All the King's Men* in 1946 and the Pulitzer Prize for poetry in 1958 and 1979. Rustin (1912–1987) worked with A. Philip Randolph on the 1941 March on Washington to end discrimination in the U.S. military. He was also the principal organizer of the 1963 March on Washington for Jobs and Freedom. Warren spoke with Rustin as part of his research for his book *Who Speaks for the Negro?* (1965).

532.3 Harlem] The Harlem race riot occurred July 16–22, 1964.

532.27 Philadelphia] The Philadelphia race riot occurred August 28–30, 1964.

532.30 Clarence Pickett] Pickett (1884–1965) was executive secretary of the American Friends Service Committee from 1929 to 1950. In 1947 the organization shared the Nobel Peace Prize with the London-based Friends Service Committee.

533.26–27 white riots . . . English riots] On Labor Day weekend in 1964 thousands of high school and college students rioted in Hampton Beach, New Hampshire. The National Guard was called in; there were over 200 arrests and considerable property damage. There was no obvious cause of the riot. In the spring of 1964 the English seaside towns of Clacton, Margate, Brighton, and Bournemouth were the scenes of fighting between members of two youth subcultures, the stylishly dressed Mods, who rode motor scooters, and the leather-clad Rockers, who favored motorcycles.

533.29 Rochester] The Rochester race riot occurred July 24–26, 1964.

533.32 Myrdal] Gunnar Myrdal (1898–1987), a Swedish sociologist, shared the Nobel Prize in Economic Sciences with Friedrich Hayek in 1974. *An American Dilemma: The Negro Problem and Modern Democracy*, funded by the Carnegie Corporation, was published in 1944.

535.2 JOHN HERBERS] Herbers (1923–2017) covered the civil rights movement for *The New York Times*, 1963–65.

535.10 J. Edgar Hoover] Hoover (1895–1972) was appointed by President Calvin Coolidge as director of the Bureau of Investigation in 1924 and became the first director of the Federal Bureau of Investigation when it was established in 1935. He served in that office until his death.

535.16 Albany, Ga.] The Albany Movement was a protest that focused on the segregation of the entire community, from lunch counters to bus stations. It lasted from the fall of 1961 through the summer of 1962. Over a thousand protestors were jailed.

535.24 Southern Christian Leadership Conference] The SCLC is an Atlanta-based civil rights organization that was founded in 1957. Its initial goal was nonviolent direct action as a method of desegregating bus systems in the South. Dr. Martin Luther King, Jr., served as the first president until his death in 1968.

535.26 Nobel Peace Prize] Dr. King was notified that he had won the prize in October 1964.

536.1–2 Warren Commission] The President's Commission on the Assassination of President Kennedy (the Warren Commission, named after its chairman, Chief Justice Earl Warren) was created by executive order on November 29, 1963. Its 888-page final report was submitted to President Johnson on September 24, 1964.

536.3 Lee Harvey Oswald] Oswald (1939–1963) assassinated President Kennedy in Dallas on November 22, 1963. Oswald, in police custody, was killed two days later by Jack Ruby.

536.28–29 tragic murder . . . in Birmingham] See note 502.8–10.

536.29–30 three murdered . . . in Mississippi] James Chaney of Meridian, Mississippi, and Andrew Goodman and Michael Schwerner, both from New York City, were killed near Philadelphia, Mississippi, in June 1964 during the Freedom Summer campaign. Nine members of the White Knights of the Ku Klux Klan were convicted on federal civil rights charges in 1967 and served relatively light sentences. In 2005 a Neshoba County grand jury indicted Edgar Ray Killen, then eighty years old, as the planner of the murders; he was sentenced to three consecutive prison terms of twenty years.

537.12 Meadville, Miss.] In May 1964 two black hitchhikers, Henry Hezekiah Dee and Charles Eddie Moore, were abducted and murdered by members of the Ku Klux Klan who thought they were civil rights workers involved in a plot to arm local black citizens. Their bodies were found during the search for missing civil rights workers Chaney, Goodman, and Schwerner (see note 536.29–30). Charges against James Ford Seale and Charles Marcus Edwards were dismissed in 1965. The case was reopened in 2005, leading to the conviction of Seale.

537.32 Leslie W. Dunbar . . . Southern Regional Council] Dunbar (1922–2017) was executive director of the Atlanta-based SRC from 1961 to 1965. He worked with Martin Luther King, Jr., of the SCLC and Roy Wilkins of the NAACP to create the Voter Education Project.

538.5 Ruby Hurley] Prior to being named director of the NAACP's Southeast Regional Branch, Hurley (1909–1980) served as the organization's youth secretary.

538.19 Student Nonviolent Coordinating Committee] See note 497.13.

538.23 Julian Bond] Bond (1940–2015), a civil rights activist, served in both houses of the Georgia state legislature, 1967–87, and later was chair of the NAACP, 1998–2010.

541.11 Nicholas Katzenbach] Katzenbach (1922–2012) served in President Johnson's cabinet as attorney general, 1964–66.

543.11–12 Chief Justice Livingston] Edwin Livingston (1892–1971) was chief justice of the Alabama Supreme Court from 1951 to 1971.

544.3–4 JAMES BALDWIN AND WILLIAM F. BUCKLEY] Baldwin (1924–1987) was a political activist and social critic. His essay collections include *Notes of a Native Son* (1955); his novels, *Go Tell It on the Mountain* (1953) and *Another Country* (1962). Buckley (1925–2008) was a political and social commentator. He founded the conservative *National Review* in 1955. *On the*

Right, his syndicated column, ran from 1962 to 2008; *Firing Line*, his weekly television program, from 1966 to 1999.

544.7 *Union president Fullerton*] Peter S. Fullerton (1943–2024) was part of a group of Conservative student politicians known as the "Cambridge Mafia." Fullerton organized and moderated the 1965 Cambridge Union debate, which was televised live by the BBC.

546.4 Gary Cooper] Cooper (1901–1961) won the Academy Award for Best Actor in 1941 for *Sergeant York* and in 1952 for *High Noon*.

547.31 Sheriff Clark in Selma, Alabama] James (Jim) Gardner Clark, Jr. (1922–2007), was sheriff of Dallas County, Alabama, from 1955 to 1966. Clark became notorious for his role in "Bloody Sunday" (see Chronology, 1965).

551.5 Johnson landslide] In the presidential election of 1964 Democratic president Lyndon Johnson won 486 electoral votes to Republican senator Barry Goldwater's 52. Johnson received 43,129,040 popular votes (61.1 percent), Goldwater 27,175,754 (38.5 percent).

552.36 *The Fire Next Time*] Published in 1963, the book contains two essays: "My Dungeon Shock," a letter to his young nephew on race in American history, and "Down at the Cross," on the relation between race and religion in America.

553.33 Watusi] Thousands of Tutsis (Watusi) were massacred in Rwanda by Hutu (Bahutu) militias from December 1963 to January 1964.

555.40 Professor Oakeshott] Michael Oakeshott (1901–1990) was a political theorist and philosopher at the London School of Economics.

556.36 Paul] Paul the Apostle (c. 5–c. 64/65 CE) spread the gospel of Jesus around the eastern Mediterranean. His epistolary contributions in the New Testament defined and clarified the theology and practice of Christianity as well as the role of its ministry.

556.39 Dachau] Nazi concentration camp near Munich, Germany, in operation from 1933 to 1945.

557.18–19 Jews and Catholics . . . as late as 1828] Catholics gained the right to vote in 1829, Jews in 1833.

559.20–21 *Beyond the Melting Pot . . . The Lonely Crowd*] *Beyond the Melting Pot*, by Nathan Glazer and Daniel Patrick Moynihan, was published in 1963. *The Lonely Crowd*, by David Reisman, Nathan Glazer, and Reuel Denney, was published in 1950.

561.7–10 Booker T. Washington said . . . prepared to vote.] In his September 18, 1895, address at the Atlanta Exposition, Washington (c. 1856–1915) said, "It is important and right that all privileges of the law be ours, but it is vastly more important that we be prepared for the exercise of these privileges."

561.12 Ross Barnett] Barnett (1898–1987) was a Democratic governor of Mississippi, 1960–64.

561.13 Adam Clayton Powell Jr.] See note 483.15.

564.3 JOHN CONYERS] Conyers (1929–2019), a Democrat, represented Michigan in the U.S. House of Representatives from 1965 to 2017.

564.4 *Voting Rights Act*] The act was signed into law by President Johnson on August 6, 1965.

564.26 journey to Selma, Ala.] See Chronology, March 21–25, 1965.

565.17–18 1957, 1960, and 1964 Civil Rights Acts] See Chronology.

567.31 Mr. RODINO] Peter Rodino (1909–2005) was a Democratic congressman from New Jersey, 1949–89. He chaired the House Judiciary Committee from 1973 to 1989.

569.2 CORE] The Congress of Racial Equality, a civil rights organization, was founded in 1942.

585.2 VINE CITY PROJECT] Also known as the Atlanta Project, it was established in February 1966 by the Student Nonviolent Coordinating Committee (SNCC).

588.1–9 How do we react . . . efforts with the Dodgers.] Mays played center field for the New York (later San Francisco) Giants and the New York Mets, 1951–73. Robinson was a second baseman for the Brooklyn Dodgers, 1947–56. Mantle (1931–1995) was a New York Yankees center fielder, 1951–68.

588.36–37 Uncle Tom or Simon Legree?] In Harriet Beecher Stowe's novel *Uncle Tom's Cabin* (1851–52), Legree is a brutal slaveowner who attempts to break Tom's spiritual faith, eventually ordering Tom to be whipped to death.

588.39 SNCC] See note 497.13.

589.2 SCLC] See note 535.24.

589.15 Niagara Movement] Black leaders held an inaugural meeting in Fort Erie, Ontario (near Niagara Falls), in 1905 to oppose the policy of accommodation offered by Booker T. Washington on segregation and disenfranchisement. Their militant comprehensive Declaration of Principles, as well as events such as the Springfield, Illinois, race riot of 1908, led to the founding of the National Association for the Advancement of Colored People in New York City in 1909.

590.14 Atlanta Project] See note 585.2.

597.2 JOHN HULETT] Hulett (1927–2006) was elected sheriff of Lowndes County, Alabama, in 1970 and served in that office for twenty-two years.

598.12 Eugene Bull Connor] Eugene (Bull) Connor (1897–1973) was commissioner of public safety in Birmingham, Alabama, 1937–54 and 1957–63.

598.12 George Wallace] See note 441.2.

598.13 Al Lingo] Albert J. Lingo (1910–1969) was head of the Alabama Department of Public Safety (including the Alabama Highway Patrol) from 1963 to 1965.

598.15 march from Selma to Montgomery] See Chronology, March 7, 1965.

598.16 Jim Clark] See note 547.31.

602.25 Richmond Flowers] Flowers (1918–2007) was Alabama's attorney general from 1963 to 1967. He opposed Governor George Wallace's racial segregation policies.

605.3 STOKELY CARMICHAEL] Carmichael (1941–1998) was a civil rights activist and one of the original Freedom Riders in Alabama and Mississippi. He served as the chair of the Student Nonviolent Coordinating Committee, 1966–67. As a revolutionary socialist he moved to Ghana and then Guinea in 1968 and worked for the Pan-Africanism movement.

605.16 Camus and Sartre] Albert Camus (1913–1960) was an Algerian-born French existentialist philosopher, journalist, and novelist. Jean-Paul Sartre (1905–1980) was a French existentialist philosopher, novelist, and political activist. Both were awarded the Nobel Prize in Literature: Camus in 1957, Sartre in 1964.

605.18 Frantz Fanon] Martinique-born French political philosopher and Marxist, Fanon (1925–1961) was the author of *Black Skin, White Masks* (1952) and *The Wretched of the Earth* (1961), key works about colonialism and racism.

605.33 Sheriff Rainey] Lawrence Rainey (1923–2002) was sheriff of Neshoba County, Mississippi, 1963–68. He was charged with helping fellow KKK members in the murders of civil rights workers Chaney, Goodman, and Schwerner (see note 536.29–30) but was acquitted in 1967.

606.1 SNCC] See note 497.13.

606.17–18 Ross Barnett] See note 561.12.

606.18 Jim Clark] See note 547.31.

607.39 Head Start . . . Upward Bound] Head Start and Upward Bound were established in 1965 as part of President Johnson's War on Poverty. The former focuses on early childhood education as well as health and nutrition programs for low-income families, the latter on improving education and academic opportunities for low-income students.

608.6 Rockefeller] Nelson A. Rockefeller (1908–1979) was Republican governor of New York, 1959–73, and vice president under Gerald Ford, 1974–77.

611.13 Rusk] Dean Rusk (1909–1994) served as secretary of state for both John Kennedy and Lyndon Johnson, 1961–69.

613.8 Brown] Edmund (Pat) Brown (1905–1996) was the Democratic governor of California, 1959–67. He was defeated for reelection in 1966 by Ronald Reagan.

613.17 Wayne Morse] Morse (1900–1974) was a senator from Oregon, 1945–69.

613.17 Eastland, Wallace] See notes 486.22 and 441.2.

614.20 Santo Domingo] Dominican Republic.

616.33 Ho Chi Minh] Ho (1890–1969) was president of the Democratic Republic of Vietnam (North Vietnam), 1945–69.

623.2 EARL WARREN] See note 342.3.

623.24 trial judge] Leon Bazile (1890–1967) was judge of the Fifteenth Circuit, 1941–65, when he ruled against Richard and Mildred Loving in support of Virginia's Racial Integrity Act of 1924.

625.32–33 descendants of John Rolfe and Pocahontas] In 1614, Jamestown tobacco planter John Rolfe (1585–1622) married Pocahontas (c. 1596–1617), the daughter of Chief Powhatan. Upon her marriage and conversion to Christianity she was known as Rebecca Rolfe. Their only child was Thomas Rolfe (1615–c. 1680).

629.4–5 Freedmen's Bureau . . . Civil Rights Act of 1866] The Bureau of Refugees, Freedmen, and Abandoned Lands was established in March 1865. Congress initially envisioned the bureau as lasting for just one year. The charter was renewed by Congress in March 1866 but vetoed by President Andrew Johnson, who argued that the bureau violated states' rights. Congress overrode the veto. Johnson's veto of the 1866 Civil Rights Act was also overridden by Congress.

629.20 *Brown* v. *Board of Education*] See Chronology, 1954.

632.2 THURGOOD MARSHALL] See note 228.2.

632.7 T. H. BAKER] Thomas Harrison Baker conducted interviews for the Center for Oral History at Columbia University.

632.12–13 Aubrey Williams . . . Youth Administration] Williams (1890–1965) led the National Youth Administration during the New Deal. He was later a civil rights activist involved with the Montgomery bus boycott (1955).

632.16 cases] The primary cases involved challenges to all-white primaries held by the Democratic Party in Texas and elsewhere in the South.

633.1 Walter White] See note 3.2.

633.18 Sam Rayburn] Rayburn (1882–1961) was a Democratic congressman from Texas, 1913–61. He served as Speaker of the House, 1940–47, 1949–53, and 1955–61.

633.25 Sweatt versus Painter] See Chronology, 1950.

633.35 Roy Wilkins] Wilkins (1901–1981) was executive secretary of the NAACP from 1955 to 1977.

636.10 Averell Harriman] W. Averell Harriman (1891–1986) was U.S. ambassador to the Soviet Union, 1943–46, and governor of New York, 1955–58. He also served as a foreign policy advisor to Democratic presidents.

638.2–3 Connie Motley] Constance Baker Motley (1921–2005) was a staff attorney for the NAACP's Legal Defense and Educational Fund, 1946–66. She then served as a judge (later chief judge) of the U.S. District Court for the Southern District of New York, 1966–86. She was also the first black woman to argue before the U.S. Supreme Court.

640.26 Ramsey or Nick] Ramsey Clark (1927–2021) was President Johnson's attorney general from 1967 to 1969. For Nicholas Katzenbach see note 541.11.

641.17 John Doar] Doar (1921–2014) served in the Civil Rights Division as first assistant attorney general, 1960–64, and as assistant attorney general, 1964–67.

641.32 Urban League] The National Urban League, a civil rights organization, was founded in New York City by Ruth Standish Baldwin, George Edmund Haynes, and others in 1910.

642.8–9 Mrs. Lavery] Blanche Hampton Nichols (1916–2012), Thurgood Marshall's secretary while he was solicitor general and for part of his tenure as Supreme Court associate justice, was first married to Charles Lavery and then to Allen DeLong. She retired in 1973.

642.30 Marvin Watson] Watson (1924–2017) was a longtime advisor to President Johnson. He served as White House chief of staff, 1966–68, and U.S. postmaster general, 1968–69.

642.38 Cissy] Cecilia Suyat (1928–2022), a civil rights activist and NAACP staff member, married Thurgood Marshall in 1955.

643.18–19 Tom C. Clark] Clark (1899–1977) was President Truman's attorney general, 1945–49, before being appointed associate justice of the U.S. Supreme Court, 1949–67.

646.19 James E. Groppi] Groppi (1930–1985) was an ordained Roman Catholic priest, community organizer, and civil rights activist. He left the church in 1976 and married Margaret Rozga, a fellow activist.

647.39 Milwaukee Mayor Henry Maier] Maier (1918–1994) was mayor of Milwaukee from 1960 to 1988.

648.5 Warren Knowles] Knowles (1908–1993) was a Republican governor of Wisconsin, 1965–71.

657.5 Danang, RVN] Da Nang is a coastal city in central Vietnam. From 1954 to 1975 it was in the northern part of the Republic of Vietnam (South Vietnam).

659.12–13 Newark and then in Detroit] The Newark race riot occurred July 12–17, 1967; the Detroit race riot, July 23–28, 1967.

664.10 Watts, and Harlem] The Watts (Los Angeles) race riot occurred August 11–17, 1965; the Harlem (New York City) race riot occurred July 23–30, 1967.

665.20–21 Kenneth B. Clark] Clark (1914–2005) was a psychologist who studied the effects of segregation on black schoolchildren.

671.23–24 Albert Reiss] Reiss (1922–2006) was a sociologist who served as research director for President Johnson's Commission on Law Enforcement and Administration of Justice (1967).

679.23 Patrick V. Murphy] Murphy (1920–2011) served as the top law enforcement official in Syracuse, Washington, D.C., Detroit, and New York City.

692.2 WHITNEY M. YOUNG] Young (1921–1971) was executive director of the National Urban League from 1961 to 1971.

692.7 THOMAS HARRISON BAKER] See note 632.7.

692.8–9 Urban League] See note 641.29.

693.23 Hugo Black] Black (1886–1971) was a Democratic senator from Alabama, 1927–37, before President Franklin Roosevelt appointed him as associate justice of the U.S. Supreme Court, 1937–71.

693.29–30 Judge Waties Waring . . . *Ivan Allen*] Julius Waties Waring (1880–1986) was a judge (later senior judge) of the U.S. District Court for the Eastern District of South Carolina, 1942–52. In his minority opinion in *Briggs v. Elliott* (1951) he stated that "segregation is per se inequality," opening the way for the ruling in *Brown v. Board of Education* three years later. McGill (1898–1969) was executive editor of the *Atlanta Constitution*, where beginning in the 1930s he reported on the negative effects of segregation. Allen (1911–2003) was mayor of Atlanta, Georgia, 1962–70.

693.40 Roy Wilkins] See note 633.34.

694.11 Hobart Taylor] Taylor (1920–1981) served as legal counsel for the President's Committee on Equal Employment Opportunities, 1961–64.

697.8 Marshall Plan] The European Recovery Program, or Marshall Plan, provided economic assistance following World War II to enable countries in western Europe to rebuild infrastructure, promote commerce, modernize industry, and counter the spread of communism.

697.35 Poverty Program] President Kennedy's New Frontier included several initiatives to assist the poor: the Area Redevelopment Act (1961), the

Manpower Development and Training Act (1962), the National Defense Education Act amendments (1963), increased Social Security benefits, extended unemployment benefits, and a pilot Food Stamps program.

698.25–26 War on Poverty] The War on Poverty of President Johnson's Great Society included initiatives such as the Civil Rights Act (1964), the Economic Opportunity Act (1964), the Food Stamp Act (1964), the Higher Education Act (1965), Head Start, Job Corps, housing assistance, and Medicare/Medicaid.

699.34 Mr. Humphrey] See note 295.2.

700.3 Kerner Report] Governor Otto Kerner of Illinois chaired the National Advisory Commission on the Causes, Events, and Aftermaths of the Civil Disorders of 1967. The 440-page report was published later in 1968.

703.24–25 General Westmoreland] William Westmoreland (1914–2005) commanded U.S. troops in South Vietnam from 1964 to 1968. He then served as army chief of staff from 1968 to 1972.

704.9 Father James E. Groppi] See note 646.19.

704.11 Denver's Crusade for Justice Center] The Crusade for Justice was a Chicano rights organization founded in 1966 by Rodolpho Gonzales. Its headquarters were at 1567 Downing Street.

704.18–19 Vel Phillips] Velvalea Rodgers Phillips (1924–2018) later served as Wisconsin's secretary of state, 1979–83.

706.26 Corky Gonzales] Rodolfo (Corky) Gonzales (1928–2005), boxer, poet, and political activist, was a leader in the Chicano Power Movement.

706.28 Poor People's Campaign] See Chronology, 1968.

707.2 SHIRLEY CHISHOLM] Chisholm (1924–2005) was a congresswoman from New York, 1969–83. She was one of the founders of the National Women's Political Caucus in 1971. President Barack Obama posthumously awarded her the Presidential Medal of Freedom in 2015.

707.29–30 Frederick Douglass . . . a struggle."] From an 1857 address delivered in Canandaigua, New York, commemorating West Indies emancipation.

711.22 Charles Hamilton] Hamilton (1929–2023) was a political scientist and co-author (with Stokely Carmichael) of *Black Power: The Politics of Liberation* (1967).

714.35 Bull Connor] See note 598.12.

717.2 NICK KOTZ] Kotz (1932–2020) was a Pulitzer Prize–winning journalist and the author of *Judgment Days: Lyndon Baines Johnson, Martin Luther King Jr., and the Laws That Changed America* (2005).

717.26–27 Burke Marshall] Marshall (1922–2003) was the assistant U.S. attorney general in charge of the civil rights division, 1961–64.

717.33 Clarence Mitchell] Mitchell (1911–1984) was the NAACP's chief Washington lobbyist for almost thirty years. President Jimmy Carter presented him with the Presidential Medal of Freedom in 1980.

718.27 Julian Bond and Vernon Jordan] For Julian Bond see note 538.23. Vernon Jordan (1935–2021) was a civil rights activist and attorney, and later a political advisor to President Bill Clinton.

719.4 1972 election] In the presidential election of 1972, Republican president Richard Nixon won 520 electoral votes to Democratic senator George McGovern's 17. Nixon received 46,740,323 (60.7 percent) popular votes, McGovern 28,901,598 (37.5 percent).

719.7 George McGovern] McGovern (1922–2012) was a Democratic senator from South Dakota, 1963–81, and the Democratic candidate for president in the election of 1972.

719.10 Andrew Young] Young (born in 1932) served as a Democratic congressman from Georgia, 1973–77, U.S. ambassador to the United Nations, 1977–79, and mayor of Atlanta, 1982–90.

719.11–12 Hubert Humphrey] See note 295.2.

721.2–3 Barbara Jordan] Jordan (1936–1996) was a member of the Texas State Senate, 1967–73, and the U.S. House of Representatives, 1973–79. In 1994 President Bill Clinton presented her with the Presidential Medal of Freedom.

721.3 Yvonne Brathwaite Burke] Burke (b. 1932) served in the California State Assembly, 1967–73, in Congress as a representative from California, 1973–79, and on the Los Angeles County Board of Supervisors, 1992–2008.

722.2 RON HUTSON] Hutson (1947–2020) won the Pulitzer Prize in journalism in 1975 and 1984 for his reporting on race issues.

723.17–18 W. Arthur Garrity Jr.] Garrity (1920–1999) was a judge (later senior judge) of the U.S. District Court for the District of Massachusetts, 1966–99. His 1974 ruling in *Morgan v. Hennigan* mandated busing to desegregate Boston's public schools.

724.38 neighborhood, extending] An unknown number of words were omitted from the text printed in *The Boston Globe* on June 27, 1974.

729.3 THURGOOD MARSHALL] See note 228.2.

729.6–7 Mr. Justice Douglas . . . Mr. Justice White] William O. Douglas (1898–1980), associate justice, 1939–75; William J. Brennan (1906–1997), associate justice, 1956–90; Byron R. White (1917–2002), associate justice, 1962–93.

732.8 which Ford inherits from Nixon] Gerald Ford became president upon the resignation of Richard Nixon on August 9, 1974.

732.16 W. Arthur Garrity] See note 723.17–18.

733.23 Edward Kennedy] Kennedy (1932–2009) was a Democratic senator from Massachusetts, 1962–2009.

733.39 Mayor Kevin White] White (1929–2012) was mayor of Boston from 1968 to 1984.

736.40 Louise Day Hicks] Hicks (1916–2003) was a member of the Boston School Committee, 1961–70, member of the Boston City Council, 1970–71 and 1974–81, and a Democratic congresswoman from Massachusetts, 1971–73.

737.29 Francis Sargent] Sargent (1915–1998) was Republican governor of Massachusetts, 1969–75.

737.32 Michael Dukakis] Dukakis (b. 1933) was governor of Massachusetts, 1975–79 and 1983–91. He was the Democratic candidate for president in 1988.

738.1–2 Edward Brooke] Brooke (1919–2015) was a Republican senator from Massachusetts, 1967–79.

739.8–11 President Dwight Eisenhower . . . in 1962] Eisenhower sent federal troops to Little Rock after Governor Orville Faubus mobilized the Arkansas National Guard to prevent nine black students from entering Central High School. Kennedy sent federal forces to Oxford to keep segregationists from preventing James Meredith from enrolling at the University of Mississippi.

740.3 BARBARA JORDAN] See note 721.2–3.

743.23–26 Thomas Jefferson . . . *but dreary things.*] From Jefferson's First Inaugural Address, 1801.

744.33–35 Abraham Lincoln . . . not be a master."] Manuscript note, c. 1858.

Index

This book is set in 10 point ITC Galliard, a face designed for digital composition by Matthew Carter and based on the sixteenth-century face Granjon. The paper is acid-free lightweight opaque that will not turn yellow or brittle with age. The binding is sewn, which allows the book to open easily and lie flat. The binding board is covered in Brillianta, a woven rayon cloth made by Van Heek–Scholco Textielfabrieken, Holland.
Composition by Dianna Logan, Clearmont, MO.
Printing by Sheridan, Grand Rapids, MI.
Binding by Dekker Bookbinding, Wyoming, MI.
Designed by Bruce Campbell.